Certified Information Systems Security Professional (CISSP®): Fourth Edition

Certified Information Systems Security Professional (CISSP®): Fourth Edition

Part Number: 093024
Course Edition: 1.0

Acknowledgements

PROJECT TEAM

Author	Production Support	Content Editor
Chrys Thorsen, CISSP	Tamara Hagen	Peter Bauer
Jason Nufryk, CFR	Brian Sullivan	

Logical Operations wishes to thank members of the Logical Operations Instructor Community, especially Kent Huelman and Andrew James Riemer, and give special thanks to John Hackmeyer, CISSP, and Belton Myers, CISSP, for their instructional and technical contributions during the development of this courseware. Join the community at **http://loic.expert/**.

Notices

DISCLAIMER

While Logical Operations, Inc. takes care to ensure the accuracy and quality of these materials, we cannot guarantee their accuracy, and all materials are provided without any warranty whatsoever, including, but not limited to, the implied warranties of merchantability or fitness for a particular purpose. The name used in the data files for this course is that of a fictitious company. Any resemblance to current or future companies is purely coincidental. We do not believe we have used anyone's name in creating this course, but if we have, please notify us and we will change the name in the next revision of the course. Logical Operations is an independent provider of integrated training solutions for individuals, businesses, educational institutions, and government agencies. The use of screenshots, photographs of another entity's products, or another entity's product name or service in this book is for editorial purposes only. No such use should be construed to imply sponsorship or endorsement of the book by nor any affiliation of such entity with Logical Operations. This courseware may contain links to sites on the Internet that are owned and operated by third parties (the "External Sites"). Logical Operations is not responsible for the availability of, or the content located on or through, any External Site. Please contact Logical Operations if you have any concerns regarding such links or External Sites.

TRADEMARK NOTICES

Certified Information Systems Security Professional (CISSP®): Fourth Edition

Lesson 1: Security and Risk Management.......................1

Topic A: Security Governance Principles...........................2

Topic B: Compliance..15

Topic C: Professional Ethics...27

Topic D: Security Documentation..................................32

Topic E: Risk Management..37

Topic F: Threat Modeling...54

Topic G: Business Continuity Plan Fundamentals...........59

Topic H: Acquisition Strategy and Practice....................71

Topic I: Personnel Security Policies..............................78

Topic J: Security Awareness and Training......................83

Lesson 2: Asset Security..89

Topic A: Asset Classification..90

Topic B: Privacy Protection..97

Topic C: Asset Retention...101

Topic D: Data Security Controls.. 107

Topic E: Secure Data Handling.. 113

Lesson 3: Security Engineering......................... 121

Topic A: Security in the Engineering Lifecycle........................... 122

Topic B: System Component Security...................................... 127

Topic C: Security Models.. 140

Topic D: Controls and Countermeasures in Enterprise Security............ 147

Topic E: Information System Security Capabilities......................... 155

Topic F: Design and Architecture Vulnerability Mitigation.................. 162

Topic G: Vulnerability Mitigation in Embedded, Mobile, and Web-Based Systems...181

Topic H: Cryptography Concepts... 190

Topic I: Cryptography Techniques.. 207

Topic J: Site and Facility Design for Physical Security..................... 220

Topic K: Physical Security Implementation in Sites and Facilities.......... 231

Lesson 4: Communications and Network Security.............. 239

Topic A: Network Protocol Security..240

Topic B: Network Components Security..................................... 262

Topic C: Communication Channel Security..................................280

Topic D: Network Attack Mitigation.. 293

Lesson 5: Identity and Access Management...................... 313

Topic A: Physical and Logical Access Control.............................. 314

Topic B: Identification, Authentication, and Authorization................. 324

Topic C: Identity as a Service.. 343

Topic D: Authorization Mechanisms.. 349

Topic E: Access Control Attack Mitigation..................................357

Lesson 6: Security Assessment and Testing...................... 367

Topic A: System Security Control Testing..............................368

Topic B: Software Security Control Testing...........................381

Topic C: Security Process Data Collection............................ 389

Topic D: Audits... 397

Lesson 7: Security Operations.............................403

Topic A: Security Operations Concepts................................ 404

Topic B: Physical Security... 410

Topic C: Personnel Security... 425

Topic D: Logging and Monitoring....................................... 429

Topic E: Preventative Measures... 436

Topic F: Resource Provisioning and Protection..................... 442

Topic G: Patch and Vulnerability Management...................... 452

Topic H: Change Management.. 456

Topic I: Incident Response.. 460

Topic J: Investigations.. 468

Topic K: Disaster Recovery Planning................................... 479

Topic L: Disaster Recovery Strategies.................................492

Topic M: Disaster Recovery Implementation.........................505

Lesson 8: Software Development Security..........................513

Topic A: Security Principles in the System Lifecycle...............514

Topic B: Security Principles in the Software Development Lifecycle........520

Topic C: Database Security in Software Development..............538

Topic D: Security Controls in the Development Environment..................545

Topic E: Software Security Effectiveness Assessment...........555

Appendix A: Mapping Course Content to (ISC)2 Certified Information Systems Security Professional (CISSP®) 2015 Exam......................565

Mastery Builders... 575

Solutions.. 617

Glossary.. 707

Index... 749

About This Course

Welcome to *Certified Information Systems Security Professional (CISSP)®: Fourth Edition*. With your completion of the prerequisites and necessary years of experience, you are firmly grounded in the knowledge requirements of today's security professional. This course will expand upon your knowledge by addressing the essential elements of the eight domains that comprise a Common Body of Knowledge (CBK)® for information systems security professionals. The course offers a job-related approach to the security process, while providing a framework to prepare for CISSP certification.

CISSP is the premier certification for today's information systems security professional. It remains the premier certification because the sponsoring organization, the International Information Systems Security Certification Consortium, Inc. (ISC)$^{2®}$, regularly updates the test by using subject matter experts (SMEs) to make sure the material and the questions are relevant in today's security environment. By defining eight security domains that comprise a CBK, industry standards for the information systems security professional have been established. The skills and knowledge you gain in this course will help you master the eight CISSP domains and ensure your credibility and success within the information systems security field.

Course Description

Target Student

This course is intended for experienced IT security-related practitioners, auditors, consultants, investigators, or instructors, including network or security analysts and engineers, network administrators, information security specialists, and risk management professionals, who are pursuing CISSP training and certification to acquire the credibility and mobility to advance within their current computer security careers or to migrate to a related career. Through the study of all eight CISSP Common Body of Knowledge (CBK) domains, students will validate their knowledge by meeting the necessary preparation requirements to qualify to sit for the CISSP certification exam. Additional CISSP certification requirements include a minimum of five years of direct professional work experience in two or more fields related to the eight CBK security domains, or a college degree and four years of experience.

Course Prerequisites

It is highly recommended that students have certifications in Network+ or Security+, or possess equivalent professional experience upon entering CISSP training. It will be beneficial if students have one or more of the following security-related or technology-related certifications or equivalent industry experience: CyberSec First Responder (CFR), MCSE, CCNP, RHCE, LCE, SSCP®, GIAC, CISA™, or CISM®.

Course Objectives

In this course, you will identify and reinforce the major security subjects from the eight domains of the (ISC)^2 CISSP CBK.

You will:

- Analyze components of the Security and Risk Management domain.
- Analyze components of the Asset Security domain.
- Analyze components of the Security Engineering domain.
- Analyze components of the Communications and Network Security domain.
- Analyze components of the Identity and Access Management domain.
- Analyze components of the Security Assessment and Testing domain.
- Analyze components of the Security Operations domain.
- Analyze components of the Software Development Security domain.

The CHOICE Home Screen

Logon and access information for your CHOICE environment will be provided with your class experience. The CHOICE platform is your entry point to the CHOICE learning experience, of which this course manual is only one part.

On the CHOICE Home screen, you can access the CHOICE Course screens for your specific courses. Visit the CHOICE Course screen both during and after class to make use of the world of support and instructional resources that make up the CHOICE experience.

Each CHOICE Course screen will give you access to the following resources:

- **Classroom**: A link to your training provider's classroom environment.
- **eBook**: An interactive electronic version of the printed book for your course.
- **Files**: Any course files available to download.
- **Checklists**: Step-by-step procedures and general guidelines you can use as a reference during and after class.
- **LearnTOs**: Brief animated videos that enhance and extend the classroom learning experience.
- **Assessment**: A course assessment for your self-assessment of the course content.
- Social media resources that enable you to collaborate with others in the learning community using professional communications sites such as LinkedIn or microblogging tools such as Twitter.

Depending on the nature of your course and the components chosen by your learning provider, the CHOICE Course screen may also include access to elements such as:

- LogicalLABS, a virtual technical environment for your course.
- Various partner resources related to the courseware.
- Related certifications or credentials.
- A link to your training provider's website.
- Notices from the CHOICE administrator.
- Newsletters and other communications from your learning provider.
- Mentoring services.

Visit your CHOICE Home screen often to connect, communicate, and extend your learning experience!

How to Use This Book

As You Learn

This book is divided into lessons and topics, covering a subject or a set of related subjects. In most cases, lessons are arranged in order of increasing proficiency.

The results-oriented topics include relevant and supporting information you need to master the content. Each topic has various types of activities designed to enable you to solidify your understanding of the informational material presented in the course. Information is provided for reference and reflection to facilitate understanding and practice.

Data files for various activities as well as other supporting files for the course are available by download from the CHOICE Course screen. In addition to sample data for the course exercises, the course files may contain media components to enhance your learning and additional reference materials for use both during and after the course.

Checklists of procedures and guidelines can be used during class and as after-class references when you're back on the job and need to refresh your understanding.

At the back of the book, you will find a glossary of the definitions of the terms and concepts used throughout the course. You will also find an index to assist in locating information within the instructional components of the book.

As You Review

Any method of instruction is only as effective as the time and effort you, the student, are willing to invest in it. In addition, some of the information that you learn in class may not be important to you immediately, but it may become important later. For this reason, we encourage you to spend some time reviewing the content of the course after your time in the classroom.

As a Reference

The organization and layout of this book make it an easy-to-use resource for future reference. Taking advantage of the glossary, index, and table of contents, you can use this book as a first source of definitions, background information, and summaries.

Course Icons

Watch throughout the material for the following visual cues.

Icon	Description
	A **Note** provides additional information, guidance, or hints about a topic or task.
	A **Caution** note makes you aware of places where you need to be particularly careful with your actions, settings, or decisions so that you can be sure to get the desired results of an activity or task.
	LearnTO notes show you where an associated LearnTO is particularly relevant to the content. Access LearnTOs from your CHOICE Course screen.
	Checklists provide job aids you can use after class as a reference to perform skills back on the job. Access checklists from your CHOICE Course screen.
	Social notes remind you to check your CHOICE Course screen for opportunities to interact with the CHOICE community using social media.

1 Security and Risk Management

Lesson Time: 5 hours, 30 minutes

Lesson Objectives

In this lesson, you will:

- Apply security governance principles.

- Plan business practices that comply with legislation and other regulations.

- Discuss professional ethics.

- Develop security documentation.

- Apply risk management concepts.

- Apply threat modeling concepts.

- Develop business continuity plans.

- Integrate security considerations into acquisition strategy and practice.

- Discuss personnel security policies.

- Apply security training and awareness objectives.

Lesson Introduction

In this course, you will explore a broad range of security concepts and best practices designed to meet the demands of increasingly specialized information systems security. Before you address specific security areas or elements, it is important that you have a plan in place for the overall management of these processes and elements. In this lesson, you will understand what comprises successful security and risk management.

TOPIC A

Security Governance Principles

When it comes to managing your security, there are several principles that you need to be aware of to truly get the most out of your high-level security efforts. In this topic, you'll be introduced to the concepts that will be the foundation of your security governance.

 Note: To learn more, view the LearnTO presentations from the **LearnTO** tile on the CHOICE course screen.

The CIA Triad

Information security seeks to protect three principles: confidentiality, integrity, and availability. This is called the *CIA triad* or triangle. If one of the principles is compromised, the security of the organization is threatened. The CIA triad permeates everything the security professional does from system security to building security and it must be kept in mind at all times.

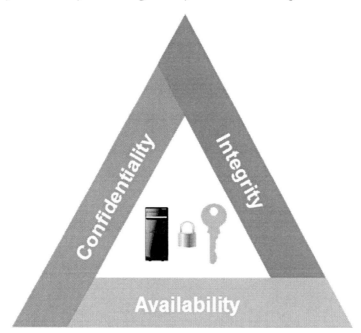

Figure 1-1: The CIA triad.

Principle	Description
Confidentiality	*Confidentiality* is the fundamental principle of keeping information and communications private and protecting them from unauthorized access. Confidentiality protects against disclosure.
	Confidential information includes trade secrets, personnel records, health records, tax records, and military secrets.
Integrity	*Integrity* is the property of keeping organization information accurate, without error, and without unauthorized modification. Integrity also protects important systems and helps to maintain those systems against unintentional changes.

Principle	Description
Availability	*Availability* is the fundamental principle of ensuring that systems operate continuously and that authorized persons can access data that they need. Availability protects against system and data destruction.
	The level of tolerable downtime really depends on the organization and the type of activity that uses the information system in question. For example, banks and financial institutions measure their downtime in minutes or even seconds. Nonprofit organizations and small business, on the other hand, might be able to tolerate system downtime for several days. This is especially true when there are paper systems in place as a backup.

Balanced Security

Confidentiality and integrity are often at odds with availability. As a security professional, you will need to always balance the need for data and system availability with the need to limit access control. In a sense, the importance of availability focuses on whether or not a system is available to the entities that actually have a right to access the system. However, narrowing availability in this manner to strengthen confidentiality and integrity is a decision that you'll have to make carefully. There's no simple strategy that will apply to every situation; it's up to you to weigh the needs of users and stakeholders to access information with the need for data to remain safe from unauthorized use. In the end, it may come down to overall impact: will it cost your organization more if sensitive data is leaked or if some users and services can't access the sensitive data at certain points in time? Keep in mind that "cost" in this case isn't always monetary, but can include reputation, legal standing, and more. Ultimately, as the business deploys new systems and you apply security measures, you should always consider the impact these changes will have on the CIA triad.

Common Security Terms

The following table is intended to establish a common language for security that is featured throughout this course and is integral to the information security industry. These terms are some of the most vital for you to understand.

Term	Description
Asset	Anything of value that could be compromised, stolen, or harmed, including information, physical resources, and reputation.
Threat	Any event or action that could potentially cause damage to an asset or an interruption of services.
Attack	The intentional act of attempting to bypass one or more security services or controls of an information system.
Vulnerability	A condition that leaves the system and its assets open to harm—including such things as software bugs, insecure passwords, inadequate physical security, and poorly designed networks.
Exploit	A technique that takes advantage of a vulnerability to perform an attack. Exploit may also refer to a packaged form of the technique, such as an application or script that automates the technique so that even an unskilled attacker can use the exploit to perform an attack.
Risk	The likelihood of a threat occurring, as well as its potential damage to assets.
Control	A countermeasure that you put in place to avoid, mitigate, or counteract security risks due to threats or attacks.
Social engineering	The practice of using deception and trickery against human beings as a method of attack.

Term	Description
Defense in depth	The practice of providing security in multiple layers for more comprehensive protection against attack.

Security Governance

Governance in an organization refers to the organization's methods of exercising authority or control as well as its system of management. In the security realm, another major purpose of governance is to mitigate the risks involved in information technology and its users. Without proper governance, your security culture will remain reactionary, and you'll find that your time is continually spent on responding to incident after incident. When you can gain greater control over the management of your security resources, your security will be much more proactive and efficient. A more proactive and efficient security program will offer stronger support to the business, ensuring that objectives are met and costs minimized with as little disruption as possible to operations.

Governance Requirements

The IT Governance Institute (ITGI), a research group established in the late 1990s, provides the global business community and enterprise leaders with valuable references, tools, and support for governing their IT-enabled business systems. ITGI suggests several expected governance activities:

*   Strategic alignment of information security with business strategies to support organizational objectives.
*   Risk management by executing appropriate measures to manage and mitigate risks, and reducing potential impacts on information resources to an acceptable level.
*   Resource management by efficiently and effectively using information security knowledge and infrastructures.
*   Performance measurement by evaluating, monitoring, and reporting information security governance metrics to ensure that organizational objectives are achieved.
*   Value delivery by optimizing information security investments that support organizational objectives.

 Note: For more information on ITGI, such as its products and services, visit **www.itgi.org**.

Security Council

Larger organizations may have ongoing security programs. You might even consider a "Security Council" or "Oversight Committee" as a way to get insight from all parts of the organization. Gathering members from multiple areas of the company not only provides necessary insight, but it can also help you garner support for security initiatives. You may decide that your group needs a vision and/or mission statement. These can be a good way to explain your efforts to management and others within the organization.

Security Council will perform the following activities:

*   Select security project initiatives.
*   Prioritize information security activities.
*   Review and recommend organizational security policies.
*   Monitor the existing security program.
*   Promote security throughout the organization.
*   Suggest areas of security requiring development and investment.

Organizational Governance Structure

In IT security, governance starts at the top with the CEO and Board of Directors who are tasked with exercising authority and control over the entire corporation. Authority of the IT security practices flows downward through the organization to the security department and to individuals who are responsible for conducting a security program based on policy.

The Chief Information Officer (CIO) and Board of Directors are responsible for ensuring that the corporation is using well-established security policies and that the security of information is protected. The essence of good security is a security policy that makes the wishes of top management known to the security organization. The policy is not a technical document, but is a high-level statement that clearly dictates expectations. Policies that support the governance activities of the board should be developed.

The CIO may oversee the security department, or it may be governed by the Chief Information Security Officer (CISO). Either way, security personnel are responsible for managing the day-to-day mechanics of security implementation. They may also draft more concentrated documentation based on the overarching goals of the security policies.

Management and the staff they manage make up the last end of the governance structure. They carry out any processes and duties that they are responsible for as per existing policy. While they may not make direct decisions about the company's security directives, they are still integral in the overall security culture.

Figure 1–2: Organizational governance structure.

The Organizational Culture's Impact on Security

The culture of an organization can have a direct impact on security. As organizations change the way they do business and realign their strategies, it is important to identify who is responsible for the various security functions and whom these people will report to. It is also important that security enhances and protects the business, and that the business will be able to react in a way that makes it competitive.

Different people within an organization are required to perform certain roles with respect to the security policy and its components. It is important to create an organizational culture that emphasizes the importance of security policies and practices. The Chief Executive Officer (CEO) and the Board of Directors are responsible for documenting organizational security goals and objectives. The security department determines how to put the established goals into practice. And finally, all staff members and employees are responsible for adhering to the goals by implementing them in their day-to-day activities.

Security and Business Alignment

Information security supports an organization by protecting its assets. It does this by implementing different types of controls. Whether the focus is more on data confidentiality (military organizations) or integrity (corporate organizations), business operations depends on the proper implementation of the CIA triad.

It is not possible to achieve a 100% security level due to cost factors and the fact that new security risks are discovered every day. Security professionals must act as risk advisers to the senior management of the organization, balancing the risk tolerance of the organization, cost to implement the security measures, and the benefits to the business. They need to keep the organizational mission in mind as they:

- Assess the risk and determine needs.
- Implement policies and controls to mitigate the risk.
- Promote awareness of the expectations.
- Monitor and evaluate the effectiveness of the controls.
- Use this knowledge as input in the next risk assessment.

A common saying in the IT industry today is "IT is the business, and the businesses is IT." Essentially this means that IT is not a separate function or cost for the business,but rather it is the very platform that the business makes money from. So it is important for both security personnel and the rest of an organization's management to recognize the mutual nature of security and business. Wise management understands that properly implemented security mitigates risk, allowing the business to innovate with less fear.

Organizational Processes

In order for the security team to properly support the business, it must understand what the organizational mission is and the processes that support it. An organization can go through phases of growth and decline, just like any living organism. The security professional must be aware of the following activities that the organization may undertake and their potential impact on security:

- Mergers and Acquisitions: When an organization acquires another organization, there is almost certainly going to be a mismatch of technology and security levels, causing security challenges. These mismatches must be rectified so that a merger does not put the entire organization at risk. Additionally, organizational changes like mergers and acquisitions will end up with some personnel being replaced by others. You should have a plan in place to transition staff gracefully, as frustrated and disgruntled people may themselves be an added risk.
- Divestitures: When a company spins off from the parent company, forming its own organization, there is a risk of information leakage, that the child organization will take with it information that does not belong to it and should stay with the parent. During a spinoff, the security professional must make sure that trade secrets and sensitive information do not leak out of the company in an unauthorized manner.
- Hiring and firing: When new staff comes on board they must be trained; when staff members leave, they must no longer be able to access company assets or information.

- Governance committees: An organization may establish committees to evaluate the effectiveness of current governance personnel and practices, as well as onboard or offboard governance board members. Committee members should have the requisite understanding of security management within the organization in order to make informed decisions that impact security.

Roles and Responsibilities

Because security management is the foundation for a dependable and protected business environment, organizational security needs to be well established. Even though senior management is ultimately responsible for security, it is important for everyone in your organization to understand and be responsible for his or her own role in maintaining security. Employing the applicable organizational goals and concepts set forth by security management will help you implement security policies and protection mechanisms in your organization.

The end user is responsible for following the security policies that have been set out by the security team with input from management. Security professionals need to help create a culture where users understand the policies and even become the eyes and ears of the organization and help to foster a secure environment.

Whatever security roles you implement in your organization, it's important to make sure that they are clear and well-defined. This will help reduce confusion and increase productivity. It demonstrates that executive management understands and properly supports information security, and it also demonstrates due diligence on the part of the company.

Every individual in the company has security responsibilities.

Role	Responsibilities
End Users	Protect information on a daily basis. They do this by adhering to organizational security policies,being mindful of security in everything they do,and watching for and reporting any security weaknesses or infractions they might observe.
Administrative Assistants	Provide a first line of defense against social engineering attacks by blocking unauthorized visitors packages. They also screen phone calls for executives.
Help Desk/Service Desk Administrators	Answer questions from users about system problems. A call to the help desk is often the first indication of security issues.
Physical Security	Provide the first line of defense for information security by protecting the physical location. Additionally, they will work with external law enforcement. With the increased automation of physical controls in today's working environments, and the need for physical control to protect information, you may also find the integration of information security and physical security into one department.
Information Systems/IT Professionals	Design security controls into information systems.
Information Systems Security Professionals	Inform executive management of security concerns and suggest solutions.
Information Systems Auditors	Determine whether or not people and systems are in compliance with the organization's security policies. The auditor checks for proper configuration and design, as well as proper implementation and operation.
Business Continuity Planners	Develop contingency plans to prepare for any incidents that might impact the organization's ability to meet business objectives.

Role	Responsibilities
Data/Information Custodians	Implement on a technical level the level of access control indicated by the data owner. Back up data to ensure recovery in the event of data loss or corruption.
Data/Information/Business Owners	Classify data and determine who has what level of access to the database.
Security Administrators	Manage access to information or systems. That person will ensure that individuals only get the level of privilege they need to do their job. Security administrator should keep a log of all requests for access, including approvals and denials. These will then be provided to the auditor as required to demonstrate compliance with policy.
Network/Systems Administrators	Keep the computing infrastructure running by managing networks and computer systems so that information is available when needed. It is they who will probably physically implement the access controls required by the data owner.
Executive Management	Protect the information assets of the organization. An organization may have one or more Chief Information Officers (CIOs), who are responsible for all information technology activities. The Chief Information Security Officer's (CISO) role focuses on information security, and often reports to the CIO.

CISO Role

The Chief Information Security Officer (CISO) is responsible for protecting all business information assets from loss or disclosure. Often this person will work with other individuals to implement and execute any policies, procedures, standards, or guidelines that the company has in place. The information security officer may also be responsible for implementing and running the organization's *computer incident response team (CIRT)*.

The CISO also provides support for expected governance activities. By reviewing the activities as stated, the CISO develops a program that reviews organizational security assets from an operational, tactical, and strategic viewpoint.

The CISO must be able to balance security needs with business objectives. For example, it may not be possible to implement all of the required security safeguards because of limitations in resources, time, and staff. Safeguard prioritization is then necessary. Prioritization decisions are not determined by the CISO; their implementation is the responsibility of the board and CEO.

CISO Responsibilities

To support the governance responsibilities of the board, the CISO is required to perform many different functions and assume numerous roles in the organization.

ISO Responsibility	Description
Understand the business	• Become knowledgeable about the business operation and goals. • Understand the vision and mission and how IT security helps to meet goals. • Be a member of the management team. • Provide insightful security guidance as it applies to the entire organization.

ISO Responsibility	Description
Stay informed	• Be up to date on the changing threat environment. • Be aware of emerging technologies that provide security solutions.
Budget	• Develop the security budget for the organization and justify expenses. • Communicate budget needs to senior management to increase the likelihood of approval. • Ask for needs rather than wants.
Develop	• Develop security policies, procedures, baselines, standards, and guidelines. • Develop security awareness programs in the corporation. • Develop security management skills within the security organization.
Train	• Ensure user and management training in information security protection. • Train security staff in new threats, new safeguards, and current operations.
Ensure compliance	• Ensure compliance to laws, regulations, and policies within areas controlled by information security. • Coordinate with the legal department as necessary.
Promote awareness	• Promote a climate of security awareness in all parts of the company. • Communicate the importance of business continuity and disaster recovery planning.
Inform	• Be the conduit for security information in the organization. • Provide frequent updates on the status of the organization's security environment. • Provide information about pending changes in advance so that adequate training can be planned.
Measure	• Measure security effectiveness by conducting penetration testing and other similar activities. • Work with internal and external auditors to determine any weaknesses in safeguards.
Assist	• Assist senior management in understanding the requirements for information security. • Assist application designers and developers in understanding how to provide security in new and existing systems.
Report	• Report security accomplishments and limitations to senior management. • Provide details regarding security violations.

Communications

Communication in the business is a two-way street; you need to know how to speak persuasively just as much as you need to know how to listen. Being adept at both will ensure that nothing serious goes unreported or unaddressed. If you lack the ability to communicate what you need to do your job, as well as the ability to learn from your colleagues and customers, your security efforts may be in vain.

It is important for security professionals to understand the business initiatives of the organization. Without understanding the business, it will be harder to protect the appropriate assets. It will also be harder to acquire the necessary resources to protect the business. As you are working to understand the business, it will also be necessary to communicate your security concerns to management, helping them to understand the risks associated with corporate initiatives. These are some of the questions that you might anticipate management asking.

- What problem are you solving?
- What is the risk to the company?
- What is the cost associated with the safeguard versus the cost of doing nothing?
- Will you completely eliminate the risk or simply mitigate the risk?
- How long will the project last?
- What resources will be required?

Regardless of who they are reporting to, security officers need to establish positive, credible working relationships with all levels of the company, from executive management to the end users.

Security Reporting Options

An information security department's reporting structure can have a significant influence on how it operates.

It is preferable for its security officer in the information security team to report to as high a level in the organization as possible. This ensures that the importance of information security is emphasized in the organization. It also helps to limit information distortion or inaccuracies that occur naturally when information is passed through several layers.

The following are examples of reporting structures and the possible pros and cons. There is no one right answer for all organizations.

Security Reporting Option	Pros and Cons
Chief Executive Officer (CEO)	**Pros:** • Top-level visibility • Accessibility to resources **Cons:** • Lack of independence
Internal audit department	**Pros:** • Develops strong relationship • Provides good feedback **Cons:** • Audit should be independent of other departments and activities • Violates separation of duties (SoD)
IT department	**Pros:** • Most security issues are IT-related • A strong working relationship is important **Cons:** • Lack of independence • Violates SoD
Administrative services department	**Pros:** • Independent of most other departments **Cons:** • Department management may not understand security requirements and needs

Security Reporting Option	Pros and Cons
Insurance and risk management department	**Pros:** • In tune with security needs • Understands risk **Cons:** • May not understand computer security risks
Legal department	**Pros:** • Knows security-related legal requirements **Cons:** • Not usually technically driven • May focus on the legal requirements, not on the risk-reduction aspects in other areas
Corporate security	**Pros:** • Security oriented **Cons:** • Focus may be physical security only • May not understand information security issues

Security Goal Categories

There are three security goal categories designed to address the short-, medium-, and long-term security goals of an organization.

Goal	Description
Strategic	These align with business and information technology goals. They have a long horizon of 3 to 5 years or more, and provide a longer view of the business security activities. Examples could include establishing security policies and ensuring all users understand their security responsibilities.
Tactical	These provide the broad initiatives necessary to support the goals of the strategic plan. These plans are much more specific, may consist of multiple projects, and usually have a 6 to 18 month time period. Examples could include things such as implementing a disaster recovery program or a customer relations management solution.
Operational	These are very specific short-term goals. They are the enactment of the tactical plan. They have milestones and dates, and ensure that individual projects are completed. Examples could include performing a risk assessment for a particular project, developing security policies for that project, training users in those policies, and monitoring compliance.

Control Frameworks

As you begin your security programs, a framework can help provide a foundation to build on. There are dozens that can be evaluated in order to find one that works for your organization. You could even create your own framework if you like.

A *control framework* seeks to minimize risk in an organization by creating a structure for the organization's security controls. Control frameworks are a subset of overall security frameworks and should meet the following criteria:

- Consistent: So security and privacy are handled the same way in similar situations.
- Measurable: So you can set goals and measure progress towards those goals.
- Standardized: So that results in one part of the organization can be compared to others.
- Comprehensive: So that it covers the minimum legal and regulatory requirements and can be extended to any organization-specific needs.
- Modular: So that you can withstand changes to the organization by only changing the controls or requirements necessary to adapt to the change.

Examples

The United States National Institute of Standards and Technology (NIST) SP 800-53r4 is a control framework of 285 controls in 19 families used by federal agencies and their contractors.

The International Standard Organization (ISO) 27001:2013 is a control framework designed to cover organizations of all sizes and types.

Due Care and Due Diligence

The legal concept of *due care* establishes the generally recognized expectations of behavior that companies or entities in a given industry must adhere to when performing normal business functions. Essentially, it is the legal definition for acting responsibly or doing what a reasonable person would do under the circumstances, also known as the prudent person or reasonable person rule. In other words, you have done all you can for security that is reasonable. You perform the legal duty. An example of due care would be to provide appropriate security training for all employees, to verify that the training was effective, and to refresh it periodically as appropriate.

If you do not provide due care, it is usually called negligence. In most countries, that is an actionable legal offense. In the United States, if a company does not provide due care, the C-level officers are personally liable.

Liability is a legal responsibility for any damage caused by one individual or company to another. Organizations must protect themselves from legal liability by complying with applicable laws and regulations, by following the prudent person rule when making decisions, and by exercising due diligence.

Due diligence is the research necessary for good decision making regarding preventive measures to avoid harm to other entities or their property. If performed properly, due diligence is the assessment and management of risk that leads to due care. Some examples of due diligence include:

- Background checks on employees.
- Risk assessments of physical security systems.
- Testing of backup services.

Liability and Due Diligence

A company that wants to acquire another company must use due diligence to prove that they looked into the company's financial and business status to ensure action in the interest of protecting their shareholders. If the company's stock fell after the acquisition and shareholders could demonstrate that the company had not performed proper due diligence prior to the purchase, it is possible that the shareholders could successfully sue for financial damages in civil court. In the computer realm, a company might be held liable for an employee's loss of personal information if the company cannot demonstrate that it practiced due care while responding to a security breach.

Guidelines for Applying Security Governance Principles

 Note: All of the Guidelines for this lesson are available as checklists from the **Checklist** tile on the CHOICE Course screen.

Use the following guidelines when establishing security governance in your organization.

- Always consider the principles of the CIA triad when securing your information and other assets.
- Attempt to balance your need for availability with your need for confidentiality and integrity.
- Establish a clear chain of governance in your organization, from top-level management to regular staff.
- Consider that security and business operations must align in order to be completely effective.
- Make sure that decision makers understand that security is not an after-thought, but a major part of doing business.
- Ensure that security is incorporated into major business processes like mergers, acquisitions, and divestitures.
- Ensure that each job role is clearly defined and positioned relative to security as a whole, as well as including each role's own security responsibilities.
- Establish the roles and responsibilities of a CISO, as this is usually the main representative of security in the organization.
- Be able communicate your security concerns to the organization's decision markers in a clear, understandable way.
- Be able to listen to the concerns and advice of others, whether management or staff, to stay aware of your organization's security climate.
- Establish a security reporting structure that makes the most sense for your organization.
- Create or adopt a security control framework to build your security mitigation efforts on.
- Always exercise due care and due diligence, and make sure that your employees do the same.

ACTIVITY 1-1
Discussing Security Governance Principles

Scenario

The Case of the Medium-Sized Training Company: Part 1

You are a security consultant working for a publicly traded medium-sized training company. Until recently, the company did not focus on the need for information security. Recently, some laptops containing proprietary information were stolen from unlocked offices, and some sensitive business information was posted on Twitter and Facebook.

After attending a business and technology seminar, the CEO announced that the organization would include information security in its daily operations. The CEO has instructed you to form a small information security group made up of tech-savvy users from the Financial Controller's office. Your group is instructed to immediately install a firewall on the company network. The Financial Controller, however, does not wish to spend the money for the firewall that you recommend, and tells you to look for a lower-cost alternative.

The next day you receive an email from the CIO of the company. The email is addressed to all employees, requesting that everyone visit the company's intranet portal, and read and comply with the corporate security policy posted there. You go to the portal to read the policy. It is a short document with generic recommendations. There's nothing in the document specific to the company you work for. You suspect the policy was copied from an online template.

After reading the policy, you look over at the receptionist and asked her if she has followed the instructions in the CIO's email. She responds by giving you a blank look and asks "What email?" You ask other employees about the email, and receive similar responses.

1. Do you think that the CIO has performed due care and due diligence in sending an organization-wide email requiring all employees to comply with the new security policy? Why or why not?

2. Based on the scenario, what gaps in the company's security governance would you immediately focus on?

TOPIC B

Compliance

A major concern of any business will be its ability to comply with the law or other established standards. In this topic, you'll look at some of the main issues of aligning the business with certain legal and industry expectations, and how you must put your due care and due diligence into action.

Compliance

Compliance refers to the awareness of and adherence to relevant laws and regulations that are set forth by and apply to a particular corporation, public agency, or organizational entity. Compliance may also refer to adherence to internal policies and requirements, but these are typically subordinate to legal compliance.

Compliance requirements evolve with the legal landscape. With the recent downfall of large corporations in the U.S., certain laws place an organization's burden of compliance at the top tier of management. Security professionals, on the other hand, are often not fully versed in compliance requirements. They should consult with legal department heads and representatives to determine if any new requirements exist and then determine the right course of action to properly comply with the changes.

Legislative and Regulatory Compliance

An organization needs to operate within the law to be considered in legislative and regulatory compliance. This requires that security professionals understand the laws and regulations of the industry or country they are in. Part of your governance and risk management needs to take these requirements into account. Regulations will list specific conditions that must be met. They might also specify what is a safe harbor (good faith) condition, a specific practice or action that is deemed not to be in violation of the law. These safe harbors can protect the organization from any penalties from a new law or regulation.

You can best remain in compliance by making sure that your organization's policies, procedures, standards, and guidelines are consistent with any laws or regulations within your industry, state, or country.

Privacy Issues

Personally Identifiable Information (PII) is a hot topic in security today. PII is any information that potentially could identify a single person. A short study of the history of epidemiology and public health policy will show that it only takes two pieces of information to be able to identify a person. Most people, including policymakers and security professionals, do not realize this. A clever person can quickly extrapolate the identity of someone through two seemingly unrelated pieces of information. It can leave that person vulnerable to attack by unscrupulous parties attempting to gain from that knowledge. A criminal could attempt to extort money from a person in exchange for silence. A campaigning politician could expose his opponent's current health or financial condition to influence public opinion about the opponent's fitness for office.

Examples of PII include, but are not limited to:

- Name, including maiden name, mother's maiden name, or alias.
- Social Security number, passport number, driver's license number, tax for identification number, financial account, or credit card number.
- Address.

- Personal characteristics including photographs, fingerprints, handwriting, or other biometric information such as retina scan, voice print, and facial geometry.

Because it can take so little to identify a person, it becomes very difficult to completely de-identify information to protect an individual's privacy. By the time you have sanitized the data to where it is not possible to identify the subjects, the data is usually no longer useful from a business perspective.

Personal privacy concerns are exacerbated by the fact that it is so easy to access information online. Of particular concern is the fact that PII has become extremely valuable for marketers. Social networking sites and consumer activities are analyzed, and then marketing campaigns are targeted at specific demographics.

U.S. Information Privacy Law

Information privacy law protects the information of private individuals from malicious disclosure or unintentional misuse. With the increased ability to collect and store personally identifying information (PII) there has grown a need to try to protect this data.

 Note: Privacy laws are becoming more common around the world and it will be important for the CISSP candidate to be familiar with some of the more common privacy laws. Privacy laws are a mixture of state common law, federal and state statutes, and constitutional law.

Information Privacy Law Act	Description
Privacy Act of 1974	The *Privacy Act of 1974* was mandated in response to the abuse of privacy during the Nixon administration. It protects the privacy of individual information held by the U.S. government. It applies to all personal information, provides for restrictions on individual access, and enforces penalties for unauthorized disclosure.
FERPA	The *Family Educational Rights and Privacy Act (FERPA)* was passed in the same session of Congress as the Privacy Act of 1974. This law protects the privacy of educational information held in any federally funded institution of higher learning. After FERPA was passed, the practice of mailing grade reports from a university or college to a student's parents was prohibited.
ECPA	The *Electronic Communications Privacy Act (ECPA)* of 1986 made it a crime to snoop into employee activities while using electronic communications devices unless the employees were notified in advance that the monitoring might take place. It also enforced the requirement for legal authorization of wiretaps and other government monitoring practices.
HIPAA	The *Health Insurance Portability and Accountability Act (HIPAA)* of 1996 was originally intended to protect people with health insurance when they transferred from one company to another. In 2003, legislation was written to modify HIPAA and add a privacy component. The privacy component now protects a class of information called Protected Health Information (PHI). PHI is any information that can identify a particular patient and includes a patient's medical record or payment history.
GLBA	The *Gramm-Leach-Bliley Act (GLBA)* of 1999 protects the privacy of an individual's financial information that is held by financial institutions and others such as tax preparation companies. A privacy standard was set and rules were created to safeguard the information and provide penalties in the event of a violation.

Information Privacy Law Act	Description
COPPA	The *Children's Online Privacy Protection Act (COPPA)* of 1998 was written to protect the online privacy of children. Restrictions provided by COPPA included the right to opt out of any information sent by a provider, to limit the amount and type of information collected from children, and to require parental consent for any information provided to children. COPPA implementation, however, has no real way of controlling childrens' access because there is no true method of identifying any user consistently when accessing the Internet.
USA PATRIOT Act	In response to the attacks of September 11, 2001, U.S. Congress passed the *Uniting and Strengthening America by Providing Appropriate Tools Required to Intercept and Obstruct Terrorism (PATRIOT) Act* of 2001. This legislation increased the governmental ability to wiretap and control financial transactions used to fund terrorism. From an information security perspective, the government could collect information from the Internet using a blanket subpoena.
SOX Act	After the accounting scandals and the failures of many large companies in the early 2000s, the *Sarbanes-Oxley (SOX or Sarbox) Act of 2002* was passed to help control how corporations report about and audit themselves. One of the major record-keeping requirements of SOX is the need to keep long-term email, voicemail, and instant messaging records in corporations.
FCRA	The Fair Credit Reporting Act (FCRA) provides consumers with the ability to view, correct, contest, and limit the use of their information in a credit report.
Federal Sentencing Guidelines	Enacted by the United States Sentencing Commission in 1991. Encourages American companies to create ethics and compliance programs. Highlights include that the organization shall: • Exercise due diligence to prevent and detect criminal conduct. • Establish standards and procedures to prevent and detect criminal conduct. • Hold the organization's high-level officers accountable for instituting an effective compliance and ethics program. • Conduct effective training programs, including refresher training, appropriate to individuals' respective roles and responsibilities. • Periodically evaluate the effectiveness of the organization's compliance and ethics program.
FISMA	The Federal Information Security Management Act of 2002 (FISMA) requires federal agencies to develop, document, and implement an agency-wide information security program.
Cyber Security Enhancement Act	Part of the Homeland Security Act of 2002. Used to access and analyze law enforcement and intelligence information from government agencies to fight terrorism.
ESIGN	The Electronic Signatures in Global and National Commerce Act (ESIGN) was enacted by the U.S. Congress in 2000 to facilitate the use of electronic signatures and electronic records in both domestic (interstate) and foreign commerce.

Information Privacy Law Act	Description
DMCA	U.S. Digital Millennium Copyright Act (DMCA) enacts two 1996 World Intellectual Property Organization treaties. Criminalizes attempts to circumvent, or dissemination of technologies that can circumvent, digital rights management of copyrighted works.
Economic Espionage Act of 1996	Makes theft of trade secrets and economic espionage a federal crime.

International Privacy Law

There are a number of international or non-U.S. information privacy regulations and laws that the security practitioner must be aware of. While it may not be obvious, your organization could be subject to these laws depending on who it serves and where its offices and customers reside.

For example, in the European Union, the European Data Protection Directive permits processing personal data only under the following conditions:

- When processing is necessary for compliance and legal action.
- When processing is required to protect someone's life.
- When the person has provided consent.
- When the processing is within the law and scope of public interest.

> **Note:** The principle EU publication covering privacy, known as Directive 95/46/EC, can be found at **www.cdt.org/privacy/eudirective/EU_Directive_.html**.

These conditions don't necessarily align with U.S.-based privacy laws, even if the differences are subtle. As many organizations do business in countries all over the world, they must be mindful of the ways in which laws and regulations diverge. What may be legal in the U.S. is not necessarily legal or accepted in another country. Some frameworks have been established to help organizations more easily transition their business operations to comply with foreign laws and regulations. For example, the US-EU Safe Harbor Protection Framework gives U.S. companies a way to comply with European privacy laws. The important thing is to be mindful of all of the jurisdictions your operations are subject to, and to exercise due diligence in researching the different requirements of these jurisdictions.

Computer Crime

A *computer crime* is a criminal act that involves using a computer as the source or target, instead of an individual. It can involve stealing restricted information by hacking into a system, compromising national security, perpetrating fraud, conducting illegal activity, or spreading malicious code. It may be committed via the Internet or a private network.

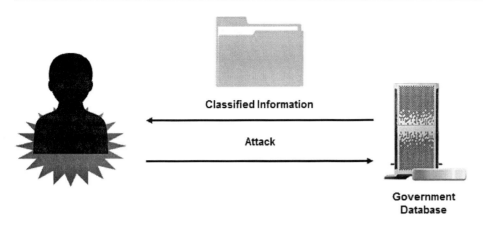

Figure 1-3: A computer crime.

Traditionally, examples of typical computer crimes have included unauthorized access to a computer or network, distributing illegal information via a computer network, and stealing classified information stored on a computer. Social engineering attacks, if they involve illegal activity, can be categorized as computer crimes.

 Note: For specific examples of modern computer crimes, consult pages 41-43 of the (ISC)² Common Body of Knowledge (CBK), Fourth Edition.

Computer Crime, Liability, and the Prudent Person Rule

Successful computer crimes may exist in areas where adequate security protections, as determined by the prudent person standard, are not in use. For example, in a high-crime area, a prudent person would ensure that doors and windows are secure before leaving home, otherwise a computer might be stolen. A prudent person would also use virus protection and firewall protection on a computer attached to the Internet.

In cases where crimes are committed and the prudent person rule is not employed, a liability may arise. For example, when magnetic tapes are transported and stolen, it is commonly known that the contained information has been leaked to the public. A prudent person would encrypt the data on the magnetic tape to protect it. If the data is not encrypted, therefore releasing personal information, the holder of the information is liable for any damages incurred to those individuals affected by the leak.

Although the concept of liability does not weigh on the facts of a crime and associated legal procedures, it does weigh on the impact to the organization when a crime is committed. Therefore, it necessary to exercise due care by complying with laws and regulations that guard against computer crimes. Likewise, you should exercise your own judgment and imagine how someone may commit a crime against your organization; this way, you can think of ways to reduce the risk of the crime succeeding, and thus avoiding liability.

U.S. Computer Crime Law

Early on, the U.S. government's main focus of protection was the area of privacy. Eventually, the use of online systems and the advent of the hacker led to computer crime law legislation.

Computer Crime Law Act	Description
CFAA	The *Computer Fraud and Abuse Act (CFAA)* of 1984 was passed to protect government systems from illegal access or from exceeding access permissions. It was amended in 1994, in 1996, and in 2001. The amendments evolved from new concerns that had developed over the intervening time period and extended coverage to new types of attacks. Final coverage addresses computers in interstate commerce. Activities that are prohibited include retrieving information without authorization, trafficking passwords, sending viruses or worms to infect computers, and so on.
CSA	The *Computer Security Act (CSA)* of 1987 was enacted when the federal legislature recognized that the government was not doing enough to protect computer systems. Key requirements of CSA were to fulfill training needs and plan developments for information and systems security. CSA was replaced by FISMA.
NIIPA	As threats to computer security expanded, the passage of the *National Information Infrastructure Protection Act (NIIPA)* in 1996 targeted some of these new threats, creating legal remedies for hacking, stealing trade secrets, and damaging systems and information. In particular, it targeted Internet infrastructure security.
FISMA	The *Federal Information Security Management Act (FISMA)* of 2002 was passed to remedy the evolutionary nature of information systems security in the federal government. Some of the act's key provisions require organizations to: • Define the boundaries of a system to be protected and then identify the types of information found within that system. • Document system information and perform a risk assessment to identify areas requiring additional protection. • Protect systems using an identified set of controls and certify systems before use. An operating approval is issued upon certification. • Continuously monitor systems for proper operation.

Federal Sentencing Guidelines

Violators of the acts protecting government information systems are subject to federal sentencing guidelines set forth by the U.S. Sentencing Commission. These guidelines specify recommended sentences. Rather than allow individual judges to set sentences for these types of crimes, specific sentence limits are provided to the judge. Additionally, the sentencing guidelines mandate that criminals have an opportunity to be informed of the risks involved in crimes against federal systems. Ignorance of the law is not a valid excuse, and if the organization fails to perform its due diligence, the Board of Directors and C-level management may be held liable.

The federal sentencing guidelines can be seen in full-text form at **www.ussc.gov**.

Data Breaches

A *data breach* is an incident that results in the release or potential exposure of secure information. Security professionals need to stay informed of the kinds of data breaches that are being faced by organizations around the globe so that they can be prepared to protect against or respond quickly to similar attacks.

Aside from harming an organization directly, data breaches are often the true test of an organization's legal compliance. It may be impractical to prevent 100% of breaches from occurring, but if the organization has done its due care to comply with laws and regulations, the breach's effects may be mitigated and the organization may avoid severe legal penalties. This is especially true when it comes to privacy laws, as the most high-profile breaches today have exposed customer PII for millions of people. If the company stores medical records, for example, and they are fully

HIPAA compliant, a breach may not actually reveal sensitive patient information. The company can therefore demonstrate it is operating within the law.

Consider the major effect that breaches have with respect to compliance failures. Although a routine audit that detects a compliance failure may spell trouble for the company, this will pale in comparison to the trouble that will visit the company should a breach be what exposes their compliance failures. The consequences are much more devastating in these situations, and the company may not be able to fully recover from them.

Data Breach Resources

There are several helpful resources that monitor data breaches:

*   www.databreachtoday.com/news
*   www.informationisbeautiful.net/visualizations/worlds-biggest-data-breaches-hacks
*   www.scmagazine.com/the-data-breach-blog/section/1263
*   http://vcdb.org

Licensing and Intellectual Property

Intellectual property law protects the rights of ownership of ideas through trademarks, patents, and copyrights, including the owners' right to transfer intellectual property (IP) and receive compensation for the transfer. It's important for security professionals to understand the various intellectual property laws for two main reasons. First, the company may end up using third-party intellectual property, like software, so it must know how it is legally able to work with this property. Essentially, the organization must comply with IP laws for any relevant IP it incorporates into business operations. The other reason is that the organization will likely have its own IP that needs protecting, and knowing how to fit its IP into the relevant laws will lend it greater legal support in case its licenses are violated.

The following table lists the various IP laws.

Intellectual Property Law	Description
Patent	A *patent* is a legal protection provided to unique inventions. The patent protects the item's creator from competition for a given period of time. Patent protection is considered to be very strong, but at the same time, it is the responsibility of patent owners to protect their patents. In the United States, patents must be filed within one year of the first production of the patented item. Patents last for 20 years in the United States. Once the patent has expired, the patent enters the public domain.
Trademark	A *trademark* is a design or phrase used to identify unique products or services. In the U.S., a trademark lasts for 10 years and may be renewed for an additional 10-year period by filing an affidavit of use. Coca Cola® is a registered trademark along with its traditional bottle shape. The ® is a registered trademark while ™ is an unregistered trademark.
Copyright	A *copyright* protects an original artistic work, such as one by an author or musician. Copyright protection is not as strong as patent protection but the length of protection is much greater. The lifetime of the copyright varies. Normal copyrights exist for 70 years past the death of the creator. Those items copyrighted by corporations, or where the identity of the original author is hidden, last for 95 years after publication, or 120 years after the first use, whichever comes first.

Intellectual Property Law	Description
Trade secret	A *trade secret* is an item that requires protection that, if lost, would severely damage the business. In order to be provided legal protection, the trade secret must be properly secured and protected. The formula for the spices used by a fried chicken company might be considered a trade secret. It is the responsibility of the organization to protect their own trade secrets. Non-disclosure agreements are a common method to enforce a trade secret.
Licensing	To use a creator's protected materials, users are generally required to obtain *licensing*. Software manufacturers protect their products by mandating and issuing licensed copies for consumer purchase. Violating the licensing provision may result in civil or criminal charges.

International Protection through WIPO

In other parts of the world, intellectual property protection is provided by general principle agreements among various countries and controlled through the World Intellectual Property Organization (WIPO). WIPO is a specialized organization under the United Nations.

International protection of intellectual property varies due to different legal systems and interpretation of laws in those jurisdictions. For example, under WIPO, a patent must be obtained before the patented product is used in commerce. There is no one-year grace period as found in the U.S. The general principle concerns first to file rather than first to invent.

For more information on WIPO, visit **www.wipo.int**.

Trans-Border Data Flow

The global economy of the 21st century is driven by the flow of information across national borders. You can have access to the best technology and services, no matter where in the world they are located. But as data flows from one place to another, it causes problems in terms of understanding how privacy can be protected and what regulations should apply. It's also not just privacy that can impact the flow of data across borders. Organizations may transmit other sensitive business data to sites or partners that cross national borders. Like with international law, trans-border data flow raises issues of how and when a company should comply with certain laws, regulations, and industry standards.

The Organization for Economic Cooperation and Development (OECD) is an international organization that has proposed some guidelines for the protection of privacy and the trans-border flow of PII. The core principles are:

- The amount of personal data collected should be limited and obtained legally with the knowledge and consent of the individual.
- Personal data is relevant to the intended purpose and should be kept up to date.
- Individuals should be notified of the reason the PII is needed at the time that it is collected and it should be used only for those purposes.
- PII should not be shared with any other entity or used for a different reason than it was originally collected unless the individual gives consent or the law demands it.
- Personal data should be protected with reasonable security safeguards against loss, unauthorized access, destruction. modification, or release.
- Developments, practices, and policies regarding personal data should be transparently communicated.
- Every individual should have the right:
  - To obtain confirmation an organization has their personal information.
  - To obtain the details of the collected data within a reasonable time, without an excessive cost, and in a form that is easily understandable.

- To be informed why a request for information was denied and the right to challenge the validity of the denial.
- To challenge the accuracy of personal data and have it corrected.

Import and Export Controls

There are limits to the level of technology that can be exported from country to country. When you do business across borders, especially when importing and exporting goods and services, you need to make sure you're in compliance with these limitations.

Security professionals should be aware of three regulations:

- *International Traffic in Arms Regulations (ITAR)*, which defined defense articles and defense services with stipulations for their import and export.
- *Export Administration Regulations (EAR)*, which allowed the President to regulate export of civilian goods and services
- The *Wassenaar Arrangement*, which was established to promote greater transparency in the transfer of weapons, technologies, and other goods.

Security professionals in all companies but particularly those that work in defense or aerospace should consult with legal counsel if they have questions or concerns about products being imported or exported.

Industry Standards

Not everything you need to consider complying with is a government mandated law or regulation. Industries have their own standards for how organizations should operate. There may not be legal consequences for failing to adhere to these standards, but a business can still suffer if it does not comply with what its industry has reached a consensus on. For example, other organizations may refuse to do business with you if you don't agree to comply with standards set by the industry.

The following table lists some of the major technological standards that are relevant to security.

IT/Information Security Standard	Description
Payment Card Industry Data Security Standard (PCI DSS)	A proprietary standard that specifies how organizations should handle information security for major card brands that include Visa, MasterCard, American Express, Discover, and JCB, all of which provide a mandate for the standard. The standard is intended to increase controls on cardholder data to reduce fraudulent use of accounts. Compliance is validated on an annual basis.
	Organizations or merchants that accept, transmit, or store cardholder data (regardless of size or number of transactions) from these brands must comply with this standard. Although not technically a federal law, organizations located in Nevada are compelled to follow PCI DSS by state law.

IT/Information Security Standard	Description
National Institute of Standards and Technology Special Publication 800 series (NIST SP 800 series)	Various publications that focus on establishing standards and models for many facets of computer security. Some publications of note include: • SP 800-12: *An Introduction to Computer Security: The NIST Handbook* • SP 800-14: *Generally Accepted Principles and Practices for Securing Information Technology Systems* • SP 800-33: *Underlying Technical Models for Information Technology Security* • SP 800-53: *Security and Privacy Controls in Federal Information Systems and Organizations*
Control Objectives for Information and Related Technology 5 (COBIT 5)	Provides a set of standards for IT management and governance. COBIT 5 promotes the following five principles: • Meeting stakeholder needs. • Covering the enterprise end-to-end. • Applying a single, integrated framework. • Enabling a holistic approach. • Separating governance from management.
ISO/IEC 27001	A joint effort by the International Organization for Standardization (ISO) and the International Electrotechnical Commission (IEC), this standard focused on information security management. The ISO/IEC 27001 covers the following topics: • Responsibilities and procedures. • Reporting information security events. • Reporting information security weaknesses. • Assessment of and decision on information security events. • Response to information security incidents. • Learning from information security incidents. • Collection of evidence.

Guidelines for Supporting Compliance

Use the following guidelines to properly comply with any laws, regulations, and standards your organization may be subject to.

• Perform due diligence by researching legal jurisdiction and industry standards that are applicable to your organization.
• Consult with the organization's legal department to get a better idea of how the laws may impact your security operations.
• Ensure that your policies and other documentation are consistent with applicable laws and regulations.
• Identify any ways in which your organization works with customer and employee PII.
• Stay current on the details of the privacy laws that are applicable to your organization, especially HIPAA, SOX, and GLBA.
• Understand that privacy laws differ based on the country in which they are based.
• Stay current on the details of the computer crime laws that are applicable to your organization, especially FISMA.
• Consider how a breach could expose your organization's compliance failures and the impact that would have on liability.

- Understand the intellectual privacy laws that govern your use of third party content services.
- Understand how these IP laws apply to your own content and services.
- Become acquainted with any import/export laws that affect your ability to move goods and services across borders.
- Research industry standards that your organization is affected by, and consider how failing to comply with them could harm your business operations.

ACTIVITY 1-2
Discussing Compliance

Scenario

The Case of the Medium-Sized Training Company: Part 2

It has been two weeks since the CIO sent out the security policy email to all employees. Since then, you have been randomly asking staff members questions to test their understanding of the company's security policy. Employees have paid little heed to the email, and don't seem to have any understanding of their role in the company's security efforts.

The CFO, concerned about allegations of potential misconduct by some of the supervisors, would like to search for evidence to confirm or deny the suspicions. He has asked you to help him access and read the supervisors' company email.

The company is also being audited by an outside firm. When the auditors request to see financial records, including relevant emails, they are informed that the company does not keep emails past 90 days, and that the records have been deleted as a matter of course during routine maintenance.

Additionally, the enrollment officer has just reported that her laptop was stolen while she was traveling out of the country. It contained financial details of all the students, including international students from other countries.

1. What compliance issues does the training company have?

2. How can you help the organization stay in compliance with regulations?

TOPIC C

Professional Ethics

In this topic, you'll explore the ethics that govern your behavior as a security professional, especially those that every CISSP must agree to follow.

The Purpose of Ethics

Ethics in a profession or an organization refers to the principles of acceptable and proper conduct as well as a system of moral values.

A code of ethics is essentially a contract between professionals that helps them cooperate and pursue their common ideals and goals. There is often pressure to behave differently than other professionals in a competitive environment, but the code helps protect against any unscrupulous behavior that could result from this pressure. It provides a guide for knowing what other security professionals will do so that they can better interact and work towards their common goals.

Organizational Ethics

When companies or governments adopt ethical codes, they often opt to document expectations for professional conduct and define responsibility standards. In doing so, determining and managing ethical behavior on an as-needed basis is less difficult. A company may also be bound to certain ethical standards by the regulatory requirements surrounding it, such as the Sarbanes-Oxley (SOX) or Payment Card Industry (PCI) standard.

Ethical code enforcement also helps regulate security by minimizing risk. Hiring and sustaining employees with high levels of ethical behavior provides valuable safeguards for reducing or potentially eliminating man-made disasters and threats.

Additionally, organizations have a responsibility to their employees, customers, suppliers, and stakeholders to operate in an ethical manner. Therefore, organizational ethics are the foundation of honorable, accountable, and reliable performance.

Regulatory Requirements for Ethics Programs

Many different types of organizations implement ethics programs. Both the American Medical Association (AMA) and the U.S. federal government are institutions that commonly enforce codes of ethical conduct. If your organization is part of these institutions or does business with them, their ethics rules could apply. You need to be aware of the codes that pertain to your organization.

Federal laws and regulations such as the Sarbanes-Oxley (SOX) Act, the Health Insurance Portability and Accountability Act (HIPAA), and the Gramm-Leach-Bliley Act (GLBA) require the adoption of ethical standards within organizations and often require an annual briefing on ethical requirements.

CSEP Policies

The Center for the Study of Ethics in the Professions (CSEP) at the Illinois Institute of Technology maintains a compiled, online catalog of approximately 1,000 codes of ethics. CSEP has collected these codes from government agencies, businesses, professional organizations and foundations, and various other enterprises and establishments.

For more information on CSEP's ethical policies, visit **http://ethics.iit.edu/ecodes/**.

Ethics Issues in a Computing Environment

The conversation on ethics can become somewhat confused by the concept of computer ethics. Remember that much of this revolves around people and processes, and the ethical concerns involved go beyond computers. The fact that a computer grants users access to a tremendous amount of information, but can seemingly also provide anonymity, can raise issues. Computer ethics are really a subset of business ethics.

Some ethical concerns are organizational in nature. For example, a company can effectively track an employee from the moment they arrive in the building until they leave at the end of the day. Systems can track usage, emails, telephone conversations, and more. It is important that employers and employees understand what is being monitored.

Other computer ethics concerns are more individual. Users that believed they could send an email anonymously because they could change the "From" address to a different user's account or perhaps even an account called "anonymous" might find out later that the employer can still trace the email back to their PC based on the IP address in the email header.

Common Computer Ethics Fallacies

As a security professional, it may help you to defend against hackers and other information security criminals if you recognize that they often consider their motivations to be neither illicit nor unethical.

Ethics Fallacy	Motivation Factor
Free information	The criminal feels the information is yearning to be free and they want to help it escape.
Computer game	The criminal feels the computer is like a game; when the criminal plays the game, they can't attain the next level if they haven't achieved the objective of the preceding level. Therefore, if the computer lets them do something, it must be okay.
Taking candy from a baby	Because it is so easy to make a copy of a file and to leave the original intact, it must be okay, so the criminal does not question about whether it is ethical.
Shatterproof	If the criminal only handles a few files, it will do minimal harm. This does not consider the larger impact of the action on those few files.
The ends justify the means	If the criminal feels that he or she is learning from this to help him or herself and society, it is unlikely a wrongful act.
Law-abiding citizen fallacy	Sometimes users believe because their actions are legal, they don't have to consider the consequences of their actions.

Internet Architecture Board Ethics

The Internet Architecture Board (IAB) views the Internet as a resource that is most valuable when its users are not performing certain actions to compromise its availability and accessibility. Therefore, IAB ethics primarily focus on unethical activities to avoid rather than ethical actions to encourage. Actions to avoid include:

• Seeking to gain unauthorized access to Internet resources.
• Disrupting intended Internet use.
• Wasting resources such as people, capacity, and computers through unprincipled actions.
• Destroying the integrity of computer-based information.
• Compromising user privacy.

Note: IAB ethics policies can be found in RFC 1087.

Ethical Minefields for Security Professionals

While one might hope that the path for ethical behavior is always clear, the reality is that often there will be circumstances that take the security professional into an ethical gray area.

Ethical minefields that security professionals will run into usually involve circumstances where there seems to be no other choice to accomplish something for the greater good. These can include:

- A legitimate need for expediency that requires the temporary suspension of proper security practice.
- The inability to find a licensed software application required for a one time purpose.
- A direct order by a supervisor or superior officer to shortcut ethics to accomplish something critical.

(ISC)² maintains that adherence to its Code of Ethics is a condition of certification. Whenever you are in doubt, remember to refer to the requirements:

- Protect society, the common good, necessary public trust and confidence, and the infrastructure.
- Act honorably, honestly, justly, responsibly, and legally.
- Provide diligent and competent service to principals.
- Advance and protect the profession.

If you ever find that you have inadvertently strayed outside the boundary of ethical behavior, be sure to immediately get back within bounds, repair any damage you might have caused, and report the breach to your supervisor or appropriate authority.

(ISC)² Code of Ethics

Before taking the CISSP® exam, the International Information Systems Security Certification Consortium (ISC)²® requires each candidate to subscribe to a mandatory Code of Ethics. Since it is a requirement, testing on this subject is likely.

Ethical Code	Goals
Preamble	The (ISC)² Code of Ethics preamble includes: • Ensuring the safety of the commonwealth and the responsibility and accountability to principals, (ISC)² committee members, and other CISSP professionals. • Requiring and acknowledging adherence to the utmost ethical values and standards of behavior. • Strictly observing this code to demonstrate compliance and fulfill the conditions of certification.
Canons	The (ISC)² Code of Ethics canons include: • Guarding the commonwealth, the infrastructure, and society. • Behaving responsibly, justly, honestly, honorably, and legally. • Providing adept, competent, and assiduous service to principals. • Improving, enhancing, and protecting the profession.

Note: A CISSP is expected to act in an ethical manner in support of employers, clients, and the computer community in general. Failure to act in an ethical manner can result in the revocation of your CISSP certification.

Additional Canon Guidance

Additional guidelines are addressed and provided for each of the four canons. Although this guidance may seem mandatory, it is merely a collection of advisory principles for ethical conduct. These guidelines are designed to help professionals assertively identify and resolve inevitable ethical conflicts and dilemmas throughout their information security careers.

For more information on the (ISC)^2 Code of Ethics, visit **www.isc2.org/InnerPage.aspx? id=558&=code+of+ethics**.

Guidelines for Upholding Professional Ethics in Security

Use the following guidelines to support an ethical career as a security professional:

- Follow a code of ethics, either external or self-imposed, in every facet of your security career.
- Document any organization-specific ethical provisions and provide this documentation to the relevant employees and customers.
- Enforce ethical codes mandated by applicable laws and industry regulations, including SOX, HIPAA, GLBA, and PCI.
- Use ethical codes to minimize risk by hiring and maintaining employees with a strong ethical background.
- Have a code of ethics for how the organization treats its employees, customers, and other stakeholders.
- Consider the unique ethical challenges posed by computers and other modern technology.
- Make sure your employees are aware of these computer-specific ethical concerns.
- Understand the fallacies that others may employ to justify attacks and other malicious behavior.
- Consult the Internet Architecture Board of Ethics (IAB) and its provisions for what actions to avoid.
- Closely study the (ISC)^2 Code of Ethics and understand that you must, at all times, adhere to this code.

ACTIVITY 1-3
Discussing Professional Ethics in Security

Scenario
The Case of the Overseas College: Part 1

You are an IT security consultant working overseas. The board of directors of a local college has just awarded you a contract to help establish IT security governance at the school. You were one of several vendors considered for the contract. A rival vendor is a good friend of the college president. The president expected to be able to award the contract to his friend, and he is disappointed that the board overrode his choice and awarded the contract to you. He is openly suspicious of your professional abilities, and regularly voices his disapproval of you—a foreigner—as a choice of vendor. At a recent meeting, he has suggested that you should not be the administrator of the college database, which includes all of the organization's financial information.

The college just received a donation of good used computers, and the small IT team is busy installing them in the library. The librarian asks if you have a copy of an AutoCAD program that can be installed on the computers for the engineering students to work on their assignments. One of the technicians recalls that her boyfriend has a copy he downloaded from the Internet and suggests that they install a copy of that software on the library computers.

---

1. How should you answer the technician's suggestion of using the downloaded software in the library?

2. How should you address the president's concern about you having administrative access to the college financial database?

3. From what you can see in the scenario, what are the larger information security issues, and how might you help the college address them?

TOPIC D

Security Documentation

Your security documentation will be the foundation on which your operations run. In this topic, you'll examine the various types of documents and how they support your efforts to keep the organization safe.

The Value of Security Documentation

Imagine an organization without any security documentation. Every individual would have to make decisions based on their own personal value system and past experiences. This kind of wild-west environment would lead to organizational chaos. Security documentation helps provide a common framework for people to work together to meet the organization's mission. It also acts as a road map to governance by providing management and other governance personnel with an official outline for how to conduct business in the most optimal way possible, especially when it comes to minimizing risk.

Security Document Types

There are generally five different documents that help define the security environment of an organization.

Security Document Type	Description
Policies	A *policy* is a document with a high-level statement of management intentions. Policies do not get into specifics, but leave that for procedures, standards, and guidelines. A policy should contain the purpose, scope, and compliance expected of the employee.
	Example: Information security will ensure the protection of information by implementing security best practices.
Standards	A *standard* describes a required implementation or use of tools. Standards help to define the requirements of a policy and can be more technical in nature.
	Example: The corporation *must* implement 802.1x security for all wireless networks.
Guidelines	A *guideline* is a recommendation or suggested action, implementation, or use of tools that is considered a best practice for meeting the policy standard.
	Example: When travelling with laptops, users *should* use safety precautions to prevent laptop theft, damage, or data loss.
Procedures	A *procedure* is an implementation document that describes the steps taken to complete an activity. Procedures help maintain compliance of policies and standards.
	Example: To implement Secure Shell (SSH) on the router, enter the **enable** mode and then enter the appropriate commands for the router.

Security Document Type	Description
Baselines	A *baseline* is a security document that specifies the minimum security required in a system or process. Security may be stronger than what is required in the baseline, but deviations to reduce security levels below the baseline require management approval. Auditing can help ensure that baselines are being met. Example: Trivial File Transfer Protocol (TFTP) must be disabled in all servers except for those specifically used for the TFTP service.

 Note: These document types are not restricted to security but are used throughout the organization to define the purpose and process of various company activities.

Guidelines vs. Standards

For a guideline to be practical, it often employs the word "should." The guideline provides non-specific guidance in a given area. The previous example relating to laptops states that users *should* employ preventative measures to acceptably safeguard their equipment and system data. This implementation may not actually mandate the use of the guideline specification. However, the guideline's strong suggestion provides input to those who may be unaware of proper laptop security maintenance.

Conversely, standards often use the word "must." For example, when traveling with laptops, users *must* use safety precautions to prevent laptop theft, damage, or data loss.

This statement clearly indicates that laptop security is a system-specific requirement that must be met by everyone while traveling.

Security Planning

Security planning efforts ensure that an organization's advanced preparations comply with security policies.

Security Planning Effort	Description
Strategic planning	*Strategic planning* is a long-range (three- to five-year) planning process that looks at required security activities, focusing on major changes or improvements in the security posture of an organization. Strategic planning must stay aligned to the business objectives. These plans need to be reviewed annually at a minimum, or more frequently if there are major changes to an organization. Mergers and acquisitions, right-sizing, or significant outsourcing could trigger a review. A strategic planning item might include a planned movement to a facial recognition system for authentication in five years when the technology has improved.
Tactical planning	*Tactical planning* is a mid-term planning process that supports strategic planning. Tactical planning might encompass the next six to 18 months, depending on corporate policy. A tactical planning item might be a move to Remote Authentication Dial-In User Service (RADIUS) for all remote and local network access authentication. RADIUS implementation is a major step for any organization and must be well planned to succeed.

Security Planning Effort	Description
Operational and project planning	*Operational and project planning* is a planning process that deals with the near term. Operational planning supports the tactical plans and includes project plans with milestones and completion dates that are communicated regularly. An operational planning item might be to plan for a penetration test in three months.

 Note: Failing to plan for security may increase the risk to corporate information because appropriate methods, tools, and practices may not be implemented in response to potential industry and threat changes.

Security Policy Objectives

Security policies can fulfill multiple objectives for an organization:

- They can inform employees about their security-related duties and responsibilities.
- They can define an organization's security goals.
- They can outline a computer system's security requirements.

The specific objective of a security policy depends on the requirements of the organization. However, all security policies have one objective in common: to disseminate standardized information to ensure that all personnel can fulfill their duties in accordance with the security requirements of the organization. Policies need to be long enough to explain but short enough to be understood. It is important that policies can be read and understood by all employees and that employees know where they can find a policy.

Security Policy Types

Senior management defines information security policies to communicate how information assets within the organization will be protected.

Security Policy Type	Description
Advisory	- Indicate certain types of actions as being more appropriate or effective than others. - Include consequences and reprimands that may be experienced if actions taken are not as indicated. - Are commonly used for indicating how to handle private documentation and money.
Informative	- Provide data to employees on a specified subject. - Include no ramifications. - Are often used as instructional instruments.
Regulatory	- Address industry regulations regarding the conduct of organizations. - Are commonly used for health care and financial organizations.

The Relationship Between Security Document Types

When applying policies, standards, baselines, procedures, and guidelines, the relationships between each of these elements must be considered.

1. The overall document environment is controlled by the policies.

2. As management creates policies, standards and guidelines are prepared to implement them.
3. To put policies and guidelines into action, procedures and baselines are created.

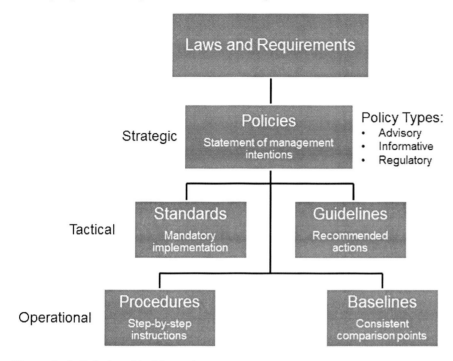

Figure 1–4: Relationship hierarchy.

Guidelines for Drafting Security Documentation

Use the following guidelines to draft effective security documentation:

- Understand how security documentation provides a common framework for everyone to work together to achieve organizational goals.
- Consider security documentation as a road map to good governance.
- Become acquainted with the various document types, and how they are different:
  - **Policies** are a high-level statement of management intentions.
  - **Standards** describe required implementation or use of tools.
  - **Guidelines** recommend or suggest an action or best practice.
  - **Procedures** document a step-by-step activity.
  - **Baselines** specify the minimum level of security for a system or process.
- Plan your security operations using three levels of planning:
  - **Strategic planning** for long-term examination of security processes.
  - **Tactical planning** for mid-term examination of security processes.
  - **Operational and project planning** for examination of security on a per-project basis.
- Meet the following objectives when drafting security policies:
  - Define the organization's security goals.
  - Inform employees about their security-related duties and responsibilities.
  - Outline a computer system's security requirements.
- Consider the relationships between the different document types and how they influence one another.

ACTIVITY 1–4
Discussing Security Documentation

Scenario

The Case of the Overseas College: Part 2

As the IT security consultant for the overseas college, you need to create some recommendations for implementing security documentation at the college.

1. What issues at the college would a security policy address?

2. How can each of the security document types help the college?

3. In what way would each document type inform (drive) the other document types?

4. How can the problem of using illegitimate software be addressed in strategic planning? In tactical planning? In operational planning?

TOPIC E

Risk Management

As your security program takes shape, one of the final steps in successful security management is analyzing and mitigating risk. Since information security risks can adversely affect an organization's business goals and technical stability, it is essential to have a structured, proactive approach to alleviate system infractions and ensure protection. In this topic, you will apply risk management techniques and strategies to your organization.

What Is Risk?

Risk is the likelihood that a threat will exploit a weakness and cause loss. It is often shown as the equation Risk = Threat × Vulnerability × Consequence. A big part of risk analysis, then, is to understand the vulnerabilities and threats that lead to risk.

- A vulnerability is defined as any weakness in a system or process that could lead to harm.
- A threat is a potential danger caused by exploiting a vulnerability.
- A *threat agent* is the agent that will expose the vulnerability and cause the harm.
- A consequence is the resulting harm that the organization could receive.

Another factor to consider is that different assets have different vulnerabilities and threats. For example, a warehouse will have significantly different vulnerabilities than an intellectual property (IP) application.

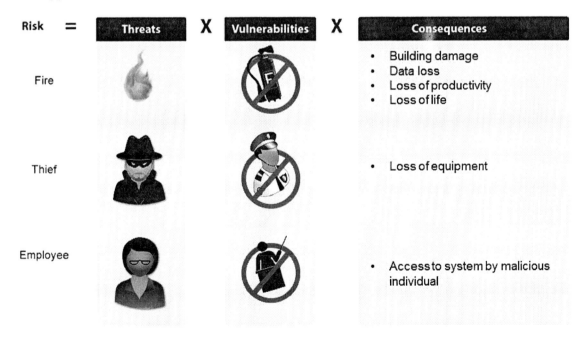

Figure 1-5: The risk equation.

Risk Management

As your security program takes shape, one of the critical steps in successful security management is *risk management*, the process of assessing risk, reducing it to an acceptable level, and implementing controls to maintain that minimal level of risk. The process for risk management can be broken down into the following parts:

- Risk analysis

- Prioritization
- Response
- Monitoring and measuring

Figure 1-6: The risk management process.

Results of Improper Risk Management

In the information management world, risks come in many different forms. If a risk is not managed correctly, any of the following could result:

- Disclosure of a critical asset
- Modification of a critical asset
- Loss/destruction of a critical asset
- Interruption of a critical asset

Understanding and reducing risk will help to minimize the impact of these losses.

Integrating Governance, Compliance, and Risk Management

Risk management is often cast as part of a three-way combination of governance, risk management, and compliance (GRC). GRC is an attempt to integrate these three elements to improve effectiveness and decrease complexity. Together, GRC helps the organization work within its own rules and acceptable risk levels, as well as external regulations. Because governance and compliance are often intertwined and crucial to the risk management process, a GRC solution that combines these processes is a helpful model for optimizing risk management in the organization.

Based on Figure 1.6 in the Official (ISC)² Guide to the CISSP CBK.

Figure 1–7: GRC.

The Risk Analysis Process

When determining how to protect computer networks, computer installations, and information, *risk analysis* is the security management process for addressing any risk or economic damages that affect an organization and are ascertained in various phases. Risk analysis is an ongoing activity that involves periodic reviews along with special reviews around significantly changed processes. Special risk analysis efforts are needed before, during, and after an acquisition.

Phase	Description
Asset identification and valuation	Identifying the assets that require protection and determining the value of the assets. Assets might include data, data systems, buildings, and employees. Determining what the assets are is generally easier than determining the value of the assets.
Vulnerability identification	Identifying vulnerabilities so the analyst can confirm where asset protection problems exist. Locating weaknesses exposes the critical areas that are most susceptible to vulnerabilities.
Threat assessment	Once vulnerabilities are understood, the threats that may take advantage of or exploit those vulnerabilities are determined.
Risk assessment	Assessing the likelihood or probability that threats will exploit vulnerabilities. This can be done quantitatively (numbers-based) or qualitatively (words-based).
Financial impact evaluation	Once the probabilities are determined, the financial impact of these potential threats needs to be evaluated.

Asset Identification

All companies have information that, if released or compromised, could have serious ramifications and jeopardize organizational goals. Remember, in today's business climate, information is a business asset. To that end, it is your job to comprehensively identify all of the assets in your organization, even ones that may not be overt. Assets might include data, data systems, buildings, and employees.

If you wait until an asset is compromised before taking stock of it, you'll have a much harder time recovering. Likewise, if you don't identify an asset, you may never even realize when it's been compromised, though you'll still feel the negative effects.

When you do identify your assets, keep in mind that it's helpful to describe them in terms of their basic characteristics, their value to the company, how they're used on a daily basis, and whether or not they're easily replaced. This will make the later assessment process much easier.

Asset Valuation

Asset valuation is the practice of determining an asset's worth to an organization. It requires taking all costs into consideration. The specific costs associated with an asset depend on the financial impact when the asset is affected by a threat. Asset valuation answers several essential questions:

1. What effort was required to develop or obtain it?
2. What does it cost to maintain and protect it?
3. How much loss in operational functionality will be sustained if the asset is misplaced or damaged?
4. What would it cost to replace it?
5. What enemies might pay for it?
6. What liability penalties might occur if the asset is compromised?

Asset Valuation Methods

Assets can be identified through different organizational systems and asset value can be determined in several different ways.

Method	Description
Asset management system	A corporate or organizational system that contains a detailed record of corporate property and similar assets. Facilities, furniture, computers, and other real property are recorded in the asset management system. Purchase prices, depreciation, and other financial asset information may also be found in the system. The asset management system provides an asset value based on accounting principles.
Accounting system	Additional asset information may be present in a general accounting system. For example, the cost to develop software packages may be expensed in the accounting system. If it is, there is a software book value that can be used to quantify the risk of damage if the original software source is lost.
Insurance valuation	Often, insurers are a good source of asset valuation. They accept the risk of loss for the assets they insure and perform an analysis of the risk associated with the policies they issue.
Qualitative valuation	Not all assets are easily described using hard numbers. It may be best to rely on word-based descriptions of the value of your assets. For example, you may describe your company's network share as absolutely necessary for the intra-company sharing of data, which adds to the productivity that the business needs to stay efficient.

Areas of Vulnerability

It is essential to ascertain the specific areas of an organization that are especially vulnerable to known risks.

Vulnerability Area	Example Threat and Risk
Physical structure	Window accessibility in a room where secure information is stored can expose vulnerabilities and create a venue for sudden intrusion threats.
Electrical	A single electrical feed that supports an entire building or enterprise can exploit an instance of vulnerability. Should that single feed fail, it will endanger the availability of system data.
Software	Worms, viruses, and Trojans are software that threaten systems.
Network	The failure to encrypt private information as it travels across a network can heighten system vulnerability. The information may be intercepted by an unauthorized user.
Personnel	If key personnel that are trained to handle situations in a critical event are not available, this can cause additional corporate-wide vulnerabilities.
Hardware	Poorly stored computer components may be stolen, costing the business money and productivity if those components are in production. Hardware may also be physically damaged beyond repair, whether through natural or man-made causes.
Documentation	Poorly written documentation may cause confusion and impair the decision making process for all levels of governance. The integrity of documents and the confidentiality of sensitive documents may also be violated.
Process	Outdated or inefficient processes can also impair business operations. Poor security processes are especially a risk to the organization, as they can weaken its defenses.

Identify Threats

System security threats come in many forms and are often categorized as natural or man-made.

Threat Type	Description
Natural disasters	Natural disasters are related to weather or other non-controllable events that are residual occurrences of the activities of nature. Different types of natural disasters include: • Earthquakes. • Wildfires. • Flooding. • Excessive snowfalls. • Tsunamis. • Hurricanes. • Tornadoes. • Landslides.

Threat Type	Description
Man-made disasters	Man-made disasters are residual occurrences of individual or collective human activity. Man-made events can be caused intentionally or unintentionally. Intentional man-made disasters include: • Arson. • Terrorist attacks. • Political unrest. • Break-ins. • Theft of equipment and/or data. • Equipment damage. • File destruction. • Information disclosure. Unintentional man-made disasters include: • Employee mistakes. • Power outages. • Excessive employee illnesses or epidemics. • Information disclosure.

Risk Assessment Methodologies

There are several types of methodologies that can be used in risk analysis:

• CRAMM (CCTA Risk Analysis and Management Method)
• Failure Modes and Effect Analysis (FMEA)
• FRAP (Facilitated Risk Analysis Process
• OCTAVE (Operationally Critical Threat, Asset, and Vulnerability Evaluation)
• Security Officers Management and Analysis Project (SOMAP)

The methodologies all have a lot of overlapping similarities, and you should determine the best method for your organizational focus.

Risk Assessment Determination Factors

Determining risk requires the evaluation of two factors:

• Likelihood: How likely is it that the threat occurs?
• Impact: What kind of damage will the threat cause?

Qualitative Assessment

Qualitative risk analysis is not based on a numerical analysis or history. It is a best-guess estimate of risk occurrence. To complete a qualitative analysis, it is necessary to gain group acceptance of the probability of risk occurrence. The group should include a wide variety of people including senior management, information security, legal, human resources, facilities, IT, and business unit owners.

The group will explore different scenarios of risk possibilities, rank the likelihood and seriousness of the threat, and the validity of possible countermeasures based on their expert opinions. An analysis could include hundreds of scenarios.

These qualitative values do not necessarily reflect experience or history, but do indicate which risks are higher priorities and which are lower priorities based on the opinion of the analysts.

Likelihood	Impact				
	Insignificant	Minor	Moderate	Major	Catastrophic
5. Almost certain	H	H	E	E	E
4. Likely	M	H	H	E	E
3. Possible	L	M	H	E	E
2. Unlikely	L	L	M	H	E
1. Rare	L	L	M	H	H

Risk
L = Low   M = Medium   H = High   E = Extreme

Figure 1–8: An example of a qualitative matrix from the Australia/New Zealand 4360 Standard on Risk Management.

Delphi Method

The *Delphi method* is a way to perform qualitative assessments of risk, especially those that do not have an accounting foundation. This method involves questioning a panel of independent experts to obtain asset value forecasts. A facilitator collects and summarizes these forecasts.

This cyclical process uses a Subject Matter Expert (SME) to answer questions about risk. The SME remains anonymous and a facilitator distributes the results. The process is repeated in two or more rounds to narrow down estimation outcomes and ensure the stability of the resulting value for the asset in question. This value is determined by calculating the median score once the final rounds are completed. This method can be especially helpful with assets that have a hard-to-ascertain value, such as brand identity.

Quantitative Assessment

Quantitative risk analysis is a numerical estimate based on the historical occurrences of incidents and the likelihood of risk re-occurrence.

Each element within the analysis (asset value, severity of vulnerability, threat frequency, impact, control costs, control effectiveness) is quantified with monetary or other numeric values. Using various statistical and mathematical tools, it is a numerical analysis that produces concrete and tangible values for risks by attaching an actual figure to each risk and the loss experienced if the risk causes harm.

Determination Factor	Description
Likelihood	The likelihood of an event occurring is stated as the *Annual* or *Annualized Rate of Occurrence (ARO)*. This is an equation percentage factor that estimates the number of times an identified event or threat will occur within a year. ARO = Event number / Years.
	If the electrical grid goes out four times a year, then the ARO will equal 4. If a flood occurs every 10 years and affects the availability of information, the ARO will be 1 in 10 years, or 10%.

Determination Factor	Description
Exposure	Not all dimensions of an asset are exposed to the same risk. You'll often have to determine the asset's *exposure factor (EF)*, or how much and what parts of the asset are vulnerable. It is typically calculated by finding the percentage decrease from the total value of an asset (AV) to its actual loss value.
	In other words, EF = loss value / AV
	For example, the asset value of a storage facility may be measured at $20,000,000, including the sensitive digital assets it stores. Because these digital assets are backed up on another site, a flood or other disaster that destroys the building may only cause $4,000,000 in damage, which is the building's physical value. So, the building's exposure factor for a natural disaster is rated at 20%.
Impact	The impact of the event is known as the *Single Loss Expectancy (SLE)*. This is also the loss value that is part of calculating exposure factor. Risk analysts calculate impact by multiplying the exposure factor by the asset's total value.
	A team estimates that a facility damaged by flooding the will incur a 20% exposure factor. The cost of the facility is $20 million. Using the formula EF * AV, the estimated SLE of the flood will cause a $4 million loss, as shown in the following equation:
	0.20 * $20,000,000 = $4,000,000
Risk	The *Annualized Loss Expectancy (ALE)* is the expected loss from each identified threat on an annual basis. It is equal to the likelihood times the impact: ALE = ARO * SLE.
	If flooding occurs once every 10 years and the damage caused by one flood is $4,000,000, the ALE equals $400,000, as shown in the following equation:
	0.10 * $4,000,000 = $400,000
	If the ALE in this example is $400,000, the organization can then spend up to $400,000 to provide safeguards for preventing flooding. Spending more than $400,000 on a yearly basis will result in higher costs to protect the asset than the estimated damage warrants. If the $400,000 will not eliminate but simply reduce the flooding, you will need to calculate a new ALE that takes into account the reduction in your SLE and/or ARO.

Prioritization

It is vital to appropriately identify the likelihood of risks and then evaluate the related potential severity of loss and probability of occurrence. In the earlier work that was done for risk analysis, it was quite likely that the impact of different risks are identified. This information will be helpful when prioritizing your risk management efforts. If impending risks are not appropriately discovered and accurately detected, your time and resource management will suffer from faulty prioritization and low profitability.

To properly assess the probability and prioritization of security risks, a series of strategic process phases should be practiced and applied to your organization's information systems.

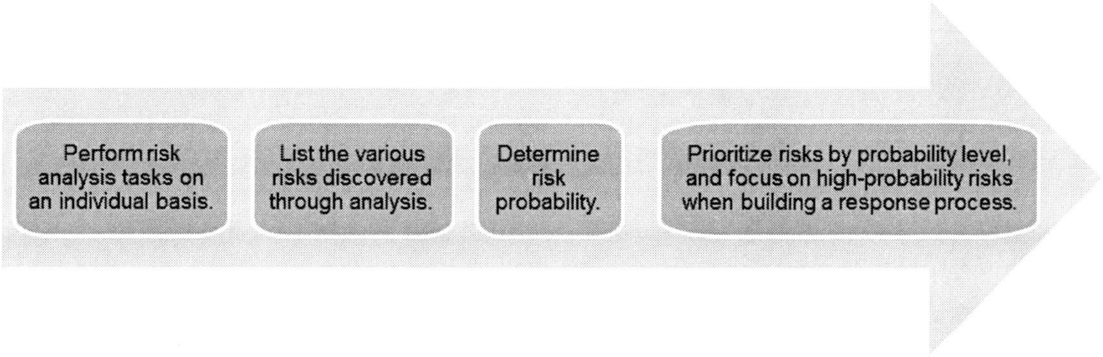

Figure 1-9: The phases in a risk prioritization process.

Responses to Risk

Once the threats and attack vector have been identified, the security professional must work with management to reduce the risk to an acceptable level. Risk responses should be based on their financial impact on the company and the likelihood that they will occur.

Response to Risk	Description
Avoidance	If the risk has a high likelihood of occurring with a huge impact on the company, you may be best off avoiding the activity (and thus the risk) altogether.
	If an office contains a large amount of computer equipment that could be removed if a window is broken, a potential risk is present. Deciding to keep the computing equipment at an alternate location will reduce the risk.
Mitigation	If the risk has a high likelihood of occurring, without a great amount of financial impact, you can use control systems to reduce the potential loss.
	The organization may choose to leave the window in place but reduce the risk of equipment theft by putting bars in front of the window. The bars will reduce—but not remove—the threat of equipment theft. The risk of loss will be minimal.
Transfer	If the risk has a low probability but a high financial impact, you can transfer all or part of the risk to a third-party. This could be done by outsourcing part of your network or system or service to a third party that specializes in only performing that type of activity, or possibly even simply taking out insurance on the system.
	The organization may choose to leave the window in place with no bars, but raise the insurance premiums to compensate for the loss should the window be broken and the equipment be stolen. The risk has been transferred to the insurance company for an increased premium.
Acceptance	If, after your risk analysis, you determine that the cost of implementing the control exceeds the benefit (do not spend $100 to protect a $10 item) and if you determine that you still need to have the system, you can simply accept the risk, monitor for incidents, and have a contingency to restore operations should the threat be realized.
	The organization may determine that intrusion barriers for the equipment storage room are firmly secured and that the window is high enough to prevent forced entry and theft. Therefore, no controls are enforced and the organization retains the risk of damages incurred upon an unexpected loss.

Control Selection Criteria

You need to determine and develop controls to eliminate or reduce risks. The controls must be economically sound and provide the expected level of protection. In other words, the controls must not cost more than the expected loss caused by threats that exploit vulnerabilities.

When you decide to mitigate a risk, the risk assessment process helps you select and apply the proper controls based on both the probable impact of a disaster and the cost of implementing the controls. The table describes three overarching selection criteria.

Criterion	Description
Cost effectiveness	Selecting cost-effective controls eliminates wasted resources. If the ALE for a given risk is $400,000, spending $500,000 annually to eliminate the risk will be ineffective. Spending up to $400,000 a year will be cost effective if it eliminates or reduces the risk to a level where the remaining risk after control selection is acceptable to the organization. It is important to account for any operational cost of the control.
Risk reduction	Controls must actually reduce risk. Selecting a control because it is new, interesting, expensive, or novel may not generate risk reduction. If the risk is related to unauthorized, individual access to a secure facility and the employed control is an inexpensive motion detection system that fails 50% of the time, it is not a valid risk-reduction defense measure. Although it may have only cost $10,000, it is ineffective.
Practicality	Controls must be practical. To ward off building floods, a high concrete wall is erected around the facility. After spending the money to build the wall, an engineer evaluates the safeguard and finds that the wall will not protect against extensive flood-induced water pressure. As an alternative, a proposal suggests building a retention pond and diversion streams to help redistribute the flood water away from the building. While the wall had originally seemed like a reasonable solution to planners, it was not a practical solution.

Once you have met the three big criterion, there are additional details to consider:

- Can the control be audited?
- Is the control from a trusted source?
- Can the control be consistently applied?
- Is the control reliable?
- Is the control independent from other controls?
- Is the control easy to use?
- Can the control be automated?
- Is the control sustainable?

Control Types

Security controls fall into different types or categories depending on their functions. Security control types break out as administrative, physical, and technical.

Security Control Type	Description
Administrative	*Administrative controls* cover a broad area of security. Beginning with security policies and procedures, the administrative control types cover personnel security, risk management, training, monitoring, user and password management, and permissions management. For example, security guards may use a printed access list to determine whether individuals attempting access without having their name on the list should be held for further evaluation. Security awareness training is another good example of an administrative control.
Physical	*Physical controls* are used to limit an individual's physical access to protected information or facilities. Locks, doors, fences, and perimeter defenses are all examples of physical access controls. Visible ID cards can also be used to identify people who are found in an unauthorized area. For example, an infrared monitoring system can detect the presence of an intruder and can signal a guard to respond when needed.
Technical / *Logical*	*Technical controls* are implemented in the computing environment. They are often found in operating systems, application programs, database frameworks, firewalls, routers, switches, and wireless access points. For example, a user sign-in process on a computer utilizes a user ID and password to verify identification. In the case of three incorrect login attempts, the system logs the incorrect attempts and locks the user account for five minutes.

Control Functions

Each control category has its own unique function and performance capability.

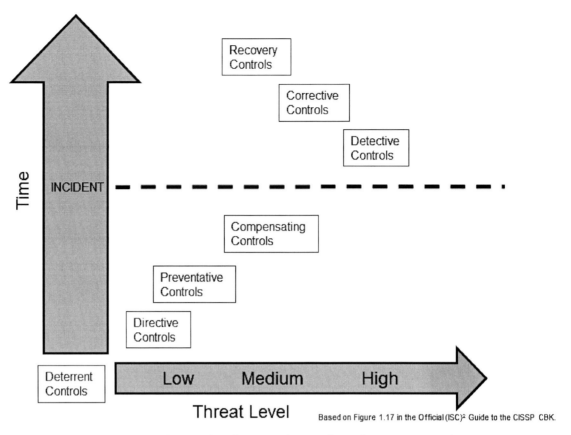

Figure 1-10: A continuum of controls relative to the timeline of a security incident.

The following table describes the categories of controls.

Control Categories	Description
Directive	A *directive control* specifies expected employee behavior and can often take the form of policies and guidelines. For example, a company may have an acceptable use policy. There may be separate policies for contractors or temporary employees.
Deterrent	A *deterrent control* discourages individuals from violating security policies because of the effort to circumvent it or the negative consequences of doing so. A notice that CCTV cameras were monitoring a site could be considered a deterrent, especially if the penalty is the loss of employment.
Preventative	A *preventative control* stops a security incident. Background screenings are an example of a preventative control.
Compensating	A *compensating control* is implemented when the system cannot provide protection required by policy in order to mitigate the risk down to an acceptable level. For example, a corporate policy might require using a smart card ID system for entry into and exit out of secure areas. At a remote site, a smart card system has not been installed. Instead, a compensating control is used where experienced security guards validate the identity of each individual using a printed roster and personal evaluation. A written log of entry and exit times is also maintained.
Detective	A *detective control* alerts the security professionals to the attempted security violation.

Control Categories	Description
Corrective	A *corrective control* responds to the security violation to reduce or completely eliminate the impact. Escorting an unauthorized visitor from the building is a corrective control.
Recovery	A *recovery control* is used to return the system to an operational state after a failure to protect the CIA triad. Changing separation of duties after an employee unexpectedly leaves the company is an example of a recovery control.

In most cases, preventative, detective, corrective, and directive controls are sufficient to maintain the CIA triad. However, deterrent, recovery, and compensating controls are additional tools used to protect systems and facilities.

Control Implementation Matrix

The access control functions are implemented in the three different access control types in the security environment.

	Administrative	Physical	Technical
Directive	X		
Deterrent		X	X
Preventative	X	X	X
Compensating	X		X
Detective		X	X
Corrective			X
Recovery	X		X

Figure 1-11: Access control functions are implemented as different access control types.

Residual Risk = (threats * vulnera * asset value) * control gap

Residual risk is the risk that remains even after controls are put into place. As comprehensive as your mitigation efforts may be, it's difficult to truly control for every possible risk. Therefore it's important to accept that no risk management system is perfect, but that you can still use even a fallible system to your advantage. Identifying the residual risk of an enterprise asset or activity will aid you in assessing the effectiveness of the controls you put in place to mitigate the risk. This gives you the chance to continuously improve your controls and optimize their effectiveness.

Monitoring and Measuring

Monitoring and measuring security control implementation is not about simple pass-fail results or generating paperwork to pass an audit. Assessment is critical to ensure that the security controls are meeting their objectives. A well-executed assessment helps determine the validity, effectiveness, and quality of the controls. In addition, it can provide information about the strengths and weaknesses of the current systems and help provide a cost-effective plan to correct any identified deficiencies.

Continuous Improvement

Continuous improvement is the ongoing effort to continually optimize policies and processes in order to identify and mitigate potential risks before they affect the organization.

As a function of risk management, continuous improvement is a never-ending process that should include the following best practices:

- Continuously seek to discover new vulnerabilities: Make sure that vulnerability assessments are run often, but be careful not to be overwhelmed by too much trivia in the report.
- Be context aware in your risk analysis: Not all vulnerabilities pose the same threat to all organizations.
- Prioritize your efforts to vulnerabilities that actually pose a significant risk: You will never have enough money or resource to address every possible vulnerability.
- Determine patchability: Test to see if patches introduce new issues, and if there is no patch available, see if other controls (such as access control, firewalls, intrusion detection/prevention) can provide an acceptable level of defense.

Continuous Improvement Process

One of the most widely used tools is the four-step cycle sometimes called the Deming Cycle:

1. Plan: Identify a policy or process with an opportunity for change, identify the objective, and make a plan.
2. Do: Put the change into effect on a small scale.
3. Check: Analyze the results of the change.
4. Act: Either implement the change on a wider scale or keep existing policy and process in place, depending on the results of the Check phase.

Risk Management Frameworks

A Risk Management framework supplies a structure that provides the foundation for designing, implementing, monitoring, and continually improving risk management. The framework will ensure risks are appropriately identified and handled within the context of:

- The nature of the risks faced by the organization.
- The organization's risk tolerance.
- The resources available to manage risks.
- The organization's culture.

Some commonly used frameworks include:

- Risk IT Framework—ISACA
- ISO 31000
- Enterprise Risk Management—Integrated Framework (COSO)
- Risk Management Framework (NIST)

Guidelines for Implementing Risk Management

Use the following guidelines when developing a risk management program.

- Construct your risk management program around a process of analysis, prioritization, response, and monitoring and measuring.
- Integrate risk management into a larger framework of governance, risk management, and compliance (GRC) to simplify and improve all three processes.
- Follow the phases of the risk analysis process to identify the impact of risk to your organization.
- Comprehensively identify all of your assets that are susceptible to risk.
- Place value on your assets using one or more valuation methods.

- Identify how each asset is vulnerable.
- Identify the threats to each vulnerable asset.
- Assess risk using qualitative or quantitative language, depending on the context of the risk and the business needs of your organization.
- Prioritize risks so that larger risks are addressed more quickly and thoroughly than smaller ones.
- Respond to risk in different ways depending on context:
    - Avoid risks that are very likely and may have a huge impact.
    - Mitigate risks that are likely but will not necessarily have a great impact.
    - Transfer risks that are unlikely but will have a large financial impact.
    - Accept risks that are unlikely and will have a minor impact, or ones that are simply not cost-effective.
- Select risk-based controls based on their cost effectiveness, practicality, and efficacy in reducing risk.
- Consider residual risk as a way to review the efficacy of your controls.
- Proactively monitor and measure the effectiveness of risk response techniques and management processes.
- Continuously improve upon your risk management program through a cyclical process of discovery, awareness, prioritization, and control implementation,

ACTIVITY 1-5
Discussing Risk Management

Scenario

The Case of a Company's Risky Business: Part 1

You are the new information security consultant for the XYZ Group, a medium-sized company that manufactures widgets. Before hiring you, the company had been plagued with security incidents that are listed below. Management has asked you to help assess the risk and conduct a cost/benefit analysis of proposed solutions.

Incident #1: Two years ago, plans for a new product were leaked onto the Internet, and as a result a competitor was able to produce a rival version of the widget and get it to market first. XYZ estimates that sales of that widget, which were expected to be at $1 million annually, were reduced by 50% due to the information leakage. Next year, the company is planning to introduce a new widget that will be a major upgrade to the previous model. It should regain the company's market share in that product line. The cost for averting a similar information leak for the new product is not yet known, but training the staff, which would cost about $50,000 per year, is expected to reduce the risk by half.

Incident #2: This year, the company had a virus attack that took half of the production floor offline for two days. Manufacturing on the production floor generates $10,000 worth of goods every day. A similar virus attack is expected to happen every year. Upgrading the antivirus would cost $20,000 in licensing annually.

Incident #3: Last year's wildfire in the surrounding hills closed access to the business for two days. Wildfires happen every year. Additionally, the area is in an earthquake fault zone. An earthquake of sufficient magnitude to severely disrupt operations for several months happens about once every 10 years.

---

1. With regard to Incident #1, the information leakage event, would training the staff be a cost effective measure to mitigate future incidents?

2. With regard to Incident #2, the virus attack, would purchasing the antivirus license be a cost effective solution?

3. With regard to Incident #3, which scenario (earthquakes or wildfires) should management devote more of its resources towards mitigating? What would be an appropriate risk response?

TOPIC F

Threat Modeling

A significant part of managing security in your organization will incorporate the threat modeling process. When you put forth the effort to discover everything you can about threats and how they target your organization, you'll be reinforcing the strength of your defenses.

Threat Modeling Process

Threat modeling is a structured process of identifying and assessing the possible threat agents and attack vectors that might be used to target systems. These models can encompass general security in an organization, or they can apply to specific systems that are the target of an attack. In addition, some threat models are attacker-focused rather than asset-focused. Either way, a threat model will assist you in evaluating the risks involved in a potential attack, as well as the best course to take to mitigate its effects.

Threat modeling is slightly different than vulnerability assessment. When you look for vulnerabilities you are looking inwards at your current systems and scanning for weaknesses. Threat modeling looks outward to determine who might want to attack you and how they might attack.

Figure 1-12: A general approach to threat modeling. The process is repeatable for each system you profile.

The basic process for threat modeling consists of six steps:

1. Identify the scope of the threat modeling process.

2. Identify threat agents and possible attack vectors. This should include both insiders and outsiders and include unintentional errors and intentional attacks.
3. Understand any controls already in place.
4. Identify vulnerabilities that the threat agents might attack.
5. Prioritize the identified risks based on likelihood and impact.
6. Identify controls that will bring the risk to an acceptable level.

Threat Agent Actions

A threat agent is an individual who could cause a threat. This could be anybody who uses or comes in contact with your computer system. It could be a well-intentioned but inept user, or a malicious hacker. Threat agents can take any of the following actions against your system or data:

- Unauthorized access.
- Misuse by authorized users.
- Disclosure to unauthorized users, competitors, or the general public.
- Modification.
- Denial of access including destruction and theft.

Threat Types

If software or a system can be created, accessed, or used, it is subject to threat. In information security, the only way to absolutely have a secure system is to have no system at all. When trying to identify threat types, educate yourself on the latest known threats (including proof of concept attacks by security companies) and then put together a team to wildly think of any other possibility. Do not discount any crazy idea that a team member may come up with. Just because it has not been done yet, does not mean that someone won't discover a way in the future (or has already discovered a way to implement that threat). Before 9/11, no one considered the likelihood of anyone flying a large jet airplane into a tall building to cause mass destruction.

Computer threats fall into the following general categories (Microsoft refers to this as the "STRIDE" classification method):

- Spoofing of user identify
- Tampering with data
- Repudiation
- Information disclosure
- Denial of service
- Elevation of privilege

There are additional ways you can categorize threats, such as:

- **Active versus passive**. Is the attack directly affecting a system, or is it focused on intelligence gathering without changing the system?
- **Human-directed versus automated**. Does the attacker need to manually execute an attack for precision, or can they launch an automated attack for more devastating effects?
- **Internal versus external**. Is the source of the threat outside of the organization, or could it be an employee who has privileged access to the network?
- **Single attack versus advanced persistent threat (APT)**. Is the attack conducted once, then stopped? Or does the attack remain covert over a long period of time before it is noticed?

Rating Threat Impact

The following risk rating system can be used to determine the potential impact of a threat (the acronym "DREAD" might help you remember the categories):

- Damage: How bad is the attack?

- Reproducibility: How easy would it be to reproduce the attack?
- Exploitability: How hard would it be to launch the attack?
- Affected users: How many people would be impacted by the attack?
- Discoverability: How easy would it be to discover the threat?

The job of the security professional is to make sure that threats are managed as effectively as possible, and that a contingency is in place to quickly bring the business back to acceptable operating levels after a security incident has occurred.

Diagramming Attacks

Diagramming possible attack vectors (the direction the attack is coming from) requires a team to really think outside the box. You should have the team imagine all possible approaches, from sophisticated code attacks to crude physical attacks, that could threaten your system. Attacks on cars, ATM machines, and baby monitoring systems have already been demonstrated. With society's paradigm shift to the *Internet of Things (IoT)*, ordinary household items such as clothing, toys, and non-electronic appliances will soon be connected to the Internet and provide possible attack vectors.

The bottom line is, if the software or system can be at all accessed, that access can be both from friendly and malicious sources. In addition, the act of creating software or a system is also fraught with attack possibilities.

Other than the general process of modeling a threat, you may also implement visual aids that more specifically outline how a threat operates. For example, assume that you have developed an app that has an instant messaging capability. As you go through your threat modeling process,you identify the threat of a malicious user intercepting messages that are not meant for them. To model this threat, you create a threat tree that identifies the threat, how the threat can occur, and how to mitigate these vulnerabilities.

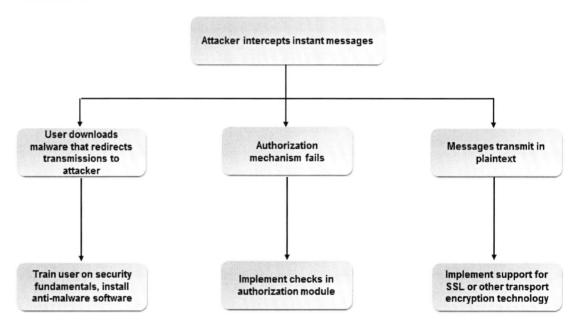

Figure 1-13: A threat tree evaluating a man-in-the-middle threat to an instant messaging feature in an app.

 Note: For a fascinating read on the latest types of threats, see the article "**10 cutting-edge security threats**" at **www.csoonline.com/article/2985867/vulnerabilities/10-cutting-edge-security-threats.html?phint=newt%3Dcso_update&phint=idg_eid%3D80aba268938a2da93b1597b0aa141204#slide2**.

Threat Remediation

Effective threat remediation involves all departments of the company and all levels of workers working together. Remediation will not merely be the implementation of technical controls, but also the implementation, management, and monitoring of good business process. IT, internal audit, compliance, and security departments should coordinate efforts to remediate risk across the organization. Threat remediation starts with a solid security policy and a comprehensive strategy for implementing the policy. The policy will reflect the organization's culture and tolerance for risk. In addition, existing strategies and controls need to be continuously evaluated for their effectiveness, with tenable, implementable recommendations made in a timely manner.

The security practitioner can refer to the following sources for best practices on threat remediation:

*   "CIS Critical Securities Controls" at **https://www.sans.org/critical-security-controls**
*   "Killing Advanced Security Threats in Their Tracks" at **https://www.sans.org/reading-room/whitepapers/analyst/killing-advanced-threats-tracks-intelligent-approach-attack-prevention-35302**
*   "Introduction to Recommended Practices" at **https://ics-cert.us-cert.gov/Introduction-Recommended-Practices**

Guidelines for Implementing Threat Modeling

Use the following guidelines when incorporating threat modeling into your security management program.

*   Understand how threat modeling differs from vulnerability assessment.
*   Follow the process for threat modeling.
*   Consider the many ways that threat agents can exploit your systems.
*   Consider classifying threats using the STRIDE model.
*   Consider classifying threats in other ways:
    *   Active vs. passive
    *   Manual vs. automated
    *   Internal vs. external
    *   Single event vs. advanced persistent threat (APT)
*   Determine the potential impact of a threat using the DREAD rating system.
*   Incorporate all personnel in the threat remediation process.
*   Consistently evaluate controls to test their effectiveness and benefit.
*   Use a visual aid like a threat tree to diagram threats and their impacts.
*   Consider structuring the threat tree to flow as follows:
    1. Identifying the threat.
    2. Identifying how the threat can occur.
    3. Identifying how to mitigate its effects.

ACTIVITY 1-6
Discussing Threat Modeling

Scenario

The Case of a Company's Risky Business: Part 2

Management of the XYZ Group attended a seminar and came back with a list of threat agents who could possibly harm the network. These are:

- The inept user
- The malicious hacker
- The corporate spy

Management is wondering if any of these might have played a role in the previous information leakage incident that has so far cost the company $500,000 in lost sales annually.

1. Which of the three threat agents might have played a role in the information leakage incident?

2. What possible threat agent actions occurred during the information leakage incident?

3. Based on the DREAD acronym, how would you rate the impact of this threat?

4. How do you think the product plans were stolen? What do you think were the possible avenues of attack?

5. What recommendations would you make to mitigate this risk for the upcoming product?

TOPIC G

Business Continuity Plan Fundamentals

Business continuity plans are important safeguards against many types of organizational threats and vulnerabilities. In this topic, you'll learn the value of planning just how your organization will resume business processes should some adverse event happen.

BCPs

A *Business Continuity Plan (BCP)* is a policy that defines how an enterprise will maintain normal day-to-day business operations in the event of business disruption or crisis. The intent of the BCP is to ensure the survival of the business entity by preserving key documents, establishing decision-making authority, communicating with internal and external stakeholders, protecting and recovering assets, and maintaining financial functions.

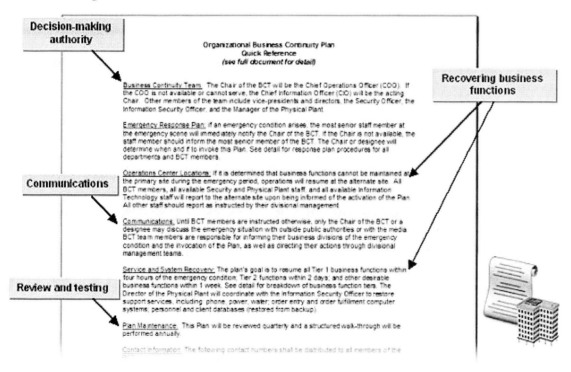

Figure 1–14: A BCP.

The BCP should address infrastructure issues such as maintaining utilities service, utilizing high-availability or fault-tolerant systems that can withstand failure, and creating and maintaining data backups.

The BCP should also account for the protection of the employees, contractors, temps, visitors, and any other people that might be present. The protection of human life will trump all other concerns.

The BCP should include information about how to communicate the details of an incident to the relevant stakeholders. This will help reduce panic and confusion, while making sure the proper personnel are told exactly what they need to know to help continue with business operations. Stakeholders may include senior management, board members, affected managers and employees, service providers, and potentially, suppliers. Clients should be informed if the disruption will noticeably affect services or product deliveries.

The BCP must be reviewed and tested on a regular basis. The creation and maintenance of a BCP is going to require senior management support. They should be fully informed of the plan and any changes to the plan.

BCP Contents

To properly implement a BCP, it should contain specific content that is consistent throughout the organization. This includes:

- A statement of policy from senior management that defines the BCP's vision and mission.
- A statement of authority that authorizes the BCP team to operate.
- The roles and responsibilities of the plan's team members.
- The plan goals, objectives, and evaluation methods.
- The applicable laws, regulations, authorities, and/or industry codes of practice.
- A budget and project schedule.
- The guidelines for records management.

 Note: For more information and general guidance on BCP content objectives, visit **www.nfpa.org/aboutthecodes**, and click the link for NFPA 1600.

Records Management

Maintaining a thorough record-keeping process is essential for two purposes:

1. It documents team activities for historical purposes.
2. It documents activities for due diligence to demonstrate that standard business processes were considered during plan development. This type of documentation would be necessary for insurance or audit purposes.

BCPs and DRPs

While some organizations consider a BCP and a Disaster Recovery Plan (DRP) the same thing, they are distinct in the CISSP material. You may consider the DRP as a component of the BCP, but they are still separate plans. The BCP is a larger over-arching document that prepares a company for disaster. The DRP is what is initiated when disaster strikes and brings the company out of the disaster. DRPs also tend to be more technically-oriented, whereas a BCP may focus more on business processes. For example, a DRP may initiate a plan of action to recover from a server's hard disk failing, whereas a BCP will outline how the organization will operate if a significant amount of key personnel fall ill at the same time.

 Note: Do not confuse a business continuity plan with the disaster recovery plan (DR). Although the two are related, the DR is actually a subpart of the BCP. The DR is focused on IT recovery, whereas the BCP is focused on recovering the overall business.

BCP Project Management

As with other projects, creating a BCP has a number of steps. These are:

1. Initiating the project.
2. Defining the project scope and plan.
3. Performing a business impact analysis.
4. Testing and evaluating your plan.
5. Maintaining the plan.
6. Implementing the plan when disaster strikes.

Management Support

All projects need support from management, but a BC project is going to need it from the highest level. Because BC projects are so encompassing of the business, and typically need flexible resources during the different phases, it will pay to have a champion in senior management. BC can be a tough sell because it definitely isn't a revenue generator. It is, however, a revenue protector, much like an insurance policy. It is also difficult to show return on investment when you have successfully avoided a disaster by having an effective business continuity plan.

To convince executive leadership of the necessity to build a BCP, you need to help them understand the risks of not having one. There are three areas of risk to the organization.

Area of Risk	Description
Financial	The company can lose money if unable to handle everyday business.
Reputation	If a company can't meet its customers' needs in a timely fashion, customers will find another company who will. This negative perception can have long-term effects.
Regulatory	The company might have fines or penalties. In addition, both the company and the individuals in senior management could be held responsible, financially or even criminally.

The Advisory Committee—BCP Team

The *Advisory Committee-BCP team* is a group of individuals from varying backgrounds within the community who assemble to create the BCP and assist in plan maintenance. The team typically includes senior management members, business partners, security and IT professionals, company personnel, and legal representatives. The team should be composed of decision makers who can influence the process objectively. When an organization has multiple satellite branches or offices, it is important to include remote business associates in the business planning process, either as part of an overall enterprise team or as a location-specific team.

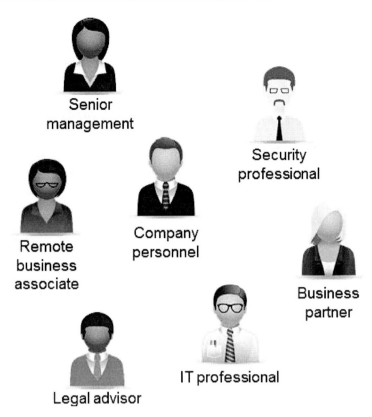

Figure 1-15: Advisory Committee-BCP team members.

BCP Program Coordinators

The *program coordinator* is the individual responsible for implementing and controlling the BCP. The program coordinator maintains the long-term plan and determines when the process modifications are required based on business operation changes. The program coordinator must receive senior management support to be effective. In addition to receiving support, the program coordinator must keep senior management informed on the progress and testing of the BCP. If seen as a low-level administrator, the program coordinator may not obtain the necessary support from the organization to complete the BCP.

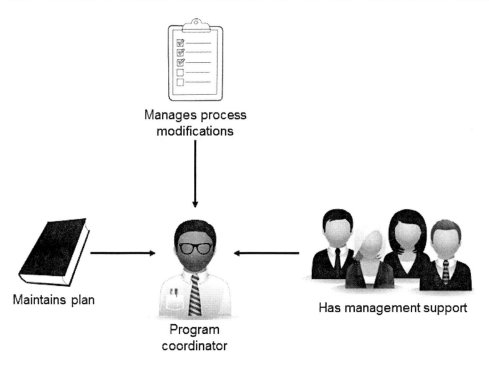

Figure 1-16: Program coordination.

Program Coordinator Duties

The program coordinator should hold periodic meetings to evaluate the BCP, and verify that copies of the BCP are available to management and staff when needed. Printed hard copies should be stored in different onsite locations as well as at a convenient offsite location for easy accessibility. BCPs should only be stored on computers as documentation, not for operational purposes.

BCP Team Responsibilities

The BCP Program Coordinator and the BCP team are responsible for an array of activities, which include:

- Determining threats and vulnerabilities.
- Providing probability estimates of threats and vulnerabilities.
- Performing a business impact analysis (BIA) based on evaluated threats and vulnerabilities, and probability estimates.
- Prioritizing recovery efforts based on critical business activities that affect the overall survival of the organization.
- Evaluating alternate sites that could be used in an emergency.
- Determining action plans in the event of a disaster.
- Writing policies, guidelines, standards, and procedures on BCP implementation.
- Testing the BCP.
- Making sure legal requirements are fulfilled during the disaster process.

Project Initiation

Project initiation is the first step in building a BC plan. A project manager should be identified to lead the project. To initiate a project, you will need to:

- Gather support of upper management.
- Define the project scope.

- Estimate the resources that will be needed. Consider both personnel resources and budgetary resources.
- Determine the timeline and the deliverables.

There is a lot of cross pollination between BC and Risk Assessment, and the teams will definitely want to work together or at least have access to each other's data.

Project Scope and Plan

The scope of the BCP defines what areas of the business are covered in this particular BCP. Or, it might define what geographical regions are covered by this particular BCP. The clearer the scope is to senior management, the fewer surprises down the road. The larger the scope, the more resources you will need from various departments.

A BCP project scope will typically include:

- Operations
- Sales
- Customer service/fulfillment
- IT
- Non-IT infrastructure and logistics (site, power, transportation)
- Personnel
- Communications and media relations
- Regulatory compliance
- Contractual obligations

Most BCPs include all aspects of either the entire company, or a self-contained business unit. For example, company XYZ might have a BCP for the entire company, or separate BCPs for the North American and European divisions.

NIST SP 800-34

In 2002 (updated 2010), the National Institute of Standards and Technology (NIST) Special Publication 800-34 Rev. 1 outlined the steps required for what they refer to as contingency planning. These steps include:

1. Developing the contingency planning policy statement.
2. Conducting a business impact analysis.
3. Identifying preventive controls.
4. Developing recovery strategies.
5. Developing an information technology (IT) contingency plan.
6. Planning testing, training, and exercises.
7. Planning maintenance.

> **Note:** For more information on NIST contingency planning, visit **http://csrc.nist.gov/publications/PubsSPs.html** and click the PDF file for SP 800-34 Rev. 1 to download.

Project Management Applications

In evaluating the contingency planning steps, it is important to note that each step contains general statements that can be applied to any project management activity. These include:

1. Starting the plan.
2. Evaluating the impact of the proposed activity.
3. Developing the project.
4. Testing and implementing the solution.
5. Maintaining the project for success.

BIA

A *business impact analysis (BIA)* is a BCP phase that identifies present organizational risks and determines the impact to ongoing, business-critical operations and processes if risks are actualized.

A BIA is designed and developed to achieve several organizational goals, which include:

- Ensuring the health and safety of employees, responders, and others.
- Enabling continuous company operations that include property, infrastructure, and facilities.
- Maintaining the continuous delivery of goods and services to customers.
- Providing a safe workplace environment should a disaster occur.

The BIA will include the following:

- A vulnerability assessment and risk analysis.
- A prioritization of critical processes.
- Estimates of tolerable downtime.
- The impact of financial loss.
- The possibility of reduced efficiency in operations.
- Resources needed to restore normal business operations.

Flood Impact Example

As a risk is identified, an organization determines the chance of risk occurrence and then determines the quantity of potential organizational damage. If a roadway bridge crossing a local river is washed out by a flood and employees are unable to reach the business facility for five days, estimated costs to the organization need to be assessed for lost manpower and production.

Critical Business Processes

A *critical business process* is an activity that, if not recovered, can lead to business loss or failure. Critical business processes are determined during the BIA by senior management based on actual impact rather than on internal political practices. The analysis should include the identification of key personnel on whom the processes depend. Critical processes may have sub-processes; if any one process or sub-process fails, the entire business may lose its sustainability and cease to operate successfully.

Of course your critical business processes will vary by company. You must also think about dependencies. What goods, services, or conditions do your critical business processes depend on? Or, what other processes depend on your critical processes? When considering your critical business processes, sketch out a map or process flow that identifies your particular processes, what each is dependent on, and things that depend on each critical process.

Example: Product Development

In a medical supplies manufacturing business, product development is a critical business process. This process may also include, and depend upon, a variety of critical sub-processes, such as:

- Ordering supplies.
- Receiving supplies.
- Managing inventory.
- Maintaining production lines.
- Controlling the quality of manufactured products.
- Warehousing.
- Shipping.
- Billing.
- Processing orders.

MTD

Maximum tolerable downtime (MTD) is the longest period of time that a business outage may occur without causing serious business failures. Each business process can have its own MTD, such as a range of minutes to hours for critical functions, 24 hours for urgent functions, 7 days for normal functions, and so on. MTDs vary by company and event.

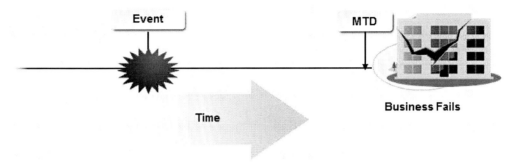

Figure 1-17: MTD.

 Note: It is quite possible you will see other similar sounding terms like maximum tolerable outage, maximum tolerable period of disruption, and others. They all essentially mean the same thing, at least as far as the CISSP material is concerned.

Medical Equipment Suppliers Example

The MTD limits the amount of recovery time that a business has to resume operations. An organization specializing in medical equipment may be able to exist without incoming manufacturing supplies for three months because it has stockpiled a sizeable inventory. After three months, the organization will not have sufficient supplies and may not be able to manufacture additional products, therefore leading to failure. In this case, the MTD is three months.

Impact of Financial Loss

You can use your BIA to determine what the potential financial loss will be based on vulnerabilities or downtime. In addition to determining the potential immediate financial loss, you'll also want to spell out any additional impact of such losses.

For example, you might determine that a natural disaster will cost your company $1 million per day in lost revenue and operational expense during a two-week immediate recovery period. In addition to the immediate financial loss, consider other losses that the immediate financial loss can cause. Most of these will be impaired operations that can cause further financial loss:

- The reduced ability to provide goods or services due to cash flow or logistics problems.
- The risk of losing customers due to the reduced ability to provide goods or services.
- The possibility of having to lay off some staff until the company can be brought back to full capacity.
- The risk of losing employees or loss of goodwill between management and staff while staff is laid off.

Possibility of Reduced Efficiency Operation

Whenever a business is attempting to recover from a disaster, it will almost always operate at reduced efficiency. This will be a reality when there are logistical or personnel issues during the disaster and recovery period. It is important that the organization have a roadmap to return to full operations to contain the impact of reduced operations.

The company will need a contingency plan to deal with any potential cash flow or logistical issues. Interim measures can include operating out of an alternate site, using alternate equipment or systems, and relocating the main systems.

The company must also be able to operate with fewer personnel and reduced infrastructure. Many staff members might not be able to report to work because roads are blocked or airports are closed. Worst yet, they might be injured or are staying home taking care of injured family members. Many staff members who would ordinarily come to work may try to work remotely, straining or overwhelming incoming network connections.

Business Plan Evaluations

The BCP development process must include an evaluation phase to ensure targeted objectives, time efficiency, and cost effectiveness. The BCP team should evaluate:

- The plan's coverage adequacy in all areas of the business.
- Threat and vulnerability identification.
- Prioritization of proper responses to business needs.
- Training and plan testing.
- Communications methods.
- BCP team staffing and time allocations.
- The frequency and methods for plan updates.

Business Plan Testing

When testing a BCP, various methods can be employed.

BCP Testing Method	Description
Reviewing contents	Because they are familiar with BCP construction, plan developers review the BCP's contents. However, because of their involvement as developers, they often have a limited view of corporate needs that can cause biased opinions.
Analyzing the business continuity solution	Senior management and division and department heads perform an additional analysis to ensure that the business continuity solution fulfills organizational recovery requirements. Because these individuals view the process from a corporate standpoint, they help to confirm that the BCP properly meets expectations.
Using checklists	Checklists confirm whether the BCP meets pre-determined, documented business needs.
Performing walkthroughs	Walkthroughs specifically focus on each BCP process phase. Planners and testers walk through the individual steps to validate the logical flow of the sequence of events.
Parallel testing	This test is used to ensure that systems perform adequately at the alternate offsite facility, without taking the main site offline.
Conducting simulations	Simulations effectively test the validity and compliance of the BCP. In a simulation, each part of the planning process is exercised, with the exception of replicating and causing an outage. Although calls are made and specific actions are taken, the real event response is simulated.
	Simulations are instrumental in verifying design flaws, recovery requirements, and implementation errors. By identifying these solution discrepancies, process improvements can be applied that help ensure high-level plan maintenance.

BCP Testing Method	Description
Full interruption testing	This test mimics an actual business disruption by shutting down the original site to test transfer and migration procedures to the alternate site, and to test operations in the presence of an emergency.

Business Plan Maintenance

Durable plan maintenance hinges on continual process improvements that are determined throughout the testing phase. To adequately maintain the BCP, it should be reviewed yearly for any necessary changes. Evaluation and test results should be included in the review process to improve any areas of deficiency. If any business units or departments have major changes in processes, products, or IT, the BCP should be updated to accommodate these modifications.

BCP Implementation During a Disaster

The business continuity process includes several steps to properly resume business operations both during and after a disruptive event. Your BCP should outline in clear detail the exact steps that should happen. This outline should be written in plain language that any intelligent person in the organization who was not involved in the BCP planning process should be able to still read and follow.

The exact steps of the implementation will depend upon the organization, but the following table summarizes the steps to follow to implement a BCP.

Business Continuity Step	Description
Assess level of disaster's impact	You will need to determine if the disruption is a temporary condition from which the business will naturally recover without incident, or if it is a disaster that will require activation of the DRP.
Begin continuity operations	The BCP should contain detailed steps regarding methods for implementing continuity operations. This is the initiation of the DRP. There will be an established process to declare the disaster and the disaster recovery team will begin their work. An operations manager should be appointed to oversee the situation and manage communications.
Notify stakeholders	Stakeholders should be informed of a significant business disruption. They may consist of senior management, board members, affected managers and employees, service providers, and potentially, suppliers. Clients should be informed if the disruption will noticeably affect services or product deliveries.
Follow the roadmap	Work as swiftly and diligently as possible to achieve the milestones in the BCP to restore the company to normal operations.
Declare the emergency over	Even though there may be some outstanding long-term recovery steps, at some point you must officially declare the disaster over. When this happens, consider holding some sort of celebratory event to help staff close the disaster on an emotional level.

Guidelines for Applying BCP Fundamentals

Here are some guidelines you can follow to implement a business continuity plan:

- Treat developing the BCP as an actual project with project management.

- Ensure that you have upper management support to develop the BCP.
- Assemble the BCP team, including an advisory committee and program coordinators.
- Go through the BCP planning steps, including project initiation, determining project scope and plan, performing a BIA, testing the plan, and maintaining the plan.
- Determine your critical business processes, and the maximum tolerable downtime for each.
- Have a contingency for managing both the immediate financial losses as well as the additional impacts of such losses.
- Have a contingency plan for working under reduced efficiency, and a clear roadmap to return to full operations.
- Ensure that your BCP is written clearly so that any intelligent member of your staff can follow and execute it, even if they were not originally involved in creating the BCP.
- Ensure that your BCP is available to all staff members, particularly during a disaster.

ACTIVITY 1-7
Discussing Business Continuity Plan Fundamentals

Scenario

The Case of a Company's Risky Business: Part 3

Your recent threat modeling activity at XYZ Group really opened management's eyes to the need for risk management. Now the company is concerned that a major incident could severely disrupt the company, or even put it out of business. The senior management team flew to an executive retreat last week where they were introduced to the idea of business continuity planning. They have just returned from the retreat, and have asked you to help them to better understand the BCP process.

---

1. What business continuity disasters do the XYZ Group face?

2. What are some of the critical business processes that XYZ needs to sustain during a disaster?

3. Which processes do you think XYZ should recover first?

4. After developing the BCP, what do you think will be the most critical exercise to perform to ensure that the BCP will save the company during a disaster?

5. How can you ensure that the BCP will be executed properly during the disaster?

TOPIC H

Acquisition Strategy and Practice

Since your organization is likely to purchase hardware, software, or services from a third party, you must understand the risks that go with such acquisitions. In this topic, you will learn strategies to help mitigate acquisition risk.

Acquisition Strategy

Security professionals need to be involved when an organization purchases hardware, software, or services. The security professional must help the organization shift its focus away from traditional supply chain vendors to cyber goods and service suppliers. The need for cyber security during all phases of the acquisition process is more important than ever. If there aren't adequate security features in the acquired product service, the risk to the organization will extend the entire lifetime of the item. To incorporate security considerations into all acquisitions, you should:

*   Create baseline security requirements as a condition for contracts.
*   Include requirements to purchase from Original Equipment Manufacturers (OEMs), authorized resellers, or other trusted sources.
*   Be aware of who is responsible for security controls when contracting with third-party service organizations.
*   Have a contingency plan for dealing with goods or services that underperform, especially if they put the integrity of your system at risk.
*   Have a contingency plan for dealing with insufficient goods or services such as inadequate numbers of items or software licenses.

Hardware and Software Acquisition

Organizations will acquire hardware, including computers, laptops, mobile devices, network devices, cabling, server room equipment, phones, and many other similar components for their operations. Since most electronic devices have an embedded operating system, the security professional must assist the organization in evaluating the security of those devices, and determine what level of configuration and patching is needed to bring the device to a suitable security level.

Software acquisition can include not only applications and licenses, but also any other electronic-based assets such as documents, source files, source code, multimedia files, and templates. As with hardware devices, software-based products (especially operating systems and applications) must also be evaluated for their security level. Security professionals must be familiar with the security vulnerabilities of the applications and operating systems that the organization is acquiring, and how to reconfigure the software or patch those vulnerabilities.

Service Acquisition

Companies are increasingly relying on network- and IT-related services to achieve their objectives. While one might initially think of physical goods and delivery logistics as being the basic components of a supply chain, your supplies could also be digital in nature. In addition to the risks to vendors and transporters, the security professional must also consider the risks of losing the digital infrastructure which today's modern commerce depends on.

The following table summarizes some of the services that the organization may contract.

Service	Description
Infrastructure as a service (IaaS)	• The service provider supplies basic computing hardware resources such as processors, memory, or storage. • The customer provides the operating system, data, and applications. • The customer provides the majority of the security controls.
Platform as a service (PaaS)	• The service provider provides the basic computing resources and the operating system or database. • The customer provides the applications and data. • The responsibility for security is shared.
Software as a service (SaaS)	• The service provider provides basic computing resources, the operating system, and the applications. • The customer provides the data. • The service provider is responsible for the majority of the security controls.

Additional Services

You should also consider security when contracting these additional services:

- **Maintenance**: You might outsource your network management or maintenance to a third-party.
- **Software development**: You might outsource software development to a third-party, or an offshore division in your company.
- **Installation**: You might outsource the installation of devices or infrastructure to a third-party, particularly if the rollout involves thousands of devices or users.

Security Questions to Ask Before Acquisition

Before the organization acquires the hardware, software, or service, be sure that the following questions are asked and sufficiently answered:

- Does the product or service meet your own security policies?
- Does the supplier have their own security policies?
- Do your policies and the supplier's policies contradict each other or dovetail?
- If there are gaps or contradictions, how will those gaps be addressed?

Acquisition Security Requirements

Requirements gathering is the first step for any acquisition strategy. Before you purchase a product or service you need to know what the "problem" is and what is required by the intended users. The document should include:

- An executive summary.
- The scope of the project.
- A statement of primary objectives.
- A description of the environment or context for use.
- User requirements that are specific and measurable.
- Any constraints.

SLA

A *service level agreement (SLA)* is a business document that is used to define a pre-agreed level of performance for an activity or contracted service. If the service is contracted and not delivered with the agreed-upon level of performance, the SLA has been violated and a penalty will be enforced.

The internal use of an SLA in an organization will assist management in determining the level of performance for each business unit.

An SLA should include the following:

- Definition of the parties involved in the agreement
- Provision for an orderly transition of the process or program to the vendor
- Scope of services
- Change order process
- Service levels and remedies
- Subcontracting
- Pricing
- Benchmarking
- Intellectual property rights
- Security, privacy, and confidentiality
- Limitations of liability
- Warranty
- Indemnities
- Provider BCP
- Dispute resolution
- Termination and transition back to owner

In some cases, you might not need a full SLA with your provider. When the product or service is simpler in nature, you might find it sufficient to use a Memorandum of Understanding (MOU). This is a less formal agreement, considered to be suitable when the acquisition is more limited in scope.

Example: Network Resource Uptime

For example, the IT department has developed and agreed to an internal SLA that requires 99.99% uptime for all network resources. The failure to meet the uptime requirement may point to many different issues that need remediation. Without the SLA, low performance levels are often difficult to determine. With the SLA, the accepted level of performance is agreed to in advance and under-performance is easily identified.

Business Documents That Support Acquisitions

There are several common types of business documents security professionals should expect to encounter in their normal duties. Many of these focus on business partnerships and alliances; since all organizations do business with other entities, there are many types of common agreements used to govern those relationships. Some of these agreements specifically deal with security and risk management, whereas others may incorporate them secondarily or not at all.

Document	Description
Interoperability agreement (IA)	This is the general term for any document that outlines a business partnership or collaboration in which all entities exchange some resources while working together.
Interconnection security agreement (ISA)	This type of agreement is geared toward the information systems of partnered entities to ensure that the use of inter-organizational technology meets a certain security standard of confidentiality, integrity, and availability. Because they focus heavily on security, ISAs are often written to be legally binding. ISAs can also support MOUs to increase their security viability. NIST provides a security guide for developing an interconnection plan, titled *Security Guide for Interconnecting Information Technology Systems Special Publication 800-47*.

Document	Description
Memorandum of understanding (MOU)	This type of agreement is usually not legally binding and typically does not involve the exchange of money. MOUs are less formal than traditional contracts, but still have a certain degree of significance to all parties involved. They are typically enacted as a way to express a desire for all parties to achieve the same goal in the agreed-upon manner. An MOU document might contain background information on each organization; the history of the relationship between the two organizations and circumstances that led to the partnership; and a general or specific timeline for collaborative business activities. Because they typically have no legal foundation, MOUs are not the most secure agreement for a partnership.
Operating-level agreement (OLA)	This agreement identifies and defines the working relationships between groups or divisions of an organization as they share responsibilities toward fulfilling one or more SLAs with their internal or external customers.
Non-disclosure agreement (NDA)	This is an agreement between entities stipulating that they will not share confidential information, knowledge, or materials with unauthorized third parties. NDAs also commonly state in which cases, if any, data may be used or processed by the receiving entity. For data acquired through public sources, an NDA is not enforceable.
Business partnership agreement (BPA)	This agreement defines how a partnership between business entities will be conducted, and what exactly is expected of each entity in terms of services, finances, and security. For security purposes, BPAs should describe exactly what the partners are willing to share with each other, and how any inter-organizational access will be handled.

Secure Outsourcing/Offshoring

As with cloud services, secure offshoring or outsourcing places some of your processes into the hands of a third-party provider. With cloud services, you usually use a self-service portal to manage your own services on the provider's website. With offshoring and outsourcing, however, you generally allow the third-party to perform daily management of your service. A common example of outsourcing is a 24-hour help desk system. When a customer calls at three in the morning, someone will answer the phone, even if they are on the other side of the world. Another common example of outsourcing is having some of your manufacturing done in a different country where labor is cheap.

Usually companies that outsource or offshore some of their processes will have some level of participation in the management of the process. Often managers are sent to oversee offshore activities. Global institutions may maintain their own offshore capabilities, thus making their help desk or manufacturing or application development department a 24-hour shop.

The following list summarizes risks to offshoring and outsourcing:

- You are dependent on someone else to do some of your work for you. You will need to make sure that you have good oversight, constant communications, and good service level agreements.
- There are likely to be language and cultural barriers, different holiday schedules, or mismatched laws and governance practices.
- Time zone differences will make timely communications difficult.
- Your offshore partner may not have the same electrical power or network bandwidth available, thus making phone communications or even their availability for communications more difficult.

- Your offshore partners are likely to have very different notions and expectations of how to conduct business, quality control and quality assurance, intellectual property, personnel and equipment safety, privacy, and Labor Relations.

The successful offshore or outsourced project or process is one in which the company is continuously, actively engaged with the offshore partner. Management teams from both sides will have to work very closely to ensure that the offshore partner provides exactly the product or service desired.

Outsourced Service Risk Mitigation

When outsourcing or offshoring, practice the following to reduce your security risk:

- Assess the risk and ask if a third party can do the task better than you can.
- Put a ring fence around the task or process to provide clear boundaries and limit its scope and maintain a clear interface with the outsource provider.
- Spend the time to actually get to know the outsource provider and the environment and conditions that they work in. Treat the outsource contract almost like a marriage. Perform your due diligence on the provider site. Observe the staff long enough to see if they try to shortcut procedure or bypass security controls.
- Verify that the provider adheres to secure working standards such as ISO 27001.
- Conduct a thorough risk assessment.
- Assign people from your own staff to remain on-site to work with the outsourced management team.
- Build the working relationship with your outsource provider.
- If your industry is constrained by federal regulation, recognize that ultimately you are liable, not your outsource provider, for adhering to these requirements.

Third-Party Assessments

A service level agreement is not enough to protect your interests. You need to assess whether the standards of the SLA are being met. This is part of your own due diligence process. When working with a third party for hardware, software, or services you should implement security assessments, inspections, and audits to confirm that they meet your security requirements. Use the following checklist when assessing a third party:

- Develop an information security assessment plan.
- Determine who in your organization will be responsible for the assessment.
- Determine the requirements for the assessment.
- Plan and allocate resources.
- If you choose a third-party assessor, evaluate that person or group.
- Ensure that your own information security policies and procedures exist first.
- Prepare documents and report templates that will be used during the assessment.
- Prepare a nondisclosure agreement.
- Allocate the team that will do the information gathering.
- Conduct the data collection.

As you conduct the assessment, you'll need to make sure that key personnel that you will be interviewing are available. As you evaluate the third party, determine if they have sufficient administrative, technical, and administrative controls in place. Be prepared to provide recommendations to cover any gaps. You may have to adjust your own policy and procedure to ensure that all gaps are covered.

Guidelines for Implementing Acquisition Strategy and Practice

Here are some guidelines you can follow when acquiring hardware, software, or services:

- Keep in mind that much acquisition today is of an information security nature, rather than physical goods or services.
- Besides evaluating functional and physical security aspects of hardware, be sure to vet any embedded operating system or application.
- Research any vulnerabilities related with software that you are acquiring, and be prepared to patch or reconfigure the software to bring it to a suitable security baseline.
- Assist the organization in transitioning to IT service acquisition including outsourcing and offshoring.
- Make sure that your SLA is comprehensive, and that it is approved by your legal department as well as your IT department.
- Spend time with your outsource service provider to mitigate risk.
- Go through a comprehensive checklist of assessing any third parties before engaging them.

ACTIVITY 1-8
Discussing Acquisition Strategy and Practice

Scenario

The Case of the Expanding Company: Part 1

You are an information security professional working for a small organization. The company is about to launch a new online product. Realizing that it will soon have to support customers in all time zones, management is considering outsourcing its help desk to provide round-the-clock customer care. Three competing vendors, two of which are offshore, are being considered for the contract. Each vendor is being championed by a different manager. You have been tasked with assisting the vetting process of the prospective vendors.

1. Of all the concepts discussed in this topic, which do you consider to be the most important when evaluating the three competing vendors? Why?

2. What items would you require in the vendor's SLA? Why?

3. Would you handle your evaluation of the offshore vendors differently from the local vendor? If so, what would you focus on the most and why?

TOPIC I

Personnel Security Policies

Human resources, while your greatest asset, are also your greatest source of risk. In this topic you will learn how to minimize personnel risk through security policies.

The Need for Personnel Security

Once security goals are in place, there are a number of concepts that can be applied to employees to reinforce security within your organization. Techniques such as personnel management are critical components to strengthening organizational security. Employing these techniques will help you increase security levels and protect your information systems from intrusive, unauthorized access.

In some ways your employees are a bigger threat than outside individuals. The individuals you hire are close to your data and might know the weaknesses of your processes and controls. Or they might simply be the weakest link and targets for social engineering attacks. You will want to carefully assess the security risks for each job position and make sure to put in place candidate screening policies and employment agreements and policies to protect your information assets.

Job Position Sensitivity Profiling

Job position sensitivity profiling is the security practice of determining an individual's need-to-know information as it relates to the individual's specific job function. The individual's required access rights to specific system information needs to be carefully assessed before authorization is granted. First, data owners must determine the need-to-know information for each organizational job function, and work with the security department to document it in a *sensitivity profile* for each job. The profiles are created based on the tasks performed, not on the individuals performing the tasks. Then, during the position-assignment process, the sensitivity profiles help administrators assign authorization permissions to individuals.

Example Sensitivity Profile for Payroll Clerk

A payroll clerk must have access to a limited amount of general, personal employee information. The payroll clerk needs to know employee names, addresses, telephone numbers, and numbers of dependents. The payroll clerk does not need to know employees' previous job performance ratings, security clearance levels, or educational degrees.

Job Candidate Screening

When hiring a new employee, it is important to match the appropriate employee with the applicable job and security responsibilities.

Hiring Practice	Description
Baseline hiring procedures	General hiring practices for all positions should include: • A personal interview to evaluate the potential employee's personality. • Education, licensing, and certification verification. • Work history verifications. • Criminal history checks. • Drug use checks. • Reference checks to verify the information provided on the application. If the potential employee is misstating facts on the application, there is a strong potential that the individual will be unreliable and untrustworthy. Be sure to conduct all history and background checks in accordance with the relevant federal, state, or other governmental fair hiring regulations that pertain to your locality. Some organizations opt to hire third-party firms that have specialized expertise in conducting these types of checks and investigations.
Position sensitivity screening	Hiring for security-sensitive positions should include: • Financial and/or credit history reviews. • Personality screenings. • Lie detector testing. • Extended background investigations. • Security clearances. Especially when you conduct more detailed and intensive security checks, be sure to comply with the relevant federal, state, or other governmental regulations that pertain to your locality.

Employment Agreements

Employment agreements are usually signed prior to or on the first day of work. The purpose of these agreements is to protect the organization while the individual is employed and after they have left the organization. They might include:

• Non-disclosure agreements to protect sensitive information.
• A code of conduct.
• Ethics agreements.
• Conflict of interest agreements.

Employment Policies

Another important consideration is the due care that you exercise after employment has begun. Implementing and enforcing policies such as those listed below will help maintain security. You should conduct periodic audits to make sure that the appropriate level of access is being maintained.

Employee Policies	Description
SoD	Separation of duties (SoD) monitors task implementation based on the specific responsibilities of authorized personnel. One person should not have the capability to implement all the steps of a security process. For example, users do not set up security profiles and security administrators do not perform system administrator functions.

Employee Policies	Description
Need to know	The need-to-know method manages individual information access based on job scope and job function requirements.
Least privilege	Least privilege helps regulate security by limiting individuals' capabilities to what is specifically needed for them to perform their jobs.
Job rotation	Job rotation involves rotating individuals between different organizational jobs so that they don't have too much control over a segment of the business for any extensive period of time. When combined with SoD, it can help prevent collusion. It can also provide individuals with knowledge about different procedures and job responsibilities. It also creates a foundation for cross-training that increases employee availability in the organization.
Mandatory vacations	Mandatory vacation policies enforce a minimum amount of consecutive vacation days each year, which allows management ample time to audit employee activities.
Regular password and access control updates	Due to the high risk potential for losing sensitive information, passwords and other authentication methods need to be changed frequently for users who have authorized access.
Frequent reviews of user privileges	Frequent reviews of account access capabilities are required to ensure that the privileges granted to a user are still required.

Termination

Employees arrive and leave organizations for many different reasons. Some of those reasons are friendly (retirement, relocation to another city) and some are unfriendly, where there is a possibility that the former employee has the means and intention to harm the organization. Programs need to be developed with the input of Legal and HR to prevent a potential disgruntled employee access to systems and data. You need to keep in mind the job position sensitivity profile and treat each type of termination with different levels of care in order to protect the organization.

Termination Type	Level of Care
Friendly	• Complete an exit interview. • Collect keys, ID cards, badges, tokens, cryptographic keys, and any other access tools. • Collect laptops, phones, company credit cards, or any other company property. • Disable access.
Unfriendly	• Disable access immediately, or even prior to notifying the employee of the termination. • Have security escort them from the building directly after the termination. • Disable access. • All passwords on all systems should be changed.

Contractors

Contractors, vendors, and consultants are often brought into the company for specific business needs. You must ensure you have adequate safeguards to protect the loss of sensitive information and mitigate any potential damage. The level of care will differ based on the nature of the relationship.

Some procedures you might follow:

- Escorting the individual if he is on site infrequently.
- Monitoring the individual virtually by screen capture technology or webcam recording.
- Requiring a non-disclosure agreement with specific sanctions.
- Investigating the security screening procedures of the third-party business who is providing contractors.
- Requiring the third-party organization to identify which individuals will be working with your company and verifying that identity on site.

Policy Compliance and Privacy

All individuals have an expectation of privacy, so you need to balance that with enforcing security policies. The balance is different in different cultures. While you might be able use a webcam to monitor individuals on site, you might not be able to do so when they are working from a home office. In most cultures it would be acceptable to place CCTV cameras in public hallways, but it would be unacceptable to have them in bathrooms. The key to maintaining this balance is clear communication about the security policies that affect privacy, including posting notices of monitoring.

Guidelines for Drafting Personnel Security Policies

Here are some guidelines you can follow for personal security policies:

- Practice job position sensitivity profiling to limit a user's access based on need to know.
- Use baseline and position sensitivity screening techniques when considering potential employees.
- Ensure that potential employees understand and agree to your employment contracts.
- Have clear employment policies in place for hiring, termination, and contractors.
- Ensure that any employment policies are in compliance with applicable laws and regulations.

ACTIVITY 1-9
Discussing Personnel Security Policies

Scenario

The Case of the Outsourced Help Desk: Part 2

Response to the company's new online product has been overwhelming. In order keep up with demand, the company must quickly expand itself. Management is using this opportunity to implement a more formal organizational structure at corporate headquarters. New roles are being created in all departments. Some employees will be promoted into new positions, and some who have not performed will be reassigned, demoted, or terminated. Many new people will be hired to fill sales, marketing, customer service, accounting, and management positions. Some staffers who used to enjoy broad privileges (particularly IT personnel) will find their new duties more focused and restrictive. The company is planning to hire contractors and temporary employees to help with the work until more permanent employees are hired.

You have been tasked with assisting management in applying personnel security best practices during the expansion process.

1. As the company prepares to rapidly expand, which personnel security practice do you think should be implemented first and why?

2. Of all the employee roles mentioned, which ones do you think require the most job position sensitivity profiling and why?

3. How would you mitigate risk when reassigning, demoting, or terminating under-performing staff?

TOPIC J

Security Awareness and Training

No one can be expected to support organizational security without adequate training and awareness. In this final topic, you will learn how to use awareness and training as a security tool.

Security Awareness

It is important for all organizations to have methods to promote security topics amongst all their employees because users are often the weakest link when it comes to security. If people are not aware of security risks or the policies and procedures in place, they can't play their role in protecting the organization.

Awareness efforts focus on attitude, motivation, and attention. The purpose is to make personnel aware of the potential threats, help them understand the impact on the well-being of the company and themselves, and to motivate personnel to follow approved practices and to pay attention to details that might point to a potential security problem. Being aware of the need for security is an important step toward changing user behavior at all levels and job roles within the organization.

All information about security awareness needs to be meaningful and easily understood by the audience. The program should include multiple methods to increase awareness. Some methods may include newsletter articles, classes, and security posters in highly visible locations.

 Note: At a minimum, all staff should attend security awareness training at least once a year. This also includes management. More frequent training may be necessary in environments where security risk is high.

Example Awareness Program Objectives

Awareness programs can have many objectives. One of the most common objectives is preventing internal personnel from accessing information that they are not authorized to access. Often, people attempt to access data that requires authorization simply because they do not know it is not allowed. Another objective is increasing the efficacy of a security policy through actual implementation of the policy. Finally, awareness programs often attempt to reduce any misuse of company resources, such as data and hardware. Awareness programs allow management to circulate the policy message to those who need it, as well as get employees involved in security awareness and accountability.

Security Training

Being aware of the risks is only half the battle—employees need to learn how to do their part to prevent the problem. Training picks up where awareness leaves off, providing personnel with skills and competencies to apply best practices, such as identifying a potential phishing scam or odd activity on their computer or mobile device, knowing how to securely save their work files, and so forth.

Improving security awareness within your organization and offering security training will help ensure that your staff is knowledgeable about the security policy and its benefits and is prepared to perform in accordance with its mandates. Your security training should include:

- A clearly identified target audience.
- Training objectives mapped to desired increases in on-the-job security practices.
- Training outcomes that can be quantified and measured.
- Variations and customizations for different job roles and levels.
- Provision for updates and refresher training sessions.

Example: Organizational Security Program

For example, while developing a security program for his organization, Sam prepares training objectives and facilitates an education initiative for management and staff. He concentrates on addressing specific security policies, threat concerns, system information protection mechanisms, and attack prevention strategies. He documents organizational security guidelines, methodologies, and best practices. He also arranges brown-bag lunch seminars, web-based training, classroom training, podcasts, email blasts, and other forums to provide effective awareness education and periodic security training.

Appropriate Levels

The level of training will vary by job role, but all employees must have at least a basic understanding of their roles. A security training program should include the following job roles.

Job Role	Training Focus
Senior management and Board of Directors	The importance of security to business objectives, legislative and regulatory requirements, and shareholder expectations.
Mid-management	Details of policies, procedures, standards, and guidelines and how to monitor their employees' compliance.
Staff	Basic computer security practices like strong passwords and avoiding social engineering attacks.
Technical employees	Technical requirements for implementing security policies.
Security professionals	Up-to-date knowledge of current threats and controls, and best practices for risk assessment, threat modeling, and business continuity planning.

Training as Part of Regulatory Compliance

Of particular interest to the security professional and management is the need to train for regulatory compliance. Your high-level officers may be liable for the effectiveness of the compliance program including staff training. This is part of due diligence as listed in the federal sentencing guidelines. For that reason, any regulatory compliance training should include the following:

* Training levels and content that are appropriate to the job role.
* An explanation of what the regulations require and the organization's plan for compliance.
* A clear map to show how training objectives and outcomes relate to the various subparts of the regulation.
* The roles and expectations for individuals in regulatory compliance.
* Directly relevant examples to demonstrate how different job roles will remain in compliance.
* A resource for further questions and clarifications.
* An objective way to measure and test the effectiveness of the training.
* A provision for updated and refresher training.

Guidelines for Developing Security Awareness and Training

To promote security awareness and provide effective training:

* Develop security awareness training points.
    * Address password protection.
    * Discuss information protection.
    * List procedures to follow if unauthorized individuals are detected in the facility.
    * Identify tactics to defeat social engineering.

- Characterize email threats.
- Analyze virus and worm prevention.
- Discuss information disclosure prevention.
- Review virtual private network (VPN) practices to protect data.
- Plan professional career development and security training.
  - Offer the necessary training so staff members can improve their skill levels.
  - Consider training offered by vendors during product announcements and product updates.
  - Invest in organizational career development to help increase staff morale.
  - Encourage organizational security memberships at the national or local level.
- Offer e-learning or instructor-led training.
  - Contract with commercial vendors for product-specific or generic security training.
  - Arrange mandatory, instructor-led presentations and seminars.

ACTIVITY 1-10
Discussing Security Awareness and Training

Scenario

The Case of the Outsourced Help Desk: Part 3

After the organization's restructuring, management is concerned that new employees, and even existing employees in new roles, don't have the adequate security knowledge that they should to keep the organization safe. Up until now, there hasn't been any formal process for getting people trained on the company's security policies, standards, and guidelines. Rather than continue to take a passive approach to people-based security, you've been tasked with planning a training program for all employees to go through.

1. What security issues need to be addressed in this training program?

2. What are the objectives and expected outcomes for the training?

3. What are the key points that your training should include for general staff?

4. Other than general staff, how would you customize the training program for different job roles/levels (e.g., board of directors, management, IT staff, security personnel, etc.)?

Summary

In this lesson, you examined security governance, ethical practice, and regulatory compliance and how they will help you efficiently manage risk exposure, minimize security breaches, and defend against system vulnerabilities. You analyzed risk management criteria as well as employing the appropriate methodology and processes for implementing business continuity plans. You also identified best practices for acquiring products and services, hiring employees and contracting with third parties, and creating security documentation, and applied the value of proactive security planning, training, and awareness.

What type of risk management and business continuity planning does your organization have in place?

What types of security policies exist in your organization and how does your organization inform and train people about the policies?

Note: Check your CHOICE Course screen for opportunities to interact with your classmates, peers, and the larger CHOICE online community about the topics covered in this course or other topics you are interested in. From the Course screen you can also access available resources for a more continuous learning experience.

2 | Asset Security

Lesson Time: 2 hours

Lesson Objectives

In this lesson, you will:

- Classify assets.

- Protect privacy.

- Discuss appropriate asset retention strategies.

- Determine data security controls.

- Discuss secure data handling.

Lesson Introduction

In the last lesson, you learned the importance of the CIA triad and risk assessment and management. Because data is such an important asset to an organization, many of these same concepts will need to be applied to it as well. As data needs become more critical and the need to access it even more real time, it has become even more difficult to protect it. Organizations have always needed to protect their physical data assets and now they need to protect their logical data assets as well. Additionally, your users are no longer willing to exclusively work at their desk; they want whenever, wherever access. This means protecting data on more devices in more places than ever before. Companies need to consider all the places they store and transmit data and look for ways to protect it.

TOPIC A

Asset Classification

When applying security to your organization's assets, the first thing you will need to know is the asset's value. When you take the time to identify and classify your data assets it will ultimately make it easier to protect those assets. In this topic, you will learn how to classify your assets for protection.

 Note: To learn more, view the LearnTO presentations from the **LearnTO** tile on the CHOICE course screen.

Asset Management

An IT asset is any hardware, software, information/data, physical system, or documentation that the company owns. *IT Asset Management (ITAM)* is not a technology, but rather a set of business functions that support IT strategic decision-making and lifecycle management of IT assets. It combines financial, contractual, and inventory activities to provide broader management support for wisely investing in and using IT assets.

The major part of IT asset management is managing the lifecycle of hardware, systems, and software. From identifying the need, to procurement, to deployment, to maintenance, and finally decommissioning and disposal, asset lifecycle requires management and security at every stage.

When designing and implementing secure asset management, be sure to address the following:

- Strike a reasonable balance between cost and need.
- Identify and distinguish between data ownership and data custodianship, especially with intellectual property.
- Clarify what data is private, and implement controls to secure the privacy.
- Have the foresight when implementing asset security to protect the organization from possible future liability, especially if an individual has been injured in some way and is suing the company.
- Identify what data is sensitive to the organization and apply classifications to the data to make it easier to implement different control types.
- Be very clear about regulatory policy requirements, and be sure to implement them in your asset management.
- In your policy, have a process in place to respond to legal requests for your data, including data discovery.

Asset Management Roles

Managing assets requires personnel to take on various roles. The following table summarizes the key points of each role.

Role	Description
Data Owner	The data owner has direct knowledge and involvement in the creation and/or acquisition of the data. They are usually involved in the usage of the data as well. They will need to understand the cost of the data whether acquired or created internally, the quality of the data, and the risk and sensitivity associated with the data. As the sensitivity of the data rises, so does the potential cost of disclosure, alterations, or unwanted destruction. All of these factors and more will be used to determine the safeguards that are needed to protect the data. The data owner will determine who has access to the data, and at what level.
	The data owner should also have input into the data retention and data destruction policies. Data owners should also be aware of any legal or regulatory issues with the data. Along with data owners, many organizations will define system owners and process owners as well. For example, in large database environments, there may be separate owners for the system that the database runs on, process owners for database design and data acquisition, but it will be important to also identify who owns the data component.
Data Custodian	The data custodian is tasked with protecting the data. This role is not the same as the data owner. The data custodian implements access requirements specified by the data owner. The data custodian is expected to apply controls, maintain, monitor, and quite likely in the end, destroy the data. The data custodian is usually a database administrator, system administrator, or some other IT department role.
System Owner	The system owner is the person or entity that owns the computer that the data (and database) resides on. Depending on the organization, the system owner may be a completely different person or group from the data owner or data custodian:
	• For example, if the sales department owns and maintains its data on its own servers, it is at once data owner, data custodian, and system owner.
	• If the sales department depends on the IT department to supply and manage the server, as well as apply access controls on the database, then the sales department is the data owner, and the IT department is both the system owner and data custodian.
	• If the sales department depends on the IT department to implement access controls on its database, and the IT department in turn depends on a third party to provide and maintain the servers, then the sales department is the data owner, the IT department is the data custodian, and the third party is the system owner
	The system owner might also need to be involved to help implement your classification on a technical level. For example, many operating systems have mechanisms for searching for and automatically classifying data based on specific criteria such as the name of the document creator, the date the document was created, or keywords in the document. It would be up to the system administrator to implement such mechanisms.

Role	Description
Business Owner	A business owner is the person or entity who owns a business or part of a business. This person makes business decisions that are implemented in an attempt to make a profit for the company. The business owner will generally not be interested in the technical aspects of the data or asset management, but instead will be interested in the financial value of utilizing such data or assets.

Classification Principles

To adequately protect information from disclosure and other threats, you need to understand the risks associated with the release or modification of the information. The risk of loss or modification is often minimized by labeling the information. Labeling schemes are often known as *classifications*. Data classification is used to support the organization's requirements for confidentiality, integrity, and availability.

One of the first things you do in classification is to determine the business value of an IT asset. Management must determine the following:

- The asset's sensitivity level (who should have access to the asset).
- The purpose of the asset.
- The value of the asset.
- The criticality of the asset.
- The owner of the asset (typically a specific department or business unit manager).

Classification Process

Once the asset has been classified, the IT department can manage its lifecycle and place appropriate access control mechanisms on it to protect it. There are six major steps for asset classification.

Step	Description
1. Identify the asset	Determine what exactly are your IT assets? Which assets are critical?
	An asset could be physical hardware, a database, any kind of file, an operational or support procedure,or any information that has been archived. An asset could also include disaster recovery and continuity plans. Your IT assets could even include services and functionality that have been outsourced to third parties. They could be communication or infrastructure services that you depend on. They could even be environmental services such as electricity, HVAC, water, etc.
	When identifying your critical assets, ask yourself which ones would destroy the business if they were lost in a fire or stolen by a hacker?

Step	Description
2. Determine who is accountable/responsible for the integrity of the asset	This is easy for tangible physical items. The person who is responsible for hardware has to make sure it's not mishandled or damaged or lost or stolen.
	Determining who is responsible for information assets is a little more difficult. Although the IT department will usually be the custodian of data, establishing and enforcing any controls as required on the data, it is the actual data owner (the business unit that will be using the data) that will determine the level of control required and must ultimately be responsible for the data's accuracy.
	For example, the IT department will make sure that the financial database is secure and available, but it is the accounting department that is responsible for what actually goes in that database.
3. Establish ownership of the asset	The data owner is usually the manager of the department that uses that data. It is this person who is ultimately responsible for the value and use of the asset.
4. Place a value on the asset	This is not simply the cost to initially acquired asset or the amount of money the asset makes for the company, but also includes the soft cost in maintaining the asset in the cost should the asset have to be replaced. Items that cost a certain amount 10 years ago might be very difficult to replace today, and thus actually have considerably more value than their initial purchase price.
5. Prepare a schema (structure) for classifying your assets	You do this by creating classification levels. The criteria can include the level of confidentiality, the value of the asset, the amount of time sensitivity of the asset, the level of access rights and authorization, and the retention required before the asset can be decommissioned or destroyed.
6. Implement the classification schema	This is actually difficult to do consistently because of the fluid nature of information.
	Imagine a behind-closed-doors session in which a top-secret formula that will cure cancer has been presented to only a few senior managers. The formula is about to go to an independent testing lab for verification. The managing director who is responsible for engaging the testing lab sends an email to her secretary, who forwards it to the various department heads and prints out a hard copy for reference at the next meeting.
	At this point, this top-secret information now exists on hard drives across the enterprise, as well as a paper copy that was left in the conference room for a few hours. While each player in the scenario had a legitimate need to have a copy of the information, had it been properly classified as top-secret, controls could have been put in place to ensure that it was always encrypted and employees instructed that no hard copy be permitted to leave the responsible party's immediate line of sight.

Classification Policies

A data classification policy provides a framework for classifying company data based on its value, sensitivity, and criticality. The policy can then be used to inform and drive all data classification procedures and activities. The policy should include:

- The different data classifications your organization uses (for example, Sensitive, Personally Identifiable, Confidential, Internal, Public, and so on.).

- Criteria for determining the appropriate classification level.
- The protection requirements of each classification.
- Roles and responsibilities of data owners, data custodians, and data users.

How users use the data can also drive your classification types. For example, if some of the data is health related and requires special handling for regulatory compliance, it might receive a special health classification, as well as being labeled "Personally Identifiable."

After the data has been classified, there should be regular reviews to see if the data has maintained the appropriate classification. If not, any discrepancies should be documented to understand how the change happened.

Examples of classification policies can be found here: **www.it.ufl.edu/policies/information-security/data-classification/**.

 Note: In addition to the security benefits of classifying data, many organizations use data classification policies to improve storage utilization, automate data retention, and improve indexing and search capabilities.

Classification Schemes

Classification schemes come in two forms: military and commercial.

Military classification is implemented by the U.S. federal government, while commercial classification is employed by non-governmental organizations. Military classification is a strictly defined and very rigid part of the mandatory access control system. Commercial schemes need to be developed to support the particular needs of the business.

Military Classification Schemes

Military classification schemes are composed of four classification levels.

Military Classification Scheme Level	Risk If Information Is Disclosed to Unauthorized Entities
Top Secret	Grave damage to national security.
Secret	Serious damage to national security.
Confidential	Damage to national security.
Unclassified	No damage to national security.

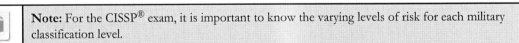 **Note:** For the CISSP® exam, it is important to know the varying levels of risk for each military classification level.

Commercial Classification Schemes

Commercial classification schemes do not use standard naming conventions, but implement levels based on the severity of loss.

Commercial Classification Scheme Level	Description
Corporate Confidential	Information that should not be provided to individuals outside of the enterprise.

Commercial Classification Scheme Level	Description
Personal and Confidential	Information of a personal nature that should be protected.
Private	Correspondence of a private nature between two or more people that should be safeguarded.
Trade Secret	Corporate intellectual property that, if released, will present serious damage to the company's ability to protect patents and processes.
Client Confidential	• Client personal information that, if released, may result in the identity theft of the individual. • Client corporate information or intellectual property. You may need to sign a non-disclosure agreement (NDA) to keep organization information about a client confidential.

 Note: The schemes listed are only samples. For the CISSP exam, it is important to understand the concept of commercial classification schemes, but not these examples specifically.

Guidelines for Implementing Asset Classification

 Note: All of the Guidelines for this lesson are available as checklists from the **Checklist** tile on the CHOICE Course screen.

Here are some guidelines for classifying your organization's IT assets:

- Recognize that IT assets can be anything the company owns, including software, hardware, data/ information, physical systems, and documentation.
- Understand that the data owner specifies the classification and access control levels of the data, and the data custodian implements those classifications and access controls.
- Implement data classification based on the value, sensitivity, and criticality of the data to the organization.
- Implement a six-stage classification process for managing the lifecycle of an asset.
- Outline the who, what, and how of your asset classification system in your classification policy.
- Apply and maintain a military classification scheme if relevant to your organization.
- Apply and maintain a commercial classification scheme if your organization is non-governmental.
- Base commercial classification schemes on the needs of your business.

ACTIVITY 2-1
Analyzing Asset Classification

Scenario

Sharon is the sales manager at a medium-sized company. There have been some recent incidents where internal proprietary information was mistakenly shared with customers. Sharon wants to make sure that her team members can indicate which documents can be shared with people outside the organization, and which documents must stay internal. She also wants Robbie, the database administrator, to put restrictions on who can read and modify data in the sales database. Sharon has heard of the benefits of data classification. She has asked you, the information security professional, to help her understand how to implement it.

---

1. What must Sharon do first in order to classify her data?
   - ○ She must determine if the access controls will be mandatory or discretionary.
   - ○ She must determine who the data owner will be.
   - ○ She must determine the sensitivity, purpose, value, and criticality of the data.
   - ○ She must determine who the data custodian will be.

2. In this scenario, which of the follow statements is true?
   - ○ Sharon is both the data owner and the data custodian.
   - ○ Sharon is the data owner and Robbie is the data custodian.
   - ○ Sharon is the data custodian and Robbie is the data owner.
   - ○ Robbie is both the data owner and the data custodian.

3. Which of the following classifications would be a good choice for Sharon's data?
   - ○ Top Secret
   - ○ Client confidential
   - ○ Corporate confidential
   - ○ Unclassified

4. What additional recommendations would you make to Sharon to help her classify her data?

TOPIC B

Privacy Protection

Now that you know the principles of asset classification, you will want to pay particular attention to a topic that has gained very serious attention: privacy protection. In this topic, you will learn how to use private data while protecting the rights of private data owners.

Privacy

The 1948 Universal Declaration of Human Rights has a clause which states "no-one should be subjected to arbitrary interference with his privacy, family, home or correspondence, nor to attacks on his honor or reputation. Everyone has the right to the protection of the law against such interference or attacks."

Since that document was written, nations have tried to write laws to protect the privacy of their citizens. But, due to the rapidly changing nature of technology, it has proven difficult. Because it is now easy to communicate and do business around the globe, it is harder to define the boundaries for privacy. Many countries either have laws or are introducing legislation to limit how much information a company can collect and retain on individuals. Security practitioners must stay abreast of legal issues in the countries their companies do business in.

As your organization identifies privacy concerns and develops privacy policies, an important component is to recognize the limits of information that will be collected. When possible, closely define:

- What will be collected.
- How collected data will be protected.
- How long private information will be kept.
- How collected data will be shared.
- How private information will be disposed of.

Data Privacy and the Internet of Things

In 2013, the U.S. Federal Trade Commission published a report titled *The Internet of Things: Privacy and Security in a Connected World*. In it, the FTC listed three potential security risks that the Internet of Things can pose to consumers:

- The unauthorized access and misuse of personal information.
- The facilitation of attacks on other systems.
- Increased risk to personal safety.

For more information on the FTC report, see the article at **https://www.ftc.gov/system/files/ documents/reports/federal-trade-commission-staff-report-november-2013-workshop-entitled-internet-things-privacy/150127iotrpt.pdf**.

Privacy Laws

Most governments have some sort of privacy laws in place, with the European Union being the most restrictive. Privacy laws are generally meant to provide private citizens more control over how their personal information is gathered, used, stored, and disseminated. Some laws, however, such as the USA Patriot Act, actually reduce privacy protections in the interest of national security and public safety.

As an information security professional, you must assist your organization in being aware of, and complying with, any relevant laws. Be sure to involve your legal department to make sure of any compliance requirements.

Private Data Ownership

It is generally acknowledged that private data is owned by the person the data is about. In other words, health information about Susie Jones belongs to Susie, and not the hospital or insurance company that has collected the data. This concept of private data belonging to the private citizen and not the company that collects the data makes compliance with privacy laws sometimes very challenging. The organization must balance the requirement for protecting an individual's privacy against the business value of utilizing that data.

For example, a nongovernmental charity that does health research in a developing nation will collect statistics on the effectiveness of their programs. Those statistics must necessarily include personal, private information that rightfully belongs to the individuals, not the organization. And yet, the organization will want to use that information to analyze the effectiveness of their programs and probably even seek donor funding.

The security professional must realize the seriousness of protecting private information, and assist the organization in not only doing what's morally and ethically right in regards to protecting individual privacy, but also likely to be required by law.

Collection Limitations

Private information also requires that only relevant and useful data is collected. If a company wants to perform a drug screening on a prospective employee, they should only be collecting information about whether or not drugs have shown up in that person's system. They should not concern themselves with the discovery that the candidate has had cancer or is a diabetic. The security professional must be conscious of what data is actually necessary for the purpose it was collected, and what data, however enticing, is not relevant to the case at hand and should absolutely not be collected.

 Note: Collection limitations fall under the personal data processing conditions put forth by the European Union's Data Protection Directive.

Databases

The risk of maintaining private data in a database is that now there is an electronic copy that could, with varying degrees of effort, be stolen and sold or used for profit. Over the years, there have been plenty of news articles about Social Security or credit card numbers stolen from a database and sold on the black market. At this point, maintaining private information on a company database makes the need to protect that database even more important. Not only does the data have a business value to the organization, but the organization will also be under additional legal requirements to protect that data from loss or disclosure.

Data Processors

A database is not useful unless somebody is processing the data in it. This exposes private data to users, systems, and processes that otherwise would have no relationship with that data and no reason for accessing it. While it may seem obvious that the person handling someone else's private data should exercise due care in keeping that data confidential, the reality is that the effort is more work. The average user will be focused on their need for and use of the data, and not its owner's privacy.

The European Union Data Protection Directive states that anyone who processes a person's private information must follow eight enforceable requirements. The data must be:

- Fairly and lawfully processed.
- Processed for limited purposes.
- Adequate, relevant, and not excessive.

- Accurate.
- Kept no longer than necessary.
- Processed in accordance with the data subject's rights.
- Secure.
- Transferred only to countries with adequate protection.

For example, if an HR person were to sit with her laptop at an Internet cafe in Paris, and work on a spreadsheet that contains private employee data, that would probably not be considered secure and thus a violation of the directive.

Although the U.S. does not have the same privacy restrictions as the European Union, the information security professional must assist organizations in complying with the spirit of data privacy and private data processing, as well as the actual letter of the law.

Data Longevity

Private data should not be retained indefinitely. Most legal requirements for collecting and using private data also specify that the data can only be kept for as long as the company legitimately needs to use it, and then it must be securely destroyed.

In today's world of social media and constant connectivity, private information ceases to be private the moment it is posted online. You will not be able to retrieve it. Not only is it available for the entire world to read, but there will also be multiple copies of it spread across the Internet. With the advent of big data analytics, your private information will not only live online possibly forever, but will also be used by both companies and the government to profile your personal habits. Additionally, as we move into the era of the Internet of Things (everyday objects that send and receive data on the Internet), we will be inundated with ordinary items that collect our private data and transmit that data to an eternal repository.

Guidelines for Implementing Privacy Protection

Here are some guidelines for protecting privacy.

- Become familiar with privacy laws that affect your organization or work environment.
- Develop a policy in your organization to specify the limits of what can be collected and how it can be processed.
- Only collect, keep, and process data in a lawful manner.
- Ensure that databases containing PII are a high security priority.
- Always keep in mind that you do not own the private data you collect.
- Securely destroy a person's private data once you are through using it.
- Recognize that once you post something to the Internet, including storing information in the cloud, you have basically granted that information eternal life.

ACTIVITY 2-2
Discussing Privacy Protection

Scenario

You are an information security professional hired by the government to work with a small application developer team in a developing nation. The team is creating an electronic health record system that will help clinicians better track and treat deadly diseases such as meningitis, and tuberculosis. The application has extensive reporting capabilities. These reports are required by the non-governmental organizations (NGOs) that need to use the data to treat patients in the field. The NGOs must provide timely and accurate reports as to the effectiveness of their efforts to continue to get funding from the U.S. government. Billions of dollars and millions of lives are at stake.

Because the accuracy of the reports is critical, and it is impossible to effectively simulate millions of patient records, the developers opt to use live patient data from the field. They know they cannot sanitize the data and still reflect the diversity and complexity of the patient population. They keep copies of the data on their laptops which they take home to work on in order to meet tight deadlines. After all, a high-level delegation is coming in one month to review the progress of the program, and the project must be able to show that the money is being well spent to save lives.

After the application has been successfully rolled out, the team is rewarded with a new set of laptops. One developer opts to donate his old laptop to a local school so it can be used in the library. He gives it away, forgetting to purge the hard drive before dropping it off at the school.

---

1. What errors were made regarding due care and due diligence?

2. What privacy laws apply to this scenario?

3. What recommendations could you make to the field office with regard to balancing security versus convenience?

TOPIC C

Asset Retention

In the previous topics, you learned about the importance of identifying data, particularly private data. You also learned how to manage private data securely. You can now widen your focus by learning how to store data securely. In this topic, you will learn how to retain your company's assets in a secure manner.

Retention

Retention is the act of storing a business asset. You will acquire, maintain, retain, and eventually discard or destroy that asset throughout its lifecycle. In the U.S., the Sarbanes-Oxley Act 2002 and the Federal Rules of Civil Procedure of 2006 both lay out requirements for records retention.

You can retain all manner of assets, including:

- Data: This can be electronic or hard copy.
- Media: This can be tape, removable drives, CDs, and DVDs.
- Hardware: Retention is part of the hardware lifecycle.
- Software: Retention is also part of the software lifecycle.
- Personnel: Retention is part of the onboarding and offboarding process.

As you consider how you will retain your assets, you must consider any organizational, legal, and regulatory requirements. These determinations must not be made by the IT team alone. Be sure to always involve upper management, your legal team, and possibly your HR department as well to ensure retention is proper and legal.

Retention Policies

All data, hardware, and software will eventually reach the end of its useful life. As such it behooves an organization to have retention policies. These are commonly referred to as record retention policies but you should in fact have policies for anything that will be disposed of. Because of these seemingly conflicting goals of keeping some data for a long time and disposing of some data very quickly, you need to make sure your policy is clear and users are well trained to follow policy.

Old equipment and old software also need to be disposed of properly so that they don't present any residual risk. Care must be taken to make sure older backup systems are kept in case they are needed to restore older tapes. Once tapes have reached the end of their life, they should be properly disposed of. NIST SP 800-88 Revision 1 offers guidelines for media sanitization.

There are eight steps you can follow to develop a record retention policy:

1. Evaluate statutory requirements, litigation obligations, and business needs: Get together with your legal department, upper management, and your IT governance committee to determine what your attention requirements actually are.
2. Classify types of records: Make sure you have determined your classification types and implement a mechanism (hopefully automatic) for classifying records.
3. Determine retention periods and destruction practices: You are not required to save absolute everything forever, but you must make sure that retention periods and destruction practices are in compliance with regulatory and business requirements.
4. Draft and justify record retention policies: Carefully vet all of the sections of your policy.
5. Train staff: Make sure that staff understands how to comply with records management, including labeling data and documents.
6. Audit retention and destruction practices: Make sure that your policy is being followed.

7. Periodically review policy: Make sure that your policy keeps up with changing business or regulatory requirements.
8. Document policy, implementation, training, and audits: Make sure that your documentation is easily understood, secure, and readily available to whomever needs it.

Retention Policy Considerations

When creating your retention policy, be sure to keep in mind the following:

- Every organization absolutely needs to have an information retention policy.
- When having to retrieve and retain information, you're not worrying just about laws and regulations; you may also have to deal with lawsuits and discovery requests.
- Make sure you can demonstrate that you have a secure storage environment for all of your electronic business.
- Make sure that your information storage mechanism allows the data to be searched and retrieved in a timely manner. This is especially true if you want to avoid huge costs related to discovery.
- Emails, instant messages, policies, procedures, and audit reports are also considered business records.
- Even though you may no longer need a record for business operations, you may still need it in the future to protect yourself against litigation or audits.
- Many people erroneously think that seven years is the maximum retention for any kind of business record. Verify requirements based on your industry, type of record, and type of organization. In some cases, your records might have to be kept indefinitely.
- The IT department should not be the sole manager of business records retention. Your legal department and an IT governance committee must also be involved.
- Do not expect users to help the company comply with retention requirements
- In case of a pending investigation, audit, or some other litigation, be extra careful to not deviate from your normal backup and retention procedures. Usually, data destruction must be suspended once you've been notified of an investigation or litigation, or you can reasonably anticipate an investigation or litigation.
- Expect that after you have destroyed data, someone in the organization will still have a copy.
- Expect that archived information might not be retrievable in a reasonable amount of time.
- Find a balance between deleting everything and saving everything. You don't want to later be accused of a cover-up, but neither do you want to have to put up massive amounts of money to store and administer unnecessary data long-term.
- Don't expect that your attorney will truly understand IT retention compliance, or the capabilities and limitations of the technologies involved.

Data Retention

Data retention is the act of continuously storing data for business or compliance reasons. One might think that the most valuable asset of a hardware store is the hardware it keeps in stock and sells. But in reality, the most valuable asset is the customer list that the company sells to, or the accounts receivable database that shows what is owed to the company and from whom. Because data is an organization's most critical (non-human) asset, it will be a priority for security professionals.

There is certain information that you are legally or contractually obligated to keep for a stated length of time. For example, financial records are usually kept for seven years. It will be important for the security practitioner and data owners to work with their legal resources to make sure they are compliant. Other data will present the opposite problem, and you will want to dispose of it more quickly. Some documents might be kept for a few months or a year and then reach their end of life.

Documentation

Consider that documentation is one form of your organization's important business data. No matter the type of documentation, it will likely hold operational information that is critical to the success of your business, as well sensitive enough to be kept company confidential. Also, like other forms of data, documentation may need to be disposed, or phased out, when it has reached the end of its lifecycle.

Media Retention

Media can be any format you store your data on, including:

- Tape
- CD/DVD
- Hard disks
- Removable flash drives
- Cloud storage
- Paper printout

Since most of your retention will be electronic, you must take good care of the media that it is on. CDs and DVDs easily become scuffed and scratched. Tapes become damaged or erased. Hard drives can crash or also become erased. It is a good idea to keep copies on different media types. As different media types become obsolete, make sure you can safely transfer your data to a new media type.

No matter what media you use for storage, you will need to determine the best way to care for that media so that the data can be retained. Typical best practices include:

- Keep media away from direct sunlight, heat, moisture, static electricity, dust, insects, mechanical impact, or anything else that might degrade its lifetime.
- If you keep backup media in a safe, remember to include silica gel packs for moisture/mildew management. Be aware, however, that some silica gel packs also have a maximum lifetime. They can absorb so much moisture then they burst open and leak all over everything. Also remember that a fire-resistant safe can still get hot enough inside during a fire to damage the media.
- Stack tapes and floppy disks (if you still have any!) on their edge, like books on a shelf. Do not lay them flat.
- If the storage medium is magnetic (tape, floppy disk, hard drive), keep it away from anything that can generate a magnetic field including fans, motors, elevator shafts, high voltage lines, and medical imaging equipment.
- Know the lifecycle of the backup tape you are using—don't overuse or retain the tape past its ability to accurately maintain the data.
- Create an authorized user list with one team for regular backups and restores, and an alternate team for disaster recovery.
- Use an automated system with bar code scanning that tracks media movement.
- Repeatedly test your backup and restore procedures.

If your backup media is the cloud, then the responsibility of maintaining the data safely has been transferred to the cloud service provider. However, always have a contingency for your data (another copy elsewhere) in case the provider has some kind of disaster they cannot recover from. Additionally, make sure your data is securely destroyed by the provider when it is no longer needed.

 Note: For more information on media retention, see the article "A Best Practices Checklist For Backup Tapes" at **www.ironmountain.com/Knowledge-Center/Reference-Library/View-by-Document-Type/General-Articles/A/A-Best-Practices-Checklist-for-Backup-Tapes.aspx.**

Hardware Retention

One factor that many overlook in their data retention policy is to include a clause about hardware retention. Hardware is an investment that companies want to make the most of. Besides getting the longest service possible out of hardware, you must also consider its role in retaining and protecting your data.

If you keep your data for 5 or 10 years or longer, will you be able to retrieve it with your current hardware? This is especially an issue if you have used tape to retain your data. The type of tape drive you used five years ago to back up your data may no longer be available today. Tape drives actually require a fair amount of maintenance.

Likewise, non-media computer components and peripherals like cases, motherboards, processors, RAM, monitors, mice, keyboards, etc., are all valuable to an organization and enable its personnel to work efficiently and without disruption. Putting a retention plan in place for these hardware items will make it much easier for your organization to service its employees' needs.

When hardware is no longer useful for its original purpose, or it becomes obsolete, you can repurpose, recycle, sell, donate, or dispose of it. Be sure to scrub any sensitive data off the device before it leaves your premises. You may also be required to properly recycle it as electronic waste, rather than just throwing it in the trash.

Software Retention

The organization may also acquire and purchase software, or it may develop its own software in-house. Either way, software, like hardware, has its own lifecycle. You should implement consistent reviews of software to determine whether or not it is meeting your business needs. If it doesn't, it may be time to dispose of it.

Software disposal may require a more complex process than simply uninstalling it from the systems that use it. Depending on what your organization uses, software is often tightly intertwined with other systems and processes within the organization, and pulling the plug on an application may cause other systems to fail. That's why you should map software dependencies in your retention policy, to ensure that you have a complete understanding of what role the software plays in your organization.

Likewise, software that works with sensitive data may require special scrubbing similar to storage media. This is especially true of third-party solutions; you may find that some applications store temporary copies of data in multiple places without your knowledge. Failing to account for this when decommissioning the software may leave sensitive data unsecured.

Personnel Retention

When considering IT retention policies, one might not think of personnel retention. But it is important to understand a common reality of business operations: that a lot of knowledge in an organization is tribal, trapped in departmental "silos," and not available to the rest of the organization. Sometimes critical knowledge is even limited to one or two individuals, and not documented at all. This is especially true with IT departments who do not have the time (or inclination) to document every procedure that they perform. While businesses will try to retain staff with competitive wages, extra perks, a great working environment or management team and other enticements, the realistic business manager understands that the longevity of an organization must never depend on any one person.

Make sure that when you are considering protecting your assets and creating your retention policies, you don't depend on being able to keep individuals who are the sole repositories of business or technical process or operations. You may be able to find replacement people with equal technical skills, but there must be a continuity of understanding business operations for that particular organization. Make sure that part of your personnel retention policy includes the time, resources, and an emphasis on documenting process, and transferring operational knowledge. Rotating duties and building multidisciplinary teams will help unlock the silos and spread the tribal knowledge.

Guidelines for Implementing Asset Retention

Here are some guidelines you can follow for asset retention:

- Always create a retention policy.
- Remember that you won't just retain data. You will also need to retain hardware, software, media, and even personnel.
- Suspend your data retention policies and practices while under investigation or litigation.
- Data will be the most important area of focus in your retention policy.
- Make sure to retain data for the length of time that is relevant to the data itself. Different data will require different retention times.
- Make sure your storage media are free from damage from natural causes, like heat and static electricity.
- Regularly test your storage media.
- Make sure that hardware can still access your data.
- Dispose of hardware components properly, depending on guidelines for electronic waste disposal.
- When disposing of software, map its dependencies on other systems.
- Make sure software is scrubbed properly.
- Ensure that no one person or small groups of people retain critical knowledge about business operations in a silo.
- Encourage documentation of processes so that knowledge is not lost upon an employee's departure from the organization.

ACTIVITY 2-3
Analyzing Asset Retention

Scenario

You are an information security professional for a small company. Management wants to ensure that the company properly retains its records for compliance and business purposes. They have a large amount of data that needs to be stored. It is critical that the archived records be easily available for data mining. Management is concerned that the organization does not have the personnel or expertise to properly care for the records. They have asked you to help them understand the process better.

1. For how long should a company retain its records?
   - ○ 1 year
   - ○ 5 years
   - ○ 7 years
   - ○ Whatever length of time is appropriate

2. What should be the very first step in drafting a records retention policy?
   - ○ Evaluate statutory requirements, litigations obligations, and business needs.
   - ○ Assign retention periods.
   - ○ Meet with data owners.
   - ○ Have the Chief Information Security Officer (CISO) announce the policy.

3. What is the most appropriate storage media for this company?
   - ○ Optical disks
   - ○ Removable flash drives
   - ○ Tape
   - ○ Cloud

4. In what ways could hardware and personnel impact records retention?

TOPIC D

Data Security Controls

In the previous topic you learned about secure data storage. But storage is not the only area where data will need protection. In this topic, you will learn about other data security controls, and how to apply them.

Data Security Control Selection

Data security controls protect the confidentiality, integrity, and availability of your data. When selecting controls to protect your data, you will need to consider the following:

* A data standard
* Baselines
* Scoping and tailoring your security implementation
* Control implementation

Some special factors to consider include:

* Data at rest
* Data in transit
* Encryption

Data Standards

A data standard is a documented agreement between organizations on the format common data should take. This will include precise criteria and technical specifications such as how the data is represented, formatted, defined, structured, transmitted, manipulated, tagged, used, and managed. Standards support data integrity by providing accuracy, clarity, and consistency. They minimize redundancy in your data, and help you document your business rules. They help you move from data that is project based to data that is enterprise based. Data standards also help you implement security controls because they give you an expectation of how different products and systems will behave.

A standard data model, or industry standard data model (ISDM), is one that is widely applied in a particular industry and shared among competitors. This allows for consistency and interoperability among products and allows the security professional to implement consistent controls across products and devices.

Data standards are typically set by standards bodies. But they can also be set by the operating system or database vendor that other vendors use for their own products. For example, many software products use Microsoft SQL Express as its small internal database. The standards defined in SQL Express by Microsoft are then used by the different vendors in their own products.

From a security perspective, data standards help vendors implement consistent security levels across their products. For example, the Payment Card Industry Data Security Standard (PCI DSS) helps vendors develop secure payment applications.

Data standards also help security professionals quickly recognize the potential scope of a security incident. In 2003, the SQL slammer worm infected nearly 75,000 systems within 10 minutes. Nearly every product that used SQL Express, as well as many competing non-Microsoft SQL databases, was subject to the vulnerability. Knowing this, security professionals were able to identify and patch potential targets before they were infected. In 2014, the Heartbleed bug made any website using the popular OpenSSL library (pre-created code module) vulnerable to disclosing users' private keys. When the advisory was issued identifying the vulnerability source, security professionals knew which systems to patch to protect their customers.

Data Standards Examples

Some examples of working data standards can be found at:

- Microsoft MSDN Examples of Standard Formats for Data Types (**https:// msdn.microsoft.com/en-us/library/office/ff867417.aspx**)
- USGS National Geospatial Program Standards and Specifications (**http://nationalmap.gov/ standards/**)
- FGDC National Data Standards Publications (**www.fgdc.gov/standards/ standards_publications/**)
- FGDC Standards Working Group (**www.fgdc.gov/standards/organization/FGDC-SWG/ index_html**)

Data Baselines

On any computer system, you can have baselines for hardware, software, and even data itself. A data protection baseline will be spelled out in a document or policy. It will typically list and define the different data sensitivity labels (such as public, private, sensitive, confidential, trade secret, etc.). It will also typically contain a table mapping controls to sensitivity labels.

Control	Public	Private	Sensitive	Confidential	Trade Secret
Read-only	Recommended	Recommended	Recommended	Recommended	Required
Encryption	Optional	Required	Optional	Recommended	Required
Data redundancy	Optional	Required	Recommended	Recommended	Required
Media sanitation and disposal	Recommended	Required	Required	Required	Required (destruction)

Figure 2-1: Baseline controls for different data types.

Baseline Resources

You can learn more about baselines with these resources:

- NIST SP 800-70 r2 National Checklist Program for IT Products
- United States Government Configuration Baseline (USGCB)

Scoping and Tailoring

Scoping determines how far reaching your security implementation will be. Any systems that fall within your security scope have to have security controls placed on them. You should have a scoping document that spells out the limits of your responsibility. Systems that fall outside of your scope will be someone else's responsibility. However, if your system interfaces with someone else's system, part of your security scope is to make sure that the other system does not compromise yours.

For example, you might be the database administrator at one site within your organization. If you make regular backups of your data to a third-party offsite database over a network connection, the scope of your security may stop at your perimeter router. The administrator at the backup site will have within their scope the security for that site as the backup data comes in. However, part of your scope must still ensure that your data is not compromised at the backup site.

With *tailoring*, you modify an existing security practice to suit your particular needs. For example, a company might have a security standards document in place that all departments are expected to follow. In a development lab environment, however, a special dispensation may be tailored to allow you to relax some of the security requirements during development since the environment is different from production.

Data Security Control Implementation

Besides protecting human life, data protection is the most critical security control you can implement in your organization. According to the security group sans.org, data protection is "best achieved through the application of a combination of encryption, integrity protection, and data loss prevention techniques."

Sans.org offers a checklist on their website for implementing data security controls. Highlights include:

*   Use approved drive encryption software on mobile devices.
*   Assess data to identify what is sensitive enough to require encryption and integrity controls.
*   If you store data in the cloud, reviewed the providers security practices for protecting your data.
*   Implement some kind of automated tool on the borders of your network to make sure that sensitive information does not leave the network. You can do this by providing filters that search for personally identifiable information, keywords, and document characteristics.
*   Periodically scan servers to see if any sensitive data (including personal, financial, health, and classified information) exists in clear text. Many server operating systems today have the ability to automatically label data based on keywords and scan for and perform actions on that data on a schedule.
*   Limit the use of USB flash drives to those that use encryption.
*   Implement network-based data loss prevention (DLP) mechanisms to automatically back up critical data and control the movement of data across your network.

 Note: Sans.org is recognized as one of the premier information security groups in the world. Based in the United States, the SANS Institute specializes in information security research and cybersecurity training.

 Note: For more information on data security controls, see the article "Critical Security Control: 17" at **https://www.sans.org/critical-security-controls/control/17**.

Data at Rest

Data can be thought of as being in two states; at rest and in transit. *Data at rest* refers to data that resides on a disk, on a CD, on a magnetic tape, or really any media that allows for long term retention. It could be there for days, weeks, years, even decades. Much of our physical data (hard copies) can also be thought of as at rest.

All data at rest needs protection. It presents a risk because of the possibility of long-term storage. The longer it is around, the longer it is exposed both to physical and logical loss. Removable media, especially small, easy to conceal data drives, present a particular concern.

A combination of physical security, data policies, retention policies, ITAM, and sound classification policies can help protect your data. Security controls you can implement to protect data at rest include:

*   Have a Data Recovery Plan (a concrete, implementable plan for restoring data after a failure or disaster).
*   Use strong encryption.
*   Implement access control (a technical or physical mechanism for limiting a person's access to a system or its data).
*   Investigate password management tools to store passwords and keys.
*   Maintain control of removable media.

- Make sure labeling policies are applied and followed.
- Removable data should be stored in a secure data-safe location.
- Document the location of removable data.

Data in Transit

Data in transit is data on the move. It is traversing the network or being moved from one type of media to another. As it crosses the wires or is sent through the air, there is risk.

In order to protect your data you must consider its exposure. The exposure on an internal network may be perceived differently than exposure on an external network. Physical cables and wireless connections present different risk. You have to consider what is the likelihood that it will be intercepted.

You can use a combination of hardware, software, and policies to protect your data in transit. One method is to use encryption to make it nearly impossible to read the bits as they go by.

When placing security controls on your data in transit, keep in mind the following:

- Web traffic should be protected with the latest versions of SSL.
- Sensitive data sent with email should be encrypted with PGP or S/MIME. Alternately, attachments could be encrypted with file encryption tools.
- Non-Web-covered data traffic should be encrypted with application level encryption.
- Connections between application servers and database servers should be encrypted.
- When application level encryption isn't available, consider a tunneling protocol.
- Encryption should be used for high sensitivity data even in protected subnets.

Encryption

Encryption is the process of scrambling data so that only authorized persons can read it. It is the single best control you can use to secure data, whether it is stored on media or moving across a network. You can encrypt data with hardware and/or software. Consider encrypting the data before storing it.

When your data is stored on media, encryption will protect it from unauthorized access, even if a person steals the system or hard drive that the data is stored on.

When your data is moving between locations, encryption can happen at any point in the network.

- The link itself could be encrypted. This will occur on high security private communication links that are owned by the organization.
- The link itself might not be encrypted, but the data sent across it might be. This is usually performed on public networks such as the Internet, or dedicated links leased to the organization by a telecommunications provider.

Guidelines for Implementing Data Security Controls

Here are some guidelines you can follow when implementing data security controls:

- Use or develop a data standard to help the data maintain clarity and reduce redundancy.
- Create a baseline of minimum security levels for different types of data, usually based on classification.
- Use scoping and tailoring to define the boundaries of where your controls will apply, as well as any customizations you might make to your current security practice.
- Implement your data security controls through a combination of encryption, integrity protection, and data loss prevention techniques.
- Keep in mind that data at rest is data that is stored somewhere. If an intruder gains access to the system or hardware storing the data, it is at risk of tampering or theft.

- Keep in mind that data in transit is data that is moving from one place to another, usually across a network. It is at risk of theft or tampering through interception or disruption of the network.
- Use encryption as your best defense for data, both at rest and in transit.

ACTIVITY 2-4
Analyzing Data Security Controls

Scenario

In this activity, you will identify key data security control concepts.

1. Which of the following are examples of data at rest? (Choose two.)
   ☐ Data being written to a backup tape.
   ☐ Files on a computer's hard drive.
   ☐ Data backed up to a cloud storage repository.
   ☐ Hard copy files being transported to off-site storage.

2. True or False? Data that is at rest is probably secure because it is most likely kept on a computer with a firewall.
   ☐ True
   ☐ False

3. Which of the following is true regarding data standards? (Choose two.)
   ☐ A data standard promotes data integrity.
   ☐ A data standard is a requirement mandated by government.
   ☐ A data standard is an agreement between organizations.
   ☐ A data standard is an enforceable guideline.

4. What are some of the potential benefits of defining and maintaining data standards?

5. What role can encryption play in a data security baseline?

TOPIC E

Secure Data Handling

In the previous topic, you learned about data security controls. Part of implementing data security controls includes maintaining security as you handle the data. In this topic, you will learn how to handle data securely through different parts of its lifecycle.

Data Policies

An organization will need a policy to drive all aspects of data management. A policy provides consistency, improves effectiveness, streamlines operations, and reduces risk. From data acquisition through data disposal, you will need to protect the confidentiality, integrity, and availability of your data. As the company changes how the data is created, how it is stored, and where it is stored, the data policies will need to evolve to provide the required structure to protect the data. Data policies will need to be flexible to meet changes in business processes as well.

Management should always be the source of any policy. Your policies should also be reviewed on a regular basis, at least annually, but that can be easily impacted by changes in the business environment. Mergers, acquisitions, right sizing, and changes of partners and vendors can all have an impact on the data. It is important that data policies, like all policies, dovetail with the business objectives and meet all of the legal obligations of the organization.

When writing a data handling policy, you should address the following:

- How it should be classified.
- Where it should be stored.
- Who will need access.
- How you will monitor and audit data access.
- How it should be retained.
- How and when the data will be disposed of.
- The impact of loss, disclosure, or corruption of the data.

Data Handling

Secure data handling ensures that your data is stored, archived, and disposed of in a secure manner throughout its entire lifecycle. It keeps your data useful by adhering to the CIA triad principles. Remember that data can be both electronic and non-electronic. It can and will exist on all manner of storage media including tape, diskette, CD/DVD, flash drives, memory cards, mobile devices, paper printouts, and more. The secret to successful data handling is to determine the value of the data and apply matching security.

As you develop data handling procedures, keep the following in mind:

- Cost: There is cost associated with acquiring and protecting data.
- Ownership and Custodianship: Specify who is the data owner and who is the data custodian.
- Privacy: Consider guidelines for what information is considered private, and how that information will be stored, managed, and used.
- Liability: Does the data or loss of the data present any liability issues? Can protection be gained with banners informing users of the importance of protecting the data? Can end-user agreements be stipulated? Is the data licensed or licensable?
- Sensitivity: If there is sensitive data, perform a risk analysis to determine appropriate processes for access.
- Existing Law and Policy Requirements: Be aware of the laws and regulations surrounding the data you have acquired.

- Policy and Process: Does this policy conflict with any existing policies? Does the policy support the CIA triad?

Safe handling and storage policies will need to be in place at all times. Safe storage is a special concern if you store data offsite. It will be the data custodian's job to make sure that it is safe in all locations. Data handling will need to comply with data retention policies and most likely lead to the need for data destruction policies.

The security professional must never assume that only authorized personnel are handling data, or that they have been trained properly on how to securely handle the data. In many cases, staff are not even really aware of the proper ways to securely handle data. Make sure you keep logs and records of how your data is being handled, including both electronic and hard copy versions.

Marking

Marking data with its sensitivity level allows automated systems to search for and act upon the data. It also allows employees to immediately know how to handle that data, including challenging any classification that seems inappropriate. The data owner must determine what the marking should be, and the data custodian will typically apply that marking. Common practices for marking data include:

- The name and address of the individual, group, or facility responsible for setting that marking.
- The date the marking was applied.
- Redundant marking on the front cover/title page, back cover, top and bottom.
- Marking that cannot be removed or modified, such as a digital signature or watermark for electronic documents, and a stamp or etching on a physical document.

Labels

To ensure secure data handling, all data should be clearly labeled either electronically or physically. Labels are the mechanism used to apply markings to your data. For electronic data, the folder it is stored in can act as one type of label. The documents themselves can contain watermarks, file attributes, or footers to specify the type of access allowed.

Once the asset has been classified by the owner, it must be labeled in a way that is consistent with the contents and makes a classification obvious to the casual observer. Proper labeling helps ensure that the data is handled securely. Follow these guidelines when labeling data:

- The asset owner must document the security classification of the asset, as well as indicate who is the asset custodian (usually some part of the IT department).
- The asset owner needs to advise the asset custodian and IT security team of the security classification of the asset so that appropriate controls can be applied.
- Make sure that all hard copies of an asset that is internal, sensitive, confidential, or otherwise restricted are clearly labeled according to their security classification.
- If the hard copy is bound, it should have an appropriate sensitivity label on the front cover, rear cover, and title page as appropriate.
- The cover sheet for a fax should also include the relevant classification label if the material is sensitive in any way.
- Any electronic communication for sensitive information must also have the proper classification level, including at the top or end of an email.

Any data that is found unlabeled should be afforded the highest protection possible until its true nature is determined. For example, if a printout is found unattended in the break room and it has no watermark indicating its classification status, it should be determined to have the highest level of protection until the data owner can be found.

 Note: Although marking and labeling are similar and may seem synonymous, labeling can be thought of as the mechanism you use to mark your data.

Note: Labels can also refer to additional keywords or "tags" that provide ancillary information about that data. Tags allow data to be more easily searched for and found by associating related words with that data. The most successful data searches are ones in which a variety of labels have been used to refer to a particular file. This gives the user flexibility in how to approach the search.

Data Storage

When handling your data securely, make sure that you store it securely. Do not allow hard copies to lie around where any passerby can pick it up or read it. Similarly, do not allow sensitive information to be stored in clear text on a hard drive. Make sure that backup media is encrypted. Send a copy to a secure off-site location, while keeping a convenient copy readily available on premises. If you do store backups onsite, place them in a fire resistant box if possible.

Data Remanence

Data remanence is a phenomenon in which information is left on storage media even after it has been erased. Unless physically destroyed, magnetic storage media such as tape and hard drives always leave some imprint of the data even after erasure. This means that sensitive data can persist and even be recovered in an unauthorized manner.

Data remanence could also be the result of sheer carelessness. A leased PC that is returned without scrubbing the hard drive, or an unencrypted backup tape that has been thrown away because the company no longer has a drive that would read the tape, would both present a data remanence scenario.

Data remanence is an issue that most users don't really understand. The user may assume that they have taken the necessary precautions by formatting the hard drive several times; they don't realize that sensitive instrumentation can still retrieve faint magnetic imprints. Most organizations concerned with high-security, particularly that of private information, will physically destroy storage media to ensure the data cannot be retrieved.

Storage in the cloud also presents a potential data remanence issue. It will be vitally important to work with your cloud vendor so they understand your concerns around data remanence. You will need assurances that if you discontinue your relationship with the cloud partner that your data will be thoroughly scrubbed.

Note: Data remanence is synonymous with the term **data remnants**. Both refer to data being left unintentionally on storage media.

NIST Remanence Resource

National Institute for Standards and Technology (NIST) SP 800-88r1 offers good information on data remanence issues.

Data Destruction

In order to remove any doubt about data remanence, special care must be used to destroy data. Special techniques will need to be used as determined by the level of protection needed. Deleting data is the least secure but it may be sufficient for non-sensitive information. When you use common tools and utilities to delete data, it is non-recoverable without special software. However, if you have a determined adversary, it might not be enough.

Information that is sensitive should be destroyed rather than simply discarded. In addition, there should be a log that describes who destroyed the data, when, and in what manner. It should also include what happened to the physical remains of the storage media.

Purging removes all data in a way that it not likely to be recovered with any currently known techniques. The table describes some common methods for purging data.

Method	Description
Overwriting	Overwriting a disk (sometimes referred to as electronic shredding) can ensure that any remnant bits on the disk have been replaced by different bits (usually all zeros), effectively erasing the original data. This leaves the physical drive intact for later reuse. One concern with overwriting is the tool may skip bad sectors on a hard drive or even skip corrupted files.
Destruction	Physically destroying the hard drive or backup media is meant to ensure that the media cannot be reassembled and the data retrieved. The physical drive is lost in the process.
Degaussing	Degaussing is a purging technique that removes all data from magnetic media. It is done on specially designed machines that create either an AC or DC field that deletes the data. It is theoretically possible that the drives could be reusable after degaussing, but frequently they are rendered useless. This presents challenges if you need to somehow verify data is deleted. It also doesn't impact non-magnetic storage like CDs or SSD hard drives. SSD drives will sometimes include their own utility for data destruction. This is good, but the validity of the utility should be verified.
Encryption	Encryption is another technique to effectively make data unavailable to unauthorized users. If you encrypt the drive or tape and then destroy the key, there will be no way to decrypt it.

Reference

The National Security Agency Central Security Service Media Destruction Guidance document provides valuable information on effective data destruction.

Quality Control

Secure data handling depends on having quality data to begin with. Data accuracy, integrity, and reliability mandate a good *Quality Control (QC)* process. The data owner needs to assure the quality of the data to data consumers. All secure data handling processes should have quality control embedded in them.

Quality control can help protect against two common types of errors that can be introduced into data: errors of commission and errors of omission. Errors of commission are committed when data that shouldn't be added is. Errors of omission are when values should be included but aren't. For example, if a data entry system allowed the user to add the value NZZ to a state field, you would have an error of commission. If, on the other hand, you build a data table with all state abbreviations and left out NY, you would have an error of omission.

A good quality control process will include comprehensive documentation on what constitutes quality data. It will also include a process for data validation. This could be built into the tools or a structured process that is performed periodically. This will vary by organization and perhaps even within an organization. Each company needs to determine for itself what level of effort they need to exercise in order to achieve the quality they are seeking. This documentation should be reviewed periodically and updated as needed. Data owners will need to be trained in the QC process.

Data quality standards help verify the reliability and effectiveness of the data. Standards can be developed for any of the following data attributes:

- Accuracy
- Precision
- Resolution

- Reliability
- Repeatability
- Reproducibility
- Currency
- Relevance
- Ability to audit
- Completeness
- Timeliness

Data Documentation

Data documentation contains information about your data. It will help you to understand your own data, as well as assist others in searching, interpreting, and understanding your data.

Guidelines for Implementing Secure Data Handling

Here are some guidelines you can follow for secure data handling:

- Always have a data policy to inform all aspects of your data handling procedures.
- Incorporate secure data handling procedures into every aspect of the data's lifecycle.
- Mark and label data to make it easier to comply with your data policy.
- Always store data, including hard copies, securely.
- When erasing data from magnetic media, keep in mind that there is usually some data remanence.
- Use the appropriate method for destroying data and avoiding remanence.
- Remember that all phases of data handling should have quality control embedded in them.

ACTIVITY 2-5
Discussing Secure Data Handling

Scenario

In this activity, you will assess your knowledge of secure data handling concepts.

1. Under what conditions do you think unqualified people might handle your data?

2. Assume you have a network share that stores files for a project another team is currently working on. The project files on this share are about an upcoming product that your organization is in the process of developing, and this product has yet to be shared with the public. The files are mostly product specifications in image and document formats.

   What sort of ways would you mark and label the data on this network share?

3. How does the rise of mobility and bring your own device (BYOD) computing affect data remanence concerns?

4. What do you think can be done to reduce the risks related to data remanence?

Summary

In this lesson, you learned about the importance of protecting your organization's assets. In protecting assets like data, it is essential to remember the importance of the CIA triad. As you develop policies and define roles, you are further protecting your assets. Understanding the importance of where your data resides and how it is classified can also add to the strength of your protection.

What are some of the asset classification types used in your organization?

As your data grows over the next few years, how do you plan to protect it?

 Note: Check your CHOICE Course screen for opportunities to interact with your classmates, peers, and the larger CHOICE online community about the topics covered in this course or other topics you are interested in. From the Course screen you can also access available resources for a more continuous learning experience.

3 | Security Engineering

Lesson Time: 6 hours, 30 minutes

Lesson Objectives

In this lesson, you will:

- Manage security in the engineering lifecycle.

- Identify security risks for system components.

- Compare security models.

- Analyze controls and countermeasures in enterprise security.

- Identify information system security capabilities.

- Determine design and architecture vulnerabilities and mitigation tactics.

- Analyze vulnerabilities and identify mitigation in embedded, mobile, and web-based systems.

- Identify cryptography concepts.

- Apply cryptographic techniques.

- Analyze site and facility design for physical security.

- Identify tools for physical security implementation.

Lesson Introduction

In the last lesson, you learned about managing assets. You learned how to classify and retain assets, as well as how to handle data securely. You also learned about the role that privacy protection plays in asset management. In order to always effect the CIA triangle, security needs to be built in to everything you do. In this lesson, you will learn about security engineering.

TOPIC A

Security in the Engineering Lifecycle

In this first topic, you will learn about security design principles, and the role security frameworks can play. You will learn about security in the engineering lifecycle.

 Note: To learn more, view the LearnTO presentations from the **LearnTO** tile on the CHOICE course screen.

Security Design Principles

Your security design should always assume that you are under attack. To be consistent in your response, you must create a framework that will consistently secure all aspects of your information system. This includes:

- Securing communications.
- Protecting your data sources and data storage.
- Hardening all systems.
- Ensuring data integrity and confidentiality through all business processes.

Every aspect of your information system must incorporate security by design. When you create a security architecture, you should not treat it as something separate, an after-thought to be added after the system is designed or created. It should instead be integrated into your entire enterprise IT architecture. Whenever you are planning to implement, upgrade, or review any system, security must be included as early as possible in the process. Your security design must allow for not only your current system, but potential future systems as well.

Security Engineering Lifecycle

There are five phases to the security engineering lifecycle as defined in the NIST publication *Generally Accepted Principles and Practices for Securing Information Technology Systems, SP 800-14.*

Phase	Description
Initiation	During this phase, you determine that you need a system and document its purpose. If your organization is a U.S. federal agency, you also conduct a FIPS-199 compliant impact assessment, which will keep you in compliance with the Federal Information Security Management Act (FISMA).
Development/ Acquisition	During this phase, you design and produce the system, either by purchasing it or building it yourself. This phase may have multiple cycles within it for development or acquisition. You also determine any security requirements, and incorporate them into your specifications.
Implementation	During this phase, you test and install the system, and implement any controls. You also perform security testing. The culmination of your testing is certification and accreditation, where the system is determined to perform as designed, and accepted by management.
Operations/ Maintenance	During this phase, the system is doing its work. You administer it and manage its security, including monitoring and auditing its operations. You install patches and updates, and apply changes in a controlled manner. At some point you will probably also add hardware and software.

Phase	Description
Disposal	During this phase, you dispose of the system, including any information, hardware, and software. This phase includes moving, archiving, discarding, or destroying the data. It also includes sanitizing or destroying any storage media.

Common Security Frameworks

The most effective way to implement good security design is to use existing standards and security frameworks. The following table summarizes the most common security principal frameworks in use.

Security Framework	Description	
NIST SP 800-14	Provides perspective at the organization level for creating new systems, policies, or practices. It identifies 8 principles in 14 practices for information technology security at the organization level.	
NIST SP 800-27 Rev A	Comprehensive set of engineering principles for system security. Provides for a structured approach to designing, developing, and implementing IT security.	

NIST SP 800-27

NIST SP 800-27 is a document published by the U.S. Department of Commerce. Its full title is *Engineering Principles for Information Technology Security (A Baseline for Achieving Security), Revision A*. It was developed by the National Institute of Standards and Technology. It is a list of 33 system-level security principles. These principles should be incorporated when you design, develop, or operate an information system.

It also contains tables to help identify where in the system lifecycle each category is applicable. The purpose of the 33 principles is to help the security professional really understand and appreciate the depth and scope of all that is necessary to properly include security design into any system lifecycle.

 Note: For more information, see **http://csrc.nist.gov/publications/nistpubs/800-27A/ SP800-27-RevA.pdf.**

Here's the complete list of the NIST SP 800-27 principles.

Category	Principles
Security Foundation	• **Principle 1**: Establish a sound security policy as the "foundation" for design. • **Principle 2**: Treat security as an integral part of the overall system design. • **Principle 3**: Clearly delineate the physical and logical security boundaries governed by the associated security policies. • **Principle 4**: Ensure that developers are trained in how to develop secure software.

Category	Principles
Risk Based	• **Principle 5**: Reduce risk to an acceptable level. • **Principle 6**: Assume that external systems are insecure. • **Principle 7**: Identify potential trade-offs between reducing risk and increased costs and decrease in other aspects of operational effectiveness. • **Principle 8**: Implement tailored system security measures to meet organizational security goals. • **Principle 9**: Protect information while being processed, in transit, and in storage. • **Principle 10**: Consider custom products to achieve adequate security. • **Principle 11**: Protect against all likely classes of attacks.
Ease of Use	• **Principle 12**: Where possible, base security on open standards for portability and interoperability. • **Principle 13**: Use common language in developing security requirements. • **Principle 14**: Design security to allow for regular adoption of new technology, including a secure and logical technology upgrade process. • **Principle 15**: Strive for operational ease of use.
Increase Resilience	• **Principle 16**: Implement layered security (ensure no single point of vulnerability). • **Principle 17**: Design and operate an IT system to limit damage and to be resilient in response. • **Principle 18**: Provide assurance that the system is, and continues to be, resilient in the face of expected threats. • **Principle 19**: Limit or contain vulnerabilities. • **Principle 20**: Isolate public access systems from mission critical resources (e.g., data, processes, etc.). • **Principle 21**: Use boundary mechanisms to separate computing systems and network infrastructures • **Principle 22**: Design and implement audit mechanisms to detect unauthorized use and to support incident investigations. • **Principle 23**: Develop and exercise contingency or disaster recovery procedures to ensure appropriate availability.
Reduce Vulnerabilities	• **Principle 24**: Strive for simplicity. • **Principle 25**: Minimize the system elements to be trusted. • **Principle 26**: Implement least privilege. • **Principle 27**: Do not implement unnecessary security mechanisms. • **Principle 28**: Ensure proper security in the shutdown or disposal of a system. • **Principle 29**: Identify and prevent common errors and vulnerabilities.
Design with Network in Mind	• **Principle 30**: Implement security through a combination of measures distributed physically and logically. • **Principle 31**: Formulate security measures to address multiple overlapping information domains. • **Principle 32**: Authenticate users and processes to ensure appropriate access control decisions both within and across domains. • **Principle 33**: Use unique identities to ensure accountability.

Guidelines for Implementing Security in the Engineering Lifecycle

 Note: All of the Guidelines for this lesson are available as checklists from the **Checklist** tile on the CHOICE Course screen.

Here are some guidelines you can follow for implementing security in the engineering lifecycle:

- When designing and building your system, always assume that it will be under constant attack.
- Create your security design to be a framework to secure all aspects of your information system.
- Use the principles in security frameworks such as NIST SP 800-14 or SP 800-27 when you design and build your systems.

ACTIVITY 3-1
Analyzing Security in the Engineering Lifecycle

Scenario

In this activity, you will assess your understanding of security in the engineering lifecycle.

1. Your company is developing a product that is being held to high security standards. At what point in the security engineering lifecycle would you attempt to certify and accredit the product?
   - ○ Operations and maintenance
   - ○ Development and acquisitions
   - ○ Implementation
   - ○ Concept and initiation

2. You're considering using security framework to help you apply security principles in your engineering lifecycle. Which of the frameworks operates at the organization level for developing new policies and practices?
   - ○ Common Criteria
   - ○ NIST SP800-27
   - ○ NIST SP800-14
   - ○ SDLC

3. You work for a government agency that is developing a secure system. At which point in the engineering lifecycle would you conduct an impact analysis to see if you are in compliance with FISMA?
   - ○ Certification and accreditation
   - ○ Testing
   - ○ Initiation
   - ○ Development/Acquisition

TOPIC B

System Component Security

In the previous topic, you got started with security design principles, frameworks you can use, and the security in the engineering lifecycle. This next topic takes you deeper into the components of a system. As you study each individual component's purpose, you will also learn about its accompanying security concerns.

System Components

Although the security practitioner does not have to be an expert in computer system components, a good working knowledge of these is immensely valuable. Any time you can understand the system or technology on its own merit, you will be in a far better position to really understand why it has security vulnerabilities, how those vulnerabilities can be exploited, and what can be done to mitigate them. From a security perspective, nearly all system components have some type of vulnerability that can be exploited.

Computer system components fall into three basic categories.

System Component	Description
Hardware	Hardware is generally defined as physical components you can touch. The computer chassis, motherboard, CPU, RAM, discs, and peripherals are all examples of hardware.
Software	Software is the instruction set that runs on the hardware. Software can be the operating system, an application, or utility (a tool such as an antivirus program). It can also include small instruction sets called drivers that allow the operating system to control hardware. Software is usually stored on storage media such as a disk or flash drive.
Firmware	Firmware is software instructions that have been burned into hardware, usually an integrated circuit (chip). Firmware is generally read only, although in many cases a voltage can be applied to a specific pin on the chip to erase the existing instructions and replace them with new instructions. In many cases, firmware on a system board contains a small, simple operating system that can be used to start the boot process of the computer. This is especially true in appliance type devices such as routers and switches. In some cases, the firmware can contain an entire operating system. The BIOS on the computer motherboard is a classic example of firmware.

TCB

With so many different hardware aspects to consider, secure information systems designers must understand the strengths and weaknesses of the hardware architecture. They need to determine if the hardware presents ways to circumvent protection schemes and to allow unauthorized access. A *Trusted Computing Base (TCB)* is one in which the hardware itself has built-in security mechanisms.

This means that the security properties of an entire system could be jeopardized should defects occur inside the TCB. The TCB is implemented in the hardware through processor rings or privileges, in the firmware through driver and resource protection, and in software through using the operating system's isolation of resources from applications.

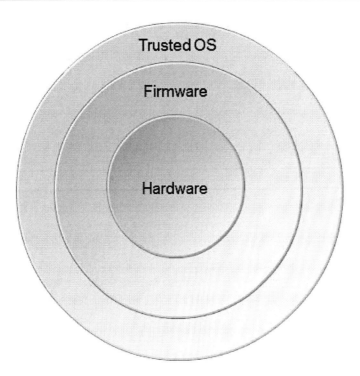

Figure 3-1: Components of the TCB.

Processors

A processor is a computer chip that performs calculations and executes instructions. The *Central Processing Unit (CPU)* is the main processor found in a computer. It resides on the motherboard (main system board) and executes instructions that allow the system to operate successfully. The failure of CPU design can lead to system failure, which then affects the availability of applications that the users need.

CPU design often includes a layered protection process. Based on the principle of least privilege, some instructions in the CPU are limited to using the operating system, while other instructions are available to the operating system and to the user programs.

When a CPU is in *supervisor state,* also known as *kernel mode,* it can execute any instructions that are available. When in *user* or *application state*, a CPU can execute only non-privileged instructions. This protects the system from unauthorized activities by user programs. These protection schemes are often implemented in rings with the most secure ring in the center, progressing to the least secure ring at the outer edge of the design.

In addition to the CPU, a computer may have other processors. The video card, for example, will typically have its own processor to handle the heavy workload of rendering graphics. The motherboard may also have a co-processor to help offload intensive numeric calculations. A network card may also have its own processor if it performs hardware-based cryptographic functions.

Processor Security Concerns

The primary security vulnerability of a processor is that it cannot by itself refuse to run the workload presented to it. This means that a malicious application could overload the CPU in a denial of service attack, keeping the CPU busy with useless activities and preventing it from doing any real work. Another vulnerability is that you might have malicious code capable of bypassing privilege level restrictions built into the hardware of the processor, thus allowing the malicious code to perform activities that would ordinarily not be allowed or steal information from another process.

Multitasking and Multithreading

In a computer system with a single CPU, the operating system divides time among the programs using a technique called *multitasking*. By giving each program a bit of time to execute, multitasking allows more than one program to run at one time.

Threading is a computing technique that enables a program to split itself into two or more concurrently running tasks. A thread is the smallest unit of executable code that runs on the CPU. It performs a single task. If a program needs to perform more than one function at a time, it may ask the operating system to help by implementing *multithreading*. This technique allows the parallel execution of multiple threads on a computer system.

Multiprogramming is an older term that may still be seen. Multiprogramming allows for the simultaneous execution of more than one program. This is very common in desktops and laptops, but is not always available in low power or low processor devices.

Multistate is the ability to run in different execution modes. Operating systems have a similar ability to run in normal mode or safe mode.

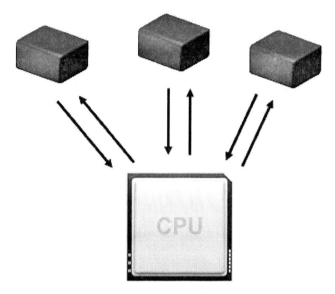

Figure 3-2: Multitasking and multithreading.

Example: Word Processing

You may need a word processing program to simultaneously spell check a document as you enter the text. When the word processor indicates to the operating system that it needs resources for spell checking, the operating system creates a new thread. Although the thread may appear as another program to the operating system, it is actually related to the word processor. The thread gets a time slice like any other program, but only when the word processor gives it something to do.

Multitasking and Multithreading Security Concerns

The biggest risk to multitasking and multithreading is that the operating system will not be able to keep the various tasks or threads separate from each other. It is possible to have a malicious process access resources (most specifically memory addresses) allocated to some other process. It is also possible that a malicious process will switch security contexts and run in a privilege level they were not originally meant to run in. Should a malicious process manage to run in system privilege level, the same as the operating system kernel, it is possible to crash the OS. It might also be possible for a malicious process to issue many threads that will take priority with the CPU over legitimate application threads. This could potentially cause a denial of service attack against the legitimate application.

Multiprocessing

Unlike multitasking, where all programs must take turns on a single CPU, *multiprocessing* permits programs to be divided among multiple physical CPUs. The OS controls all of the processors in such a way that the system's optimum performance is reached. Motherboards found in servers can have up to 32 or more CPUs. The version of the operating system will dictate how many processors can be used at once.

Another technique that is essentially the same as having multiple CPUs is to have multiple cores on a single CPU. A single CPU chip might have 2, 4, 8, 16 or more cores that act as independent CPUs on the same physical chip. CPUs with multiple cores appear to the operating system as multiple CPUs. Processes can then be split across the cores by the operating system in the same way that they would be split across physical CPUs.

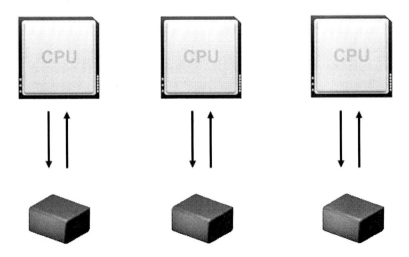

Figure 3–3: Multiprocessing.

Multiprocessing Security Concerns

Multiprocessing systems have similar security concerns to multitasking and multithreading systems. The multiple CPUs share parts of memory. Threads running on one CPU could access the memory of another CPU. Additionally, the different processors communicate with each other to stay coordinated. They are susceptible to replay attacks on the data cache of each CPU. A replay attack is the act of capturing and replaying a transmission as if you are the originator of that transmission, in order to bypass authentication mechanisms. In this case, the replay attack masquerades as a legitimate request message between CPUs to gain unauthorized access to another CPU's data cache. There could also be attacks on the integrity of the control messages between CPUs. Putting a counter on each request issued effectively places a unique identifier on data messages so that replay and integrity attacks between CPUs will be unsuccessful.

Memory

Memory is a type of storage that allows the CPU to keep track of all the tasks it is working on. Instructions are loaded into memory, fetched by the CPU, and executed. The results are then stored again in memory to be presented to the user or saved for later use.

There are a number of different types of memory that can be found in a computer. First and foremost is *Random Access Memory (RAM)*. This is what we typically refer to when we speak of computer memory. A "stick" of RAM is a collection of chips on a small card. Its job is to remember (temporarily store) instructions that the CPU is currently working on. the operating system, applications that you open, and any files that you open are loaded into RAM. The instruction sets from these programs or files are then fetched from the CPU, processed, and an output is returned.

The output can then be displayed on a monitor, played on a speaker, sent to a printer, sent across the network, or stored on disk, or used in whatever capacity required.

The data in RAM is temporary. It is only stored as long as power is applied to the chip. If the power is shut off, the data in the RAM is lost. A significant implication of this is that if malicious code is running on the computer, it is most likely going to exist at that moment in RAM. If you suddenly shut off the power, that code will disappear. While this is sometimes a way to eliminate a virus that has not yet written itself to disk, it also is a quick way to destroy any evidence of malicious activity. If you're performing a forensic investigation on a computer, you will want to preserve what is running in memory before you shut the computer down.

Another common type of memory found in the computer is *Read Only Memory (ROM)*. This is typically in the form of firmware. The BIOS on the motherboard is an example of ROM. The data stored in ROM is not volatile. When the power is turned off, the data remains. This data is used during the initiation, or boot, process of a computer.

Because memory is an information storage location that is immediately available, it is often called *primary storage*. A special category of RAM is cache memory. This is a small amount of memory that is built into the CPU. It is used to expedite access to instructions that are repeatedly used by the CPU.

 Note: Do not confuse memory with memory card. Today's cameras and mobile devices use the term "memory card" to refer to removable storage. A memory card is actually a flash disk on a small flat card used for storing images, videos, and other files. It does not assist the device to run processes on the CPU.

Memory Security Concerns

While memory is designed to keep the code of different applications segregated from each other, malicious code might be able to steal information from another application by reading its memory address. As with the CPU, you could also have a denial of service attack that consumes all of the available memory in a system, rendering it unable to perform any real work. In addition, a poorly written application could have a memory leak. This is a condition in which an application continues to consume memory without releasing it back to the system, to the point where no more memory is available and the operating system slows almost to a halt.

Virtual Memory

A special category of storage is *virtual memory*. Virtual memory is essentially hard disk space masquerading as real RAM. It is used when there is not enough real RAM to perform all of the tasks running on the system.

Virtual memory has been around throughout most of computing's history. Every application you launch, and every file that you open, requires a certain amount of memory. When the system runs out of memory, it will refuse to open any more applications or documents.

In the early days of computing, RAM was very expensive. The workaround was to extend the capabilities of RAM by putting some of the instructions on disk. Nearly every operating system provides virtual memory capabilities. When there is insufficient RAM, the least recently used code (instructions) in RAM gets "paged out" (temporarily transferred) to a page file (a special file on disk used to capture this code). When those instruction sets are required again, they are fetched from the page file and restored to RAM for use.

Virtual memory still exists in nearly every system today. Most operating systems assign a virtual memory structure to every application that launches, in order to give the application a consistent, reliable amount of memory resources. The application may never need to use the virtual memory, but the structure is still there for convenience.

Although virtual memory seems to be a very convenient mechanism for opening more programs and documents then you actually have physical RAM for, it has its drawbacks and limits. Paging dramatically slows down the system. This is because the access speed of RAM is typically 8 nanoseconds (billionths of a second) while the access speed of a hard drive is about nine milliseconds (thousandths of a second). This means that RAM is a million times faster than a hard drive. Also, there's a practical limit as to how much the operating system can use a page file on disk as opposed to real RAM. There comes a point at which a larger page file will gain you no benefit.

Virtual Memory Security Concerns

The drawbacks of virtual memory are more performance related than security related. Virtual memory can allow a system to appear to have a large amount of RAM when, in fact, it has limited RAM and uses disks to store swapped information temporarily. This swapping, or paging, of programs and data can seriously impact performance if the system has to wait for the disk's input/output to complete. In addition, if you run out of both RAM and pagefile space, the system will become extremely slow or halt altogether as it will not have any place in memory to store running code. Like real RAM, virtual memory has its limits. If an application has a memory leak, virtual memory may help the system function a little longer, but will not address the real problem. A memory leak can eventually consume all of virtual memory once the real RAM has been exhausted. The security professional should recognize that a poorly performing system may also be a security hazard if it cannot perform security-related functions.

Storage

Besides the primary storage of memory, a computer can use *secondary storage* to store data more permanently. Originally, secondary storage was a floppy disk. This was then replaced by the internal hard disk.

Today, secondary storage can refer to any hardware or media that can store data without power. There are two types of secondary storage: fixed and removable. Fixed storage is installed inside the computer, and is usually a hard drive. Hard drives are magnetic-based. They store data by imprinting magnetic 1's and 0's on small metallic platters that spin inside the disk. A set of small readers move on an arm across the platters as they spin, reading or writing to the disk.

Removable storage can be a flash disk, a memory card, a CD or DVD, a floppy disk, a tape, or some other media that is temporarily plugged in or inserted into the system and then removed. The removed storage can then be inserted into a different system, thus allowing the user to transfer data from one system to another.

Solid-state drives (SSD) are basically large flash drives. Flash drives are approximately 100 times faster than traditional hard drives, so they can dramatically improve the performance not only of your storage but also of your virtual memory. The only caveat of solid-state drives is that they are currently still very expensive, and they do not have nearly the storage capacity of a traditional hard drive.

Storage Security Concerns

From a security perspective, removable storage is the most common way to spread a virus. In the early days of computers the worst offender was the floppy disk. In today's modern systems, the removable flash drive is the most common virus carrier. Some flash drive vendors have responded to this vulnerability by using digital signatures and encryption built into the firmware to prevent malware from overwriting the flash drive's functionality or data. As with CPU and RAM, storage can also be consumed by a malicious process to the point where the system cannot perform its intended service.

It is possible to damage or destroy the data by passing any magnetic media, including a hard drive, through a strong magnetic field. From a security perspective, even erasing or overwriting a hard drive or tape can still leave a faint magnetic imprint that a sensitive enough reader can read and reveal the original information. For this reason, organizations that want to be completely secure will physically destroy hard drives before discarding them. You can physically destroy a hard drive by drilling holes through it or by shredding the metal.

Peripherals

A peripheral is any hardware device that can be plugged into the computer to provide it with extra functionality. The device can be "internal" or "external." If the device is internal, the computer is opened and the device is plugged into a slot on the motherboard. If it is external, the computer is not opened, and the device is simply plugged into a port such as a USB, audio, or video port.

Examples of peripherals include (but are not limited to):

* Keyboard
* Mouse
* Printer
* Plotter
* Camera
* Image capturing device
* Human interface device (mouse or keyboard substitute)
* Joystick
* Scanner
* Speakers
* Microphone
* Headset
* External CD/DVD drive
* USB modem
* Network adapter

 Note: While flash drives and external hard drives are technically peripherals, they are also storage.

Peripheral devices that provide input to the computer system and output from the computer system are also called *input/output (I/O)* peripheral devices. Keyboards, monitors, mice, sound cards, scanners, printers, and network interfaces are all I/O devices.

I/O devices are attached to computer systems via cabling or are directly connected to the computer bus.

Security Concerns for Peripherals

From a security perspective, peripherals are often a source of vulnerability. The peripheral itself might not be secure. Or a user could plug a specialized device into a port for malicious purpose, such as capturing keystrokes, secretly recording audio or video from a user, redirecting network traffic, or stealing data.

 Note: In July 2013, a security group named Mactrans demonstrated how even the power adapter for an Apple iOS 6 device could be used to compromise the phone. For more information, see: **www.cnet.com/news/apple-power-adapter-security-flaw-to-be-patched-in-ios-7/**.

Computer Bus

In computer architecture, a *computer bus* is the set of physical connections between devices that are attached to the computer's motherboard, or primary circuit board. Buses can be serial with components connected one after another in a daisy-chain fashion or parallel with multiple communication pathways.

Parallel buses include three different physical pathways to transfer information between a CPU and an I/O device. One pathway is the *data path*. Another pathway is the *instruction path*, and the last pathway is the *addressing path*.

The CPU sends a request via the instruction path to a device identified by an address sent on the addressing path. In return, the I/O device returns the information to the CPU via the data path.

Computer Bus Security Concerns

The architecture of some computer buses can potentially allow an attacker to gain control of a computer system. For example, a Direct Memory Access (DMA) attack could allow a malicious device that uses the DMA bus to bypass operating system security mechanisms and take control of the system's memory, stealing any data that passes through RAM. Similarly, because users can and do plug all manner of peripherals into the Universal Serial Bus (USB), it is often used as an attack vector. Users frequently plug infected flash drives into their systems, thus bypassing any network-based security mechanisms. A user could (knowingly or unknowingly) plug other compromised or maliciously built devices into a USB port to attack the system.

Drivers

A *driver* is a small set of software instructions that allows an operating system to talk to and control a specific hardware component. Every piece of hardware, including all peripherals and components on the motherboard, requires a driver to work. Drivers are not only device specific, but they are also operating system specific. Most operating systems ship with drivers for the most common hardware makes and models. Most devices come with a CD that contains drivers for the most popular operating systems. If your computer does not have a driver for a specific device, you can usually download that driver from the manufacturer's website.

Security Concerns for Drivers

As with any other software, a driver has to be well written in order to not crash, compromise, or otherwise negatively impact the computer it is installed on. Drivers that are not well-tested may make the operating system unstable. It is also possible to obtain a driver that has been altered with malicious code. Microsoft and other operating system vendors test drivers for the most popular peripherals. Make sure that any drivers you install have been tested and certified by the operating system manufacturer. Make sure also to only install drivers that have been digitally signed by the manufacturer. This guarantees that the driver is authentic and has not been modified in any way.

Firmware

Firmware is a chip designed to hold a small set of instructions to assist devices. Motherboards, network interface cards (NIC), printers, smartphones, and many other devices rely on these special chips to perform a variety of tasks. These are frequently referred to as Read Only Memory (ROM) chips, but in fact, many of them are not technically read only. So, a more technically accurate term that should be used is Electronically Erasable Programmable ROM (EEPROM).

Firmware code can be updated through a process known as flashing.

The Basic Input Output System (BIOS) is a common use for firmware. When the PC is turned on, the BIOS will perform a power-on self-test (POST). Once the POST is complete, it will locate the boot sector, which contains instructions on loading the operating system. The BIOS may also provide an option for authentication and require the user to provide a password, thus providing another layer of security, one that is enforced even before the loading of the operating system.

One of the newest uses for firmware is the Trusted Platform Module (TPM). It has a Rivest, Shamir, Adleman (RSA) key burned into it and can be used for storing and creating other cryptographic keys, for pseudo random number generation, and for binding and sealing of data.

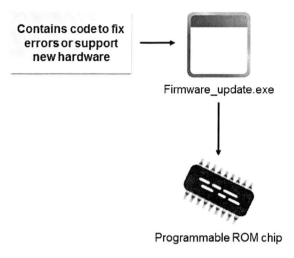

Figure 3-4: Updating firmware code.

Firmware Security Concerns

Because firmware has instructions built into it, it is potentially an avenue for attack. If the attacker is able to modify the instructions on the firmware, that malicious code could be executed without the knowledge of the operating system. Or, the firmware could simply not perform properly, thus rendering functionality on the motherboard useless or inaccessible to the operating system.

The instructions on firmware can be altered to make the system unstable or insecure. Some operating systems, such as Apple IOS, check the integrity of the firmware before allowing the system to boot. The security professional should not allow users to jailbreak or root their mobile devices. This is a popular technique for bypassing the built-in security mechanisms on a mobile device's firmware. Users do it so they can have administrative privilege on the device, or install unapproved software. The risk, however, is that much of the software (particularly games) that a user might install can also contain malicious code.

Operating System Software

The operating system manages all the hardware and software in a computer system. It is in itself a type of software, and is the first thing that is installed on a bare metal box (brand-new computer). The computer will not run without some form of operating system. Popular operating systems today include:

- Microsoft Windows
- Linux
- Free BSD
- Mac OSX/iOS
- Unix

Computers are not the only devices to have operating systems. Switches, routers, firewalls, mobile phones, tablets, gaming consoles, and even some household appliances have their own operating system.

Many systems, especially network devices such as switches and routers, have miniature operating systems burned into their firmware. This allows the device to boot up in a limited fashion, sufficient functionality to install a full operating system.

Every operating system has had different versions that were released in history. Some versions have more vulnerabilities than others. Typically, when a vendor wants to provide a lot of extra functionality to users, the risk of also introducing extra vulnerabilities increases. The security professional must recognize that every single operating system has some form of vulnerability, and must be hardened to make it more secure.

Note: For more information on operating system vulnerabilities, see the National Vulnerability Database at **https://web.nvd.nist.gov/view/vuln/search**.

 Note: For more information on the currently most vulnerable operating systems, see the article "Most vulnerable operating systems and applications in 2014" at **www.gfi.com/blog/most-vulnerable-operating-systems-and-applications-in-2014/**.

Operating System Security

An operating system, with its millions of lines of code and numerous user functions, is the single biggest source of a computer's security problems. While every operating system vendor will have their own recommendations for hardening their systems, the basic steps are the same:

- Disable all unnecessary services.
- Disable all unused accounts, including default accounts.
- Remove all unnecessary executables and registry/configuration entries.
- Apply appropriately restrictive permissions to files, shares, services, end points, and registry entries.
- Provide users and services with the least privilege level necessary to perform their task.
- Change all default passwords.
- Only permit remote administrative access through an encrypted connection, or disallow it altogether, particularly across a public network such as the Internet, or an easily accessed network such as wireless or Bluetooth.
- When possible, change default ports.
- Apply the latest vendor patches.
- Run vulnerability assessment software and procedures against the system on a regular basis. Make sure the tool you use is updated to look for the latest vulnerabilities.

Application and Utility Software

Besides the operating system, there are two general types of software: applications and utilities.

An application is any type of program the user wants to run on the computer. Running applications is the primary reason for having a computer. A few examples include:

- Games.
- Office productivity programs.
- Multimedia editing programs.
- Drafting and design programs.
- Health monitoring programs.
- Accounting programs.
- Customer relations management programs.
- Software or systems development programs.
- Industry- or business- specific programs.

A utility is a software-based tool. Utilities are used mostly by IT support personnel to maintain the functionality and integrity of a computer system. Examples of utilities include:

- Antivirus/antimalware programs.
- Data and system backup programs.
- System performance and health check programs.

Application and Utility Security Concerns

Any software program can introduce vulnerabilities into the system. Users frequently download and use programs with little real knowledge of how those programs were created and by whom. Much of the software that is traded illegally on peer-to-peer networks is infected by viruses. Hackers take advantage of human nature by offering free copies of otherwise expensive or difficult-to-find programs. Users, eager to have the software, then download and use it, not realizing that it has been compromised for the hacker's gain.

The security professional must make sure that the only software an organization uses is original, well-tested, properly licensed, and digitally signed (digitally guaranteed) by the manufacturer. If the software is downloaded from the Internet, you can often check the file integrity by running a checksum against it using the MD5 hash (expected integrity results) provided by the manufacturer.

Guidelines for Ensuring System Component Security

Here are some guidelines for ensuring system component security:

- Approach system component security with the attitude that *everything* has a vulnerability, even if it is not yet been discovered or exploited.
- Educate yourself on the latest hardware and software vulnerabilities and how to remediate those vulnerabilities.
- Ensure that any system has sufficient hardware resources and is properly maintained by IT support personnel.
- Make sure that any peripherals you install have been tested by the operating system manufacturer for compatibility.
- Only use legitimate, licensed copies of software.
- Only install software that has been digitally signed by the manufacturer.
- Do not permit anyone to install unsigned or unnecessary software on servers or other critical devices.
- Keep antivirus systems up-to-date.
- Make sure that antivirus software automatically scans any removable storage the instant it is plugged into the computer.
- Do not permit users to root or jailbreak their mobile devices.

ACTIVITY 3-2
Analyzing System Component Security

Scenario
In this activity, you will assess your understanding of system components security.

1. What is the greatest security concern with regard to storage?
   - ○ Viruses from removable drives
   - ○ Information leakage across the network
   - ○ Hardware crash
   - ○ Media sanitization before disposal

2. What rule can you follow to minimize the risk of using any new software?
   - ○ Ensure that it is clean and paid for.
   - ○ Ensure that it is installed from original media.
   - ○ Ensure that it was not downloaded from the Internet.
   - ○ Ensure that it is properly licensed and digitally signed.

3. What is the greatest security concern regarding device drivers?
   - ○ They could contain malicious code.
   - ○ They could be applied to the wrong hardware.
   - ○ They could be poorly written and destabilize a critical system.
   - ○ They could damage the device.

4. You just installed a new application on a computer in a hospital radiology department. The application controls a digital X-ray machine. The X-ray machine uses a USB serial cable to plug into the computer. The application sends a signal out the USB port to command the X-ray generator to transmit X-rays onto the patient. The application then captures the resulting image in a digital picture format. The application is supposed to run in non-privileged user mode. The application is multithreaded, and the computer has multiple CPUs. When you start the application for the first time, however, the computer crashes. You reboot the computer and start the application again. Again, the computer crashes.

   What do you think might be causing the problem? (Choose two.)
   - ☐ The application driver that controls the X-ray machine was not well-written.
   - ☐ The application is using the wrong computer bus to access the CPU.
   - ☐ The application should not be using an X-ray machine as a peripheral.
   - ☐ The application is launching in system privilege level, and then becoming unstable.

5. You have a server that monitors your network for suspicious activity. You install a software utility you downloaded from the Internet onto the server. It is supposed to help the server inventory all of the network devices that are being monitored. The application seems to work fine. After awhile, however, you notice that the server has started slowing down. You check the server's monitoring logs and see that no new entries have been logged for the past half hour. You know that there has been activity on the network that should have been logged. Large amounts of disk space seem to have been consumed on the server. Eventually, the operating system seems to stop. You move the mouse, and it takes a full minute before the pointer on the screen moves.

What do you think may have happened?

○ You have run out of disk space.

○ The server is too busy monitoring the network to respond to the mouse.

○ The application is replicating itself across the network.

○ The application has consumed all of the server's memory and virtual memory, causing a denial-of-service attack on the server.

6. A user brings a mobile device to you that is behaving strangely. It was running fine for weeks, but its performance suddenly became very poor. Upon examining the device, you notice that several unauthorized games have been installed on it. You ask the user how those games got on the device, and he answers that his daughter had borrowed the phone several times and must have installed the games at some point. The device is locked down and should not permit the installation of unauthorized software.

What do you think may have happened?

○ The daughter figured out her dad's device password.

○ The device needs more RAM to run the games properly.

○ The daughter rooted the device to bypass firmware security controls.

○ The games were designed to be played on a laptop, and not a mobile device.

TOPIC C

Security Models

In the last topic, you learned about the individual components that make up a computer system, and the potential vulnerabilities that each component has. In this next topic, you will learn how security models are used to address potential system vulnerabilities.

Theoretical/Mathematical Security Models

Security models provide different approaches for protecting the confidentiality, integrity, and availability of information on devices or networks. Unlike security frameworks, which provide an overarching approach to incorporating security throughout the enterprise, security models are concerned with how to implement access control and CIA on a specific system.

The four theoretical/mathematical models that form the basis of other models are summarized in the following table.

Types of Security Models	Description
Lattice	The *Lattice Model* is a conceptual model where data (objects) is classified or labeled and users (subjects) are cleared for access. Lattice Models provide strict rules on what is allowed or not allowed between subjects and objects.
Information Flow	The *Information Flow Model* controls the direction of data flow among the various security levels when allowed. It is based on an object's classification and a subject's need to know. This model is useful for detecting unauthorized data flows, or communications paths, called *covert channels*.
	Information Flow Models are not a category unto themselves but are a collection of other models that control information flow. By analyzing sources and information destinations controlled by Information Flow Models, it is possible to discover covert channels that may leak information between different levels of security. BLP and Biba are both information flow models.
Non-Interference	The *Non-Interference Model* is a very strict mathematical security model that prevents covert channels. It limits the interference between elements at different security levels. Non-Interference Models create barriers between levels so that information cannot inadvertently leak between them.
State Machine	The state of a system is a single point in time. The *State Machine Model* is a theoretical model that monitors the system as it moves from one state to another. More specifically, it looks at what operations are allowed or not allowed as the system moves from one state to the next. A security policy will provide the rules for the system. BLP is an example of a state machine.

Security Models

These models are based on the theoretical/mathematical models.

Security Models	Description
BLP	The *Bell-LaPadula (BLP) Model* was developed by the U.S. Department of Defense. It was the first mathematical model to address multi-level security policy. It is a state machine that uses the lattice concept to maintain confidentiality. BLP uses mandatory access control to limit the access to classified objects to those subjects with equal or higher clearance. This model is primarily used for maintaining confidentiality. The intent is to prohibit classified information from being moved to a lower classification level. Access modes described in the BLP Model include the Simple Security Property, which is equivalent to the read property; the * Security Property, which is generally referred to as the star (*) or write property; and the Strong * Property, where read and write are at your level.

In BLP, subjects cannot read up to objects with a higher classification and information cannot be written down, or moved down, to a lower classification level. Simply stated, BLP implements no read up or no write down policies. It is important to remember that BLP is primarily concerned with the confidentiality of documents. |
| Biba | The *Biba Model* is a model that uses a lattice to describe integrity at information trust levels. It enforces the lattice through mandatory access control. Information with high trust needs to be protected from the insertion of information with a low trust level. Like BLP, access modes described in Biba include the Simple Integrity Axiom (read property) and the * Integrity Axiom (write property).

In Biba, subjects cannot read down to objects with a lower integrity level and information cannot be written up, or moved up, to a higher integrity level. Simply stated, Biba implements no read down or no write up policies. Biba reverses BLP and is sometimes referred to as upside down BLP. It is important to remember that Biba is primarily concerned with the integrity of documents. |
| Clark-Wilson | The *Clark-Wilson Model* extends Biba. It is an integrity model that relates trust to the integrity of the processes surrounding the data. Clark-Wilson features three essential tenets:

• No changes are made by an unauthorized subject.
• No unauthorized changes are made by an authorized subject.
• No mistakes are made in making any changes.

It also has two types of objects. A constrained data item (CDI) can only have changes made to it by a well-formed transaction or program called a transformation procedure (TP). An unconstrained data item (UDI) can be directly manipulated by a subject. An integrity verification procedure (IVP) is a program that runs periodically to check the consistency of CDIs. |
Graham-Denning	The *Graham-Denning Model* deals with creating and deleting objects and subjects, as well as the reading, granting, deleting, and transferring of access rights. It specifies rules of how a subject can execute basic commands on an object.
Harrison-Ruzzo-Ullman	The *Harrison-Ruzzo-Ullman Model* is a variation of the Graham-Denning model and deals with changing access rights and creating and deleting subjects or objects. It also addresses situations where you do not want a subject to gain permissions.
Brewer-Nash	The *Brewer-Nash Model* relates to the control of the conflict of interest. It addresses security issues that can arise where there are dynamic changes in access rights. If a user is accessing Client A data, then the user cannot access any other client information until Client A's access is discontinued. Brewer-Nash can be implemented at the system level and extend into the process level. Brewer-Nash is sometimes called the Chinese Wall model.

The Impact of Biba

The concepts surrounding the Biba Model are often difficult to understand because most governmental systems deal with confidentiality, not integrity. In Biba, an integrity label is used. For example, a policy is built indicating that data is labeled based on trust using L1 through L4, with L1 being no trust and L4 being the highest level of trust.

A military scenario works well to illustrate this model. Rumors of enemy activity heard on the street are trusted at L1 because there is little or no supporting information. Rather, intelligence gathered about enemy activity by trained intelligence officers who actually viewed the movements are trusted at L4. For example, an intelligence officer with an L3 rating cannot read down to L1 or L2 information and bring it into an L3 storage area because the information with lower trust levels would pollute the L3 information. The same officer cannot write up information from L3 to L4 because it would give the L3 information more credibility than it deserves.

Access Control Categories

Many of these models will support the concepts of either discretionary, non-discretionary, or mandatory access control (MAC). There are four access control categories, each giving the system administrator a different amount of control over implementing access control. The categories are summarized in the following table.

Access Control Category	Description
Discretionary Access Control (DAC)	Each user (Creator/Owner) has control over his or her own data. The data owner can grant different access levels to that data. This is the most commonly used form of access control in a desktop operating system.
Mandatory Access Control (MAC)	This is the strictest form of access control. Access levels are enforced by the system, and cannot be changed by a user or system administrator. Objects (computer resources) are assigned security labels. These labels indicate the classification (top secret, confidential, unclassified, etc.) of the resource as well as its category (department, project, or management level). Subjects (users) are given security clearance levels. A subject can only access an object if the subject's security clearance level matches the object's classification and category level.
Role-Based Access Control (RBAC)	This is a type of DAC in which users are assigned to roles based on need or job function, and the access level of the role is determined by the system administrator. The roles are typically implemented as groups. If a user belongs to a certain group, that user can access whatever the group can access. Microsoft Windows Server is an example of an operating system that uses both DAC and RBAC.
Rule-Based Access Control	In this type, access is granted based on rules set by the administrator. It doesn't matter who the subject is; access is only granted if the activity matches the rule. This type of access control is most commonly used on firewalls and routers to control network traffic. For example, a rule might state that only web browser traffic, and no other type of traffic, may exit the corporate network and enter the Internet.

Note: Sometimes Rule Based Access Control also uses the acronym RBAC, even though it does not refer to the same thing as Role Based Access Control RBAC. Be careful not to confuse the two.

TCSEC

Trusted Computer System Evaluation Criteria (TCSEC) is a standard security evaluation framework used to assess the security level of a computer system. It was first published by the U.S. Department of Defense in 1983. Frequently referred to as the "Orange Book," it was used to help identify which products provide a baseline of security for military and government computer systems.

It introduced the concept of a Trusted Computing Base (TCB) as part of its rating system. The rating system uses divisions to designate the security level of a system. Because the use is intended primarily for military and government systems, the focus of the security was confidentiality. The more rigid and formal the testing process that the system passed, the higher its rating would be. The divisions are summarized as follows.

TCSEC Division	Evaluation Class	Description
A: Verified Protection	A1	Highest. Equivalent to B3, but also includes formal accreditation and acceptance. Used in military computers.
B: Mandatory Protection	B3: Security Domains	Satisfies Reference Monitor requirements. Excludes code not essential to security policy enforcement. Automated intrusion detection and response.
	B2: Structured Protection	DAC and MAC on all subjects and objects. Security policy model clearly defined and documented. Covert channels identified and analyzed.
	B1: Labeled Security Protection	Introduces labels and mandatory access control. DAC and MAC over some subjects and objects.
C: Discretionary Protection	C2: Controlled Access Protection	Individual login and password, auditing, accounting, and resource isolation. Suitable for everyday nonclassified government use.
	C1: Discretionary Security Protection	Has basic discretionary access control.
D: Minimal Protection	D1	Evaluated, but did not meet security requirements.

The Rainbow Series

The Orange Book was part of a series of publications called the Rainbow Series. The Red Book focused on network security. The Green Book focused on password management.

Note: For more information on the Rainbow Series, see **https://en.wikipedia.org/wiki/Rainbow_Series**.

Examples of System Ratings

An example of a C2 rated system is Microsoft Windows NT 4.0 Server SP6a (plus hotfixes). Trusted XENIX 4.0 is an example of B2. Examples of A1 systems include Aesec's GEMSOS, Boeing's SNS Server, and Honeywell's SCOMP.

ITSEC

Taking lessons learned from TCSEC, the European community offered its own evaluation framework in 1990 called the *Information Technology Security Evaluation Criteria (ITSEC)*. Not as strict as TCSEC, ITSEC allows the vendor or consumer to choose from a list to specify their requirements.

The choices would be organized into a Security Target (ST). The product being evaluated was known as the Target of Evaluation (ToE).

ITSEC divided its labeling into two sets, functional (F) and security effectiveness (E). It addressed a wider range of security needs than TCSEC, adding integrity and availability to the confidentiality requirements. It also uses the concept of assurance levels, or E levels. This means that the vendor not only provides a certain level of assurance with the current product, but will also continue to provide that same level of assurance in the future.

The following table compares ITSEC to TCSEC ratings.

TCSEC	ITSEC
A1	F-B3 E6
B3	F-B3 E5
B2	F-B2 E4
B1	F-B1 E3
C2	F-C2 E2
C1	F-C1 E1
D	E0

ITSEC also has the following ratings that have no equivalent in TCSEC:

- F6: High integrity
- F7: High availability
- F8: High integrity during data communications
- F9: High confidentiality during data communications
- F10: Networks with high confidentiality and integrity

Operating System Examples

Microsoft NT 4.0 SP3 is an example of E3 F-C2. Banyan Vines is an example of E2 F-C2. Sun Solaris CMW 1.2 is an example of E3 F-B1.

CTCPEC

The Canadian Trusted Computer Product Evaluation Criteria (CTCPEC) was published in 1992 by the Canadian System Security Centre (CSSC) to address gaps in the Orange Book. CTCPEC addresses a variety of systems: monolithic, networked, distributed systems, subsystems, databases, and others. It separates functionality from assurance requirements. Its functionality criteria are divided into four major categories:

- Confidentiality
- Integrity
- Availability
- Accounting

These categories are further divided into Security Services. Assurance requirements are included across the entire product, with dependencies between functionality and assurance included as well.

Common Criteria

Common Criteria was released by the International Standards Organization (ISO) in 1997. Common Criteria has largely superseded TCSEC, ITSEC, and CTCPEC.

It has two types of security requirements: functional and assurance. Functional requirements describe what a system does, as well as its security capabilities. The security requirements used in the system's evaluation are known as the Security Target (ST), which are organized around the concept of TCB entities. The system and its controls are defined in a Protection Profile, and include:

*   Physical and logical controls.
*   Startup and recovery.
*   Reference mediation.
*   Privileged states.

The Target of Evaluation (ToE) is the system being tested. Assurance is categorized into eight Evaluation Assurance Levels.

CC Assurance Level	Description
EAL 7	Formally verified, designed, and tested
EAL 6	Semiformally verified, designed, and tested
EAL 5	Semiformally designed and tested
EAL 4	Methodically designed, tested, and reviewed
EAL 3	Methodically checked and tested
EAL 2	Structurally tested
EAL 1	Functionality tested
EAL 0	Inadequate assurance

Operating System Examples

An example of a high level, EAL 6 operating system is the Integrity 178B by Green Hills software. It is used in jet fighters and other critical devices. Windows Server 2008 R2, HP-UX, AIX, FreeBSD, RedHat, and SUSE Enterprise Linux are examples of EAL 4.

Guidelines for Implementing Security Models

Here are some guidelines you can use for implementing a security model:

*   Use existing security models as examples to help you understand how to create or choose your own security model.
*   Use Common Criteria if you wish your product to be evaluated for its security level.

ACTIVITY 3-3
Discussing Security Models

Scenario

In this activity, you will assess your understanding of security models.

---

1. What security model do you use in your current work environment and why?

2. Under which conditions would it be preferable to use mandatory access control? Discretionary access control?

TOPIC D

Controls and Countermeasures in Enterprise Security

In the prior topic, you learned about using models to address potential system vulnerabilities. In this next topic, you will learn how to use security controls to protect an enterprise environment.

ESA

Enterprise Security Architecture (ESA) focuses on implementing information security across an entire organization, rather than a single system or application. It emphasizes consistent application of a strategic design that can be used by multiple applications, systems, and business processes.

Keep in mind that the larger the organization, the more likely that large parts of its infrastructure will be virtualized. Make sure that you have a consistent security policy that extends across both the physical and virtual infrastructure.

With enterprise security architecture, you're trying to establish a long-term strategy for providing security services across your entire enterprise. You do this by establishing priorities when developing your security services. You design and implement security services that are consistent across the enterprise, and can be used by all lines of business.

Some processes and lines of business will have greater security needs than others. For that reason, you will need to identify the different security requirements of each, and organize them into zones, each with their own privilege levels and boundaries.

ESA Goals

The goal of an enterprise security architecture is to provide a single unified vision and high-level, long-term view of all of your security controls. It allows you to see your security system in its entirety as a holistic entity. This helps you identify potential gaps in your controls, with a long-term mechanism for mitigating risk and improving the architecture.

ESA has the following goals:

- Provide a long-term, simple view of your controls.
- Provide a unified vision for common security controls across the organization.
- Maximize existing technology investments.
- Be flexible in addressing current and future threats.
- Always support the core needs of the organization.

As you evolve your security controls, your architecture should permit you to use existing technology when possible. This allows the company to realize as much return on investment as it can.

Your architecture should also be flexible enough to address current and potential future threats while servicing the needs of the business.

Your security architecture should support your security program. Different data, processes, and departments will have different security needs. These needs are not expected to be of equal importance to the business, nor will they maintain the same value or risk in their lifetime. Your security architecture should support a security program that uses the most effective technology to protect business assets. Technical controls should be combined with quality business processes to help reduce risk to acceptable business levels. Your architecture and security program should also include a mechanism for assessing and constantly improving information security controls in your enterprise.

ESA Benefits

The benefits of having a clearly defined and integrated enterprise security architecture include:

- Outlining general security strategy.
- Providing guidance when making technical decisions.
- Providing decision-makers with good guidance to make security related design decisions and investments.
- Limiting future technological needs to a realistic set of proposed services.
- Being able to implement industry standards and best practices.
- Managing risk consistently across the enterprise.
- Reducing costs by providing reusable common security services.
- Aligning the overall security strategy to support business goals.

ESA Building Blocks

When building your ESA, there are five security services that form the foundation for your architecture.

- Boundary control services.
- Access control services.
- Integrity services.
- Cryptographic services.
- Auditing and monitoring services.

These services become the building blocks for designing your enterprise solution. In this context, security services are functionalities within an operating system and are applied automatically.

Boundary Control Services

One of the most basic security services that you can define for your ESA is boundary control. The boundary control service focuses on how and when information is allowed to move from one system to another, or from one state to another. Boundaries can be defined at the physical, network, or process level.

In order to effectively use boundaries, you need to identify security zones. Each zone has a different level of trust. Security zones help the solution architect to group assets and systems that have the same security needs together. With each security zone, you can apply different policies and configure appropriate measures for that zone. You then separate the zones using boundary control to ensure that sensitive information does not leak from a more secure zone to a less secure zone.

As each zone connects to the other, and users or information moves from one zone to another, you want to control the movement across those boundaries. You would do this by having specific, controlled points of entry from one zone to another.

Boundary Level	Description
Physical	For example, you could have a physically secure zone where only authorized employees are allowed to enter and use specific machines. You could have a highly secure zone, in which a computer is in a room that requires biometric access and is not even connected to the network.
	Boundaries can be created through the use of separate areas, locked doors, fencing, different facilities, or some other method of physically separating systems.

Boundary Level	Description
Network	At the network level, you could have an internal network zone where employees are allowed to freely use different services on the network. This kind of zone is considered to be trusted. You could then have a perimeter network zone where the general public enters to access your services from the Internet. This zone, while protected, is still not considered to be trusted because the general public can access it. Finally, you could have the Internet zone, which is your connection to the Internet and is the least trusted of all.
	Boundaries are achieved by using devices such as firewalls, routers, proxies, access control lists, and gateways to protect sensitive assets and processes in the more trusted zones from less sensitive assets and processes in the less trusted zones.
Process	At the process level, you could have controls that determine which processes can access which resources, or when a process can change state. A state refers to the privilege level a process is currently running in.
	The security kernel restricts which processes are permitted to access which resources on a system. The Reference Monitor enforces process access control at the security perimeter, the boundary that separates a zone of trusted processes (such as core operating system processes) from a zone of untrusted processes (such as user-launched applications).

Access Control Services

The next most common ESA security service is that of access control. Access control refers to any mechanism (physical or electronic) for limiting access to data or a system to only authorized users, systems, and processes. At its most basic level, access control includes:

- Identification: Initially determining who or what this subject is that is attempting to access a resource.
- Authentication: Sufficiently proving that the subject really is who or what it claims it is.
- Authorization: Once authentication is completed, specifying exactly what the subject is allowed to access.

The security professional must realize that if multiple access control systems are implemented, the user will have to pass all of them to access the intended resource. For example, you could put share and file permissions on a folder in Microsoft Windows. If the share permission is read-only, and the file permission is full control, the user will have to get past both access control mechanisms to access the file across the network. In this case, the user will only be able to read, because one of the access control mechanisms (the share permissions) only permits reading.

Additionally, if multiple authentication and authorization systems are involved, they will have to be coordinated so that the user can sign in once to obtain access.

Integrity Services

Integrity services are a critical ESA building block to maintain the authenticity of the data or systems. They check for corruption, offer antivirus protection, provide checksums, filter content, maintain file integrity, white list or blacklist, and help prevent intrusions.

Because the first and foremost principle of information security is the CIA triangle, you will want to make sure that your data does not change in an unauthorized manner. Integrity services focuses on keeping your data and your systems correct and free of corruption. Integrity services should function automatically, regularly checking for and detecting unauthorized alterations. Antivirus, digital signatures, hashing, and cyclical redundancy checks (CRC) are common examples of integrity services.

Maintaining the integrity of data or a system will always require a level of work, and thus reduce the performance of the system. A certain amount of CPU time and memory needs to be applied to regularly verify the consistency and integrity of the items you're trying to protect. Antivirus programs can noticeably slow down the performance of the system that does not have sufficient hardware to perform both the antivirus scan and normal user work.

The security professional should be alert to the fact that these performance slowdowns might induce a user to reduce the amount of scanning, thus reducing the level of protection. This is particularly true if an antivirus system is configured to inspect email messages or file access in real time. Users will often turn these features off so that they can have quicker access to the data they need.

Cryptographic Services

Once you have provided for the integrity of systems and data in your ESA, you will naturally want to provide for confidentiality. This is the function of cryptographic services. While you can apply access control lists to prevent unauthorized users from accessing data, the most secure mechanism you can use to keep that data confidential is to encrypt it. In this case you must balance the type and level of encryption with the need for availability. You may also have regulatory requirements for your industry that require you to use certain encryption types or levels. The security professional must work with both the technical teams and the legal department to ensure that the cryptographic services are satisfactory.

Auditing and Monitoring Services

There is no guarantee that an automated system will completely perform all of the functionality you desire. Additionally, you will want to see what attempts are made against the systems and data you're trying to protect. For this reason, another building block of your ESA must be auditing and monitoring. Most operating systems, applications, and security oriented network devices have the ability to log access attempts, both successful and unsuccessful. Intrusion detection systems (IDS) are the most common examples of monitoring. However, most operating systems and applications will log activity. Additionally, most access control systems (even physical) log activity.

The risk of logging activity, whether it be physical access control or processes in a system, is the sheer volume of information that will be captured. One only needs to look at a Windows event viewer log to see that the user can be quickly overwhelmed by trivia that is not important at the moment. For any logging to be useful to the security professional there must be an automated way to parse (read through) the log, pick out relevant events, and present these events clearly. The best auditing and monitoring services will provide a convenient console where security personnel can tell at a glance what is going on. Potential security incidents are flagged and easy to identify. The security operators should be able to click the incident for more information, and possibly take remediating action.

It is also important to centralize where all of that logging information goes. Individual systems should automatically forward their logs to a central system that collects, collates, and analyzes these logs. This not only makes it convenient for the operator, but it also protects data from being lost should one system become corrupted or compromised.

Even with centralized collection and automated log parsing, enterprise organizations will employ entire departments to monitor and audit security events from these logs.

Critical Security Controls

A control is any safeguard or countermeasure used to counteract risk. Controls need not be electronic (technical). They can also be procedural (administrative) or physical.

Note: Not all of the below listed security controls have primary or secondary focii.

Sans.org lists the following 20 critical security controls (with primary and secondary focii and recommended solutions) on its website. Almost all can be implemented technically; some are also administrative:

1. Inventory of Authorized and Unauthorized Devices.
2. Inventory of Authorized and Unauthorized Software.
3. Secure Configurations for Hardware and Software on Mobile Devices, Laptops, Workstations, and Servers.
4. Continuous Vulnerability Assessment and Remediation.
5. Controlled Use of Administrative Privileges.
6. Maintenance, Monitoring, and Analysis of Audit Logs.
7. Email and Web Browser Protections.
8. Malware Defenses.
9. Limitation and Control of Network Ports, Protocols, and Services.
10. Data Recovery Capability.
11. Secure Configurations for Network Devices such as Firewalls, Routers, and Switches.
12. Boundary Defense.
13. Data Protection.
14. Controlled Access Based on the Need to Know.
15. Wireless Access Control.
16. Account Monitoring and Control.
17. Security Skills Assessment and Appropriate Training to Fill Gaps.
18. Application Software Security.
19. Incident Response and Management.
20. Penetration Tests and Red Team Exercises.

Note: For more information on the top 20 critical security controls, including a downloadable PDF and wall poster, see the article "Critical Security Controls" at **https://www.sans.org/ critical-security-controls/**.

ESA Frameworks

The challenge of implementing an ESA is that organizations have different security needs and security architects have different approaches to satisfy those needs. A framework is a common structure that allows you to develop a broad range of different solutions with consistency, using proven best practices. It provides consistent tools and a common vocabulary, as well as recommended standards.

There are many security frameworks and models to choose from, but one of the largest considerations in choosing one is to make sure it will work with your organization's business objectives and that it has the support of upper management. It is important not to look at these tools as confining or constraining your efforts, but rather as a method that can be used to consistently address security. Rather than create piecemeal, reactive security policies or products, a better approach would be to have a consistent framework that supports your business and your security.

Some of these frameworks and models are not unique to security but are used in risk analysis and project management as well.

ESA

Frameworks

Framework	Description
Zachman	Named for John Zachman, the *Zachman* framework is designed to get the different groups working on a project to communicate with each other. It also helps to define what the different groups expect the project to deliver. The Zachman framework was not originally designed for security, but it has been widely adopted to help build secure systems. The Zachman framework is commonly associated with the who, what, when, how, where, and why of information security. These objectives are matched with the roles of planner, owner, designer, builder, programmer, and user. There is also a concern with mapping technology projects to business objectives.
ISO/IEC 27001	*ISO/IEC 27001* is concerned with the standardization of a company's Information Security Management System (ISMS). Because it is a formal standard, the company can elect to be audited to assure its compliance. ISO/IEC 27001 frequently uses the security controls put forth in ISO/IEC 27002 though it is not a requirement. ISO/IEC 27001 came from ISO 1799, which came from BS 7799.
COBIT	*Control Objectives for Information and related Technologies (COBIT)* is a framework for security governance best practices. There are 34 high level objectives that are divided into the four domains, Plan and Organize, Acquire and Implement, Deliver and Support, and Monitor and Evaluate. COBIT works to help companies realize value from IT initiatives. COBIT was developed by the Information Systems Audit and Control Association (ISACA).
PCI-DSS	Payment Card Industry Data Security Standard (PCI-DSS) was developed by the PCI Security Standards Council to promote payment card security. Similar to COBIT and ISO 27002, it provides a framework for the secure processing, storage, and transmission of cardholder information.
ITIL	IT Infrastructure Library (ITIL) was developed by the Central Computer and Telecommunications Agency (CCTA) as a collection of best practices for IT governance. The five key areas of focus for ITIL are Service Strategy, Service Design, Service Transition, Service Operations, and Continual Service Improvements.
TOGAF	*The Open Group Architecture Framework (TOGAF)* is an open framework seeking to provide common terms and methods that can be followed to create a secure organization. TOGAF was developed in the mid 1990s. It is based on earlier work done by the U.S. Department of Defense. TOGAF has evolved to version 9, which was released in February 2009. It provides design, planning, implementation, and governance modeled at four levels or domains. The levels are Business, Application, Data, and Technology. The inclusion of an Architecture Development Method (ADM) is important as it gives guidance on how to develop an enterprise architecture that meets the business and IT needs of a company.

Guidelines for Implementing Controls and Countermeasures in ESA

Here are some guidelines you can use when creating your enterprise security architecture:

- Design your architecture to have a unified security vision with common security controls across the entire organization.
- Base your ESA on an existing framework that is appropriate for your organization.
- Extend your policy to cover both the physical and virtual infrastructures.

- Ensure that your ESA includes the five building blocks of boundary control services, access control services, integrity services, cryptographic services, and auditing and monitoring.
- Use the 20 critical security controls provided by sans.org.

ACTIVITY 3-4
Discussing Controls and Countermeasures in ESA

Scenario

In this activity, you will assess your understanding of controls and countermeasures in enterprise security architecture.

1. Your organization is attempting to start a security project involving many different groups. The groups come from different organizations that have never worked together before, but would like to create a security product that can benefit all of them. Of the various ESA frameworks you have studied, which framework would be a good choice to use and why?

2. You are implementing your company's Information Security Management System. The desired end result is formal verification of compliance. Which of the ESA frameworks that you have studied would be an appropriate choice in this case?

3. Of the five ESA building blocks, which provide both physical and logical controls? (Choose two.)
   - ☐ Integrity
   - ☐ Cryptography
   - ☐ Auditing and monitoring
   - ☐ Boundary control

TOPIC E

Information System Security Capabilities

In the last topic, you learned about security controls that are used to protect enterprise environments. In this topic, you will learn about built-in security capabilities that can be found in an information system.

Information System Security Overview

There is a wide (and often daunting) range of technologies that can be used to implement information system security. Ideally, a system should be able to defend itself from any attack. The reality is, however, that most systems require additional protection from other devices, good design, and an alert system administrator.

In order to protect itself, an information system should at the very least be able to do the following:

- Distinguish one person or process from another.
- Distinguish between the subject (person or process trying to gain access), and the object (data, asset, or resource you are trying to protect).
- Assign an identifier to both the subject and the object.
- Authenticate and authorize all subjects before they access an object.

The strength and verification of these capabilities is what allows an information system to be considered a Trusted Computing Base. When you have a system in which no subject can access any object without authorization, you have what is known as complete remediation. This means your information system can protect itself and all of the processes running on it from malicious attack.

Most information systems have the following security capabilities:

- Memory and process protection.
- Virtualization.
- Trusted platform module.
- Interface protection.
- Fault tolerance.

Memory and Process Protection

As mentioned earlier, memory is considered to be the primary storage mechanism in a computer. Although volatile in nature, memory is the place where instructions the CPU is currently working on reside. From a security perspective, storage (both primary and secondary) must be protected the most. If the data in memory or disk is disclosed, becomes damaged or corrupt, you have lost confidentiality and integrity, and likely compromised your system.

A secure information system should have good memory management. It should protect processes from each other by prohibiting processes from accessing each other's allocated memory.

In theory you could separate subjects by assigning each process a different thread and allocating it a specific block of memory addresses. The reality is that processes get their memory from a common pool. Once the application is finished with its process, it must destroy its thread and release its memory back to the general pool. If this did not happen, the system would quickly run out of available memory. The system must be able to distinguish between subjects and objects, the memory allocated to each, the areas of memory used for execution of code, and areas of memory used for storing result sets once that code is finished executing. With a single system multitasking between many processes, it is quite possible for a malicious process to break out of its restrictions and access the memory of another process.

Memory use in a computer is a very dynamic system, with memory allocation being assigned and unassigned constantly. The risk is that any allocated memory can become compromised by a malicious process. Applications tend to set up the same structure within the memory that is assigned to them. A hacker can study this memory structure and identify key points of entry in both the application and operating system that would allow malicious code to be inserted.

Memory and Process Protection Techniques

Techniques that can be used to help keep subjects isolated from objects and isolated from each other include the following.

Technique	Description
Different processor states	System code is kept separate from user code. The system code runs in a supervisory state or mode. It is fully trusted and has full access to the operating system and hardware. User code runs in a less privileged state (also known as a problem state) and is not permitted access to other running processes or hardware. The operating system is able then to give resource priority to the supervisory state, and limit resource access to the user state.
Layering	Interactions between more privileged and less privileged processes are controlled on the CPU. The layers are hierarchical, with each layer able to access only the layer immediately above or below it.
	The way this is enforced on a CPU is through the concept of ring protection. On an Intel processor, there are four rings, or levels of protection. These can be conceptually visualized as a series of concentric rings (like a bull's eye) with Ring 0, the most privileged layer, in the center. Ring 0 is where the kernel and the most privileged operating system processes run. Ring three, the outermost layer, is the least privileged, and is where user processes run. Rings can be used to control the interaction between different execution domains (the range of objects available to a particular subject) with the level of privilege assigned.
	Through the use of an *application programming interface (API)*, a less privileged process can request services of a more privileged process running in a different ring. The API is a sort of connection point for a process. It allows a process to offer its services to another process in a controlled and limited manner.
Process isolation	Processes running at the same ring level are provided specific and distinct address spaces in RAM to prevent them from accessing each other's area of memory. The allocation of memory areas is randomized and mapped to make it more difficult for malicious processes to find the memory locations. You can also encapsulate a process as an object, using only APIs for access to the functions within, to help provide isolation.
Data hiding	Activities running on the CPU are kept separate from each other, effectively hiding the data at one security level from being seen by processes running in a different security level.
Abstraction	The removal of details about an object so that only its essential functions are exposed. This technique is used in both database design and programming to protect a module of code or a database table. It does so by hiding, or abstracting, the internal details from the outside world.
ASLR	In *Address Space Layout Randomization (ASLR)*, data areas are randomly arranged in memory to make it harder to identify vulnerable parts of the structure.

Virtualization

Virtualization provides many management and security advantages. A virtual machine (VM) is an operating system running as an application within another operating system. The VM is called the guest, and the computer running the virtual machine is called the host. The guest VM has no knowledge that it is running inside of another operating system. It is isolated from other virtual machines as well as the host processes. This is known as sandboxing. The VM has its own allocated CPU and RAM (which are actually portions of the host CPU and RAM), and its own network and port interfaces (internal connections to the host's network and port hardware).

With virtualization, an application or even an entire operating system is run as a separate process on a host machine, isolated from other processes. One great feature of virtualization is that the guest operating system need not be the same type of operating system as the host. For example, a Windows host could run on Linux guest and vice versa. Additionally, the guest is not dependent on the host to use any connected hardware. As long as the virtualization platform permits it, the guest VM can communicate directly with any device plugged into a port on the host. This means that, even if the host has no driver (software instructions) to work with a particular camera, printer, external hard drive, etc., as long as the guest itself has that driver, the guest can use the device even if the host cannot.

Virtualization makes it easy to manage entire network services, and consolidate systems onto a single computer. Rather than allocating a separate physical computer to an email server, a database server, a file and print server, domain controller server, etc., they can all be grouped together as virtual machines onto a single physical machine. While one might wonder if any real advantage is gained by doing this, the actuality is that most physical servers are underutilized in terms of CPU and memory usage. The system's power supply still has to consume electricity whether work is being performed or not. The computer also takes up floor space or rack space. Rather than the CPU of a single system running at a typical 17% utilization, several virtual machines can run together on that computer, bringing the utilization closer to 70% or 80%. Virtualization also saves in physical space and power consumption. Large organizations have saved 1,000,000 square feet of data center space and millions of dollars in electricity usage through virtualization.

From a security perspective, virtualization allows operators to more conveniently manage and isolate systems, quickly shut down a malfunctioning or compromised system, and replace it with a known good copy. Virtualization makes it easy to backup and restore whole systems, reducing a process that would normally take hours down to a few minutes.

The risk of virtualization is that it has already been demonstrated that guest processes can break out of their sandbox and access the host or other guests. The security architect must realize that the convenience of virtualization carries with it a trade-off of this potential risk. Currently the risk is not very high. Nonetheless, this may change in the future, so contingencies must be planned for in case of an incident.

TPM

The *Trusted Platform Module (TPM)* is an international standard for implementing a secure crypto processor. This is a dedicated chip on the motherboard designed to secure hardware using cryptography. It has RSA encryption keys burned into it, allowing the hardware itself to be authenticated.

TPM can provide the following services:

- Platform Integrity: If the hardware is fundamentally changed, the operating system can refuse to boot.
- Disk encryption: The entire hard drive can be encrypted and remain encrypted even during use. This is useful if someone steals the hard drive from a computer and attempts to install it in a different machine to access the data.
- Password protection: The user cannot boot the system without the user entering a password. Since the user's password will be combined with the TPM key to create a larger authentication password, the user's part of the password can be simpler and easier to remember. Although that

part will be weaker, when combined with TPM key, the overall authentication password will remain strong. To assist the user part of the authentication, many enterprises will make the user's part of the password a combination of a pin combined with a one-time, six-digit number generated by an RSA token. The token generates a new code every 60 seconds, so it effectively can only be used once.

- Digital rights management (DRM): Content can be encrypted using a key from a particular systems TPM, and thus only be able to be played back on that same system.
- The protection and enforcement of software licenses: As with digital rights management, a software license can be tied to a specific system and not reusable on other systems.
- Prevention of cheating in online gaming: The user would only be able to use the authorized system to play.

The purpose of a TPM is to guarantee the integrity of a system. Most modern motherboards have TPM capabilities. The security professional should insist that the enterprise use TPM capabilities, particularly on laptops.

 Note: The Microsoft Windows implementation of whole hard drive encryption is known as BitLocker.

Interfaces

An interface provides a single point of access to a system or process. This allows it to be used as a choke point, controlling data flow through that interface. An interface can be physical or logical. An application programming interface (API) is a logical set of functions that a process can use to access the hidden functionality of another process. It exposes only specific functions of a software module to other modules.

A physical interface on a computer is also known as a port. It restricts what type of devices can plug into it, but by itself is not designed to stop a malicious device. However, rules can be placed on the interface by the operating system or security software to restrict which devices can plug in (by manufacturer or serial number) as well as what data can flow through the interface.

Fault Tolerance

All of the previously mentioned security capabilities are highly useful. However, any one of them can fail at some point. The final protection capability of an information system is the ability to recover from an undesired non-functional or compromised state to a desired, functional state. While fault tolerance is generally considered a function of availability, if you have a system such as intrusion detection responsible for a security function on your network, if that system goes down you lose that security function.

One can manually recover by restoring backups (assuming backups were created and checked for validity). However, restoring a backup is time-consuming, and the service will be unavailable during that time.

Fault tolerance uses redundant hardware, software, communication links, or entire systems to allow the service to quickly recover. You can implement fault tolerance at any level, including:

- Extra power supply.
- Spare hard drives.
- Redundant network links.
- Redundant peripherals.
- Redundant computers.
- Redundant servers or server services.

Preferably, your fault tolerance should be designed to provide automatic failover. It should be able to detect a failure, and immediately switch to a hot spare (duplicate device waiting on standby), or re-route traffic through a different link or to a different system. From the user perspective, the failover would be seamless and go unnoticed.

Hot spares are considerably more expensive to implement. An organization may instead opt for implementing manual failover, where a cold spare remains in storage until there is a failure. The trade-off of using cold spares is that the service will be down until personnel can manually retrieve the cold spare from storage, remove the failed original device, and put the cold spare in its place. The risk of using cold spares is that the cold spare will not be configured the same as the hot spare. Perhaps when the cold spare was first obtained its configuration was set to match the original, but over time that configuration changed on the original and the cold spare was not updated. Additionally, if the data resides on the hot spare, and the hot spare is damaged to the point where the data cannot be retrieved, the cold spare will be of little value.

The best practice for implementing any kind of fault tolerance is to make sure that the data is separate from the device, so that it is not dependent on a single device for access.

Server Fault Tolerance Techniques

You can make your servers fault-tolerant through a number of techniques. These are summarized in the following table.

Technique	Description
Clustering	In clustering, two or more servers run the same service while sharing a common data storage. Typically, one server is actively providing the service while the other is in a standby (passive) mode. The passive node (server) listens to the heartbeat of the active node. If the heartbeat stops for any preconfigured length of time, the passive node takes over. Since both nodes are connected to a common data storage structure such as a RAID array or a storage area network (SAN), the data is up to date when the passive node becomes active. The failed node can then resume control when it comes back online.
	Clustering is an excellent choice where the data changes constantly, such as in a database server or email server.
Network load balancing (NLB)	Network Load Balancing is very similar to clustering, except that each node has its own copy of the data. Instead of one node being active for the other remains passive, in NLB all nodes are actively servicing client requests, dividing the load amongst themselves. Should any one node in an NLB fail, the others will shoulder its load. Because of their load-balancing capabilities, NLBs are resistant to denial of service attacks.
	NLB is an excellent choice when the data seldom changes, such as in a web server that acts as a front end for a database behind it. It is common to put multiple Web servers in a network load balance configuration, while the database server behind the Web servers is clustered.
Virtualization	Virtual machines are an excellent way of providing system redundancy at a reduced cost. You can create a VM as a backup copy of a server. You can also have multiple VMs online at the same time, providing the same service together. Virtual machines and/or their host computers can be clustered just like physical servers. An NLB can contain either physical or virtual servers.

Technique	Description
Redundancy and Replication	Some services including database, email, and directory service servers can also provide fault tolerance by replicating their database to other servers. The replication can happen on a regular schedule, whenever there is a change, or whenever the system is relatively free. Where this is very useful is when the copy servers exist on other networks, safely away from each other.

Guidelines for Assessing Information System Security Capabilities

Here are some guidelines you can follow for assessing information system security capabilities:

- Verify that the system provides common memory and process protection techniques.
- Choose a system that natively provides virtualization.
- Determine if a system or program provides limited interfaces to protect it from outside programs or systems.
- Use hardware and server fault tolerance techniques to improve resilience.

ACTIVITY 3-5
Analyzing Information System Security Capabilities

Scenario

In this activity, you will assess your understanding of information system security capabilities.

---

1. How do you think virtualization could benefit security in your own environment?

2. How can implementing TPM benefit security in your own environment?

3. Server fault tolerance techniques might you use to enhance security in your own environment?

TOPIC F

Design and Architecture Vulnerability Mitigation

In the last topic, you learned about security capabilities that already exist in information systems. But those capabilities did not appear by accident. They were engineered into system design. In this next topic, you will learn about potential vulnerabilities in design and architecture and how to mitigate those vulnerabilities in your design.

Architecture Vulnerabilities

While most security vulnerabilities arise from a weak implementation of a good design, there are some systems that are vulnerable because of poor architecture (design) itself. Common architecture vulnerabilities include:

- Failure to include the 5 ESA building blocks in your design.
- Failure to leverage system security capabilities in your design.
- Insufficient redundancy/single point of failure.
- Allowing emanations and covert channels.
- Leaving potential client- or server-based vulnerabilities unaddressed in your design.
- Leaving common database vulnerabilities unaddressed in your design.
- Failure to consider potential issues that can arise in larger, distributed systems.

Since most threats are well known (or can be easily researched) the security architect must take responsibility for ensuring that the design of a system appropriately addresses all known security concerns. This of course will have to be balanced against making sure that the system can also function at an acceptable level. During risk analysis, the security team will determine which controls are worth implementing to mitigate risk to an acceptable level.

While the security practitioner might not be the solution architect, especially when it comes to software development, the security practitioner must be aware of all aspects of the design, development, and implementation process and insist that security is always a priority from the beginning. As we move to larger, more diverse distributed systems in our daily lives, the security practitioner will need to stay educated on emerging vulnerabilities and threats.

Single Point of Failure

With the prevalence of virtualization, the practice of aggregating virtual machines onto a single host now presents a new risk: the virtualization host as a single point of failure. The most common single points of failure include:

- Single point of connectivity to your data, especially to network-based storage.
- Single point of connectivity to the general network.
- Single host server.
- Single virtual server.
- Single instance of a critical service or application.
- Single power supply or other infrastructure capability.

Single Point of Failure Mitigation

As with any other fault-tolerant solution, the virtualization host itself, as well as the storage medium that the virtual machines are located on, must also be redundant. The security professional should work with the server and network virtualization teams to ensure that there is no single point of failure throughout the network. The following table summarizes areas to focus on to prevent a single point of failure.

Area of focus	Recommendation
Data Connectivity	Implement multiple host bus adapters (HBAs). Also implement multiple paths to access the storage area network (SAN). A SAN is an area of your network used to centralized storage.
Network Connectivity	Configure at least two different network interface cards (NICs) on a server or virtual machine. Maintain redundant switches, routers, links, Internet connections, virtual private network (VPN) servers, firewalls, proxies, and other network devices.
Clusters	Place the cluster shared volume on a redundant storage system such as a RAID 5 (multiple disks that act as a single fault-tolerant unit) or SAN. Make sure the cluster is configured to restart an application or service in case of failure. Maintain multiple communication paths both to the cluster as well as between the nodes in the cluster.
Application Availability	Install critical applications and services in either cluster, network load balance (NLB), or other redundant configuration. Both clusters and NLBs use multiple servers to give a specific service fault tolerance.
OS Availability	Install redundant operating systems as virtual machines, and if available, configure the VMs to automatically migrate from one physical computer to another in case of failure.
Infrastructure	Maintain redundant power supplies and power sources such as uninterruptible power supplies (UPS) and backup generators. Maintain redundant facilities in case an entire facility or access to that facility fails.

Emanation

Emanation is an attack where protected information is leaked through the natural process of electrons passing through a wire or over the radio. These electrons can be detected by sophisticated monitoring devices, and then be captured and turned into information that can be used by an attacker. Keyboards, cathode ray tube (CRT) monitors, cabling, and computers are all subject to emanations. Wireless is practically emanation by design.

Another emanation example is the vibration of window glass caused by the human voice. With the use of a monitoring device, the vibrations can be captured and the speech recorded from a distant location.

Although most emanations are electronic in nature, this is actually a physical vulnerability. Your devices or your work area are not shielded enough to prevent this leakage.

 Note: If you have ever heard the noise created by a nearby smartphone on your television speakers, you have heard the effect of emanation.

Emanation Mitigation

The traditional method for restricting emanations is to block it by surrounding the room completely with steel, or by the use of a Faraday cage. A Faraday cage is a large wire mesh cage that completely encases the entire room, or at least the area where the computer is. The distance between the wires in the mesh is tuned to the frequency of the emanation. In other words, the wires are spaced appropriately apart to be smaller than the wavelength of the emanation, thus trapping them and not permitting them to pass.

You can also use distance and reinforced thick concrete walls to reduce emanations.

 Note: You can see a modern example of a Faraday cage by looking at a microwave oven front door. Notice that inside the window on the glass door is a fine steel mesh that you look through. That is a Faraday cage.

Covert Channel

A covert channel is a software design vulnerability that provides access to information in an unintentional way. Historically, there have been two types: *covert storage* and *covert timing*. In covert storage, a file saved by one process should be unavailable to another, but the second process may be able to learn information just by seeing that a file exists, or by reading some attribute of the stored file. In covert timing, the watching process observes the order or timing in which processes access a shared resource. For example, it could monitor traffic or CPU utilization, and even though it cannot read the information, it can make determinations based on the amount or type of traffic it sees, as well as the order in which it is accessed.

More recently, a covert channel can also take the form of innocent looking packets on the network that a firewall or intrusion detection system would ordinarily ignore. It often works by embedding extra, seemingly unimportant, content in the header or body of a network packet.

 Note: For more information on network-based covert channels, see the article "Intrusion Detection FAQ: What is covert channel and what are some examples?" at **https:// www.sans.org/security-resources/idfaq/covert_chan.php**.

Covert Channel Mitigation

Covert channels are difficult to mitigate because they use unconventional methods for carrying data. When developing software or systems, one way to mitigate covert channels is to require every process to declare what resources it needs before it is allowed to execute. You could then require that only one process at a time can actually access the resource so that there is no sharing, and thus no possibility of a covert channel. Although complete isolation would be effective in theory, it is not practical to implement. Another way to mitigate covert channels would be to obscure the type and amount of resources a process uses. Both methods would degrade system performance.

The most effective countermeasures currently in use against covert channels focus on making the covert channel less effective by limiting its capacity. It's usually accomplished by adding randomness to obscure any regularity of process access to shared resources. If the covert channel is hiding malicious code inside of innocent-looking network packets, use a firewall or some type of intrusion detection system to inspect the contents of your network traffic to look for hidden payloads.

Client-Based Vulnerabilities

A network has two basic types of computers:

- A server: A dedicated computer that provide services.
- A client: A computer or process to use the services provided by the server.

Of the two, clients are by far the greater security threat. This is because you generally don't have as much control over the condition of the clients that access your server, especially if your server is a public Web server.

The possibilities for client-based vulnerabilities are endless. The most notable include:

- The inadvertent or intentional abuse of full administrative privileges granted to users on their client machines.
- Clients that are unpatched.
- Clients that are loaded with viruses and malware.

- Malicious applets (small executable programs) embedded in web browser pages that clients process.
- The deliberate abuse and manipulation of legitimate web browser applets by hackers.
- The deliberate abuse and manipulation of locally cached data on a client by hackers.

Client-Based Vulnerabilities Mitigation

Because client computers and mobile devices are subject to endless numbers of vulnerabilities, from hardware to software to patching to user error, you will need to institute all the standard best practices for keeping the devices in a healthy state and educate the users to minimize their risk. In your own environment, you have a lot of control over vulnerability levels of client computers and mobile devices.

You can require computers to join your directory service and apply policy through the directory service to maintain acceptable antivirus, patch, and configuration levels. For mobile devices or client operating systems that cannot join the directory service, you can limit their access within the internal network.

[handwritten: GPO Group Policy Object in AD]

For remote users working from home or on the road, you can use mobile device management and network access control (NAC) to require mobile devices and client computers to receive service packs and patches, security configurations, and antivirus updates, and maintain required firewall settings before they can connect to your network. You can also disallow devices from remotely connecting to the network if they cannot first pass a health check.

You can also harden your servers and web applications to check any input received from clients. You can require clients to make secure connections to servers, and require both users and client machines to authenticate before those connections are permitted.

Vulnerabilities from External Clients

Although you have a lot of control over clients that are part of your own organization, it is far more difficult to protect your network from clients and users that are outside your control. These will mostly be the thousands or even millions of home computers and mobile devices that customers use to access your website.

One vulnerability is malicious hackers. According to security group **Sophos.com**, "over 30,000 legitimate small business websites are hacked every single day." The Ponemon Institute estimates that a company that depends upon its website for revenue can lose up to $3.4 million per hour if that website is knocked out by a malicious attack, and that the average website data breach in the United States costs $5.4 million.

Not all attacks are intentional. Many are caused by systems where the user is unaware that their home computer or mobile device has been compromised.

External Client-Based Vulnerability Mitigation

Because you cannot control the health of external clients that connect to your publicly available servers, all of your defense must be put on the server side. You must design your website (or any other publicly accessible computer) with the assumption that external client devices will be infected, and that many connection attempts across the Internet will not be by customers with legitimate business to conduct on your system, but by hackers or unauthorized persons with malicious intent.

Do the following to protect your system from external client-based vulnerabilities:

- Develop web applications using secure coding practices.
- Patch your server.
- Harden your servers as much as possible, locking them down to permit only the barest minimum necessary to provide service to external clients.

- Keep your public facing servers in a protected network (demilitarized zone) away from both the Internet and your internal network.
- Pre-screen traffic using a firewall or reverse proxy (a service that fetches server information on behalf of an external client).
- Use deep inspection on your firewall to look for known malicious traffic signatures.
- Ensure that your web applications run sanity checks and other tests to verify the legitimacy of clients requests.
- Use intrusion detection to constantly monitor traffic to your public facing servers.

Server-Based Vulnerabilities

Since it is your servers that provide business services and products to your users and customers, it is your servers that you must protect the most from vulnerabilities. Any of the following could provide an avenue for attack:

- Remote access by users.
- In-band (using the existing network) remote access by administrators.
- Out of band communications (using an alternate network such as cellular) for emergency remote access by administrators.
- Weak authentication mechanisms.
- Inherent vulnerabilities associated with making a server available to the public.
- Insufficient vulnerability assessment.
- Insufficient security management capabilities of the organization.
- Inconsistent mechanisms and controls for updating code, installing software, and change management.
- Insufficient or nonexistent business continuity, fault tolerance, and disaster recovery requirements of the server and its services.
- Insufficient controls over data flow.

Server-Based Vulnerability Mitigation

When addressing server-based vulnerabilities, be sure to include the following:

- Require strong authentication by remote access users.
- Require even stronger authentication by remote access administrators.
- Attempt to shield your out of band communication system from being discovered by outsiders.
- Use strong authentication mechanisms, including multifactor authentication, to prevent brute force attacks or key logging.
- Place any public facing servers and services behind a firewall, or within a DMZ or perimeter zone.
- Regularly conduct vulnerability assessments on the servers.
- Regularly assess the security management capabilities of the organization.
- Regularly assess and standardize mechanisms and controls for updating code, installing software, and change management.
- Ensure that business continuity, fault tolerance, and disaster recovery requirements of the server and its services exist.
- Ensure that data flow is controlled at all points.
- Realistically determine whether or not the organization has the ability to protect the server, or if the service should be transferred to a third party provider.

Cloud Services

A cloud is simply a collection of servers that offer a service. The servers are virtual machines hosted on many powerful computers. They reside in a data center and are owned and maintained by a cloud service provider. Customers connect to these cloud services across the Internet. Rather then purchasing, installing, configuring, and maintaining their own servers, the customer can simply rent a little time off the provider's servers. All you have to do is connect to the provider's website portal, place the services you want into a shopping cart, pay. and enjoy. Within a matter of minutes, your infrastructure will be provisioned and ready to use. The service can be anything, but common cloud services include:

* Web, database, and email hosting.
* Storage.
* Online applications (such as Microsoft Office 365).
* Blank servers or unconfigured services that customers can use as they please.
* Telephone systems.
* Directory services.
* Remote monitoring and management.
* Mobile device management.
* Entire network infrastructures.

The benefit of cloud services is that you don't have to pay for and maintain your own computer systems. You have transferred the risk of security and the cost of maintenance to a third party who specializes in delivering these services. Also, since cloud services are accessible across the Internet, you can access your service from virtually anywhere.

In addition to the well-known cloud services of SaaS, PaaS, and IaaS, a cloud can also offer the following:

Cloud Service	Description
Identity-as-a-Service (IDaaS)	This is an authentication infrastructure that can be thought of as cloud-based single sign-on.
X-as-a-Service (XaaS)	This refers to "anything service" or "everything as a service." It refers to the growing number of services that can be delivered via the cloud.
Malware-as-a-Service (MaaS)	Naturally anything that can be profitable for legitimate business can be lucrative for criminals as well. Organized Criminal Gangs (OCGs) offer their MaaS sites on the Dark Web—anything from hacking to illegal drug deliveries to assassinations.

Note: For more information on the Dark Web, see the article "What is the Dark Web? How to access the Dark Web..." at **www.pcadvisor.co.uk/how-to/internet/what-is-dark-web-how-access-dark-web-deep-3593569/.**

Cloud Services Vulnerabilities

Cloud service comes with its own security risks:

* Your security is dependent on the security practices of the cloud service provider.
* You don't have direct immediate control over the systems, which is undesirable for very sensitive or secret data.
* Your virtual machines are hosted on the same computer as other customers' virtual machines.
* Additionally, if the virtual machine of another customer manages to escape its sandbox, it could potentially attack your virtual machine or the host that both of you are on.

It is for these reasons that many organizations opt to not place their most sensitive information into cloud services. Large financial institutions prefer to host their own internal cloud services. They provide internal departments and business units with the convenience and rapid response of ordering servers and services on the company intranet, while maintaining strict control over their data.

Cloud Services Risk Mitigation

To mitigate the risk of using cloud services, follow these precautions:

*   Do not use someone else's cloud service to host your most critical data.
*   Make sure that the cloud service provider has an excellent service level agreement (SLA) that describes exactly how they will protect your data, including their own incident response, business continuity plan, and disaster recovery procedures.
*   Make sure your connection to the provider's cloud is protected by strong encryption and authentication, not only between systems, but also between users and systems.
*   Have contingencies in place in case the provider is breached and your data is compromised.

Database Security

In addition to the standard vulnerabilities of a server, its operating system, or a database management system, a database has other security concerns:

*   Inference
*   Aggregation
*   Data Mining
*   Data Analytics
*   Data Warehousing

 Note: Caution: the nature of these vulnerabilities is such that you may not be able to completely eliminate the risk. In such a case, your risk management strategy might have to be "accept."

Data Inference

Inference is the ability to deduce (infer) hidden information by observing available information, and making a deduction based on that information. For example, by discovering medications that a person takes, one can infer the person's illness. Alternatively, massive shipments of military equipment to an overseas location might indicate preparation for some type of engagement.

Inference is a common attack used against databases. It can best be understood through an example. In the following illustration, a database is used to keep track of military shipments. Pvt. Smith queries the shipping database and only sees the unclassified information.

This seems okay so far, but if the private becomes curious about any other potential cargo, she could attempt to run other queries to deduce the existence of hidden records. She could run a query against guns to find the record's primary key (unique entry number in a table). By discovering and comparing the primary keys of the other shipments, she notices that there is a gap in the numbering between grenades and uniforms. From here, she deduces that there is a secret entry that she cannot see. Additionally, she notices that she cannot see what is scheduled to go in cargo area C.

Since it is a large cargo area that has previously been used to carry conventional missiles, she speculates on the type of cargo that might go into such a hold. She wonders whether it might be another type of missile, but one that is not conventional? Continuous cross-referencing information across the shipping database or other databases might help turn up more information to help Pvt. Smith infer the type of cargo.

Flight #	Cargo Area	Cargo Description	Classification
1142	A	Guns	Unclassified
1142	B	Grenades	Unclassified
1142	C	Nuclear missiles	Top Secret
1142	D	Uniforms	Unclassified

Figure 3-5: Military shipping database example.

Data Inference Security Concerns and Controls

The following table summarizes the concern and controls related to database inference attacks.

Concern	Controls
This is a difficult threat to control as it deals with legitimate, often publicly available peripheral information that a clever person or program may be able to glean data from.	This requires deep understanding of the data, how it is used, how people will access it, and what peripheral information is visible. • Organize a team including the database architect to examine what combinations of accessible data might allow a person to infer hidden or privileged data. • After identifying the possible attack vectors, see if the database can be reorganized to minimize the risk.

Data Aggregation

Aggregation is the combination of nonsensitive data from separate sources to create sensitive data. To better understand how this works, consider a real life example:

A woman is the only person in her age group to give birth at a particular clinic during a particular month (this is common knowledge to all of her friends and family). Now combine this knowledge with a report that the clinic is required by law to publish, that lists the percentage of TB-infected women who delivered by age group by month. Each of these pieces of information by themselves is relatively low value from a security perspective. Together, they form a breach of privacy and a real concern.

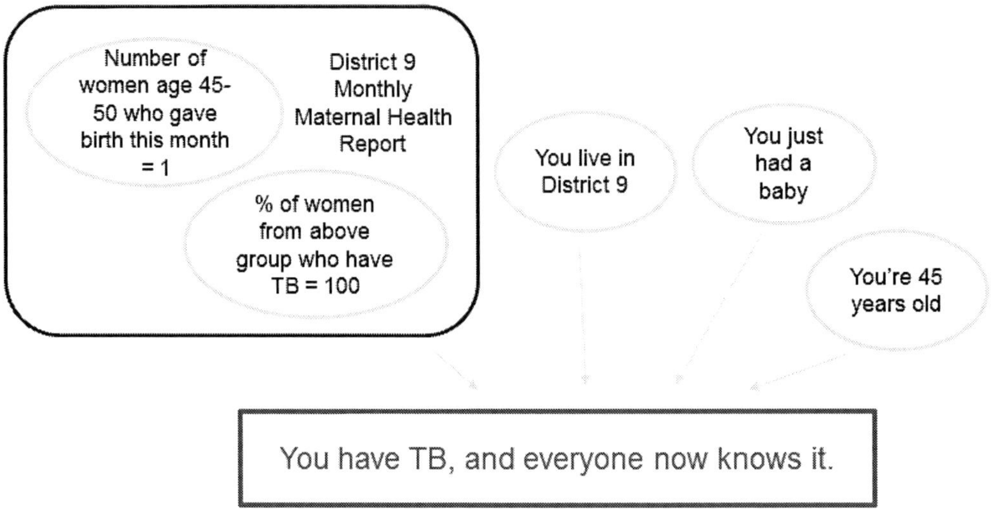

Figure 3-6: Aggregation.

Data Aggregation Security Concerns and Controls

The following table summarizes the concern and controls related to aggregation attacks.

Concern	Controls
Combined data sensitivity is often greater than the sensitivity of individual pieces of data.	• Work with the data architect to understand the different fields and types of information that you can find in the database. • Put together a team that can analyze this and look for possible combinations that escalate the sensitivity of the combined data. • Determine if any appropriate actions can be taken.

Data Mining

Data mining uses queries run against databases in a data warehouse to discover information. It reveals hidden patterns, relationships, and trends that cannot be found in a single database. It is a common, very useful tool for business analytics and marketing. It also causes serious breaches of privacy.

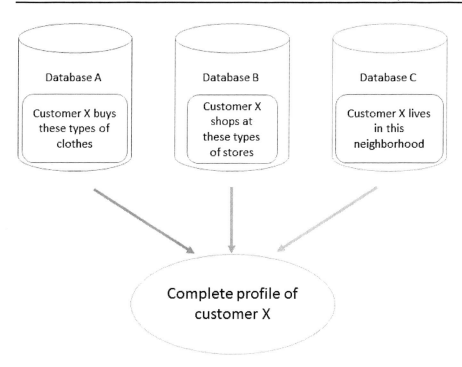

Figure 3-7: Data mining.

Data Mining Security Concerns and Controls

The following table summarizes the concerns and controls related to data mining.

Concern	Controls
• The amount of detail that can be discovered about individuals can create a privacy violation. • The risk is increased if this private information is stored on a Web server or some other unprotected area of the network, making it more vulnerable to unauthorized access. • Data mining can also produce inaccurate data relationships or patterns, resulting in data contamination.	Use the integrity models of Clark-Wilson and Biba to guide your data mining security procedures.

Data Analytics

The expected next step from data mining is data analytics. Data analytics uses data mined from different sources to predict an outcome.

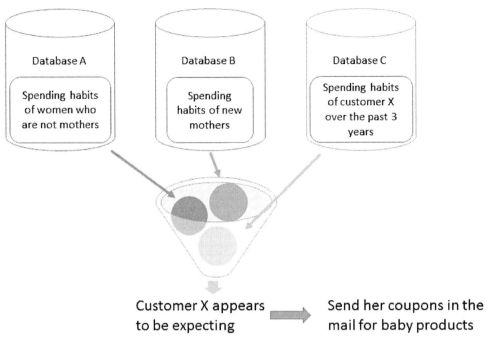

Figure 3-8: Data analytics.

Data Analytics Security Concerns and Controls

The following table summarizes the concerns and controls related to data analytics.

Concern	Controls
• Attacks will have much farther-reaching consequences to reputation, legal liability, and may even cause a company financial ruin. • Moving data to the cloud could inadvertently remove permissions or confidentiality restrictions on the data. • Privacy is at greater risk than ever before.	• Plan and monitor for any new legislative and regulatory requirements, especially across multiple jurisdictions. • Implement privacy best practices directly into the logic of your analytics programs. • Implement transparency and accountability in your data analytics.

Data Warehousing Security Concerns and Controls

A data warehouse is a repository for data collected from various sources. It comprises many databases housed together in a single facility. The focus of a data warehouse is on analytics rather than company operations.

Concern	Controls
The data warehouse is a single repository, the sum of everything the company knows. • It's a potential single point of failure. • It's a much more valuable target, a one-stop shop for a hacker.	Pay extra attention to the design and implementation of access control and disaster recovery.

Distributed Systems

Massive amounts of data require large systems with a lot of computing power to analyze them. A more practical (and popular) approach is to divide a large workload among multiple computers. This is known as a distributed system. A software application is installed across all the participating machines, coordinating efforts between the machines by passing messages across the network.

An example of a distributed system is an intrusion detection system where data collected from the network is analyzed at the collection point, rather than forwarded to a central management console for analysis. This allows the entire system to be faster and more responsive, with nodes that are closer to the incident or malicious traffic source able to respond quickly. The results of that analysis and the response would then be forwarded to the central console.

From a security perspective, distributed systems create special challenges. The fact that the systems must coordinate via messaging across the general network is in itself a security risk. The messages could be intercepted or compromised, or the application or service permitting the application to communicate could be compromised. In the early days of network management, the SNMP protocol was originally not encrypted. It could be intercepted and even have false messages injected into the network by a malicious actor. Even the act of a client logging onto a server across the network provides an opportunity for passwords and other secret data to be captured.

The notorious Blaster worm of 2003 is also an example of the vulnerabilities of a distributed system. The worm was based on a vulnerability that permitted a buffer overflow (insertion of malicious code into another application's memory address) of the Microsoft distributed component object model (DCOM) service that distributed applications used to communicate with each other across a network. The buffer overflow then permitted malicious code to run in system-level privilege, performing any action the intruder desired.

Grid Computing

Grid computing is a type of distributed system that coordinates and shares computing resources across a dynamic and geographically dispersed organization. The resources can be applications-, data-, storage-, or network-based. The grid structure gives individual users the ability to access extremely large sets of data across many locations around the world. The data is not housed in any one system or location. Instead, it is divided up and distributed across the various regions. There may be redundant copies of the same data in different locations as well. Each region is administratively independent of the other regions. Database middleware organizes the content from these regions into a superstructure. When a user (from anywhere in the world) requests information or a service, the data is retrieved from the relevant location and presented to the user.

Conversely, a grid system could be one in which a large number of individual computers work together on a single computationally intensive project. Individual computers participate sporadically when they have spare CPU time and available network bandwidth.

The SETI@home project is an example of a grid system in which the general public can participate. In this ongoing scientific experiment, approximately 2.5 million home computers are currently connected via the Internet. They collectively examine vast amounts of radio-telescope data, searching for evidence of extra terrestrial life. Each person's computer analyzes a small portion of the data, reporting any findings back to the SETI main servers.

Peer–to–Peer Systems

Peer-to-peer is another type of distributed system. In peer-to-peer, a single computer can download a file from a group of other computers. Each computer in the group has a complete copy of the file, but is only required to provide a portion of the file to the receiving peer. In this way, the workload and necessary bandwidth required to share the file is divided between multiple computers. The more computers that participate as peers, the better the speed, availability, and performance of the download. Once the receiving peer has downloaded a complete copy of the file, it in turn joins the source group for the next individual who needs to download.

The most common use today of peer-to-peer distributed systems is for illegal file sharing. Much of what is shared illegally is also virus infected. There are, however, legitimate groups who also use peer-to-peer to distribute large open source files to the community.

BitTorrent Peer-to-Peer Example

BitTorrent is the most popular peer-to-peer system today. Many different software programs (clients) exist that can participate in BitTorrent. When a user wants to download a file via BitTorrent, he or she performs an Internet search, and downloads the torrent, which is a small file containing the necessary instructions to download that particular file. All of the peers that participate in providing the file are collectively referred to as a swarm. The individual computers in a swarm are called seeders. An individual who downloads a file, but does not then also participate as a seeder, is derogatorily referred to as a leacher.

Distributed System Risk Mitigation

To mitigate the risk of using a distributed system, particularly one that provides peer-to-peer file sharing, do the following:

- Keep your antivirus system up to date.
- Download and use the hash (integrity check results) provided by the file's author to verify that the shared file has not been modified or compromised.
- Do not use a distributed system to download illegal copies of software, movies, music, or other files.

To mitigate risks to your own distributed system, implement these approaches:

- Apply redundancy and fault tolerance to critical parts or computers in the distributed system.
- When possible, configure systems to authenticate using certificates.
- Implement authorization to different member computers based on levels of trust, by verifying the authenticity and reliability of the member computer and/or its data sources.
- Ensure that the distributed application grants participating systems the least privilege possible to perform the task.
- Make sure that participating systems are also patched and security hardened.
- Implement intrusion detection and intrusion prevention on the network to monitor for malicious activity.

Large-Scale Parallel Systems

Large-scale parallel systems take distributed processing to a whole new level. A parallel system is one in which computations are carried out across multiple systems simultaneously. Today's scientific and industrial applications require enormous amounts of data for analysis. Large-scale parallel systems satisfy those requirements.

Large-scale parallel systems, and the masses of data they are expected to process, are taking us into uncharted waters with regard to security and privacy. The risks and vulnerabilities of these systems are as yet largely unknown. Whatever the impact, it is a certainty that we cannot escape it or reverse the trend. In a study published by data management company EMC(2), the digital universe will grow exponentially to the point where by the year 2020, there will be over 44 zettabytes of data, the equivalent of 6.2 terabytes (TB) of data for every man woman and child on earth. **Computerworld.com**, in an online article, puts this in perspective by saying this is "estimated to be 57 times the amount of all the grains of sand on all the beaches on earth," and that the majority of the data "will not be produced by humans but by machines as they talk to each other over data networks."

Note: For more information, see:

www.emc.com/leadership/digital-universe/index.htm

www.computerworld.com/article/2493701/data-center/by-2020--there-will-be-5-200-gb-of-data-for-every-person-on-earth.html

Large-Scale Parallel System Vulnerability Mitigation

What security challenges and solutions large-scale parallel systems will bring is yet unknown. As a security professional, besides implementing the known best practices for server, client, and network security, you must stay educated on the subject. Be alert to potential vulnerabilities, and implement countermeasures as soon as you know what they are.

Big Data

The advent of large-scale parallel systems allows for the new phenomenon known as Big Data. *Big Data* is a general term that refers to data sets that are so huge and complex that they cannot be processed through traditional means. They must be run on large-scale parallel systems. The data has to be captured, curated, analyzed, searched, shared, stored, transferred, and visualized in a way that is both useful and timely.

Big Data is too big to be managed by traditional database structures such as SQL. Instead, a new style of database dubbed NoSQL has emerged to organize and store Big Data. It's actually a broad term that encompasses a number of database technologies that are nonrelational in structure. These organize data in graph structures, key-value pairs, collections of whole columns as opposed to single rows, or complex structures known as documents.

You have probably already encountered Big Data by using any of the following:

- Google
- Facebook
- Netflix
- Amazon

Big Data is not limited to very large companies. Many organizations from retailers to political groups use Big Data and Big Data analytics to target their audiences. Many providers now offer Big Data services for customers.

From a security perspective, Big Data as a technology has a lot of security limitations. These include: privacy concerns, insufficient security on the raw data itself, cost, bad analytics, and flat-out bad data. It wasn't originally designed for security. Its focus has been to inform business about customers' critical buying decisions and habits. This is sensitive information, however, and carries with it a greater risk of security breaches. When securing Big Data, the security practitioner will need to protect both the organization's and the customer's data.

Note: For an interesting read on recent uses of Big Data and Big Data analytics, see the following articles: "How Companies Learn Your Secrets" at **www.emc.com/leadership/digital-universe/index.htm**, and "Obama's White Whale" at **www.slate.com/articles/news_and_politics/victory_lab/2012/02/project_narwhal_how_a_top_secret_obama_campaign_program_could_change_the_2012_race_.html**.

Big Data Vulnerability Mitigation

At the moment, Big Data has no unified security model. Like the Internet of Things, Big Data is cutting edge and well ahead of any regulations, laws, or even consistent security controls. Companies that implement Big Data are essentially on their own with regard to security.

At the moment, the cost of a Big Data security breach has not been estimated. The security architect will have new challenges in the areas of privacy, trust, verification, trust-based denial of service attacks, content leakage, and general security with large-scale parallel systems and Big Data. As with the Internet of Things and cloud services, the security practitioner must stay abreast of the latest developments and guide the organization accordingly.

The best practices at the moment are to:

- Implement attribute-based encryption. This is a type of public key encryption in which decryption is possible only if the attributes (any descriptive information) of the user's key match attributes of the encrypted data. (For example, both the user and the data have to be associated with the same project committee in the same university department in the same city.)
- Implement additional access controls and limit who has access to the servers.
- Use role-based authentication, and if possible. encryption between nodes.
- Realize that your Big Data server clusters will not be a single physical entity but hundreds or even thousands of individual computer nodes connected together.
- Understand that servers will be automatically meshed together to form a cluster, share data, and provide query results.

Industrial Control Systems

An Industrial Control System (ICS) is a command-and-control center of systems on a network designed to support and manage an industrial process. They control and monitor large complex distributed infrastructures, such as electricity generation plants, transportation systems, oil refineries, manufacturing, and chemical plants.

While an ICS can have the same vulnerability as any other computer-driven system, from an architectural perspective its biggest vulnerability is that it is meant to be a far-flung network of thousands of devices/machines scattered across the countryside. These machines are often located in remote, unsupervised, and relatively unprotected areas.

To compound matters, utility companies and others that use ICS systems have so far not demonstrated the same seriousness and effort in protecting their cyber infrastructure as other IT-dependent companies have.

The U.S. Department of Homeland Security (DHS) recently published a report identifying the five most common weaknesses on an installed ICS:

- Improper input validation.
- Security configuration and maintenance.
- Credentials management.
- Improper authentication.
- Permissions, privileges, and access controls.

Additional vulnerabilities can include:

- Unauthorized use of remote maintenance access.
- Attacks via the office or enterprise network.
- Attacks on Commercial off-the-shelf (COTS) components used in the ICS network.
- Denial of service or distributed denial of service attacks.
- Human error or sabotage.
- Malware introduced via removable media or external hardware.
- Clear text communications.
- Unauthorized access to ICS resources.
- Standard network attacks.
- Technical malfunctions.
- Force majeure (extreme weather or natural disasters).

ICS Risk Mitigation

The DHS makes the following recommendations for vendors to mitigate ICS risk:

- Train developers in secure coding practices, especially input validation, authentication, and integrity checks.
- Quickly test and provide security patches for affected customers.
- Test and implement strong authentication and encryption.
- Increase the robustness of your network parsing code.
- Create firewall and IDS rule sets, including custom protocol parsers.
- Engage third parties to conduct security source code audits.
- Develop advanced cyber test suites to detect and address production line security issues.
- Incorporate encryption in the graphical caches for data storage and communications.

The DHS makes the following recommendations for ICS asset owners to help mitigate risk on their side:

- Redesign networks to take advantage of firewalls and VPNs.
- Use a layered network topology that places critical communications in a secure and reliable layer.
- Restrict physical access.
- Deploy security patches in a timely manner.
- Customize your intrusion detection systems for the ICS host 10 networks.
- Restrict user privileges, using role-based access control.
- Implement a strong password management plan.
- Change default passwords.

Guidelines for Mitigating Design and Architecture Vulnerabilities

Here are some guidelines you can follow to mitigate design and architecture vulnerabilities:

- If you are designing the system yourself, design it to leverage ESA security services and built-in system security capabilities.
- Eliminate potential single points of failure in your design.
- If your system is likely to produce or be susceptible to emanations, use shielding, thick construction materials, or distance to minimize the emanations.
- Design your database to be resistant to inference and aggregation.
- Do not use a third party's cloud services for critical data.
- Educate yourself on emerging vulnerabilities and countermeasures for large-scale parallel systems and Big Data.
- If your network uses ICS, take your infrastructure and network security seriously, and implement the recommendations as put forth by the U.S. DHS.

ACTIVITY 3-6
Discussing Design and Architecture Vulnerability Mitigation

Scenario

In this activity, you will assess your understanding of design and architecture vulnerability mitigation.

1. You are the information security consultant for a state run utilities company for a small nation. Recent droughts and soaring temperatures have caused water levels at the nation's hydroelectric plant to run dangerously low. As a result, the government had to resort to rolling blackouts to conserve and manage what little electricity is available to provide power to its citizens. Personnel at the Ministry of Energy were excited to deploy new equipment that would allow their department to monitor and better manage electricity distributed throughout the land. In a gala event attended by the news media, staff proudly showed off new monitoring and remote control systems that would allow them to use a central console to dynamically analyze, reroute, and load balance electricity throughout the country.

   What potential architecture vulnerabilities do you think may exist in the system, and how would you mitigate them?

2. After working for several weeks with the Ministry of Energy to harden its ICS system, you felt pretty good about the nation's power infrastructure and went on a well-earned vacation. You were in the middle of enjoying a sightseeing tour when you suddenly received an emergency priority one call. Something happened, causing the electrical grid in a major province to completely collapse. The entire region has been without power for two days. Panicked ministry officials have pleaded with you to come back at once to resolve the problem. When you arrive at Ministry headquarters, you notice that many computers in the main operating plant had torrent clients installed on them. Workers, taking advantage of the available Internet bandwidth at the job site, were busy downloading movies. You notice that those computers, which are connected to the ICS command and control center, are running very slowly. You also notice that the ICS control consoles are not responding.

    What do you think happened? What are the gaps that allowed this situation to happen?

3. After cleaning the torrent clients off the production computers, you decide to examine network traffic to look for anomalies. You notice that an unusually high number of ICMP packets are being sent to some of the production computers. When you capture a sample of these packets, they do not have the usual alphanumeric pattern expected in a packet of this type. Instead, the packets seem to be filled with random characters.

    What do you think is going on? Could these unusual packets be a security risk?

4. The security failures you've uncovered so far at the power plant have you suspicious that there could be more undiscovered issues. You interview plant personnel to get a better sense of how the network is being run. You learn that some of the managers work from home, making remote connections from their laptops into the network.

    What additional security risks do you think the managers could be introducing into the network? What evidence would you look for to validate your concerns?

5. Newspaper reports of the power failure have caused a political scandal. One of the local rags published internal emails between Ministry members and plant management. In the memos, the Minister of Energy ordered plant managers to erase evidence of personnel using BitTorrent on government computers. The Minister is furious that the memos were leaked to the press and is trying to blame the leak on dissident engineers. You've been asked by a special investigative committee to help uncover the source of the leak. You want to review the email logs, but are having trouble locating the email server in the server room. You ask the local IT team where the email server is. The technicians are new to their job, and are not sure where the email server is located. One technician remembers hearing a manager saying something about "that cloud provider across town."

    If the emails were not leaked by plant personnel, how could the newspapers get copies? How can future risks be mitigated?

6. Figuring out that hidden data exists in a database, even though you cannot see it, is known as:
    - ○ Data mining
    - ○ Aggregation
    - ○ Data analytics
    - ○ Inference

7. Using multiple data sources to figure out what is likely to happen is known as:
    - ○ Data mining
    - ○ Aggregation
    - ○ Data analytics
    - ○ Inference

8. Which statement best describes the security concerns of a distributed system?
    - ○ Multiple computers could crash simultaneously
    - ○ Messages between participating systems could become compromised
    - ○ An overall profile of an individual can be created from many sources
    - ○ A consumer's spending habits can be predicted before the actual event

9. What is currently the biggest risk associated with Big Data?
    - ○ Shared files are likely to have viruses
    - ○ Lack of standard public key encryption could compromise the data
    - ○ The ability of computers to automatically mesh together could form bottlenecks
    - ○ There is no unified security model

TOPIC G

Vulnerability Mitigation in Embedded, Mobile, and Web-Based Systems

In the last topic, you learned about mitigating security vulnerabilities in system design and architecture. With society's paradigm shift to being always online and always connected, whole new avenues of vulnerability and exploits have appeared. In this next topic, you will learn about mitigating vulnerabilities in mobile, embedded, and web-based systems.

New Technology Brings New Challenges

New technologies and their widespread adoption have brought a whole host of new security challenges. Remote users, mobile devices, embedded systems, the high prevalence of web applications, and the soon-to-be very pervasive Internet of Things will bring a level of connectedness, social enjoyment, and productivity never before seen in human history. They will also bring never before seen security challenges that the security practitioner must prepare for. Some vulnerabilities have already been discovered, but not all, and mitigation is often far less clear than in the past.

Risks from Remote Computing and Mobile Workers

Organizations often make the mistake of assuming that when an employee works remotely and connects to the corporate network through virtual private network (VPN), they are secure. Actually, VPNs do not ensure that the remote computer is free from software, hardware, or configuration vulnerabilities. There is also no guarantee that the end user is actually the employee, as opposed to a family member. An employee's laptop could be used by a child to play online games and thus become infected with the virus. That virus will then be securely transmitted across the VPN to the corporate network.

Remote workers might work from home or on the road. Remote computing can have the following risks and issues:

*   The user's identity at the other end is not guaranteed.
*   Laptops are sometimes lost or stolen.
*   Allowing laptop to connect to the LAN as opposed to the DMZ. If the remote device becomes compromised, the connection is already past the firewall.
*   No network access control solution with remediation in place to prevent infected machines from connecting until they are cleaned.
*   The organization might have insufficient or improperly implemented controls that can be easily bypassed by hackers or malware.
*   Multiple device synchronization including password management in the cloud presents the risk of data leakage.

Mobile Device Vulnerabilities

In the past few years, society has shifted to being always online and always connected via the mobile device. The modern mobile phone is actually a small computer with an operating system, CPU, memory, and disk space. Most mobile devices have ports, Bluetooth, near-field communications (NFC), wi-fi wireless, or some other method of connectivity besides the cellular network. In addition, most mobile devices have global positioning system (GPS) capability that is always on.

In the era of bring your own device (BYOD), companies must struggle with finding a balance between allowing users to use their own mobile device (the one they're comfortable with) and ensuring that the plethora of mobile device types, makes, and models do not compromise company network security.

The single biggest security risk to a mobile device is when a user roots (Android) or jailbreaks (iPhone) the device. When you do that, you have bypassed all of the integrity checking mechanisms built into the device's firmware, thus allowing all manner of malware to be installed, including replacing parts of the operating system itself. Users root/jailbreak their devices primarily to be able to install any software they want on the device. The trade-off of having that freedom is that you also have the freedom to install compromised software.

The following is a list of potential vulnerabilities for mobile devices:

- Physical access.
- Social engineering.
- Rooted or jailbroken devices.
- Bluetooth, Wi-Fi, infrared or other short range wireless connectivity.
- Email.
- SMS.
- Third-party applications.
- USB or memory cards.
- Operating system vulnerabilities.
- MySQL database vulnerabilities.
- GPS/location information.
- Camera and microphone.
- Cached credentials.
- Downloads.

 Note: Because it uses MySQL as a tiny onboard database system, Apple iOS 7 is still vulnerable to the SQL slammer worm even though that threat first appeared 12 years ago.

Mobile Vulnerability Mitigation

All of the powerful functionality in a small handheld device has opened up whole new avenues of security challenges. From a security perspective, mobile devices need to be treated like other computers. To mitigate mobile device vulnerabilities, be sure to implement the following:

- Mobile device management.
- Remote wipe, remote lock, and remote power down for the GPS location services in case the device is lost or stolen.
- Anti-malware and endpoint protection (personal firewall).
- A secure connection (VPN) to the workplace.
- Strong authentication.
- Digitally signed third-party software.
- The ability to separate personal data from work data.
- Protection from theft and data loss.
- Protection of the data and company network in case the device is lost or stolen.

Do not allow applications from unknown or untrusted sources to be installed. Disallow users from rooting or jailbreaking their device, as this will also bypass your other security mechanisms. Be sure to also record the electronic serial numbers (ESN) of your devices, and have these numbers handy if you have to report a stolen device to law enforcement.

 Note: For more information on securing mobile devices, see the NIST Special Publication 800-124 "Guidelines for Managing the Security of Mobile Devices in the Enterprise."

Mobile Device Management

You can also use mobile device management (MDM) to track, secure, and control all of the mobile devices in your enterprise. The MDM can be web-based, but can also be part of a larger in-house systems management service. A typical MDM solution provides the following:

- Device provisioning in the enterprise, including enrollment and authentication.
- Remote device lock or wipe.
- Account management.
- Turn on/off device features.
- GPS, Wi-Fi, and cellular device location.
- Remote software deployment.
- Updates of the OS, application, and firmware.
- Application management.
- Secure backup and information archiving.
- A secure, encrypted container on the device to segregate organizational access and data.
- Jailbreak or root access protection.

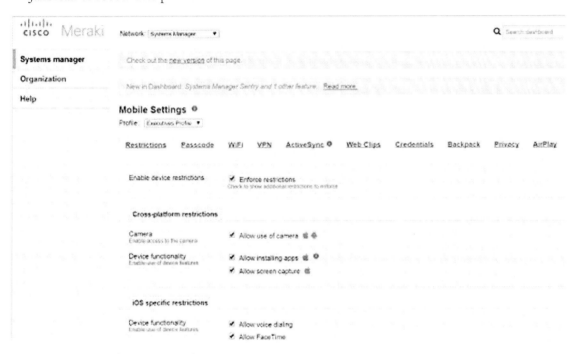

Figure 3-9: Typical MDM console.

Embedded Devices/Cyber Physical Systems

An *embedded device*, or cyber-physical system, is a small computer system that performs a dedicated function in a physical device. It exists within a larger electrical or mechanical system. It is typically a combination of hardware and software that performs a specific task for that particular device. Many types of products use embedded systems, including medical equipment, traffic lights, ATMs, airplane controls, point-of-sale (POS) terminals, GPS navigation systems, cameras, household appliances, toys, industrial machines, automobiles, vending machines, early cell phones, and many more.

Embedded systems use some form of limited operating system. Examples include:

- Embedded Java.
- Embedded Linux.
- Symbian.

- Blackberry OS.
- Palm OS.
- Windows Mobile.

We've entered the era of the Internet of Things (IoT). This is a major paradigm shift in which physical objects, or things, are now embedded devices that have electronics, software, sensors, and network connectivity. They can connect, collect, and exchange information. The potential positive uses of the Internet of Things are fantastic. We could have artificial clams and sea creatures monitoring coastal shelves and coral reefs. Thousands of devices micro-monitoring geologically unstable areas could dramatically improve earthquake and volcano early warning systems. Embedded devices in bridges and roads could provide an unprecedented level of infrastructure management and emergency response coordination. Farming, water conservation, manufacturing, energy—the list is endless. But as with all technology, the capabilities area two edged sword—the same widespread micro-monitoring capability that could provide near instantaneous real-time information and response could also be used for malicious or destructive purposes. A nation's power grid or air traffic control system could be hijacked by an enemy. The real-time micro movements of a peaceful assembly including details of every participant could be monitored and swiftly acted upon by an oppressive regime.

Vulnerabilities in Embedded Devices/Cyber Physical Systems

One immediate vulnerability of embedded devices is that since they are so small and have such minimal processing power, they often rely on distributed control, remote commands from another system, to perform their tasks. An example of this is a modern automobile. It contains a large number of processors that monitor and manage everything from airbags to brakes. All of these processors communicate together to perform complex tasks for the car's handling and performance. If the communications can be disrupted, hijacked, and controlled in a malicious fashion, the performance or functionality of the system (or even the safety of its operator) could be compromised.

Most of the vulnerabilities of embedded devices come from poor programming techniques. According to NIST, 92% of reported vulnerabilities in 2011 occurred at the application level. Code injection is currently the largest issue with embedded devices. As with most applications, the embedded device will take input and process it. If an attacker can insert malicious code into normal data input, the embedded application may, while processing the normal input, also execute the malicious code. Since the software on the device most likely runs with the highest privilege level possible, the malicious code will be run with the same level of privilege, potentially completely controlling the device.

One great risk that has always existed in programming is that many developers use the C programming language, which by itself is riddled with potential vulnerabilities. C does not have built-in protections against malicious input. The programmer must write protections into the code, line by line, against malicious input. Many programmers, under deadline to produce a working product, do not have the time for this cumbersome task. A great many other programmers do not know the best practices for writing secure code.

Initially, embedded devices ran on their own, with no network connectivity. For this reason, they ran in relatively safe environments. With the prevalence of the Internet of Things, not only is there a dramatically increased risk of malicious actors remote controlling everyday devices, but there is also a very great privacy risk. Since embedded devices have IP addresses (with the Internet of Things, this will be IPv6 addresses) and they are discoverable, the information they sense and gather could be added to a big data repository. Heart monitors and tennis shoes could provide health information about the owner. Toys, games, and household appliances could provide demographic information or even personal habits about the people living at that house.

Everybody, everywhere is continuously online, and everything they do can be collected, analyzed, potentially known to anyone, and vulnerable to exploit. The implications of this have yet to be fully revealed, but one thing is clear: as a society, we will have to find whole new ways in which to maintain public safety and personal privacy. The security practitioner will have to stay on top of these new trends and developments that appear almost daily, and help the organization to adapt.

Embedded Device Vulnerability Mitigation

Currently, the best way to mitigate embedded device vulnerabilities is through design. Ideally, the programmer would develop the embedded device application in a programming language that does not have the inherent vulnerabilities of C. This, however, may not always be feasible. In that case, the developer must write his or her code to always validate input, to protect against malicious code injection. The developer must become familiar with and implement secure coding practices. Management must also provide developers with the time and resources necessary to write secure code. Any required remote control of the embedded device must include a secure channel between the controller and the device.

Although it is possible to apply a patch to an embedded device, in most cases it would be very cumbersome. If a flaw is discovered in an automobile or a pacemaker, for example, most consumers would find it quite onerous to return to the dealer or a hospital to have this patched, especially if the vulnerability did not immediately manifest itself.

Companies and application developers must therefore do everything possible to ensure that the code is secure before the product is sent to market. Programmers need to use testing suites to identify as many application security issues as possible upfront. Security flaws must be reported and remediated as quickly as possible, and all testing must be done against unknown security standards.

Vulnerabilities in Web-Based Systems

Although web-based systems have all of the vulnerabilities of any other, they are particularly vulnerable because of their high public accessibility. Companies that have large numbers of mobile users typically place web servers in the perimeter network to provide services to those mobile devices. These services can provide any number of conveniences to the mobile user, including downloading device updates and patches, uploading and downloading files from/to an internal file server or database, posting time sheets and vacation requests via the mobile device, and using the mobile device to remotely participate in video and audio conferences.

Most web services are placed in a semi-protected perimeter network or demilitarized zone (DMZ) between two firewalls. Such networks are considered untrusted because they are public-facing. In most cases, some level of communication and data sharing must go on between the trusted internal network and the web service in the untrusted DMZ.

Whether the web-based system services traditional computer clients, mobile devices, or both, they typically have these vulnerabilities:

- The web app was written without sufficient security.
- Communications between the web app and a back-end database or file server are not sufficiently secured.
- The web service that the web app runs on is not sufficiently secured.
- The web system is located on an insufficiently protected operating system or hardware.
- The web application, web server, or operating system has inadequate authentication requirements.
- Failed logon attempts are not being properly monitored or controlled.

In addition, web-based systems use languages that have their own vulnerabilities. These are summarized in the following table.

Language	Vulnerability description
XML	Extensible Markup Language (XML) is the de-facto World Wide Web Consortium (W3C) standard for expressing data in a neutral format that is independent of the application or its database. It is at risk, however, of having its content be manipulated and misinterpreted by the XML parser (the process that reads and interprets the XML). It is also at risk of injection attacks, where malicious code is inserted into the middle of ordinary data.
SAML	Security Assertion ~~Market~~ Language (SAML) is a standard based on XML for exchanging authentication and authorization information. It is platform neutral, and does not require user information to be synchronized across directories. SAML is inherently secure, but its risk lies in improper implementation. For example, if your application leaves out the identifier of the authorization request, or the identity of the recipient, an attacker could access a user's account without proper authorization.

Web–Based System Vulnerability Mitigation

When addressing Web server vulnerabilities, include the following:

- Ensure that the developer addresses inherent vulnerabilities of any XML-based languages that are used.
- Institute an assurance sign-off process before putting the server or web application into production.
- Harden the OS.
- Perform extensive vulnerability scans prior to deployment.
- Secure or remove entirely administrative interfaces.
- Only permit access from authorized hosts or networks using certificates or multifactor authentication.
- Never hardcode authentication credentials into the application itself.
- Use account lockout.
- Use extended logging and auditing.
- Encrypt all authentication traffic.
- Verify that the interface is at least as secure as the rest of the application.
- Use a web application proxy/firewall.

Tools for Securing Web Applications

There are additional tools the developer can use to help secure a web application. These are summarized in the following table.

Tool	Description
OAuth 2.0	An authentication protocol that allows a user to approve an application to act on the user's behalf. With OAuth 2.0, the user does not have to share their password with the application.
OpenID Connect	An authentication mechanism built upon OAuth 2.0. It allows a wide diversity of client device types to identify an end user using an authorization server. It lets developers authenticate users without having to store and manage passwords.
OWASP	A non-profit organization dedicated to improving software security. Their website provides extensive guidance and software security testing help for developers.

 Note: For more information on OWASP, see **https://www.owasp.org/index.php/ Main_Page**.

Guidelines for Mitigating Vulnerabilities in Embedded, Mobile, and Web-Based Systems

Here are some guidelines you can use to secure embedded, mobile, and web-based systems.

Embedded Systems

To protect embedded systems:

- If possible, develop your embedded app in a language other than C.
- Employ secure coding practices when developing the system, specifically being on the lookout for potential injection flaws.
- If the system depends on remote control, always ensure that there is a secure channel between the controller and the embedded device.
- Use testing software that is specifically designed to look for embedded device vulnerabilities.

Mobile Devices

To protect mobile devices:

- Implement a comprehensive mobile device security policy.
- Require the use of a passcode/passphrase/pattern to login to the device.
- Automatically lock the device after 10 minutes of inactivity.
- Never store highly confidential or secret data on the device.
- Use the highest level encryption possible (at least 128 bit) to protect the data.
- Prefer to use a cellular network over Wi-Fi as it will be typically more secure.
- Use a VPN client if you connect to the corporate network via Wi-Fi.
- Report a lost or stolen device as soon as possible.
- Record ahead of time the device electronic serial number (ESN) and keep the number available to assist law enforcement with recovering a stolen device.
- Utilize a tracking service to help find stolen devices.
- Use mobile device management software to remotely lock or wipe them in case of a security breach.
- Only install digitally signed applications from a trusted source.
- Do not jailbreak or root the device, which allows the user to bypass security mechanisms to install unsigned third-party software.
- Disable any options or applications you do not require, including GPS.
- If you use Bluetooth, do not allow the device to be discovered automatically, and secure it with a password.
- Regularly back up the data from the device, and store the backups in encrypted format.
- Apply updates and vendor patches in a timely manner.
- Limit others from using your device.

Web-Based Systems

To protect web-based systems:

- Use OAuth 2.0 and OpenID Connect in your web app to simply and securely manage user authentication and authorization.
- Take advantage of resources such as OWASP to verify you are employing secure coding practices.
- Use best practices to harden all of the underlying technologies that your web application depends on including the Web server, database and database management system, operating system, hardware, network, and so on.

ACTIVITY 3-7
Discussing Vulnerability Mitigation in Embedded, Mobile, and Web-Based Systems

Scenario

In this activity, you will assess your understanding of vulnerability mitigation in embedded, mobile, and web-based systems.

---

1. **Use this scenario for Questions 1-3.** At a recent weapons trade show, a vendor proudly unveiled its new computer-aided automatic machine gun targeting system. The system, with its embedded operating system and software, uses fast, wide-range laser scanners to help a soldier quickly acquire and lock on a target. The new system garnered a lot of attention and excitement among the press and trade show attendees. Meanwhile, a blackhat security conference was underway across town. Intrigued by the media attention the targeting system was getting, a contingent of blackhats went to see the targeting system for themselves. At the booth, they asked the vendor about the risk of "friendly fire." They identified themselves as security experts, and pointed out what they felt were potential security vulnerabilities in the targeting system. The vendor, however, was dismissive of the blackhats, implying that they didn't know what they were talking about. The vendor went on to assure the onlooking crowd that the wireless capabilities the targeting system could sense and communicate with other nearby systems, identifying and thus avoiding soldiers that were "on the same side." Disappointed, and stung by the attitude of the vendor towards them, the blackhats returned to their hotel room. They determined to hack the system and prove the vendor wrong. The next day, while the vendor was busy demonstrating to an even larger crowd, the blackhats returned and managed to hack the system through its wireless connection, gaining control of the device. They turned the gun away from its acquired target and aimed it elsewhere, pointing it at a different target (though not any humans). While the vendor struggled to gain control of the gun and explain the anomaly to the crowd, the blackhats revealed that it was they who hacked and gained control of it. They explained how they used a wireless connection to inject malicious code into the embedded application, thus taking control of it. They also reminded the vendor that, had they had any truly malicious intent, they could have pointed the gun at the crowd. Instead, they simply wanted to show that the product indeed had the security flaws they warned about. That night the vendor's legal department, citing a variety of legal claims, filed a lawsuit against the blackhats and obtained a restraining order barring the blackhats from coming within one hundred yards of the vendor's stand. The vendor also issued a public statement asserting that the tracking system was "quite safe" and "does what it was designed to do." It also stated that, "since the system does not connect to the Internet, it could not be remotely compromised. Any potential hacker would have to be physically with the user, which would not happen on a field of battle."

   What are the risks in this scenario, and how would you mitigate them?

2. What are the ethical considerations in this scenario?

3. If you were in the blackhats' position, and had discovered how to compromise the targeting system, how would you as a CISSP have handled the situation?

4. From a security perspective, why is jailbreaking or rooting a mobile device the most damaging thing you can do to that device?

5. In what way do web-based systems increase the risks associated with mobile devices?

6. How do OAuth 2.0 and OpenID Connect work together to protect web apps?

TOPIC H

Cryptography Concepts

In the previous topic, you learned about security vulnerabilities in new mobile, embedded, and web-based technologies. Because the CIA triangle must always be the foundation of information security, you will need to understand the role cryptography plays in securing systems and information. In this topic, you will learn cryptography concepts.

Cryptography Concepts

Cryptography is the analysis and practice of information concealment for the purpose of securing sensitive data transmissions. It uses techniques such as encryption and decryption to control the privacy and legibility of valuable information. Cryptography is used extensively in computer security and other technical applications, such as ATM cards and electronic commerce.

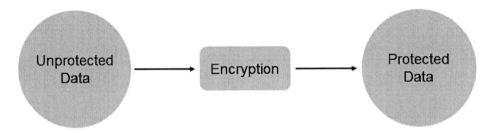

Figure 3-10: Cryptography.

Example: Removable Media

When removable media such as flash drives or magnetic tape are transported from one location to another, the information stored in them should be encrypted to safeguard the information stored on them. That way, even if someone stole the drive or tape, they still wouldn't have access to the data. The processes used to encrypt and decrypt the information are the result of the study of cryptography.

Encryption and Decryption

Encryption is a security technique that converts data from an ordinary, intelligible state known as *cleartext* or *plaintext* form, into coded, or *ciphertext* form. Only authorized parties with the necessary *decryption* information can decode and read the data. Encryption can be one-way, which means the encryption is designed to hide only the original message and is never decrypted. Or, it can be two-way, in which the encoded message can be transformed back to its original form and read.

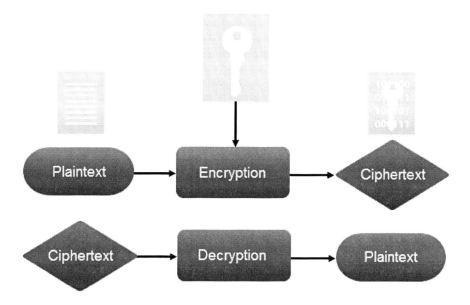

Figure 3–11: Encryption and decryption.

Encoding

Encoding is sometimes included in discussion on encryption but it really is something different altogether. Encoding is simply changing the format of information not in order to hide it, but to make it easier to transport or store. One of the best examples of encoding is Morse code. Even though "… --- …" might seemed encrypted, anyone that knows Morse code can easily understand it and translate it to "SOS." It is only changed into dots and dashes to make it easier to send across the wire.

A Simple Encrypted Message

The following example demonstrates how the content of a plaintext message cannot be easily determined once the message is encrypted.

- Plaintext message: Attack at Dawn
- Encrypted message:
  ```
  i8xfe zieam 5e3xy
  ```

Confidentiality

Confidentiality is the primary goal of encryption. When you encrypt something, only someone who has access to the decryption key (presumably an authorized user) will be able to decrypt the file and see its contents. The military is mostly focused on the confidentiality aspect of encryption.

Integrity

While confidentiality guarantees that a message being sent from one person to another cannot be read by others, it does not guarantee that the message was not altered since being sent. Integrity guarantees that a file or transmission has not changed in an unauthorized manner. Unlike confidentiality with the military, integrity is the primary focus of commercial business.

When you create a file, document, or transmission, you can run an encryption algorithm on that file and make the results of that encryption available for the recipient. The recipient can then run the same algorithm on his or her copy and compare it to the one you published. If the result is the same, then we have mathematically proven that the file has not changed and that integrity was maintained.

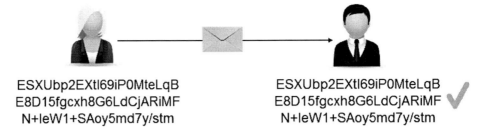

Figure 3-12: The receiver verifies the encrypted message's integrity.

Non-repudiation

Non-repudiation is the goal of ensuring that the party that sent a transmission or created data remains associated with that data and cannot deny sending or creating that data. You should be able to independently verify the identity of a message sender, and the sender should be responsible for the message and its data. Protocols and algorithms that provide non-repudiation do so by cryptographically binding the identity of the person to the transaction.

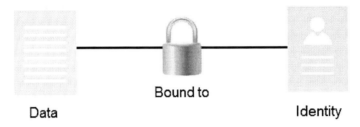

Figure 3-13: Non-repudiation.

Ciphers

A *cipher* is the rule, system, or mechanism used to encrypt data. It is also known as an encryption *algorithm*. Algorithms can be simple mechanical substitutions, but in electronic cryptography, they are generally complex mathematical functions. The stronger and more complex the algorithm, the more difficult it is to break the encryption. In symmetric and asymmetric encryption, the algorithm is used with a key (essentially a long number) to accomplish the encryption or decryption.

Algorithms are often based on very large prime numbers, also known as prime factors. A prime number is a number that can only be divided by itself or 1. Since it cannot be broken down by smaller numbers (such as 2, 3, 5, etc.) the lack of any repeat pattern makes it much harder to analyze and figure out. The RSA encryption algorithm, which we use in e-commerce, uses prime numbers. It is based on the idea that while it is easy to take two factors and multiply them to produce a result, it is extremely difficult to take a very large number and figure out the two (and only two) prime factors that were used to create it.

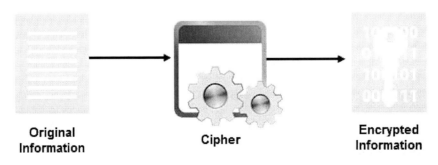

Figure 3-14: Ciphers.

A Simple Encryption Algorithm

A letter-substitution cipher, in which each letter of the alphabet is systematically replaced by another letter, is an example of a simple encryption algorithm.

The Avalanche Effect

The *avalanche effect* is a process found in a cipher that causes a very small change in the plaintext to produce a very large change in the ciphertext.

Keys

A cryptographic *key* is a specific piece of information that is used with an algorithm to perform encryption and decryption. Generally the algorithm published is well-known. It is the key that is secret and known only to authorized individuals. Although some keys contain letters or phrases (particularly in wireless implementations), a key ultimately is something that can be converted to a number. The number is then used along with the algorithm to perform the encryption.

Keys have various lengths depending on the cryptographic algorithm used and the amount of protection required for the encrypted data. A different key can be used with the same algorithm to produce different ciphertext. Without the correct key, the receiver cannot decrypt the ciphertext even with a known algorithm. The more complex the key, the stronger the encryption.

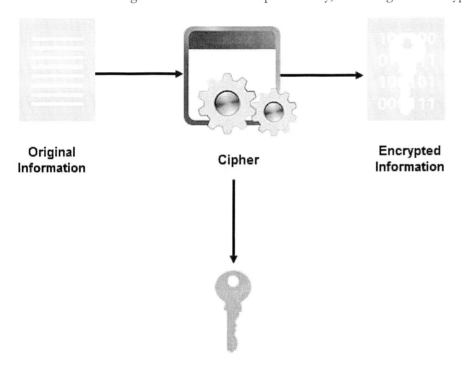

Figure 3-15: Cryptographic keys.

A Simple Encryption Key

In a simple letter-substitution algorithm, the key might be "replace each letter with the letter that is two letters following it in the alphabet." If the same algorithm were used on the same cleartext but with a different key—for example, "replace each letter with the one three letters before it"—the resulting ciphertext would be different.

A 128-Bit Key

The following example represents a 128-bit key.

01000100001000111110100101011010000111110001011101100010101100011

01111101101000111000100101011010010100010001011101100010101100011

Because this is difficult to read, it is frequently represented with text that looks like this:

- d8Zxin7T92mH4jpz

With 8 bits in each character or byte, 16 characters are used to represent a 128-bit key.

In general, the longer the key, the more secure the encryption. On the other hand, the longer the key, the more computationally expensive the encryption will be. Also, different types of encryption will need significantly different key lengths to be sufficiently secure. While 256-bit symmetric encryption is very secure, you would need key lengths approaching 2,048 in asymmetric encryption for the same level of assurance.

Key Clustering

Key clustering is the phenomenon of two different keys producing the same ciphertext, from the same plaintext, using the same algorithm. This is not desirable, as a good algorithm should produce different ciphertext regardless of the key length. Even if the keys are very short in length, different keys should still produce different outputs.

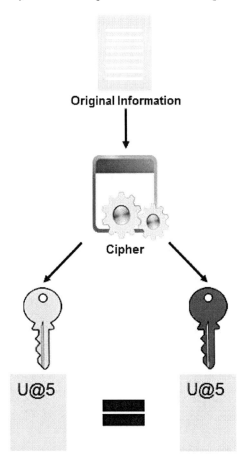

Figure 3-16: Different keys producing the same ciphertext.

Key Management

Regardless of the kind of encryption you implement, one of your biggest concerns will always be key management. Because the key holds the secret to decryption, you must make sure that the keys are stored safely so that they cannot be stolen or compromised. In addition, keys should have a limited lifespan. The longer you use the same key, the greater your chance of that key being cracked (discovered). Many keys (particularly those in digital certificates) have a default lifespan of only one or two years.

Ensure that you have a policy regarding the mechanism for safely keeping keys. Most operating systems and applications that use encryption have built-in mechanisms for storing keys. However, it is possible to export the keys out of the system. When this is done, the keys are simply stored on a file that can be read or stolen. The key is just a number contained in a small file. It would be very easy to attach it in an email or copy it to a flash drive.

If you must export your keys (and sometimes it is necessary for system administrators to do so), make sure that the key file is itself encrypted with a password that is not easy to guess. Preferably use a certificate-aware program such as the Certificates snap-in in Microsoft Windows to back up your keys in a secure manner so that they can be both protected from theft and easily recovered in case the system crashes beyond repair and must be reinstalled.

In an enterprise network, use key management services to securely issue, store, backup, renew, revoke, expire, and ultimately destroy the keys your organization uses.

Key Management Factors

There are various factors of the key management process that you should be aware of.

Key Management Factor	Description
Key control measures	Determine who has access to keys and how they are assigned.
Key recovery	Recovers lost keys.
Key storage	A secure repository for key assignment records.
Key retirement/destruction	How keys are removed from use and how they are destroyed.
Key change	The process of changing keys to systems on a periodic basis.
Key generation	Generates random keys for better data protection.
Key theft	What to do when keys have been compromised.
Frequency of key use	Limits the time that keys are used and the frequency of key reuse.
Key escrow	Provides law enforcement and other agencies authorized access to encrypted information; keys may have to be stored at other locations. To do so, key escrow is used. *Key escrow* involves splitting the key into multiple parts and storing each part with a separate escrow agency. When a law enforcement agency receives approval to obtain the escrowed keys through a court order, the agency contacts the key escrow agency and acquires each of the parts. An additional escrow method called *Fair Cryptosystems* allows the key to be split into "N" parts. All "N" parts are required to re-create the initial key, but each "N" key can verify that it is part of the original key without divulging its information.

 Note: For more information on the key management process, consult pages 393-408 in the *Official (ISC)² Guide to the CISSP Common Body of Knowledge (CBK), Fourth Edition.*

Cipher Evolution

Cryptography, or at least the use of ciphers and codes to protect secrets, has been around for thousands of years. Until recently, however, it was based on pen and paper, or some simple mechanical means. It wasn't until the electronic age and the advent of the computer that modern cryptography was born. The following table summarizes the evolution of cryptography and ciphers.

Cipher Era	Description
Early or manual ciphers	Early ciphers were implemented manually. For example, in ancient Sparta, the Spartans wrapped paper or leather around a staff and then wrote a message on the paper or leather down the length of the staff. When the paper or leather was unwrapped, the message was hidden. To decrypt the message, it was wrapped around a staff of an identical diameter and made readable again.
Mechanical era	Hardware-based cryptosystems are implemented without the use of software. The use of mechanical cypherdisks like those found in the Enigma marked the beginning of the mechanical era. During this period, devices sped up the encryption and decryption processes.
Software or modern era	Software-based cryptosystems rely on computer software to implement a cryptographic process. In the past, it was often necessary for those doing the encryption and decryption to understand the process, even with mechanical assistance. Today, the software era allows the process to be performed with little or no user knowledge. By following simple instructions, the user can perform the encryption and decryption processes.
The future	The future of cryptography is *quantum cryptography*. Although it might not be ready to have its own era named after it, there is a lot of excitement about quantum cryptography. It is based on the idea that any time you measure something, you have in fact made slight alterations to the object. By measuring light particles as they pass through a device, nearly impossible-to-break keys can be created.

Substitution

Substitution is one of two overall cipher techniques that replaces parts of a message or cryptographic output to hide the original information. Substitution occurs during processing within the cipher algorithm, where predefined bit patterns in the intermediate output are replaced with substitute patterns. When decrypted, the substitute patterns are identified and the original patterns are reinstated.

As an example, consider the plaintext message "Keep this secret." If the substitution key is to move each letter three places down in the English alphabet, then the ciphertext of the message becomes "Nhhs wklv vhfuhw." The algorithm is the alphabet, and the key is the instruction "shift down three."

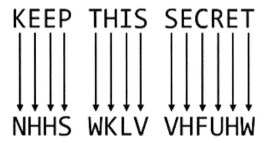

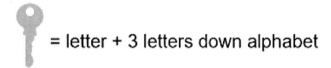

= letter + 3 letters down alphabet

Figure 3-17: A substitution cipher.

Transposition/Permutation

Transposition, or permutation, is the process of rearranging parts of a message or cryptographic output to hide the original information. The original message or key may be the subject of the transposition process. Transposition may also occur during the operation of the cipher algorithm.

With an input value of "Begin attack" and a transposition rule of 1, 7, 11, 5, 3, 2, 10, 6, 9, 4, 8 your transposed value will be "Btkng ecaait."

The characters in the input value are transposed, or reorganized, based on the rule provided. The first character in the input is the first character in the output, the eighth character in the input is the second character in the output, and so on. While this example illustrates character-based transposition, most algorithms use a bit-based transposition process.

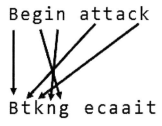

```
Begin attack

                    Transposition Rule
                    1 7 11 5 3 2 10 6 9 4 8
Btkng ecaait
```

Figure 3-18: A transposition cipher.

Stream Ciphers

A *stream cipher* is a type of symmetric encryption that encrypts data one bit at a time. Each plaintext bit is transformed into encrypted ciphertext. Stream ciphers generate a keystream that is Exclusive ORed (XORed) with each bit to output the ciphered text. These algorithms are very fast to execute, making stream ciphers ideal for realtime communications. The ciphertext is the same size as the original text, which can aid the cryptanalyst in breaking the cipher. This method produces fewer errors than other methods, and when errors occur, they affect only one bit.

For a stream cipher to be effective, the key stream should be as random as possible and should not have repetitious patterns. If the key stream values do repeat, they should be long enough to dismiss easy guesswork. Modern stream ciphers are extremely fast and can be implemented in hardware modules.

RC4 is the most common example of a stream cipher. Created in 1987 by Ron Rivest, it can use a key from 8 bits to 2,048 bits with a usual keysize of 40 to 256 bits.

 Note: For an online live demonstration of different symmetric ciphers, see **http://symmetric-ciphers.online-domain-tools.com/**.

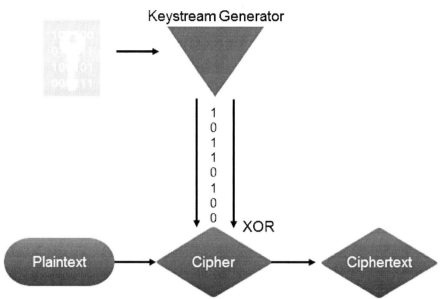

Figure 3-19: Stream cipher.

XOR

XOR is a binary math operation that tests to see whether two inputs are the same as or different from each other. The result is 0 if the inputs are either both 0s or both 1s. The result is 1 if one input is a 0 and the other is a 1. The following table shows this logic.

Because the XOR operation has fast performance, it is used in stream ciphers.

Text	10010101
Key	01010101
Cipher text	11000000

Block Ciphers

A *block cipher* encrypts data a block at a time, often in 64-bit or 128-bit blocks. It is usually more secure, but is also slower, than stream encryption. Block ciphers are best used for large amounts of data kept in storage.

Without using techniques such as transposition and substitution, cleartext blocks with identical content may be encrypted to produce identical ciphertext. For this reason, block ciphers are strengthened by using an iterative process where multiple rounds of substitution, diffusion, and other functions are performed from four to 32 times. Or they may be strengthened through *chaining*, in which the results of one cipher step change the encryption process for the next cipher step.

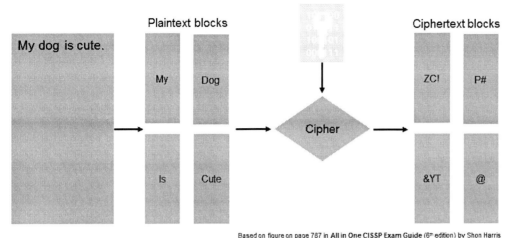

Based on figure on page 787 in **All in One CISSP Exam Guide** (6ᵗʰ edition) by Shon Harris

Figure 3-20: Block cipher.

Block Cipher Examples

The Digital Encryption Standard (DES) is an example of a block cipher. A 64-bit block of plaintext is encrypted with a 64-bit key, resulting in a 64-bit block of ciphertext.

Other examples of block ciphers include:

- IDEA: Using 64 bit blocks and a 128 bit key. Until 2012 was considered immune (under certain assumptions) to a cracking technique known as differential cryptanalysis, which studies how differences in input can affect the resultant difference at output.
- RC5: Created by Ron Rivest in 1994. It uses a simple algorithm and variable block and key sizes. Unless at least 18 rounds of computations are performed, it is susceptible to differential cryptanalysis.
- 3DES (triple DES): An algorithm that applies DES three times using three 64-bit keys to a block of data.
- AES (advanced encryption standard): Based on the Rijndael ("rhine-doll") algorithm. It has a fixed block size of 128 bits and a key size of 128, 192, or 256 bits. After a five-year competition, AES was chosen by NIST in 2001 to replace DES as the national standard.
- Blowfish: Released as an open standard in 1993, it uses a 64 bit block size with variable key length. It provides good encryption in software and to date no effective cracking technique has been proven against it when it employs full rounds of encryption.
- Twofish: A finalist in the NIST AES competition, it uses 128 bit block and key sizes up to 256 bit. Like Blowfish, Twofish is in the public domain. It is used in the OpenPGP standard, but its use is not as widespread as Blowfish.

Block Cipher Modes

Modes of operation define how a block cipher will repeatedly encrypt single blocks of data in a secure manner. Some common block cipher modes are as follows.

Block Cipher Mode	Description
ECB	The *Electronic Code Book (ECB)* mode breaks the plaintext down into 64-bit blocks and then encrypts each block separately. Duplicate plaintext blocks cause the same encryption result. This is beneficial for encrypting small amounts of data, which are seen in electronic transactions.

Block Cipher Mode	Description
CBC	In *Cipher Block Chaining (CBC)* mode, 64-bit plaintext blocks are XORed with a 64-bit IV and then encrypted using the key. The resulting ciphertext is then chained to the next ciphering round, where it replaces the IV and helps to mask the contents of the second data block. This process is continued until the last block is encrypted. A potential concern with CBC is that errors will propagate.
CFB	In *Cipher FeedBack (CFB)* mode, the IV is first encrypted using the key and then XORed with the plaintext to create the ciphertext. In the second step, the ciphertext from the first step is encrypted with the key. The resulting encrypted information is XORed with the second plaintext block, and the ensuing ciphertext is chained to the third step, where it is encrypted. CFB is a stream mode technique.
OFB	In *Output FeedBack (OFB)* mode, the IV is encrypted with the key and then chained to the next block's encryption step. Each encryption step encrypts only the result of the first IV's previous encryption.
CTR	*Counter (CTR)* mode uses a counter to provide the IV. The counter encryption can be performed in parallel, rather than serially, because the numbers used for the IV can be predetermined. Errors do not propagate. The 802.11i standard for wireless encryption supports AES in CTR mode.

Steganography

Steganography is an alternative cipher process that hides information by enclosing it in another file such as a graphic, movie, or sound file. Where encryption hides the content of information, but does not attempt to hide the fact that information exists, steganography is an attempt to obscure the fact that information is even present. Steganographic techniques include hiding information in blocks of what appears to be innocuous text (or even blank spaces in a text file), or hiding information within images either by using subtle clues, or by invisibly altering the structure of a digital image by applying an algorithm to change the color of individual pixels within the image. In an audio file, steganography can hide information in the form of small amounts of noise in the sound, or by slightly shifting the phase of individual waveforms. Data that has been hidden through steganography also typically uses some form of encryption or password to further protect the information from discovery.

Besides being used for deceptive purposes, steganography is also commonly employed in the form of digital watermarking to protect copyrighted materials from unlawful use.

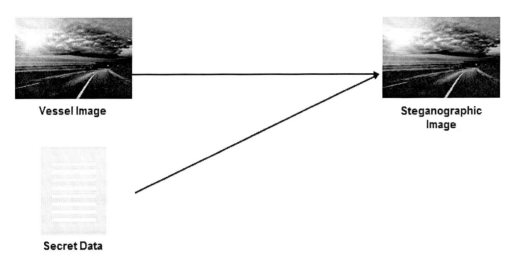

Vessel Image

Steganographic Image

Secret Data

Figure 3-21: Steganography.

Cryptographic Lifecycle

History has demonstrated that all cryptosystems eventually outlive their usefulness. Algorithms that were originally thought to be unbreakable (see Enigma) eventually succumb to new cryptanalytic attacks, or sheer brute force computing power:

- The Electronic Frontier Foundation (EFF) created a DES Cracker machine for under $250,000 that could crack DES in 4.5 days.
- WEP, a weak implementation of RC4 used for years in wireless devices, can now be broken by a single laptop in a matter of minutes, spawning a whole movement towards WPA and WPA/2-based wireless security.
- Even one of the toughest algorithms today, 4096 bit RSA, was successfully broken into by using a microphone to listen to acoustic variations in the sound produced by a CPU while performing calculations with the algorithm. This "side channel" attack demonstrates that even strong encryption can have vulnerabilities in unexpected ways.

Although conventional methods of brute forcing an algorithm (trying every possible combination until the key is discovered) assure us that it would take thousands of years to break our best encryption algorithms, the security practitioner must never become complacent. A weak implementation of a good algorithm, or some currently unknown side channel attack, may be discovered and exploited.

 Note: For more information on how 4096 RSA was broken, see **www.extremetech.com/ extreme/173108-researchers-crack-the-worlds-toughest-encryption-by-listening-to-the- tiny-sounds-made-by-your-computers-cpu**.

Cryptosystems

A *cryptosystem* is the general term for the hardware and/or software used to implement a cryptographic process. Cryptosystems implement ciphers to encrypt and decrypt sensitive information.

Early on, cryptosystems were based in hardware. Today, they can be implemented more efficiently in software due to the complexity of algorithms. However, the software still requires a hardware platform to operate.

Cryptanalysis is the study of cryptosystems with the intent of breaking them, and by extension the security services the cryptosystem supports.

The *work factor* is the amount of time needed to break a cryptosystem.

Note: *Cryptology* is the study of both cryptography and cryptanalysis.

Example: The Enigma

During World War II, the Germans used a hardware device called the Enigma to encrypt and decrypt messages.

During this period, the United States had their own encryption device called SIGABA and the Japanese had the Purple machine. Each country had huge cryptanalysis efforts during the war. The United States and Great Britain had some success breaking the Enigma and Purple machines. SIGABA was unbroken and remained classified until 1996.

Figure 3-22: The Enigma.

Encryption-Based Attacks

There are several common encryption-based attack categories.

Encryption Attack Type	Description
Birthday attack	A *birthday attack* exploits a paradox in the mathematical algorithms used to encrypt passwords. This type of attack takes advantage of the probability of different password inputs producing the same encrypted output, given a large enough set of inputs. It is named after the surprising statistical fact that there is a 50% chance that any two people in a group of 23 will share a birthday.
Rainbow attack	A *rainbow attack* automates password guessing by comparing encrypted passwords against a predetermined list of possible password values. A rainbow attack is based on the much simpler *dictionary attack*, in which an automated tool simply goes through a long list (dictionary) of possible passwords in the hopes that the actual password is on the list. Both rainbow and dictionary attacks are only successful against fairly simple and obvious passwords, because they rely on a dictionary of common words and predictable variations, such as adding a single digit to the end of a word or substituting numbers for similar looking letters.

Encryption Attack Type	Description
Replay attack	A *replay attack* can be used to bypass the encryption protecting passwords while in transit. If the encrypted password can be captured and then replayed, the attacker may be able to gain access to a system without ever having access to the password itself. WEP cracking (spoofing a wireless access point into eventually revealing the WEP key) is based on a replay attack.
Side channel attack	A *side channel attack* targets the cryptosystem by gathering information about the physical characteristics of the encryption and then exploiting them. For example, by timing the transfer of encryption key information, an attacker might be able to determine the length of the key.
Factoring attack	A *factoring attack* attempts to determine the prime numbers used in asymmetric and symmetric encryption as a means to break cryptosystems. This attack theory was discovered by RSA Laboratories when it developed the RSA Factoring Challenge as an effort to research and explore computational number theory and integer factorization using semiprimes, or numbers with two prime factors. Although the challenge was discontinued in 2007, it was extraordinarily successful in testing the cryptanalytic strength of both asymmetric- and symmetric-key algorithms.

Cryptanalysis Methodologies

Cryptographic attackers can employ several variants of man-in-the-middle attacks to determine encryption keys and break cryptosystems.

Cryptanalysis Methodology	Description
Ciphertext-only	The attacker has several ciphertext samples of messages encrypted with the same algorithm and, possibly, the same key. The intent is to find the encryption key. Once the key for one message is determined, the other messages may be decrypted.
Known plaintext	The attacker has a copy of the plaintext and ciphertext for one or more messages. The intent is to find the correct key. Messages often have a common format with salutations and closings. With this knowledge, the attacker can use a limited amount of information to figure out the encryption key.
Chosen plaintext	The attacker has a copy of the plaintext and ciphertext for one or more messages, but chooses to work with only a selected part of the plaintext when attempting to break the system. The intent is to find the correct key. By manipulating the key, a portion of the message may be decoded and eventually the entire key may be recovered.
Chosen ciphertext	The attacker has a copy of the plaintext and ciphertext for one or more messages, but chooses to work with only a selected part of the ciphertext when attempting to break the system. The intent is to find the correct key. By manipulating the key, a portion of the message may be decoded and eventually the entire key may be recovered.

Frequency Analysis

Frequency analysis is a method for breaking encryption when simple substitution algorithms are used. Letters used in a particular linguistic alphabet appear in certain words based on a given frequency. For example, in English, the most often used letter is E. If an encrypted document contains a number of Vs approximately equal to the frequency of E in typical plaintext samples, the V may be replaced with E in all instances to derive the original message. Other frequency replacements may be used.

Guidelines for Applying Cryptography Concepts

Here are some guidelines you can use for understanding cryptography concepts:

- Remember that the purpose of encryption is to provide confidentiality, integrity, and non-repudiation.
- Keep in mind that cryptography requires both an algorithm and a key to encrypt something.
- Choose algorithms that do not permit key clustering.
- Use block ciphers to encrypt large amounts of data at rest.
- Use stream ciphers to encrypt real-time data transmissions.
- Recognize that, as technology and computing power advance, all cryptosystems have a limited lifespan, and will eventually be replaced by stronger systems.
- As you study cryptanalytic attacks, you can choose to start your attack with known amounts of either the plaintext or the ciphertext.

ACTIVITY 3-8
Analyzing Cryptography Concepts

Scenario

In this activity, you will assess your understanding of cryptography concepts.

---

1. **Why are encryption methods used for data in transit often not suitable for data at rest?**

   ○ They require other networking protocols for support.

   ○ Encryption methods for data in transit always rely on weak keys.

   ○ Data in transit is vulnerable for a very short time (i.e., the life of a packet), but data at rest may be around for a long time, increasing the chance that the cryptographic methods used may be defeated as technology progresses.

   ○ Such distinctions are a myth—encryption technologies are always equally appropriate for data at rest and data in transit.

2. **Which answer choice best describes the process of digitally signing a message?**

   ○ The sender requests the public key of the recipient. The sender generates a symmetric key and uses it to encrypt a message. The sender encrypts the symmetric key with the recipient's public key. The encrypted symmetric key and message are sent to the recipient.

   ○ The sender creates a message. The sender creates a hash of that message. The sender encrypts the hash of the message with his/her private key. The message, the encrypted hash, and the sender's public key are sent to the recipient.

   ○ The sender creates a message. The sender creates a hash of that message. The sender encrypts the hash of the message with the recipient's public key. The message and the encrypted hash are sent to the recipient.

   ○ The sender creates a message. The sender creates a hash of that message. The sender encrypts the hash of the message with his/her public key. The message, the encrypted hash, and the sender's private key are sent to the recipient.

3. **How can key escrow protect against abuse of decryption keys?**

4. **When would you choose to use a stream cipher over a block cipher?**

   ○ When you need to quickly encrypt large files on your hard drive.

   ○ When you need to quickly encrypt data in realtime.

   ○ When you need to run multiple encryption permutations over the same file.

   ○ When you need to introduce randomness into your encryption process.

5. **In what way could steganography aid a terrorist group?**

6. Why must a security professional never assume that even a strong cryptosystem will remain unbroken indefinitely?

7. Why does cryptography so often depend on prime factors?
    - ○ Because very large numbers are harder to guess.
    - ○ Because RSA set a precedent using prime factors that the rest of the world followed.
    - ○ Because prime factors are easy to multiply and divide.
    - ○ Because prime factors have no internal repeat pattern, making them harder to analyze.

8. Does a replay attack require that the password ever be discovered?
    - ○ Yes, this is what allows the replay to occur.
    - ○ Yes, because that is the ultimate goal of a replay attack.
    - ○ No, because there is a 50% chance that two different inputs will produce the same result.
    - ○ No, because the attacker uses data that has already been authenticated.

TOPIC I

Cryptography Techniques

In the previous topic, you learned about cryptography concepts, including various individual parts of a cryptosystem. In this topic, you will learn techniques to implement cryptography.

DRM

Digital Rights Management (DRM) is a set of services used to protect intellectual property. It encrypts a document such that you must have the correct key to read the document, or perform some task on the document such as print it or forward it in an email. The key must be obtained by the vendor, often for every single use, and cannot be transferred. Moreover, a copy cannot be made of the document to evade the encryption. Only the original (including the required key) can be used.

A few examples of products that use digital rights management include:

- Adobe Acrobat.
- Microsoft Office.
- Microsoft Money.
- Music and video files.

Symmetric Encryption

Symmetric encryption or *shared-key encryption* is a two-way encryption scheme in which encryption and decryption are both performed by the same secret key. The key can be configured in software or coded in hardware. Then, the key must be securely transmitted between the two parties prior to encrypted communications.

This need for secure key exchange leads to the largest challenge of symmetric encryption. Symmetric encryption is relatively fast and suitable for encrypting large data sets, but it is vulnerable if the key is lost or compromised. Adding to the confusion, a symmetric key is sometimes called a secret key or private key because of the absolute need to protect the key from exposure.

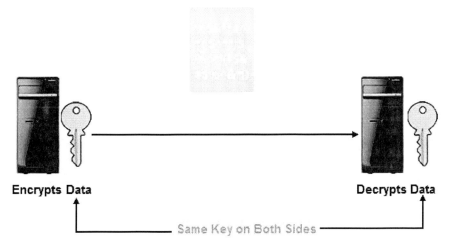

Encrypts Data   **Decrypts Data**

──────── Same Key on Both Sides ────────

Figure 3-23: Symmetric-key cryptography.

Symmetric Encryption Algorithms

The following are algorithms used for symmetric encryption.

Symmetric Algorithm	Description
Data Encryption Standard (DES)	A block-cipher symmetric encryption algorithm that encrypts data in 64-bit blocks using a 56-bit key with 8 bits used for parity. The short key length makes DES a relatively weak algorithm, though it requires less performance overhead.
Triple DES (3DES)	A symmetric encryption algorithm that encrypts data by processing each block of data three times using a different key each time. It first encrypts plaintext into ciphertext using one key, then encrypts that ciphertext with another key, and lastly encrypts the second ciphertext with yet another key. 3DES is stronger than DES, but also triples the performance impact.
Advanced Encryption Standard (AES)	A symmetric 128-, 192-, or 256-bit block cipher developed by Belgian cryptographers Joan Daemen and Vincent Rijmen and adopted by the U.S. government as its encryption standard to replace DES. The AES algorithm is called Rijndael (pronounced "Rhine-dale") after its creators. Rijndael was one of five algorithms considered for adoption in the AES contest conducted by the National Institute of Standards and Technology (NIST) of the United States. AES is considered one of the strongest encryption algorithms available, and offers better performance than 3DES.
Blowfish	A freely available 64-bit block cipher algorithm that uses a variable key length. It was developed by Bruce Schneier. Blowfish is no longer considered strong, though it does offer greater performance than DES.
Twofish	A symmetric key block cipher, similar to Blowfish, consisting of a block size of 128 bits and key sizes up to 256 bits. Although not selected for standardization, it appeared as one of the five finalists in the AES contest. Twofish encryption uses a pre-computed encrypted algorithm. The encrypted algorithm is a key-dependent S-box, which is a relatively complex key algorithm that when given the key, provides a substitution key in its place. This is referred to as "n" and has the sizes of 128, 192, and 256 bits. One half of "n" is made up of the encryption key, and the other half contains a modifier used in the encryption algorithm. Twofish is stronger than Blowfish and offers comparative levels of performance.
Rivest Cipher (RC) 4, 5, and 6	A series of algorithms developed by Ronald Rivest. All have variable key lengths. RC4 is a stream cipher. RC5 and RC6 are variable-size block ciphers. RC6 is considered a strong cipher and offers good performance.

Asymmetric Encryption

Although using a single key to encrypt a message is a good form of security, it has its drawbacks, such as ensuring that both parties agree to and know the key. If the key gets compromised, all communications encrypted with that key have also been compromised, and a new key has to be issued, with both parties communicating ahead of time to agree upon the key.

Asymmetric encryption was a response to the challenges of symmetric key exchange. It is based on the concept of having two keys (a key pair) that are mathematically related. One key is called the public key. The other key is called the private key. If you encrypt with one key, you must use the other key to decrypt. You cannot use the same key to both encrypt and decrypt.

You freely give away the public key, but you carefully guard the private key. Anyone who has your public key can use that key to encrypt a file or a transmission before they send it to you. Since you are the only possessor of the private key, you are the only one who has the ability to unlock that encrypted file or transmission. The nice thing about asymmetric encryption is that the two parties don't have to agree ahead of time on what the encryption key will be. You just have to trade public keys.

Notice that asymmetric encryption only works in one direction, if you only have one person's key pair. If Bob and Sue want to trade encrypted messages, then they will need to trade public keys. Bob will need to get a copy of Sue's public key, and Sue will need to get a copy of Bob's public key. Bob will use Sue's public key to encrypt the message and send it to her. Sue will then use her private key to decrypt it. In return, Sue will then use Bob's public key to encrypt the response, and send it to Bob. Bob will then use his own private key to decrypt the message.

 Note: To see an example of a public/private key pair, try the online RSA key generator at **http://travistidwell.com/jsencrypt/demo/**.

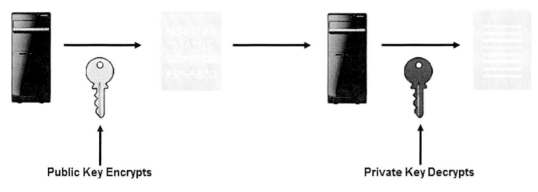

Public Key Encrypts   **Private Key Decrypts**

Figure 3-24: Asymmetric-key cryptography.

Asymmetric Encryption Techniques

The following table lists some of the techniques and algorithms used in asymmetric encryption.

Asymmetric Algorithm	Description
Rivest Shamir Adelman (RSA)	Named for its designers, Ronald Rivest, Adi Shamir, and Len Adelman, RSA was the first successful algorithm for public key encryption. It has a variable key length and block size. It is still widely used and considered highly secure if it employs sufficiently long keys.
Diffie-Hellman (DH)	A cryptographic technique that provides for secure key exchange. Described in 1976, it formed the basis for most public key encryption implementations, including RSA, DHE, and ECDHE.
Elliptic curve cryptography (ECC)	An asymmetric, public key encryption technique that leverages the algebraic structures of elliptic curves over finite fields. ECC is used with wireless and mobile devices.
Diffie-Hellman Ephemeral (DHE)	A variant of DH that uses ephemeral keys to provide secure key exchange.
Elliptic Curve Diffie-Hellman Ephemeral (ECDHE)	A variant of DH that incorporates the use of ECC and ephemeral keys.

Hashing

Hashing is one-way encryption that transforms cleartext into ciphertext. The resulting ciphertext is never decrypted and is called a *hash, hash value,* or *message digest*. It may seem odd that it is never decrypted, but it can perform its function just the same. Because the cleartext can be hashed again at any point in time and be compared to the original hash, you will know if there has been any change to the integrity of the cleartext. The input data can vary in length, whereas the hash length is fixed.

For example, a 128-bit hashing algorithm always produces an output that is 128 bits long. Note however that the output of most hashing algorithms is actually expressed in hexadecimal format.

It is possible to break a hash through brute force. With a large password or a large file, the likelihood of finding the correct password for file contents through brute force is improbable.

The message digest can be either keyed or non-keyed. When keyed, the original message is combined with a secret key sent with the message. When non-keyed, the original message is hashed without any other mechanisms.

You can further protect the integrity of the hash by using a hashing algorithm such as Hash-based Message Authentication Code (HMAC) that includes your private key. This not only guarantees the integrity of the file, but also authenticates the message by clearly identifying its source.

 Note: A *collision* occurs when a hash function generates identical output from two different inputs.

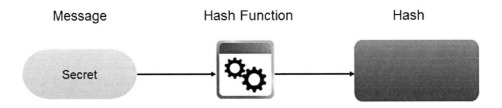

Hashing is one-way encryption

Figure 3–25: Hashing.

Hashing Encryption Algorithms

The following are algorithms used for hashing encryption.

Hashing Algorithm	Description
Message Digest 5 (MD5)	This algorithm produces a 128-bit message digest. It was created by Ronald Rivest and is now in the public domain. MD5 is no longer considered a strong hash function. In 2004, it was demonstrated that it is not collision resistant. Its predecessors were MD2 and MD4.
Secure Hash Algorithm (SHA)	This algorithm is modeled after MD5 and is considered the stronger of the two. Common versions of SHA include SHA-160, which produces a 160-bit hash value, whereas SHA-256, SHA-384, and SHA-512 produce 256-bit, 384-bit, and 512-bit digests, respectively. Performance-wise, SHA is at a disadvantage to MD5.
NT LAN Manager (NTLM)	NTLMv1 is an authentication protocol created by Microsoft® for use in its products and released in early versions of Windows® NT. It is based on the MD4 hashing algorithm. NTLMv2 was introduced in the NT 4.0 SP4, and is based on HMAC-MD5.
RACE Integrity Primitives Evaluation Message Digest (RIPEMD)	This is a message digest algorithm (cryptographic hash function) that is based along the lines of the design principles used in *MD4*. There are 128-, 160-, 256-, and 320-bit versions called RIPEMD-128, RIPEMD-160, RIPEMD-256, and RIPEMD-320, respectively. The 256- and 320-bit versions reduce the chances of generating duplicate output hashes but do little in terms of higher levels of security. RIPEMD-160 was designed by the open academic community and is used less frequently than SHA-1, which may explain why it is less scrutinized than SHA.

Hashing Algorithm	Description
Hash-based Message Authentication Code (HMAC)	This is a method used to verify both the integrity and authenticity of a message by combining cryptographic hash functions, such as MD5 or SHA-1, with a secret key. The resulting calculation is named based on what underlying hash function was used. For example, if SHA-1 is the hash function, then the HMAC algorithm is named HMAC-SHA1.

Salting the Hash

A salt is a random number added to the input of a hashing function to add randomness. If two identical pieces of plaintext were hashed without a salt, they would generate the same hash value. In cryptography, consistently getting the same result is undesirable because it makes it easier for a hacker to figure out what the original plaintext was. By adding random data with the original plaintext, the system will generate unique hash values every time.

Hashing in Password Protection

Hashing is used in a number of password authentication schemes. When a password is entered into a computer system for user authentication, rather than store the password in readable form, most systems use a one-way hashing function to encode the password for system storage. Although a hash is created from the raw data, that data cannot be obtained from the hash.

Because hashing algorithms are publicly known, the protective nature of the hash is its one-way function. When a user attempts to access the computer with a specific password, the password is hashed using the same algorithm and the stored hash value is compared to the new hash. If the values match, the password is correct. If they do not match, the password entered is incorrect. Because hashing does not require the use of keys, there is nothing to share.

Hashing in File Transmission and Verification

If a 20-gigabyte (GB) file needs to be transported to another location, it is critical to ensure that the file contents are correct. This can be accomplished by first encrypting the file prior to forwarding, and then decrypting it once it arrives at its destination. Successful decryption indicates that the file has not been modified in the transmission process. An excessive amount of time is required for file encryption and decryption.

To limit the time frame for content verification, a message digest can be computed. Using a hashing algorithm, a 168-bit hash can be generated that represents the entire 20-GB file. The hash and the file are then transmitted to the desired destination. Once received, a new hash is created and, if the original hash and the destination hash match, it can be assumed that the file was not modified during transmission.

IVs

An *initialization vector (IV)* is a specific way in which encryption algorithms are salted. It is a string of bits that may be used with either a block or stream symmetric cipher and a key to produce a unique result when the same key is used to encrypt the same cleartext. The IV is used to reduce the likelihood that identical ciphertext will be created when the identical cleartext is encrypted. IVs may be calculated using time factors, such as synchronized clocks, or by using a pre-shared value. The IV may be as large as a block in a block cipher or as long as the key in a stream cipher.

IVs gained notoriety in the security world when a weak implementation of RC4 opened nearly every existing wireless network at the time to attack. The Wired Equipment Privacy (WEP) algorithm used a 24-bit IV to help lengthen the key in wireless security. 24 bits, however, is a relatively short length. When coupled with a replay attack that would provoke a wireless access point to issue new IVs at an accelerated rate, the key would eventually be reused and could be cracked. More sophisticated cryptanalysis developed a little later allowed the attacker to break the WEP key after collecting a fraction of the IVs, without going through the entire 24-bit cycle. The use of initialization vectors, however, is not limited to wireless. It is still a sound concept for introducing randomness in symmetric ciphers.

IV Implementation

Using the key `abcdefghijklmnopqrstuvwxyz`, the plaintext message "Attack at Dawn" will be encrypted as `i8xfe zieam 5e3xy`. If encrypted again, the message "Attack at Dawn" will result in the same encrypted message.

If an IV is used with the key, the resulting encrypted message will be different. For instance:

* Plaintext message: Attack at Dawn
* IV: `i8j3k0x12axejq9drfwxyqkdszzy` (generated using a time base such as a clock)
* Key: `abcdefghijklmnopqrstuvwxyz`
* Encrypted message: `aqn7e zy8n2 qplm5`

Hybrid Cryptography

Hybrid cryptography combines the convenience and security of public key encryption with the speed and efficiency of symmetric key encryption. A symmetric key is first used to encrypt the data. Symmetric encryption is faster and better suited for encrypting large blocks of data. Then, to protect the symmetric key that was used to encrypt the data, an asymmetric public/private key pair is used. The public key is used to encrypt and protect the symmetric key. Only the possessor of the private key would be able to unlock the symmetric key, which in turn can unlock the original data.

Examples of hybrid cryptography can be found in:

* SSL/TLS website connections.
* Microsoft Encrypting File System.

PKI

A *public key infrastructure (PKI)* is a cryptographic system that is composed of a Certification Authority (CA), certificates, software, services, and other cryptographic components for the purpose of enabling the authenticity and validation of data and/or entities. The CA is the server that issues a certificate (a public key embedded in a file).

PKI can be implemented in various hierarchical structures, with a root CA at the top of the hierarchy. Any number of subordinate CAs can exist below the root to help offload the work of issuing certificates. The root CA issues certificates to the subordinate CAs, which in turn issue certificates to end users and devices. The end users and devices then use the certificates to authenticate or encrypt files and transmissions.

All certificates, at any level, form a chain of trust that points back to the original root CA. With PKI, users and systems never need to meet ahead of time to trust each other. They only need to trust the original root CA that issued their certificates.

It is very common to implement an internal, private PKI system within the organization. Most server operating systems have certificate services built into them. You can turn a server into a certificate authority with minimal effort. The CA service is typically not taxing to a server with a moderate work load. Implementing your own CA saves money because you will not have to pay an external provider for every certificate your users and devices use. To make your CA's certificates accepted by the outside world, configure your own internal CA to be subordinate to a well-known commercial root CA. You can pay a fee to have a commercial root CA issue a certificate to your own CA, thus setting up a chain of trust that outside systems will accept.

There are a number of commercial root CAs available on the Internet. We refer to these as Trusted Root Certification Authorities or trusted roots. Their public keys come preinstalled in most operating systems, including mobile devices, and can be viewed by any user. Of course, should a root CA become compromised, every single certificate that it and its subordinates have issued also are compromised. The certificates must be revoked and re-issued. For this reason, commercial root CAs are highly protected, and typically left offline until needed to minimize the possibility of attack.

While PKI is the basis for all modern e-commerce, it can also be installed and maintained privately by an organization. In that case, if you want users or devices outside your organization to trust your root CA, you must export its public key and make it available to those users and devices.

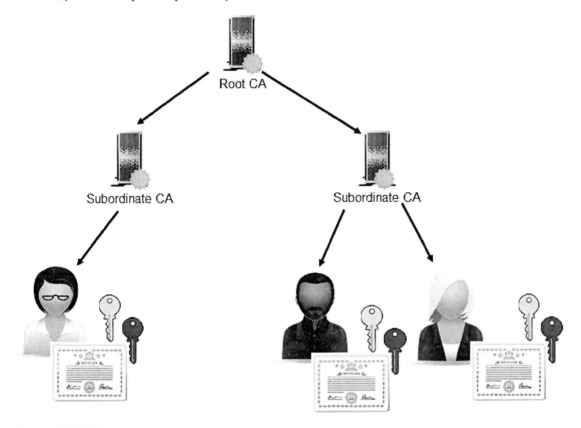

Figure 3–26: PKI.

PKI Components

A PKI contains several components.

- Digital certificates: Files that contain a public key, used to verify the identity of an entity, or encrypt data that only that entity can unlock.
- One or more CAs, to issue digital certificates to computers, users, or applications.
- A *registration authority (RA)*, responsible for verifying users' identities and approving or denying requests for digital certificates.
- A *certificate repository database*, to store the digital certificates.
- A *certificate management system*, to provide software tools to perform the day-to-day functions of the PKI.

The PKI Process

When using the PKI, the first step is to obtain a public and private key pair from the CA. The public key is retained by the CA and a certificate is then issued to the individual. That certificate, standardized as an X.509 version 3 certificate, is also available to anyone who wishes or needs to verify that the public key provided is the actual key of the individual supplying it. The CA certifies the identity.

The steps include:

1. User 1 asks CA to issue certificate.
2. CA validates identity and issues certificate.
3. User 1 presents certificate to User 2.
4. User 2 doesn't know User 1, so asks CA to verify identity.
5. CA checks certificate is valid.
6. CA tells User 2 certificate is valid.
7. User 2 now trusts User 1.

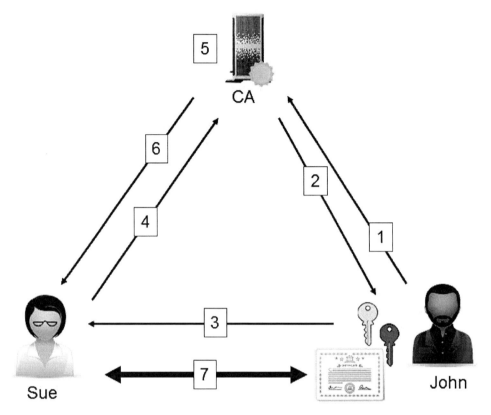

Figure 3-27: The PKI Process.

Certificate Information

Certificates contain the following information:

- Version
- Serial Number
- Algorithm ID
- Issuer
- Validity
- Not Before
- Not After
- Subject
- Subject Public Key Info
- Issuer Unique Identifier (Optional)
- Subject Unique Identifier (Optional)
- Extensions (Optional)
- Certificate Signature Algorithm
- Certificate Signature, to determine certificate validity

Certificate Revocation

The PKI process also includes procedures for revoking certificates when they expire or when the security of the private key is in doubt.

A *Certificate Revocation List (CRL)* is a list of certificates (or, more accurately,their serial numbers) that have been revoked, are no longer valid, and should not be relied on by any system user. The list enumerates revoked certificates along with the reason or reasons for revocation. The dates of certificate issue, and the entities that issued them, are also included. In addition, each list contains a proposed date for the next release. When a potential user attempts to access a server, the server allows or denies access based on the CRL entry for that particular user.

A CRL is generated periodically after a clearly defined time frame, and may also be generated immediately after a certificate has been revoked. The CRL is always issued by the CA, which issues the corresponding certificates. All CRLs have a (often short) lifetime in which they are valid and during which they may be consulted by a PKI-enabled application to verify a counterpart's certificate prior to its use. To prevent spoofing or denial of service (DoS) attacks, CRLs are usually signed by the issuing CA and therefore carry a digital signature. To validate a specific CRL prior to relying on it, the certificate of its corresponding CA is needed, which can usually be found in a public directory.

An alternative to CRL is the Online Certificate Status Protocol (OCSP). It is a newer method for obtaining the revocation status of a digital certificate from a server using an HTTP request. OCSP requests use less bandwidth and provide faster confirmation on the validity of the certificate.

Digital Signatures

A *digital signature* is a message digest that has been encrypted again with a user's private key. The digital signature is appended to a message to identify the sender and the message. When the message is received, the digital signature is decrypted, with the user's public key, back into a message digest. The recipient then rehashes the original message and compares it to the sender's hash. If the two hash values match, the digital signature is authentic and the message integrity is confirmed.

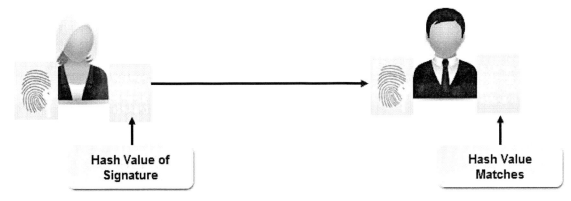

Hash Value of Signature

Hash Value Matches

Figure 3-28: A digital signature.

Encryption of the Hash

It is important to remember that a digital signature is a hash that is then itself encrypted. Without the second round of encryption, another party could easily:

1. Intercept the file and the hash.
2. Modify the file.
3. Re-create the hash.
4. Send the modified file to the recipient.

Digital Signature Non-Repudiation

Determine the information source by signing a hash or any other data with a private key. If it is possible to decrypt the information with the sender's public key, the sender has been verified, thus resulting in non-repudiation. Non-repudiation exists when the sender cannot deny his or her association with a data transmission.

If you digitally sign something, you cannot later disavow that action. This is because you are presumed to be the only predecessor of the private key that performs the digital signature. With a digital signature, you use an encryption key that only you possess to mark the file as originating from you.

The use of a digital signature is very often legally binding. If your private key is ever stolen or compromised, someone else could use it for malicious purposes and you could be held accountable. For that reason, private keys must be protected very carefully, including never being exposed in clear text, and if put on removable media, it must be physically controlled to minimize theft.

Digital Certificates

A *digital certificate* is an electronic document that associates credentials with a public key. Both users and devices can hold certificates. The certificate validates the certificate holder's identity and is also a way to distribute the holder's public key. A server called a *certificate authority* (CA) issues certificates and the associated public/private key pairs.

Note that a digital certificate is only the public key half of an asymmetric key pair. When the certificate is issued, it is accompanied by the private key, which is in the form of an encrypted file. The private key remains encrypted on the computer's hard drive, even after installation. This is to protect it from accidental or malicious disclosure.

 Note: You can view a certificate by opening Microsoft Internet Explorer. Once the browser is open, open **Settings→Internet Options→Content→Certificates**. Most of the tabs will contain one or more certificates, which you can double-click to examine.

PFS

Perfect forward secrecy (PFS) is a characteristic of session encryption that ensures that if a key used during a certain session is compromised, it should not affect previously encrypted data. This is a very desirable trait, as long-term keys, such as public/private key pairs, shared keys, and others, are at risk of exposing all data encrypted with them if the key is compromised.

In cryptographic systems without PFS, data that was previously captured by an attacker can be vulnerable to decryption at any point in the future if the long-term keys used during the communication are compromised.

Two real-world examples of this include:

- Decryption of previous HTTPS traffic through the compromise of a web server.
- Decryption of previously sent and received emails through the compromise of a user's desktop or laptop.

Obtaining PFS requires that long-term keys are only used to derive ephemeral (per-session) keys and that the same ephemeral key is never used twice to generate other keys. By never using the same key twice, an attacker who compromises a session key or long-term key can only decrypt one piece of information, such as one packet of a network stream or one conversation.

PFS is a standard function of the SSH and Off-the-Record Messaging (OTR) protocols and is optional in the IPSec and TLS protocols. Despite its significant benefit to security, the vast majority of websites that use TLS do not fully incorporate PFS. There is minor overhead involved in PFS communication, but it is usually not prohibitive enough to justify leaving it out of a TLS-enabled website.

Heartbleed and the Importance of PFS

In April 2014, a member of Google's security team discovered that OpenSSL, a popular open-source implementation of the SSL/TLS protocol, had been vulnerable to a devastating exploit for more than two years. An attacker could use this exploit to retrieve plaintext user names, passwords, and even the cryptographic keys themselves.

This bug was named Heartbleed, and it affected hundreds of thousands—or about 17%—of the Internet's trusted, secure web servers. Although it would not have solved the problem and attackers would still be able to glean sensitive information, PFS would have greatly mitigated its effect. Any keys an attacker could have gleaned with the exploit would only be valid for that particular session. Without PFS, an attacker could use these keys to unlock encrypted communications from the past, putting a great deal more information at risk.

Guidelines for Applying Cryptography Techniques

Here are some guidelines you can use when implementing different cryptography techniques:

- Use DRM to restrict data leakage out of your organization.
- Use symmetric encryption algorithms to encrypt files stored on disk.
- Use asymmetric encryption to protect symmetric keys and authenticate users, especially online.
- Use a hash to verify the integrity of a message.
- Use a salt or initialization vector to add randomness to the encryption or hashing process.
- Use hybrid cryptography to take advantage of the speed of symmetric encryption, and the key protection of asymmetric encryption.
- Use a PKI system if you wish to use digital certificates for authentication and encryption.
- If you implement your own private PKI, export the certificate of your trusted root, and give that certificate to all partners who need to trust certificates issued by your PKI CAs.
- Use digital signatures to authenticate or prove authenticity.
- Issue digital certificates to all users, services, and devices that need to participate in PKI authentication and encryption.

ACTIVITY 3-9
Analyzing Cryptography Techniques

Scenario

In this activity, you will assess your understanding of cryptography techniques.

1. Which of the following statements is true?
   - ○ Symmetric encryption is faster than asymmetric encryption.
   - ○ Asymmetric encryption is faster than symmetric encryption.
   - ○ Symmetric and asymmetric encryption have equally fast performance.
   - ○ Both symmetric and asymmetric encryption have slow performance.

2. Moo and Lily use asymmetric encryption to send secret messages to each other. If Moo wants to send Lily a message that only Lily can read, which key should he use?
   - ○ Moo's public key
   - ○ Moo's private key
   - ○ Lily's public key
   - ○ Lily's private key

3. How does a salt improve a hash?
   - ○ It makes the key longer.
   - ○ It adds randomness.
   - ○ It makes the output longer.
   - ○ It doubles the algorithm strength.

4. What role did the initialization vector (IV) play in the eventual downfall of WEP as a wireless protection mechanism?
   - ○ It used a keyspace that was too short.
   - ○ It slowed down the encryption process enough that a hacker could exploit the delay.
   - ○ It facilitated replay attacks against the wireless access point.
   - ○ It was especially susceptible to dictionary and rainbow attacks.

5. What is the benefit of making your own CA subordinate to a commercial trusted root CA?
   - ○ You can request the trusted root to issue end user certificates on your behalf.
   - ○ You can obtain substantial cost savings by issuing certificates on behalf of the trusted root.
   - ○ You can save money by not having to install your own trusted root CA.
   - ○ You can save money by freely issuing any number of certificates that will still be trusted by the outside world.

6. How is a digital signature different from a digital certificate?

   ○ A digital signature is a message digest created by using a private key to ensure the authenticity of a file or transmission, whereas a digital certificate is a public key embedded into a file.

   ○ A digital certificate is a message digest created by using a private key to ensure the authenticity of a file or transmission, whereas a digital signature is a public key embedded into a file.

   ○ There is no real difference. They both refer to the same thing.

   ○ Digital signatures are based on symmetric encryption, whereas digital certificates are based on asymmetric encryption.

7. What consideration(s) must you weigh when deciding whether or not to use Perfect Forward Secrecy (PFS) on your website?

   ○ You have to determine if the benefit of using PFS is worth its licensing cost.

   ○ You have to decide if the additional performance overhead of PFS is substantial enough to restrict its use.

   ○ You have to decide if you have the resources to support a proprietary technology.

   ○ You have to decide if you have the resources to support an open-source technology.

TOPIC J

Site and Facility Design for Physical Security

In the previous topics, you learned about the logical aspects of building security into an information system. No security engineering lesson would be complete, however, without including the physical aspects of information security. The first step is to understand how to include security into the design of a facility. In this topic, you will learn about site and facility design for physical security.

Physical Security Overview

Physical security refers to the implementation and practice of various control mechanisms that are intended to restrict physical access to facilities. In addition, physical security involves increasing or assuring the reliability of certain critical infrastructure elements such as electrical power, data networks, and fire suppression systems. Challenges to physical security may be caused by a wide variety of events or situations, including:

- Facilities intrusions.
- Electrical grid failures.
- Fire.
- Personnel illnesses.
- Data network interruptions.

What is a Site?

The site is a physical facility that your organization uses. It can be an office building, a warehouse, a manufacturing plant, or any other location where you conduct business. It can comprise a single building or campus of buildings. It will have any number of people working at it, and may or may not be open to the general public. But regardless of its purpose, most sites will have the same things in common. They will need to be able to accommodate whatever operations are conducted at that location, provide security and safety for personnel, and most likely include some form of network and communications infrastructure.

Site Planning

As you prepare to move into, or renovate, a site for your facility use, you will need to conduct some site planning. The single most important goal in sight planning is to protect life, property, and operations. While all planning should be based around this concept and should not be compromised, your planning will need to also pay attention to convenience, accessibility, functionality, and attractiveness. A holistic approach can be taken to ensure that security and functionality are integrated and achieve a balance.

For example, providing a straight path between two locations may be the quickest way to allow people to move, but it also introduces the risk of a vehicle with too much speed and becoming a safety issue. Do not create a direct path straight to your front door. Use parallel roadways, winding paths, bollards (cement posts), or other blocking mechanisms to reduce the risk of a driver attempting to deliberately ram into the building, or panicking if the gas pedal sticks.

You could use an earthen berm (a raised bank or path), high curbs, trees, and other impediments to help keep vehicles from leaving the roadway. You could add barriers, swing gates, wide lawns, etc. to keep vehicles away from the building or travel more slowly as they approach.

Crime Prevention Through Environmental Design

Crime Prevention Through Environmental Design (CPTED) is a technique that uses landscape design and physical layout to reduce crime. You use elements such as water features, vegetation, and landforms to make the space attractive and welcoming, but also for enhancing security. Use open spaces to make it easy for anyone to see suspicious activity. You don't permit dense vegetation close to a building to the screen illicit activity. Similarly, you don't permit transformers, trash bins, and the like to provide areas of concealment. To use CPTED effectively without creating a poor image or fortress-like appearance, do the following:

- Treat gates or grills as public art.
- Make perimeter fences look attractive.
- Use thorny shrubbery.
- Use open grill designs and internal shutters instead of roller shutter blinds.
- Use toughened or laminated glass as an alternative to types of grills.
- Make all walkways naturally lead to the front entrance or guard shack.
- Direct all visitors through one entrance where a receptionist can greet the visitor and determine the purpose of their visit.
- Create shared community areas with seating that are attractive. If employees use these commonly, their presence will act as a good deterrent. Additionally, employees will have a community sense of ownership over the area and will be more alert to intruders.
- Use trees to help make shared areas feel safer.
- Design defensible spaces to have a single egress point so that potential intruders will be afraid of being trapped.
- Use closed-circuit TV cameras to extend guard presence.

Factors to Consider When Designing or Renovating a Site

When planning a new facility or performing significant renovations, there are several factors that should be considered. One issue involves the availability of critical infrastructures and services, such as electrical power, communications connections, and water supply. Although it may seem more efficient from an initial cost perspective to have all utilities and services enter the building in the same place and to have all controls for these systems in the one location, you need to plan for potential disaster scenarios, including:

- Install separate lines to the building for utilities.
- Ensure there are redundant lines for utilities.
- Install a backup power supply or generator.
- Use separate routes for utility lines and communications lines within the building.
- Make sure that the HVAC system in the building is adequate to keep employees comfortable and equipment safe.

Site Survey

When performing a site survey, you examine architectural drawings and do a physical walk-through of the facility to identify possible areas of vulnerability. You should also interview on-site personnel to obtain additional insight.

The survey should be performed by a team rather than a single individual. The survey should produce a report identifying the state of the site, including physical security strengths and weaknesses, and areas for improvement.

Your site survey should address the following key security concerns:

- Control of facility security before, during, and after hours of operation.
- Personnel security policies and procedures.
- Personnel employment screening.

- Site and building access control.
- Video surveillance.
- Natural surveillance.
- Incident response protocols.
- Degree of integration of the various building systems into overall security.
- Shipping and receiving security.
- Property identification and tracking.
- Proprietary systems and information security.
- Computer and network security.
- Personnel safety and workplace violence prevention.
- Mail screening and handling.
- Parking lot security.
- Data center security.
- Communication security.
- Executive and management protection.
- Business continuity procedures.
- Evacuation procedures.

The site survey report should include the following:

- A comprehensive overview of the entire facility including physical security controls, policy, procedures, and personal safety.
- The expected location of where you will place assets that need protection.
- A list of all discernible threats (both man-made and natural), their nature, and their approach vectors.

Fundamental Resources

There are several fundamental resource areas in an organization that require a high level of protection. Create a threat matrix listing each fundamental resource, the probability of attack (very low, low, medium, high, very high), and the consequence of loss. This is similar to a qualitative analysis, and will help you prioritize your security efforts.

When performing a site vulnerability assessment, keep in mind the following:

Fundamental Resource	Description
Physical plant	The physical plant area of protection is spread across an entire facility. In most cases, there are central control areas that require protection in addition to systems that encompass entire buildings or even a campus. Areas to be protected include: • Heating, ventilation, and air conditioning (HVAC) systems. • Electrical sources and lines. • Fire detection and suppression systems. • Lighting. • Doors. • Windows. • Fences. • Plumbing.
Computer facilities	Computer facilities include server rooms and data centers. Maintaining security in these areas by limiting access to only authorized individuals is a vital component of an overall security policy.

Fundamental Resource	Description
Data network	The data network protection area includes network hardware and wiring and the areas in which they reside. Network hardware includes routers, switches, firewalls, cabling, and wireless access points. This hardware should be protected in the same manner as other computer facilities to provide security against various attack vectors.
Personnel	People are a key asset that should be protected in any circumstance when physical security is involved. **Safety of personnel is a key issue for the CISSP® test.** In addition to protecting personnel, one must also form a defense against both electronic and physical attacks from authorized and unauthorized personnel.

Physical Threats

The physical threats a security specialist faces can come from many different areas.

Physical Threat	Description
Internal	Carnegie Mellon University (CMU) and the Central Intelligence Agency (CIA) have reported that 85% of security problems, whether they are physical or logical threats, come from within the organization. Although most were accidental, some were intentional. It is important to always consider what is happening inside of the organization, especially when physical security is concerned. For example, disgruntled employees may be a source of physical sabotage of important security-related resources.
External	When conducting a risk analysis of your physical security, attempt to determine all likely external threats. Are you close to an airport and therefore at risk of a plane crash? Is it possible that a car driving down the street could skid out of control, jump the curb, and smash into the front of your building? Could a domestic terrorist driving a truck laden with explosives pull up to your front door? Are the train tracks behind your building close enough that if the train derails it could run into your building? It is impossible for any organization to fully control external security threats, but you can work to mitigate the risks. Complete a thorough site survey, pay attention to security site planning, and use CPTED.
Man-made	Whether intentional or accidental, people can cause a number of physical threats. Man-made threats can be internal or external. A fire could be intentional or accidental. A sprinkler system may go off due to accident or negligence. A backhoe operator may accidentally dig up fiber optic cables and disable external network access. On the other hand, a disgruntled employee may choose to exact revenge by cutting the fiber optic cable on purpose.

Physical Threat	Description
Natural	Although natural threats are easy to overlook, they can pose a significant threat to the physical security of a facility. Is your building located in a floodplain? Are you in an earthquake, tornado, hurricane, typhoon, or other natural disaster zone?
	You might not be able to move your location, but buildings and rooms that contain important computing assets should be protected against likely weather-related problems. For example, after hurricane Sandy, financial institutions in New York moved their data centers to the fourth floor, rather than leaving them on the ground floor.
	Make sure that employees are trained in what to do in case of a natural disaster. Establish a communication system as well as an assembly area. Designate responsible parties to ensure that all personnel in their department have managed to evacuate safely.

Everyday Environmental Threats

In addition to the occasional natural disaster, your facility will have ordinary everyday environmental threats. These are internal threats caused by missing or inadequate environmental controls inside the building. They are summarized in the following table.

Threat	Description
Heat	Heat is the natural enemy of electronic equipment. Server rooms in particular need to be temperature controlled. The preferred temperature for a server room is between 65° and 70°F.
Dust	Dust is also another great enemy of electronic equipment. It will clog fans and eventually degrade electronic and mechanical system performance. In some regions where dust has a high iron content, it can actually corrode circuit boards, creating additional unwanted electrical paths between circuit board components. In addition to dust, hair, fibers, pollen, lint, and other airborne contaminants can collect in systems and clog air intake vents and fans.
Water	Water and excessive moisture can also pose a risk to your server room and computer equipment. Computers actually like to have cool temperatures and up to 50% humidity to prevent static electricity from damaging them. However, if a computer system is exposed to the elements or a very humid room, the humidity can actually become a problem. Always protect computer equipment from the risk of flooding, rain, fire sprinklers, excess humidity, condensation, dripping HVAC systems, or other sources of moisture.
Static Electricity	Static electricity is a natural result of contact with and friction against synthetic materials. It particularly happens when the air is cool and dry such as during the wintertime. Although static electricity is only a nuisance to humans, it is quite damaging to delicate circuit boards. Discharging static electricity into electronic components, especially while you are servicing them, can degrade the life expectancy of the device.
Caustic chemicals	Besides the risks associated with a chemical spill, caustic chemicals are often airborne and can collect in areas to eventually corrode and ruin electronic parts, circuit boards, and connectors. This is especially true around photographic dark rooms (including film-based x-ray labs), and areas where spray paint, solvents, cleaning chemicals, or any other kind of aerosols are frequently used.

Power Disruptions

Even in a region with a good power grid, power interruptions can and do happen. During normal operations, available voltage from the utility company will vary. Japan and the Americas use 110 volts, with the acceptable range being 105 - 127 volts. The rest of the world uses 220 volts, with the acceptable range being + or - 10% (198-242 volts).

The following table summarizes the different types of power disruptions.

Power Disruption Type	Description
Sag	Voltage briefly drops below acceptable operating range. Sags are also known as dips.
Spike	Voltage briefly rises above acceptable operating range. On a typical power grid, spikes can be as high as 30,000 volts, but they are so brief that they are successfully absorbed by a surge protector. Spikes are also known as transients.
Brownout	A prolonged sag. The obvious indicator is that incandescent lights dim, and fluorescent lights flicker. Motors might slow down, and some equipment might malfunction. Computer equipment might repeatedly restart. Brownouts happen when there is more demand on the electrical grid than the utility company can handle.
Blackout	Power is completely off. Blackouts can occur for any number of reasons including planned load shedding by the utility company, power grid failures, or even a neighborhood transformer that explodes.
Lightning strike	Lightning can strike a power grid, sending a tremendous surge of energy (millions of volts) through power lines. These strikes have destroyed televisions, computers and other electronic equipment in whole neighborhoods. They have been known to physically blow telephones off the walls in people's houses. The power surge from a lightning strike can also enter server rooms and data centers, jumping past UPSes and destroying equipment.

[handwritten note: Surge: Long spike]

Most server operating systems and network equipment can recover from a sudden interruption of power. However, where a power interruption can be truly disruptive or even destructive, is if an operating system or database management system is interrupted while writing a record to its file system or data store. In that case, the data can become corrupted and the transaction lost. Also, if the power briefly flickers on and off several times, an operating system that is continuously interrupted during its boot process can become corrupt. This is even true of advanced networking equipment such as Cisco routers and switches, which now use operating systems based on Linux, as opposed to a single binary image.

Another risk of a sudden power interruption is the disruption of the various services hosted on a server. Some services including network infrastructure, virtualization, and communications may not be able to automatically recover from a sudden power outage, requiring manual intervention by the administrator once the network is back up.

Critical Areas

Your facility may have several critical areas that require extra consideration to adequately protect them. They are summarized in the following table.

Area	Description
Wiring Closets	Wiring closets are often at risk because they are placed in communal areas in the building. Many offices in a single building might share a common wiring closet, leaving their data and communications systems vulnerable. A technician working on the phone system for one company might leave the door propped open for the entire floor while going to retrieve tools from his truck. He might also accidentally damage your phone connections while working on your neighbor's.
	If possible, insist on having your own dedicated wiring closets that are not shared with other building tenants.
Server Rooms	Server rooms are among the most critical areas in the building that you must protect. Consider putting cipher locks, biometric, or card access controls on the door. Don't forget to look for ways to circumvent the security, including lifting ceiling tiles to climb into the ceiling and over the wall. Also ensure that your server room has good dedicated electrical power sufficient to supply the machines, as well as its own HVAC.
	If you electronically protect the door entrance to the server room, you must also consider what will happen in the case of a power outage. In a developed nation with a redundant and advanced power grid, the likelihood of the power going out for any length of time is minimal. However, in a developing nation, where power goes out every day, consider having some kind of failsafe mechanism that allows for emergency access into the server room without the benefit of the electronics. This usually means that you have to have a physical key to unlock the door. Make sure this key is of the sort that cannot be duplicated, and that it is in possession of and protected by a failsafe operator.
	Also make sure that your server room has other forms of security including cameras, physical intrusion detection, and environmental monitors. A physical attack such as cutting off the power, turning off the AC, or setting off the sprinkler system would be a crude but potentially effective form of denial of service against the server room.
Media Storage Facilities	If you have a tape backup library, special care must be included in its implementation and design to protect the backup media. Make sure that where you store your backup media, you are protecting the tapes from electromagnetic fields (especially from motors, radiographic equipment, and elevator shafts), excessive heat or sunlight, dust, excessive moisture, or unauthorized access. Make sure that stored media is properly labeled, and stood upright on its end (like books on the shelf) as opposed to stacked flat. Be sure to have strict protocols for checking in and checking out backup media, logging all activities and access. The tape librarian should be the only person permitted to directly access the backup media.
Evidence Storage	If you have a security incident that may lead to a criminal investigation, you must be especially careful if you are storing evidence. Any system that is considered evidence should be photographed, documented, and bagged and tagged, with a log that carefully tracks the chain of custody of that item. There should be no gaps in the log as to where that item is at any one time. If you dedicate an area to evidence storage, make sure that it is secured and does not permit tampering or other evidence contamination.

Restricted Work Areas

You may need to implement extra security in some areas to protect the content of information stored in those areas. You can implement a variety of security options to create a restricted work area when this protection is needed.

- Secured areas should be restricted to authorized individuals with the proper level of access or clearance.
- Access control and closed-circuit television (CCTV) systems may be used to further safeguard secured areas.
- Simple options for securing areas include adding additional locks or lighting, and keeping an entry and exit log.
- More advanced protection for secured areas includes strengthened walls, stronger floors and ceilings, heavier doors, and other hardening to protect the area's contents.
- The use of mobile phones, smartphones, personal digital assistants (PDAs), cameras, and external computing devices can also be restricted or denied depending on the circumstances.

Example Restricted Work Area

Consider an area where national security documents are stored and used; by controlling physical access, the disclosure of information is limited to only those with access to the controlled area. When access is limited, it is easier to trace the source of unauthorized disclosure. If the list of people with access privileges was larger, it would be more difficult to locate the origin of disclosure. In many secured areas, it is difficult to transport unauthorized information into or out of the space.

Data Center Security

A data center is a dedicated facility specifically for computer operations. It is likely to have many large server racks with hundreds of virtual machines running on powerful servers, high-speed network links, high security, and integrated security and environmental controls.

Many organizations choose to build small data centers in a dedicated area on their premises. It might be a building on a campus, a floor in a building, or even a single room. Large data centers, however, are entire facilities. A typical global company will have several data center sites in separate geographical regions to provide redundancy and fault tolerance. These data centers are backups to each other, hosting mirrored copies of the data that are updated in real time. They are very expensive to operate, but can mean the difference between a company staying in business or going out of business. For example, during hurricane Sandy, financial companies on Wall Street were unable to access local data centers. They re-routed all data processing and network operations to remote data centers in other parts of the U.S., or even overseas.

The value of having a data center is that you can concentrate your systems, storage, and data into a single location. Your data center security then can be highly focused on providing appropriate controls for servers and networks, with less concern for other types of operations.

In terms of site security, the data center is the single most important physical location your company can have. Follow these best practices when implementing data center security:

- Use a multi-layered approach to security:
  - Start with perimeter controls—fences, gates, guards, lighting, and CCTV.
  - Institute increasingly restrictive rings of security leading to the actual server room.
  - Use biometrics and access control cards to limit and log entry.
  - Put cameras everywhere.
  - Ensure that physical security controls cannot be bypassed.
- Limit movement around the data center by limiting on-site personnel to those required for maintenance and security.
  - Do not advertise the purpose of the facility.
  - Prohibit the general public from visiting the data center.

- Prohibit your own employees from visiting the data center, unless they have legitimate business there.
- Monitor and manage the data center remotely through a separate Network Operations Center (NOC).

Guidelines for Designing Site and Facility Security

Here are some guidelines you can use when designing physical security for your site or facility:

- Conduct a site survey and do some site planning to identify and mitigate potential vulnerable areas and security risks before you occupy the facility.
- Consider all physical aspects of your site including HVAC, power and other utilities, fire suppression, windows, and physical access.
- Always remember that your first priority in designing site security is to protect human life.
- Recognize that most threats will come from within, either malicious or inadvertent.
- Use natural design and physical access controls to mitigate external threats.
- Have backup power systems such as UPS and standby generators.
- Control everyday environmental threats such as heat, dust, moisture, and static electricity.
- Control other common environmental threats such as lightning strikes from electrical storms and airborne contaminants and caustic chemicals.
- Pay special attention to securing critical work areas such as wiring closets, server rooms, media and evidence storage rooms.
- If necessary, provide extra physical security by creating restricted work areas for machines that handle sensitive data.
- If your organization is larger, you can concentrate your network and system security efforts by grouping your servers and storage into a central data center.
- Consider having more than one data center for fault tolerance.

ACTIVITY 3-10
Discussing Site and Facility Design for Physical Security

Scenario

In this activity, you will assess your knowledge of site and facility design for physical security.

---

1. **Use this scenario for Questions 1-2.** Your client is considering moving its warehouse and distribution operations to a different location in Southern California. The property's price has been slashed, and your client is eager to take advantage of any savings. They have asked you, a security consultant, to go on a site survey with them to help assess the location's existing physical security. The site is in an industrial area of town, about 2 miles from the airport. A raised freeway passes by the building, with the front of the building almost underneath the freeway's edge. You drive underneath the freeway, between concrete pylons covered in graffiti, and pull straight up to the building's front door. A six-foot chain link fence encircles the small parking lot in front. The parking lot has a single 20 foot lamp post in the middle. There is no guard shack outside. The warehouse is large, with side doors that open to surrounding alleys that are actually part of the property. The alleys don't seem to have been used much. Fresh graffiti can be seen on the alley walls, and the outside doors that lead to the alleys are not well lit. Bars cover the lower windows, some of which are broken. A train track runs parallel to the back of the building, 100 feet from the loading dock. The realtor points out the easy freeway access, adding that the train track is a plus. She explains that the previous owner had an agreement with the railway company to load goods directly from the dock onto the train, thus saving a considerable amount of money in trucking fees.

   From the scenario, what external threats do you identify?

2. **What natural threats do you identify?**

3. You enter the building and take a look around, looking for a suitable place for the data center. The entire indoors is one large open manufacturing area. There are no interior walls, just cubicles off to one side. The loading dock can be seen at the back. A short flight of stairs leads to a few small offices built overhead along one wall. The offices have large windows that overlook the open space of the production facility below.

   Is there any suitable place for the data center, restricted work area, or to house critical equipment?

4. You step out onto the loading dock. Off to the corner, you notice a large power generator housed in a cage. The generator looks like it has been used for several years. It appears to be in pretty good shape. You ask the realtor if power is a problem in the area. She says that she is not aware of any problems.

   Do you think that power disruptions are likely at this location?

---

5. Does the building appear to have any environmental conditions that could threaten computer equipment?

TOPIC K

Physical Security Implementation in Sites and Facilities

In the previous topic, you got started with physical security. You learned about physical threats to a facility, and how to include security in its design. You will now complete your knowledge of security engineering by studying how to implement physical security at a site. In this topic, you will learn about physical security implementation in sites and facilities.

Physical Security Implementation

Physical security implementation involves a wide range of techniques and disciplines. You can start by focusing on common features necessary to make any location safe and functional for human activity. These features include power, environmental control, secure windows, and fire prevention/suppression.

Generators and UPS

A power generator and an uninterruptible power supply (UPS) are both an excellent short term line of defense against power disruptions. A generator is a gasoline or diesel powered engine that generates electricity while running. A UPS is basically a battery with a power inverter. The outlet from the wall charges the battery. The battery then supplies the inverter, which in turn supplies the computer. Since the UPS is always plugged into the wall, its battery is continuously charging as long as normal electrical power is available.

Not all backup power generators are designed to start automatically. Some must be manually started and the power cut over. Additionally, a generator will run out of fuel unless continuously supplied. Being an engine, it requires regular maintenance and oil. Smaller generators are only designed to run for 8 - 10 hours, and then must rest for a few hours to cool down before they can be restarted again.

Similarly, a UPS will not run indefinitely. Most UPSes are designed to supply power for one half hour to two hours; just long enough to finish existing tasks and allow a server to shut down gracefully. Most UPSes have a serial or USB port that the server can connect to so that it can receive a shutdown signal when power is lost. This requires that you install an application (provided with the UPS) on the server to watch for that signal. Some devices, particularly switches and routers, do not have the ability to be alerted by the UPS. The risk of leaving such devices on the UPS is that they will continue to run until the UPS battery drains completely. When the power comes back on, smaller UPSes that are not configured properly may get stuck in a cycle of constantly trying to shut down and restart. They will click and beep loudly as they try to resume normal operations. If you are in an area that experiences regular power outages, configure your UPS to expect poor quality power.

A large UPS found in a server room will generally require its own dedicated circuit (sometimes 40 amps or more) and will be hardwired into that circuit (not plugged into a normal power outlet). UPSes by design use specialized AC cables that disallow devices from being plugged directly into a wall.

Biometric and access control lock systems should also have their own backup batteries. You must decide whether or not, in the case of a prolonged power failure, you want such locks to fail safe or fail secure. A fail safe lock can be opened, at least from the inside. A fail secure lock cannot. Most biometric and access control systems can have a break glass emergency switch that allows personnel to leave the room, locking the door behind them.

HVAC

A *heating, ventilation, and air conditioning (HVAC) system* controls the environment inside a building.

Most experts recommend that temperatures in a computer facility should be in the range of 65 to 75 degrees. In an effort to save energy and money, this number is rising. Vendors are now testing equipment to run in data centers with temperatures as high as 85. This would be uncomfortable for humans, but many data centers are unoccupied or lightly occupied. Some server racks have self-contained airflow mechanisms. Rather than cooling an entire room, sheets of plastic surround the rack, restricting airflow to the rack itself. Cool air is directed into the front of the rack, drawn across the equipment mounted inside, and is exhausted out the rear and back up into the cooling system. In this way, the equipment can be protected while the rest of the data center stays warmer.

The relative humidity in the facility should be between 40% and 60%. High and low temperatures and humidity can damage equipment. Low humidity causes static electricity; high humidity causes corrosion.

Positive air pressure is a must. Air should be forced from the data center and server rooms to keep contaminants out. Filters on HVAC systems keep dust to a minimum and must be changed regularly. Ultraviolet (UV) light is used to fight bacteria, germs, and viruses. Intakes for the HVAC systems should be hard to access and protected with filters to prevent the introduction of contaminants.

To ensure that HVAC systems are running properly, it is important to monitor them both locally and remotely.

Windows

Windows are easy to break into, making them targets for intruders. They are a potential vulnerability that needs to be addressed. When installing exterior windows, special attention should be paid to the glazing, the frames, anchoring the frame to the building structure, and types of glass to minimize the chance of a break-in as well as minimize any hazardous effects of flying glass in case of impact or explosion. Consider using steel frames that are securely fastened or cemented into the surrounding structure.

A window should not be placed adjacent to a door. If the window is broken, the intruder could reach in and unlock the door. Use laminated glass instead of conventional glass, and install window guards such as grills, screens, or meshwork across the opening to protect against entry. Windows on the ground floor should not be able to be opened. Windows up to the fourth floor should have alarms that will sound if the window opens.

You can also use glass break sensors as an intrusion detection method for buildings that have a lot of glass windows or doors.

The following table summarizes the different types of glass.

Glass Type	Description
Tempered glass	This is similar to glass installed on car windshields. It can resist breakage and if smashed will disintegrate into small cubes with no sharp edges. Use tempered glass for entrance doors and adjacent panels.
Wired glass	Wired glass has a wire mesh embedded into it to make it resistant to impact from blunt objects. It's harder to break this type of glass. This is good for small utility windows on the ground floor where ventilation is needed but aesthetics are less important.
Laminated glass	This is two ordinary sheets of glass that are bonded together with a middle layer of resilient plastic. If the glass is struck, it may crack into many small pieces, but the pieces will stick to the plastic of the inner material, leaving the sheet of glass largely intact. This is a good choice for human safety.

Glass Type	Description
Bullet resistant glass	This type of glass uses layers (standard being 1 1/4 inch thick) to protect the glass from a 9 mm round. This type of glass is used in high risk areas such as banks.

Fire Prevention

The first rule of fire protection is fire prevention. Local fire codes specify the fire prevention practices required or expected by the community. Periodic fire drills are one typical requirement. Other requirements might include:

* The elimination of storage items and trash in fire stairwells.
* Not storing fuel or volatile chemicals near paper or rags, or in a closed area where combustible fumes can collect.
* The specifications of fire extinguisher types used in a facility.
* The type of fire suppression system used in a building.
* Maximum permitted occupancy in a room.
* Leaving exits unblocked.
* Leaving emergency exit doors unlocked during business hours.

Fire Suppression

Fires in computer facilities are especially dangerous. The damage done to computers is extremely expensive, and the chemicals used in the machines may emit toxic substances. The insulation on data cables will either be made of polyvinyl chloride (PVC) or some form of plenum-grade materials (special plastic or Teflon). PVC cables are cheaper, but give off toxic fumes when they burn. Plenum-grade cables are more expensive, but will not give off toxic fumes. Unless plenum-grade cable is required by local fire code, most companies will opt for PVC.

It is not practical to fight these fires with small extinguishers or to douse fires with water. Special gasses are used to extinguish fires in computer facilities. The gasses are typically discharged at high velocity from special vents under a raised floor to quickly displace oxygen in the room and put out any fire.

If an electrical fire breaks out in a server room or amongst your computer equipment, the first thing to do is to cut the power. This will immediately stop feeding the source of the fire, which is the high electrical current that generates enough heat to burn circuits and wiring. Immediately unplug the offending device or turn off the power breaker. Large UPSes have an emergency kill switch to assist with this. If necessary, use a class C fire extinguisher on the electrical fire. If the fire is small, limited to a single box or wire that you can easily access, it may not be necessary to use a fire extinguisher. Just make sure that there is no open flame, or risk of a fire starting from a superheated component. If possible, remove the affected device from the room where it cannot cause any additional damage or set off a smoke detector.

Always practice good safety when dealing with electrical fires. Do not put yourself or others in danger.

Fire Extinguishing Gasses

The first fire extinguishing gas used in large-scale computer fires was Halon. Halon, however, is full of chlorofluorocarbons, which are ozone-depleting substances. The Montreal Protocol of 1989 banned production and installation of Halon systems effective January 1, 1994. Systems already in place could continue to use Halon but it is becoming increasingly difficult to find it to replenish the system. New substances are available that can replace Halon for large computer fires, including FM-200, Inergen, argon, and FE-13.

Hand-Held Fire Extinguishers

In some cases, small fires may be extinguished using hand-held fire extinguishers. All fires are caused by the presence of fuel, heat, and oxygen. They join together to create a chemical reaction. Extinguishers are designed to remove one or more of those components so that the fire goes out. However, because all fires are not fueled in the same way, fire extinguishers are not universal. They vary according to the type of fire and extinguishing agent used. Since class A, B, and C can be put out using the same type of powder, it is possible to manufacture an extinguisher to address all three types. All fire extinguishers should be inspected on a regular basis.

Make sure the personnel know how to properly use a handheld fire extinguisher, pointing at the base of the fire, not into the flames, sweeping from side to side until the fire is out. Also make sure that personnel know how to choose an appropriate extinguisher depending upon the fire type. For example, you do not want people using a water-based extinguisher on a grease or electrical fire.

Extinguisher Classes and Fire Types

The following table describes the class of extinguishers and the types of fires they are meant to extinguish.

Class	Type of Fire	Agent Used	How to Remember
A	Common combustibles like wood, paper, and so on	Water, soda acid, multipurpose dry powders	Common combustibles create Ash
B	Liquids and fuels	CO_2, gas, foam, multipurpose dry powders	Liquids are stored in Barrels
C	Electrical fires	CO_2, gas, multipurpose dry powders	Electricity moves in Circuits
D	Combustible metals	Class D dry powder	Metal fires are Dangerous
K	Kitchen fires	Wet chemical	K is for Kitchen

Water-Based Extinguishers

Water-based systems of various types are used to extinguish fires in most areas of a building. These are commonly known as sprinkler systems, because a water sprinkler is mounted in the ceiling of the room. Sprinkler systems are used to contain class A fires and protect human life. They should not be used in data centers and server rooms, as they will destroy your equipment. The following table summarizes the various types of water-based systems.

Water-Based System Type	Mode of Operation/Considerations
Wet pipe	**Mode of Operation:** Water is stored in the pipes at all times. When a given temperature is reached, a heat-sensitive vial in the sprinkler head will break, releasing the water. Different vials with different sensitivities can be used in different areas. **Considerations:** Pipes may leak due to corrosion or freezing. If a sprinkler head malfunctions, water can damage the surrounding area.

Water–Based System Type	Mode of Operation/Considerations
Dry pipe	**Mode of Operation:** Pipes are filled with compressed air. If there is a loss of air pressure, the valve will open, filling the pipe with water. Because pipes are not filled with water until a fire is detected, there are fewer concerns with freezing or accidental leaks. Sprinkler heads are individually activated like the wet pipes. **Considerations:** No leakage and no unexpected discharge unless the fire system malfunctions.
Preaction	**Mode of Operation:** Preaction requires two separate actions to happen before discharging. First, a fire is detected. Second, an alarm is activated. There may be a short delay between the alarm and the release of the water to allow time for people to leave the area. **Considerations:** Same considerations that apply to dry pipes. Incurs higher costs to purchase and install.
Deluge	**Mode of Operation:** High output sprinklers in wet or dry pipe systems that saturate the affected area. The sprinklers are always open and when the system is activated, it delivers water to all sprinkler heads. **Considerations:** Not used in computer facilities due to high water output. May be appropriate in areas where extensive fire damage is expected.

[handwritten annotation: thermal fusible link]

Guidelines for Implementing Site and Facility Security

Here are some guidelines you can follow for implementing site and facility physical security:

- Make sure that you have standby power available such as UPS or backup generator.
- Make sure that HVAC systems are set to an appropriate temperature for your equipment.
- Make sure that appropriate window types are installed to resist break-ins.
- Make sure that you have appropriate fire prevention and suppression systems in place such as sprinkler and gas systems.
- Make sure that fire extinguishers supplied around electronic equipment are class C.
- Make sure that personnel know how to choose and use a fire extinguisher appropriately.

ACTIVITY 3-11
Discussing Site and Facility Physical Security Implementation

Scenario

In this activity, you will assess your understanding of site and facility physical security implementation.

1. When would it be useful to deploy both a backup power generator and a UPS for your server room?

2. How do you think that a data center can benefit from racks that have self-contained air cooling systems?

3. What type of glass would you use in a restroom window at your facility?

4. You have a small server room in your facility. The server room has a high-capacity UPS that is directly wired to a 40A circuit. Management has insisted that, for security's sake, yours is the only fingerprint that can unlock the biometric lock on the server room door. You are not always at the facility. You are worried that a fire in the server room could spell disaster for the rest of the building if you are not available to immediately open the door.

   What steps can you take to maintain security while minimizing the risk in case of fire?

5. In what ways can hand-held fire extinguishers and sprinkler systems enhance fire suppression in a data center?

6. If you choose to install a water-based system at a data center, which one would be appropriate?

Summary

In this lesson, you learned about engineering security into an information system. You started with including security in the engineering lifecycle, examining models and frameworks that are used to ensure a consistent security approach. You went on to study individual system components, their vulnerabilities, and how to mitigate those vulnerabilities. You continued by learning about the risks associated with new technologies and how to manage those risks. You then learned about cryptography, a bedrock of the CIA triangle. Finally, you learned about site and facility physical security.

What cryptography techniques do you use in your own organization?

Of the new technologies you just learned about (such as Big Data, Cloud Services, mobile devices, embedded systems, etc., which do you think will provide the greatest security challenges to your organization, and why?

Note: Check your CHOICE Course screen for opportunities to interact with your classmates, peers, and the larger CHOICE online community about the topics covered in this course or other topics you are interested in. From the Course screen you can also access available resources for a more continuous learning experience.

4 | Communications and Network Security

Lesson Time: 4 hours, 30 minutes

Lesson Objectives

In this lesson, you will:

- Analyze network architecture security.

- Analyze security of network components.

- Identify communication channel security risks and mitigation.

- Identify mitigation tools and tactics for network attacks.

Lesson Introduction

In the last lesson, you learned about mitigation against vulnerabilities in system components, multiple architectures, and physical security. Many of those topics are pervasive to the CISSP material, and you will see many of them throughout the course. Topics like defense in depth, cryptography, and network design will present themselves in Communication and Network Security as well. The network is changing, which means additional security measures are necessary. Voice and video are now delivered across the network, where before those were separate networks. Because the network has become such an important part of the business, protecting it has become critical.

TOPIC A

Network Protocol Security

Networking technologies use many different protocols, and each one comes with its own challenges to security. In this topic, you'll learn about some of the major networking protocols and their vulnerabilities, along with ways to mitigate them.

 Note: To learn more, view the LearnTO presentations from the **LearnTO** tile on the CHOICE course screen.

Network Security Overview

Network security is one of the most critical and complex topics in IT because so many rapidly changing technologies are involved. The security professional must know how to secure each technology separately and handle interoperability issues. You need to know the basics (routers, firewalls, TCP/IP, cabling, etc.), but you also need to understand such topics as web security, virtualization, cloud computing, social networking threats, and wireless technologies. Networks no longer have clear-cut boundaries, because users are often on the road or working from home. As the complexity of the network increases, the number and type of threats increases as well.

OSI Model

The evolution of data networks began in the early 1970s. At that time, each vendor created its own unique communications protocols with little or no interoperability. Beginning work in 1977 and publishing in early 1980, the International Organization for Standardization (ISO) implemented the *Open Systems Interconnection (OSI) model* for data communications. The intent was to provide a framework for all communications systems. The ISO committees were well aware of the various networking efforts. The goal was to create interoperability in networking products, as well as a way to reference networking topics. As part of this effort, they promoted encapsulation at the layers to allow for a certain amount of independence. The different layers operate independently and are isolated on a technical level. The headers established for the layers allow for layer identification and communication. Abstraction is also part of this process. Abstraction attempts to hide header information from all but the immediately adjacent layers.

Today, the OSI model is used to describe the various functions provided in an information network without regard for any specific implementation. Consisting of multiple layers, it is a reference model for how data is exchanged between any two points in a network. Although one might think that the OSI model is a bit dated, its principles still hold true to networking today. The layers are still referenced frequently in documentation and by product vendors to indicate the function of devices; a Layer 3 switch, for example. Most network engineers, when troubleshooting network problems, also refer to the problem or solution by its OSI layer.

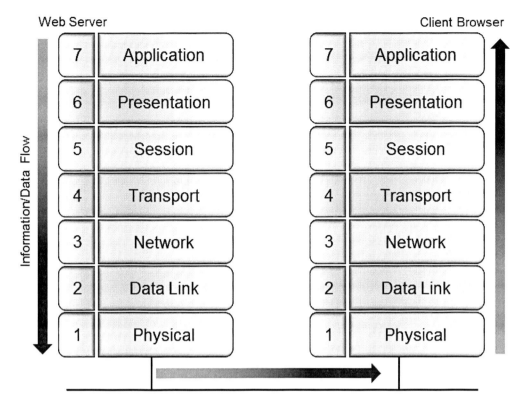

Figure 4-1: Data flow from a web server to a client browser through the OSI model layers.

OSI Model Layers

The OSI model encompasses seven different layers or functional differences.

OSI Model Layer	Function
Layer 7: Application	The *Application layer* is where applications send information into the communications network. Application interfaces built into the operating systems provide a portal for sending and receiving information.
	Examples of Layer 7 protocols include Simple Mail Transport Protocol (SMTP), Post Office Protocol version 3 (POP3), File Transfer Protocol (FTP), and the Hypertext Transfer Protocol (HTTP), among others. Many of the layers include a *Protocol Data Unit (PDU),*which is a unit of data as it appears at each layer of the OSI model. The PDU at Layer 7 is the data.
Layer 6: Presentation	The *Presentation layer* ensures that the receiver can properly interpret the transmitted information. Early issues included the translation from the Extended Binary Coded Decimal Information Code (EBCDIC) used on mainframe systems and the American Standard Code for Information Interchange (ASCII). Today, data representations such as MPEG, GIF, JPEG, and others are tagged when included in web pages, emails, or other documents to ensure the correct display of information. The Presentation layer can provide compression and encryption services as well.

OSI Model Layer	Function
Layer 5: Session	A *network session* is a persistent, logical connection between two hosts or nodes. When an application requires the creation of a session for any reason, the *Session layer* is used. Session startup, session continuation, and session termination are all functions of this layer.

The Session layer allows for the transmission of information in three different modes:

- *Full-duplex*—Simultaneous two-way data communication. A phone call is a full-duplex conversation with both parties able to talk at the same time.
- *Half-duplex*—Two-way data communication over a single channel; conversations with walkie-talkies are half-duplex with only one person being able to talk at a time.
- *Simplex*—One-way data communication only; a radio station provides simplex communication.

The network file system (NFS) and remote procedure calls (RPCs) use the Session layer.

OSI Model Layer	Function
Layer 4: Transport	As application information is delivered to the *Transport layer*, an application identifier is added to the data so that the receiving device knows which application is to receive the information. This application identifier is commonly implemented as a port number. The Transport layer accepts information and then creates smaller units called *segments* to control information flow, making sure it is more acceptable to the Layer 3 and 2 networks. The Transport layer may also implement some type of flow control so that information is not lost due to buffer overflow or other network problems. The Transport layer builds on the work done by the Session layer to create end-to-end connections between hosts.

Examples of protocols that function at Layer 4 include Transmission Control Protocol (TCP) and the User Datagram Protocol (UDP). The protocols are functionally equivalent, but TCP is connection-oriented whereas UDP is connectionless. The decision regarding which of those two protocols to use is usually determined by the application, with a possible override by the user or an administrator. The PDU at the Transport layer is a segment.

Firewalls, gateways, and Layer 4 switches are all Transport layer devices.

OSI Model Layer	Function
Layer 3: Network	The *Network layer* is where the concept of logical networking is introduced. Layer 3 networks use a component of the logical addresses to represent networks. The logical address will be an IP address in most modern networks. In the past, it might have included Novell® IPX™ or Apple® AppleTalk®. In allowing the forwarding of packets and datagrams, Layer 3 can connect different physical networks by augmenting the Data Link layer information. The ability to move information between different physical networking structures gives data networks flexibility. At Layer 3, devices are grouped together in networks by a common network address. Each device must have a unique device within a network. A Layer 3 function called *routing* allows the devices in one network to send information to and receive information from other logical network devices. This requires the use of a *routable* protocol such as Internet Protocol (IP). Not all early protocols were routable because they had no way to distinguish unique networks. An example of a Layer 3 address is the IP address used in networks, such as the Internet, that are based on the Transmission Control Protocol/Internet Protocol (TCP/IP). An IP address, along with its subnet mask, can uniquely identify the network and the node of any device on the network. Routers and gateway devices support Layer 3. Routers can use dynamic routing protocols like Routing Information Protocol (RIP) and Open Shortest Path First (OSPF) to help discover available networks. The PDU at the Network layer is either packet or datagram, with packet being the most common term.
Layer 2: Data Link	The *Data Link layer* is where bits are organized into frames. Most Data Link layer protocols define the structure of a frame and introduce the use of Media Access Control (MAC) addresses. The MAC address is a 48-bit hexadecimal number that identifies the Organizationally Unique ID (OUI) and the serial number of the device. When transmitting a frame on the media, most protocols include a MAC address to indicate the sending and receiving devices. Transmission error detection is often included in a Data Link layer protocol. Ethernet uses a *Cyclical Redundancy Check (CRC)* function to discover errors. The CRC is included in a trailer or footer of each frame and is checked by the receiver. If the receiver's CRC calculation does not match the sender's, the receiver knows the frame no longer has integrity. At Layer 2, all network devices are considered to be on the same physical network. The Data Link layer was later split into two sub-layers, the Logical Link Control (LLC) and the MAC layers. LLC interfaces with the Network layer above and the MAC with the Physical layer below. Bridges and switches support Layer 2. The PDU at the Data Link layer is a frame.
Layer 1: Physical	The *Physical layer* is where bits are transmitted across a physical medium. This layer describes the type of wire, fiber, or wireless communication medium and the transmission of bits. Connectors and physical network termination are also part of the Physical layer. Examples of Layer 1 items include Ethernet signaling, cabling, RJ45 connectors and jacks, and wireless access point frequencies. Repeaters, network interface cards (NICs), and hubs support Layer 1. The PDU at the Physical layer is a bit.

Mnemonics and the OSI Model

Remembering the OSI layers is an essential task required of every CISSP® candidate. People often use the following mnemonics as a memory tool to help recall the order of layers.

- Please Do Not Throw Sausage Pizza Away (PDNTSPA) identifies the order of Layer 1 through Layer 7.
- Please Don't Nudge The Sleeping Porpoises Again (PDNTSPA) identifies the order of Layer 1 through Layer 7.
- All People Seem To Need Data Processing (APSTNDP) identifies the order of Layer 7 through Layer 1.

TCP/IP Model

The *TCP/IP model* represents a collection of communications protocols used to govern data exchange on the Internet. It was developed in the late 1960s from a project sponsored by the Defense Advanced Research Projects Agency (DARPA) to design the Internet's protocols. Not only is TCP/IP the *de facto* protocol suite for the Internet, but many vendors have adapted it for their default protocol as well. For example, Microsoft and Novell both now use TCP/IP as their networking protocol. Nearly all the work done on TCP/IP is documented in request for comments (RFCs).

TCP/IP Model Layers

The TCP/IP model is simple and specifies four different layers in the communication function.

TCP/IP Model Layer	Function
Application	The *Application layer* is similar in function to the Session, Presentation, and Application layers of the OSI model. At the Application layer, application programs begin the process of sending information, and end the process at the destination device or application.
Host-to-Host	The *Host-to-Host layer* is similar in function to the Transport layer of the OSI model. At the Host-to-Host layer, the TCP and UDP protocols support application-to-application information transfer using port numbers to identify the applications. These port numbers become very important for firewalls and other network devices to identify traffic on the network.
Networking	The *Networking layer* creates logical networks using IP network addresses. It is similar in function to the Network layer of the OSI model.
	IP is the networking protocol used in this model.
Network Access	The *Network Access layer* covers the physical networking requirements of generating frames on a cable, fiber, or wireless network. It is often compared to the Physical and Data Link layers of the OSI model.
	Ethernet is an example of a Network Access layer protocol that is used on the local area network (LAN). Frame Relay, X.25, and Asynchronous Transfer Mode (ATM) are examples of Network Access layer protocols used on the Wide Area Network (WAN).

OSI and TCP/IP Model Comparison

The OSI model and the TCP/IP model are not related but their functions are often compared.

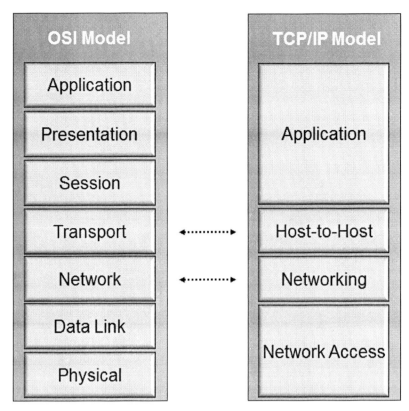

Figure 4-2: Comparison of the OSI and TCP/IP models.

TCP/IP Protocols

There are several primary communications protocols that constitute the TCP/IP protocol suite.

TCP/IP Protocol	Description
IP	*IP* is used to move information between nodes on an IP network. It supports logical addressing in the form of an IP address and subnet mask combination. The IP protocol establishes encapsulation and support for the data delivered from the upper layers. IP is a connectionless protocol but it does check for header integrity with a checksum. IPv4 provides 32 bits for addressing. IPv6 provides 128 bits for addressing.
TCP	*TCP* is a connection-oriented protocol used in the TCP/IP model. TCP features a session establishment process, process identification using port numbers, a data accounting feature, data segmentation to meet network frame size limitations, error detection, retransmission of lost segments, flow control, and a session termination process.
UDP	*UDP* is a connectionless protocol that supports process identification using port numbers and error detection.

TCP/IP Protocol	Description
DHCP	The *Dynamic Host Configuration Protocol (DHCP)* is used to assign IP addresses to devices in an IP network. This occurs in the following four-step process using a DHCP server: 1. Clients request the services of a DHCP server. This request will be sent as a broadcast, called a *discover*, to the entire network, as the client does not have a server's IP address to which it could send a unicast. 2. When a client request is received, the server will send an offer. This offer will go out as a broadcast, as the client does not have an IP address at this time. 3. When the client receives the offer, it will return a request for an address. The DHCP server manages a group of addresses known as a pool for each network. Addresses are assigned on a first come, first served basis. 4. The server returns an acknowledgement with the assigned address. Addresses are provided for a given period of time using a lease process.
DNS	*Domain Name Service (DNS)* is a protocol that is used to resolve or translate device and domain names into IP addresses using a central repository of device names and IP addresses in each organization, and a locator function in the Internet to locate the organizational repositories.
ICMP	The *Internet Control Message Protocol (ICMP)* is used by operating systems and network devices to send error messages or relay messages back to devices that a device is unavailable. Ping and Traceroute use ICMP to help system administrators discover network congestion.
ARP	The *Address Resolution Protocol (ARP)* is used in the TCP/IP model to resolve known IP addresses to unknown MAC addresses. By resolving the IP address of a device to an address that can be used to send information over the local LAN, IP devices are able to communicate over the Ethernet network.
RARP	The *Reverse Address Resolution Protocol (RARP)* is used when a device knows its MAC address but needs to request an IP address from a server. It can be used by diskless workstations in high-security environments.
FTP	The *File Transfer Protocol (FTP)* transfers files from one device to another over TCP/IP. It operates in a client-server architecture, where one or more devices host data that client devices request. Standard FTP offers little security, but similar protocols like FTP over SSH and File Transfer Protocol Secure (FTPS) offer encryption services with data transfer.
HTTP	*Hyper Text Transfer Protocol (HTTP)* is a TCP/IP protocol that enables clients to connect to and interact with websites. It is responsible for transferring the data on web pages between systems. HTTP defines how messages are formatted and transmitted, as well as what actions web servers and the client's browser should take in response to different commands. By default, HTTP is not secure; HTTPS is a secure alternative that incorporates SSL/TLS encryption.
SMTP	The *Simple Message Transport Protocol (SMTP)* is a standard for email delivery. SMTP is used for outbound mail and for mail between messaging servers. Much of its earliest success was attributed to the store and forward method it used for delivering mail between systems.

TCP/IP Protocol	Description
POP and IMAP 	Both the *Post Office Protocol (POP)* and *Internet Message Access Protocol (IMAP)* are considered mail retrieval protocols. IMAP generally leaves the messages on the server, allowing the user to check mail from several different hosts. POP generally pulls the mail down to the host the user is using. If the user checks email from multiple hosts, there is the potential for mail to be located on multiple machines.
LDAP 389	The *Lightweight Directory Access Protocol (LDAP)* is a directory access protocol that runs over TCP/IP. LDAP clients authenticate to the LDAP service, and the service's schema defines the tasks that clients can and cannot perform while accessing a directory database, the form the directory query must take, and how the directory server will respond. An alternative is Secure LDAP (LDAPS), which implements SSL/TLS encryption to prevent eavesdropping and tampering attacks.
NetBIOS	*Network Basic Input Output System (NetBIOS)* is an interface that allows applications to properly communicate over different computers in a network. NetBIOS has three basic functions: communication over sessions, connectionless communication using datagrams, and name registration.
NFS	*Network File System (NFS)* is an older file sharing network protocol that is predominant in communicating with Linux/UNIX environments. Secure NFS (SNFS) implements DES-based encryption.
IGMP	The *Internet Group Management Protocol (IGMP)* is used with IP multicasting to indicate when a device is joining a multicast-enabled application data stream.

X.500 (handwritten annotation)

> **Note:** For a complete listing and description of protocols, visit **www.protocols.com/pbook/ tcpip1/**.

IP Networking

The Internet Protocol (IP) is a Layer 3 protocol that is responsible for nearly all network traffic. It is used in both public and private networks. Part of what accounts for its near ubiquitous presence is that it is a non-proprietary routable protocol. There were other Layer 3 protocols and other routable protocols but IP has become the *de facto* standard. The term has developed a usage beyond the Layer 3 protocol and is frequently used to describe the entire network stack.

It comes in two versions, IPv4 and IPv6.

IP Version	Description
IPv4	IPv4 provides 32 bits for addressing. The subnet mask is a required element of an IPv4 address. The subnet mask is what determines the routing of the IP address as it divides the IP address into two components. The first part will be the network address and the second part will be the node address.
	For example, in the IP address of 192.168.10.10 with a subnet mask of 255.255.255.0, the first three octets of the initial IP address of 192.168.10 is the network portion and the final octet of .10 would be the node address.

IP Version	Description
IPv6	It became apparent in the mid to late 1990s that the IPv4 address was going to run into issues particularly around availability. Although mathematically a 32 bit number provides approximately 4.2 billion numbers and that was considerably more hosts than existed at the time, it wasn't too hard to see that it wasn't going to be enough in the future. Therefore, IPv6 was proposed as a 128 bit number. This creates an absolutely huge number (340 undecillion) and should provide sufficient growth for the foreseeable future. It also provides for more efficient routing and has support for security and quality of service built in.

Protocol Vulnerabilities

None of the original TCP/IP protocols can be considered secure. In the early days of networking, engineers were simply trying to make the system work. Security was not even a consideration. As a result, newer protocols (such as IPv6) had security designed into them. To maintain interoperability, however, the older protocols were mostly left as is. Since we still use those protocols today, we have had to add security in other ways.

Nearly all protocols have had or currently have vulnerabilities that should be understood. Anytime risk analysis is done for networks or networking products, you will need to be very clear on what protocols are being used.

TCP/IP Protocol	Vulnerability and Threat
IP	IP has no mechanism for verifying the actual identity of the sender or the receiver. For that reason, IP addresses can be easily spoofed without the user's knowledge, so that packets are sent to or received from a machine other than the intended destination or source. Additionally, IP packets are often fragmented by a router so that they can be transmitted over a particular media segment. An attacker can craft malicious IP packet fragments that cannot be reassembled by the receiving computer. This will cause that computer to waste time attempting to reassemble the packets, thus causing a denial of service attack using very few packets.
TCP	An attacker can predict the incrementing sequence number of a TCP session, push the legitimate client or server out of the way and take its place, and thus hijack a session that has already been authenticated and authorized.
UDP	Because UDP requires no acknowledgment, the source or destination of UDP packets can easily be spoofed.
DHCP	Because DHCP is broadcast in clear text: • An attacker can plug directly into a network jack and receive an IP address. • An attacker can masquerade as a DHCP server without the client knowing.
DNS	• An attacker can manipulate DNS and divert, intercept, or deny end-user communications. • An attacker can carry out an unauthorized zone transfer between primary and secondary DNS servers and gain information on the entire network. • An attacker can send inaccurate information about DNS mapping because when a server receives a response to its request, it does not authenticate the sender.

TCP/IP Protocol	Vulnerability and Threat
ICMP	• An attacker can send an ICMP redirect telling it to use the attacker's machine as a default route. • An attacker can insert data inside an ICMP packet, which will be passed through routers and firewalls under the assumption that it is just a status message. • An attacker can send oversized ICMP packets and overwhelm the system.
ARP	ARP is vulnerable in that it is sent in clear text by broadcast, with no way to verify the identity of the sending computer. An attacker can poison a system's ARP table cache, which contains hardware addresses and associated IP addresses, and receive packets intended for another computer.
RARP	Because RARP is broadcast in clear text (like ARP and DHCP), it can also be spoofed.
FTP	Standard FTP may provide plaintext password authentication, but it offers no actual encryption. This opens the protocol up to man-in-the-middle attacks, compromising both the confidentiality and integrity of the data transfer.
HTTP	Standard HTTP sends information through plaintext and without authentication, so an attacker may intercept sensitive information a user is entering into a web form, for example.
SMTP	There is no authentication or encryption. Fake email servers use SMTP to flood the Internet with spam. Additionally, a sniffer could capture someone's email since it is in clear text. Most email servers now require clients to send SMTP using a modified version that uses a different port and is encrypted. However, SMTP sent between servers on the Internet is still in clear text on the original port.
Telnet 23	All transmissions, including user authentication, are in clear text.
POP and IMAP	POP and IMAP, like SMTP, have no authentication or encryption. Messages are sent in clear text and can be sniffed and read by an unauthorized person. Most email servers and clients now use a modified form of POP and IMAP, which uses a different TCP port and is encrypted.
LDAP	LDAP provides weak authentication based on DNS. If DNS is compromised, LDAP will be easy for an attacker to compromise as well. Additionally, standard LDAP sends messages in plaintext, which can be easily intercepted and read by attackers.
NetBIOS	Attackers can exploit NetBIOS by obtaining information about a system, including registered name, IP addresses, and operating system/applications used.
NFS	Older versions of NFS do not include any encryption mechanisms to prevent eavesdropping or tampering of data being transferred.
IGMP	Malformed IGMP packets can cause a buffer overflow in denial of service on a receiving host.

Protocol Vulnerability Mitigation

To maintain compatibility, none of the original TCP/IP protocols have been revised to address security problems. Instead, security was added on as an option.

For example, online email servers can require clients to use alternate ports, authentication, and encryption when sending and receiving mail. Partner organizations can also require authentication and encryption between email servers. But most email servers on the Internet do not use such mechanisms so they can remain compatible with other systems. Instead, they rely on blacklists, DNS TXT file verification of the server, firewalls, and hiding unnecessary machine identification during a handshake to protect the server from rogue email servers.

A similar situation has arisen with DNS, which is a clear-text protocol that by its very nature must be available to the public. To protect DNS servers from having their databases corrupted by malicious attackers, the DNSSEC (DNS Security) standard arose. With DNSSEC, each DNS record is accompanied by an additional file that contains a digital signature for that record. It sounds like a great idea, but it is an add-on solution that must be implemented universally by every DNS server and client to be effective.

As long as the world uses IPv4, protocol vulnerabilities will continue to plague security professionals. IPv6 has mandatory security built into it, but there is no requirement for the world to switch to IPv6 by a specific date. Instead, it is expected that countries and organizations will adopt IPv6 as opportunity permits and in their own time. The IPv6 community recognizes that this could take decades. Meanwhile, the security practitioner must use every practical additional security measure to keep existing protocols as safe as possible.

Use the following techniques to mitigate protocol vulnerabilities:

- Use firewalls and intrusion detection to monitor protocol abuse and suspicious traffic.
- Harden and patch servers and workstations to mitigate risks associated with TCP/IP protocols.
- Use TCP wrappers on Linux/UNIX computers to verify incoming connections to a host.
- Configure personal firewalls on all computers.
- Configure routers to disallow/filter:
    - Source routing: Can potentially be used for spoofing.
    - Subnet broadcasts: Can potentially be used for denial-of-service.
    - ICMP: Filter ICMP by message type, only allowing PING to and from trusted hosts.
    - IP fragments: Deliberately malformed fragments could be used as a denial of service technique.
    - IP options: Excessive use of these could result in router CPU denial of service.
    - IP packets entering the network with low time-to-live (TTL): These could be used for denial of service.
- If practical, implement DNSSEC in your environment.
- If practical, implement authentication and encryption between servers, not only in your enterprise, but also with partners.
- When possible, use authenticated/encrypted alternatives to clear text protocols, including:
    - SSH (port 22) instead of telnet (port 23).
    - HTTPS (port 443) instead of HTTP (port 80).
    - SMTPS (port 465) or MSA (port 587) instead of SMTP (port 25).
    - IMAPS (port 993) or IMAP-SSL (port 585) instead of IMAP (port 143).
    - SSL-POP (port 995) instead of POP3 (port 110).
- When possible, change the default port of a service to an unexpected port number.
- When possible, encrypt and digitally sign the payload.

Ethernet

Ethernet is a networking protocol that supports communication between devices at the Physical and Data Link layers of the OSI model. Ethernet is supported by addresses assigned to each Ethernet interface. The Media Access Control (MAC) address is a 48 bit number that uniquely identifies each Ethernet interface.

CSMA

Carrier Sense Multiple Access (CSMA) is a protocol used to determine if there is anyone else on the network as it gets ready to transmit data. Methodologies like Ethernet make no effort to determine which nodes will send data at any given time and it is assumed that there will be more than one node, hence the term Multiple Access. To make sure that all nodes don't transmit simultaneously, a node will first listen (carrier sense) to see if any other nodes are currently communicating. If the node hears traffic on the network, it will wait a small amount of time and then listen again to see if it is clear. Because computer traffic tends to happen in bursts, there is as good chance that it will be able to send. CSMA is a non-deterministic protocol. This is sometimes also referred to as a probabilistic protocol. Its opposite would be something like Token Ring, which is a deterministic or non-probabilistic protocol.

CSMA with Collision Detection

Ethernet uses *Carrier Sense Multiple Access/Collision Detect (CSMA/CD)*. In CSMA/CD, nodes listen for traffic before transmitting. It is quite possible that two different nodes could listen for traffic, and hearing none decide to send their frames onto the wire. When this happens, you have a collision. That's OK; it has been accounted for and is even expected. When there is a collision, there will be a spike in voltage and all nodes will sense that a collision has happened, not just the two senders. All nodes will then go into a random wait period, and then start the whole process over when their wait period has expired. It sounds a little bit like chaos but it worked very well for the early years of Ethernet.

Today, switches have mostly eliminated collisions. Each node that is plugged into a switch has separate transmit and receive wire pairs. In most cases, the switch port uses both pairs of wires simultaneously (full duplex mode). With only one node on the other end of the cable, there is no opportunity for collisions, and the network is utilized very efficiently.

CSMA with Collision Avoidance

With *CSMA/CA*, there is an additional component. When the node has listened to make sure that no one else is transmitting and hears nothing, it will send out a jam signal to essentially tell everybody else to wait so that it can send. The jam signal has the effect of avoiding collision rather than dealing with them like CSMA/CD does. CSMA/CA is used in 802.11 wireless networking and legacy AppleTalk networks.

Multi-Layer Protocols

Multi-Layer protocols are those that span more than one layer in the OSI model. There are a number of examples that have been used for many years: Ethernet, Asynchronous Transfer Mode (ATM), X.25, and various cellular system protocols.

One example that is in very wide use, but hardly noticed by security professionals, is *Distributed Network Protocol 3 (DNP3)*. It sits on top of IP (OSI Layer 3), spanning the next three OSI layers. DNP3 is used to carry communications for industrial machinery like that used to run power plants and manufacturing facilities. These systems were traditionally run with proprietary systems that were written as a solid stack rather than a layered model like OSI or TCP/IP. The *Supervisory Control and Data Acquisition (SCADA)* system is one common example.

A SCADA network typically supports critical infrastructure facilities such as electric, gas, and water utilities. It is the most common form of industrial control system (ICS). It works by sending remote control signals through Distributed Network Protocol (DNP3) to industrial assets used by these utilities. The SCADA also receives information about the state of these assets to analyze or troubleshoot any problems they may be experiencing. For example, an engineer may use a SCADA system to receive information about the pressure and volume of water in a tank at a treatment plant, while also using the SCADA to adjust those factors to run the tank more efficiently.

Because these systems were typically self contained and didn't interact with other systems, they were thought to be secure. Over time, there has been a desire to run these on top of TCP/IP, which has led to vulnerabilities. Compounding the issue is that traditional anti-virus software does not work with these proprietary systems.

DNP3 Vulnerabilities

DNP3 already has 25 known vulnerabilities that have been published by CERT.gov. Most have to do with inadequate input validation or malformed packets that can result in denial of service attacks against the SCADA master or end devices. The vulnerabilities can be exploited remotely over an IP-based network, or locally through a direct serial connection between two devices. Since the vulnerabilities are two-way, potentially any sewage lift pump box in a local neighborhood, or an oil pump out in a field, could be a backdoor for attack into a utility's infrastructure.

IP Convergence

Convergence is bringing together the formerly separate data network and voice network. Now you can carry both types of traffic on an IP network. This presents some challenges as IP was not designed to have the guaranteed delivery that is necessary for voice traffic. Data traffic can generally be delayed by a second or two, but voice traffic generally needs to arrive within milliseconds. Any delays over 100 milliseconds can result in voice traffic becoming unacceptable to the users. The most common converged IP product at this point is Voice over IP (VoIP). With more demand for multimedia applications, you can expect to see more video over IP as well. While voice is very sensitive to delays, it is not a big consumer of bandwidth and makes a good candidate for convergence. Video, on the other hand, is as sensitive to delay as voice but consumes significantly more bandwidth. Because of this, you must approach video convergence projects carefully. With class of service, and quality of service, these projects are becoming more viable.

The benefits of IP convergence include:

- Improved support for multimedia applications.
- Easy to maintain.
- Flexible.
- Scalable.
- Efficient use of resources.
- Lower operating and maintenance costs.

There are several converged protocols. Some of the major ones include:

- FCoE.
- iSCSI.
- MPLS.
- VoIP.

FCoE

Fibre Channel over Ethernet (FCoE) allows traditional Fibre Channel protocols to use high-speed Ethernet networks to transmit and store data. This protocol decreases the infrastructure cost of cabling, as well as lowers the amount of physical hardware devices that are required, like network interface cards (NICs) and switches. Likewise, power and cooling costs may be reduced. FCoE is designed to allow all of the functionality provided by the upper OSI level Fibre Channel packets, but packages and ships them over an Ethernet infrastructure rather than Fibre Channel hardware. Standard Ethernet, however, is not suited for this kind of data. Only the latest versions of Ethernet with upgraded standards to provide low latency, better quality of service (QoS), and other features that are typically associated with a protocol like Fibre Channel are adequate.

FCoE has the following security implications:

- **Eavesdropping**: Now that all traffic (TCP/IP and Fibre Channel) is passed over Ethernet, there is only one wire to monitor for intruders. This can be a concern because, in many default Fibre Channel configurations, the data crosses the network unencrypted and an intruder could rebuild data from captured frames.
- **Denial of Service (DoS)**: Another concern associated with the shared Ethernet standard is the potential for a DoS. Typically, the completely segmented Fibre Channel SAN is very difficult to attack. Now that Fibre Channel and TCP/IP are sharing one network, an intruder simply has to execute a TCP/IP-based DoS attack, and it will impact all network bandwidth.

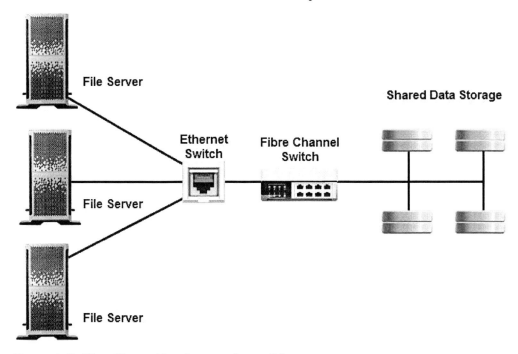

Figure 4–3: Fibre Channel implemented over Ethernet.

Use the following guidelines to mitigate FCoE security concerns:

- Use strong authentication on the FCoE switches to limit administrator access.
- Use role-based access control (RBAC) to limit user access to the data.
- Use FCoE network devices that have policy-based security services that can span multiple devices and operating systems.
- Configure switches to snoop for and filter out unwanted DHCP requests on the network.
- Use network devices that can verify host IP addresses (IP source guard).
- Use network devices that can prevent switch fabric reorganization when a new switch is plugged in (BPDU Guard).

iSCSI

The *Internet Small Computer System Interface (iSCSI)* is a protocol implementing links between data storage networks using Internet protocol (IP). This protocol is designed to extend across wide area networks without needing any new infrastructure. Users can enter commands and remotely manage data servers from great distances, and iSCSI can centralize data storage so that the information is not bound to individual servers. Although useful primarily for smaller organizations, iSCSI implementations can't match the speed and efficiency of an infrastructure-overhauling storage technology like Fibre Channel.

An iSCSI architecture comprise *initiators*, which are iSCSI client machines, and *targets*, which are iSCSI storage devices or applications. Each iSCSI client is assigned an *iSCSI Qualified Name (iQN)*, which is an initiator node name similar to a Media Access Control (MAC) address that is used to identify each client in the architecture.

Security concerns of iSCSI include:

- **User permissions**: Users accessing the data should only be given permission to access data that is essential to their tasks and no more (least privilege). User accounts need to be appropriately guarded, passwords need to be secure, and permissions should always be carefully assessed.
- **Encryption**: iSCSI operates as a cleartext protocol, which means data is not encrypted as it moves. Since it uses Ethernet standards to transmit data, an unauthorized user may be able to eavesdrop on the iSCSI network and capture and reconstruct traffic. Therefore, you should implement encryption at other layers of the protocol stack, such as by using Internet Protocol Security (IPSec).
- **Authentication**: Devices on an iSCSI SAN verify each other by means of their iQN, but this process can easily be spoofed. One way to decrease the risk is by implementing Challenge Handshake Authentication Protocol (CHAP), which requires initiators and targets to supply a correct user name and password before a connection will be made. While this alleviates some of the risk, CHAP is not a wholly secure protocol and is vulnerable to a variety of attacks.
- **Isolation**: In most scenarios, the only thing separating the iSCSI SAN from the rest of the network is some form of physical or virtual network segmentation. Since both the SAN and the regular LAN use the same protocols for communication, if someone were to misconfigure the network setup in some manner, the SAN could become easily accessible to the regular network, and this change could go undetected. You should consider segmenting the iSCSI SAN physically from the rest of the network to prevent this issue from arising.

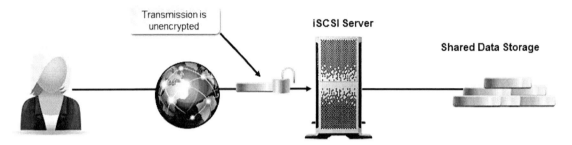

Figure 4-4: A client connecting to iSCSI storage facilities over the Internet.

MPLS

Multi-Protocol Label Switching (MPLS) is a protocol that operates between Layers 2 and 3 of the OSI model. It is commonly used in metropolitan area networks. In a typical IP network, a packet is sent to the next router in a path, which looks up IP addresses to determine the next destination in the path. This process repeats until the packet reaches its ultimate destination. In an MPLS, the first device in the path will do the lookup, but instead of finding the next destination, it will find the ultimate destination. It also determines the path from the device to the ultimate destination and affixes this label to the packet. Rather than each destination along the path performing an IP lookup, the devices will simply forward the packet to the next node based on the label. So, the first device does the Layer 3 routing, whereas the rest of the devices along the path do Layer 2 switching.

The advantage this provides is that it reduces the load of routers performing constant lookups, when only one edge router needs to perform this lookup in an MPLS system. Modern technology has made the performance impact of IP lookups mostly negligible, but MPLS is still used by network administrators to help shape traffic on the network.

The most pressing security concern of MPLS is ensuring the availability of communications. There are several implementations of MPLS—for example, Virtual Leased Line (VLL) delivers data over MPLS to connect two different media types. These lines are difficult to load balance because the transmission's payload isn't visible. On the other hand, Virtual Private LAN Service (VPLS) using MPLS is easier to load balance because the payload headers are exposed.

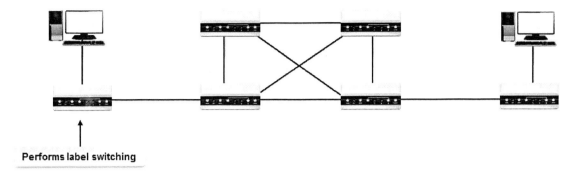

Performs label switching

Figure 4-5: MPLS performs multi-service label switching using Layer 3 routers.

VoIP

Voice over Internet Protocol (VoIP) is a technology that enables you to deliver telephony communications over a network by using the IP protocol. Many VoIP solutions allow users to communicate through a single application, and some solutions allow users to call landline or cellular phone numbers from a computer application, or vice versa. In all implementations, your voice is converted to data packets that are sent to the receiving device over a network. These packets are generally compressed using various codecs, and when the packets reach their destination, the recipient device decodes them. Each codec has its own performance and quality specifications that will have an impact on the speed and quality of communications.

VoIP solutions are based on the Session Initiation Protocol (SIP), which manages voice and other multimedia connections. Early versions of VoIP had no encryption, so VoIP calls could be sniffed and recorded like any other clear-text IP traffic. Most implementations of VoIP have eliminated this concern. SIP supports encryption mechanisms like SSL/TLS and MD5 to ensure confidentiality and integrity. One risk of SIP involves a client on a call also acting as a server; like any software-based server, this makes the machine vulnerable to certain threats, such as memory overflows.

There are some additional security concerns of using VoIP technology, most of which concern availability:

- **Packet loss**: Unlike other data transfer protocols, VoIP can't simply wait for dropped packets to arrive, so the VoIP solution must essentially fill in the blanks to maintain the call's reliability. Filling in the gaps is called interpolation, and is often implemented using a technique called Packet Loss Concealment (PLC). Every network is different, so the nature of VoIP calls and their errors will differ as well. So, you should implement the proper technique of PLC that aligns with your network's levels of congestion, packet loss, and similar characteristics. *+ Latency*
- **Jitter**: Similar to packet loss, a VoIP call experiences jittering when packet delays vary in a connection. When there is too much variation, callers will experience delays and the quality of the call will degrade. To prevent jittering, you can try and reduce packet delays in the network by putting priority on VoIP traffic. Preventing the packet buffer from exceeding 150 ms of delay by using algorithms that keep the buffer under control can also alleviate the symptoms of jittering.
- **Sequence errors**: Like packet loss, an out-of-sequence packet in a VoIP call presents a problem that other data transfer protocols may not have. Improperly sequenced packets may make the call incomprehensible. Sequence errors typically occur because packets take different routes through a network, and packet one may show up after packet two. This is usually mitigated by a buffer, but the buffer may be reduced to avoid the jittering problem as described above. Essentially, the best practice to mitigate sequence errors is to ensure that VoIP packets are following consistent routes.
- **Codec quality and bandwidth usage**: As mentioned above, codecs may compress audio packets in a variety of different ways. Some favor quality over speed, whereas others guarantee the opposite. Codecs that favor quality take up more of your network's bandwidth, and many upstream Internet providers will throttle this bandwidth. So, you must choose the right codec that won't exceed your network's or provider's capacity, while ensuring that the codec offers sufficient quality of voice.

To assist with VoIP security and availability, implement VoIP in its own virtual LAN (VLAN) and grant VoIP traffic priority using Quality of Service rules on the router.

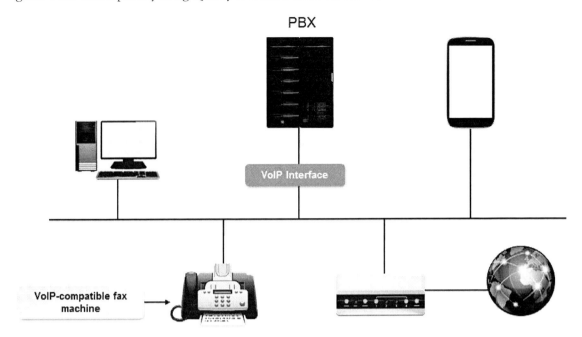

Figure 4-6: VoIP transmits voice signals over IP networks.

Wireless Technologies

With wireless networking, the air is used as the media as opposed to any sort of cable. It is not uncommon to hear the term unbound for wireless as compared to bound for cabled networks. Infrared, Bluetooth, 802.11, and a lot of other technologies fall under the wireless umbrella. Within each of the wireless types there are likely many standards. For example, Bluetooth has Class 1, 2, and 3, which offer different powers to cover different distances. There are also different versions within Bluetooth that can affect the security of the devices as well. The same is true with the 802.11 family of Wi-Fi standards.

Wireless Technology	Description
Wi-Fi	Uses IEEE 802.11 WLAN standards to allow devices to connect wirelessly over a network. Devices connect to wireless access points that can transmit data up to about 70 feet indoors. The 802.11 standard defines communication over the 2.4, 3.6, 5, and 60 GHz frequency bands. There are several protocols in the standard, and new protocols are continually being developed to improve the speed and reliability of Wi-Fi communications. For example, IEEE 802.11ac was published in 2014 and has a throughput of at least 500 Mb/s on a single link.
Bluetooth	A short-range wireless radio network transmission medium usually used between two personal devices, such as between a mobile phone and wireless headset. The typical maximum range of Bluetooth is around 30 feet.
WiMax	WiMax is similar in function to Wi-Fi, but has much longer ranges of about 50 miles. WiMax has variable throughput, which often degrades over long distances. WiMax is typically used in very large networks that reach users across long distances, whereas Wi-Fi is more for home and normal business use.

Wireless Technology	Description
Spread Spectrum	Spread spectrum is a simple technique that spreads the wireless conversation over multiple frequencies, making it more difficult for someone to intercept a message. There are several types: • Frequency Hopping Spread Spectrum (FHSS) • Direct Sequence Spread Spectrum (DSSS) • Orthogonal Frequency Division Multiplexing (OFDM) • Vectored Orthogonal Frequency Division Multiplexing (VOFDM) It is important to note that this technique is not encryption and doesn't offer that level of protection; it only provides resistance to interception. Because it also offers some improvements in performance, it is still used even when encryption is used.
Cellular/Mobile	Mobile communication protocols use orbiting satellites and terrestrial towers to communicate across global distances. Mobile networks are typically used for telephony purposes, but also have data sharing capabilities. Mobile networks often employ the following channel access methods: • Frequency Division Multiple Access (FDMA) • Time Division Multiple Access (TDMA) • Code Division Multiple Access (CDMA) • Orthogonal Frequency Division Multiple Access (OFDMA)

Wireless Security

Because the traffic is no longer bound to a physical cable but is rather unbound and travelling through space, it becomes vulnerable to devices that might try to intercept the signal. There have been many attempts to protect wireless signals with different mechanisms from how the signal is transmitted to using encryption.

Wireless security protocols need to evolve in order to adequately safeguard and protect network data. Due to the unbound nature of wireless, it is a tempting target.

Wireless Security Protocol	Description
WEP	*Wired Equivalent Privacy (WEP)* was the first attempt at securing wireless transmissions over the 802.11 networks. As the name implies, the level of security provided by WEP was equivalent to a wired network. WEP, however, has been shown to be vulnerable to attacks and can now be compromised in minutes. This is because WEP relied on a stream cipher using a 24-bit initialization vector (IV). Attacks on the IV can easily predict this relatively short value. WEP is therefore obsolete and should not be used.
WPA	*Wi-Fi Protected Access (WPA)* is a security standard that provides additional encryption capabilities for wireless transmissions. WPA introduced the *Temporal Key Integrity Protocol (TKIP)* as an improvement to the number of keys and usage of keys. However, attacks have shown TKIP to be vulnerable to the transmission and decryption of arbitrary packets on the network. As such, WPA is also obsolete and should not be used.

Wireless Security Protocol	Description
802.11i or WPA2	*802.11i,* also known as *WPA2,* is the latest advancement in the wireless protection protocols. It includes stronger encryption types than were available when WPA was introduced, particularly the CCMP encryption protocol that uses the AES standard. Enterprise implementations of WPA2 also use a centralized authentication server called a RADIUS server. Small versions of WPA2 (WPA2 personal) use a pre-shared key (password). The biggest known vulnerability of WPA2 is the potential for administrators to secure their network with a weak password. WPA2 is the current best choice for Wi-Fi security.

When implementing wireless security, use these recommendations:

- Select WPA2 (even WPA2 personal) over WEP or WPA.
- When possible, use a RADIUS server for wireless authentication.
- If you must use a pre-shared key, make the password complex and change it regularly.
- If necessary, enter the MAC addresses of all devices that are permitted to connect to the wireless network into the access point.

Network Encryption Protocols

Although many of the protocols used in your network have inherent vulnerabilities, some network protocols are designed specifically to apply a measure of security to your communications. These protocols typically use some form of encryption to offer assurances of confidentiality, integrity, and authentication. The following table lists some of the most common network encryption protocols.

Network Encryption Protocol	Description
SSL/TLS	*Secure Sockets Layer (SSL) and Transport Layer Security (TLS)* are security protocols that combine digital certificates for authentication with public key data encryption. SSL/TLS offers guarantees of authenticity, integrity, and confidentiality. Because of these security guarantees, SSL/TLS has become the *de facto* protocol for protecting HTTP traffic through web browsers.
SSH	*Secure Shell (SSH)* is a protocol used for secure remote login and secure transfer of data. To ensure security, the entire SSH session, including authentication, is encrypted using a variety of encryption methods. SSH is the preferred protocol for working with File Transfer Protocol (FTP) and is used primarily on Linux and UNIX systems to access shell accounts. The encryption that SSH provides will secure communications from any eavesdropping.
DNSSEC	*Domain Name System Security Extension (DNSSEC)* is a set of specifications to provide an added level of security to DNS, which was not originally designed with strong security features. DNSSEC provides origin authentication of DNS data, authenticated denial of existence, and data integrity. DNSSEC also supports zone signing, which uses digital signatures using public-key cryptography and a chain of trust to provide end-to-end protection to domain name data.

Network Encryption Protocol	Description
PGP	*Pretty Good Privacy (PGP)* is a publicly available email security and authentication utility that uses a variation of public key cryptography to encrypt emails: the sender encrypts the contents of the email message and then encrypts the key that was used to encrypt the contents. The encrypted key is sent with the email, and the receiver decrypts the key and then uses the key to decrypt the contents. PGP also uses public key cryptography to digitally sign emails to authenticate the sender and the contents. GNU Privacy Guard (GPG) is a free, open-source version of PGP.
S/MIME	*Secure/Multipurpose Internet Mail Extensions (S/MIME)* is another email-based encryption standard that adds digital signatures and public key cryptography to traditional MIME communications. MIME defines several advanced characteristics of email messages that had previously been unavailable, including the ability to send text in character sets other than ASCII and the ability to send non-text file attachments. S/MIME provides assurances of confidentiality, integrity, authentication, and non-repudiation, and is built into most modern email clients.

Guidelines for Implementing Network Architecture Security

 Note: All of the Guidelines for this lesson are available as checklists from the **Checklist** tile on the CHOICE Course screen.

Here are some guidelines for securing network protocols:

- Understand the layers of the OSI and TCP/IP models and how your network technologies fit in those layers.
- Pay attention to the vulnerabilities of each networking protocol that your organization implements.
- Understand the vulnerabilities associated with multi-layer protocols, especially when it comes to SCADA systems.
- If you implement FCoE, be aware of the threat of eavesdropping and denial of services attacks since Fibre Channel and TCP/IP are sharing a network.
- If you implement iSCSI, be aware that it is not encrypted by default.
- Ensure that any MPLS implementations provide for proper load balancing to defend against DoS threats.
- Incorporate VoIP in your network in a way that reduces packet loss, jittering, and other issues that could affect availability.
- Use WPA2 to encrypt your Wi-Fi network, and always secure it with a strong password.
- Implement network encryption protocols where possible to provide confidentiality, integrity, and authentication of communications in your network.

ACTIVITY 4-1
Analyzing Network Protocol Security

Scenario
In this activity, you will assess your understanding of network protocol security.

1. On 802.11-based wireless networks, what method is used to prevent nodes from transmitting at the same time?
   - ○ CSMA/CD
   - ○ Token-passing
   - ○ CSMA/CA
   - ○ POTS

2. Which statement best describes the primary purpose of the OSI model?
   - ○ It allows network gear manufacturers to target their products to specific network types.
   - ○ To facilitate interoperability between networking products.
   - ○ It serves as a platform-independent reference detailing how network applications and devices communicate.
   - ○ While once a useful tool, the OSI model serves no purpose in modern networks.

3. At which layer of the OSI model does segmentation occur?
   - ○ Layer 4: Transport
   - ○ Layer 3: Network
   - ○ Layer 3: Transport
   - ○ Layer 4: Network

4. How are the OSI model and the TCP/IP model related?
   - ○ While they share similarities (for example, an Application layer) and are both used as frameworks for understanding network communications, they are distinct models that are not related to each other.
   - ○ The TCP/IP model is used for networking in Microsoft Windows networks. The OSI model is used with non-Windows networks.
   - ○ The OSI model is used by hardware designers. The TCP/IP model is used exclusively by software developers.
   - ○ The TCP/IP model may be viewed as a simplification of the OSI model, since the layers in the TCP/IP model may be mapped to layers within the OSI model.

5. What are among the benefits of IPv6 networking? (Choose three.)
   - ☐ Integrated security
   - ☐ Improved media streaming
   - ☐ Improved routing
   - ☐ Very large address space
   - ☐ Faster network speeds
   - ☐ Eliminates anonymous traffic

6. What are the steps involved with automatic IP addressing using DHCP on IPv4 networks?
    ○ Discover – Request – Offer – Acknowledge
    ○ Find – Request – Offer – Accept
    ○ Discover – Offer – Request – Acknowledge
    ○ Request – Lease – Acknowledge – Renew

7. What is the best definition of "Convergence"?
    ○ Combining formerly distinct voice and data networks on a single IP network.
    ○ Reducing network traffic by eliminating duplicate transmissions.
    ○ Combining many smaller networks into one larger network.
    ○ The migration of IPv4 networks to IPv6.

8. Which of the following protocols are connectionless? (Choose two.)
    ☐ DNS
    ☐ TCP
    ☐ IP
    ☐ UDP
    ☐ SMTP
    ☐ ICMP

9. What is the primary difference between FCoE and iSCSI?
    ○ While they both can save money, iSCSI is suitable for long distances over existing infrastructure.
    ○ FCoE cannot use an Ethernet network, whereas iSCSI can only travel on Ethernet.
    ○ iSCSI is meant for distances under 30 meters, whereas FCoE can travel much greater distances.
    ○ They are both basically the same; choosing between them is mostly a matter of preference.

10. What is the primary advantage of MPLS?
    ○ Improved performance on a LAN
    ○ Improved performance on a MAN
    ○ Improved performance on an FCoE link
    ○ Improved performance on a VoIP network

11. What made WEP such a weak wireless security mechanism?
    ○ Its use of weak passwords.
    ○ The fact that it used only 40 bit encryption.
    ○ Its poor use of signaling efficiency.
    ○ Its use of a short-length initialization vector.

12. While cryptography and encryption are valuable tools for securing network communications, what other factors should be considered to ensure a sound approach to communications security?

TOPIC B

Network Components Security

How you design your networks and the types of equipment you use will certainly have an impact on their security. The topology types implemented might also have advantages and/or disadvantages in terms of speed, efficiency, reliability, redundancy, and cost. In this topic, you will learn about different topologies, different media, and the various hardware components of a network.

Networking Hardware

There are various components that make up the network architecture of a computer system.

Network Hardware	Description
Router	A *router* is a networking device used to connect multiple networks that employ the same protocol. Routers send data between networks by examining the network addresses contained in the packets they process. Routers can work only with routable protocols, which are network protocols that provide separate network and node addresses. Routers in turn use special routing protocols like RIP, EIGRP, Border Gateway Protocol (BGP), and OSPF to exchange information about routes between themselves. They then use this information to build routing tables. Routing protocols help establish the distance and/or cost to get from one network to another. They will also recalculate the routing tables if the network topology changes. A router can be a dedicated device, or it can be implemented as software running on a node, typically with two network interface cards. Routers can also be used as security devices because they can be configured to limit traffic entering or leaving different networks. Routers help to optimize network traffic by segmenting it into broadcast domains to reduce the number of stations competing for access to a particular network segment. Routers are Layer 3 devices.
Wireless router	*Wireless routers* act as both routers and wireless access points. Like a traditional router, wireless routers send data between networks using routing protocols that operate at Layer 3. Wireless routers typically support the IEEE 802.11 standard of Wi-Fi communications, and also usually have physical Ethernet ports for wired switching. As is the nature of wireless networking, wireless routers are a much easier and more frequent target of attack, as no physical access is necessary. This is why it's essential to harden your router with a strong encryption password, as well as a strong password for access to administrative settings. Tactics such as filtering out unwanted MAC addresses from connecting, as well as turning off service set identification (SSID) broadcast, offer minimal security.

Network Hardware	Description
Switch	A *switch* is an interconnecting network device that forwards frames to the correct port based on Media Access Control (MAC) addresses. A *MAC address* is a unique, hardware-level address assigned to network access devices, such as Ethernet cards, by its manufacturer.
	Switches work with pairs of ports, connecting two segments as needed. Most switches can work with multiple pairs of ports simultaneously to improve performance.
	Switches can be used as security devices by shutting down unused ports, by restricting port use to authorized devices, and by building virtual local area networks (VLANs) to isolate workgroup traffic on the same switch.
	Switches can optimize network traffic by segmenting into collision domains to reduce the number of stations competing for access to a particular network segment.
	Unless otherwise indicated, switches are Layer 2 devices. Modern switches may be capable of working at Layer 3 and even Layer 4, but they will be identified as such.
	Bridges are similar to switches, the difference being that they are older and software based, whereas switches are newer and hardware based. Switches are typically thought of as multi-port bridges.
	Switches introduce security risks to the network when you fail to implement port security, or fail to harden the switch itself from unauthorized access. Configure the switch to shut down unused ports, restrict the number of MAC addresses on a single port (to prevent users from adding devices by plugging hubs into a switch port), and to segregate traffic into VLANs. Harden the switch from unauthorized access by requiring authentication on the switch. Do not permit unsecured remote administration of the switch.
Hub	A *hub* is like a switch, only it is dumb in the sense that it transmits signals to *every* node in the network. This makes them inefficient and potentially insecure, as anyone with access to the hub can essentially see all traffic on the network. Hubs are obsolete for these reasons, and have been surpassed by switches and routers. Hubs are basically thought of today as multi-port repeaters. To minimize the risk of eavesdropping and reduced network performance, disallow the use of hubs whenever possible.
Gateway	A *gateway* is a device, software, or a system that converts data between incompatible systems. Gateways can translate data between different operating systems, between different email formats, or between totally different networks.
	Gateways can work at many different layers, from Layer 2 all the way to Layer 7.
Modem	A *modem* converts digital signals to analog signals, and vice versa. This is often used in modern computing to transmit digital signals between traditional analog cabling, like phone lines, and digital signaling used in computer networks. Because modems often translate signals received from the public Internet, they can be used to remotely access a network. To prevent an attacker from using this to their advantage, you should tightly control the use of modems in your network.

Network Hardware	Description
Multiplexer	A *multiplexer* combines multiple signals into one. This can make the transmission of the signal more efficient than if they were sent separately. Before the advent of broadband and VPNs, multiplexers were used to maximize the use of a dial-up modem. Today, the most common use of a multiplexer is the CellMux, where multiple cellular connections (often from different carriers) are aggregated together to give more bandwidth to a single call. This is used by news reporters, especially those on foot. The biggest current risk for multiplexers today is malicious code (buffer overflow) that can destabilize the system. This can only be mitigated by patches released by the vendor.
Concentrator	A *concentrator* connects multiple links to a signal destination. Concentrators help to perform load balancing between connected devices.
Front-end processor	A *front-end processor* is placed between an input or output device and the computer's central processor. This helps to lighten the load on the main processor when it comes to I/O activities like a user typing on a keyboard. This is because I/O activities are typically much slower than normal CPU processes, so if the CPU handles them, its throughput may be negatively affected.
Repeater	*Repeaters* are used to amplify signals as they normally degrade over long distances. This can increase the physical size of a network considerably.
Firewall	A *firewall* is a software program or hardware device that protects networks from unauthorized data by blocking unsolicited traffic. Firewalls allow incoming or outgoing traffic that has been specifically permitted by a system administrator, and enable incoming traffic that is sent in response to requests from internal hosts. Firewalls use complex filtering algorithms that analyze incoming packets based on destination and source addresses, port numbers, and data types. Firewalls can be found from Layer 3 through Layer 7.
Proxy	A *proxy* is a software- or hardware-based device that fetches content from the outside network (usually the Internet) on behalf of an internal client. For example, if a client wants to download a web page from a website on the Internet, it will request the proxy to fetch the page for it. The proxy will consult an administrator-configured list of rules to see if that particular client is permitted to obtain that particular content. If it is allowed, the proxy puts the client session on hold and downloads the page for the client. It then delivers the downloaded page to the client. It also keeps a cached copy of the content for a pre-determined amount of time. In this way, if similar requests for the same content are made by other permitted clients, the proxy can simply give them a copy from its cache, rather than use bandwidth on the Internet link to fetch the same page. Proxy rules can be based on user, client, website, content type, time of day, key words, or other similar criteria. Proxies are also very useful for reducing the load on a limited Internet link. The downside of using a proxy is that cached content can become stale very quickly, especially if retrieved from a news site or some other website that constantly changes its content.
Reverse Proxy	A *reverse proxy* works in the opposite direction of a regular proxy. It is a type of proxy that fetches internal content for external clients. For example, if a user on the Internet wants to download a web page from the company's web server, a reverse proxy will put the external client on hold while it retrieves the content from the company website. In this way, the general public is never allowed to directly access the web server. The reverse proxy always fetches the content for requesting Internet clients. Most firewalls have reverse proxy capabilities.

Network Hardware	Description
Appliance	The term *appliance* refers to any dedicated hardware device that performs a specialized network function. An appliance can be contrasted with a server. Both might perform the same task, but the server is general purpose in nature. The server uses software to perform the task, along with many other tasks that are configured on it. An appliance, on the other hand, is not general purpose. Its functionality is limited to the specific task it was designed for.
	One example of an appliance is a bandwidth-limiting device. To better serve many different traffic types, it may be necessary to limit the amount of bandwidth used by one traffic type to allow other traffic to flow more readily. A *traffic shaper*, or *bandwidth limiter*, may restrict the amount of instant messaging traffic so that Voice over Internet Protocol (VoIP) traffic may use more bandwidth.
	Another example of an appliance might be a storage area-networking data repository. You could also have appliances that are spam filters, authentication servers, proxies, VPN servers, and more.
	Appliances are available for every OSI layer.

Note: It is important not to confuse a gateway with the default gateway in TCP/IP, which just forwards IP data packets. In the earliest days, routers were called gateways and they were the default route from one network to the next.

Data Network Types

Many types of data networks are commonly employed to allow users to share resources such as files, printers, and email.

Data Network Type	Description
LAN	A *local area network (LAN)* is a network established within a limited scope. Depending on the LAN protocol used, LANs are often implemented within workgroups, or a single building, floor, or room. In most cases, LANs are implemented using copper-based wiring systems or wireless components.
	An Ethernet LAN is an example of a data network. Ethernet network interface cards (NICs), wiring, switches, router interfaces, and driver software all make up the Ethernet network.
	Wireless LANs (WLANs) implement a local network using primarily wireless access points rather than typical Ethernet cabling.
	The greatest risk for a LAN or WLAN is the relative ease by which unauthorized devices can make a connection. This can only be mitigated by implementing port security on switches, requiring strong device and user authentication, or even configuring switches and wireless access points to only accept certain device MAC addresses (hardware addresses).

Data Network Type	Description
CAN	A *campus area network (CAN)* is used to connect buildings within a campus setting, such as a university or enterprise campus. Due to the extended distance between the network elements, CANs are often implemented using fiber optic media.
	The biggest risk to implementing a CAN is that the network is physically larger, with more opportunities for rogue devices to connect. Implement the same security on the CAN as you would the LAN. Just ensure that there is no corner of the network that you have forgotten to secure.
MAN	A *metropolitan area network (MAN)* is used within a metropolitan area, such as a provider-supplied network encircling a major metropolitan network. MANs are often implemented as Synchronous Optical Networking (SONET) rings. Metro Ethernet is becoming much more common. The biggest risk to implementing a MAN is damage to buried fiber optic cables by careless workers digging nearby. Attempt to physically protect your cable and to alert others of its presence.
WAN	A *wide area network (WAN)* is used to connect physically distributed networks over long, geographical distances. A WAN may use a provider service or may be a dedicated service created by the enterprise. WAN protocols are usually not the same as the protocols used in LAN, CAN, or MAN networks.
	A WAN includes technologies such as X.25, frame relay, High-Level Data Link Control (HDLC), ATM, PPP, and so on.
	The biggest risk to implementing a WAN is that as an end consumer, you have no control over the network. Implement strong authentication and encryption on traffic that travels over a WAN.
PAN	*Personal area networks (PANs)* are very small and might include small office home office (SOHO) networks, or just a mobile phone and a headset. Bluetooth is often used in a PAN. Bluetooth is a wireless technology operating in the 2.4 GHz spectrum.
	There are three classes of Bluetooth. Class one devices can work up to 100 meters, Class two is 10 meters, and Class three is less than 10 meters. Bluetooth security has been shown to be vulnerable and should be disabled if not needed.
	The biggest risk of implementing a PAN is that Bluetooth, especially version 3, can so easily make connections (pair) with surrounding devices. This can happen without your knowledge. Once another device has paired with yours, an attacker could try to steal your data. Require a PIN for Bluetooth pairing, or even turn off Bluetooth if not needed.
SAN	*Storage area networks (SANs)* are high-speed, private networks of storage devices all linked together to create one large storage resource. Numerous storage devices including hard disk arrays, tape libraries, and optical devices can be combined to act as storage for other systems. To the servers that use it, however, the SAN just looks like another local drive, as if it was just another hard drive in the machine. The server simply hands data off to the SAN and allows the SAN to manage the storage of that data behind the scenes. The devices in a SAN communicate and rearrange data among one another and the entire process is unknown to the original server. SANs use FCoE and iSCSI as their primary protocols. You can address SAN security vulnerabilities by requiring authentication between devices, and addressing protocol vulnerabilities.

Data Network Type	Description
VLAN	A *virtual local area network (VLAN)* is a logical grouping of switch ports. It is used to provide Layer 2 security on a switched network, and to limit the impact of broadcast traffic. Nodes connected to a VLAN can only communicate with other nodes in the same VLAN.
	The VLAN is created on the switch, given a VLAN ID (a number), and then ports are associated with the VLAN. One switch can have many VLANs on it, but each switch port can only belong to one VLAN at a time. Ports belonging to a particular VLAN on a switch do not have to be physically next to each other.
	If desired, the same VLAN can also be extended across multiple switches through the use of trunk ports. When switches are trunked together, they can assign some or all of their ports to belong to the same VLAN. In this way, you could have a department spread across multiple buildings on a campus. Users in the same department could be plugged into different switches in different buildings and yet be grouped together.
	When properly implemented, each VLAN is also assigned its own IP subnet. VLANs that need to communicate with each other are connected via routers. Routers can then use access control lists to allow or disallow traffic from one VLAN to reach another VLAN.
	The biggest risk associated with VLANs is improper implementation. In a few cases, you might also have a switch that has an unpatched vulnerability that allows traffic in one VLAN to intrude into another VLAN. Learn how to properly implement VLANs, including routing between them and restricting routing with access control lists. Make sure your switch is properly patched against any VLAN vulnerabilities.
Switched networks	Switched networks forward traffic between segments using a single type of network protocol, such as Ethernet. Switched networks provide traffic isolation services and forward frames at the Data Link layer of the OSI model.
Routed networks	Routed networks connect similar or dissimilar physical networks based on the existence of logical networks at Layer 3 of the OSI model. Routers may be used to connect various LANs or to connect LANs to CANs. A router is required when connecting a LAN to a WAN.

 Note: Depending on the device, it is possible to have one switch port be associated with two VLANs, one for a VoIP phone and one for the PC plugged into the phone.

WAN Technologies

Here is a resource for future study on WAN technologies: **http://en.wikipedia.org/wiki/ HDLC**.

Network Topologies

A *network topology* is the physical and logical arrangement of nodes in a network. The physical arrangement describes the physical connections of cables and nodes. The logical arrangement describes the logical patterns of data flow. The most common types of data network topologies are star, bus, ring, and mesh. Networks can be cabled or wireless.

It is important to remember that the physical and the logical topology do not need to match. For example, a network could be a physical star and a logical bus. Every combination has been tried at some point and they all have conceptual advantages and disadvantages.

The biggest vulnerability with regard to any network topology is that they all offer the opportunity for unauthorized devices to tap into the network. When possible, configure network devices to disallow rogue computers. Also configure monitoring such as intrusion detection to watch for suspicious activity.

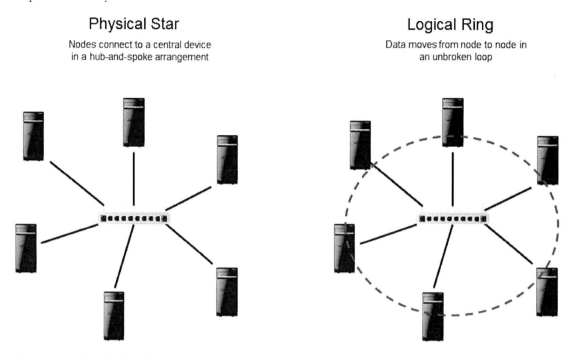

Physical Star
Nodes connect to a central device
in a hub-and-spoke arrangement

Logical Ring
Data moves from node to node in
an unbroken loop

Figure 4-7: Physical and logical network topology.

Data Network Topology Types

The various topology types implemented have differing advantages in terms of speed, efficiency, reliability, redundancy, and cost.

Data Network Topology Type	Description
Point-to-point	A *point-to-point topology* is simply a link between two devices. This topology offers dedicated communication between these two devices.
	Because of its simplicity, point-to-point topologies are not very practical in most situations. The speed and reliability it offers is offset by its limited size and distance.
Star	A *star topology* is a network topology in which all devices are connected to a central device that performs a traffic distribution function.
	In this topology, problems with cabling are usually isolated to a single device. But, you will need to run cable for each device back to the central collection point, resulting in a much larger amount of cable than in a bus, for example.
Bus	A *bus topology* is a network topology in which all devices are connected to a single, linear communication path that is shared by all.
	The amount of cable is small, but a single break in that cable can result in the entire network being unavailable.

Data Network Topology Type	Description
Tree	A *tree topology* is a network topology in which all devices are connected to a branching cable. Every node receives all the transmitted traffic and processes only the traffic destined for that node.
	Damage to one node will not affect the rest of the network, but a cable failure will result in the entire network being unavailable.
Ring	A *ring topology* is a network topology in which all devices are connected to a single, circular communication path with a structure that requires each node to connect directly to two other nodes.
	The amount of cable is only slightly more than a bus, but it can still suffer an outage if the ring is broken. Some implementations saw the use of dual rings to help provide resiliency, but this requires more cabling. Rings might also suffer from the delay of waiting for a token to make its way around the ring in order for you to communicate.
Mesh	A *mesh topology* is a network topology in which all devices, such as nodes, are directly connected to all other devices.
	This provides great resiliency, but can require an enormous amount of cabling and interfaces. It is usually only found on critical devices in the data center. The formula for determining the number of cables is $(N * (N - 2)) / 2$, where N is the number of devices.

Circuit-Switched Networks

In a circuit-switched network, two nodes set up a dedicated connection to one another before they actually communicate. This guarantees a consistent bandwidth, reliability, and quality of service of the communications channel. Once the circuit is established, only the caller and receiver have access to it. The original circuit switch network concepts were developed by Bell Labs for AT&T. In the very early networks, a human operator would complete the circuit for the caller; eventually, equipment was developed that could do it automatically. This is sometimes still referred to as the *Plain Old Telephone System (POTS)* or the *Public Switched Telephone Network (PSTN)*.

One of the foremost systems for circuit switching is the *private branch exchange (PBX)* system. PBX is a phone system used in larger organizations that have their own switching network and control lines for both internal and external communications. PBX alleviates the need for each user to have his or her own line that goes to the telephone company's central office. PBXs are vulnerable to *phreaking*, in which an attacker can identify the tones used to route long distance calls, enabling them to switch calls and use long distance services for free.

More generally, circuit-switched networks are vulnerable in the sense that they can't assure availability when you need to send large amounts of data to multiple endpoints. Circuit switching is more efficient when it only has a limited amount of endpoints to send data to, as there is a significant cost involved in establishing more communication channels over more circuits. This is why it's used primarily for time-sensitive telephony, not time-insensitive data transfer.

Packet-Switched Networks

In packet-switched networks, the data is first assembled into a packet or a frame, then the most efficient route is determined and the data is sent on its way. The next bit of data could easily take a different route even if the destination was the same. As the network experiences congestion and delays, it will look for new ways to deliver the data. The packet will contain a header and a payload. The hardware used to move the packets will need to be able to identify the header in order for it be routed. In an IP network, it is your IP address.

Compared to circuit switching, packet switching is more efficient for large data sets that need to be transmitted to multiple endpoints, because it does not need to wait for a dedicated line to become available in order to transmit data. The channels are shared among multiple users. This, however, can become a problem when the number of users exceeds the network's capacity. This can cause delays in packet reception. Likewise, packets may arrive out of order, causing corruption of the data. However, modern protocols can address this issue and offer a more reliable transmission of data. Because bandwidth in a packet-switched network is dynamic, the amount provisioned to each communication channel can adapt to the needs of the overall network. Packet switched network providers implement traffic shaping in their networks. You may need to pay for a committed information rate or premium service to guarantee bandwidth at all times.

Cell Switching

One alternate method of packet switching is called cell switching. In cell switching, the packets are actually constructed of a small, fixed length—a cell, in other words. This form of switching is used by Asynchronous Transfer Mode (ATM) networks to provide high bandwidth as well as low latency. It essentially combines the strengths of both circuit switching and packet switching. A virtual circuit is established before data transfer is allowed, and the transfer uses the fixed-length packets (cells) to hold the data. Therefore, it can be used for voice, video, file transfers, and just about any data transmission.

Transmission Media

There are two main types of data network media.

Data Network Media Type	Description
Wired	If your network is connected with physical cabling, it is referred to as wired. Then, depending on the topology in use, the cabling of the network may be simple or complex. A star network is wired similarly to an enterprise telephone system, with all wiring going from a wall jack to a central location on a floor in a building. A mesh network is most complex because all devices must be connected.
	The type of cable you choose will also affect the security of the network. Copper cables will typically be more susceptible to interference and potential eavesdropping. Twisted pair cabling uses four pairs of wires twisted around each other. It can be either shielded twisted pair (STP) or unshielded twisted pair (UTP). The twist helps to prevent signals from one wire interfering with another, a phenomenon known as crosstalk. The wire also need not be made of metal. It could be fiber optic cabling that carries one or more beams of light.
	A cabled network is also referred to as a bound network.
Wireless	Wireless networking reduces the cabling burden for any topology. Most wireless devices today work as if they were wired in a star configuration with a central access point for the wireless network.
	Wireless networks can greatly increase the chance for eavesdropping as the signal is being propagated through the air. Wireless networks will typically use some sort of frequency hopping as a way to prevent eavesdropping or enhance quality. However, because these signals are being freely propagated through the air, some type of encryption is nearly mandatory.
	A wireless network is also referred to as an unbound network.

Router Vulnerabilities

Routers are a key network component. They connect networks to each other and to the Internet. If a router is compromised, the attacker could use it in a man-in-the-middle attack, misdirecting traffic to a useless destination, or redirecting traffic to another destination across the Internet, resulting in information disclosure. This is analogous to planting a bug in a room so you can listen remotely to a conversation. A hacked router could also be used to launch denial-of-service or other attacks against the internal network.

First and foremost, your router must be protected physically. If the attacker can physically access your router, it's not your router anymore. If they physically remove it, you will lose access to all the networks that router provides connectivity for. If they turn it off, the result will be the same. If they reboot it, they can quite possibly change the password(s) and now they have logical access as well. This could lead to them reading router configurations and possibly setting up a redirect of traffic to a compromised network.

Routers are also subject to logical attack. The attacker will try to use a network attached to the router to gain access. This might involve trying to log into the router using remote management tools like telnet or Secure Shell (SSH). The attacker may also try to set up a DoS attack and swamp the router with ping packets or other traffic that will effectively keep the router from doing its job.

Router Security

Routers are continuously sharing route information with other routers. The techniques vary between routing protocols, but it is important to protect that information so it isn't intercepted. Early routing protocols had no provisions for even password protecting the exchange of information between routers. All routing protocols since RIPv2 have provided an authentication method, but initially it wasn't widely adopted. Now companies are taking much more aggressive steps to protect their routers, not only with strong password policies, but better access control and encryption as well.

To protect your router, implement the following security measures:

- Deploy the router in a secure, locked area to limit physical access.
- Disable all unnecessary services on the router, including any web-based administrative interface.
- Disable any unnecessary routing protocols.
- Harden the router per the manufacturer's recommendations.
- Prefer encrypted secure shell (SSH) over clear-text telnet when making a remote administrative connection to a router.
- Create access control lists to limit remote administrative connections to the router.
- Require strong authentication with a username and complex password when making an administrative connection to the router.
- Configure the router to limit the number of permitted administrative connections and to log out an inactive session after a few minutes.
- On higher-end routers such as Cisco, require authentication to a centralized server at every opportunity, including console access, virtual terminal remote connections, and escalated privileged levels.
- If possible, create custom administrative accounts with limited privileges for support personnel.
- Ensure that passwords are stored in an encrypted format in the router's configuration file.
- Configure the router to forward all security events to a central syslog server.
- Monitor activity on the router, and watch for suspicious behavior.

Boundary Routers

A boundary router is a router that sits at the edge of your network. It connects your network to a different autonomous system (another network under someone else's administrative control), usually the Internet. If you are an ISP, your boundary router connects you to another ISP. Boundary routers are also referred to as border routers.

Security Perimeter

Historically, we have always tried to identify a perimeter to define the zone we are trying to protect. Whether it was a wall, a moat, or even just circling the wagons, we drew some sort of physical or imaginary line around what we needed to protect. Different physical locations would have different levels of trust, from the open air market outside the castle, to the courtyard behind the drawbridge, to the audience hall just inside the castle, to council chambers and private quarters deep inside the castle. Each of these areas can be thought of as its own zone with different security requirements. Once you define the various zones and draw boundaries around those zones, you control the access points with gates, locked doors, bridges, security personnel, and the like to limit traffic in or out.

The same concept can be applied to your network. You must identify zones in your network, and determine the level of security required for each. The following table summarizes typical network security zones.

Zone	Description	Perimeter Security Control
Internet	Least trusted. The point where your network connects to your ISP.	Firewall.
Perimeter	Untrusted. A separate network connected to an additional interface on your firewall. Analogous to the side yard of a house. Public-facing servers such as web, email, or DNS servers are placed here.	Firewall.
Demilitarized zone (DMZ)	Untrusted. A separate network sandwiched between two firewalls. The outside firewall connects to the Internet. The inside firewall connects to your internal network.	Two firewalls. Alternatively, a packet filtering router could replace the outside firewall.
Intranet	Trusted. Your organization's private, internal network. Usually placed behind a firewall.	Firewall.
Extranet	Semi-trusted. A server or perimeter network provided for partners, vendors, contractors, customers, and the like. Typically requires a VPN connection or a login to a website.	Firewall, VPN server, or SSL-protected web server.
Remote Access	Usually a VPN or dial-up server placed outside the company's firewall. Typically has a secure connection that bypasses the firewall into the intranet. Remote users make secure connections to the server, and then are permitted to connect through it into the private network.	VPN or dial-up server. Can use multiple servers connected to Internet links for fault tolerance and load balancing. The Remote Access server must be locked down with the same care given to a firewall.
Virtual Local Area Network (VLAN)	Trust level depends on the purpose of the VLAN. A group of switch ports that are logically separated from the rest of the switch. Nodes on a VLAN can communicate with each other, but cannot directly communicate with other VLANS or networks. A router must be used to forward traffic in and out of a VLAN.	Switch, router.

Zone	Description	Perimeter Security Control
Secure Internal	Highly trusted. Any internal network that is separated from the rest of the intranet, and given a higher level of security. Often implemented as a virtual local area network (VLAN). In a military installation, will be a separate physical network with no connection to other networks.	Internal router or switch.

Network Partitioning

Network partitioning is a generic term that describes any method used to divide a network, physically or logically, into smaller separate networks. It is done for security, performance, or management reasons. You identify and implement boundaries based on:

- Security zone.
- Customer requirements.
- Administration/traffic management requirements.

Although you will end up with many smaller networks, they are actually easier to manage than a single large unwieldy network.

Network partitioning can be approached two ways:

- Using physically separate networks.
- Using virtualization.

Physically separate networks have their own cabling, switches and routers. An example is the U.S. Department of Defense SIPRNet (sipper-net) that is used to carry classified and secret transmissions, NIPRNet (nipper-net) for unclassified transmissions, and JWICS (Jay-wicks) for top secret transmissions. A common implementation of a physically partitioned network is a secure room that contains separate computers. Each computer is connected to its respective network. There is no connection between the computers, and any attempt to bridge the networks is technically not feasible. Operators with security clearance for all of the networks enter the room and simply switch computers, depending on the network they need to use. In some cases an operator that has security clearance to use some but not all of the networks is still allowed to enter the room, but cannot log on to the restricted computers.

You can also use VLANs to logically partition a network. An example of this is a business that separates each department into its own VLAN, or a university that separates each classroom into its own VLAN. Network administrators routinely use VLANs to create any number of separate network zones including server network, storage area network, VoIP network, guest network, wireless network, extranets, quarantined remote client network, perimeter networks, and DMZs. They are also used to add multiple switch ports to a single Internet connection to allow a separate device to monitor incoming and outgoing Internet traffic.

The risk of network partitioning is that you will do it incorrectly or ineffectively. Be sure to really understand how to implement network partitioning to support security. Cisco and other network equipment vendors have extensive documentation including use cases and configuration examples that they make freely available to the general public.

Firewalls

Firewall configuration and deployment comes in many different forms, depending on the purpose of the firewall. It pays to think about the layers of the OSI model at which different types of firewalls operate. Packet filtering and stateful inspection firewalls look at the information in Layer 3 and Layer 4 headers. Proxy and application layer firewalls look at Layers 5 through 7.

Firewall Type	Description
Packet filtering firewalls	These firewalls make decisions on packets as they move through the firewall. Each packet is treated individually and oftentimes the firewall is simply making decisions on the Layer 4 port number. The firewall generally starts by blocking all ports and then, as business needs dictate, certain ones are opened up. For example, the company may decide that it needs SMTP (25) and HTTPS (443) traffic to be allowed through.
Stateful inspection firewalls	These firewalls are a bit more sophisticated than packet filtering firewalls and will actually be able to determine the state of the packet. These firewalls can determine if the packet being evaluated is related to an earlier packet and if the conversation was initiated inside or outside.
Proxy firewalls	Proxy firewalls are devices that act as intermediary servers or gateways. They will terminate the connection and then re-initiate it if the traffic is warranted. A proxy firewall also has the added benefit of hiding the identity of the original sender, as it now appears that the conversation is coming from the proxy firewall.

Use the following recommendations when implementing your firewall:

- Take the time to really learn and implement the capabilities and limitations of your particular firewall product. While many administrators spend a great deal of time configuring the firewall, many other administrators leave firewalls in a default configuration, which might not be optimal.
- Recognize that your network has many other possible points of entry besides the firewall. Thee include wireless access points, VPN servers, dial-up modems, and even sneakernet (users physically transporting data on removable media, plugging devices into the network behind the firewall). Use as much care securing these alternate points of entry as you would your firewall.

Additional Firewall Terms

Additional firewall terms include the following:

- A *bastion host* is any server exposed to the Internet. This could be a public-facing server in the DMZ such as a web, DNS, or email server. It could also be a server that has proxy, firewall, or VPN services installed on it. By removing all unnecessary services from the bastion host, the device becomes less vulnerable to attacks and protects itself. Servers presented to the Internet should be configured as bastion hosts for the greatest level of protection.
- *Dual-homed firewalls* have two network ports. One port faces the Internet, or the untrusted part of the network, and the other port faces the trusted part of the network. These often form the inner and outer perimeters of networks.
- A *screening host* is a firewall with limited capabilities, such as a router that protects the trusted part of the network with ACLs.
- A *demilitarized zone (DMZ)*. The DMZ is a small network that sits between two back-to-back firewalls. It contains resources (servers) that are made available to Internet users. The outside firewall is directly connected to the Internet, while the inside firewall is directly connected to the internal network. The DMZ is considered to be an untrusted network because it contains bastion host devices that provide service to Internet users. These devices are typically web servers, DNS servers, and email relay servers. Internal users will also use DMZ resources, particularly the web server. A DMZ is often referred to as a *screened subnet*.
- A *perimeter network* is an alternate type of DMZ. With a perimeter network, the organization does not have two back-to-back firewalls. Instead, it has a single firewall with three interfaces. One interface connects to the Internet, one connects to the internal network (intranet), and one connects to the perimeter network. The bastion hosts are then placed in the perimeter network. As with a traditional DMZ, the perimeter network is considered untrusted.

- An *extranet* is an area of the network reserved for vendors, partners, and contractors. These people must log in to access its resources. It is typically a website, but it could also contain several servers that are accessed through a VPN. Extranets are often placed in a DMZ or perimeter network.
- *Network Address Translation (NAT)* is frequently the firewall's job. A NAT device translates a private IP address used inside networks, as defined by RFC 1918, to a public IP address that is routable on the Internet. *Port Address Translation (PAT)* is a type of NAT that uses port numbers, as a means of providing uniqueness, to allow hundreds of internal users to be serviced by a single, exterior IP address.

Endpoint Security

An emerging concept that has become an industry buzzword is *endpoint security*. Endpoint security, or endpoint protection, refers to a comprehensive solution that secures laptops and mobile devices as they remotely connect to the organization's network. It protects the corporate network by ensuring that each remote device, which is a potential entry point for attack, is in itself clean and healthy, and can only make a secure connection to the company network. Endpoint security software is installed on each device to enforce the security health of the device. This software is usually a multi-layered combination of firewall, VPN client, antivirus, antimalware, data encryption, and other security features.

The model for endpoint security is typically client/server, with a central server on the corporate network sending updates to the mobile clients, and controlling their access to the company's intranet. Endpoint security is considered to be a more comprehensive solution than mobile device management (MDM). Many endpoint security solutions include MDM as a feature.

CDN

A *content delivery network (CDN)* is a large distributed system of servers that serve web content to end users via the Internet. The servers are *proxy servers* that cache (temporarily store) content obtained from the original source server(s). These proxy servers can number in the thousands. They are strategically placed in data centers around the world, each servicing end users in their geographical region. The goal is to provide the best possible end user experience, serving multimedia content with high availability and high performance.

The most common deployment of CDNs are the streaming media servers used by online news outlets, Internet portals, and social media sites. Online retailers and financial services also depend on CDNs to provide the best possible customer experience on their websites. CDNs provide a large percentage of the Internet content we enjoy today. They deliver any combination of text, graphics, scripts, audio, video, files, software, and documents.

Although most CDNs are deployed publicly on the Internet, companies can also deploy their own private CDNs on their internal network. A company can use a CDN to deliver internal news, live video streams, teleconferences, documents, and software across the enterprise.

CDNs do not introduce any new or exotic security risks, but rather the same vulnerabilities that show up in other systems. The most prevalent CDN vulnerabilities include:

- Lack of sufficient input validation: These can result in malicious requests made to random CDN proxy servers to bombard the original source server with requests for content refresh, causing a distributed denial of service attack against the company's source server.
- Lack of good user session management: Then coupled with malicious input, can result in system hacking or abuse.
- The acceptance by humans of self-signed certificates from unknown publishers (read: malicious hackers). Content that is self-signed is still accepted as trustworthy because it uses a certificate, even though the origin of that certificate is unknown. This means that hacked, malicious content can masquerade as being legitimate, and be distributed by the CDN.

The security practitioner can use the following methods to mitigate CDN vulnerabilities:

- Scan for malware.
- Filter out unwanted/dangerous content.
- Deploy security systems that intelligently scan the content, looking for potential threats, and to detect and block problematic traffic.
- Install endpoint protection and security controls on end-user devices in your enterprise.
- Educate your users to make good choices about accepting content that is digitally signed by an unknown publisher.

 Note: Content delivery networks are also known as content distribution networks.

Physical Devices

When we think of physical devices, we tend to think of computer-type devices and networking hardware. However, there are other types of physical devices that play a role in network security. As such, they should be given careful consideration when deployed in your environment. They are found in most server rooms, and include (but are not limited to):

- Equipment racks.
- Cabinets.
- Patch panels.
- PC and laptop mounting hardware.
- Cable trays and cable management.
- Keyboard-Video-Mouse (KVM) switches.
- Power strips/power adapters.
- Fiber optic to Ethernet media converters.
- Telecom smart jacks.
- Power-over-Ethernet (PoE) power injectors.

The security practitioner can use the following methods to secure non-computer physical devices:

- Physically secure all devices against tampering or accidents.
- Lock cabinets and rack doors.
- Use cable locks on laptops and small PCs.
- Mount power adapters, smart jacks, media converters, and other miscellaneous devices to a plywood backboard on the wall, off the ground, where they can be easily monitored and serviced.
- Consider using a lights out approach to server management, where there is no convenient keyboard, mouse, monitor, or KVM connected to the server for an intruder to use.
- Rather than letting non-rack-mountable equipment sit at the bottom of an equipment rack, place it on boltable trays above the rack floor.
- Route all cables both inside racks and in the ceiling in managed bundles and cable trays, using looping and other strain-relief methods, so that they do not obscure your view, strain the cable or equipment, or cause a safety hazard.

Guidelines for Implementing Network Components Security

Here are some guidelines you can use to secure network components:

- Harden routers, switches, firewalls, and other networking components based on the manufacturer's recommendations.
- Use VLANs to partition your network and segregate traffic.
- Use physical network partitioning in high-security environments.
- Use firewalls to protect your internal network from the Internet.

- Deploy public-facing servers such as web, email, and DNS servers in a DMZ or perimeter network.
- Lock down your remote access server with the same care and attention you would give to your firewall.
- Use endpoint security to provide comprehensive protection for (and from) remote users.
- If you use a CDN, ensure that it is protected against malware, insufficient input validation, and poor session management. Also educate users to not automatically accept content that uses self-signed certificates.
- Secure any non-computer physical devices against tampering or accidents.

ACTIVITY 4–2
Analyzing Network Components Security

Scenario

In this activity, you will demonstrate your understanding of network topologies, networking media, and networking devices.

1. How can a hub help a hacker eavesdrop on the network?

   ○ It could be used to capture and redirect traffic flowing through it to a single unauthorized destination.

   ○ It repeats all traffic out every port.

   ○ It can intelligently forward traffic to the port the hacker is using.

   ○ It has a MAC address table of all devices that the hacker can easily download.

2. Your network comprises a wired Ethernet network and one wireless access point (WAP). When clients access resources on the wired LAN after connecting through the WAP, what is the most appropriate term to describe the role of the WAP?

   ○ Firewall

   ○ Switch

   ○ Choke Point

   ○ Gateway

3. Which statements about network hardware are correct? (Choose two.)

   ☐ Routers use protocols like RIP, BGP, and EIGRP to communicate with client systems.

   ☐ Routers operate at Layers 2 through 4 of the OSI model.

   ☐ Firewalls may be implemented as hardware or software, and may operate at Layers 2 through 7 of the OSI model.

   ☐ Switches use Media Access Control (MAC) addresses to forward frames to destination ports.

4. Which statement best describes a physical star-logical bus topology?

   ○ All nodes are connected by a singular, linear data path, but all communications are distributed through one central device.

   ○ All nodes are connected to a central device, but communications between nodes are as if they are all connected to a singular, linear data path.

   ○ Each node connects directly to two other nodes, but communications between nodes are as if they are all connected to a singular, linear data path.

   ○ All nodes are connected to a central device, but communications are as if all nodes are directly connected to all other nodes.

5. Which statement is true regarding circuit-switched and packet-switched networks? (Choose two.)

   ☐ Of the two, a circuit-switched network is more secure.

   ☐ Of the two, a packet-switched network is more secure.

   ☐ In terms of bandwidth utilization, a circuit-switched network is more efficient.

   ☐ In terms of bandwidth utilization, a packet-switched network is more efficient.

6. A security zone that allows some hosts within it to be accessible from the Internet is called which of the following? (Choose two.)
   - ☐ DMZ
   - ☐ Proxy firewall
   - ☐ NAT
   - ☐ Screened subnet
   - ☐ Bastion host
   - ☐ PAT

7. True or False? Stateful Inspection Firewalls are the basis of many web application proxy servers.
   - ☐ True
   - ☐ False

8. How could a router be used to eavesdrop on a network?
   - ○ It could be used to capture traffic into a log file for later unauthorized review.
   - ○ It could be used to block legitimate traffic so a sniffer can capture that traffic.
   - ○ It could be used to capture and redirect traffic flowing through it to an unauthorized destination.
   - ○ It can be planted like a bug on the network.

9. You are the network security consultant for a small college. Recently, students have been hacking into the school's database to change their records. How can you use VLANs to help mitigate this?
   - ○ You can use VLANs to encrypt the database.
   - ○ You can use VLANs to isolate the database from the rest of the network.
   - ○ You can use VLANs to apply sensitivity labels to your data.
   - ○ You can use VLANs to facilitate intrusion detection on your network.

10. How can you use a content delivery network to conduct a denial-of-service attack on a company server?
    - ○ You can configure CDN servers to bombard Internet root DNS servers with requests for lookups to the original content server.
    - ○ You can configure CDN servers to withhold lookup results from clients.
    - ○ You can configure CDN servers to bombard the source server with random content requests.
    - ○ You can configure CDN servers to withhold client lookup requests from the source server.

11. What is the purpose of a switch?
    - ○ Connects multiple networks that share common protocols.
    - ○ Delivers frames to destination ports based on MAC addresses.
    - ○ Analyzes traffic against rules based on source and/or destination address, port numbers, and/or protocol type.
    - ○ Converts data between disparate systems.

TOPIC C

Communication Channel Security

This topic is an extension of what you learned about data in transit in Lesson 2. As more and more of your users are working from multiple devices and multiple locations, you certainly have a lot of data in transit. Thinking about how your users are accessing and using systems can be the first step in protecting those systems.

Communication Channel Overview

When two nodes talk to each other on a network, their communication channel may need to be secured from tampering or interception. On a normal data network, this is generally not considered necessary. There are several cases, however, where extra security steps should be taken:

- During voice, conferencing, and collaboration sessions.
- When a user works remotely.
- In high security installations such as military or government.

The most common way of securing a communication channel is to encrypt it. If the organization owns all of the cabling and network equipment end-to-end, the link itself could be encrypted using hardware-based encryption at the two ends of the channel. In most cases, however, encryption is performed at a higher level so that the encrypted traffic can traverse any network, including the Internet.

Voice Vulnerabilities

Since the invention of the telephone, making a phone call has been an inherently insecure process. From early party lines where callers could hear other people's conversations, to governments tapping phone lines to eavesdrop on citizens, to cellular phone calls being intercepted, voice communications has had its fair share of vulnerabilities. Unfortunately, much of the security vulnerabilities have also been traditionally ignored.

Now that many companies have upgraded their internal phone systems to VoIP, voice calls also have the same security concerns as any other data transmission, including unauthorized access, spoofing, denial-of-service, hijacking, man-in-the-middle, and capturing/recording.

The following table summarizes common security issues with voice communications.

Issue	Description
Eavesdropping	Unauthorized listening can occur at any number of points along the path of the phone call, if the system is POTS, VoIP, or cellular. In the early days of VoIP, packets were sent unencrypted across the network. They could thus be intercepted. The entire phone conversation could be recorded, reconstructed, and played back.
Wiretapping	This is a form of eavesdropping where phone lines are physically tapped into with additional wiring and a listening device.
Phreaking	Phone hackers known as phreakers have found many ways over the years to hack public phone booths or break into a company's phone system to make free long distance phone calls. A lot of phreaking occurred because companies did not bother to change the default administrator password on their PBX. The phreaker would dial the company's main number, then press a series of buttons to gain administrative access to the PBX. From there, the phreaker could use the company's internal phone system to make long distance or international calls.

Issue	Description
Wardialing	A hacker uses a software program that automatically dials a long list of telephone numbers, in the hopes that one would have a dial-up modem or remote access server at the other end. If the receiving end answered with the correct signal, then the war dialing program would make note of it for the hacker to use later. In some cases the software would even attempt to log in using a list of common user names and passwords.
IMSI-catcher	This telephony eavesdropping device performs man in the middle attacks on cell phones, also tracking the mobile device's movements. It does so by capturing the phone's unique identifier known as the international mobile subscriber identifier (IMSI). IMSI-catchers are usually implemented as rogue cell towers, placed in plain view of the public. However, a reasonably skilled hobbyist can build a smaller version for only a few thousand dollars. Mobile devices that are within the IMSI-catcher's vicinity are lured to connect to it because of its relatively higher signal strength. The IMSI device instructs the mobile phone to not use encryption. In this way the phone call can be eavesdropped on as the call is forwarded to a legitimate cellular carrier.

 Note: For more information on phreaking, visit **www.2600.com.**

 Note: To read an interesting article on IMSI-catchers, see **https:// www.washingtonpost.com/world/national-security/researchers-try-to-pull-back-curtain-on-surveillance-efforts-in-washington/2014/09/17/f8c1f590-3e81-11e4-b03f-de718edeb92f_story.html**.

Securing Voice

Initially, voice networks were considered secure because they were a separate network provided by a separate carrier. Because calls were circuit switched with only a temporary connection, it was pretty hard to intercept a phone call. Wiretapping was usually done at the customer or home premises, outside of the phone company's view.

Phone carriers have long since moved to a digital infrastructure. The ability to packet switch or cell switch voice traffic makes it considerably easier for carriers to manage their networks. It also adds a whole host of considerations to securing voice. The following table summarizes countermeasures to the issues listed earlier.

Vulnerability	Countermeasure
Eavesdropping	When possible, encrypt all phone communications from end-to-end. Configure the PBX/PABX to disallow internal users from listening in on incoming phone calls that they have transferred to another user.
Wiretapping	Since wiretapping can now occur anywhere, including at the carrier's switching station, when possible encrypt voice traffic from end-to-end to make intercepted calls unintelligible.
Phreaking	Change the default administrative passwords on your company's PBX/PABX. Use the manufacturer's recommendations to harden the PBX/PABX just as you would any other network device.
Wardialing	If you must use a dial-up modem, make sure the number is unlisted and not in the same block of phone numbers used by the rest of the company. This will make it harder for a hacker to identify the number as belonging to you. If possible, configure the modem to only answer calls from certain numbers.

Vulnerability	Countermeasure
IMSI-catcher	If possible, use phones that do not negotiate the encryption level with their cell tower. Currently, phones that provide such end-to-end strong encryption are expensive. Some tech companies are creating products that can detect unusual cellular activity patterns or the fingerprints of known IMSI-catcher devices. This is a new field, however, so be cautious about vendor claims that all IMSI-catching activity can be discovered.

In addition to the points listed above, use the following network techniques to add security to voice:

- Segregate all voice traffic into its own VLAN.
- Only use VoIP products that encrypt the call (most products nowadays have encryption built in).
- Design redundancy into your VoIP network, including a spare PABX, redundant links, and redundant switching/routing.
- If external administrative access is permitted to the PABX across the Internet, change the default port to something random, and require strong authentication.

Collaboration

As employees and project teams become more geographically distributed, there will be a special need for collaboration products that work across the local area network as well as the wide area network.

Collaboration refers to the use of technology to conduct virtual meetings between two or more participants, usually in different locations. Depending on the product used, collaboration can include any or all of the following features:

- **Audio/video conferencing**: Uses cameras, microphones, and monitors (often large, high-definition TV screens) to create virtual meetings. Participants can belong to the organization or not. They can join the meeting from all over the globe to see and hear each other. PowerPoint slides, spreadsheets and other documents are often shared and simultaneously viewed during the conference. Participants can also share a whiteboard that they can draw on together. They can even share their own desktops for others to view. These tools can also be used to support webinar-style presentations.
- **Peer-to-peer file sharing**: End users are able to send files to each other by dragging and dropping the files into their collaboration session window.
- **Remote meeting**: A form of conferencing in which the organization's employees connect while working from home. They make a remote connection into the corporate network to join a conference.
- **Instant messaging**: End users are able to hold conversations with each other primarily using text, but also with images and video. This makes it easier for users to quickly communicate when speaking in person is not feasible.

A collaboration session can be as small as two people sitting at different desks in the same department, or as large as hundreds of people attending an online town hall meeting. Individual users can participate using an application on their computer or mobile phone. Some desktop phones have collaboration capabilities built in as well. Elaborate systems can accommodate an entire room full of people using multiple cameras, microphones, and televisions, giving participants a panoramic view of life-sized moving images in high definition.

Collaboration products can make your teams more productive if used well but they can also present vulnerabilities. Like all software, it is important to follow manufacturers' recommendations and to maintain updates as necessary. And as always, it is important to train your users in the proper usage of the tools and to make sure they follow all applicable policies.

Note: Do not confuse collaboration peer-to-peer file sharing with BitTorrent-style distributed peer-to-peer file sharing. In BitTorrent, multiple sources "swarm" together to collectively provide a file. Much of what is traded on BitTorrent is illegal and virus infected.

Collaboration Security Concerns

The following table summarizes common collaboration methods and security concerns.

Collaboration Type	Security Concerns
Audio/Video Conferencing	Much A/V conferencing equipment is not hardened properly, or is accessed via a public IP address with little or no firewall protection. Many systems are also configured to automatically answer an incoming video call request. This allows a hacker to start a video conference from the outside, even though there is no one else in the room at the other end. The system's microphones and cameras can then be used to spy around the room, or listen in on nearby conversations. Compromised systems can also be used to launch an internal attack on the organization. The riskiest part of A/V conferencing is that senior management uses it the most, frequently discussing topics that are highly sensitive. Additionally, many user-initiated conferences are not configured properly to keep uninvited parties from joining the conference.
Peer-to-Peer File Sharing	Although it is less likely for files shared within an enterprise to be infected with a virus, it is of course still possible. The risk increases with participants who are making a remote connection from outside the enterprise, and are thus outside the control of the enterprise IT team. It is also possible for excessive file sharing to consume too much bandwidth, especially if the Internet link is slow.
Remote Meeting	The primary concern associated with a remote meeting is that if you don't configure the system properly, you cannot prevent unauthorized people from joining your meeting. Unauthorized attendees might also be able to exploit the meeting to attack the internal network.
Instant Messaging	Instant messaging is a standard feature of collaboration. It is also a common vehicle for social engineering. Send someone what they think is going to be a picture or video, and really it's malicious code. They double-click it and now the virus is inside the network.

Note: For an interesting report on hacking video conferencing systems, see the article "Board Room Spying for Fun and Profit" at **https://community.rapid7.com/community/metasploit/blog/2012/01/23/video-conferencing-and-self-selecting-targets**.

Securing Collaboration Solutions

Use the following guidelines for securing your collaboration solutions:

* Spend the time actually learning how to configure security settings on your collaboration devices and software.
* Always require authentication for users and devices to participate in collaboration.
* Place collaboration systems behind a firewall that is intelligent enough to map incoming calls to specific devices.
* Use manufacturer recommendations to implement specific security settings.
* Keep patches updated, especially for the collaboration software itself.

Terminal Emulation

Terminal emulation refers to any technology that allows you to open a remote console connection to a device using a window on your computer. Many network devices including routers, switches, firewalls, and other appliances have no provision for you to plug in a monitor, mouse, or keyboard. They don't provide a graphical user interface,only a command prompt for administration. To access that command prompt, you plug a USB or other serial cable to a console port on the device. You then plug that cable into your PC. You access the console of the device by opening a terminal emulation program (terminal emulator). The terminal emulator presents the device's console inside a window on your computer.

Most terminal emulator programs also allow you to make Telnet or SSH connections across the network to administer the device. If the device is configured to permit it, you specify the IP address of the device to make the connection and obtain its command prompt.

Screen scraping is a form of terminal emulation that allows you to access legacy programs on newer hardware. For example, you might use screen scraping software to connect to an old program running on a mainframe. The screen scraper presents the program in a window on your PC. This lets you continue to use the program without having to find or develop a modern replacement.

From a security perspective, terminal emulation is really useful in that it allows administrators to access network devices without having to enter the server room. There is a risk, however, that if you do not put restrictions on the devices and require strong authentication, unauthorized users could also access your devices, even across the Internet.

Remote Access

Remote access refers to the ability to connect to the company network from a remote location, such as your home, a hotel, an airport, or a coffee shop. Unlike simply connecting to a public-facing server such as a web server, with remote access you access internal services on the company network as if you are physically there. You can connect to file and print servers, database servers, email servers, even the computer at your desk.

Initially remote access was used by telecommuters and road warriors who needed access to files, databases, and email from the internal network while away from work. A remote access connection allowed them to participate on the company network as if they were there plugged into it. The connection was slower because of the distance and technologies used, but they could do everything they normally would as if they were sitting at their own desk in the office.

Eventually remote access became more sophisticated, allowing users to take remote control of a specific machine inside the company network. You could see and interact with a computer's desktop from a remote location as if you were sitting at that computer. Administrators routinely used this capability to work on servers, routers, and switches without going to the server room. The Help Desk also quickly adopted the technology as it allowed them to help users without going to the user's desk.

There are two ways to make a remote access connection:

- Dial-up: You make a connection over a telephone call. Today that call can be made over a landline or cellular network. The connection speed is slow, and you are probably paying for the long distance call or minutes of airtime. However, it is convenient when you don't have Internet access, or you would like to make a remote connection to a server outside the normal network.
- Virtual Private Network (VPN): You make an encrypted connection across the Internet. This does not incur any additional costs besides your Internet access. It is also usually much faster, provided your Internet connection speed is good.

Regardless of the type of remote access connection you make, there needs to be a remote access server (RAS) waiting to receive your connection at the other end. In the early days of remote access, this was a server that had a dial-up modem attached to it. The modem was plugged into a telephone line. You made a phone call to the server. It would answer the call, and let you make a connection. With the advent of broadband, most people started using VPN connections across the Internet rather than paying for long-distance phone calls. Most dial-up remote access servers had the ability to accept VPN connections as well. No matter which way you contacted the server, you could enter the network through it.

Remote Access Security

The risk of using an RAS has always been that it bypasses the firewall. You make a connection on the outside, and then pass through the RAS to the inside. An even greater risk is that administrators have paid far less attention to securing the RAS than they have securing the firewall. A lot of effort is usually put into securing a firewall, but security on an RAS (particularly the dial-up part) is often very lax. Since an RAS is a public facing server, not protected by a firewall, it is an easy target for hackers.

When deploying an RAS, be sure to do the following:

- Require strong authentication for all users, preferably using certificates.
- Require two-factor authentication for administrator connections.
- Harden the RAS as much as possible, eliminating unnecessary services and protocols, especially file and print, web, database, and other common server services.
- Change default passwords and default configurations.
- Install a good security suite on the operating system.
- Turn on the software firewall on the RAS.
- Lock incoming user accounts after three bad login attempts.
- Install intrusion detection on the network directly behind the RAS.

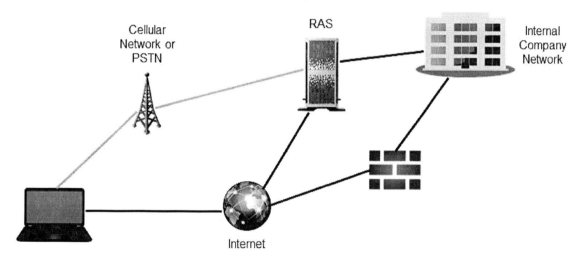

Figure 4–8: Connections to an RAS bypassing the firewall.

VPN

VPNA *Virtual Private Network (VPN)* is a remote access connection across a common network, usually the Internet. The encrypted connection is called a tunnel. Each user packet is hidden inside another packet, encrypted, and then sent across the network. Even if the packets are intercepted, the encryption makes it difficult to see the contents of the packet. The packets arrive at the company VPN server. They are removed from their outer protective packets and decrypted. They are then sent into the private network as normal traffic.

 Note: A user's connection across the Internet is analogous to a long line of cars forming a convoy on a highway. In the case of a VPN, the cargo in each car is hidden, locked, and secret.

The risk of using VPNs is that you might implement yours inadequately, especially through misconfiguration or the use of weak passwords. Be sure to use strong authentication and encryption when you configure your VPN.

Different VPN types use different protocols to encapsulate (hide), encrypt, and authenticate the packets. The following table summarizes the most popular types of VPNs.

VPN Type	Description
Point-to-Point Tunneling Protocol (PPTP)	A Microsoft proprietary VPN type. It encrypts the data, but does not digitally sign the packets, so packet integrity and authenticity is not guaranteed. Only the user is authenticated. Neither the client computer nor the server have to prove their identity. PPTP was popular for many years because it was easy to set up, and could pass through a firewall or network address translating router without breaking the tunnel.
Layer 2 Tunneling Protocol (L2TP)	This VPN type requires that every packet be digitally signed, and that both the client and server authenticate to each other. It is not concerned with user authentication; only machine authentication. It uses a vendor neutral protocol that can carry payloads other than IP. LT2P does not natively encrypt the data, so it is often coupled with IPSec for encryption. It is considerably more secure than PPTP and was long a popular choice for commercial VPN clients.
IP Security (IPSec)	This VPN type uses two protocols, one for authentication and one for encryption. Both protocols digitally sign the packet. Either or both can be used to form the tunnel, depending on the requirement. IPSec is the single most popular VPN type in existence. It is used not only in client/server connections, but also site-to-site VPNs between routers.
SSL VPN	While not technically a VPN (there is no encapsulation), SSL VPNs have nonetheless become very popular because they require no special software on the client end, and can easily go through a firewall. As with an ordinary SSL web connection, only the payload (contents) of the packet is encrypted, not the packet itself. SSL VPN clients are typically ordinary web browsers, though you can also use a separate client application that is SSL enabled. The client connects to a specially configured web server that acts as a portal into the corporate network. Like other bastion hosts, it sits behind a firewall. Permitting SSL through a firewall is very easy. Most firewalls are already configured to permit such connections.

> **Note:** For more information on SSL VPNs, see
> **www.cisco.com/c/en/us/td/docs/ios/12_4t/12_4t11/ htwebvpn.html#wp1053815.**

 Note: Technically, a tunnel does not have to be encrypted. You can encapsulate one protocol inside another for compatibility reasons, such as hiding IPv6 inside of IPv4 packets for transmission across the Internet. With VPNs, however, the tunnel is always encrypted for security.

IPSec

Internet Protocol security (IPSec) is a set of two open, non-proprietary protocols that can be used to secure IP traffic as it travels across the network or the Internet. It works at OSI Layer 3, encapsulating, digitally signing, and optionally encrypting the packet.

The two protocols that make up IPSec are:

- Authentication Header (AH): This digitally signs the IP header, providing machine authentication, integrity, and non-repudiation. AH does not encrypt the packet.
- Encapsulating Security Payload (ESP): This inserts an extra digitally signed UDP header in front of the payload, and then encrypts the payload.

You can use one or both protocols to protect your traffic, but remember that AH only digitally signs; it does not encrypt. Also remember that IPSec is concerned with authenticating machines, but not users.

The risk of using IPSec is that you might use weak passwords or you might not use ESP when you need to encrypt. Be sure to use the strongest authentication and encryption possible when implementing IPSec.

IPSec Modes

IPSec has two modes of operation:

- Transport mode: The tunnel is created between two endpoints. It is used to create a client/server VPN. The data is protected from the moment it leaves the client's or server's network interface card, remaining encapsulated until it reaches the other machine.
- Tunnel mode: The tunnel is created between two routers. It is used to create a site-to-site VPN. Traffic inside a site is unaffected. Any traffic bound for the other site becomes encapsulated and encrypted as it leaves the router and enters the Internet. Once it arrives at the other site, the router at that end de-encapsulates and decrypts the packet, passing the packet into that site as normal traffic.

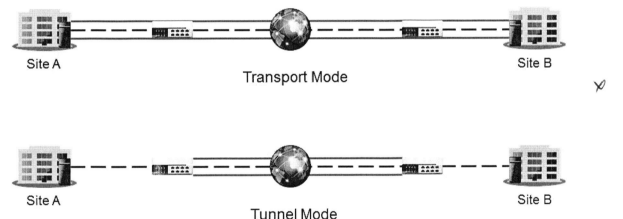

Figure 4-9: IPSec modes of operation.

Before an IPSec tunnel is created, the two ends must first agree on the level of service. The agreement is made during a process called the Security Association (SA). Two different SAs are required: one for sending and another for receiving. The Security Association includes:

- Negotiating the time limit for the SA.
- The mode (tunnel or transport).
- The ESP encryption algorithm, key, and initialization vector (IV).
- The ESP authentication algorithm and key.
- The AH authentication algorithm and key.
- A sequence number counter.

Periodic renewal of the security association ensures that both ends stay connected so the communication may continue.

The IPSec Process

The two IPSec protocols work together to achieve the desired result. It is hybrid encryption using a combination of hashing, symmetric, and asymmetric encryption.

Whether transport or tunnel mode is used, IPSec requires that certain processes occur to be successful. IPSec uses two capabilities to deliver confidentiality and integrity. Confidentiality is provided through the use of an Encapsulated Security Payload (ESP) header, which provides information about the encrypted part of the IPSec messages. Integrity and authentication are handled by the Authentication Header (AH). However, it is important to note that ESP can also handle authentication and integrity. In fact, ESP could be used by itself to provide all three services (confidentiality, integrity, authentication), making the AH optional.

Before IPSec can connect between the two ends of a connection, it must first agree on the services to provide. The agreement is made during a process called the Security Association (SA). Two different SAs are required: one for sending and another for receiving. The Security Association includes:

- Negotiating the time limit for the SA.
- The mode (tunnel or transport).
- The ESP encryption algorithm, key, and initialization vector (IV).
- The ESP authentication algorithm and key.
- The AH authentication algorithm and key.
- A sequence number counter.

Periodic renewal of the security association ensures that both ends stay connected so the communication may continue.

SDNs

Software Defined Networking (SDN) separates network control (decisions about where to send data traffic) from data forwarding (the underlying mechanism that actually delivers the data to its destination). It divides the network into three basic layers in order to have a more adaptable environment:

- **Application**: How the data is used.
- **Controller**: Software defining how the data is sent.
- **Data plane**: Physical network components (for example, switches and routers) that actually move the data.

The application explicitly and programmatically sends its network requirements to the controller. It tells the controller how it wants the network to behave. The controller then translates the application's requirements, sending them down to the data plane.

The data plane consists of generic switches and routers, also known as whitebox switches. These physically look like traditional Layer 2/3 (multi-layer) switches, but they receive their intelligence from the controller. Rather than the whitebox switch building its own forwarding/routing table (as in traditional systems), the controller uses an application programming interface (API) to program the forwarding table of the whitebox switch. It dictates how the whitebox switch should route the traffic to achieve the application's requirements.

Both cloud computing and virtualization can benefit from SDN. Both functions need:

- Better traffic management.
- Scalability.
- Reliability of critical data delivery.
- Increased bandwidth.
- Faster provisioning of network services.

SDN is able to implement higher-level policies to control network traffic based on the shifting needs of users, devices, and applications. The down side of SDN is that you would have to deploy new network devices in order to separate the control plane from the data plane.

From a security perspective, SDN architecture enhances network security because the controller has a central view of the network. It can collect statistics from the data plane, and then apply an algorithm to detect any anomalies. If any unusual behavior is detected, the controller can reprogram the data plane to respond. This makes the SDN more resilient in the face of distributed denial of service (DDoS) attacks, botnets, and worms. It can also implement moving target defense (MTD) algorithms that periodically hide or change key properties of the network, thus making it harder to analyze for attack. It can also randomly fake open, closed, and filtered ports on different hosts, making the reconnaissance (scanning) phase of a hacking attack less useful.

 Note: SDN architecture also includes subcomponents and interfaces between the major components. For more information, see **https://en.wikipedia.org/wiki/Software-defined_networking#Architectural_components**.

Virtualized Networks

The term virtualized network can refer to a number of different things, all of which can be used to create security on a communication channel.

The risk of implementing virtualized networks is that you will not properly configure them to adequately separate the networks. Make sure you take the time to really understand the underlying technologies and how to implement them properly. Cisco and other network vendors provide extensive free online resources for configuring virtualization in your network.

Virtualized Network Type	Description
Physical networks combined into a logical structure.	An example of this would be combining a data center network and a wide area network into a single cohesive logical unit that can be administered from a single console.
Networks in a hypervisor-based virtual machine environment.	Virtual machines connect to each other (and the outside world) by connecting to virtual switches that are also part of the virtual environment. This type of virtualization even allows virtual machines to connect to physical storage area networks (SANs) through the use of virtual storage area networks (virtual SANs). These virtual SANs are actually software connections that form a bridge between the virtual machine and actual SAN hardware.
Network virtualization (NVs) with NFVs and SDNs.	A virtualized network can also refer to a series of connections that are laid on top of a physical network. This type of connectivity is called *network virtualization (NV)*. It is a sort of tunnel that directly connects one part of the physical network with another part, without interacting with the parts in between. It's especially useful because administrators can create a network without having to physically wire the parts together. NVs are used a lot to connect virtual machines across a physical network.
	NVs work with two associated technologies:
	• Network Functions Virtualization (NFV): This is a Layer 4-7 function such as a firewall or intrusion detection/prevention. After creating the NV, you can immediately assign an NFV virtual firewall or IDS to one or both ends of the NV.
	• Software Defined Network (SDN): Makes the network programmable through the use of the SDN application and controller.

Virtualized Network Type	Description
VLANs and PVLANs.	As mentioned before, VLANs logically group switch ports together, creating multiple smaller, separate networks out of a single larger network. VLANs limit communications between devices on a network.
	A variant of the VLAN is the Private VLAN (PVLAN). PVLANs are actually smaller VLANs inside of a larger VLAN. Nodes in a PVLAN are restricted so that they can only connect to a specific uplink (connection that allows them to exit the VLAN). That uplink is a switch port that leads to a central resource such as a firewall or router to an ISP. PVLANs also allow you to reuse IP addresses within the same VLAN.
	An example of PVLANs can be seen in a hotel. Each floor in the hotel might be its own VLAN. Then, each hotel room on that floor is its own PVLAN. Multiple devices in that room can connect together, and they all can connect to the room's uplink to the Internet. But the room PVLANs are kept separate, so that devices in one room cannot see devices in another room, even though all of the rooms are in the same VLAN.

Guidelines for Implementing Communication Channel Security

Here are some guidelines you can use to implement communication channel security:

- Always keep voice communications encrypted.
- Configure collaboration systems so that unwanted or unauthorized users cannot initiate or participate in a session.
- When high security is required, use IPSec (both AH and ESP) as your preferred VPN type.
- Use SSL VPNs when you need the convenience of being able to connect through a firewall without adding new firewall rules.
- Use IPSec transport mode when you want to create a secure end-to-end connection between nodes, such as a client and a server.
- Use IPSec tunnel mode when you want to create a site to site tunnel between two routers.
- Use software-defined networks when you want the flexibility to immediately and programmatically change your network connectivity and routing.
- Choose the appropriate virtualized network type depending on your communication channel security needs.

ACTIVITY 4-3
Analyzing Communication Channel Security

Scenario

In this activity, you will demonstrate your understanding of secure communication channels.

1. Your security policy states that all internal network traffic must be encrypted. It also requires authenticated connections between devices. To meet these requirements, you decide to implement IPSec. Which features of IPSec may be used to meet the policy requirements? (Choose two.)

   ☐ AH only

   ☐ ESP only

   ☐ AH and ESP

   ☐ ESP to send, AH to receive

2. What steps may be taken to secure collaboration products? (Choose two.)

   ☐ Keep the collaboration software updated/patched.

   ☐ Run collaboration products on Honeynets.

   ☐ Use CSMA/CD.

   ☐ Train users on the proper use of the collaboration products.

3. What aspect of remote access makes it particularly vulnerable to attack?

   ○ It is usually deployed in a DMZ or perimeter network, instead of behind the internal firewall

   ○ It mostly accepts dial-up connections with no firewall.

   ○ It is usually deployed in parallel to the firewall, thus bypassing firewall protections.

   ○ The fact that it uses older technology that is less secure.

4. What feature of an SSL VPN makes it easier to deploy? (Choose two.)

   ☐ It uses an SSL connection, which most firewalls are already configured to permit.

   ☐ It allows clients to use browsers to connect.

   ☐ It allows administrators to use existing routers to terminate the connection.

   ☐ It uses PPTP protocols, which are already built into most client and server systems.

5. What feature of a software-defined network makes it more intelligent than traditional networks?

   ○ It decentralizes switching and routing decisions, making the network more responsive.

   ○ It uses an architecture that monitors and manages traffic from a higher level.

   ○ It uses whitebox switches that can work with any system.

   ○ It uses generic components that are cheaper, thus allowing you to deploy a fuller infrastructure for the same amount of money.

6. **What is the fundamental difference between a VLAN and a PVLAN?**

   ○   A PVLAN is a VLAN that has its own IP addressing scheme.

   ○   A PVLAN is a type of VLAN that has been specially designed for hotels and other customer-facing implementations.

   ○   A PVLAN is a virtual network implementation, whereas a VLAN is a physical network implementation.

   ○   A PVLAN is a subdivision of a VLAN.

TOPIC D

Network Attack Mitigation

It would be impossible to describe all the different attacks that might take place. But if you learn the concepts and look at the big picture, you can begin your understanding of attack types.

Attackers

A hacker tries to discover and exploit weaknesses in a network or computer system. Hackers are motivated by a wide range of reasons: intellectual curiosity, the desire to improve security, profit, protest, challenge, or fun. The following table summarizes the various types of hackers.

Attacker Type	Description
White hat	Someone who breaks computer security for non-malicious purposes, usually to improve the security of that system. Also known as an ethical hacker. Named after the good guy in old western movies who always wore a white hat.
Black hat	Someone who breaks computer security for malicious reasons or personal gain. Also known as a cracker. Named after the bad guy in old western movies who always wore a black hat.
Grey hat	Someone whose ethics lie somewhere between white and black. This person may illegally break into systems to alert the company about weaknesses found. They might offer to fix the vulnerability for a fee. But they usually are more interested in learning how something works than hacking for malicious or personal gain.
Blue hat	A hacker employed to find security bugs in software so they can be patched before product launch.
Elite hacker	A highly skilled hacker. Almost always a programmer.
Hacktivist	Someone who hacks to support a cause.
Script kiddie	Someone who uses hacking tools written by others, with little or no understanding of the underlying technology.
Newbie	A beginner. Also known as noobie or noob.
Nation state	A country's cyberwarfare operatives.
Organized crime	A group that carries out organized criminal hacking for profit.

Attack Overview

Networks are subject to a number of different attacks that jeopardize their ability to support confidentiality, integrity, and availability. Due to the often secretive nature of hacking, most notably with the rise of selling zero day exploits (those with no existing patch) on the Dark Net (Internet black market), the true number of hacking exploits that exist in the world cannot reliably be determined. Offensive Security's exploit database currently boasts about 35,000 archived exploits This is the same number as are available in the exploit archives at Packetstormsecurity.com. NIST lists almost 75,000 known vulnerabilities in the National Vulnerability Database.

Many of the network attacks take tools and protocols that you use everyday, and turn them around to use them for nefarious purposes. Classic examples are TCP SYN floods and Smurf attacks. In both cases, normal networking operations are abused to cause denial of service attacks against a server.

The greatest risk associated with network attacks is that companies still don't take network security seriously enough. Almost every single organization in existence has either experienced a network security breach, or will experience one. Most of these breaches go undetected, unreported, and unmitigated.

Methodology of an Attack

The goal of any hacking attack is to compromise a system. The attacker might wish to steal data or other resources, use the hacked system as a platform for staging further attacks, make the system unusable for others, or simply prove a point.

Although the exact steps will vary, most attacks go through three basic stages:

* **Reconnaissance**: Look for potential weaknesses in the target.
* **Penetration**: Exploit any discovered weaknesses to gain access.
* **Control**: Once access is gained, use the system in an unauthorized manner.

In some cases, such as a denial-of-service, the penetration stage is skipped as there is no attempt to actually break into the system, only to control the availability (or unavailability) of the network or system.

Some attacks can be used at more than one stage. For example, social engineering can be used for either reconnaissance or penetration purposes. Sniffing can be used for penetration or control purposes.

Reconnaissance

Reconnaissance is the act of studying and analyzing your target. The goal of reconnaissance is to find a weakness that will permit you to launch an attack. Reconnaissance can be broken down into the following sub-stages:

* **Footprinting**: Conduct research to learn about your target:
  * Techniques are non-intrusive, mostly done online.
  * Create an overall profile of your target.
  * Look for ways to intrude into the environment.
  * Search for locations, business activities, names, titles, addresses, phone numbers, email addresses, IP addresses, policies, technologies the company uses—anything that might suggest an avenue for attack.
* **Scanning**: Discover systems and the services they offer on the target network:
  * Use automated tools to discover IP addresses, protocol, and ports used on the target's network.
  * This technique disguises itself as a series of legitimate client requests, eliciting responses from available systems.
  * Scan results provide a profile of operating systems and services on the network, and help narrow the scope of the next attack stage.
* **Vulnerability scanning**: Discover which systems/services respond to specific hacking techniques:
  * Send non-disruptive malicious code to an open port to see how the service responds.
  * Response type indicates whether or not the target is vulnerable to a known exploit, or if it has been patched.
  * If the target has not been patched, you can later attempt a full attack.
  * This step is an inquiry: You're not trying to break in yet.

Reconnaissance Techniques

The following table summarizes the most common reconnaissance techniques.

Technique	Description
Whois search	A type of footprinting, and a good starting point to research your target. You can find out basic domain registration information about the company, including its address, contact information, DNS servers, and possible network IP addresses.
Website mirroring	A type of footprinting in which you (slowly and stealthily) download a complete copy of a target's website. You then take your time combing through the copy thoroughly for names, titles, email addresses, phone numbers, job postings, etc. Using an offline copy ensures that your repeated queries to the website will not alert the company's webmaster.
Google hacking	A type of footprinting in which you use advanced Google search queries to discover additional information about the target, including files the company may have posted online.
Job board search	A type of footprinting in which you search for online job offerings by the company to discover what technologies they use, and what current staffing weaknesses they have.
EDGAR search	A type of footprinting in which you search the Electronic Data Gathering, Analysis, and Retrieval (EDGAR) online public database to discover additional information about the company.
Social engineering	The use of persuasive human interaction (phone calls, face-to-face, emails, social network postings, chat, etc.) to gain access and discover insider information about the company.
IP scanning	A type of scanning in which an attacker sends a ping request to every address in a subnet (block of IP addresses) to see which ones respond. A response indicates there is a computer or other device on the network that could be attacked.
Port scanning	A type of scanning in which an attacker sends a number of packets to a single IP address, each destined for a different port, to see which ports respond. A response indicates that there is a service on that device listening on that port for incoming client connections. You can analyze which port numbers have responded, including how they have responded, to build a profile and patch level of the target operating system. A patient hacker will run a port scan very slowly to evade detection.
Vulnerability scanning	A type of scanning in which different non-disruptive commands are sent to a port to see how it responds. The type of response indicates whether or not the system has been patched or is still vulnerable to attack.

Reconnaissance Countermeasures

Use the following countermeasures to minimize the risk of hacker reconnaissance against your network:

- Restrict information posted online to content you would be comfortable giving to a hacker.
- Immediately remove content of a sensitive nature from your website.
- Go to **www.google.com/remove.html** to request that Google remove from its cache any material that should not be online.
- If you cannot remove sensitive information from the Internet, take steps to make it irrelevant or less useful to a hacker. If you cannot, then take extra measures to protect the asset that information might expose.
- Change your web server error messages to limit the amount of server information that can be returned.

- Keep systems patched and up-to-date.
- Protect systems using firewalls and intrusion detection/prevention.
- Monitor who is scanning your systems.
- Harden all public-facing systems.
- Require strong authentication when possible.
- Deploy decoy systems to confound scanners.
- Configure intrusion detection to search for sniffers.
- Encrypt transmissions.
- Transfer the risk by using third-party providers to mirror your public servers.

Penetration Techniques

Penetration is the act of actively breaking into a system or the network. The goal of penetration is to take control of the system. The following table summarizes common penetration techniques. Most of the virus-type penetration attacks also carry a malicious payload that if opened immediately takes the attack into the control stage.

Penetration Technique	Description
Sniffing	*Sniffing* is the network equivalent of planting a listening device in a room. The sniffer records packets as they pass by in an attempt to obtain information about the network or its systems. You can also use a sniffer to capture passwords during network authentication, make copies of transmitted files, read or listen in on any transmission that is not encrypted such as email, telnet sessions, VoIP calls, network management messages, etc.
Password Cracking	*Password cracking* is a systematic attempt to figure out someone's password. The attempt is almost always done with an automated tool. There are three types of password cracking: • *Dictionary attack*: Trying thousands of common passwords in a list (dictionary) in the hopes that the user's password is in that list • *Rainbow attack*: Using a dictionary (rainbow table) that contains the encrypted form (pre-computed hash) of the passwords. Rainbow attacks are much faster than traditional dictionary attacks. • *Brute force attack*: Trying different combinations of characters until the password is discovered.
Keystroke Logging	*Keystroke logging* is a type of spying that captures every keystroke that a user types. The keystroke logger can be software installed on the system, or a physical device that looks like an adapter placed between the computer and the keyboard.
Malicious Code Attack	A *malicious code attack* is a type of code injection where an attacker injects (inserts) some type of malicious software, or *malware*, into the server or user's system to disrupt or disable the operating system or an application. A malicious code attack can also force the target system to disrupt or disable other systems on the same network or on a remote network.

Penetration Technique	Description
Buffer Overflow	A *buffer overflow* is a combination of malicious code injection and privilege escalation that exploits applications that do not perform input validation. Meaningless input is used to flood the input buffer (allocated memory space for input) of the application, eventually replacing part of the application's real code with malicious code. The application then runs that malicious code (usually in system-level privilege) as if it was a legitimate part of the application's code. Usually, an application that has had a buffer overflow attack will destabilize or crash. Restarting the service or rebooting the machine is the only way to restore functionality. Buffer overflows usually do not show up in any log. If you suspect a buffer overflow, use a vulnerability scanner to see if your system is susceptible.
Spam	While *spam,* sometimes referred to as unsolicited commercial email (UCE), usually does not cause a failure, it can cause network over-utilization by filling networks with unwanted email messages. It also has the ability to fill email server storage systems to capacity and block needed emails in lieu of the spam content. As a network attack, spam is a general nuisance to users, help desk personnel, staff, and administrators.
Virus	A *virus* is a malware or malicious program that attaches itself to another program. When the target program executes, the virus takes over and circumvents the security features of the system. Viruses can be used to steal data or cause a system failure.
Worm	A *worm* is a malware program that does not require the support of a target program like a virus. A worm is independent but is capable of duplicating itself to other devices in the network.
Logic Bomb	A *logic bomb* is malicious software that stays hidden and dormant on a system until an event such as a date or remote command detonates it. A disgruntled employee might leave a logic bomb to destroy files weeks or months after that person has safely left the company.
Ransomware	*Ransomware* is a particularly malicious type of virus that encrypts the victim's drive and then extorts the user for money to decrypt the drive. The device is completely disabled. The virus is designed to make it seem like the only way to restore functionality is to comply. Variations include placing pornographic images on the victim's machine, impersonating law enforcement, or targeting businesses. This type of attack has become increasingly sophisticated. Unfortunately, even when compromised users pay the ransom, functionality is often not restored. Ransomeware is usually delivered via suspicious websites, clicking an infected advertisement, or occasionally by email. Many antivirus vendors offer removal tools on their websites.
Trojan horse	A *Trojan horse* or *Trojan program* is unauthorized software that masquerades as legitimate software. It is usually malicious code embedded inside a normal application. Downloading a shareware program to clean a disk drive may look harmless, but if the program cleans the drive by reformatting it, the harm is obvious.

Penetration Technique	Description
Rootkit	A *rootkit* is a hacked version of a core operating system file. It is usually implanted into an operating system by virus or worm. It replaces the original file to perform malicious activity in the background. Rootkits are hard to detect, as they operate at a lower level than what is usually monitored by auditing software.
ARP poisoning	*ARP poisoning* is a type of spoofing that misdirects network traffic at Layer 2 to a hacker's machine, rather than the intended target. It is often used to facilitate man-in-the-middle attacks.
Hijacking	*Hijacking* is the act of taking the place of a client in a client/server session after the client has authenticated to the server. The server is unaware that the client has been replaced by a malicious actor. The client simply thinks it has lost connectivity with the server.
Man-in-the-middle	A *man-in-the-middle attack* occurs when an attacker interposes a device between two legitimate hosts to gain access to their data transmissions. The attacker captures and reads each packet, responds to it, and forwards it to the intended host, so that both the sender and receiver believe that they are communicating directly with each other. This deception allows attackers to manipulate the communication rather than just observe it passively.
Spoofing	*Spoofing,* or masquerading, comes in many forms wherein the attacker assumes an electronic identity to conceal his or her true person. **Internet Protocol (IP) address spoofing:** • Creates IP packets with a forged source IP address to mask the sender's identity. The attempt is to make it appear as if the packet came from a legitimate and trusted source. **Media Access Control (MAC) address spoofing:** • Intercepts frames by sending false Address Resolution Protocol (ARP) packets to a router or a switch. • ARP frames containing the MAC address of an attacker's machine replace the correct entries in the router and switch with the attacker's incorrect addresses. • The router and server send the frame to the attacker's MAC address where the information in the packets can be intercepted and modified. **Domain Name System (DNS) spoofing:** • Substitutes a different IP address for a domain name or host name within the DNS system. • Corrupts the lookup database of a local DNS server, replacing correct IP addresses with false information, thus redirecting clients to fake web servers. This type of DNS spoofing is also known as *DNS cache poisoning.*
Fake Wireless Access Point	A fake wireless access point is a device that masquerades as a real access point. Its relatively strong signal induces clients to connect to it, rather than legitimate access points. It will usually relay the client's traffic to the final intended destination so as not to arouse suspicion. As it is relaying the traffic, it is also capturing usernames, passwords, and other information. A commercially available fake access point called a *pineapple* can be easily obtained on the Internet.

Penetration Technique	Description
Fake Website	A fake website uses a combination of spoofing and social engineering. An attacker creates the fake website to trick the user into entering private information, or clicking something that will infect their computer. The website looks legitimate and may even borrow elements from the real website it is modeled after.
Cookie Stealing	A *cookie* is a text file that a browser downloads from a website. The text file is used to later identify the same browser when the user visits the site later. It can be used to extend the validity period of a user's login to the website, or to send targeting advertisements and marketing to the user. Cookie stealing is used to impersonate an already authenticated user to a website, such as an online shopping site. Since the site thinks the user has already logged on, the attacker can make purchases, transfer funds, or perform other activities posing as the user.
Cross Site Scripting (XSS)	*Cross-site scripting* is the act of injecting malicious code into input that you then post to a website (such as a social networking site or forum). As others view the post, they unknowingly download and execute the malicious code.
Cross Site Request Forgery (XSRF)	*Cross-site request forgery (XSRF)* embeds malicious code into a website a user trusts (often through cross-site scripting) to further exploit the user.
Clickjacking	*Clickjacking* is the act of taking control of a user's system by embedding malicious code in a web page. When the user clicks on normal controls on the page such as buttons, the malicious code runs in the background.
SQL Injection	SQL injection is a technique that nearly every SQL database management system was vulnerable to in 2003. It exploits an input validation bug in which a specially crafted query can trick the SQL server into running arbitrary commands. The notorious SQL slammer worm was based on this vulnerability. Although most vendors have patched the vulnerability, it still exists. To date, Apple iOS 7 mobile apps using the MySQL database are still vulnerable to SQL injection.
Social Engineering	Social engineering can also be used to trick users into revealing passwords and other sensitive information. Hackers try to gain the user's sympathy or trust, often posing as some sort of authority figure such as help desk personnel or a company director. One common social engineering technique is to scatter infected flash drives in the company parking lot.
Phishing	Phishing is a type of social engineering in which a fake email is sent to a large number of recipients. The email uses free offers or scare tactics to induce the user to click on a link or open a malicious file, thus infecting their machines with a virus. Phishing has variations: • Spear phishing: Phishing that targets specific companies or users. • Pharming: Using the Internet to automatically collect thousands of pieces of information and passwords. • Vishing: The act of using a phone to scam a user. Often performed by call centers overseas. • Smishing: SMS phishing, the act of using text messages to scam a user.
NFS Attacks	*Network File System (NFS)* attacks take advantage of poorly configured Linux computers. Hackers connect to these systems to steal data that has been shared on the network.

Penetration Technique	Description
Physical Attacks	An attacker might simply sit at an unguarded machine and attempt to log on or do something else such as install a keystroke logger or physically remove the hard drive from the computer.

 Note: This list is by no means exhaustive. For more hacking techniques, see **https://packetstormsecurity.com/**.

Penetration Countermeasures

Use the following countermeasures to minimize the risk of hacker penetration into your network:

- Physically protect devices and systems.
- Keep patches up-to-date.
- Keep antivirus up-to-date.
- Disallow script execution on browsers, or install anti-script plugins such as NoScript.
- Harden systems based on the manufacturer's recommendations.
- Require strong authentication.
- Require two factor authentication for administrators.
- Include input validation in your application's source code.
- Educate users to protect themselves.
- Regularly scan for rogue wireless access points.
- Lock user accounts after three or five bad login attempts.
- Monitor for malicious network or host activity.
- Keep all critical systems and data backed up.

Control

Control is the act of performing any desired action on a compromised system. Control can include any of the following activities:

- Gain control of a system.
- Escalate privilege.
- Steal, delete, or corrupt data.
- Denial-of-Service.
- Use the compromised system to stage additional attacks on other networks or systems.
- Plant a back door for further attacks.
- Eliminate evidence of the attack.

Control Techniques

The following table summarizes the most common control techniques.

Control Technique	Description
DoS	A *denial of service (DoS)* attack is a crude but effective way of taking down a system or network for a temporary amount of time. It goes straight to the control stage with little or no attempt to compromise a system through penetration. It focuses on the availability aspect of the CIA triad. DoS can target network devices, bandwidth availability servers, applications, and workstations. Most DoS attacks last for several hours or even days.
DDoS	*Distributed denial of service (DDoS)* uses multiple source machines (sometimes thousands) to perpetrate a coordinated DoS against a chosen victim. This is often done using previously compromised PCs that have been organized into a *botnet*.
Syn flood	A *SYN flood attack* is a type of denial of service that uses bogus client connection requests to keep a server too busy to service legitimate clients. An attacker sends multiple SYN messages initializing Transmission Control Protocol (TCP) connections with a target host. Since most servers are configured to handle only a limited number of concurrent client requests, the SYN flood uses up all of the available connections.
IP fragmentation attack	An *IP fragmentation attack* is one in which specially crafted pieces of an IP packet (IP fragments) are sent to the target. The target attempts to reconstruct the pieces into a single packet but cannot, because the pieces are malformed. This usually results in the target crashing or at least being extremely busy for awhile.
Ping of death	A *ping of death* is a type of IP fragmentation attack. In the attack, fragments of an oversized ping packet are sent to a target, causing the target to crash as it tries to reconstruct the pieces.
Smurf attack	In a *smurf attack*, multiple pings (ICMP echo requests) are sent to many computers. The source IP address, however, is spoofed to contain the address of the real target. The machines send their ping responses to the target, temporarily overwhelming it with traffic. Another common technique for a smurf attack is to ping the broadcast address of an IP subnet through the router. The router forwards the pings to all hosts on the target subnet, severely congesting the network.
Fraggle attack	A fraggle attack is a variation of a smurf attack that uses UDP instead of ICMP. UDP packets are sent through a router to the broadcast address of a subnet. The router will forward the UPD packets to all hosts on that subnet, severely congesting the network for awhile.
Arbitrary code execution	Exploiting software bugs in various applications to execute unexpected commands.
Remote code execution	A type of arbitrary code execution. Once the target has been compromised across the network, the attacker sends any command he or she wants to the compromised system. This is often done through a firewall. The compromised system makes a connection out of the corporate network to the hacker's machine to receive the commands. Most firewalls permit such outbound connections.

Control Technique	Description
Source routing	Source routing is a normal part of the IP protocol specification. With it, the sender specifies how a packet should be routed, rather than allowing a router to make that decision. Hackers exploit this as a form of spoofing. A specially crafted IP header requests a trusted host to relay the packet to the target. From the target's perspective, the packet is coming from the trusted host, not the hacker behind it. The hacker can thus have a conversation with the user on the target machine without the user being aware of the spoof.
Snarfing	Snarfing is the act of stealing a large file in the background from a computer or mobile device without the user being aware of the transfer.
Defacing	Defacing is the act of changing a website to contain an unwanted message from the hacker.
Backdoor	A backdoor is a convenient method, usually a newly created administrator account, that allows the hacker to return later to the compromised machine.
Covering tracks	When covering tracks, the hacker erases evidence of the attack, including selectively deleting log entries and command histories. This makes it difficult for the administrator or forensic investigator to find any evidence of wrongdoing.

Control Countermeasures

Use the following measures to minimize the risk of hacker control in your network:

- Keep system patches up-to-date.
- Implement endpoint security, especially on mobile devices.
- Turn off unnecessary network services that might permit unauthorized connections in the background, such as Bluetooth or Wi-Fi.
- Implement IDS/IPS.
- Configure your router to disallow source routing or broadcasting.
- Regularly check for unknown user accounts, especially administrator accounts.
- Forward all logs to a central log collection server.

IDS

An *intrusion detection system (IDS)* is a hardware or software solution that passively monitors for potential attacks on a computer (host) or the network. It is analogous to placing cameras around the facility. An IDS is considered to be a technical, detective control. It can monitor for known malicious patterns of activity, or detect new activities not previously seen on the network. The activity can be based on the use of ports, protocols, and application payload types. It can also be based on authentication attempts, file access, or privilege use on a single host.

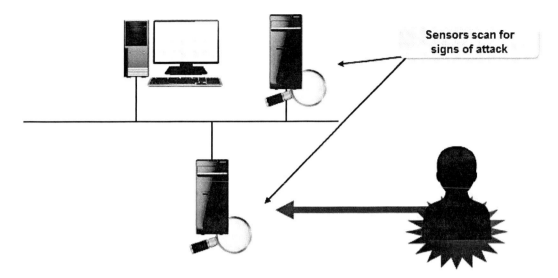

Figure 4-10: IDS is a technical, detective control.

IPS

An *intrusion prevention system (IPS)* is an IDS that proactively responds to potential attacks. It is considered to be a technical, preventive control. The IPS is inserted in-line into the traffic stream. Any traffic that violates the restrictions found in the signature file or anomaly database is blocked, thereby preventing damage to the system or network. It is analogous to placing guards at entry points in your facility.

Initially, IPSes were built as separate devices and were placed directly behind the firewall. Now their functionality is integrated into next generation firewalls (for enterprises) or unified threat management systems (for small to medium sized businesses).

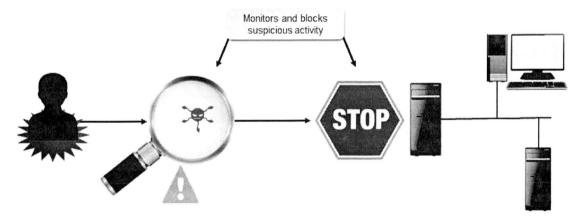

Figure 4-11: IPS is a technical, protective control.

IDS/IPS Scope

Regardless of whether your system is passive (IDS) or active (IPS), there are two approaches you can use to categorize its functionality. The first category is by scope, whether it monitors the network or a single host. The second is by detection method.

The following list compares IDS/IPS scope types:

- **Host-based Intrusion Detection System (HIDS)**: An IDS or IPS capability (almost always software) installed on a workstation or server to protect that single device. Host-based systems are only concerned with activities on that host. They watch for bad logon attempts, file access, privilege use, and changes to the host's configuration. HIDS are not concerned with network activity, even if that activity is targeted at the host (such as a port scan). The activity must be taking place internally on the host to fall under host-based scope. Most host-based systems are a combination of IDS/IPS. Once you install the HIDS on the system, it is almost impossible to remove it without damaging the operating system.

- **Network-based Intrusion Detection System (NIDS)**: IPS or IDS systems or appliances that monitor network traffic and restrict (IPS) or alert (IDS) when unacceptable traffic is seen. NIDS systems are not concerned with what goes on internally on a computer, such as file access or configuration change. They are focused on traffic on the network. They might, however, detect unauthorized network-based logon attempts if the network packets used for the logon attempt contain malicious patterns in their payload. Some NIDS focus on specific protocols or application payload types. For example, you might implement a NIDS in front of your web server that is focused on threats that are specific to web applications.

IDS/IPS Detection Method

The second category is by its detection method, whether it is signature-based, anomaly-based, or a combination of both (hybrid). Many modern systems are a hybrid of both methods.

IDS Category	Description
Signature-based	An IDS/IPS solution that uses a predefined set of rules provided by a software vendor to identify traffic that is unacceptable. The IDS/IPS must periodically download a signature file provided by the vendor. The signature file contains profiles of known threats that are compared to data sequences seen by the IDS. The signature file, like a virus scanner signature file, must be updated frequently to keep up with current threats.
Anomaly-based	An IDS/IPS that compares activity with a baseline of acceptable patterns. When first installed, the IDS/IPS learns what is normal and then detects variations (anomalies). Anomaly-based systems are dynamic and create a database of acceptable traffic flows during their implementation process. The administrator can also add acceptable patterns to the database.

Deciding on Monitoring or Prevention

The decision to monitor (IDS) or prevent (IPS) attacks or unacceptable traffic is based on risk. The risk of using an IDS is that it cannot proactively protect the network. It can only alert you that an attack has already happened or is underway. There are several risks associated with an IPS:

- **False alarms**: An IPS can easily overreact, cutting off legitimate traffic. For example, you might implement a new video conferencing system that uses ports that were not originally captured by the IPS as part of the normal network traffic baseline. If this traffic moves through the firewall during a remote videoconference, the IPS might misinterpret it as an attack, and instruct the firewall to block the ports.
- **Malicious activity seen as normal**: If you have malicious activity that is captured as part of the baseline, that traffic will then be considered "normal" and will not be reported on.
- **Performance bottlenecks**: Since an IPS is a choke point on incoming network traffic, it might not be able to process traffic fast enough in real time, causing performance problems.
- **Cost**: An IPS is generally far more costly than an IDS.

If the traffic profile of your network does not change significantly, and there is a high risk of damage to the network from a DoS or zero day attack, an IPS is the most appropriate choice. An IDS is best employed when experience shows that little or no threat exists to network security, and a warning of possible problems is sufficient.

SIEM

Security Information and Event Management (SIEM) is a combination of Security Information Management (SIM) and Security Event Management (SEM) techniques. It is the collection and analysis of security event logs from a wide variety of devices including servers, routers, IDS, and IPS. It provides real-time monitoring and analysis. It correlates events and issues notifications to a centralized console. SIEM involves using system logic to reduce the tens of thousands of log entries into a manageable number.

SIEM is used as a vulnerability management and compliance tool. It can be implemented in software or as a hardware appliance. One of its main purposes is to monitor and help manage privilege use by users and services. SIEMs track system configuration changes and provide auditing and incident response review.

 Note: SIEM is pronounced as "sim." The three terms SIEM, SIM, and SEM are often used interchangeably. There are nearly 100 SIEM systems available on the market today.

Big Data as a Security Tool

One new (and growing) use for Big Data is to use it not for marketing, but to enhance IT security itself. Some IT departments are finding traditional SIEM output to be too cumbersome and expensive to manage, Big Data is becoming a popular replacement for SIEM. It can provide a single data store and analysis center for:

*   Mining and analyzing security events.
*   Spotting trends.
*   Predicting security breaches before they happen.
*   Gleaning otherwise hard-to-discover information out of vast stores of security and system log information.

Defense in Depth

Defense in depth is a risk concept that is used to mitigate security threats at multiple levels within the networks and systems. Defense in depth employs a layered approach to keep hackers and malware out of a network. Physical security reduces the risk of attackers directly accessing the system. A router can have access control rules to pre-screen traffic before it reaches the firewall. The firewall blocks certain traffic types, inspecting packets for malicious payloads. Network zones guide the level of control applied to that part of the network. Hardening the operating system reduces its vulnerability to attack. Hardening the application that manages the resource (such as a database management system or email service) further protects the resource from attacks that the operating system alone might not recognize. The resource itself, usually data in a file or database, can be protected through encryption. All the while, an IDS or IPS can monitor and react to malicious traffic patterns and activity.

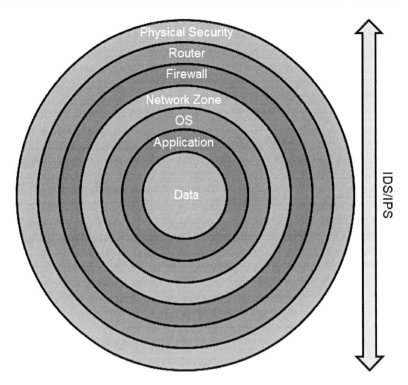

Figure 4-12: Defense in depth.

The 80/20 Rule

The 80/20 rule, or Pareto principle, states that for most events, 80% of the effects come from 20% of the causes. In terms of information security, you can mitigate 80% of your vulnerabilities by focusing on the top 20% of your available technical controls. This allows an organization to spend its money wisely. You can spend 20% of your effort to manage 80% of your problems.

Applying the 80/20 rule becomes even better when you implement defense in depth. If you apply the 80/20 rule at each layer, the cumulative security coverage is not simply left at 80%. Instead, each layer has a narrower focus as it comes closer to the resource you are protecting. The overall attack surface shrinks with every layer you apply.

From an implementation perspective, your top 20% focuses on three things:

*   Removing anything unnecessary, including services, protocols, and defaults.
*   Keeping patch levels current.
*   Implementing strong authentication and access control.

If you implement these three things at every layer in a defense in depth model, you will shrink your attack surface to something small and manageable.

Guidelines for Mitigating Network Attacks

Here are some guidelines you can use to mitigate attacks on your network:

*   Follow the 80/20 rule for hardening networks and systems.
*   Pay attention to securing and monitoring all possible points of entry for the network including firewall, VPNs, wireless access points, switch ports, dial-up modems, and sneakernet.
*   Keep patch levels current.
*   Remove all unnecessary services, protocols, and user accounts.
*   Change default configurations.
*   Implement strong authentication and access control.

- Follow manufacturer recommendations for hardening specific devices and systems.
- Automate your monitoring with IDS/IPS as much as possible.
- Implement defense in depth.

ACTIVITY 4-4
Discussing Network Attack Mitigation

Scenario
In this activity, you will discuss ways to mitigate attacks.

---

1. Your Monday morning starts with numerous calls from users urgently asking for your help. When you go to investigate, you notice that they all have a message displaying on their screens. The message appears to come from the FBI. It states that they have violated the law and must now pay a fine or go to prison. It includes a phone number and a link to resolve the matter. Frightened users are asking what they should do.

   What do you think happened, and how can this issue be resolved?

2. Network traffic to your company's website is unusually heavy one night. When you check the logs, you notice GET requests coming from the same IP address, downloading nearly every page on your site. It looks like your entire website was downloaded within an hour.

   Is this legitimate traffic to your website, or should you be concerned?

3. You placed a sniffer next to your critical servers and reviewed its logs a week later. You notice that the servers received numerous client connection requests on various ports. These connection requests never seemed to complete. When the server acknowledged the connection attempt, the client did not respond in kind. Then, perhaps an hour later, the same client attempted to start another connection on a different port, again not completing the connection. This went on for a week, with the same client attempting to make connections to perhaps a hundred different ports.

   What do you think is going on, and what can you do about it?

4. Several high ranking officials in your company have complained to you that their account keeps getting locked out. It has happened to each of them several times in the last few days. When you investigate, you notice that they each had a high number of failed login attempts. When you ask them about it, they deny that they had unsuccessful logins. They each assert that they know their password very well, and they usually have no trouble logging in. The logs seem to back up the officials' claims.

   What is going on, and how can you mitigate the problem?

5. You notice that your web server has been crashing a lot lately. When you check the logs, there seems to be no indicator as to what happened. You notice, however, that some administrator accounts have mysteriously appeared on the computer. Your firewall also shows that the web server has been initiating connections to overseas IP addresses.

    What do you think is happening, and what can you do about it?

6. The marketing department at your college uses social media to generate buzz and recruit students. Lately, the marketers' machines seem to be having a lot of problems. Their browsers are getting hijacked, taking them to strange websites, and viruses keep appearing on their computers. Their machines are running very slowly. They are the only members of staff who seem to be having this problem. You watch their online behavior to see if you can determine what is going on. They do a lot of reading and posting to websites and chat rooms.

    What do you think is happening, and how can the problem be addressed?

7. You have a server that keeps exhibiting strange behavior. At odd intervals, it seems to totally freeze up. When you move the mouse, or tap a key on the keyboard, it does not respond at all. A few minutes later, it behaves normally again. This has been going on all day at random times. You check and CPU, memory, disk, and network utilization on the server have been pretty low all day. Whenever the server freezes, the CPU utilization shoots to 100%, though the other resources remain under-utilized. The server does not have any pending tasks that it needs to run.

    What do you think could be causing the slowdown, and how would you fix the problem?

8. You are a security consultant for the Air Force. Base command has received an alert that there will be a high risk of a terrorist attack during the upcoming holidays. The general has decided to institute war games to verify personnel readiness. You participate by calling random staff members. In an authoritative voice, you tell each person that the general wants to know if they are in compliance with the base computer network password policy. You then demand that they prove their compliance by telling you their logon password so you can verify that it meets complexity requirements. A number of staffers, wishing to be cooperative, immediately tell you their password.

    Did the troops pass the test? If not, why not, and what can be done?

9. In a highly publicized scandal, a celebrity had all of the contacts stolen off her mobile phone and published on the Internet. Your boss, a high-powered CEO who regularly interacts with movie stars and high-ranking politicians, is worried that the same thing could happen to her phone. She wants you to configure her phone to protect her from that risk.

   What steps can you take to protect the phone?

10. Your company maintains valuable customer information in a database on a server in your network. The server is in a restricted security zone, has endpoint security installed, and the network zones are protected by stateful inspection firewalls. Your Information Security Officer (ISO) believes an Intrusion Detection System (IDS) may help safeguard the customer data.

    Would you recommend a Network-based or Host-based IDS? Why? What factors may influence the effectiveness of an IDS solution?

11. **Discuss the potential benefits and drawbacks of adopting a Defense in Depth approach to security.**

Summary

In this lesson, you analyzed the models and topologies, services and technologies, and protocols and attack methodologies that apply to network systems and telecommunications. This information will help you effectively build networks that provide a secure environment to share and distribute information. Securing your network systems properly will limit system attacks, ultimately ensuring the reliability of stored and transmitted data.

What are the biggest network security challenges that you face in your environment?

In your environment, what types of hacker attacks give you the most problems?

 Note: Check your CHOICE Course screen for opportunities to interact with your classmates, peers, and the larger CHOICE online community about the topics covered in this course or other topics you are interested in. From the Course screen you can also access available resources for a more continuous learning experience.

5 | Identity and Access Management

Lesson Time: 3 hours, 30 minutes

Lesson Objectives

In this lesson, you will:

- Analyze physical and logical access control.

- Identify methods of identification, authentication, and authorization.

- Analyze Identity as a Service

- Evaluate the strengths and weaknesses of authorization mechanisms.

- Identify access control attacks and mitigation.

Lesson Introduction

A very large part of maintaining the confidentiality, integrity, and availability of your data and your systems depends on identity and access control. By properly identifying the user or systems that are trying to gain access, you can determine how much, if any, control to grant them. This keeps unwanted entities out of your systems, while ensuring that the proper entities have exactly what they need, and no more.

TOPIC A

Physical and Logical Access Control

By breaking down the term access control, you can identify the goals of nearly any implementation either physical or logical. You are controlling who or what has access to the data, the system, the building, and so on.

 Note: To learn more, view the LearnTO presentations from the **LearnTO** tile on the CHOICE course screen.

Access Control

Access control is the process of allowing only authorized users, programs, or other computer systems such as networks to observe, modify, or otherwise take possession of the resources of a computer system or physical facility. It is also a mechanism for limiting the use of some resources to authorized users.

In access control, the term *subject* is given to the entity requesting access and the term *object* is given to the entity being accessed. The subject can be a person, system, or process. The object can be any type of resource, including another process. The access control process limits the subject's access to objects using pre-defined rules, roles, or labels. It is possible for a program or process to be both a subject and an object. Whether it is acting as a subject or object will depend on whether it is requesting access to objects or providing access to subjects.

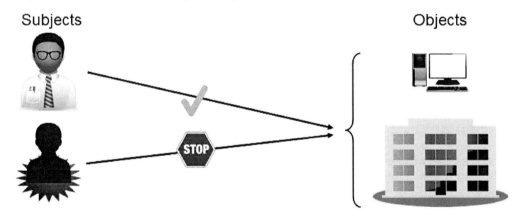

Figure 5-1: Access control.

Entities

The term *entity* is used to identify multiple things. A user is an entity when requesting access to a computer program, and the computer program is an entity when it requests access to a computer database, file, printer, or communication process.

Types of Access Control Services

There are several categories, or types, of access control services that support the phases of access control implementation.

Access Control Services	Description
Identification and authentication (I&A)	Provides a unique identifier for each authorized subject (user) attempting to access the object (system) followed by a method or methods to ensure the identity of the subject (authentication). I&A is typically administered with some type of Identity Management System and the support of a directory.
Authorization	Determines the capabilities or rights of the subject when accessing the object.
Audit	Creates a log or record of activities on the system.
Accountability	Reports and reviews the contents of the log files. Each subject identifier must be unique to relate activities to one subject.

The importance of uniqueness is hard to overstate as all auditing will rely on unique subject identifiers. It is also important in the identification mechanism that the systems that support access control services are reliable, scalable, and capable of the highest levels of confidentiality and integrity.

Access Control Services Implementation

Access control services implementation is required for all systems, regardless of the access control system type. Once the access control rules are provided and implemented, the system must then limit access based on those rules.

Implementing access control services involves:

1. Identifying the individual or entity attempting to access an object.
2. Verifying or authenticating the individual's identity.
3. Evaluating the rules and/or roles to see what the individual is permitted to do.
4. Creating an audit trail by writing each access attempt and function performed to a log file.
5. Reviewing the log to see what was completed when and by whom. This review is performed by managers and supervisors and helps to create accountability in the system access process.

Reference Monitor

A *reference monitor (RM)* is a conceptual component that determines if a subject can access an object. RMs are found in operating systems and network access control systems. The *security kernel* implements the RM in an operating system, allowing the system to enforce access controls. This RM implementation depends on the access control methods used, and it must possess specific characteristics:

- It must be tamper proof.
- It must always be invoked.
- It must fail closed: All processing tasks are stopped and all packets are denied.
- It must be compact and verifiable.

To ensure proper access control, the RM must not be manipulated and cannot be bypassed. It has to be small so the code inside can be analyzed for weaknesses.

In all RM implementations, assume that subjects are not allowed access to objects by default. Subjects may be allowed access if the rules have been configured to allow it.

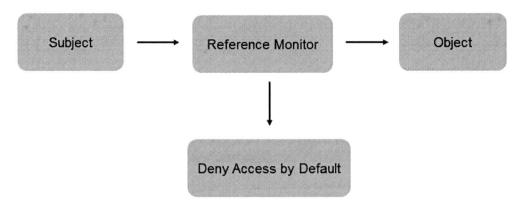

Figure 5-2: A reference monitor.

Access Control Administration

There are three significant access control administration methods.

Access Control Administration Method	Description
Centralized	Centralized access control involves administering access controls at a centralized site. All requests for access are handled by a single group of administrators.
	When administered centrally, requests are handled uniformly by the staff. Centralized access control is often administered using protocols specifically designed for this type of process, such as Remote Authentication Dial-in User Service (RADIUS), Terminal Access Controller Access Control System (TACACS), and Diameter.
Decentralized	In decentralized access control, the administration of the access control elements are in distributed locations throughout the enterprise. By moving this administrative process to localized parts of the enterprise, it is placed closer to the individuals requesting access. This often eliminates the bottlenecks found in centralized administration, where requests may be delayed due to workload. Local administrators are often more aware of critical situations and can react quickly when necessary.
	Nevertheless, decentralized administration does have a few disadvantages. Occasionally, the local administrator can be coaxed into doing something that does not comply with policy. Also, if the local administrator is sick or on vacation, work can be delayed unless others are trained in the processes.
Hybrid	It may be possible to implement access control using a centralized function with local administration. For example, a local administrator has access to the centralized RADIUS system to establish new accounts and manage existing accounts.
	The benefits of both types of access control administration are found in the hybrid system. A disadvantage is the lack of a control mechanism to specify which administrators are allowed to update which accounts. Changes made by a local administrator may be modified by a centralized administrator, or vice versa.

Identity and Access Provisioning Lifecycle

Part of administrating access controls in your organization, whether logical or physical, is to adhere to a lifecycle of provisioning, review, and revocation.

*   **Provisioning**: This is where you determine that a new or existing entity requires new access control parameters. In provisioning access controls to an entity, you should be mindful of the principles of least privilege and separation of duties—does the entity absolutely *need* a certain level of access based on their current job role? Likewise, you should consider how such new access may be revoked in the future, rather than waiting until a later date to determine this.

*   **Review**: You should implement continuous monitoring and auditing of access controls to determine their effectiveness at reducing risk. Any hardware or software that you are using or considering should be capable of at least minimal levels of auditing. In fact, systems are so good at it, and collect so much information, it is easy to become overwhelmed with data. The problem is that if you have too much to review, the job becomes daunting and is left undone. There are tools you can use that will help the audit process by looking for known issues.

*   **Revocation**: At some point, you'll need to remove the access control provisions you've made from certain entities. For example, an employee may be terminated or demoted and should no longer have access to sensitive systems. Periodic reviews and audits should help determine when revocation is necessary, and to what degree. Some revocation is only temporary and coincides with job rotation. Either way, the revocation process should not be delayed, as it is crucial in avoiding the risk of unauthorized access.

Access Control Policies

With the lifecycle in mind, you can begin writing access control policies. You should start out with administrative policies; that is, policies that are written by the security team with input from management, frequently HR and legal. Once an administrative policy has been designed, it is often reinforced with technical policies; that is, policies applied through the interface of a particular system. For example, once a logon policy is written, it can be reinforced with a Windows Group Policy. That policy could reinforce the length of your password, the number of days you can use a password, and how many wrong passwords you could attempt before the system locks you out. Nearly all of your system hardware, and much of your software, will have the ability to implement some form of access control based on the policies you have written.

Password Policy Example

Here is an example of a policy that establishes a baseline for password use:

*   All passwords must be at least seven characters long using three different types of characters.
*   A user's identity must be verified before IT staff can reset that person's password.
*   There must be a process in place to suspend or deactivate a user account in case of employee termination, account compromise, or infection.
*   An inactive user account must be disabled after 60 calendar days.
*   The user account will be locked out for 15 minutes after three bad logon attempts.
*   No users are permitted to have local administrative privileges on their computer unless approved by their manager.
*   Existing local administrative privilege will be reviewed annually.
*   All administrator accounts must use two factor authentication to log on to the network.
*   All workstations must implement a screen lock after 15 minutes of inactivity.
*   Access to administrator systems must be reviewed annually.
*   IT staff may not use administrator accounts for general purpose.
*   Vendor and contractor access list to be approved, monitored, and limited to the length of the contract.
*   Default administrator passwords must be changed before the system goes into production.
*   Default ports for administrator access must be changed when possible.

- Administrative access cannot be accomplished through a public interface.
- Each new user account will receive a unique first-time password that must be changed upon first use.
- Any reset passwords must be set to unique value for each user and changed upon first use.

Facilities Access

You need to consider logical threats to facility access.

Logical Access Concern	Mitigation
One concern is an electronic intrusion into your network. For example, if your Wi-Fi signal extends too far past the facility grounds and extends onto the public sidewalk, an attacker may have an easier time of sniffing traffic without even needing physical access to the building.	Establish a logical perimeter around your facilities.
You may also need to consider how attackers can hijack any networked utilities or devices operating under an industrial control system. If an attacker gains access to critical facility systems like the HVAC system, they can cause considerable harm.	These networked utilities should be hardened with protocols that mandate strong authentication and authorization.
Attackers may also be able to remotely tamper with networked doors, mantraps, and other physical access control mechanisms.	Continuous monitoring of access granted by these networked mechanisms is crucial.

There are also physical access concerns for your facility.

Physical Access Concern	Mitigation
Unauthorized people entering the facility.	You need to establish a physical perimeter around your facilities. Determine how employees will be able to enter and exit your facilities, while keeping unauthorized users from entering at all. For example, guards and entrance and exit checkpoints can determine if a person is authorized to enter the building.
Unauthorized people attempting to enter the facility.	In addition to guard checkpoints, security cameras placed prominently in key areas could deter attackers that fear being identified.
Unrestricted access to all areas within the facility.	Once inside, you need to handle access to certain areas within the facility. Access needs to be divided by room, sector, etc. Some employees may be authorized to enter Sector C, a low security area, but Sector D may be designated a high security area, and not open to general staff. Guards can once again control access to these areas, or locked doors that can only be opened with the proper identity cards are also a potential solution.

Systems Access

You need to consider logical threats to system access.

Logical Access Concern	Mitigation
Attacker access to configuration consoles.	Systems that provide services to your customers and employees will need configuring by administrators. Do not use default administrator passwords.
Remote access to a critical system by an attacker.	Establish authentication and authorization in remote services.

There are also physical access concerns for your system.

Physical Access Concern	Mitigation
An attacker could physically damage a server in order to take down some mission-critical services, like a network share that employees use every day.	Even servers that don't host databases need to be segmented from the rest of the employee populace in closely guarded rooms.
Networking equipment can also be physically damaged. It is also a greater physical risk as it often needs to be positioned in certain key areas to ensure coverage. It can't be separated in closely guarded rooms.	In this case, there are equipment lockers of various sizes that are a more portable solution than constructing locked rooms around where the equipment needs to be.

Device Access

You need to consider logical threats to device access.

Logical Access Concern	Mitigation
Attacker accessing the configuration console.	Make sure that all devices are configured with strong user names and passwords, and not left to their defaults.
Unrestricted access to workstations.	Users need authentication and authorization to use their own workstations, as employees in different departments may have different levels of access. Directory services like Active Directory are common ways to control user access to devices in an organization.
The phenomenon of mobility and BYOD has made securing devices even more of a challenge, since they're now so portable and often pass beyond the perimeter.	Administrators can implement some form of mobile device management on users' mobile devices to mandate authentication every time the user wants to work the device. If this is too intrusive, you can still implement policies that require users who bring their personal devices to work to use some kind of PIN or other lock mechanism.

There are also physical access concerns for your devices.

Physical Access Concern	Mitigation
Devices are always at risk of theft, whether they remain on premises or not.	If there are frequent guests that make their way through the offices, it may be wise to force users to lock their laptops or other devices when they're not physically near them.
Loss of a device can prompt a malicious person to access it and read sensitive company information stored on that device.	Once again, mandating procedures for locking phones, tablets, and so on, is a good way to prevent accidental leakage of information. Require a PIN to access device.
Mobile devices have the additional security risk of nearby malicious devices making wireless connections in the background to steal information.	If you do not require services such as Bluetooth, Near-Field Communications (NFC), geo-locating, and other mobile device conveniences, consider turning them off.

Information Access

You need to consider logical threats to information access.

Logical Access Concerns	Mitigation
Databases containing sensitive company information are prime targets for intruders.	They should be isolated from the rest of the network whenever possible, and in all instances, protected with authentication and authorization mechanisms afforded by database management systems.
Users remotely connect to databases to update them. How can you ensure that these connections are from authorized users?	Rather than just protecting access at the database endpoint, you may also implement remote authentication protocols to add more layers to your defense.
If every account has full access, that's more attack surfaces that someone else can exploit.	The information itself may require certain degrees of access. Some employees may only need read access, whereas others will need write access in order to make changes. Keep in mind your provisioning policies so as not to give one account more access than is needed.

There are also physical access concerns for your information.

Physical Access Concern	Mitigation
External and internal attackers simply walking out with a bunch of servers.	Protecting the hardware that contains the databases is crucial, so any rooms or data centers that hold this hardware should be locked and monitored.
Sensitive information that exists in hard copy form that can be stolen.	Any such documents should be sealed in locked filing cabinets or safes that only authorized personnel should have the key or know the combination to.

Guidelines for Planning Physical and Logical Access

 Note: All of the Guidelines for this lesson are available as checklists from the **Checklist** tile on the CHOICE Course screen.

Use the following guidelines when planning physical and logical access controls:

- Draft access control matrices to get a better view of how access is provisioned for each of your systems.
- Verify that your operating system's security kernel uses an effective reference monitor to enforce access control between subjects and objects.
- Choose between centralized, decentralized, or hybrid access control administration depending on your business needs and capabilities.
- Follow the identity and access provisioning process, remembering to periodically review access and come up with a plan for revoking access.
- Draft access control policies at an administrative level that can be easily translated into technical policies.
- Create a logical and physical perimeter around your facility to keep intruders from gaining access.
- Create points of access within your facilities, like locked doors, to maintain differing levels of access within the organization itself.
- Consider implementing deterrent controls to prevent attackers from even trying to gain access.
- Make sure that critical utilities like HVAC are using modern authentication and authorization protocols if they're networked.
- Make sure databases storing sensitive information employ access control, as well as any communication channels they use.
- Provide degrees of access to information, such as read access versus write access.
- Consider that information may be stored physically on servers containing databases, or hard copy documents, and that either one may be the target of attack.
- Make sure that remote access to systems is tightly controlled.
- Ensure that networking equipment is stored safely in locked containers to prevent theft and damage.
- Implement directory services to provide access control on user devices.
- Consider the challenges of mobile devices and the BYOD phenomenon with respect to attackers gaining access to personal devices that contain company information.

ACTIVITY 5-1
Analyzing Physical and Logical Access Control

Scenario
In this activity, you will assess your knowledge of physical and logical access control.

---

1. Which statement is true regarding subjects and objects?
    - ○ An entity can be either a subject or an object, but not both.
    - ○ An object can be any entity attempting to access a subject.
    - ○ A subject can be any entity attempting to access an object.
    - ○ Subjects can be people and processes, but not systems.

2. Your company is a rising star in the world of remote data storage and has been going through a period of rapid growth. If trends continue, you will outgrow your current data center and office space within 18 months. Senior management has announced plans to relocate both the data center and the office to a newer, larger leased floor of an office tower. The office tower is one of the most popular in the area, and houses numerous high-profile tenants. Senior management selected the location because they felt it would bring the company greater visibility and prestige.

    Which of the following choices best represent special concerns to address when considering physical access controls in the leased space? (Choose two.)
    - ☐ The presence of smoke detectors and sprinkler systems.
    - ☐ The availability of a front desk attendant and tenant list.
    - ☐ The architecture may not adequately isolate the leased space.
    - ☐ Emergency stairwells have push-bar doors.
    - ☐ Stairs and elevators start in the lowest parking levels.
    - ☐ Elevator riders may currently stop on any floor.

3. Which one of the following is generally considered to be the first physical layer of defense in a layered protection scheme?
    - ○ Device locks
    - ○ Secured area access
    - ○ Facility access
    - ○ Perimeter access

4. Which of the following is not a physical security control?
    - ○ Employee entrance
    - ○ Encrypted hard disk
    - ○ Chain link fences
    - ○ Device cable locks

5. Which of the following is not a valid access control service?
   - ○ Identification
   - ○ Activation
   - ○ Authentication
   - ○ Audit

6. Which statement best describes a characteristic of centralized access control administration?
   - ○ A single group of administrators handles requests at a single site.
   - ○ Access control decisions occur closer to the subjects requesting access.
   - ○ It leverages centralized functions with local administration.
   - ○ Local administrator actions may be overridden by central administrators.

7. A local administrator persuaded to violate policy is a risk of which access control method?
   - ○ Centralized
   - ○ Local
   - ○ Decentralized
   - ○ Convergent

8. True or False? Access control monitoring is often called auditing.
   - ☐ True
   - ☐ False

9. Why should you periodically review your organization's access controls?

10. Why is it a good idea to isolate your database from the rest of the network?

11. Why would you follow an administrative access control policy with a technical access control policy?

TOPIC B

Identification, Authentication, and Authorization

The importance of identification and authentication is hard to overstate. So many of your systems are built on the idea of authorization based on the identity of the requesting entity, be it a user or system. Without unique identities that can be shown to be authentic, your systems would be woefully vulnerable to exploit. These are the mechanisms that make sure your confidential data stays confidential, that your data has integrity, and that the systems will be available when and where they are needed.

Identity Management

Identity management is the process of controlling how users and other entities are recognized in various systems. Identity management helps to maintain information about entities such as account names, passwords, profiles, access rights, and more. Implementing a management process is crucial because digital identities are becoming more and more prolific, and affect a wide variety of systems both within and without the organization. The organization needs to consider identity in the context of the many interactive parts that make up the whole; for example, a user may have a set of credentials for accessing a customer records database, but what about accessing an archival database? Or perhaps another type of system altogether, like a network share? Should the user names and passwords be the same? Should they be separate? How do you shape each user's level of access across the different systems? Identity management attempts to answer these questions and provide a framework for ensuring that every entity gets access to what it needs, while at the same time minimizing unauthorized access that could compromise the business.

Common identity management tasks include:

- Assigning and changing user access.
- Resetting user passwords.
- Tracking user activities.
- Creating and de-provisioning IDs.
- Synchronizing multiple identities.
- Enforcing policies.
- Maintaining compliance with government regulations.

Identity Management Process

There are three steps in the process of identity management:

1. Identification: Assertion of a unique identity.
2. Authentication: Proving the person is who they say they are.
3. Authorization: Provide access to allowed resources.

Identification Types

For identification to be useful, each identity must be unique. Using "guest" as an identification is not appropriate, because it is impossible to identify which guest performed which operation in the auditing and accountability processes. In addition to the identities being unique, it is necessary to have a way to prove the identity of the user.

An identification is often claimed by entering a user ID during a system login function or by presenting an identity card at an access portal.

Identification Type	Description
ID Cards	An ID card or badge is a physical device that often contains a picture of the subject, the subject's name, and other identifying characteristics. Matching the picture on the ID card to the carrier is one way of providing identification. ID cards might also include a mechanism to provide electronic access to systems or facilities.
User IDs	A user ID is a string of characters, unique to one individual, used to provide identification of the user to the system being accessed. Traditionally, user IDs have not been kept secret from others, but the disclosure of a user ID may lead to attempts to access a system without permission. If user IDs are standardized based on employee names, they may be easy to guess. An account number might also be used to provide uniqueness and thereby serve as a user ID.
Email Address	An email address is often used as a user ID, particularly for web commerce sites, because it is globally unique. When a person registers for a site, the site will send a confirmation email to that address and wait for a reply before completing the registration process. This validation method is based on the assumption that the person in control of the email address is a legitimate user.
Account Number/PIN	An account number or PIN provides a unique identifier for a specific user within a system.
MAC Address	A Media Access Control (MAC) address is a 48-bit number that uniquely identifies a computer.
IP Address	An IP address provides the logical location of a device on a network.
Radio Frequency Identification (RFID) tag	A RFID tag uses radio signals to track people and devices.

Identification Type Weaknesses

Along with the different identification types comes some weaknesses.

Identification Type	Weakness
ID Cards	An ID card can be copied or re-created easily using modern computer printing techniques. Security can be added to the card by using smart card technology with embedded logic or applying a corporate logo image with a hologram.
User IDs	The user ID is also subject to attacks such as social engineering techniques and shoulder surfing.
Email Address	There are no technical restrictions preventing someone from using another person's email address as an identifier. Email addresses are easily spoofed.
Account Number/PIN	An account number is difficult for humans to memorize, so its use as an identifier may be limited. PINs are typically a short sequence of numbers, which may be brute forced if granted an unlimited number of attempts. People often use personal information (like an important calendar date) as a basis of PINs, and this information is often publicly available and easy to guess.
MAC Address	MAC addresses are no longer embedded in hardware, but are set by software. Therefore anyone with administrative access to a device can change the MAC address, which means it is not a truly global unique identifier. Attackers can also spoof MAC addresses from their own devices.

Identification Type	Weakness
IP Address	An IP address is assigned by software and can be identical across subnets. IP addresses may also be spoofed by malicious users.
Radio Frequency Identification (RFID)	RFID tags are considered dumb since they listen and respond to any request signal, without any means of verifying authorization. They are vulnerable to skimming (eavesdropping), traffic analysis, spoofing, and DoS/DDoS attacks.

Authentication Types

Once an identity has been claimed, the subject is then required to prove the identity through authentication. This is an extremely important step. The information used for authentication is typically protected, because the identification component might be commonly known. The methods used to authenticate identity have been broken down into three distinct areas:

- Something you know.
- Something you have.
- Something you are.

Something You Know

Something you know as an authentication factor includes the use of passwords or other pieces of information that the user must remember. An individual assigned a user ID establishes a password in the system as part of the authentication process. Passwords, properly protected, also need to be modified periodically so that techniques such as password guessing cannot be used over a period of time to gain unauthorized access.

Something you know is the most common example of single factor authentication, where only one type of authentication method is required for access. Passwords, while the simplest authentication method to implement, are considered to be the weakest. They can be communicated to coworkers or disclosed through bad practices, such as writing them down where they can easily be found.

 Note: Something you know is sometimes referred to as authentication by knowledge.

There are several types of passwords that can be used in "something you know" authentication.

Password Type	Description
Password	A password is a string of numbers, letters, and/or special characters used to authenticate an identity. Longer passwords are more secure than shorter passwords due to the number of different character combinations available.
Passphrase	A passphrase is sometimes termed a *virtual password*. A long phrase is known to the individual and is entered into the password administration system.
	It is easier for most people to remember a passphrase than a password. On the other hand, the passphrase is longer and takes more time to enter. It is helpful if the password system allows spaces so users can use favorite lines from songs, movies, or books. If the passphrase "It was the best of times, it was the worst of times," is used, it is a very long 51 character password.
PIN	PINs are short passwords, typically numeric, used with certain systems such as ATMs and voicemail. Using a four-digit numeric PIN, there are only 10,000 unique combinations, which make PINs the most vulnerable of the password types. Most systems allow for longer PINs; however, users are slow to change them.

Password Type	Description
Graphical password	Graphical passwords use images instead of alpha-numeric characters. A graphical password might require the user to select the correct image from a set of images. You can increase complexity by using a series of image sets, requiring multiple image selections in the correct sequence.
	Another type of graphical password uses a single image, and requires the user to select specific regions of the image, or draw a series of specific shapes on the image.

Defending Against Keystroke Loggers

In high security areas, where there is a concern that a keystroke logger might be able to capture users typing in their password, an organization may present an onscreen keyboard. This allows users to click on letters with a mouse rather than type them. Keystroke loggers typically do not capture the coordinates of mouse clicks so password capture is avoided.

This can also be useful in a situation where the repeated entry of a PIN could show wear on the device and reveal helpful information to an attacker. In this case, a small screen can be used to scramble the numbers so even though the same PIN is entered, variable wear patterns will be created.

Password Administration

Passwords should be changed frequently. In some organizations, passwords are changed weekly, and in others, passwords are changed every six months. There should be an administrative policy dictating how often passwords should be changed. It might also include password length, the reuse of older passwords, and the need for special characters. The administrative policy is then followed up with a technical policy.

The more frequently passwords are changed, the more likely they are written down. The less frequently passwords are changed, the more likely that password-cracking techniques can be employed to gain access. In the end, it is up to the users to protect their passwords. Security administrators should have no knowledge of any user password, other than for the initial setting when a new account is created or a password is lost.

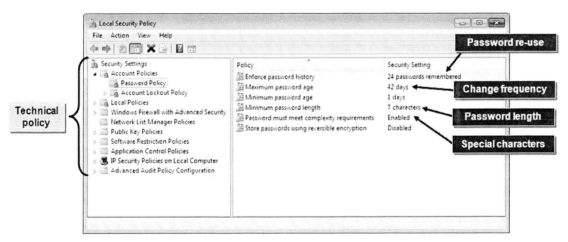

Figure 5-3: A Microsoft Windows security policy showing password settings.

Something You Have

In a something you have method, the individual possesses a physical device of some type that provides authentication capabilities. Devices in this category include magnetic stripe cards, proximity cards, smart cards, Radio Frequency Identification (RFID) cards, or token devices.

 Note: Something you have is sometimes referred to as authentication by possession.

In each case, the individual possesses the device and uses it for access when necessary. One potential downside is that theft of the devices prohibits access by the authorized user and may, in some cases, allow access by an unauthorized user.

Most of these devices also require the use of another form of authentication. Requiring you to use a PIN or password along with a smart card or token is also known as two-factor authentication. Two-factor authentication has long been considered the most secure authentication method available. The theft of a device must be combined with the theft of the associated PIN to complete an unauthorized authentication. This is an important consideration, and all users should be trained in the proper use and protection of their device or devices.

Cards and Tokens

The following table lists some of the devices that enable something you have authentication.

Device	Description
Magnetic stripe cards	*Magnetic stripe cards* store authentication data on a strip of magnetized metal that is swiped through a magnetic reader. Magnetic stripe cards are easy to duplicate and therefore are being phased out.
Smart cards	*Smart cards* are typically credit-card-sized devices that contain a chip that can provide storage and intelligence to the authentication process. The chip can store data such as certificates and it can read and write a small amount of data to provide basic authentication functions. This makes them a good replacement for magnetic stripe cards.
	From a security standpoint, smart cards also present the opportunity to perform authentication at the end point as opposed to at a central server. This can help prevent the attack of authentication information in transit. Because smart cards are flexible and yet have chips embedded in them, they can be subject to high failure rates. If a card is unable to function, it can prevent a legitimate user from gaining access.

Device	Description
Tokens	An *asynchronous token system* establishes a challenge response scenario. After an initial connection is made, the system will generate a challenge which the user will enter into a token device. The token will generate an appropriate response. If the user does not possess the token device, they will be unable to generate an appropriate response.
	A *synchronous token* also presents information to the authentication server. This information may be based on time or a counter mechanism. The information that is presented will typically include a PIN that the user knows. This information will be checked against the information the authentication device is expecting and is thus considered synchronous. With synchronous tokens, all information is included with the initial authentication request, whereas in asynchronous tokens, there is a need to establish communication before the challenge is delivered.
	Synchronous tokens typically display a number that changes frequently— usually every 60 seconds—and the number is only good during that window of time. For counter-based tokens, once a token is used, it will increment to the next token.

Something You Are

The something you are method uses biometric measurements or personal attributes for authentication. These attributes are unique to the individual seeking to authenticate identification. Examples include fingerprints, hand geometry, retina scans, iris scans, facial recognition, and behavioral characteristics such as voiceprints. To make authentication comparisons, individuals must be registered or enrolled in the biometric system. This enrollment should take no more than two to three minutes per person. The subsequent authentication should take no more than five to 10 seconds.

 Note: Something you are is sometimes referred to as authentication by characteristic.

Fingerprint Scanner

Figure 5-4: Biometric authentication.

Types of Biometric Devices

There are several types of biometric devices used for "something you are" authentication. They can be divided into those measuring physiological traits or behavioral traits.

Physiological Biometric Device Type	Description
Fingerprint	Capturing and comparing fingerprints of the individual with previously captured fingerprints to determine a match.
Hand geometry	Comparing the hand structure of an individual to a previously captured hand structure to determine a match.
Iris scan	Comparing the patterns of the colored part of the eye to previously captured iris images to determine a match.
Retina scan	Comparing the blood vessel patterns in the back of the eye to previously captured patterns. This method can be affected by pregnancy, diabetes, and diseases of the eye.
Facial recognition	Comparing the facial structure to a previously captured facial structure to determine a match. Facial recognition can be applied individually and it has also been applied to crowds. Casinos have used this technology for years and it has become more popular at large events to protect against terrorism.
Voiceprint	Comparing a spoken phrase to a registered phrase previously spoken by the individual.

Traditional biometrics have been based on a physical attribute of a person; a fingerprint or hand geometry, for example. Behavioral biometrics is based on a unique way that each individual would perform a function; walking or typing, for example. These are newer and not as well-tested, but they will likely be included in future biometric systems.

Behavioral Biometric Device Type	Description
Keystroke recording	Capturing the unique way individual users would type a common phrase can be used to uniquely identify a user.
Touch screen movement	Capturing the unique way individual users manipulate touch screen interfaces can also be used to uniquely identify a user.
Signatures	Capturing the speed, acceleration, and pressure applied while signing a pressure sensitive interface and comparing it to previously captured information.

Biometric Acceptance

Some biometric measurements are readily accepted by the user community. For example, fingerprints, voice analysis, and facial recognition are often associated with law enforcement and personal privacy.

Of all the authentication types mentioned so far, biometrics incurs the most user reluctance. There are concerns ranging from ideals of civil liberties to the practicalities of sanitation that need to be considered with any implementation. For example, retina scans and iris scans are not well-accepted because of health concerns.

Regardless of the methods employed, not all users will be satisfied with the results, and the risks associated with unauthorized access should be weighed against the users' concerns. Therefore, implementing a more balanced approach is ideal.

Biometrics products continue to mature and new ones will be developed. Although biometrics provide very robust authentication, they have also been known to fail. All systems should be tested periodically.

Biometric Errors

Any measurement process will suffer from some type of error. Biometrics are not immune to errors. Two types of errors occur when biometrics are used for authentication.

In one case, individuals are excluded when they should be allowed access because the biometric measure says they are not allowed access. The other type of error occurs when the biometric measure allows individuals access when they are not authorized. In the first case, the individual who is denied access is delayed, and in the second case, the system or facility is under threat from the unauthorized individual given access.

Type I errors, also known as *false rejection rates (FRRs),* exist when an authorized individual is denied access. Systems with high sensitivity levels often result in Type I errors because they tend to reject authorized individuals more often.

Type II errors, also known as *false acceptance rates (FARs),* exist when an unauthorized individual is given access. Systems with low sensitivity levels often result in Type II errors because they allow more unauthorized access because they lack sufficient detection capabilities.

Most organizations will consider Type II errors more serious. However, it is important to remember that Type I errors can keep legitimate users from getting their work done.

Most systems will allow for a certain amount of sensitivity tuning.

The point at which the two errors intersect on a graph is called the *crossover error rate (CER),* and this affects both error types. The biometric measurements with the lowest CERs provide the best protection.

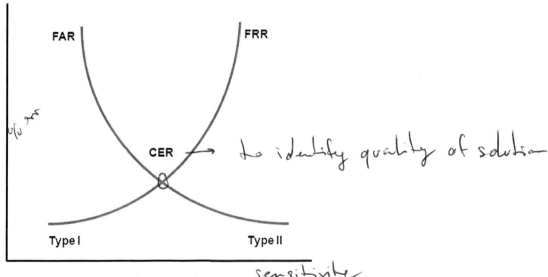

Figure 5-5: A CER graphic example.

Multi-Factor

Multi-factor authentication is a system wherein more than one type of authentication is used in accessing a system or facility. Using a fingerprint scanner device with a PIN is a simple example of two-factor authentication. In this case, something you are is matched with something you know to gain access. There is also three-factor authentication where you might also have to present an ID badge. All of these are sometimes called strong authentication, but that term is considered ambiguous and is falling out of favor.

It is important to make the distinction that using the same type of authentication twice is not multi-factor authentication. For example, being prompted for your password to log in and then prompted for another password to access an application uses the same type of authentication twice. You need to use two different authentication types for it to be multi-factor.

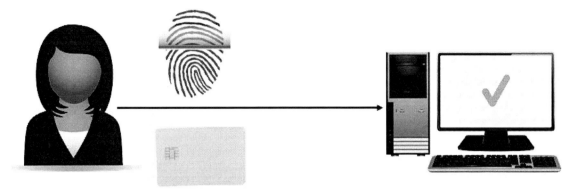

Figure 5-6: Multi-factor authentication.

Authorization

Authorization determines the capabilities or rights of the subject when accessing the object. This is where the rubber hits the road, so to speak. After identification and authentication have happened, the next and perhaps most critical step is to find out what the entity is allowed to do. What can the user or the system access, what can they change, and what can they execute? These are sometimes referred to as rights or permissions, and nearly all systems have some mechanism to allow authenticated users the authority to make such changes as apply to them. This is a huge component of deciding who has the ability to view and change data; ergo, modify the confidentiality and integrity of documents.

Accountability

Accountability is the concept of determining what entity can be held responsible for what action. This is similar to non-repudiation, which ensures that entities cannot deny having performed a certain action. This is an important supplement to identity management because it ensures that users are being properly identified with respect to the tasks they carry out. If actions can't be traced back to particular identities, it becomes more difficult to correct access control issues or support an investigation in case of an intrusion. The following processes are integral for accountability to be useful to the organization:

- **Identification** must support the ability to tie an action back to an entity.
- **Authentication** must be strong enough so that a perpetrator of account abuse can't shift the blame to weak authentication practices.
- **Training and awareness** must be available and mandated for all users so that they understand good account practices and also the penalties for account abuse.
- **Continuous monitoring** ensures that account abusers can be held accountable quickly and reliably.
- **Audit logs** are necessary for keeping a record of actions that can be traced back to users.
- **Organization policies** should also support accountability so that implementation is consistent and fair.

Session Management

Session management describes how a single instance of identification and authentication is applied to a resource or group of resources, like an operating system desktop. Typically, when the identification and authentication process is complete and the entity has been authorized, the result is a session. In most cases, once the permissions/rights have been established, they won't change for the duration of that session. So, a user can initiate one desktop session and maintain that while starting up a completely different desktop session.

There are various ways of controlling desktop sessions, including through screensavers. The original function of screensavers no longer applies to modern LCDs, but screensavers are still used to lock a user's desktop session down. The user might activate the screensaver when they temporary leave their computer to ensure that no one else uses it. Their session is still active, the user is still logged on, and all of their apps are running in the background, but no user can change the state of the session without either unlocking the computer or shutting it down, which will terminate the session.

Likewise, most modern operating systems include settings that will automatically lock the computer after a certain time period without activity from the user—in other words, the computer will timeout and lock itself to preserve the session and minimize unauthorized access. Users may be able to set their timeout settings, or you can apply your own restrictions based on established access control policy.

Registration and Proofing of Identity

In order for an organization to create an identity for an individual, particularly an electronic identity, the organization will often need to initiate a process for actually proving that this person should be attached to this identity. This comes before the identity is actually created, because the organization needs to be absolutely sure that the individual is who they claim to be. The process of proving and registering an identity may include the following:

- An in-person interview.
- Face-to-face verification of a driver's license or other picture ID.
- Verification of birth certificate, social security number, or other documents with the relevant governmental agencies.
- An interview with the subject's friends, family members, and past colleagues.

The lengths you need to go to prove identity will vary based on the sensitive nature of your organizations. Federal organizations are particularly thorough in verifying a prospective employee's identity due to regulations like FIPS 201-2. This regulation includes two sections on Personal Identity Verification (PIV) that have requirements such as:

- The agency must obtain a Nation Agency Check with Written Inquiries (NACI) or equivalent investigation.
- The candidate must undergo a check for fingerprint history with FBI criminal databases.
- The candidate must appear in person at least once before a PIV official.
- The candidate must provide two unique forms of identity from a list of acceptable documents.

Credential Management Systems

The staggering amount of credentials in today's connected world demands a more robust system for managing these critical pieces of identification. Users will likely have more than a dozen unique credentials for many more systems, some of which interact on a daily basis. This overwhelming amount of credentials leads to poor security practices—reusing passwords, choosing short, simplistic passwords that are easy to remember—and makes it harder for administrators to maintain the integrity of credentials in the organization.

This calls for more robust credential management systems that can tackle the ever-increasing complexity of identification and authentication in the modern business landscape. Some necessary features of credential managers include, but are not limited to:

- Keeping an archive of user passwords.
- Generating complex passwords for users so they don't have to.
- Encrypting credentials to keep them from being accessed by unauthorized parties.
- Providing granular access control to specific information and systems.
- Implementing failover systems to ensure that credentials are always active.
- Auditing successful and unsuccessful credential use.

As useful as a credential management system is to addressing identification and authorization complexity, it does have some risks that you should be aware of. For example, the credential manager may become a single point of failure; if attackers take control of it, then this could have devastating implications. In the event that a credential manager is compromised, rebuilding credentials can be a painstaking and time consuming process. Also, even when credential management systems are kept secure, the impact they have on financial cost and resource overhead may outweigh their benefit.

Federated Identity

A *federated identity* is a single identity and its characteristics that are linked across many different identity management systems. Federated identities encompass all of the policies and protocols that contribute to an identity. This provides a centralized identity management structure that eliminates the need for superfluous identity information. Federated identities not only relieve some of the strain on the host, but also streamlining a single account for multiple use cases can be, in certain contexts, much more practical and efficient than needing many different accounts.

For example, an enterprise might have several domains or closely integrate with different companies; federating the identity of users across these domains will alleviate the need for each domain to manage its identity separately. This can reduce cost and even lower risk, since account information is centralized instead of replicated across several different domains.

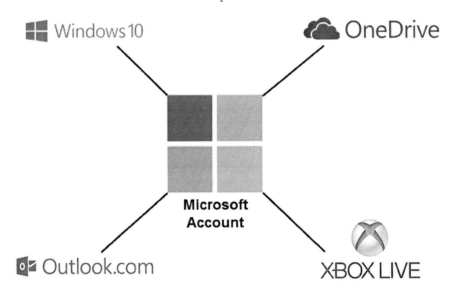

Figure 5-7: A Microsoft account can be used across many different systems.

Directory Services

A *directory service (DS)* is a centralized authentication system used to provide a consistent and scalable mechanism to control access to applications, services, and systems. Directory services are often deployed by enterprises to more easily manage the entities in their network. The most common directory services are X.500, LDAP, and Active Directory.

Many directory services contain access control mechanisms such as user identifications and authentication methods. The goal being that you can create a user centrally and then multiple systems or applications can use that information to provide authentication, authorization, and auditing. Many directory services also support federated identities.

LDAP

The *Lightweight Directory Access Protocol (LDAP)* is a standard directory access protocol that runs over Transmission Control Protocol/Internet protocol (TCP/IP) networks. LDAP clients authenticate to the LDAP service, and the service's schema defines the tasks that clients can and cannot perform while accessing a directory database, the form the directory query must take, and how the directory server will respond. The LDAP schema is extensible, which means you can make changes or add on to it. Because it is a standard for querying a directory service, LDAP-compliant systems can use LDAP to communicate with each other. This makes it convenient when you want to synchronize two different directory services together so that both contain the same set of usernames and passwords.

Secure LDAP (LDAPS) is a method of implementing LDAP using SSL/TLS encryption protocols to prevent eavesdropping and man-in-the-middle attacks. LDAPS forces both the client and server to establish a secure connection before any transmissions can occur, and if the secure connection is interrupted or dropped, LDAP likewise closes. The server implementing LDAPS requires a signed certificate issued by a certificate authority, and the client must accept and install the certificate on their machine.

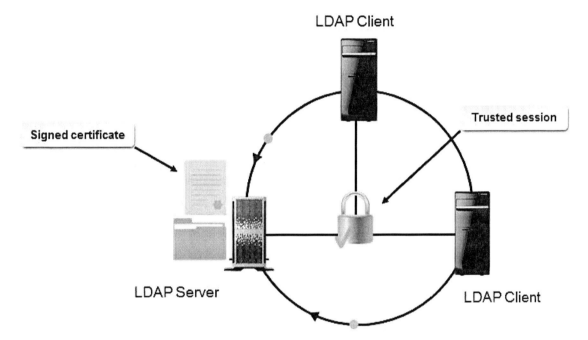

Figure 5-8: LDAP clients communicating with an LDAP server over SSL/TLS.

Active Directory

Active Directory (AD) is Microsoft's LDAP-compatible directory implementation. It structures objects within an organization into a hierarchy. An object is a single entity, such as a printer, a user, a computer, or a group, and the attributes for that entity. Objects are grouped into domains, and all the objects for a single domain are grouped and stored on one database. Active Directory allows administrators to centrally manage and control access to objects using access control lists (ACLs). AD allows users to find resources anywhere on the network. It also has a schema that controls how accounts are created and what attributes an administrator may assign to them.

For example, you can grant permissions to a group object to a shared resource like a printer. The users in that group are now authorized to access that printer, and any users outside of the group must also be granted the permissions before they can access the shared printer.

Active Directory allows you to subdivide the domain into *organizational units (OUs)*. OUs are analogous to folders on a hard drive. They are logical containers that can contain any number of users, groups, computers, printers, etc. OUs are especially convenient for applying different policies to different users, and delegating control of parts of the domain to other administrators. OUs typically represent departments, business units, job functions, office locations, user or computer types, or any other logical grouping.

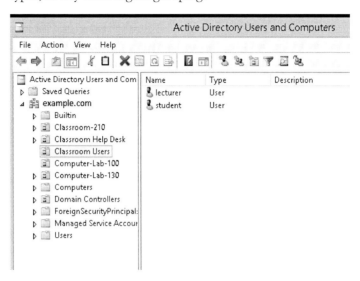

Figure 5-9: User objects stored in an Active Directory database.

 Note: Microsoft Active Directory is a directory service that is both LDAP and X.500 compliant.

Kerberos

Active Directory implementations always use *Kerberos,* an authentication service that is based on a time-sensitive ticket-granting system. It was developed by the Massachusetts Institute of Technology (MIT) to use a single-sign on method where the user enters access credentials that are then passed to the authentication server, which contains an access list and allowed access credentials. You can use Kerberos to manage access control to many different services using one centralized authentication server. Kerberos' mutual authentication between client and server will help protect the users in your domain from man-in-the-middle or replay attacks.

The Kerberos Process

In the Kerberos process, there are three primary systems. The user enters access credentials that are then passed to a Key Distribution Server, which also acts as an Authentication Server (AS), which contains the allowed access credentials. The AS verifies the credentials and passes a Ticket Granting Ticket (TGT) back to the requesting user. When a user requires the resources of another object, they use their TGT. That ticket contains a verification of the user's credentials, and it is then passed to another element of the system called the Ticket Granting Server (TGS). The TGS then verifies the request to access a given system or application and provides access rights.

A Service Ticket (ST) is then returned to the user. The ST is sent to the application server or network resource, which verifies that the user is allowed access to the system and that the user is authorized to use the system.

These tickets are only valid for a limited period of time (typically 8 - 12 hours, depending on the configuration). Additionally, the clocks of Kerberos servers and clients must be synchronized to the same source. By default, Kerberos can only tolerate a 5 minute difference (adjusted for time zone) between the clocks of participating devices. This narrow time window reduces the risk of replay attacks.

Kerberos can suffer from denial of service (DoS) attacks if there is only a single server. Overwhelming the AS or TGS restricts the number of users who can authenticate or get authorization. An AS or TGS failure also presents a single point of failure. No access will be given if the AS or TGS fails.

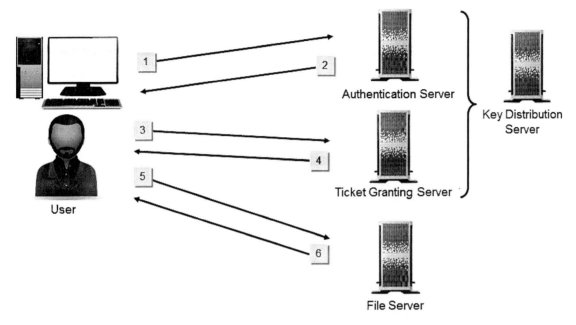

Figure 5-10: The Kerberos Process.

SSO

Single sign-on (SSO) allows a user to authenticate once and receive access to a number of related but independent software systems, without having to sign in again when accessing each specific system. For example, if the Active Directory® service is deployed in a Windows® environment, the user is not prompted to re-authenticate because Active Directory-aware applications retrieve Kerberos service tickets automatically. SSO is often considered a subset of identity federation, as an SSO identity can stay logged on to multiple disparate systems without needing to sign in more than once.

SSO has several benefits to an enterprise over traditional separate login systems, and the roaming authentication provided by SSO is performed transparently to the user. The first benefit of SSO is that compromised credentials can be quickly regained by a single action. Similarly, the burden of logging and monitoring user logins can be greatly reduced by having a central server delegate credentials and approve access. Although the process of logging in may seem instant, a large enterprise with many employees will lose time if the employees constantly need to log in to access separate systems. This also makes it easier on the user, as they aren't required to remember as many passwords.

The use of SSO requires a number of security considerations, though, as a compromise of a single set of credentials can lead to access to a number of systems instead of just one. Likewise, if authentication servers become unavailable, the entirety of a system may be unavailable as well. Secure SSO setups, particularly those that are Internet-facing, require multiple levels of authentication before providing full access. Common examples of such authentication include the use of hardware devices such as dongles or smart cards.

RADIUS

Remote Authentication Dial-In User Service (RADIUS) is an Internet standard protocol that provides centralized remote access authentication, authorization, and auditing services. When a network contains several remote access servers, you can configure one of the servers to be a RADIUS server, and all of the other servers as RADIUS clients. The RADIUS clients will pass all authentication requests to the RADIUS server for verification. This relieves the local remote access servers from having to maintain the user authentication database. User authentication, authorization, configuration, remote access policies, and usage logging (accounting) can be centralized on the RADIUS server.

You can configure RADIUS servers using a number of different authentication protocols described in the following table.

Authentication Protocol	Description
Password Authentication Protocol (PAP)	A protocol that sends user IDs and passwords as plaintext. It is generally used when a remote client is connecting to a non-Windows server that does not support strong password encryption. When the server receives a user ID and password pair, it compares them to its local list of credentials. If a match is found, the server accepts the credentials and allows the remote client to access resources. If no match is found, the connection is terminated. Because it lacks encryption, PAP is extremely vulnerable and has been largely phased out as a legacy protocol.
Challenge Handshake Authentication Protocol (CHAP)	An encrypted authentication protocol that is often used to provide access control for remote access servers. CHAP was developed so that passwords would not have to be sent in plaintext. It is generally used to connect to non-Microsoft servers. CHAP uses a combination of message-digest 5 (MD5) hashing and a challenge-response mechanism, and it accomplishes authentication without ever sending passwords over the network. It can accept connections from any authentication method except for certain unencrypted schemes. For these reasons, CHAP is a more secure protocol than PAP. However, CHAP is also considered a legacy protocol, particularly because the MD5 hash algorithm is no longer suitably secure.

 Note: Microsoft's version of CHAP is MS-CHAP and MS-CHAPv2.

Authentication Protocol	Description
Extensible Authentication Protocol (EAP)	A framework that allows clients and servers to authenticate with each other using one of a variety of plugins. Because EAP does not specify which authentication method should be used, it enables the choice of a wide range of current authentication methods, and allows for the implementation of future authentication methods. For example, Microsoft provides EAP use with MS-CHAPv2 in virtual private networks (VPNs). EAP is often utilized in wireless networks and can also be used in wired implementations.
Protected Extensible Authentication Protocol (PEAP)	An extension of EAP, an open standard developed by a coalition made up of Cisco Systems, Microsoft, and RSA Security. PEAP encapsulates EAP in an encrypted Transport Layer Security (TLS) tunnel to strengthen its authentication communications. This protects the authentication exchange from man-in-the-middle attacks.
Lightweight Extensible Authentication Protocol (LEAP)	Cisco Systems' proprietary EAP implementation. LEAP features mutual authentication between the client and RADIUS feature, as well as generating Wired Equivalent Privacy (WEP) keys used in wireless communication encryption. LEAP clients can reauthenticate frequently in order to lower the lifespan of the key; however, because WEP is insecure and obsolete, you should avoid using LEAP with WEP.

 Note: These protocols may also be used outside of RADIUS.

Diameter

Diameter is an authentication protocol that improves upon RADIUS by strengthening some of its weaknesses. For example, Diameter has a failover mechanism because it is Transmission Control Protocol (TCP)-based, and RADIUS does not have a failover mechanism because it is User Datagram Protocol (UDP)-based. Additionally, RADIUS does not mandate confidentiality per packet, whereas Diameter does by requiring IPSec and TLS. The name "Diameter" comes from the claim that Diameter is twice as good as RADIUS. Diameter is a stronger protocol in many ways, but is not as widespread in its implementation due to the lack of products using it.

NPS

Network Policy Server (NPS) is a Microsoft Windows Server 2012 implementation of a RADIUS server. It helps in administrating VPNs and wireless networks. NPS was known as Internet Authentication Service (IAS) in Windows Server® 2003.

NAP

Network Access Protection (NAP) is a Windows Server technology that uses RADIUS to evaluate the health state of a host client. Health requirements could mandate that a host be running a particular operating system version, that the host has the latest anti-malware signatures installed, that the host's firewall is enabled, and so on.

Guidelines for Applying Identification, Authentication, and Authorization

Use the following guidelines to assist in the identification, authentication, and authorization process:

- Become acquainted with the different types of identification and how each one is potentially vulnerable.
- Understand the differences between the authentication factors: something you know, something you have, and something you are.
- Draft administrative policy to dictate how often passwords are changed, their minimum length, and other restrictions.
- Make sure administrators don't know individual users' passwords except during initial creation to generate a temporary password.
- If using a card system for authentication, use smart cards rather than older magnetic stripe cards for increased security.
- Consider applying a biometric system as an authentication factor, but be aware of potential errors arising in this still-evolving area of technology.
- Whenever possible, mandate the use of multi-factor authentication for users and administrators.
- Make sure your identity, authentication, and authorization systems support accountability.
- Apply desktop session management practices like screensaver locks and timeouts to maintain session security.
- Adopt a process for proving identity before actually provisioning the identity.
- Implement credential management systems to streamline the process, but be aware of the its risk as a single point of failure.
- Implement a directory service like LDAP or Active Directory to facilitate authentication and authorization across your organization.
- Implement RADIUS for remote authentication using a secure protocol like PEAP.

ACTIVITY 5-2
Analyzing Identification, Authentication, and Authorization

Scenario

In this activity, you will assess your knowledge of identification, authentication, and authorization.

1. What are the three steps of identity management?
   - ○ Authentication, Authorization, Accounting
   - ○ Authentication, Authorization, Auditing
   - ○ Identification, Authorization, Accounting
   - ○ Identification, Authentication, Authorization

2. Which protocol is most often associated with Challenge and Response?
   - ○ RADIUS
   - ○ RDP
   - ○ CHAP
   - ○ TACACS

3. What is a potential weakness of using email for identification?

4. What types of attacks represent specific weaknesses to identification? (Choose two.)
   - ☐ Shoulder surfing
   - ☐ Bluejacking
   - ☐ Social engineering
   - ☐ Worms

5. Your organization recently updated its security policies, requiring all users to be issued new ID cards that carry digital certificates. Card readers are being installed at each workstation, and in the server room. Users will still be required to enter a user ID and password, but will also insert the smart card into a reader before logon will be successful. This is an example of what?
   - ○ Single sign-on
   - ○ Two-factor authentication
   - ○ Something you have authentication
   - ○ Something you know authentication

6. Which of the following are not typical biometric authentication methods? (Choose two.)

   ☐ Retinal scan

   ☐ Facial recognition

   ☐ Fingerprint

   ☐ Geolocation

   ☐ Signature

   ☐ Hand geometry

7. When is it permissible to share your password with another?

   ○ When you need them to do some work on your behalf.

   ○ When they are your boss.

   ○ When they are a system administrator.

   ○ Never.

8. Which statement is true regarding biometric crossover error rate (CER)?

   ○ Of false acceptance and false rejection, CER is the lower of the two.

   ○ Of false acceptance and false rejection, CER is the higher of the two.

   ○ CER is the intersection of false acceptance and false rejection rates.

   ○ CER is the lowest point of either false acceptance or false rejection errors.

9. True or False? Smart cards cannot be used for authentication at an endpoint.

   ☐ True

   ☐ False

10. Which term refers to methods that allow a single instance of identification and authentication to be applied to many systems or services?

    ○ Session Layer

    ○ Split-token

    ○ Session Management

    ○ Multi-factor

11. Which statement best describes a federated identity?

    ○ Using a single identity across your enterprise.

    ○ Using a single identity across multiple identity management systems.

    ○ Using a user name and password implemented in one system, and a smart card implemented in another system.

    ○ Using the same authentication server to authenticate users in different organizations.

12. What is the value of using a directory service?

13. What value does LDAP add to a directory service?

14. How might you use organizational units in Active Directory to enhance security?

15. What is the value of using time-sensitive tickets in Kerberos?

16. Under what conditions could Single Sign-On become a security risk?

17. How can the use of RADIUS enhance remote access security?

TOPIC C

Identity as a Service

Your users are no longer content to simply work from their desk anymore, and they really don't like the hassle of supplying different usernames and passwords for the myriad systems they use. As your organization embraces the work anywhere, at anytime, from nearly any where, the identification and authentication tools you use will need to accommodate them.

IDaaS Functionality

Identity as a Service (IDaaS) moves the identification and authentication (I&A) function to the cloud. IDaaS can provide an entire authentication, authorization, and accounting (AAA) function, or it might provide a subset of functionality for a particular system or application. IDaaS can be used for internal resources, or other cloud based resources like Software as a Service (SaaS) or Infrastructure as a Service (IaaS).

IDaaS should include functionality for the following:

- **Identity governance and administration**: This includes the ability to create accounts and/or synchronize accounts.
- **Access**: Allows for user authentication, and authorization perhaps providing SSO.
- **Intelligence**: There is still a need for logging and I&A audits.

Additional features that might be part of an IDaaS offering:

- SSO.
- Support for Federations.
- Granular Authorization Control.
- Tools to support administration.
- Integration with internal Directory Services.
- Integration with external services like SaaS, PaaS, IaaS, and so on.

Cloud Identity

With cloud identity, the user's account identity is created in the cloud for a particular application or site. It is used for a single purpose and no synchronization is required. Office 365 is an example of cloud identity when it is used as the sole point of authentication, and is not synchronized with any other directory.

Cloud identity effectively shifts the burden of maintaining directory services entirely to the provider and is a common choice for smaller organizations or those that don't want to take on the added effort of managing account information internally.

Cloud Security

There is much to like about the cloud, but you must maintain the same vigilance in the cloud as you do in your internal networks. But now you have another vendor to work with. You need to make sure they take security as seriously as you do. By setting clear goals and providing an option for audits, you can help protect your assets in the cloud.

Cloud identity and access management has its own set of problems:

- **APIs**: Providers might offer some interfaces, but likely not all of them that are needed.
- **Authorization mapping**: How users are granted privileges may need to change as identity is managed by the cloud provider.

- **Audit**: Requesting logs from providers may be difficult, as the provider must be careful not to disclose logged data from other clients that share virtual machine tenancy.
- **Privacy**: Sensitive user information is being sent over the Internet and stored on servers that you don't personally maintain. This can be a huge risk to the organization.
- **Latency**: Configurations may take time to push out to the cloud. A delay in user rights changing may incur risk.
- **App identity**: Apps won't necessarily check a client's identity, which can be a problem if you want to make sure your cloud-based users' identities aren't using unauthorized apps.
- **Mobile**: Cloud providers often have mobile services, which adds another system and attack surface you need to defend.

Federated Identity and Trust

Until fairly recently the whole process of I&A was pretty much limited to within a single organization. You worked for company A, you logged into company A's PC, and you had access to company A's resources.

But what if you could extend the I&A process to Company B, or take advantage of SSO with websites or web hosted applications? This is the idea of federation; extend the usefulness of your existing user name and password to gain access to resources far beyond your company's borders. This will sound like a big win for employees who no longer have to remember different passwords for different sites, but there is a lot of work that needs to be done to support federated services. There will need to be a method for establishing trust between the user and the resource. This trust needs to start at the corporate level and then is supported with a federated services implementation.

When organizations want the ability to access information in their partners' systems but do not want to create accounts on those systems, it would be beneficial if they could take advantage of their own account stores for authentication. With federated trust, you create a resource domain and an account domain that trust each other. As an account is making requests for resources, the authentication request is processed by the account partner. This implies a series of trusts should be in place. Also it typically involves certificates and public key infrastructure (PKI).

In a federated environment, each organization in the federation agrees to a common set of policies regarding user identification and authorization. There are two common models:

- **Cross-certification trust**: Each organization individually certifies every other organization in the federation. This is also known as a peer model of trust.
- **Third-party certification trust**: Each organization trusts a third-party organization to manage the trust. This is also known as a hierarchical model of trust.

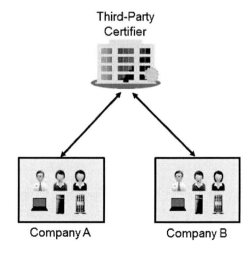

Figure 5-11: Federated identity models.

Identity Federation Methods

There are several different identity management methods that you can implement for a federated environment. The following table lists some of those methods.

Identity Federation Method	Description
Security Assertion Markup Language (SAML)	SAML is an XML-based framework for exchanging security-related information such as user authentication, entitlement, and attributes. This information is communicated in the form of assertions over a secure HTTP connection, which conveys the identity of subjects and authorization decisions about the access level of the subjects. SAML contains components such as assertions, protocol, and binding. Authentication assertions contain information about any acts of authentication or user identity validation, attribute assertions contain information about users, and authorization assertions contain information about the level of access for each user. Clients request assertions from SAML authorities and get a response from them using the protocol defined by SAML. The single greatest feature of SAML is that single sign-on can be achieved across enterprises through non-proprietary web browsers. SAML is based on an explicit trust between your organization and the identify provider. It is vulnerable to spoofing by attackers posing as actual users.
OpenID	OpenID is a method of authenticating users with certain sites that participate in an OpenID system. Like SAML, it uses browser-based single sign on. This allows users to retain a single account for all participating sites. A user registers with an OpenID system in a given domain like they would with any other account. A site under this OpenID domain then gives the user the option to sign in using this system. The site then contacts its external OpenID provider in order to verify that the login credentials supplied by the user are correct. OpenID is used by Microsoft®, Facebook®, Google®, Yahoo!®, PayPal®, Symantec®, and others. OpenID is vulnerable to spoofing, both on the client and the provider side.
Shibboleth	Shibboleth is a federated identity method based on SAML that is often employed by universities or public service organizations. In a Shibboleth implementation, a user attempts to retrieve resources from a Shibboleth-enabled website, which then sends SAML authentication information over URL queries. The user is then redirected to an identity provider with which they can authenticate using this SAML information. The identity provider then responds to the service provider (the Shibboleth-enabled website) with the proper authentication information. The site validates this response and grants the user access to certain resources based on their SAML information.
Where Are You From (WAYF)	WAYF is an SSO implementation that is centered around asking users what institution they are from before they are allowed access to a service provider. In WAYF, a user connects to a web resource, which then refers to a WAYF identity management system. The system asks which institution the user is from, which mandates that the user log in to their institution if they are not already. After the user is successfully logged in to their own institution, the WAYF informs the user what identity information will be sent to the service provider. The user must consent before this information is sent. The service provider then decides, based on this information, whether to allow the user access.

Directory Synchronization

Directory synchronization involves syncing a cloud identity with another directory; for example, your Active Directory. This gives users the ability to use a familiar login to access cloud resources. As users are created in AD, they will need to be synchronized with the cloud provider. The synchronization can be done with a directory synchronization tool, a PowerShell script, or a cloud provider's API.

An example of directory synchronization would be your own Active Directory domain synchronizing users, groups, and passwords and other objects with Microsoft Azure or Google Cloud services. After an initial synchronization, any changes to your directory services are regularly synchronized with the cloud provider. Users can then use the same username and password to access local or cloud resources.

Directory synchronization helps enable federation across your internal identity management service and the third party services that you employ in the organization. When directories synchronize, they can also enable single sign on capabilities so that users can access internal and cloud resources without needing to log in twice.

Granular Authorization Control

Granular authorization control allows you to have users with different levels of access. A system will start with an administrator account. The administrator account will then be able to create accounts that have less privilege on the system. For example, some users may have read-only permissions; some may have read and change, but only to certain areas of the system. It will be important to add accounts carefully, and to audit these accounts periodically. This is especially true of federated accounts.

Consider, for example, an account that's been federated across two different systems, both controlled by the organization. You want the person using this account to have write access on System A, but only read access to the resources on System B. Simply setting an authorization role of "write" on the user's account will cause issues with System B. Only when you implement more granular authorization rules will you be able to cover all scenarios and uphold your access control policy. In this example, you may need to implement authorization rules at the system level so that a user's propagated identity will only have the access that each particular system deems necessary.

Guidelines for Implementing IDaaS

Use the following guidelines when implementing IDaaS:

- Incorporate an IDaaS system with administration, access, and intelligence capabilities.
- Consider offloading identity services to a cloud provider, especially if internal solutions prove too costly.
- Keep in mind, however, that cloud services introduce a whole host of security issues.
- Ensure that you understand the risks to privacy, auditing, and app integration that cloud identity and access management services provide.
- Implement identity federation to streamline user interactions and identity management within the enterprise.
- Implement identity federation to reduce the cost and the risk associated with multiple identity management systems.
- Establish a cross-certification or third-party certification trust model in federated systems, depending on your organization's needs and capabilities.
- Use a SAML-based federation framework like Shibboleth to securely manage individual identities.
- Ensure that identity propagation has fine-grained control over whose identity gets propagated where so you conform to access control policies.

- Likewise, ensure that propagated identities are obeying the principle of least privilege in every system they touch.

ACTIVITY 5-3
Analyzing Identity as a Service

Scenario

In this activity, you will assess your knowledge of identity as a service.

1. What is the primary trade-off in using IDaaS?
   - ○ You are trading your existing centralized system for a vendor's decentralized system.
   - ○ You are giving up control in exchange for convenience.
   - ○ You are reducing cost in exchange for security.
   - ○ You are increasing complexity in exchange for security.

2. What is required for a federated trust to work?
   - ○ A reciprocal agreement between participating organizations.
   - ○ A trust between the root CAs of the federated partners.
   - ○ A third party certifier that both sides recognize.
   - ○ A single directory service that the federated partners share.

3. Which SAML-based authentication system is often used by universities?
   - ○ OpenID
   - ○ SAML
   - ○ WAYF
   - ○ Shibboleth

4. You are the security consultant for a county health department. The county has a special program that uses community volunteers and contract health workers to provide health services to poor and underprivileged communities. The county maintains a number of different databases that keep information on the thousands of clients (health care recipients) that receive services.

   How can granular authorization control assist with this program?
   - ○ It can use different databases to keep information about the clients separate from information about the service providers.
   - ○ It can provide different types of service providers (volunteers, contractors, internal county employees, etc.) levels of access appropriate to their role.
   - ○ It can provide clients with access to information about the program.
   - ○ It can provide policy makers with access to information about the program.

TOPIC D

Authorization Mechanisms

Once a user or system has been identified and authenticated, they will need to be authorized to perform an action or function within the systems or data they are accessing. Authorization follows as the next step in the I&A process. In fact, the process is sometimes referred to as AAA for Authentication, Authorization, and Accounting. Many older systems and documentation use the term AAA, and you will want to be familiar with it.

Authorization Mechanisms

Each authorization mechanism model has a place in security planning just as each model has benefits and drawbacks. You must choose which model(s) are the most appropriate for your organization based on its operational needs and potential risk or benefit to the organization. The three primary access control models are:

- Discretionary access control.
- Mandatory access control.
- Non-discretionary access control.

In the earliest days of computer security, physical controls were the most important controls. If you could not access the computer facility, you could not access the information stored there. Eventually, when multiple users could access computer systems, the security requirements changed. Direct access terminals were the first connections used. Shortly thereafter, the users' rights to the data on computers needed to be limited. The first instance of technical controls came with the advent of the access control matrix. As you continue to change how and where you do computing, the need to reevaluate how and where you will apply security will be ongoing.

MAC

Mandatory access control (MAC) is a means of restricting access to objects based on the sensitivity (as represented by a label) of the information contained in the objects and the formal authorization (for example, clearance) of subjects to access information of such sensitivity. MAC is employed in cases where high levels of security are required and information needs to be protected based on its sensitivity, and it is the most restrictive access control model.

Top Secret government information requires a high level of protection and is classified accordingly. Only users with a Top Secret clearance may access Top Secret information. The formal authorization to access Top Secret information for an individual is determined by the system based on labels and categories. Within classifications, categories can be used to group information within a specific topic or project area.

Because MAC offers the most restrictive access control, its primary disadvantage is that it is difficult to make changes to. A system owner can't simply grant access to a file on a user-by-user basis; they must ensure that the user has the proper security label for the exact file they are trying to access. So, while MAC is often necessary in governmental organizations, commercial businesses may find it too strict for their purposes.

Example Classification Table

Depending on the mandatory access requirements, only users with Top Secret clearance have access to Top Secret files. The security clearance and classification levels are therefore enforcing principles. A subject with a given clearance level may only access an object with an equal or lower classification level.

	Security Clearance
John	Top Secret
Brian	Secret
Carla	Classified

File Name	File Classification Level	Who Has Access?
Budget.xlsx	Classified	John, Brian, Carla
2016 strategy.pptx	Secret	John, Brian
International treaty.docx	Top Secret	John
Field report.docx	Top Secret	John
Research report.docx	Secret	John, Brian

Figure 5-12: User security clearance and file classification level determine who has access.

DAC

Discretionary access control (DAC) is a means of restricting access to objects based on the identity of the subjects and/or groups to which they belong. Assigning a user ID and password to an individual user is an exemplary case of DAC. The controls are discretionary in the sense that a subject with certain access permissions is capable of passing those permissions (perhaps indirectly) on to any other subject (unless restrained by another access control method).

DAC is less restrictive than MAC, because a data owner can change a user's assigned permissions in order to accommodate any changes that have been made to the data or user. On the other hand, the system owners must place a certain amount of trust in the discretion of every data owner who has the power to change permissions. If even one mistake is made in authorization, it could compromise the CIA of data.

Discretionary Access Levels

The owner of a file database, Larry, has assigned the following access levels to each relevant user in the organization.

User	Database Access Level
Peter	• Read
Matt	• Read • Write
Sue	• Read • Write • Delete

Figure 5-13: Larry's access control matrix for his file database.

As a the database's owner, Larry can adjust these levels at any time. If Peter is promoted, for example, Larry can add write access to his account.

Non-Discretionary Access Control

Non-discretionary access control differs from discretionary access control in that only certain system administrators are allowed to change access permissions on data, rather than the individual owners of that data. This may help limit the risk of data owners incorrectly interpreting or applying company access control policy and create fewer surfaces for attackers to exploit.

 Note: The term non-discretionary access control is not commonly used in information security, and some sources draw no distinction between it and mandatory access control.

Access Control Matrix

The *access control matrix* is a technical access control consisting of a tabular display of access rights. It uses the concepts of need to know, least privilege, and SoD to assign rights to users. It shows the users who can access the system, the resources to access in the system, and the rights assigned.

Permissions indicate the subject's access capabilities to the object. The lack of assigned permissions in the access control matrix dictates that a user has no access to the file and is an implicit deny. Many systems also allow for an explicit deny that trumps all other permissions.

In a discretionary system, it is the owner who has the right to set permissions. The owner can grant or deny anyone access, including administrators. In some discretionary systems, however, the administrator has the right to take ownership.

Permissions are also cumulative in nature. If you belong to three different groups, you have the permissions of all of those groups combined. Effectively, you have the most permissive permissions. The exception to that is deny, which overrides any other permission. If any one of your permissions is deny, you will not be able to perform that particular activity, even if you are an administrator.

Permission Codes in an Access Control Matrix

Depending on the system implementation, the permissions are indicated by a capability to read, write, execute, or have owner status of the file, as shown here:

- r = read
- w = write
- x = execute
- o = owner

Other rights such as delete (d), list (l) for directories, and modify (m) are used in different operating systems.

A Simple Access Control Matrix

In this very simple example of an access control matrix, the subjects, or users, are seen in the left-hand column of the matrix. The names of the files to be accessed are seen in the first row of the table. Bob and Alice work together and need to access the file parts used for manufacturing operation. The access limits for these two users are different. Alice can query the file, but Bob can update and change the access rights to the file since he is the file owner.

Natasha is the manager of the personnel and payroll departments. She is the data owner and has allowed Boris to edit the payroll and people files. She has also allowed Alice and Bob to view the personnel file, so they can view which staff is available for manufacturing from time to time. However, the control file can be viewed by Bob and Natasha but can only be updated by Alice.

	Pay1	*People1*	*Part1*	*Control1*
Bob		r	rwo	r
Alice		r	r	rwo
Boris	rw	rw		

	Pay1	*People1*	*Part1*	*Control1*
Natasha	rwo	rwo		r

Consider the challenge of using an access control matrix in a large system with 3,000 users and 30,000 files. For each user, the matrix row is established and permissions are configured. In most cases, users have very limited access to files. Although the matrix is very large, the areas it uses are small. In the end, this option can take a lot of administration work for very little benefit.

> **Note:** Microsoft NTFS file system permissions expand upon the basic rwxo permissions. It also includes *delete*, *change* (the ability to change permissions but not take ownership), and *full control* (the ability to change permissions and take ownership). There is also *special*, which can refer to any combination of permissions, but usually means the user has the right to change the permissions themselves. In addition, there is *deny*. This applies to any single permission, and cannot be overridden, even if the user is an administrator. For example, a user can have *read* permissions but *deny write*, meaning they can read a file but cannot modify it under any conditions.

RBAC

Role-based access control (RBAC) is implemented when the subject's access to objects is based on the job performed by the subject. In RBAC, administrators create groups that represent different roles. Groups are assigned permissions, and users are assigned to the groups. If the user is removed from a group, that person no longer has that associated permission. Rather than working with each individual user's permissions, the group permission and group membership simplifies administrative overhead.

Sometimes RBAC is used when a limited duration assignment to a job exists. For example, a hospital uses nurses from a pool of available staff. When a nurse comes in for a shift, that individual is assigned to a group with visiting nurse capabilities, and then when the shift ends, that individual is removed from the group.

RBAC is an attractive solution because it's often easy just to assign rules based on each person's existing role in the organization. Someone in the Marketing department might be assigned the Marketing role and have access to the organization's promotional materials. If a user leaves or moves to a different apartment, it's simply a matter of changing their role. However, RBAC may prove inadequate in situations that require more granular division of access control; each person in a department might require their own unique level of access, so assigning a role becomes nearly pointless. Likewise, access to some systems cannot be simplified into roles, but require a heavier focus on the object rather than the subject.

RBAC can accommodate a single user belonging to many roles. This can also lead to unexpected complexity and confusion. If a single user belongs to multiple roles, then that user's final permission is a combination of all role permissions together. For example, if a user belongs to three groups, one of which can read, the other write, and the last execute, then the user's cumulative permissions are read, write, and execute. Where the complexity comes in is if one of the roles is denied a specific permission. If the user's three groups have read, write, and deny write permissions, then the user can only read. Deny overrides any other permissions for that particular activity.

RBAC Architectures

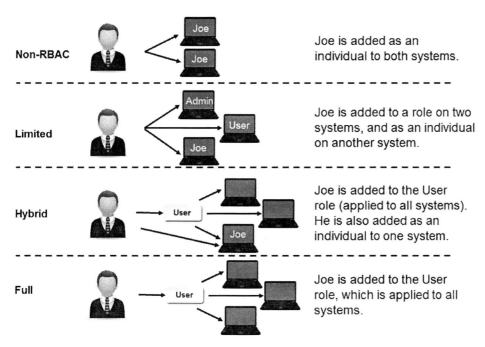

Figure 5–14: User and administrator roles applied to different systems in each RBAC architecture.

There are four basic RBAC architectures.

Architecture	Description
Non-RBAC	This refers to mapping access control to each individual user, rather than assigning the user to an actual role.
Limited RBAC	In this architecture, each system has its own roles that users are assigned to. Rather than an organization-wide role, the user has a role only within that particular system, and may have a completely different role in a different system.
Hybrid RBAC	In this architecture, the user has a role that applies to multiple systems, but at the same time each system may apply a different or complementary role.
Full RBAC	In full RBAC, roles are organization-wide and proliferate through every system. Individual systems or groups of systems do not assign their own roles.

Rule-Based Access Control

Rule-based access control is based on a set of operational rules or restrictions. For example, a set of firewall-based port restriction rules is a type of rule-based access control. While a DAC may specify that user John can access a database server, a rule-based control may block his access if he tries connecting to the database using a remote desktop protocol whose port is blocked on the firewall.

Rule sets are always examined before a subject is given access to objects, so even though in the previous example John already has his level of access set by the DAC, he must still pass a rules check before that access is truly granted.

Rule-based access control therefore offers a more granular option for authorization. As useful as this seems, keep in mind that overly complicated and restrictive rules may reduce your systems' availability, frustrate users, and overall make your access control services much more complex and difficult to manage.

Rule-Based Access Control Techniques

The following are some examples of rule-based access control techniques.

Rule-Based Technique	Description
Context dependent	*Context dependent access control* will determine the context of the request before processing the request.
	For example, a stateful inspection firewall can determine if the packet request came from the inside or outside the network and use that context information to determine whether to route it or drop it.
Content dependent	*Content dependent access control* limits the subject's access to objects by examining object data to see if the subject has access rights.
	An attempt to access the CEO's payroll information by a payroll clerk may be denied when the system checks the clerk's access rights against the CEO's salary level. This is because not all clerks can see the CEO's payroll information; only those with special access capabilities are permitted.
	Content dependent access controls put extra overhead on the process because object information must be accessed to determine if the subject can see the information.
Constrained interfaces	*Constrained interfaces access control* limits access to information by constraining the interface.
	An ATM machine is a perfect example because there are a limited number of keys, a limited screen display, and limited functions that can be performed on an ATM.
Time-based	*Time-based access control* limits when an individual can access the system.
	In some organizations, users are allowed access to their workstations between 8:00 a.m. and 5:00 p.m., and access outside of those hours is denied. Individuals who do not have authorized access through those workstations will also be denied.

Guidelines for Implementing Authorization Mechanisms

Use the following guidelines when implementing authorization mechanisms:

- Use mandatory access control (MAC) when your organization needs to exercise tight control over highly sensitive materials, especially in a governmental context.
- Make sure access levels are thoroughly defined for all subjects and corresponding objects in a MAC system.
- Implement discretionary access control (DAC) when you need to empower data owners to make their own decisions on access control, especially if those parameters are constantly changing.
- Keep in mind that these data owners may be a risk to the organization if they do not properly follow policy, or if their accounts are compromised.
- Implement role-based access control (RBAC) when your organizational structure is closely tied to how you need to delegate access.
- Keep in mind that RBAC by itself may not offer a sufficient level of granularity when it comes to setting access control levels.
- If you implement RBAC, evaluate and select the appropriate architecture (limited, hybrid, full).
- Complement your existing authorization mechanisms with rule-based access control for a more fine-grained approach.

- Consider the different rule-based techniques, like time-based and content dependent, and apply ones that fit your particular business operations.
- Avoid making rules needlessly complex so as not to put a strain on access control management.
- Ultimately, choose whichever model or combination of models is most appropriate for your business needs.

ACTIVITY 5-4
Discussing Authorization Mechanisms

Scenario

In this activity, you'll discuss the advantages and disadvantages of various authorization mechanisms.

1. You have a folder with the following access control permissions assigned to it: Bob has no explicit permissions (he is not listed in the folder's ACL). The Sales group can read. The Managers group can write. The Marketing group has the deny read permission assigned.

   If Bob belongs to all three groups, what is his effective permission on the folder?

   ○ He can only read.

   ○ He can only write.

   ○ He can read and write.

   ○ He cannot access the folder in any way.

2. Why is mandatory access control not widely deployed in private, commercial organizations?

3. Why is discretionary access control not widely deployed in the military?

4. What is the primary difference between role-based access control and rule-based access control?

5. In what situations would non-RBAC be a preferred architecture model?

6. In what situations would time-based access control be useful?

TOPIC E

Access Control Attack Mitigation

Despite your efforts to implement a robust access control system, attacks can and will happen. It's important that you understand the various ways that attackers can gain authorized access to your organization, and the ways you can defend against these attacks.

Access Control Attacks

There are many different methods you can use to attack an access control system. However, there are two basic goals involved: gaining access that you're not authorized for, and preventing authorized users from gaining access. An attacker may be attempting to reach one or both of these goals. With either goal in mind, access control attacks generally take the approach of targeting software components, targeting the human element, or targeting physical entities.

These attacks can vary in scope, complexity, and impact. For example, an attacker may be able to simply steal a user's credentials by guessing them. If the user is an administrator, the attacker can wreak havoc on key operational systems. On the other hand, an attacker may need to spend a great deal of time and computing power to brute force their way into an account with credentials that aren't easily guessable. It's important to recognize that access control attacks are not always parallel with one another, requiring you to think more creatively about how your systems are vulnerable and how threats to access control can be disarmed.

Software-Based Access Control Attacks

Some access control attacks are software based.

Software-Based Attack Method	Description
DoS and DDoS	Denial of service attacks can limit or eliminate the user's ability to access the network and/or data. A simple example of a DoS attack involves parking a car in the drive-through lane of a bank so cars cannot get through.
Buffer overflow	Buffer overflows can cause access control mechanisms in systems or software to fail, enabling an attacker to bypass these controls.
Malicious software	Malicious software is a type of attack that causes system failures or malfunctions. Malware, viruses, and worms are all examples of software gone bad. *Spyware* is another form of malicious software that is secretly installed on a user's computer to gather data about the user and relay it to a third party.
	All of these programs can cause serious system failures or malfunctions that an attacker can take advantage of beyond just limiting availability. Malware may be able to capture users' credential input, for example, so that an attacker doesn't even need to guess their user name and password.
Mobile code	Mobile code is software that is transmitted from one device to another and then executed on the new host. It is different from traditional software in that it does not need to be installed but can execute nonetheless. JScript and ActiveX are common examples. Not all mobile code is malicious. It is dangerous because it can circumvent normal software restrictions and checks.

Software–Based Attack Method	Description
Brute force password attack	Brute force is a type of password attack where an attacker uses an application to exhaustively try every possible alphanumeric combination to try to crack encrypted passwords and circumvent the authentication system. Creating complex passwords can increase the amount of time it takes for a brute force attack to succeed. Using brute force to crack a wireless network may result in access capabilities to many corporate resources.
Dictionary password attack	A dictionary attack uses a set of predefined words from a dictionary to crack a password. Creating a dictionary of pre-hashed passwords can provide a *rainbow table* to speed up the password attack.
Sniffing	Sniffing involves using special monitoring software to gain access to private communications on the network wire or across a wireless network. This type of attack is used either to steal the content of the communications itself or to gain information that will help the attacker later gain access to your network and resources. This type of attack is also known as eavesdropping. Encryption of data in transit can help prevent sniffing.
Emanation	Emanation is an attack where protected information is leaked through the natural process of electrons passing through a wire or over the radio. These electrons can be detected by sophisticated monitoring devices, and then be captured and turned into information that can be used by an attacker. Keyboards, cathode ray tube (CRT) monitors, cabling, and computers are all subject to emanations. Wireless is practically emanation by design.
Object reuse	As a software attack, *object reuse* is the act of reclaiming classified or sensitive information from media once erroneously thought to have been erased or overwritten. Hard drives and other forms of read/write devices may end up with data left on them unintentionally. For example, ribbons from impact printers have been used to recover information. Print queues hold a copy of a file for a short time, and an unscrupulous administrator might have the ability to read those files before they are cleaned up.
Data remanence	Occasionally, deleted information remains available due to an electronic property known as data remanence, where faulty information is left on media during the file erasure and deletion process. Applications will store information in memory where it may be left for another process to find. Sophisticated means are necessary to actually erase information during this process.
Trapdoor, backdoor, and maintenance hook	A *trapdoor attack* is where a hidden entry point into a program or operating system bypasses the normal identification and authentication processes. A *backdoor attack* is a type of software attack where an attacker creates a software mechanism called a *backdoor* to gain access to a computer. The backdoor can be a software utility or an illegitimate user account. Typically, a backdoor is delivered through use of a Trojan horse or other malware. Backdoor software typically listens for commands from the attacker on an open port. The backdoor mechanism often survives even after the initial intrusion has been discovered and resolved. The terms trapdoor and backdoor are frequently used interchangeably. *Maintenance hooks,* on the other hand, are frequently created by the developer of the application or hardware device. They are intended for use by technicians during development and should always be removed before the product is shipped so that they cannot be exploited. Trapdoor and backdoor activities are not included in the audit trail so there is no accounting for what happens.

Software-Based Attack Method	Description
Spoofing	Spoofing, or masquerading, comes in many forms wherein the attacker assumes an electronic identity to conceal his or her true person. Using IP, MAC, or DNS spoofing, an attacker forces a system to recognize a false identity, potentially allowing the attacker greater access based on this identity.

Note: Although emanations are listed here as a software-based attack method, they are more precisely a phenomenon of electrons and electronic systems.

Social Engineering Access Control Attacks

Social engineering is a type of attack that uses deception and trickery to convince unsuspecting users to provide sensitive data or to violate security guidelines. It exploits weaknesses in human judgment and is often a precursor to another type of attack. Because these attacks depend on human factors rather than on technology, their symptoms can be vague and hard to identify. Social engineering attacks can occur through a variety of methods: in person, through email, or over the phone.

The following table lists some examples of social engineering attacks that can compromise access control.

Social Engineering Attack	Description
Shoulder surfing	*Shoulder surfing* is an attack where the goal is to look over the shoulder of an individual as he or she enters password information or a PIN number. This is much easier to do today with camera-equipped mobile phones.
Dumpster diving	*Dumpster diving* is an attack where the goal is to reclaim important information by inspecting the contents of trash containers. This is especially effective in the first few weeks of the year as users discard old calendars with passwords written in them.
Tailgating	Also known as piggy backing, *tailgating* is a human-based attack where the attacker will slip in through a secure area following a legitimate employee. The only way to prevent this type of attack is by installing a good access control mechanism and educating users not to admit unauthorized personnel.
Spoofing	Spoofing can occur in human-based form if employed in email, where various email message headers are changed to conceal the originator's identity. The attacker then solicits the victim to provide their credentials under the guise of helping them. For example, the email may claim to come from the user's bank, telling the user that their account has been compromised. In order to set things right, the email claims, the user must provide their user name and password so they can be reset. If the user complies, the attacker now has access to that user's financial services. This is also called *phishing*.

Social Engineering Attack	Description
Baiting	*Baiting* exploits the human tendency toward curiosity by planting physical media in an area where someone will find it and then promptly use it. For example, a social engineer might install malware on a removable Universal Serial Bus (USB) drive, then place that drive on the ground in a parking lot outside of a corporate office. An employee who arrives for work may notice that drive, pick it up, then promptly insert it into their workstation. If their workstation has autorun enabled for removable media, the malware will immediately infect the host and may then spread to other hosts in the corporate network. A similar virtual attack occurs when a user is enticed to download free software, which an attacker has packaged with a Trojan horse.

Human-Based Access Control Attacks

Some access control attacks are directed against or take advantage of people, but don't necessarily involve deception.

Human-Based Attack Method	Description
Guessing	Guessing is an attack where the goal is to guess a password or PIN through brute force means or by using deduction. For example, PINs are often the last four digits of a person's Social Security number or the four digits of his or her birth month and day.
Theft	Theft is an attack where the goal is to blatantly steal information and resources in order to bypass physical or technical access controls. This usually requires unauthorized access or collusion with a disgruntled employee.
Threatening	Threatening is an attack that involves placing a victim in a state of duress in order to take advantage of their identity and authorization. The duress may come from threats of bodily injury or death to the self or loved ones, or it may come from blackmailing the victim into helping the attacker gain access.

Physical Access Control Attacks

Some access control attacks target physical systems.

Physical Attack Method	Description
Physical breach	A physical breach involves bypassing doors, locks, gates, and other physical controls. The attacker may do this covertly, e.g., sneaking in through an unguarded back door; or the action may be more covert, e.g., an attacker kicks down a locked door to the server room.
Tampering	Attackers can use tampering to configure a physical system in order to enable a breach, or they can tamper with the system to shut down all authorized access. For example, an attacker may be able to use special tools to cut through the barbed wire at the top of a perimeter fence, allowing the attacker to more easily climb the fence and gain entry to the premises.

Physical Attack Method	Description
Physical harm	Attackers may physically harm personnel that act as access control mechanisms in order to render them ineffective. This mainly comes in the form of intruders attacking and incapacitating guards, allowing the intruders to move past a checkpoint unabated.
Destruction	Destruction of physical systems involves directly attacking hardware or facility systems that provide access control services. For example, an attacker is able to gain access to a server room and locate the servers that hold the organization's Active Directory domain. If the attacker smashes the server hardware, then the servers will become inoperable, and directory services in the organization will fail to serve and validate identity.

General Mitigation Strategies

No matter the type of attack, there are some general mitigation strategies you should use when implementing access control:

- Choose an authorization mechanism and make sure you aren't lax in its implementation.
- Continuously monitor access from both object and subject perspectives. Be on the lookout for anomalous or dubious behavior.
- Routinely audit access control mechanisms to ensure their effectiveness.
- Keep all staff well-trained on security policies and best practices.

In addition, a defense-in-depth approach with multiple control types are often used to protect systems. While this is very valuable, it is also necessary to constantly monitor for effectiveness. It is important for users to upgrade skills and protection mechanisms, but it is also important to periodically audit protection mechanisms to maintain security. There is a wealth of information in the audit logs and you need to ensure that they are being reviewed.

Guidelines for Mitigating Access Control Attacks

Use the following guidelines to mitigate access control attacks.

Mitigate Software-Based Access Control Attacks

To mitigate software-based access control attacks:

- Implement load balancing systems at key points in your network infrastructure to mitigate the effects of a DoS attack.
- Ensure that passwords are encrypted using a strong hashing algorithm, and that the resulting hashes are stored securely in a password database.
- Tightly control access to password hash databases.
- Ensure that applications use password masking. This displays asterisks (*) instead of the actual password when the user types it.
- Thoroughly test all software implementations of access control to catch memory overflow vulnerabilities.
- Ensure that network hosts have anti-malware solutions that actively monitor for malicious software.
- Make sure malware definitions are always up-to-date.
- Enforce password policies with technical controls that make brute forcing attempts unfeasible.
- Properly wipe drives with sensitive data, especially stored credentials.
- Implement vulnerability scanning and assessment for any systems likely to be the target of an attack.

- Implement intrusion detection systems to continuously monitor your network and hosts for unauthorized access attempts or other anomalous behavior.

Mitigate Socially Engineered Access Control Attacks

To mitigate social engineered access control attacks:

- Ensure that staff at all levels have adequate training to enable them to identify the various social engineering attacks.
- Write a policy that stipulates how users should and should not use communications; for example, they shouldn't send credential information in any email correspondence.
- Clearly define the roles in your organization with regards to data ownership in security. A general staff member doesn't need access to all of the company's sensitive information, and if they become a victim of social engineering, the impact will be lessened. In other words, follow the principle of least privilege.
- Plan a social engineering penetration test to detect any weaknesses within your employees' awareness of end user security. Keep in mind that such a test has ethical implications, and that you should abide by rules of conduct at all times.
- Thoroughly destroy all hard copy documents that contain sensitive information before throwing them out.
- Educate users on reporting suspicious behavior to the appropriate members of the IT or security team.
- Mandate the use of multi-factor authentication for critical systems to reduce the chance of a social engineer gaining access.

Mitigate Human-Based Access Control Attacks

To mitigate human-based access control attacks:

- Train users as to why certain passwords are weak and easy to guess. They should know to avoid using PII like birthdays in their passwords, as this information is often publicly available.
- Enforce account lockout policies on your systems, preventing an attacker from making many incorrect guesses in succession.
- Display last logon information to users so they can verify that no one has accessed their account since they used it last.
- Ensure that all sensitive hardware is locked down or kept isolated from the main facilities. Small devices are particularly easy to steal.
- Ensure that all sensitive information is encrypted in storage and transit, so that any virtual theft will prove useless to the attacker.
- Ensure that all staff can quickly and easily contact law enforcement in case they are faced with threats.

Mitigate Physical Access Control Attacks

To mitigate physical access control attacks:

- Make sure all locks and doors are properly maintained. Replace old equipment before letting it become a vulnerability.
- Routinely verify the integrity of fences and other perimeter access control mechanisms.
- Ensure that physical access control devices have tamper protection. An intruder shouldn't be able to breach a gate by cutting power to a generator that's placed outside that very gate.
- Include hostage alarms and hostage key patterns to cipher locks and access control systems. In this way, should someone be forced to open a door under duress, a silent alarm can be triggered.
- Place surveillance cameras at key entrances and exits to deter intruders.
- Ensure that guards and other security personnel have direct access to central security or law enforcement in the event of a violent confrontation.
- Place critical hardware in access controlled rooms, safes, or lockboxes.

- Ensure that cameras or guards monitor large equipment that would compromise operations if it were damaged.

ACTIVITY 5–5
Discussing Access Control Attack Mitigation

Scenario

In this activity, you'll discuss the various ways to mitigate access control attacks.

1. Your organization just upgraded all of its laptops and mobile devices. After erasing the hard drives, the IT department sold the lot of it to a used equipment dealer. A few weeks later, some private (and embarrassing) emails by company executives were posted on social media.

   What do you think happened, and how can this be avoided in the future?

2. Your school has been using access control cards to track student attendance. When a student holds their card up to the reader, the door unlocks, admitting access to a classroom. When you review the attendance logs collected by the access card readers, the numbers are dramatically lower than expected. You are quite sure that more students have been attending school than are showing in the logs.

   How is it possible that the access control system is not accurately tracking student attendance?

3. After a nice relaxing weekend, you come into the office expecting a typical Monday morning. Frantic users rush out to meet you in the parking lot. The entire network, including the phones, seem to be down. You go straight to the server room to see what the matter could be. The door is locked as usual, but when you enter the room, you notice that the rack has been disturbed. Upon closer inspection, you notice that the router is missing. The cables that connected to it are just hanging down. When you look around the room, you see that some ceiling tiles next to the wall are not sitting quite right in their hanging frame. There is dust on the floor below those ceiling tiles. You climb up on a ladder to peer into the ceiling, and observe that the entire floor has a drop ceiling, with sufficient space to crawl between the rooms. When you go into the restroom next door, you observe that the ceiling tiles above the sink have also been disturbed. There is dirt on the sink below. Additionally, the restroom window is open. The window is large enough for a small person to squeeze through.

   What do think has happened, and how could this have been prevented?

4. Your organization stores information in a secure area that is of very high value to criminals. The security team is discussing ways to reduce the risk of armed criminals forcing personnel to open locked doors under duress.

    What methods might you suggest to mitigate the risk?

5. You worked late at the office the other night. When you finally went home, you noticed some strange people loitering around the trash bin outside. They did not look like ordinary scavengers. You're afraid they might be dumpster diving for credit card numbers or other valuable information.

    What can you do to mitigate the risks associated with dumpster diving?

Summary

In this lesson, you learned about identity and access management. Identity and access management is a fundamental part of your organization's security. Frequently it is the starting point for what stands between the users and the information they need. However, it is also what stands between your data and malicious users.

With which types of access control systems are you most familiar?

Have you ever experienced an access control attack on your information systems? How did you or your organization respond to the known attacks? What methods or techniques were implemented to prevent attacks?

 Note: Check your CHOICE Course screen for opportunities to interact with your classmates, peers, and the larger CHOICE online community about the topics covered in this course or other topics you are interested in. From the Course screen you can also access available resources for a more continuous learning experience.

6 Security Assessment and Testing

Lesson Time: 2 hours

Lesson Objectives

In this lesson, you will:

- Identify system security control testing techniques.

- Identify software security control testing techniques.

- Evaluate security process data collection methods.

- Facilitate auditing of your systems.

Lesson Introduction

In the previous lesson, you learned the importance of identification and access management. In this lesson, you will learn the importance of security assessments and testing to verify the security of your organization. It is only when you have done a thorough risk assessment of both your physical and logical assets that you can begin the work of protecting the organization. This lesson will delve further into vulnerability assessments, penetration testing, log reviews, all around testing, and validating your security.

TOPIC A

System Security Control Testing

Until you thoroughly evaluate your systems, you should not consider them sufficiently secure. Outlined in this topic are the various approaches to testing that can give you much-needed perspective when it comes to your security operations.

 Note: To learn more, view the LearnTO presentations from the **LearnTO** tile on the CHOICE course screen.

Security Assessment

Since security controls are designed to minimize risk to your company's assets, it is critical that you periodically test the effectiveness of these controls. Security assessment is the process of evaluating how successfully a system, person, process, network, and so on, is meeting the organization's security requirements.

Security assessment is more than simply running a vulnerability scan against your network. Remember that a control can be administrative (actions people take), or technical (carried out by computer systems). As such, your test strategy should include testing both administrative and technical security controls. It should examine the entire security posture of the organization, starting with the security policy (if it exists) as well as the organization's culture and management's attitude towards security. An expensive firewall is of little value to an organization if people regularly circumvent it with unsecured wireless access points in the LAN.

There are several risks to conducting a security assessment:

- Testers might focus only on technical assessments, ignoring administrative controls, policy, and culture.
- The testing process may disrupt normal operations.
- The resulting data will not be properly interpreted.
- Recommendations will be ignored, or improperly or insufficiently implemented.

Security Test Strategies

To have an effective test strategy, you must know the level of security you wish to achieve beforehand. You must then test your entity to see if it achieves those objectives.

The steps to assessing your security are:

1. Create a security assessment policy.
 2. Create a security assessment methodology.
3. Assign testing roles and responsibilities.
4. Determine which systems you will test.
5. Determine how you will approach the testing, addressing any logistical, legal, and policy considerations.
6. Carry out the test, addressing any incidents that may arise during/because of the test.
7. Maintain the CIA principles while handling the data through all phases of the test, including collection, storage, transmission, and destruction.
8. Analyze the data and create a report that will turn technical findings into risk mitigation actions to improve the organization's security posture.

Note: For more information on security testing as well as recommendations and guidelines, see NIST 800-115 "Information Security Testing and Assessment" at **http://csrc.nist.gov/ publications/nistpubs/800-115/SP800-115.pdf**.

Administrative Assessment Test Output

Your security assessment will produce test output. Test output is the raw data collected after an action is taken against a system and the system's response. That raw data is then analyzed to determine the effectiveness (or even the lack of presence) of a control.

Test output from an administrative assessment can include any of the following:

- Responses by management and users to security-related questions.
- A list of existing or non-existing procedures or documentation.
- Recorded observation of user or management activities.
- Recorded observation of user or management adherence to existing procedures and policies.

These test outputs can then be used to determine the effectiveness (or even the nonexistence) of your controls.

Technical Assessment Test Output

Test output from a technical assessment can include any the following:

- The current firewall configuration of each system.
- The antivirus patch level of each system.
- A list of known or potential vulnerabilities found on each system.
- A list of default configurations found on each system.
- A list of unused user accounts found on each system.
- A list of user privilege levels on each resource or system.

Vulnerability Assessments

A *vulnerability assessment* is an evaluation of a system's security and ability to meet compliance requirements based on the configuration state of the system, as represented by information collected from the system.

Essentially, the vulnerability assessment determines if the current configuration matches the ideal configuration. The process consists of the following steps:

1. **Collect** a predetermined set of target attributes (such as specific parameters or rules for a firewall).
2. **Store** the collected sample for reference.
3. **Organize** the data to prepare it for analysis and comparison.
4. **Analyze** and document the differences between the current configuration and the baseline.
5. **Report** on the results.

Perform vulnerability assessments when:

- **You first deploy new or updated systems**. This provides a baseline of the systems' security configurations.
- **New vulnerabilities have been identified** (through penetration tests, or based on general information from vendors, vulnerabilities database, or other sources). A vulnerability assessment can reveal systems that are subject to the vulnerabilities, where you need to focus your remediation efforts.
- **A security breach occurs**. The vulnerability assessment can help you identify possible attack vectors and determine whether they have been exploited.

- **You need to document the security state of systems**. For example, you may be required to do this to satisfy a regulatory audit or other oversight requirements.

Vulnerability Scanning

Although the vulnerability assessment process could be conducted manually, vulnerability assessments are typically accomplished through automated vulnerability scanning tools, which examine an organization's systems, applications, and devices to determine their current state of operation and the effectiveness of any security controls. Typical results from a vulnerability scan will identify misconfigurations and missing security patches or critical updates.

The tools available to you are numerous, and hackers likewise have access to them. Some of the more common types of scanning tools include the following.

Vulnerability Scanning Tool	Description
Port scanner	A device or application that scans a network to identify what devices are reachable (alive), what ports on these devices are active, and what protocols these active ports use to communicate. A port scanner typically relies on the most common network protocols (for example, Transmission Control Protocol [TCP], User Datagram Protocol [UDP], and Internet Control Message Protocol [ICMP]) to retrieve this information. The port information revealed in a scan can help you pinpoint vulnerabilities in your network, as attackers will often use open ports as an intrusion vector.
Protocol analyzer	Decodes and analyzes the traffic sent over a network communication session. By presenting the conversation to the end user in an easily understood manner, this decode process simplifies the interpretation of the protocols used in the traffic. Protocol analyzers are useful for diagnosing network connectivity issues, detecting anomalous network behavior, and gathering traffic statistics that can be used to assess which protocols are most vulnerable in a network.
Packet analyzer	Captures and decodes the actual content of particular network packets sent using various network protocols. This can be useful for filtering certain packets to keep them from communicating across the network, as well as verifying that security controls, like firewalls, are working as intended.
Network enumerator	Gathers information on users, groups, and services on a network without authenticating to the device. Network enumerators often use protocols like ICMP and Simple Network Management Protocol (SNMP) to discover network hosts and retrieve the information.
Intelligence gathering	Gathers information regarding a target organization before actually conducting the attack for the purpose of discovering key information and vulnerabilities without being detected. Methods include taking advantage of people exposing too much on social media sites, using the Whois domain lookup to retrieve Internet registration information, and mapping a network's topology.
Vulnerability scanner	This automated tool tests a system for known weaknesses by sending malicious commands to its open ports. If the system responds in kind, it is considered to be vulnerable to that exploit.

Note: Most commercially available vulnerability scanners do not cause any damage to the system they scan. However, there are some vulnerability scanners (most notably Metasploit and Core Security) that can be used to actually compromise a machine. Metasploit uses the true exploit (such as the original buffer overflow) and can destabilize the target machine. Core Security is written in the Python programming language. It exploits the vulnerability, but is carefully engineered to not cause any real damage.

Penetration Testing

A *penetration test*, or pen test, uses active tools and security utilities to evaluate security by simulating an attack on a system. A penetration test will verify that a threat exists, then will actively test and bypass security controls, and finally will exploit vulnerabilities on the system. Such vulnerabilities may be the result of poorly or improperly configured systems, known or unknown hardware or software flaws, or operational weaknesses in processes or technical countermeasures. Any security issues that are found in the test and can be exploited are presented to the organization with an assessment of the impact and a remediation proposal.

Penetration tests are less common and more intrusive than basic vulnerability assessments. Penetration tests tend to be driven by an organization's desire to determine the feasibility of an attack and the amount of business impact a successful exploitation of vulnerabilities will have on an organization. One of the major differences between penetration testing and typical vulnerability assessments is that the rating assigned to a vulnerability during a vulnerability assessment is subjective, whereas a penetration test will exploit a real vulnerability to test it. Penetration testing also tends to combine multiple vulnerabilities together to provide a more holistic understanding of an organization's vulnerability state.

It is important that penetration testing follows a method that is similar to what a real attacker would use, including phases in which the attacker prepares and learns what he or she can about the target. The difference between the execution of a real attack and a penetration test is that of intent, and you should have the explicit permission of the target organization before you begin the test. You should make sure that the organization is aware that the test should not stop until the attack has been fully carried out. Otherwise, the results of the test could be skewed, or the live systems themselves may be damaged.

Keep in mind that the ultimate purpose of a penetration test is to provide some sort of deliverable to the organization. This deliverable is typically in the form of a report that details the steps undertaken by the pen tester in attacking the organization. The reports also clearly outline any weaknesses discovered in this process, as well as recommendations for how to correct them.

 Caution: While the information gained from a penetration test is often more thorough, there is a risk that the system may suffer actual damage because of the security breach.

Penetration Test Preparation

Before you can begin penetration testing, you need to take a few preliminary steps. These steps can be thought of as answers to the following questions:

- **Who will commission the test?**

  Executive security personnel, like a CISO, will generally take the initiative in planning the test. The security executive needs buy-in from the CEO or Board of Directors so that they understand both the risks and benefits involved in a pen test. The security executive must accept responsibility for the test from start to finish.

- **Who will conduct the test?**

  This will differ based on organizations, as many will prefer to rely on a third party organization that specializes in pen testing. This offloads the burden of testing from internal security staff, and it may also benefit the organization if the third party is much more skilled and experienced in pen testing. However, some organizations will identify too much of a risk in handing off this sensitive task to even a reputable third party, so they'll use in-house security personnel to do the job. In this case, security professionals should be well-trained and have a pen testing policy or framework to follow.

- **How will the test be conducted in the enterprise?**

  There are various techniques and components that can make up a penetration test, and the planning stage is the best time to make a decision regarding these. What you choose will depend greatly on what you actually expect to get out of the test, as well as what you can and cannot afford (both financially and operations-wise) to do.

- **What are the test's limitations?**

  Planning for a pen test should clearly define both the scope and rules of engagement for pen testers. This will prevent the tester from overstepping certain bounds and causing actual harm to the organization. For example, you might forbid the tester from attacking mission-critical servers with the intent of wiping the data.

- **What tools will be used in the test?**

  There are many tools out there that are used by pen testers and malicious users alike. You should evaluate a fair number of the most common and trusted tools to get a sense of how they might fit into your pen testing process. For example, Kali Linux is an entire operating system dedicated to penetration testing, as it includes hundreds of open source security tools.

The Penetration Test Process

Penetration testing requires a multiphase approach.

1. **Reconnaissance**

   The tester must gather as much information as possible about the target organization and its systems. This is done before the actual attack and involves passive intelligence gathering tactics.

2. **Scanning**

   The tester will begin actively scanning the systems they have identified in the first phase to enumerate those systems. This gives the tester a more complete picture of the target.

3. **Exploitation**

   This is where the tester begins their attack, targeting whatever vulnerabilities they have identified in the previous phases.

4. **Maintaining Access**

   Once the tester breaches the organization's systems, they can install backdoors, rootkits, and other exploits that allow them to maintain access in the future. This helps illustrate vulnerabilities that can harm the organization over the long term, even after an active breach has been identified.

5. **Reporting**

   The tester must conclude their operations by reporting their findings to the appropriate personnel. The report is the primary deliverable of a pen test. Reports are vital in debriefing these personnel on the vulnerabilities found in the test, the risks these vulnerabilities pose to the organization, and any suggested ways to mitigate these problems. Include an executive summary that managers can understand, along with very specific technical results for the IT staff.

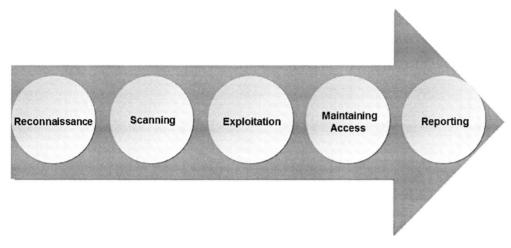

Figure 6-1: The phases of a typical penetration test.

Penetration Test Approaches

When it comes to the reconnaissance phase of the pen test, there are three possible approaches:

- The *black box* approach, which simulates an outside attacker who would know nothing about the target. The pen tester must do their own reconnaissance.
- The *grey box* approach, which simulates an inside attacker who knows something about a target, but not everything. The pen tester must do additional reconnaissance beyond what has been provided to them.
- The *white box* approach, which simulates an inside attacker who would have extensive knowledge about the target. The pen tester does not need to perform their own reconnaissance, as this is provided for them.

Each box type has its own benefits and pitfalls. Black box approaches are the most effective at evaluating the organization's defenses from a real-world perspective, but they take more time and effort to perform. Another issue with the black box approach is secrecy—who should know about the test? A real attacker likely won't have the trust of everyone in the organization, or even any contact whatsoever. To preserve the black box nature of the test, you may need to inform only key personnel of the test, which could lead to significant issues if something goes wrong during the test.

With the white box approach, you have a much more broad perspective of organizational systems. You may be able to evaluate more than you would have if given less than total information about the target. However, the environment in a white box may be *too* simulated; that is, you only end up strengthening your defenses against more pen tests, not actual attacks. Because attackers are usually limited in their knowledge, they need to think creatively—and a white box test may fail to account for this.

Finally, a grey box test attempts to combine the best of both worlds. The tester should have enough information upfront to feel like the test will be comprehensive, but enough should be withheld so that the test is more reflective of reality. Striking this balance is difficult, however, and you may find that choosing a white or black approach is preferable to overly complicating the test's parameters.

Penetration Test Components

The following table lists components that often make up a penetration test. Note that not all pen tests will include all of these components, as context will dictate what is and is not necessary for the test.

Penetration Test Component	Description
Network scanning	*Network scanning* uses a port scanner to identify devices attached to the target network and to enumerate the applications hosted on the devices. This function is known as fingerprinting.
Social engineering	Attempts to get information from users to gain access to a system. This tests for adequate user training. For example, you might impersonate a help desk employee and see if any other staff members take unsolicited help as bait. If enough do, this might suggest that more training is needed for the organization as a whole or for individuals. Keep in mind that deceiving people has ethical implications that you should be mindful of. You don't want to undermine your employees' trust in you or their trust in their coworkers.
War dialing	*War dialing* uses a modem and software to dial a range of phone numbers to locate computer systems, Private Branch eXchange (PBX) devices, and heating, ventilating, and air conditioning (HVAC) systems.
War driving	*War driving* locates and then attempts to penetrate wireless systems. If your wireless signals leak out onto public property, like a sidewalk, then you may be able to connect to the network from outside the company's physical perimeter.
Vulnerability scanning	Vulnerability scanning exploits known weaknesses in operating systems and applications that were identified through reconnaissance and enumeration. This is not just a major step in vulnerability assessment, but can also assist the pen tester in discovering weaknesses to exploit.
Blind testing	*Blind testing* occurs when the target organization is not aware of penetration testing activities. Security administrators may respond to penetration testing as if an actual attack is underway. For example, a port scan alert generated by an IDS may prompt security personnel to disconnect the targeted host from the network.
Targeted testing	*Targeted testing* occurs when the target organization is informed of the test. There is less disruption to the organization due to a more controlled climate. The security professional, for example, may take no action in the event of the IDS alert other than recording that it happened.

 Note: NIST Special Publication 800-42 provides documentation on different components of penetration testing.

Event Log Review

An *event log* contains detailed information about system and application performance and problems. While many administrators use event logs to troubleshoot functionality or performance issues, you should also review event logs as part of your security control test process. An automated tool can help you identify and analyze security events from the masses of information stored in an event log.

In Microsoft Windows, these logs are viewable in the Event Viewer. In Linux, they are collected in a series of text files that can be read with any text reader.

Network devices also report system and security events to their console, though you may have to configure them to capture the desired level of detail into a log. Nearly all applications, particularly server services, produce logs as well.

Common activities that are logged include:

- Authentication requests, both successful and unsuccessful.

- New user or group creation.
- Group membership changes.
- User privilege level changes.
- Resource access, such as opening, changing and deleting files and folders.
- Client requests for server services.
- The number of transactions per hour of a particular service.
- Application or service shutdowns and restarts.
- System shutdowns and restarts.
- Service or system component errors and failures.
- System policy changes.

The challenge with using event log collection is the sheer volume of information collected. A single day will garner 100s or even 1000s of events. A single action on a computer, such as opening a document, actually involves a number of background steps by several processes. A typical Windows System Event Log can easily contain 50,000+ entries.

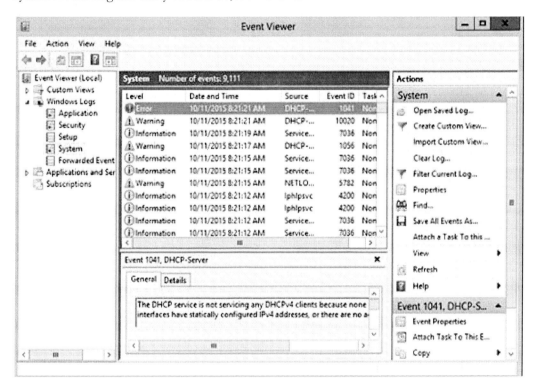

Figure 6-2: Windows Event Viewer Security Log.

Log Directory Locations

Each operating system has a specific directory where system logs are stored:

- Windows - %systemroot%\System32\config
- Linux - /var/log

Log Management Infrastructure

A *log management infrastructure* is a software application that consolidates logs from all devices. It must be able to collect, analyze, present, archive, and eventually purge event logs from all critical servers and network devices. It must provide an intuitive dashboard to the user, make it easy to further investigate an event (dig deeper into the log), and offer response options.

Your network may have dozens or even hundreds of critical devices generating logs. Logs generated by different device types and vendors are typically not compatible with each other. For example, your network may have a Windows server, a Linux server, a Cisco router, a firewall, and a spam filter. You would need an event log collection service that can handle all of these formats simultaneously, combining them into a single dashboard.

A good log management infrastructure must do the following:

- Centralize event log collection. Have all servers, firewalls, routers, switches, security appliances, and other important devices forward their logs to a central location. This is done by having agents installed on the devices report regularly to a central console. The central console can be a Linux syslog server, a Microsoft System Center Operations Manager server, or other third-party product. Centralization simplifies log management and analysis, and makes it harder for a hacker to cover his or her tracks.
- Use an automated tool that will parse (read and analyze) the log, pick out noteworthy events, summarize findings for you, and provide actionable next steps.
- Back up, archive, and purge older log entries to clear disk space.
- Provide easy-to-read reports with trends analysis.

 Note: Not all centralized event collecting consoles work with all types of devices. Check with the documentation of your servers and devices to see what types of event collection services they are compatible with.

Log Management Policies

In order to make log management effective and consistent, the organization will need to have a log management policy with procedures in place. Your policy clearly defines the purpose of gathering the logs, what type of logging is mandatory, and how to manage the logs. Most organizations struggle to find a balance between limited resources for effective log management and the ever-growing size of their event logs.

Your log management policy should:

- Prioritize requirements and goals based on your perceived risk reduction in the expected resources needed to perform log management functions.
- Define log management roles and responsibilities for key personnel.
- Create and maintain in log management infrastructure.
- Specify resources and management support for the log management system.

Log Management Procedures

Your log management procedures should include the following:

- Monitor the status of all log sources.
- Monitor log rotation, backups, and archiving processes.
- Check for upgrades and patches for logging software, and test and deploy these upgrades.
- Maintain clock synchronization between devices in the logging console.
- Regularly review logs for effectiveness based on any policy or technology changes, and reconfigure logging as needed.
- Document and report any anomalies in log settings or processes.
- Ensure logs are consolidated to a central repository.

Synthetic Transactions

A synthetic transaction imitates a single, real action on a system or the network. It is usually a short software routine that mimics normal (or abnormal) client behavior. Synthetic transactions give the administrator the ability to inject specific events into a system in a controlled manner, and observe the system response.

Because a synthetic transaction is crafted by the tester, and its inputs are known, it has expected outputs. Examples of synthetic transactions include:

- A client request to a server.
- A VoIP phone call.
- A video conference call.
- A security or performance event.
- An outside connection attempt.
- The injection of malicious traffic into the network.

Most of the time, administrators use Real User Monitoring (RUM) to monitor actual transactions and gauge the user experience on a system or network. Synthetic transactions are used when the administrator wants to investigate system response to specific activities or what-if scenarios.

Guidelines for Implementing System Security Control Testing

 Note: All of the Guidelines for this lesson are available as checklists from the **Checklist** tile on the CHOICE Course screen.

Use the following guidelines when testing the security of your systems.

General Security Testing

When conducting any type of security test:

- Test every one of your controls, whether administrative, logical, or physical.
- Understand the risks of conducting a security assessment, especially the risk that it may disrupt business operations.
- Adopt a security test strategy that can comprehensively support all of your organization's security needs.
- Make sure your test output is robust and can truly be useful in evaluating the effectiveness of your security controls.

Vulnerability Assessment

When conducting vulnerability assessments:

- Follow a process of collecting, storing, organizing, analyzing, and reporting assessments.
- Perform vulnerability assessments routinely and in response to security incidents when they arise.
- Implement a vulnerability scan to detect weaknesses or misconfigurations in systems.
- Choose from a number of scanning tools, such as port scanners and network enumerators, that will help you identify system issues.

Penetration Testing

When conducting penetration tests:

- Keep in mind that the purpose of pen testing is to deliver a report on the state of the systems and how they can be improved.
- In preparing for a pen test, outline who will conduct the test, how they will do so, and any limitations that need to be imposed on the test.
- Following a process of recon, scanning, exploitation, maintaining access, and reporting for pen tests.
- Understand the advantages and disadvantages of white, black, and grey box testing approaches.
- Use a combination of several components, like war driving and vulnerability scanning, in your pen test.

Log Reviews

When conducting log reviews:

- Review system event logs to identify security incidents.
- Configure event logs to capture a feasible level of detail that won't overwhelm the reviewer.
- Keep track of common security-related activities that get logged, including failed login attempts or system policy changes.
- Institute a log management infrastructure that can centralize and streamline logs from many systems across the organization.
- Draft log management policy to outline the how, what, and why of capturing logs.

ACTIVITY 6–1
Discussing System Security Control Testing

Scenario
In this activity, you will assess your understanding of system security control testing.

---

1. **What is the single most important output of a security assessment?**
   - ○ A comprehensive analysis of the vulnerability state of the network.
   - ○ A report on the overall security posture of the organization.
   - ○ A report that turns technical findings into risk mitigating actionable items.
   - ○ A complete list of IP addresses, ports, and protocols in use on the network, as well as the results of a vulnerability scan of every system.

2. **With regards to an administrative assessment, what is the security relationship between policy/documentation and observed activity?**

3. **Why would unused user accounts present a security vulnerability?**

4. **Why should you perform a vulnerability assessment when you first deploy a new system?**

5. **When conducting a penetration test, why is it necessary to outline the rules of engagement first?**

6. **Why would a pen tester want to install a backdoor in a vulnerable system as part of the test?**

7. **Why is a blackbox approach to penetration testing so effective?**

---

8. How can having a system event log actually hurt security efforts?

9. How can having a centralized logging system help reduce an attacker's ability to hide evidence of the attack?

10. How can log management policy and procedures help increase network security?

11. How could a synthetic transaction be used in a penetration test?

TOPIC B

Software Security Control Testing

Aside from a system-wide testing program, you'll need to also consider the unique case of software security testing. Whether the software is developed in-house or licensed from a third party, you need to ensure that it meets your security standards.

Code Review

Code review is a systematic, manual review of a developer's code by another person. Functionally similar to proofreading, code review attempts to find and fix problems that the developer overlooked. The reviewer is typically a fellow developer or the developer team lead, but can also be a third party outside the organization. Code review is also known as peer review.

Common Software Vulnerabilities and Exploits

The following table describes the various ways in which software is vulnerable to compromise or exploits.

Software Vulnerability	Description
Error and *exception handling*	Software developers cannot reasonably account for every possible way a user or attacker may interact with an application that could result in an error. This is why the key defense mechanism for any application is how it responds to unexpected errors, which is a technique called exception handling or error handling. Because errors can cause app failures, they can lead to holes in the security of an app. An attacker may attempt to execute a Structured Query Language (SQL) injection or buffer overflow on your app by targeting inputs. If your app lacks proper exception handling, it is vulnerable to these threats.
Improper storage of sensitive data	The types of sensitive information applications may have access to include passwords, credit card numbers, account records, customer data, and even proprietary company information. The most popular method for securing this sensitive information is through encryption. The popularity of encryption in application libraries and languages has made integrating encryption into applications simple, but developers still tend to make mistakes in their implementations. The amount of protection offered by standard encryption functions can sometimes be overestimated or misunderstood, leading to implementation weaknesses or missing security controls.

Software Vulnerability	Description
Buffer overflow	A buffer overflow vulnerability occurs when an application copies the data input by users into an allocated memory buffer that is not large enough to accommodate it. The destination buffer overflows, which results in adjacent memory being overwritten with the user's data. Depending upon the type of buffer being overflowed, an attacker may be able to exploit a buffer overflow vulnerability to gain control of the application and execute arbitrary code. The attacker could use this arbitrary code execution to perform unauthorized actions, such as adding a user to a system, opening up a socket connection to a system shell, or crashing the application. One of the most recognizable buffer overflows is a stack overflow. A stack-based buffer overflow involves overwriting the return address of a function on the system stack to alter the execution of an application.
Integer overflow	In an integer overflow, an application attempts to store a number in a variable type that is not large enough to store that number. For example, you know that computers can only process and store binary data represented as a 1 or 0. An 8-bit integer means that the computer has allocated eight spots for this integer to be stored and is represented by the maximum value of 11111111, or 255 (in decimal). If you attempt to store an integer with a value greater than 255 at this location, the buffer will overflow, causing the registers to roll over. Like standard buffer overflows, integer overflows can cause an app to over-allocate memory and eventually crash.
Memory leaks	A memory leak is the result of an application allocating memory and then not cleaning that memory up by freeing it when it is no longer required for usage by the application. Memory leaks are a common programming error in unmanaged code programming languages like C and C++, as the application developer is responsible for managing allocated memory within the application. Memory leaks are not as prevalent in managed code programming languages such as Java, as these languages have built-in memory management and garbage collection functionalities. If identified by an attacker, they can exploit a memory leak through a Denial of Service (DoS) attack so that users are not able to access the app or the system it runs on.
SQL injection	Almost every web application employs a database backend to store whatever kind of information it needs to operate. To gain access to the information stored within the database, the application may use *Structured Query Language (SQL)* to communicate. SQL is one of the most widely used languages that applications utilize to speak to the database to perform four basic functions. These functions are: selecting data from the database, inserting data into the database, deleting data from the database, and updating data within the database. In a SQL injection attack, an attacker can modify one or more of these four basic functions by adding code to some input within the web app, causing it to execute the attacker's own set of queries using SQL.

Software Vulnerability	Description
Session fixation	Session fixation is forcing a user to browse a website in the context of a known and valid session. An attacker attempting a session fixation attack needs to force an already known session onto the targeted user. To carry out this attack, an attacker can manipulate the methods sessions normally assigned to a user, such as providing alternative inputs to web applications via GET requests. Some web applications assign these values via GET requests directly to the user's cookie for backward compatibility reasons. An alternative, and more popular, method for carrying out a session fixation attack is to use a cross-site scripting (XSS) attack to set the session cookie directly with a client-side scripting language such as JavaScript.
Session prediction	Session prediction attacks focus on identifying possible weaknesses in the generation of session tokens that will allow an attacker to predict future valid session values. If an attacker can guess the session token, then the attacker can take over a session that has yet to be established.
Cross-site scripting (XSS)	In an XSS attack, an attacker takes advantage of scripting and input validation vulnerabilities in web apps to attack legitimate users in three different ways: • In a *stored attack*, the attacker injects malicious code or links into a website's forums, databases, or other data. When a user views the stored malicious code or clicks a malicious link on the site, an attack is perpetrated against the user. • In a *reflected attack*, the attacker crafts a form or other request to be sent to a legitimate web server. This request includes the attacker's malicious script. The attacker sends a link to the victim with this request, and when the victim clicks on this link, the malicious script is sent to the legitimate server and reflected off it. The script then executes on the victim's browser. • In a *Direct Object Model (DOM)-based attack*, malicious scripts are not sent to the server at all; rather, they take advantage of a web app's client-side implementation of JavaScript to execute their attack solely on the client.
Cross-site request forgery (XSRF)/(CSRF)	In an XSRF attack, an attacker takes advantage of the trust established between an authorized user of a website and the website itself. This type of attack exploits a web browser's trust in a user's unexpired browser cookies. Websites that are at the most risk are those that perform functions based on input from trusted authenticated users who authenticate automatically using a saved browser cookie stored on their machines. The attacker takes advantage of the saved authentication data stored inside the cookie to gain access to a web browser's sensitive data.

Software Test Techniques

Carrying out security testing on software generally includes the following high-level techniques:

• **Black box/white box testing**: The idea behind these box types is similar to how they're used in penetration testing. In a software testing context, black box testers do not have access to the software's inner-workings. White box testers have full access to an application's components, including its source code. Like with pen testing, the amount of knowledge the tester has will likely have a significant impact on their findings.

- **Manual/automated testing**: In a manual test case, a human being is primarily responsible for running the test. Automated testing involves tools that specialize in testing other software. While automated tools ease the burden of enormous and complex tasks, a human eye is often needed in the testing process to catch certain esoteric issues.
- **Static/dynamic testing:** Static tests are meant to analyze the software when it is not in a state of execution. In a dynamic test, the tester executes the application and observes its behavior while it runs. Testing an application while it runs is a good way to gain perspective as to how the application will fail for certain use cases, but there may too many variables in the execution process that take too much time to test. That's why static testing is an alternative—it usually involves looking directly at source code to detect any root problems.

Software Test Types

You should test your software at all stages of the development process. The following table summarizes the different levels for testing your code.

Test Type	Description
Unit test	The developer writes a simple pass/no pass test for a small piece of code, typically an individual function that is run alone and isolated. This is done to ensure that a particular block of code performs the exact action intended, and provides the exact output expected. Ideally, there should be one unit test for every complete line or block of code. Although most developers consider unit testing to be a bother, it is the most effective way to minimize software bugs.
Integration test	Individual components of a system are tested together to see if they interact as expected. This is important because developers typically each work on a different component or module in the application, and a test is necessary to see if the two modules work together as expected.
Interface test	A type of integration test that focuses on the interface between two systems/applications. If the systems are applications or software modules, the interface will be an API. The interface could also be a user interface, or a physical interface such as a port.
Functional test	This tests a specific functionality in an application. It simulates a specific user interaction with the system to see the system's response and performance.
System test	This tests a complete, integrated system to verify that it satisfies the original specified requirements.
Acceptance test	In this test, end users try the completed software to see if they like it, can easily use it, and if it satisfies their business requirements.
Regression test	The running of the same set of tests after some component of the application has been changed or updated. This is done to make sure any updates or fixes don't break other functionality.
Misuse test	This test identifies vulnerabilities and weaknesses in applications by validating the input that the app accepts, as well as any other ways that an attacker could exploit the app's behavior.

Test Cases

A test case is a set of conditions (scenario) in which a specific test will be performed. When writing test cases, you are presumed to have knowledge of the source code, and an expectation of how the application will behave. The test checks to make sure the application works as expected. When you enter a specific input, you have an expected result. This is known as positive test cases or the happy path. An example of a happy path is as follows: The user inserts a bank card into an automated teller machine (ATM) and enters an incorrect PIN. The ATM machine then notifies the user that the PIN is invalid and prompts the user to enter the PIN again.

Notice that happy doesn't necessarily mean that the user is happy. It means that the software behaved exactly as expected. For a specific input, there should be a specific output.

Test cases are used to ensure that the software being developed addresses all of the pre-defined business requirements. There should be at least one test case for each business requirement.

A test case is usually spelled out in a test case document that lists:

- The test name.
- The test description.
- Test data.
- Pre-conditions.
- Expected results.
- Post-conditions.
- A mapping or reference to the exact business requirement the software will satisfy.

Code-Based Testing

Code-based testing seeks to identify and make up for gaps in the positive testing process. The main principle of code-based testing is to test every reachable, functional element of the code within practical time and cost constraints. This is done by using unit tests to check every statement in the program. Wherever the code has not been tested, you create additional test cases to cover those gaps. Code-based testing challenges the logic decisions made by the application, looking for dead code that is never used.

Interface Testing

In the context of security, interface testing assures that information passed from one software component to another is done securely. This is crucial especially when it comes to connection-based software like web apps. The app needs a way to gracefully recover from an interrupted or terminated connection, especially if the user was in the middle of a sensitive transaction. Another element that needs careful consideration is the client's own software or configurations. In the web app example, you typically don't control which browser the user is accessing your app with. Therefore, you need to perform interface testing for all major browsers to ensure that their differing behavior doesn't compromise your app's effectiveness.

Some more scenarios that require interface testing include:

- How your app handles general errors and exceptions.
- How your app handles copy and paste functionality.
- How your app handles resuming paused downloads.
- How your app handles third-party extensions, like browser plugins.
- Whether or not your app supports encryption in all necessary contexts.
- Whether or not your app supports cross-platform interfaces.

Misuse Testing

Misuse testing is the opposite of using test cases for testing. It is also known as negative testing or the unhappy path. It is a test type that determines if an application can gracefully handle invalid input or unexpected illegal user activities, including potential hacker attacks. In misuse testing, there is no expected result. The result is discovered when invalid input is entered. It forces developers to consider what might happen to their code in a less-than-ideal world, and embed security (especially input validation) into their code during the development process. You write negative test cases to see if you can deliberately crash or break into the application. Misuse testing is a good way to enhance your threat modeling process.

Examples of misuse testing include:

- Input validation techniques, such as:
  - Entering illegal values or characters in an input field (such as letters in a U.S. zipcode field, a negative number in an age field, or an image in a text field).
  - Deliberately leaving required fields empty.
  - Attempting to exceed the allowed number of characters in an input field. For example, if you limit the first name text box to 20 characters, attempting to enter a name that is 21 characters long.
  - Entering data that exceeds the limits of the data type defined for that field (for example, if the data type for a field is defined as byte (8 bits of data), attempting to enter 9 bits).
  - Pressing unusual or unexpected key combinations while the software is executing.
  - *Fuzzing*, or inputting massive amounts of random data in an attempt to make the system crash.
- Repeatedly opening and closing the soft keyboard in a mobile phone app.
- Editing client side JavaScript in a web page and then submitting that page to the web server.
- Attempting to open a web page without first performing a required login.

When you write negative test cases, you do it from the perspective that you have no prior knowledge of the source code, and therefore no expectation of how it will react to the unexpected.

Misuse testing can also be applied to computer systems and hardware as well as software. This is done to ensure that the system can continue to perform under stressful conditions.

To be really effective, misuse testing should include deliberate misuse and abuse by not only software developers and test personnel, but also by end users.

Test Coverage Analysis

While ideally every single line of code in your application should be tested, this is usually not practical. Test coverage refers to how much of your code is actually tested, often through the use of automated unit tests. Most software development environments (programs that developers use to write and test their code) have built-in code testing suites.

Many organizations like to target a specific number (such as 80%) to measure their code coverage. Effective test coverage, however, should focus on how much of the logic and functionality of your code has been tested, rather than a specific percentage number. For example, 50% coverage would be acceptable if the 50% of code you tested contains all the application's logic.

Guidelines for Conducting Software Security Control Testing

Use the following guidelines when testing software security controls:

- Ensure that software developers are trained on the importance of incorporating security into the development process, rather than as an afterthought.
- Implement code reviews for all software your organization writes or integrates with.
- Become familiar with the various software vulnerabilities that are common to many apps.
- Consider the advantages and disadvantages of the various software testing techniques and how they might be best used in your organization.
- Consider the different test types and how they might help you evaluate software security.
- Outline thorough test cases that address business requirements.
- Implement interface testing to ensure that information flows securely from software component to software component.
- Use input validation and similar techniques to test for misuse cases.

- Create a baseline for test coverage analysis, ensuring that your testing processes cover the most important elements of source code.
- Ensure that any software acquired by a third party vendor is up-to-date.
- Don't be overly verbose in error messages displayed to users, so as not to give an attacker a vector to exploit your software.
- Separate systems testing software from those running production software.

ACTIVITY 6-2
Discussing Software Security Control Testing

Scenario

You work as an information security officer for a large financial institution. The bank has partnered with a cellular carrier to provide mobile money financial services. Cellular customers can use their mobile phones to send and receive money even if they do not have a bank account. The bank will process the financial transactions for the cellular company. The bank will also extend its own services to allow its customers to send mobile money via an automated teller machine (ATM) transaction. The bank's developer team has developed the ATM software and is ready to test it. The developer team lead asserts that the code has 70% test coverage.

1. What concerns, if any, do you have regarding the test coverage? What else might you require of the developer team?

2. What testing needs to be performed to make sure that the bank's system works with the cellular provider's system?

3. What positive test cases might you write for the bank's ATM application?

4. What negative test cases might you write for the bank's ATM application?

TOPIC C

Security Process Data Collection

An important component in assessing your security programs is continuously collecting data. Without this up-to-date data, you can't possibly have a complete and accurate view over all of your security operations. As you manage your security systems, you must not only collect data on security events, but also on how your security systems themselves are performing. The security practitioner must help the organization regularly evaluate and fine-tune its own security processes.

ISCM

Information Security Continuous Monitoring (ISCM) is the ongoing process of identifying controls, vulnerabilities, and threats as they relate to the organization's risk management policies. It is a comprehensive, hierarchical system of data gathering, reporting, and response.

ISCM accomplishes the following:

*   It maps risk to tolerance.
*   It adapts to ongoing needs.
*   It actively involves management.

ISCM data comes from both manual processes and automated tools. Automated tools can include intrusion detection systems (IDS), operating system event logs, inventory and asset control systems, firewalls, configuration and change management systems, and anything else that can automatically collect information that has security implications. Manual processes can include results recorded from training exercises, BCP/DR test results, analyses from management or staff, and any other correlations that are not created by a system.

ISCM Data Collection

In order to set up an ISCM program, top management must determine what security information needs to be collected. You determine your metrics based on specific objectives that will help the organization maintain or improve its security posture. Typical data collected includes:

*   Physical asset location.
*   Logical asset location (IP addresses and subnets).
*   Numbers of identified MAC addresses.
*   Violations of network policy.
*   Number and severity of vulnerabilities discovered.
*   Number and severity of vulnerabilities that have been remediated.
*   Number of unauthorized access attempts.
*   Variances in configuration baselines.
*   DR/BCP plan testing dates and results.
*   Number of staff that have successfully completed security awareness training.
*   Risk tolerance thresholds that have been exceeded.
*   Risk scores for specific systems.

Security data is collected and analyzed as often as needed in order to continuously manage risk at each tier in the organization. You set thresholds that, when exceeded, trigger an alert to the next level. An example of a threshold might be if a computer is stolen, or if the number of unauthorized devices detected on the network exceeds 1% of the total number of devices. Everyone must be actively involved in responding to these alerts, from top management providing governance and strategy, to middle management determining if improvements are necessary, to users that will implement the improvements.

ISCM Tiers

An ISCM divides the business into three tiers. Tier 3 is made up of individual users or systems involved in daily operations. Reporting typically comprises security alerts, security incidents, identified threat activities, and remediation efforts. The data that is collected at tier 3 is correlated and analyzed. Reports are then sent up to tier 2.

Tier 2 is made up of departments and lines of business. It is at this level that the mission or business processes are implemented. Middle management analyzes the security reports from below to determine if current security is adequate for the business processes. If it is not, then additional tools and resources are provided down to tier 3. If it is not possible to provide tier 3 with additional resources, then at least those who manage the business processes at tier 2 are aware of the risks and can make decisions accordingly.

The departments at tier 2 similarly analyze aggregate security effectiveness for their business processes. They roll up security reports to top management at tier 1. Top management uses these reports to determine if more tools and resources need to be given to tier 2. It is tier 1 that provides governance, policy, and strategy. Tier 1 sets the overall security posture for the organization. It determines the organization's risk tolerance level, which is then realized in the responses, controls, and resources that the upper levels provide to the lower levels.

Based on Figure 2-1 in NIST SP 800-137

Figure 6-3: Organization-wide ISCM.

 Note: For more information on ISCM, see the article "Continuous Monitoring Program" at **www.fedramp.net/continuous-monitoring-program.**

ISCM Implementation

Implementation of your ISCM must be driven by the following goals:

- Have visibility into all of your assets.
- Detect anomalies and changes in your operating environment and information systems.
- Be aware of your vulnerabilities.

- Update your knowledge of threats, the effectiveness of your security controls, your overall security status, and your overall compliance status.

Your organization-wide ISCM rollout must included the following:

- Active involvement by upper management.
- Configuration management and change control processes throughout your SLC/SDLC.
- Security impact analyses on your information systems, monitoring for any changes to those systems.
- Continuous assessment of your security controls, with controls on the higher-impact and more volatile systems being assessed more frequently.
- Accurate and up-to-date security status communications and alerts to management.
- Management response.

NIST SP 800-137

NIST SP 800-137 is a publication that provides guidance for ISCM deployments in the United States federal government. It points out that a successful ISCM strategy cannot depend on either manual or automated systems alone. An organization should use both, using a strategy that includes:

- Understanding the organization's tolerance for risk.
- Defining and implementing meaningful metrics for measuring security status at all organizational tiers.
- Continuous assessment of the effectiveness of your security controls.
- Verification of compliance.
- IT asset management.
- Effective change control.
- Continually updated awareness of threats and vulnerabilities.

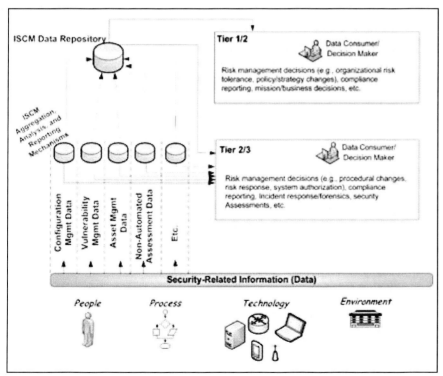

Figure D-2 in NIST SP 800-137

Figure 6-4: Typical ISCM Deployment.

Image reproduced from NIST SP 800-137.

An ISCM program that incorporates these strategies can shift the focus of an organization's risk management processes from being compliance-driven to being data-driven. This makes the organization's IT process proactive and mature.

Process for Establishing an ISCM

NIST SP 800-137 also recommends that organizations wishing to establish an ISCM follow these steps:

1. Define your ISCM strategy.
2. Establish your ISCM program.
3. Implement the program.
4. Analyze data and report on findings.
5. Respond to findings.
6. Review and update your ISCM strategy and program.

 Note: For more information on NIST SP 800-137, see **http://csrc.nist.gov/publications/ nistpubs/800-137/SP800-137-Final.pdf**.

KPIs

A *key performance indicator (KPI)* is a quantifiable unit of measure (metric) that an organization uses to gauge its own performance. Organizations use KPIs to determine if they are meeting strategic and operational goals. Since a KPI is a key performance indicator, it will measure something that management considers vital to the success of the company.

KPIs are typically aggregated data that are presented in a visual way (often using colors) in a dashboard. Many organizations publish the dashboard on their company intranet portal (internal website). Senior executives use the KPI dashboard to view trends and to see at a glance which areas or departments are under-performing. Executives also use KPIs to evaluate levels of risk in the organization based on established metrics.

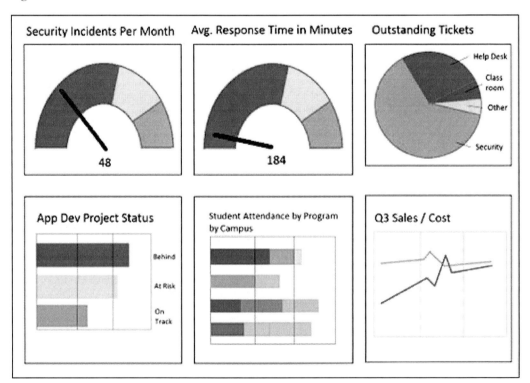

Figure 6-5: KPI dashboard.

KPIs can further report statistics based on additional criteria such as time of day, day of the week, business hours vs. non-business hours, department, location—any division that is useful. You must make sure, however, that you actually have that data. If your data has no timestamp, for example, you won't be able to divide an indicator into day and night time periods.

Most KPI reporting software allows a user to drill down to see the details behind a particular KPI. For example, if a KPI is used to report overall software test coverage and the current status across the company is amber (warning), the manager can click a link to drill down deeper into the data and discover that of the 10 teams developing software, 5 are "green" and 5 are "amber." The manager can then drill down further to find out which individual applications for each department do not have sufficient test coverage, and are thus causing the amber status—all the way down to which blocks of code in a particular application have not yet been unit tested.

Security KPIs

Security KPIs can come from any number of security monitoring systems. Although the data can be collected and processed manually, it should ideally come from automated systems that provide continuous updates. These automated systems can include your IDS, code testing software, your help desk ticket system, our SIEM, or any other service with automated logging capabilities. The automated systems should then be "spot checked" by manual processes to ensure their accuracy and completeness.

The number and type of KPIs monitored will depend on the organization. Common metrics in a KPI include:

- The number of vulnerabilities, by service level, that have been discovered and remediated.
- The number of failed logins or unauthorized access attempts.
- The number of systems currently out of compliance with security requirements.
- The number of security incidents reported within the last month.
- The average response time for a security incident.
- The average time required to resolve a help desk call.
- The current number of outstanding or unresolved technical issues in a project or system.
- The number of employees who have completed security training.
- Percentage of test coverage on applications being developed in-house.

Security Awareness and Training

Tracking staff training levels is one of your most important KPIs. Other KPIs, such as preventable user-level incidents, can help indicate how successfully staff have assimilated the concepts presented in your training programs. Even gauging simple awareness of security issues can help you discover risks that are latent in your organizational culture. Collecting and analyzing this human-focused data will help you in mitigating one of the weakest links in any organization's security.

Establishing awareness programs with clear objectives will assist in the data collection process. One of the most common objectives is preventing internal personnel from accessing information that they are not authorized to access. Often, people attempt to access data that requires authorization simply because they do not know it is not allowed. Another objective is increasing the efficacy of a security policy through actual implementation of the policy. Finally, awareness programs often attempt to reduce any misuse of company resources, such as data and hardware. To achieve these goals, programs use methods like presentations, incentives, posters, and newsletters. These allow management to circulate the policy message to those who need it, as well as get employees involved in security awareness and accountability. You can then measure real-world performance against these objectives and determine areas that need improvement.

Data Collection Process Components

The following are additional important components of the data collection process.

Component	Description
Account Management	A major part of any security data collection process is account management. There are two aspects to this: • Monitoring user account data including active users, login attempts, group memberships, and privilege levels. • Monitoring and managing which accounts have the right to collect and report on user data. You will want to regularly review both user account data and the accounts that collect that data.
DR/BCP	Disaster recovery and business continuity plan (DR/BCP) data should also be a part of your security data collection process. Remember that the purpose of DR/BCP is to return to normal operations as quickly as possible after an incident. For that reason, you will want to monitor how effective your DR/BCP plans and processes are. An organization can expect to have periodic small DR/BCP incidents throughout the year. How quickly DR teams respond to these minor incidents are an indicator of team readiness for larger events. You should include DR response/resolution time as part of your normal KPI dashboard.
Backup Verification	Successfully restoring a backup is almost always the bottom line contingency plan for any security program. Backups are used to cover the residual risk, those disaster possibilities for which there is no cost-effective solution. For that reason, it is essential that you make sure that your backups are successful and kept up-to-date. Any issues related to backups and restores should be tracked as part of your key performance indicators.
Management Review	Your security process data collection system should not be a set-and-forget model. It needs to be reviewed regularly by management for its effectiveness in shaping security policy and making wise security decisions. Since your ISCM is based on actively engaging management, make sure that management regularly reviews the entire system for its business value.

Guidelines for Collecting Security Process Data

Use the following guidelines when collecting security process data:

• Recognize that you must help the organization to regularly fine-tine its security processes.
• Implement an ISCM process that takes on an ongoing stance in identifying controls, vulnerabilities, and threats.
• Ensure that your ISCM program has the involvement of upper management.
• Implement configuration management and change control processes through the system's lifecycle.
• Incorporate NIST SP 800-137 strategies for continuous monitoring.
• Use key performance indicators (KPIs) to measure the effectiveness of security processes, like the number of incidents reported in a certain time span.
• Use KPIs that reflect user awareness and training to measure these programs' effectiveness.
• Establish awareness programs with clear objectives to facilitate the data collection process.

ACTIVITY 6-3
Discussing Security Process Data Collection

Scenario

A local college was recently bought by an investment firm that specializes in academic capacity building. The school just moved into a newly renovated building where a good amount of money was spent on IT infrastructure. Of the 19 classrooms, 5 are computer labs filled with new equipment. There are 30 administrative users and 40 academic staff. 300 students roam the halls at any one time, with a total of 1800 enrolled. Wireless access points exist on all floors, providing Internet for students and staff alike. Every office has a VoIP phone.

Card-based access control is about to be implemented to track student attendance. In the past, the paper-based system made it impossible to be sure how many paid students were actually attending class. With the new system, as students enter a classroom, they will tap their badge to a card reader outside the door. The card reader will record the student ID and time of entry. If students fail to do this, they do not get credit for attending that day. The card readers are all connected to the network. Management particularly wants to know if the night classes are profitable for the college.

Every classroom now has a brand new projector. These projectors are also connected to the network, and can play streaming video content from any source. Management is hoping to maximize this feature by having world-renowned guest lecturers occasionally tele-teach from different parts of the globe. During these remote teaching sessions, live audio/video will be streamed into the classroom, with local staff facilitating.

Within a few weeks of the school's Grand Opening, it was clear that the local two-person IT team could not possibly manage the network. The investment company has hired your IT consulting firm to take over all aspects of network administration including help desk, classroom support, phones, network management, and network security. Anything to do with IT is now in your hands. They have asked you, the head of the firm, to provide monthly reports as part of the IT governance plan. They are particularly concerned that security measures are adequate. Already there has been some petty theft with some mice, keyboards, patch cables, and even a computer stolen during business hours. As a result, security is about to be beefed up. IP cameras will be installed in key locations and guard presence will be increased. The board of directors is open to spending more money on security at your recommendation.

Management has asked how you will measure the effectiveness of any new security measures. They have also asked you to describe what key performance indicators you will include in your reports to not only help with cost/benefit analysis, but to also show that there is continuous improvement in the IT process. They want to make sure that the network has sufficient capacity to handle all of the traffic throughout the day. They are also keen to see return on investment after all the money they spent.

---

1. What key performance indicators should be included in your monitoring process?

---

2. You have decided to train staff to maximize utilization of the new equipment.

   What training KPIs could you include?

3. Will you implement an ISCM as part of your monitoring process?

4. Would you use NIST SP 800-137 to guide your ISCM implementation?

5. Do you see a need for collecting/reporting on data from DR/BCP and backups?

TOPIC D

Audits

Another necessary component of any assessment and testing platform is auditing. When you facilitate auditing practices in your systems, you'll be much more likely to catch security issues or compliance violations before they bring unacceptable risk to your organization.

Internal and External Audits

The following table describes internal and external audits.

Item	Description
Internal	An organization's audit department is an important ally in the detection of computer crimes. Internal audit departments review processes, logs, and transactions to ensure compliance with generally accepted principles of operational and regulatory requirements. Organizations like banks, savings and loans, and security traders are required to comply with federal, state, and local laws and regulations. An important function of the audit department is to verify compliance.
External	Certain enterprises are also required to submit to an audit by an external auditing organization. The purpose of the external audit is to again validate and verify compliance and provide additional oversight. Recently, the use of external auditors associated with the accounting firms used by the organization has caused insurmountable problems. The problems could be traced back to a lack of separation of duty. Consequently, regulations have been devised that enforce the use of external auditors not directly affiliated with the accounting firm used by a particular organization.

Audit Preparation

Before an audit begins, there are some first steps that the auditor and organization need to take. These steps are collaborative in nature, and both parties should be clear and sign off on all points before proceeding with the audit in earnest.

- Define the scope of the audit and the expected time period it will take place in.
- Identify any security controls in place.
- Review the organization's audit readiness.
- Offer recommendations to address any issues found while reviewing audit readiness.
- Discuss the preferred approach in performing the audit and receiving results.

Foundation Documents

Whether internal or external, the audit process will include documents that contain federal and state requirements. These documents are often in checklist form. Auditors use these checklists to verify compliance with the stated requirements.

The actual form these documents take will vary between regulation/standard. For example, PCI DSS v3 takes the following appearance in an Excel spreadsheet.

PCI DSS Requirements v3.0	Milestone	Status *Please enter "yes" if fully compliant with the requirement*	If status is "N/A", please explain why requirement is Not Applicable	If status is "No", please complete the following		
				Stage of Implementation	Estimated Date for Completion of Milestone	Comments
Requirement 1: Install and maintain a firewall configuration to protect cardholder data						
1.1 Establish and implement firewall and router configuration standards that include the following:						
1.1.1 A formal process for approving and testing all network connections and changes to the firewall and	6					
1.1.2 Current network diagram that identifies all connections between the cardholder data environment and other networks, including any wireless networks	1					
1.1.3 Current diagram that shows all cardholder data flows across systems and networks.	1					

Figure 6-6: PCI DSS prioritized approach milestones.

In PCI DSS, each requirement fulfills a milestone, and each milestone is basically a check to see if the organization is meeting the standard's overarching goals. For each requirement, the auditor records whether or not the requirement is being met, or if the requirement is not applicable. If the requirement is applicable but not met, the auditor indicates the current stage of its implementation, the estimated date that the milestone will be met, and any additional comments.

Audit Best Practices

The audit process is typically accompanied by a set of best practices. Best practices are often documented in industry publications and books related to the operation of networks, computers, auditing, and the like. Hardware and software vendors also provide best practice guidance to their customers on websites or in other forms of documentation.

Some examples of auditing best practices are as follows:

- Have an overall plan for the auditing process.
- Collect data in advance of on-site auditing to save time.
- Meet with key data handlers and owners involved in the auditing process.
- Conduct tests on the necessary systems.
- Analyze the on-site information off site.
- Issue regular reports, usually weekly, about the status of the auditing process.
- Have management review a draft of your report before finalizing it.
- In the report to management, include recommendations for fixing any outstanding issues.

 Note: Most financial audits include an IT audit. The CISSP can benefit from also being a Certified Information Systems Auditor (CISA). For more information on the CISA certification, see **www.isaca.org/Certification/CISA-Certified-Information-Systems-Auditor/Pages/default.aspx**.

SOC

A *service organization control (SOC)* is an accounting standard used to assure customers who outsource their services to service providers. SOC reports address security, privacy, and availability concerns that customers may have. They assert that the providers have appropriate controls in place over their own environments. There are three types of SOCs:

- **SOC 1**: In this report, the service provider describes its objectives and any controls that may impact users' financial information. SOC 1 reports are limited in scope to financial reporting. They include classifying transactions, procedures for processing and reporting on transactions and related events, managing accounting records, and preparing user reports.
- **SOC 2**: These reports extend beyond just financial interests and focus on the CIA of information as well as general security and privacy concerns. There are many operational topics covered in SOC 2 reports, including configuration management, disaster recovery, information disclosure, accuracy of information, use and retention of PII, and much more.

- **SOC 3**: This is a short version of SOC 2, omitting detailed descriptions of test controls and related results. The overall scope remains the same, however. SOC 3s are therefore more easily distributed to several parties.

SAS 70

SOCs have replaced the outdated Statement on Accounting Standards (SAS) 70, which focused only on financial reporting.

SOC 2/3 Trust Services Principles

SOC 2/3 reports are based on five core trust services principles. Each principle has a set of criteria that must be met in order for that principle to be fulfilled.

Principle	Sample Criteria
Security	• The organization documents security policy. • The organization communicates its policy to relevant parties. • The organization implements procedures that support policy. • The organization monitors systems to ensure they comply with policy.
Confidentiality	• The organization documents policy for protecting the confidentiality of information. • The organization communicates breaches of confidentiality to affected clients. • There are procedures in place to ensure information is only disclosed to authorized parties. • There are procedures in place to restrict access to physical and logical assets. • The organization periodically reviews its confidentiality policies and procedures.
Processing Integrity	• The organization has a policy of identifying and responding to violations of integrity. • The organization communicates the expected state of goods and services to its clients. • The organization provides warranty information for clients. • There are procedures in place to restrict access to authorized systems. • The organization monitors accuracy, completeness, and timeliness of goods and services.
Availability	• The organization assesses risk to availability periodically. • The organization provides business continuity services. • Changes to availability are communicated to management. • There are procedures in place for backing up mission-critical data. • The organization implements ongoing identification of issues related to availability.

Principle	Sample Criteria
Privacy	• The organization has a management framework for its policies and procedures. • The organization provides privacy policy notices to clients, including how personal information will be used. • The organization informs clients of their choices and obtains consent to handle their personal information. • The organization collects information only for the purposes outline in the notice. • There are procedures in place for the use, retention, and disposal of personal information. • Clients are able to access and review their own personal information. • The organization discloses personal information only in accordance with the notice and with the client's consent. • The organization prevents unauthorized access to personal information. • Client information is kept accurate and complete. • The organization implements continuous monitoring or privacy compliance.

 Note: For more detailed information about SOC criteria, visit **www.aicpa.org/InterestAreas/ InformationTechnology/Resources/SOC/TRUSTSERVICES/ DownloadableDocuments/FINAL_Trust_services_PC_Only_0609.pdf.**

Guidelines for Conducting Audits

Use the following guidelines when conducting audits:

- Use internal audits to verify compliance with organization policy and established industry principles of security.
- Understand that you may be subject to external audits, especially when it comes to legal and regulatory compliance.
- Take steps to prepare for an audit of your systems, such as determining the scope of the audit and identifying current security controls.
- If conducting audits internally, use a foundation document as a checklist, comparing a list of requirements against the current state of the organization.
- Incorporate best practices into the auditing process, such as collecting data ahead of time and issuing regular reports during the process.
- Consider using SOC 1 if your organization primarily deals with financial reporting.
- Consider using SOC 2 for a more comprehensive and detailed accounting of organizational security.
- Consider using SOC 3 to report to a more general audience that doesn't require a lot of detail.
- Review the principles and criteria of SOC 2 and SOC 3.

ACTIVITY 6–4
Discussing Audits

Scenario

You are an information security consultant. A local lending company has engaged you to assist them with their payment processing system. The company outsourced some of its transaction processing to a third party to provide web-based online payment capabilities for its customers. With the loan industry under increasing scrutiny by federal and state regulators, the company wants to make sure that it is in compliance with any applicable laws. The company's attorney has asked you to help them conduct an internal IT audit. They want to make sure that their servers and IT processes follow industry best practices. You have already told them that you are not an information systems auditor, but you have agreed to help verify the technical aspect of their IT equipment and process. You are about to go into a meeting with management to discuss scope and expectations for this audit. You have already downloaded a checklist of specific technical recommendations for a business of this sort.

1. What topics should be addressed in the pre-audit meeting?

2. With regard to the web-based payment processing system, what specific standards should be implemented for the audit?

3. Would this company benefit from an external audit?

4. When conducting the internal IT audit, what steps will you include?

Summary

In this lesson, you discussed the importance of developing a security assessment and testing platform. The platform has several components, including system and software security control testing, security process data collection, and auditing. Together, these components can help ensure your organization is meeting its security requirements and not leaving open any vulnerabilities for attackers to exploit.

Do you conduct penetration tests in your organization? If so, what type of tests do you perform? If not, what other testing do you do on systems and security?

What sort of KPIs do you use in your organization to measure security performance?

 Note: Check your CHOICE Course screen for opportunities to interact with your classmates, peers, and the larger CHOICE online community about the topics covered in this course or other topics you are interested in. From the Course screen you can also access available resources for a more continuous learning experience.

7 | Security Operations

Lesson Time: 6 hours, 30 minutes

Lesson Objectives

In this lesson, you will:

- Identify foundational security operations concepts.
- Identify physical security mechanisms.
- Analyze best practices for protecting personnel.
- Evaluate logging and monitoring capabilities.
- Evaluate preventative measures in stopping attacks.
- Follow best practices for resource provisioning and protection.
- Evaluate patch and vulnerability management processes.
- Identify the importance of change management in the organization.
- Create an incident response plan.
- Follow the forensic investigation process.
- Plan for disaster recovery.
- Review disaster recovery strategies.
- Discuss disaster recovery implementation.

Lesson Introduction

Security operations is a concept that encompasses two basic ideas: to ensure that day-to-day activities that support the business are protected against risk and to deeply integrate security processes within those day-to-day activities. Recognizing the importance of both of these ideas is a necessary step in ensuring that the organization functions without any impairment.

TOPIC A

Security Operations Concepts

Before you begin diving into specific security operations, you need to become acquainted with some foundational concepts.

 Note: To learn more, view the LearnTO presentations from the **LearnTO** tile on the CHOICE course screen.

Security Operations Overview

There are four main themes that recur in security operations.

Focus	Description
Maintain Operational Resilience	Keep core business functions operating even when a negative event occurs. You will need to anticipate these events and make sure that you have a backup plan to minimize disruption.
	The best way to determine which processes are most important to the business is to ask the managers of the different departments or lines of business. IT people are often not the correct person to determine what is operationally important to a business unit. An IT person might assume that keeping the database server online is the most critical focus to keep the business unit functioning. The manager, however, might instead say that having a working phone system to call customers is more urgent.
Protect Valuable Assets	Security operations must protect a wide range of assets and resources, from data to equipment to human. In order to do so, you'll need to maintain the controls that were put into place to protect those assets.
Control System Accounts	It's particularly important to control users who have access to critical business systems. Operations security must provide the checks and balances required to prevent misuse of system privilege.
Effective Security Services Management	Any business unit requires strong management to ensure that it is effective. Security operations is no exception. You'll want to make sure that strong leadership is in place to keep security operations services consistent and effective. Good management also ensures that there is continuous process improvement.

Least Privilege

Least privilege is one of the most foundational concepts of security. Giving a user exactly what they need to do their job, and no more. Particularly in an IT department, you'll find that privilege slowly escalates, with people becoming administrators and super users who don't really require the capability. In addition, users may be shifted to other roles or leave, but their group memberships may still remain. Even users who don't have direct access to privileged information may be able to aggregate lower-level information in order to learn something more sensitive in nature. Transitive trust levels can also erode access security, as even if you don't explicitly give a user access to a system, that system may be configured to implicitly give the user access if both entities trust the same third party.

Because of these issues, you cannot set and forget permissions levels. These must be reviewed regularly, to make sure that users who once had specific privileges and no longer need them are removed from those permission sets. On a technical level, it is good to set limits to how long someone can maintain a privilege level. For example, you can set expiration times for user accounts. You can also set policies that automatically review members of administrative groups, removing users who should not be in those groups.

Besides internal misuse of privilege, you do not want others to misuse someone's user account. For example, executives and department heads will have access to critical resources. It can be very damaging to the organization if a malicious user logs in as that manager and accesses that resource in an unauthorized way. Similarly, an IT administrator who regularly uses a privileged account for mundane activities such as printing or answering email runs the risk of having a background malicious process use that privilege level to access the system. For this reason, most IT personnel are assigned two user accounts: one for common end-user tasks, and another for administrative tasks.

Figure 7–1: Least privilege example.

Need to Know

Similar to least privilege is the idea of need to know—a high ranking staff member may have high-level permissions overall, but they don't necessarily need to be able to access certain documents that are beyond their job scope. This prevents even users with major permission levels from being another vector of attack for certain information should the user's account be compromised. Need to know is most often used in a military setting to restrict the amount of people who are entitled to know the details of an operational plan.

Separation of Duties

Separation of duties is a common technique to limit how much power a single user has. The goal of separation of duties is to require at least two people to perform a complete cycle of a task. This means that malicious activity would require collusion between at least two people. It also minimizes mistakes by preventing the same people who created or implemented something from auditing or testing it. Examples of IT duties that you would separate include:

- Backup and restore.
- Enter and delete data.
- Receive inventory and log the receipts.
- Create policy and enforce policy.
- Develop software and deploy software.
- Creation and destruction of records.

User Account Special Privileges

There are typically six types of user accounts. Each has a different privilege level, as summarized in the following table.

Account	Description
Root/Built-in administrator	An all-powerful account that can perform any action on a device or system, including taking ownership of files and processes, and further escalating its own privilege. This account cannot be deleted or locked out, nor can any of its base privileges be changed or revoked.
	Best practice dictates that administrators do not login using the roots or built-in administrator account, but rather belong to administrative groups. If possible, disable any generic administrator accounts and instead put individual user accounts in administrative groups. This permits auditing to identify individuals who use or misuse system privilege.
Service	This is usually used by an application such as an email or database server service to access the computer at system level. Originally, such an account had considerable privilege levels on a system. Most operating systems today have mitigated that risk, minimizing the privilege level to be essentially the same as an ordinary user, with the added privilege of being able to log on locally to a server.
	The challenge of service accounts is that most services do not know how to regularly change their password. Traditionally, this meant that you had to configure the account with an unchanging password. If someone should discover the password, they could abuse it and logon to that service. Some operating systems, such as Windows server 2012, have password management policies in place where the system can automatically change the service password on a regular basis without human knowledge or intervention.
User-created administrator groups	This is an ordinary user account that is a member of one or more administrator groups. The administrator groups will vary in scope. Some might be enterprise-wide. Some might be limited to a specific system, task, or service. Most operating systems permit you to create such groups and specify the tasks that members of the groups can perform. Using user-created administrator groups is a good way to implement least privilege for IT and technical support staff
Power user	This is a user who has certain privileges above that of an ordinary user, but not quite that of an administrator. Power users are usually limited to a specific system. Typically, a power user can install software, manage printing, and make some configuration changes to the computer they are working on.
Ordinary user	This is a regular user account. Ordinary users can generally run programs but not install or modify them. They usually have the right to create folders and files within their own profile, manage their own print jobs, and change their own passwords. They're usually allowed to log on locally to their own desktops, but not to servers. They must connect across a network to access server services and centralized resources, and can only access what they have been given permission to access.
Guest	This is a limited account that can be enabled to give visitors restricted access to a system. Guest users do not have their own account, and therefore use the guest account to do things such as print or get online.

Job Rotation

Like separation of duties, job rotation is a common technique to minimize fraud and abuse. If one person stays in a single position for too long without oversight, it is very common for that person to begin to abuse their privilege. If a user with privileged access knows that someone else will come in behind them, accessing and managing the same systems, any fraud or misuse will be exposed.

Similar to job rotation is the concept of mandatory vacations. Users knowing that they will be forced to go on vacation on a regular basis will be less likely to perform malicious activities for fear of discovery.

Information Lifecycle

Information has its own lifecycle. At some point, it will no longer have any value to the company. The information lifecycle consists of three stages:

1. Creation
2. Use
3. Destruction

The security professional needs to be aware of the security aspects of each stage of the information lifecycle. When information is created, someone in the organization will have to be responsible for it. The data owner is usually NOT someone in the IT department, but someone who has to use the data for business purposes. This is usually a business unit or department manager. This data owner is the person who has the right to decide who is permitted to use the data. For example, a sales manager will own the sales database, and will be the person to determine who has access to what tables are in that database.

Generally, the data owner will not be the data custodian. That is the job of the database administrator who then grants or revokes rights to specific users based on what each department manager requires.

When creating information, the data owner works with the data custodian to ensure that controls are in place and only authorized users have access to that information.

Throughout the life time of the information, the requirements for its usage will probably change. It is up to the data owner to then communicate this requirements to the data custodian. For example, if the sales department hires 10 new salespeople, the department manager needs to let the database administrator know that these 10 new people require access to specific tables.

When it is time to retire the data, it must be archived or destroyed in a way that does not compromise business process or security. Typically company policy or regulatory requirements will mandate that the information be archived for a certain retention period. Since the IT team (which includes the database administrator) will be the data custodians, proper archiving and records retention will be their responsibility. Retention policies should be clear and retention schedules well documented. At some point, nearly all information will cease to be valuable to a company and must be destroyed or deleted in a secure manner.

SLA Metrics

SLAs are very important to day-to-day business operations. Whether they apply externally or internally, they often form the foundational expectations of one or more organizations. They very clearly outline responsibilities, expectations, and metrics with regard to the service being provided. Having this clearly written in black and white means that when a service level is not provided as expected, neither party can claim that it was not aware. Both parties would have the same understanding of all requirements.

Some of the key metrics to monitor in your operations in order to support your SLAs include:

- **Availability**: How often the service can be used, and any specific times that the service is or is not available. Different industries will require different uptimes.

- **Defects**: Any errors in service or delivered products, or any missed deadlines for providing these.
- **Technical quality**: Whether or not a service or product meets a baseline expectation of quality established in the SLA.
- **Security**: Other than availability, measuring the success of organizational systems in upholding confidentiality, integrity, and so on.

"Nines" and Service Level Availability

In IT, service levels are usually measured not only by performance levels, but also by uptime. There's a common scale of "nines" in use. "One 9" means that the service is available 90% of the time. "Two 9s" means of the services available 99% of the time. "Three 9s" means that the services available 99.9% of the time. "Four 9s" means 99.99% of the time. And "Five 9s" means of services available 99.999% of the time. While five nines is the gold standard of service availability, it is generally impractical in most applications. It would require that the system cannot be down for more than five minutes in an entire year. Except for financial and emergency institutions, many companies are content if their service level reaches two or three nines.

Guidelines for Applying Security Operations Concepts

 Note: All of the Guidelines for this lesson are available as checklists from the **Checklist** tile on the CHOICE Course screen.

Use the following guidelines when building a foundation for your security operations.

- Focus on four main areas of security operations:
    - Maintaining operational resilience.
    - Protecting valuable assets.
    - Controlling system accounts.
    - Managing security services effectively.
- Always adhere to the principle of least privilege.
- Constantly monitor and evaluate permission levels; don't set and forget them.
- Practice separation of duties for key operations, including data backups, policy enforcement, and software deployment.
- Pay close attention to the different types of user accounts and how they differ with regards to access.
- Implement job rotation so no one employee has control over certain systems for too long.
- Incorporate security throughout the three general stages of the operations lifecycle: creation, use, and destruction.
- Ensure that your service level agreements (SLAs) outline expectations with regards to day-to-day business operations.
- Track key metrics to support the requirements outlined in SLAs.

ACTIVITY 7–1
Discussing Security Operations Concepts

Scenario

In this activity, you will assess your understanding of foundational security operations concepts.

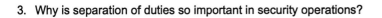

1. Why is maintaining operational resilience a core theme of security operations?

2. Why is it that you cannot set and forget permissions levels?

3. Why is separation of duties so important in security operations?

4. What are some risks associated with service accounts?

5. How is the security benefit of job rotation different from that of separation of duties?

6. What are some security concerns associated with the destruction phase of the information lifecycle?

7. Why should security be a key metric in an SLA?

TOPIC B

Physical Security

Your business operations need logical security controls, but these controls will be useless if an attacker can just compromise your physical systems. That's why no security operations program is complete without controls that focus on the objects both inside and directing surrounding your facilities.

Perimeter Security

Perimeter security is the first level of physically protecting the outermost boundary of a facility. It should include:

- Gates, fences, walls, doors, and other barriers.
- Locks.
- Guards.
- Perimeter intrusion detection such as infrared, fence vibration sensors, normal light and infrared CCTV, sound and motion detectors, and any other system that can detect the presence of an intruder.
- Alarm systems.
- Logging and reporting of all physical access attempts.

Internal Security

Internal physical controls begin at the building and can include access control and monitoring at any point. The level of access control depends on the value of the area being protected. The goal of access control is to minimize the opportunity for committing a crime. Your internal physical controls can include:

- Access controls like card readers, locks, and mantraps.
- Safes, vaults, and other secure storage containers.
- Guards.
- Surveillance systems.
- Alarm systems.
- Logging and reporting of all physical access attempts.

Internal physical controls should be applied to sensitive or high-risk areas such as:

- Street level entrances.
- Lobbies.
- Loading docks.
- Elevators.
- Server rooms.
- Telecommunication closets.
- Filing systems/records storage.
- Operations centers.
- Equipment lockers.
- Any area that contains sensitive information or valuable assets.

Layered Protection

In physical security, *layered protection* is a mechanism that begins from the perimeter and continues inward through the building grounds, entry points, and interior of the building. It uses multiple layers of physical access controls to deter, detect, delay, or respond to unauthorized access. Rather than working in isolation, the advantage of layered protection is that multiple physical controls, both perimeter and internal, are working in tandem to defend the entire premises.

One major concern of physical security and your layered defense strategy is inadequate design. For example, imagine your company purchased a building and had very little input on its design. In this instance, you will need to account for the inadequacies and reinforce them where you can. On the other hand, perhaps you are in a multi-tenant building and have very little or no control of the perimeter of the building. Then, you will need to pay extra attention to your internal design choices.

There are three areas that are often involved in a layered protection plan.

Layered Protection Area	Description
Perimeter access	The perimeter is the first layer of defense. At the perimeter, fences, gates, lighting, intrusion detection devices, dogs, and guards are among the techniques that can be used as protective measures. Perimeter security is a visible and immediate deterrent to casual troublemakers, while more advanced perimeter security measures can provide a significant and delaying obstacle for determined attackers, giving security and police more time to respond.
Facility access	Restricting facility access to authorized personnel has become a standard practice in most industries. Like paper financial records, computers and networks are at their most vulnerable when an individual can gain direct, physical access to the sensitive information or hardware. Controlling access to the entire facility limits potential access to vital or important information or hardware that may not be within a secure area and enhances the personal security of employees and visitors. Facility access is controlled by using guards, locks, access devices, man traps, gates/doors, and good design.
Secured area access	Within the facility, specific areas should be designated as secured areas. These areas are home to highly sensitive and vital business information and/or technology assets. Admission to these areas should be tightly controlled and monitored at all times. Access to secured areas is controlled by secured doors, locks, strengthened walls, and other similar methods.

Note: If an unauthorized person can bypass one physical control layer, like the perimeter of a building, the next control layer should provide more deterrence for access. Each layer should implement its own physical access controls. In addition, multiple levels can implement the same physical access control, such as locks for building, office, server, and similar entry points.

Note: Layered protection in physical security is the equivalent of defense in depth in logical or organizational security.

Physical Access Barriers

Barriers are protective devices in a number of categories that seek to limit physical access to a space. Barriers are primarily perimeter controls, but they can also be placed inside a building at key points.

Physical Access Barrier	Description

Fencing	The first barrier that is often considered is a fence.
	
	 • A fence that is 3 to 4 feet high does not eliminate access but can be used to clearly mark a property line. It may keep trespassers out of the area but will not dissuade determined attackers.
	
	 • A fence that is 5 to 6 feet high may not keep determined attackers out of the area; however, the difficulty of overcoming a barrier of this height will serve as a deterrent for most people.
	
	 • A truly deterrent fence is 8 feet high and has barbed or razor wire at the top. Few people will attempt to cross this type of barrier.
	
	 • Very high security areas may provide multiple fences with a no-man's land in between. The area between may also be filled with razor wires and sensors. Strain-sensitive cabling can also be wound into the fence to detect an intruder climbing or cutting the fence. This will keep out all but the most determined intruders.
	
	 • Fences need gates. These gates will be perceived as a weak spot. Make sure your gates match the security level of your fencing. Gates are evaluated as Class I through IV by Underwriters Lab (UL) 325.
	
	    • Class I: Residential usage; covering one to four single-family dwellings.
	    • Class II: Commercial usage where general public access is expected; a common application would be a public parking lot entrance or gated community.
	    • Class III: Industrial usage where limited access is expected; one example is a warehouse property entrance not intended to serve the general public.
	    • Class IV: Restricted access; this includes applications such as a prison entrance monitored either in person or via closed circuitry.

Walls	External and internal walls should be constructed in such a way that they prevent individuals from trying to gain access through them. Solid concrete walls with embedded reinforcements are excellent barriers and are well suited to use as external walls. Walls have the added advantage/disadvantage that they obstruct views. This can be an advantage because it keeps people from seeing into an area, but can quickly turn into a disadvantage if the intruder has breached the wall and is no longer visible. Internal walls, especially those surrounding a secure area, need to be solid and difficult to penetrate. Standard drywall is considered inadequate for security but it can be improved by including mesh between two layers of drywall. Fire codes often define the fire protection levels for walls, and most walls should have the protection capability to withstand a fire for at least one hour.
Doors	Doors must have sufficient locks to defeat penetration attempts. Secure areas should have solid doors that meet the same fire protection level as the walls.
Windows	Windows present a number of different security issues. Ideally, secured areas will not have windows. They can break easily, and even with protective wire meshes or unbreakable glass, it is not difficult to access a space using a window. If windows are necessary, the strongest possible protection must be provided. Be sure to take into account local fire codes.

Physical Access Barrier	Description
Lighting	Lights are not a true barrier; however, the visibility that they provide represents a deterrent control against entry into an area. Lights can be used to illuminate large areas, such as the perimeter of a building or a fence.
	The lights that are present should allow either a video camera or a guard to see potential intruders. Lights should also be used in entryways, easing the identification of an individual at a door.
	Lighting can also act as a detective control. The amount of lighting will vary by area. For example, the areas around buildings should meet the illumination requirement of producing two foot candles of light at a height of 8 feet. This guideline is known as the 2x8 rule or the 8x2 rule. Lighting in a parking facility might be as high as 5 foot candles.
	Lighting is also important for video surveillance purposes. In this case, it should shine outwards from the building to illuminate the intruder's face. Lighting that points back towards the building can cause glare and reduce the effectiveness of cameras.
	Lighting may also be triggered by a perimeter IDS. If the system identifies an attacker, trip or glare lights are activated in the area of intrusion. Because of their brightness intensity, these lights tend to momentarily blind and disorient an intruder.
Bollards	*Bollards* are obstacles designed to stop a vehicle. They are strategically placed to provide a physical barrier. They may be as simple as a concrete post or large concrete planters. Designs that are more sophisticated might include carefully planted trees and even sculptures designed to withstand impact.

Lock Types

Locks are one of the most obvious and necessary methods of securing various facilities and objects, such as doors, windows, gates, computers, and network equipment.

Lock Type	Description
Key lock	Key locks require keys to open them. They are easily picked by experts, but may include a ward, or obstruction, in the keyhole to prevent uncut keys from opening the locks. Key locks typically use pin tumblers, interchangeable cores, or wafers under springs used for tension. The body and bolt of the lock should be made of substantial materials to withstand bolt cutters and hack saws.
	Physical key protection is essential to control manual lock security and safeguard entry systems. Keys are often marked with a "do not duplicate" indicator that informs key manufacturers to ensure key protection.
Deadbolt lock	Deadbolt locks are keyed locks that incorporate a bolt into the door frame for added security when used with an alternate type of lock. If the same key is used as the tumbler lock in the door, the protection against lock picking is minimal. Additional protection is gained by making it harder to kick down the door.
Keyless lock or cipher lock	Keyless locks do not require keys to unlock them. A keyless lock typically has a keypad or push buttons that open the lock when the correct access code is entered. These are not very secure because they frequently have a small number of combinations and can show wear patterns that reveal the combination.

Lock Type	Description
Combination lock	Combination locks are keyless locks that use a sequence of numbers in a specific order to open the lock. The combination may be provided at the time of lock manufacturing or may be programmable by the user. A combination lock may be electronic and can include a digital display.
	Combination values should be protected to control combination lock security and safeguard entry systems.
Intelligent keys	Keys that have chips embedded provide higher levels of protection. The lock can recognize the key and provide access control decisions based on user, time, and more.
Device locks	Device locks protect mobile and desktop computing devices and peripherals that are easy to steal without detection. Device locks include cable locks to anchor laptops and peripherals to desks, chairs, and so on; power switch control covers; port controls; and slot locks or brackets. Device locks can be keyed or keyless.
Biometric or access card locks	These use a biometric or access card reader to release an electric strike or magnetic lock on the door.

Key Control

A lock is only as good as the security of the keys that unlock it. If too many keys are floating around or unknown keys exist, security is greatly compromised. In many cases, master keys exist to unlock many different locks. Master keys must be controlled very carefully. Knowing exactly which locks they will and will not affect is very important. High security areas will need to use locks with different, or no, master keys.

Key control systems should take into account factors like key identification, key issuance, key returns, no-returned keys, and master keys. This is clearly defined in policies, procedures, and guidelines. To make sure keys can be accounted for, it is necessary to perform key audits.

Access Controls

Advanced systems are available to provide physical access controls beyond simple barriers and locks.

Facility Control Device	Description
Automatic access control	Automatic access controls may use cipher keypads, access control cards, or other types of controls to identify authorized users. The door lock may be electrically activated or may be manually activated by turning a handle. Automatic systems can also log the access events of those who pass through a door or gate.
Card entry systems	Card entry systems use cards that may be similar in size and shape to a credit card to identify the individual attempting access. These cards have a magnetic stripe containing identifying information. This magnetic stripe is read by the reader as the card is swiped through it. Proximity cards transmit radio signals containing the card ID to a receiver when held close to the receiver.

Facility Control Device	Description
Biometric entry systems	Biometric identification systems utilize unique facets of individuals to identify them. Examples of biometric identification systems include retina or iris scanners, fingerprint scanners, or hand geometry sensors. These devices require a central system that contains a database of unique identification information for each individual in the system. Once the biometric scan is completed and the identity has been verified, an automatic door lock may be opened.
Man traps	A *man trap* is a physical entry portal with two doors, one on each end of a secure chamber. An individual enters a secure area through an outer door. The outer door must be closed before an inner door can open. Identity is sometimes verified before an individual enters the secure area through the first door, and other times while they are confined to the secure area between the two doors.

Secure Storage

Even when internal access controls are in place, leaving sensitive items inside a building may not offer suitable protection. You have several options to securely store valuables and other key physical items, adding another layer of protection.

Secure Storage	Description
Container	Containers are similar to filing cabinets, but have more advanced locking mechanisms and are more resilient to forced entry. Containers are often used by military and government agencies to hold hard copies of sensitive files.
Safe	Safes, typically made of steel, are more reinforced than containers and are harder to break into. Safes are also resilient enough to protect against natural threats like floods and fires. Organizations and individuals use safes to store physical currency and small valuable objects. The access mechanism used on a safe is usually a key or a combination lock.
Vault	Vaults are much larger than safes and containers, being an entire room a person can walk around in. This is particularly useful for organizations that need to store huge quantities of physical currency, like a bank, or particularly large valuable objects. As such, vaults are heavily reinforced with thick steel that covers the floor, the ceiling, the walls, and especially, its door. For a vault door to be adequately protected from physical attack, it must be resistant to cutting torches and other such tools. Vault doors usually have a combination lock or a biometric lock.

Guards

While not sophisticated electronic systems, security guards can monitor critical checkpoints and verify identification, allow or disallow access, and log physical entry occurrences. They also provide a visual deterrent and can apply their own knowledge and intuition to potential situations.

Although guards are effective resources for controlling facility security, maintaining security guard patrols requires a considerable amount of investment. Patrol times can be lengthy, and shift costs as well as uniform and equipment expenses can be high.

Due to the expensive nature of security patrol implementations and the possibility of unreliable guard behavior, an organization may consider precautions and counteractive measures. Many facilities require guards to use devices that record their locations and activities to ensure and verify proper surveillance practices.

PIDS

In a layered protection strategy, securing the facility's perimeter is the first line of defense. A *perimeter intrusion detection system (PIDS)* senses changes in an environment, such as an individual approaching a building or touching a vehicle.

Although perimeter controls such as fences help to delineate physical boundaries and deter attacks, they can be penetrated. In other cases, it may be impossible to install fencing or other security measures due to local building codes or community standards. A PIDS can supplement other perimeter security controls or provide a strong level of security in the absence of other security measures.

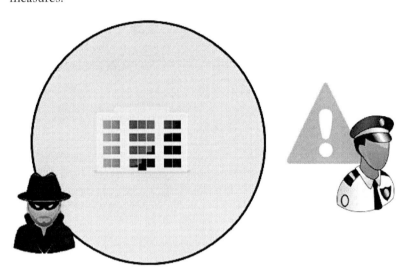

Figure 7-2: A PIDS example.

PIDS Types

There are several types of PIDSes that help monitor security disturbances.

PIDS Type	Description
Motion sensor	A *motion sensor* uses movement to detect a perimeter approach or a presence inside a controlled area. It can detect human and animal movement, and be unintentionally triggered by natural events like wind.
	Many motion sensors are implemented using a beam of light or radio signal. A sensor that is positioned opposite the signal emitter detects a break in the beam and generates an alert.
	Motion sensors come in two forms:
	• *Infrared devices*—Emit a beam of infrared light that is sensed by the receiver. These devices have a limited distance of operation.
	• *Microwave systems*—Emit a narrow beam of low-intensity radio signals that are sensed by the receiver. These systems are used in situations where the coverage areas are too large for effective infrared device detection.
Pressure-sensitive sensor	A *pressure-sensitive sensor* detects pressure when weight, such as a human or animal body, is applied to the device. Pressure sensors often have the capability to set low- and high-sensing thresholds. In a highly secure area, a perimeter fence is commonly surrounded by crushed gravel within its interior zone. If the fence is defeated, pressure-sensitive sensors are typically embedded in the gravel as a second line of defense.

PIDS Type	Description
Heat detector	A *heat detector* is installed to measure temperature increases emitted from a heat source such as a human, fire, or animal. It can detect a fire before it flames, it does not require a line-of-sight to the monitoring area, and it is not susceptible to wind or natural events.
Proximity detector	A *proximity detector* is installed to emit a calculable electrical field while in use. Also called a capacitance detector, it measures the change in the electrical field caused when an individual or animal approaches the sensor. Typically, it sounds an alarm if triggered and protects specific objects, such as artwork, cabinets, or a safe, rather than an entire space.
Vibration detector	A *vibration detector* is installed to measure vibrations caused by breaking glass, collisions with solid objects, or footsteps. It may be unintentionally triggered by natural events like wind.
Magnetic detector	A *magnetic detector* is installed to measure changes in a magnetic field. It reacts to conductors like keys or coins. For example, a wand used in airport security screening is a magnetic detector.
Photometric detector	A *photometric detector* is installed to detect a change in the light level in a designated area, specifically a windowless room or area. It emits a beam that is expected to hit a receiver. If it does not, an alarm sounds.

Surveillance Systems

A *surveillance system* is a physical security mechanism that monitors designated internal and external areas of a facility for unusual behavior or a potential intruder. In external scenarios, surveillance systems are often a component of a PIDS rather than a distinct system. Video surveillance occurs through visual human detection or through visual recording devices. Audio surveillance occurs through sophisticated listening devices. Both of these methods are used to detect abnormal activity or undesirable conditions.

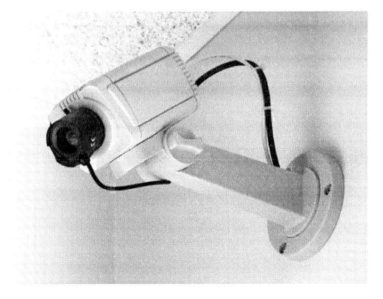

Figure 7-3: A video surveillance camera.

Types of Surveillance Systems

There are several types of surveillance systems that effectively monitor the physical security of a facility.

Surveillance System Type	Description
Video	Most of today's video monitoring systems have switched from videotape to complete digital archival and retrieval systems. The key to successful video surveillance, however, is in assessing the total facility security needs to ensure the most effective placement of cameras, lighting, and recording devices.
	Closed-circuit television (CCTV) is a visual recording device that uses video cameras to transmit images to monitors and video recorders. CCTV surveillance levels include detection, recognition, and identification.
	A CCTV system typically consists of a camera (or cameras), transmission media, and a monitor. In addition, lenses of various lengths are available to provide wide-area coverage for physical security and surveillance. Security camera lenses have several features that you must choose from, depending on your requirements. These are: focal length, depth of field, f-stop, and manual/auto iris.
	With focal length, you determine if you want a wide view or a zoomed-in narrow view. Lenses with a short focal length give a wide view. Lenses with a long focal length zoom in on a distant object to the exclusion of surrounding objects, giving a narrow view. Lenses can be a fixed length for reduced cost or can zoom the focal length in or out for more control.
	Depth of field is the distance between the nearest and farthest objects that stay in focus. A camera lens can only be focused on a single spot. You can include an area in front or behind this single spot to also remain in focus. The smaller the aperture (opening of the lens), the greater the depth of field. This comes at a price, however. A smaller aperture lets in less light. If lighting conditions are low, such as at night, objects that move will be blurry. The larger the aperture, the shallower the depth of field, but more light will enter the lens and moving objects will remain clearer. The lens aperture is measured in f-stops. An f-stop of f/2.8 will give you an extremely shallow depth of field. An f-stop of f/11 will give you a very large depth of field. Another word for aperture in cameras is iris. You can choose whether or not the aperture (iris) can be adjusted automatically or manually. Lenses might have automatic irises to allow for changing light levels. This is especially important if guards have the ability to raise light levels if they sense an intrusion. Otherwise, the increased light might make the cameras ineffective.
	Zoom is most helpful when guards are able to manage it remotely. Pan Tilt Zoom (PTZ) cameras provide the most control but at a much higher cost. Today's sophisticated digital cameras require less lighting to illuminate the monitoring area and generate highly visible images. CCTV systems may include video motion sensors, pre-programmed computer activation, and alarms.
Guard stations	Highly secure facilities, such as military installations and prisons, have guard stations with armed security personnel at all times to provide surveillance, deterrence, and security enforcement. They are equipped with monitoring devices, alarm systems, and so on.

Surveillance System Type	Description
Security dogs	Dogs provide an effective, rapid response mechanism against trespassers or other disturbances. Barking dogs are helpful in identifying threats to alert security guards who need to respond. While dogs cannot actually remove suspicious individuals, they employ scare tactics that encourage intruders to vacate the premises or delay escape until human guards can respond to a particular situation.
Audio	Audio surveillance includes recording systems or listening devices that provide eavesdropping capabilities. Military, government, and law enforcement agencies all use different forms of audio surveillance. Surveillance transmitters, surveillance recorders, audio monitoring equipment, covert room transmitters, and listening devices can be used to monitor and collect evidence on suspected intruders or suspicious activity. • Lithium transmitters have features such as remote activation and voice activation. • Digital transmitters can send data bursts via encryption, voice, or computer. • Concealable transmitters can be used for undercover surveillance and tracking capabilities. • Phone transmitters can monitor phone and room conversations.

Alarm Systems

Alarm systems are used to alert responders; depending on the alarm, systems can be triggered manually, passively, or by PIDS/surveillance system notification.

Alarm System Type	Description
Lights	Trip and glare lighting deters intruders. Flashing indicators and revolving lights are used to attract the attention of responders to problematic locations. High-intensity strobe lights are very effective for identifying and startling intruders.
Bells and sirens	Bells and sirens promptly alert responders to security disruptions. Specific sounds are associated with certain disturbances that provide triggers for individuals to respond accordingly. For example, when a fire alarm sounds, most people are conditioned to exit a building through the closest marked exit. Alert bells and sirens related to non-fire activities should include a different sound identifier than a fire alarm.
Local activation/ local response	Alarm systems in this category are triggered by a local event and have local responders present. An intrusion detection alarm caused by the unauthorized opening of a door could sound a local alarm; a local responder would then be responsible for researching the problem and providing a remedy. An example would be the doors to jet ways at airports. Each door is alarmed. If someone opens the door without using the keypad, a local alarm is sounded at or near the door. Airport police would respond to secure the door.
Local activation/ remote response	A residential home alarm could be considered a local activation/remote response system because the alarm is activated locally, in the home, and it immediately generates a remote response when the alarm company calls the home owner to follow up on the triggered alarm.

Alarm System Type	Description
Remote activation/ local response	In some cases, a local problem will be reported from a remote location. An alarm management system may be installed off site that requires remote monitoring by company staff or a third party. When a problem occurs in the facility, the alarm is sounded at the remote site, and a message or call is placed to local responders.
Remote activation/ remote response	Alarms and responses can also be handled remotely. For example, in a campus setting, the organization might have an agreement that all alarms from the on-campus fire detection system are sent directly to the municipal fire department. The fire department can then respond directly to the site of the alarm. Campus personnel do not need to call in the alarm or take any action other than evacuating the area.

Physical Access Logs

Physical access logs are maintained by access control systems and by security guards. These logs record individual entry to and exit from facilities and controlled areas. Security guards can maintain logs on paper or through a special computer application; facility control systems create logs automatically. In addition to entry and exit logging, some organizations use radio frequency identification (RFID) or other technologies to track individuals as they move around monitored facilities.

A physical access log should clearly identify:

- The name of the individual attempting access.
- The date and time of access.
- The access portal or entry point.
- The user ID entered to attempt access.
- The location of access to internal spaces, if required.
- Unsuccessful access attempts, including those during unauthorized hours.

One advantage to activity logging is that it can help to control bad habits by exposing individual behavior to security personnel. A related potential threat is known as tailgating, whereby an individual closely follows someone else into a secure environment with the intent of avoiding authentication by the control system. When the unauthorized individual attempts to leave, the control system can flag the incident as unusual and alert security personnel.

Guidelines for Implementing Physical Security

Use the following guidelines when implementing physical security.

- Introduce protection in layers (both perimeter and internal) to more successfully delay or stop an attacker.
- Implement physical access barriers like fences to keep intruders outside of your building perimeter.
- Choose an appropriate lock type for the physical assets you're trying to protect.
- Implement physical access controls like man traps to keep attackers out of the building even if they've breached the perimeter.
- Lock up valuables, sensitive hard copy documents, and physical money in secure storage like a container or safe.
- Use guards for a human-based control to both perimeter and internal security.
- Implement a PIDS for comprehensive monitoring of your perimeter.
- Implement surveillance systems as a component of a PIDS or as part of the building's internal security.
- Use various types of alarms so that security personnel are alerted to potential attacks.

- Ensure that all physical access attempts are properly logged.

ACTIVITY 7-2
Discussing Physical Security

Data Files

C:\093024Data\Security Operations\XYZco-new-building-concept-diagram.pdf

Before You Begin

Open and study **XYZco-new-building-concept-diagram.pdf**. Examine it from a physical security perspective.

Scenario

You are the information security consultant for XYZco, a company that develops custom software for a variety of clients. In order to accommodate increased demand, the company has hired more programmers and sales staff. The old facility has become too crowded, and management is considering moving operations to a new building. They just received the concept diagram from the architect, and have asked you to make physical security recommendations. Some of the software that XYZco develops is highly confidential in nature. XYZco has certain government and military clearances that allow it to create software that will process sensitive or classified data.

The building is in an upscale neighborhood with a low crime rate. There is currently no fence or security surrounding the property. The following list describes the different activities that would occur in each area of the building:

- Admin: Human resources, payroll, accounting.
- Offices: Executive director and Chief Technology Officer private offices.
- Sales: Sales and Marketing.
- Records: Printed project designs, paper records, office supplies, final copies of completed software projects.
- Conference Room: Meetings, product team brainstorming sessions with customers.
- Prod Area 1, Prod Area 2: Software development.
- Test Area: Product testing.
- Server Room: Databases, network devices, servers, virtual machine hosts, telecom, incoming data and phone lines.
- Basement storage (downstairs): Miscellaneous equipment and furniture storage.

---

1. Does the physical layout of the facility lend itself to good layered security?

2. What type of fencing would you install?

3. Where would you place lighting?

4. Are bollards necessary?

5. Which internal areas do you think are sensitive or high-risk?

6. Where would you place cameras?

7. Would you install any other types of surveillance?

8. What security recommendations would you make regarding any windows and doors?

9. On which doors might you put a biometric/card access lock?

10. Would you place a cipher lock on any of the doors?

11. Do you think a mantrap would be useful anywhere?

12. Where might you post guards?

13. Would you install a PIDS anywhere?

14. What types of secure storage would you provide for copies of completed products?

15. What type of alarm system might you install?

16. How can you automatically update and maintain physical access logs?

TOPIC C

Personnel Security

It's not just inanimate object that need your protection—your personnel are the lifeblood of your organization. They need to know that they're safe from threats both physical and psychological as they perform their duties.

The Importance of Personnel Safety

Your greatest company assets are your human resources. Without people, all other systems are valueless. Likewise, when your people are put in jeopardy, so goes your business. That's why organizations like the International Information Systems Security Certification Consortium, or (ISC)$^{2®}$, highlight in their publications that personnel safety is the primary goal of physical security. Organizational security policies and procedures should clearly stress the vital importance of keeping valuable personnel resources safe in any emergency situation. Your policies should state and enforce specific personnel safety priorities.

When it comes to keeping personnel safe, it's not just about keeping them away from physical harm. It's just as important that they have a healthy mental well-being. With that in mind, consider some of the following personnel safety concerns:

- How to retain privacy.
- How to travel safely and securely.
- How to avoid poor judgment as a result of duress.

Personnel Privacy

Although it varies by culture, all individuals have some expectation of privacy. The security professional must be aware of the limits, both legal and ethical, of monitoring individuals. For example, it is perfectly acceptable to place cameras in server rooms, hallways, entrances, elevators, and places where people handle money. On the other hand, it is generally not considered acceptable to place cameras in locker rooms, restrooms, or other private areas. Some areas are more difficult to assess. For example, is it acceptable to place cameras in a classroom? A private office? A home office if it is used for company business? The answer depends on perspective and the security goals of the company.

In some cases, the level of expected privacy is well-established. For example, most employees today understand that company email is not private, and that websites you visit on company time using company equipment can also be monitored. The company's legal department should be involved to provide guidance on what is both legal and acceptable. A company may also set expectations among its employees by prominently posting notices that email and company equipment are not private, and may be monitored. A company may also require employees to sign agreements as to the level of expected privacy.

Companies may also encourage users to take their privacy into their own hands by training them on best security practices. For example, you might present certain scenarios to your employees and ask them whether or not it's wise to give out their personal information. You can then gauge their answers and help correct any misconceptions they may have. This way, you further engender a culture of security by involving even general staff.

Failure to include these measures may get the company in trouble, and be grounds for a lawsuit. The security professional must help management understand the potential ramifications of invading personal privacy.

Travel

Monitoring employees while they travel, and attempting to ensure their safety while they are overseas, presents a lot of challenges. For one thing, many of the controls that an organization has in its own facility will not be available while an employee is abroad. The security professional must find other mechanisms including training and technical controls to protect both the employee and the company. Countries have different concepts of personal privacy and human rights.

Use the following security tips for when you are abroad:

- **Preparation**
    - If it is sensitive and you do not need it, do not take it with you. This includes contact information.
    - Back up all of your data and leave the backup at home before you leave.
    - If possible, use a different mobile phone from the one you usually use. Remove the battery when you do not need the device.
    - Prepare your device using strong passwords, updated OS and application patches, and up-to-date antivirus/anti-spyware protection.
    - Encrypt sensitive data on your devices, but be warned that some countries will not allow you to enter with encrypted information.
    - Update your browser to use strict security settings.
    - Disable infrared, Bluetooth, and other connectivity mechanisms and features that you do not need on the device.

- **While Traveling**
    - In most countries, you should have no expectation of privacy in hotels, offices, public places, and Internet cafés. In many countries, hotel business centers and phone networks are routinely monitored. Hotel rooms are often searched by government agents posing as hotel staff.
    - Expect that any information you send electronically, by fax, mobile device, computer, or telephone can be intercepted. Your wireless device will be especially vulnerable.
    - Realize that both security services and criminals can track your movements by monitoring your mobile phone even when you think it's off. They can hijack your device, inserting malicious software, to capture pictures of you or places you have been, or even turn on your microphone. To prevent this from happening, remove the battery from the device.
    - Malware can be transferred to your devices through flash drives, computer disks, or other gifts.
    - While corporate executives and government officials are most at risk, others can also be targeted. Do not assume that you are too insignificant to be of value.
    - Security services and criminals are good at phishing, pretending to be someone you would ordinarily trust in order to obtain information from you.
    - If a customs official demands to see your computer or mobile device, or if your room is searched without your presence, assume that your hard drive has been copied.
    - Avoid transporting electronic devices in checked baggage.
    - Do not leave electronic devices unattended in your baggage, even behind the front desk or in the care of hotel staff.
    - Do not use thumb drives that are given to you as gifts. They may be compromised.
    - Shield passwords from view, and be aware of who is observing you.
    - Do not use remember me password features on websites. Clear your browser cache, history, and cookies after each use.
    - Terminate connections when you are finished using them.
    - Do not open emails or attachments from unknown parties. Do not click on links in emails.
    - Empty your trash and recent folders after every use.
    - Avoid Wi-Fi networks if you can.

- If your device or information is stolen, immediately notify your organization back home as well as the local U.S. Consulate.
- Obtain official cyber security alerts from **www.onguardonline.gov** and **www.us-cert.gov/cas/tips**.
- When you return, change your passwords and have your own security team examine your phone and/or laptop for malware or signs of compromise.

Duress

When a person is under duress, that person does things that he or she would ordinarily not do because they are under threat of harm. A classic example of this is the bank teller being told by a robber to put money in a bag. The robber threatens to shoot the teller if he or she does not comply. Another example could be an intruder breaking into an office and threatening to shoot the receptionist if the manager does not open the server room door.

In duress, the situation happens quickly. Good training is crucial to ensure personnel safety while still taking action to stop the criminal. In the case of the bank teller, while the teller appears to be complying, he may slip a dye pack into the bag with the money. The dye pack will explode, marking all of the money and hopefully the robber as well. The teller may also press a silent alarm button alerting law enforcement that there is a robbery in progress. In the case of the data center, a manager or administrator may be forced at gunpoint to open the server room door. In such a case, there should be a simple hostage situation cipher lock combination pattern that person can press without arousing suspicion to alert the police.

Examine the scenarios that may occur in which an intruder will attempt to force personnel to provide access to resources. Put together a team to talk out or even act out the duress scenario to try to identify potential safety mechanisms that you can easily teach personnel, and that they will remember and use. Be sure to then train all personnel thoroughly in these procedures, so that responses are automatic even when panicked.

Remember that duress situations are volatile and extremely dangerous, even deadly. The information security professional should always seek assistance of law enforcement and other experts who are familiar with dealing with duress situations, especially when a real incident is in progress.

Guidelines for Ensuring Personnel Security

Use the following guidelines to keep personnel safe and secure.

- Ensure that all personnel understand their level of privacy with regards to their activities at work.
- Write policies to establish privacy baselines and involve legal counsel, if necessary.
- Post prominent notices that specify what equipment or areas may be monitored.
- Train users on best practices for maintaining privacy.
- Prepare your devices for travel by hardening their security settings and backing up any data you can't afford to lose.
- Use careful judgment when using electronic devices during travel. For example, don't connect to public Wi-Fi networks.
- Determine what potential attack situations might cause your personnel duress.
- Identify ways for personnel to resolve or mitigate duress during an attack should it arise.
- Always seek out law enforcement when dealing with dangerous situations.

ACTIVITY 7–3
Discussing Personnel Security

Scenario

In this activity, you will assess your understanding of personnel security.

1. In addition to physical well-being, what is the other goal of personnel safety?

2. How is scenario-based training useful in raising privacy awareness in a company?

3. Why should corporate travelers be wary of using technology gifts they have received abroad?

4. Why should an organization involve law enforcement or other experts when training staff to deal with duress?

TOPIC D

Logging and Monitoring

Unless you can track issues when they arise, you'll constantly be trying to catch up to the attackers that threaten your organization. Being able to monitor your systems and record the results of that monitoring will turn your security operations from reactive to proactive.

Continuous Security Monitoring

Security monitoring falls into two categories:

*   Passive: Events are logged and examined after they occur.
*   Active: Events are both logged and responded to continuously in real-time.

Continuous security monitoring has become the norm for effective security operations. Organizations that are serious about security can no longer afford to occasionally scan their logs or only scan the logs after an event is detected. Security monitoring must be constant, with the vast majority of the effort automated to ease the burden on administrators.

Your organization will probably implement both passive and active monitoring. The vast majority of your monitoring should be automated, but there should always be manual monitoring and oversight of automated monitoring systems by humans. If you depend only on automated systems, you run the risk of false reporting by systems that are not properly configured or updated.

IDS/IPS Implementation

As stated earlier, an intrusion detection system is a passive system that logs unauthorized activities on both the network and hosts. An intrusion prevention system (IPS) is an IDS that proactively responds to suspicious activity. The most common IPS response is to block the offending traffic. The network administrator, however, must ensure that legitimate traffic is not accidentally blocked. You should implement both network and host-based intrusion detection/prevention as part of your security operations.

Implementing an IDS/IPS has four points of concern:

*   True positive.
*   True negative.
*   False positive.
*   False negative.

	Alarm	*Silence*
Intended Function	True Positive: Alarm sounds during actual incident.	True Negative: Alarm silent, and there is no incident.
Broken Function	False Positive: Alarm sounds although there is no incident.	False Negative: Alarm does not sound even though there is an actual incident.

In a false positive, you have a false alarm. The problem with these is that too many false positives will cause the operator to belittle the alarms and eventually ignore them. In the midst of the false alarms, a real alarm could happen and yet go undetected. With false negatives, the system gives you a false sense of security by not reporting events that are actually happening.

IDS/IPS Placement

Strategically placing IDS/IPS probes and sensors is straightforward: place the probes where interesting traffic occurs:

*   Directly behind (at the inside interface of) firewalls, dual-homed proxies (those with two network cards), routers, and VPN servers.
*   Right next to single-homed proxies, servers, and wireless access points.

Most intrusion detection systems can forward their logs to a centralized console. Make sure that the central console is in a protected area where hackers cannot access it. Also make sure that any communications between IDS/IPS sensors and their console are encrypted.

The following diagram shows a typical IDS/IPS infrastructure.

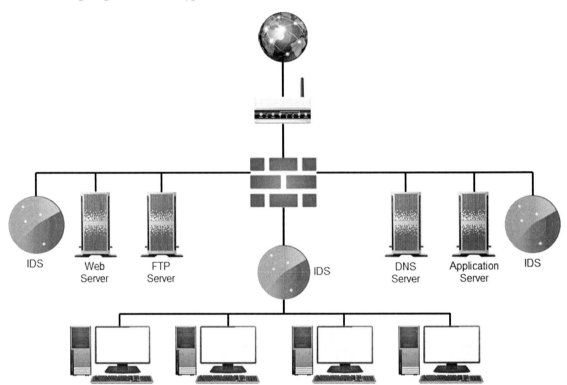

Figure 7–4: Placement of IDS/IPSes behind firewalls and next to servers.

DLP

Data loss prevention (DLP) is a strategy for making sure that users do not accidentally or deliberately send sensitive information outside the organization. DLP products are software based solutions that help the network administrator control what data end users can and cannot transfer to others. The DLP will monitor, detect, and block data that you categorize as sensitive in any or all of the following states:

*   The data is at rest (stored on a hard drive).
*   The data is in motion (being transmitted across the network).
*   The data is in use (actively being used on a user's machine or other endpoint).

Standard DLP mechanisms can include:

*   Firewalls.
*   IDS/IPS.
*   Antivirus software.

More advanced DLP tactics may include machine learning and reasoning algorithms to detect abnormal user access to data. They may include:

- Abnormal email exchange.
- Keystroke monitoring for systems that are not online.
- User and system activity monitoring.

Monitoring email is the most common implementation of advanced DLP. The DLP might strip out attachments, or block the transmission of an email that contains "Reply All" or specific words in the subject line or body of the email. The user is then prompted to either approve the transmission or is notified that the transmission has been blocked.

Egress Monitoring

Egress monitoring is the most important aspect of data leakage prevention. Any time a user attempts to send an email, upload a file, post to a website, or any other activity that could potentially send data out of the organization, the action is temporarily blocked while undergoing analysis. If the activity fails the data leakage test, the activity is permanently blocked and the attempt, including the user's identification, is logged. The system can also be configured to send an alert to the user's manager, describing the blocked attempt.

Typically only pre-screened and pre-authorized servers (such as email, DNS, patch management, and proxy servers) should be allowed to make connections out to the Internet, and only through the firewall. While some servers (Web, FTP, VPN) may accept incoming connections from the Internet, most of these servers have no legitimate reason for initiating their own connection out to the Internet, and should therefore be disallowed. Some servers (database, directory service, DHCP) should not be allowed to access the Internet at all.

In addition to controlling connection attempts in and out of the network, only specific protocols (such as HTTP, HTTPS, DNS, SMTP, SIP, IPSec, L2TP) should be allowed to exit the network as well, especially to the Internet.

End users generally should have no direct connection to the Internet. Instead, all end-user activity should go to the Internet through a proxy server.

Finally, content that is sent out to the Internet (especially email and uploads/posting to websites) should be inspected for disallowed keywords, attachments, and prohibited destinations. Activities containing those disallowed items can be blocked, or a warning sent to users requiring authorization override. Devices that prevent this type of egress are typically placed between the Internet and the internal network.

Watermarking

Digital watermarking is a mechanism that uses steganographic techniques to embed data within media to enforce copyright protection. Data is embedded in a file so that certain hardware or software platforms can validate its authenticity. The hidden data may include information about its source for identity purposes, such as the copyright owner and the media distributor.

Watermarking can help an organization monitor its copyrighted or sensitive materials to prevent them from leaving the network. For example, if a user attempts to send an email attachment that is an image of a confidential product schematic, the egress monitoring system will detect the watermark in this image and block the email.

Egress Monitoring Evasion

Even with robust egress monitoring in place, a user can still circumvent such controls. Several common ways include:

- Steganography: Although the organization can use steganographic techniques to prevent data leakage, an attacker may also be able to use steganography to their advantage. Freely available tools can hide sensitive data within other media, and if the egress monitor doesn't know what to look for, the attacker may be able to successfully exfiltrate this data.

- Encryption: If the contents of a network packet are encrypted, and then embedded into an allowed protocol such as HTTPS, then an IDS/IPS will not be able to perform an inspection of the packet to disallow it.
- *Sneakernet*: This is the process of physically carrying removable media such as thumb drives and DVDs into or out of the network. A technical egress monitoring system won't stop a physical attack like this.

The most common way to mitigate the risk of egress monitoring evasion is to issue company-owned laptops and computers that are locked down, and require users to use them. These devices can be configured to disallow any removable media, as well as disallow users from installing any software on them. Both steganography and encryption require special software to hide the data. Any attempts to install such tools are prohibited automatically and logged by the security system. To prevent users from using their own devices, the company-owned devices are pre-registered with the network access control (NAC) system. If an unrecognized device is plugged into the network or tries to connect to a wireless access point, its connection attempt will be quarantined and disallowed.

SIEM Implementation

The principle behind having a SIEM is the idea that having a single view of all security events from all devices makes it easier to spot trends and recognize patterns that are out of the ordinary. SIEM systems allow an organization to more quickly identify, analyze, and recover from security events. They also help compliance managers confirm that the organization is fulfilling any legal or internal compliance requirements.

SIEM systems work by having multiple agents installed on the various devices collect event data from that device. The agents are deployed in a hierarchical manner to collect data from desktops, servers, network equipment, and security products such as firewalls, antivirus programs, and IDS/IPS systems.

At its simplest, a SIEM can simply use a set of rules and matching patterns to look for events. At a more sophisticated level, a SIEM can cross-correlate events from the various sources to establish relationships and confirmation of security incidents. In larger SIEM deployments, edge devices such as firewalls and routers can pre-process their events, filtering out the noise and only forwarding relevant entries. The risk of this approach is that the subtler aspects of an attack might be filtered out too soon, and thus go unnoticed.

SIEM systems are typically expensive to implement and complex to operate. Originally, PCI DSS was a major driver for SIEM adoption in the credit card industry. Since then, most large organizations have adopted SIEM technology as the backbone of their security monitoring. Many smaller organizations, wanting the benefits of SIEM, look to managed security service providers (MSSP) to provide SIEM functionality for them.

 Note: Because a SIEM device will potentially correlate a large amount of key information about your systems, it should be placed behind the firewall, and not in a public-facing zone such as the DMZ or perimeter network.

Guidelines for Logging and Monitoring

Use the following guidelines when logging and monitoring your systems:

- Implement a continuous monitoring program to support proactive security in your organization.
- Be aware of the danger of false positives and false negatives in intrusion detection systems.
- Place IDSes directly behind firewalls, dual-homed proxies, routers, and VPN servers.
- Place IDSes next to single-homed proxies, servers, and wireless access points.
- Implement egress monitoring with data loss prevention (DLP) to stop sensitive data from leaving your network.

- Implement a proxy server that will handle internal users attempting to access the Internet.
- Ensure that servers that don't need Internet access (for example, databases) aren't public-facing.
- Be on the lookout for egress monitoring evasion techniques like steganography, encryption, and sneakernets.
- Configure company-issued computers to block the installation of evasion tools.
- Implement a SIEM solution in your organization to correlate logs across multiple devices.
- If a SIEM is too expensive to implement and maintain, consider relying on a third party SIEM provider.
- Place SIEM devices behind the firewall so that they're not public-facing.

ACTIVITY 7-4
Discussing Logging and Monitoring

Data Files

C:\093024Data\Security Operations\School-logical-network.pdf

Before You Begin

Open **School-logical-network.pdf**. Examine the diagram from a security perspective.

Scenario

You are the new information security consultant for a local school. After some recent high profile incidents where hackers changed student grades, management has decided that it needs to monitor the network for malicious activity. If possible, they would like hacker activity to be stopped as it happens. They have given you the current network diagram and have asked for your recommendations.

The school has several network zones:

- Wireless: Providing wireless access for 150 students.
- Classroom: A collection of 10 classrooms, each containing 20 computers.
- Production: 7 servers used to provide services to both end users and classrooms.
- End User: 50 desktops and VoIP phones for administrative staff and faculty.
- Perimeter network: Contains the public-facing web server and email server.

The firewall has three interfaces on it:

- Untrusted: Connected to the edge router, which is connected to the ISP.
- Trusted: Connected to the backbone switch in the internal network.
- Perimeter: Connected to the perimeter network (which is also considered untrusted).

In addition, there is a traditional VPN server that has been deployed in parallel to the firewall. Faculty and administrative staff sometimes connect to the VPN server from home.

---

1. Should the school use passive monitoring (intrusion detection) or active monitoring (intrusion prevention)?

2. What is the biggest concern with implementing an IDS?

3. Where would you place IDS sensors on the network?

4. In addition to the firewall, where might you implement data loss prevention?

5. Where should egress monitoring be implemented?

6. How might a hacker evade egress monitoring?

7. If you were to implement a SIEM system, where would you put the central console and where would you place the data collection agents?

TOPIC E

Preventative Measures

Another element of proactive security operations is implementing preventative measures. These measures will help stop an attack before it can cause real damage.

Types of Prevention

Security controls attempt to minimize or prevent security incidents from happening. As such, nearly all security controls have some aspect of prevention to them. They can either be used directly for prevention (or at least mitigation) or can be used to inform and configure prevention systems. The following is a list of controls that have some element of prevention:

• IDS and IPS.
• Blacklisting and whitelisting.
• Sandboxing.
• Honeypots and honeynets.
• Anti-malware.
• Third-party security services.

IDS and IPS for Prevention

As you've seen, an IDS or an IPS can detect anomalous behavior in your networks or on your hosts. An IPS is obviously preventative in the sense that it can actively block attacks.

You can also use a more passive IDS as a preventative measure. A properly configured IDS will alert administrators immediately to a potential attack, and the administrator can use their own judgment before blocking the attack themselves.

Every IDS/IPS needs a useful system for generating alerts so human operators aren't in the dark about any abnormal activity that's been identified. An IDS/IPS alert system has three components/phases:

• **Sensor**: This is the mechanism that actually detects the unwanted or unexpected behavior. It's important to tune the sensor so that it doesn't produce too many false negatives and, at the same time, not over-tune the sensor so that it produces too many false positives. After it's tripped, the sensor produces the alert.
• **Communication**: Once the alert is produced, it needs to be transmitted to the proper recipient. The communication mechanism determines whether the alert gets send to a specific administrator over email; if it triggers a text message sent to a security professional; and whatever other communication scenario is appropriate for the organization.
• **Enunciator**: This system adjusts the alert based on a number of factors. For example, it might change the alert depending on who will receive it. The network admin might receive a technically detailed explanation of the alert, whereas the CISO might receive a more streamlined version. The enunciator can change other characteristics of the alert as well, such as its timing and its format across different transmission media.

The nuances involved in this alert process highlight how important it is to configure detection systems in a number of ways. In order for your IDS/IPS to truly be effective as a preventative measure, it must get the right information to the right people at the right time. Only then can security personnel stop the attack before it becomes a significant problem.

Whitelisting and Blacklisting

Blacklisting is the process of blocking known applications, services, traffic, and other transmission to and from your systems. Blacklists are created when the organization knows the source or mechanism of a potential risk and determines that this risk can be shut out from the organization entirely. This prevents the risk from ever being an issue, and your security professionals will have one less attack vector to watch for.

Blacklists are useful in many cases, such as keeping track of known malicious websites that internal users are prevented from visiting. However, they have two fundamental weaknesses: the first is related to an IDS/IPS false positive. You may end up adding a website, IP address, or whatever it may be to the blacklist that actually has legitimate uses. This can end up being a sort of collateral damage in an attempt to defend against too large of an attack vector scope.

The other main weakness of blacklisting is everything that you don't know. You can't possibly know every single malicious attack vector out there, and the ones on the list might not be comprehensive enough. You're essentially running the blacklist from a limited perspective, one that can't possibly catch up to the ever-changing world of threats.

Whitelisting is a good response to this problem of what you don't know. In a whitelist, you block everything *except* what you trust. In the website example, you have a list of websites that users are allowed to visit, and any site not on this list is blocked. It's much easier to account for what you know is safe or acceptable.

Whitelists are therefore more secure than blacklists, but they're not flawless. They can be incredibly restrictive, preventing users and systems from transmitting data to new or changing recipients. They need to be constantly fine-tuned in order not to interfere with business operations, which can be cost and time prohibitive for some organizations.

Sandboxing

As mentioned previously, sandboxing is the most fundamental security concept underlying virtualization. It is the primary preventative measure offered by any virtualization deployment. Since every virtualized operating system, application, and desktop runs in its own sandbox, it is prevented from accessing and interfering with other virtual machines as well as the host.

One way to securely deploy end user desktops is to run them as virtual machines across the network. The user's computer has a basic operating system that hosts the virtual desktop, but does not keep any of the user's applications or data on it. When the user logs on, the computer connects across the local area network to a server that contains the actual user desktop. The desktop itself is actually a software environment with various configurations such as wallpaper, application shortcuts, and documents. These are downloaded to the host computer and presented for the user to use. When the user logs off, the local copy of the virtual desktop top can either be cached for off-line use or simply discarded.

Alternatively, the desktop might never truly be downloaded to the user's computer. Instead, the user might only be seeing a streaming video representation of the desktop that is actually kept on the server. The local machine allows the user to interact with this presentation by sending mouse clicks and keyboard strokes up to the server. When the user logs off, the connection to the server is broken, and the desktop remain safely on the server.

Another way to use sandboxing in virtualization is to virtualize each application that the user runs. Rather than actually installing an application on the user's computer, it is streamed live from a server into its own sandbox on the user's desktop. This allows the user to run incompatible applications side-by-side on their computer, because the applications are not truly running on the local machine, but rather as virtual machines that are visually streamed to the user's computer.

Honeypots and Honeynets

A *honeypot* is a decoy computer used to distract would-be hackers from attacking the real network. Similarly, a *honeynet* is a decoy network. Honeypots look real but they are not. They are hopefully challenging enough to keep the hacker busy and away from the real servers. Honeypots are typically placed outside the firewall, or in the organization's perimeter network (demilitarized zone). The goal of a honeypot is to keep a would-be intruder busy enough so that information can be collected about that intruder and deterrent actions taken.

Honeypots and honeynets raise the issue of enticement and entrapment. Although the two may seem similar, there is a legal distinction between them. With enticement, you are luring an attacker into providing enough information about them after they have already committed a crime. With entrapment, you are actively soliciting someone to break into your network where they originally had no intention of doing so. Enticement is legal. Entrapment is not. Many system administrators will use the information gathered by a honeypot or honeynet not for legal ends, but to simply block the intruder or take some other preventative action.

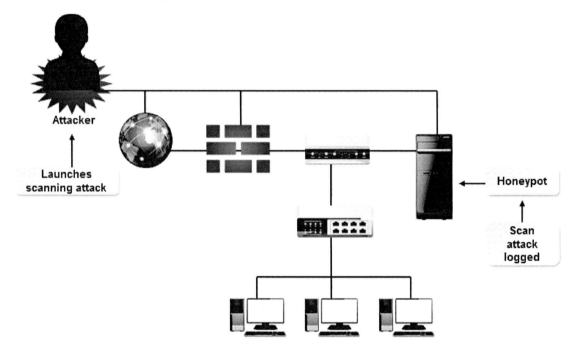

Figure 7-5: A honeypot logging a scanning attack.

Anti-Malware

Because so many hacking attacks are automated using malicious software, one of the most basic preventive measures you can take is to install antivirus/anti-malware software and keep it up-to-date. The challenge of installing such software is that historically no one system has proven to be completely impervious to attack. Different products throughout different periods in time may have been the most effective against malware, but this leadership position has shifted from product to product as new attacks have surfaced.

The problem is that antivirus software requires a certain level of control over the operating system to be effective. This means that by its very nature it will not allow other antivirus or anti-malware products to coexist on the same system. Some organizations have made the mistake of thinking that by installing two antivirus products on their desktops, they will have greater coverage. The reality is that their systems then become very slow under the burden of two products that compete for control over that system.

Some enterprise-wide antivirus products successfully use multiple antivirus products at once. The vendors who have developed such products have worked in cooperation with the antivirus companies to incorporate multiple antivirus scanning engines into the same console. These antivirus products work in harmony together to provide more comprehensive protection for desktops and servers.

Firewalls for Attack Prevention

A firewall is of course a very basic preventive measure that can be installed both as a hardware device at the edge of your network, as well as a software solution on each individual computer. All organizations should insist that user computers and servers maintain software firewalls. Mobile devices can also have software-based firewalls. These are usually bundled together with antivirus, VPN, and other protective apps. The bundle is then known as endpoint protection.

Most hardware-based firewalls have a starting configuration that disallows any traffic in or out of the network. The administrator must then create rules to permit certain kinds of traffic (whitelisting). A common approach is to make a "permit all" rule that allows all outbound connections from the internal network out to the Internet, but disallows any unsolicited inbound connections originating from the Internet. Additional rules can then be added to block users from going to specific sites on the Internet, or from using protocols other than HTTP or HTTPS on the Internet (blacklisting).

Software-based firewalls typically permit all outbound connections from the host to the network, but drop all inbound connection attempts from external hosts. Servers that provide services such as database, file and print, email, and the like, make specific exceptions so that these services can accept incoming client connections across the network. Additionally, client computers should make exceptions in their personal firewall rules to allow servers to connect and manage them.

Most organizations implement both hardware firewalls on the edge of the network as well as software firewalls on every single computer.

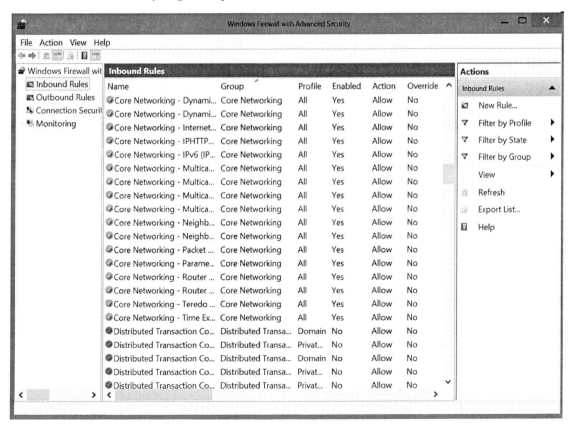

Figure 7-6: Windows Firewall.

Third-Party Security

You can outsource your information security to a third party. Usually this means engaging a Security-as-a-Service (SECaaS) provider. Businesses typically outsource their security when it is more cost effective to do so. Many businesses prefer to let a third-party handle the cost of purchasing, configuring, and maintaining authentication systems, antivirus, security event management, and other security related systems.

Security as a Service provides the following benefits:

- Continuous antivirus updates that are not dependent on user compliance or local configuration management.
- Greater security expertise than is available in the organization.
- Faster user provisioning.
- Outsourcing of administrative tasks.
- A web interface that allows customer in-house administration of security activities.

Guidelines for Implementing Preventative Measures

Use the following guidelines to implement preventative measures in your organization:

- Ensure that all alert systems on IDS/IPS are properly tuned and configured to your computing environment.
- Ensure that alerts contact the right people at the right time so they can work fast to stop an attack.
- Consider blacklisting certain websites, services, and so on.
- Understand the limitation of blacklisting—can't protect against what you don't know.
- Implement a whitelist for a stricter preventative measure.
- Understand that a whitelist may be too strict, negatively affecting business operations.
- Deploy virtual machines to separate their running processes from the underlying host.
- Create honeypots or honeynets to distract attackers and keep them away from real targets.
- Understand the legal difference between enticement and entrapment when it comes to honeypots/nets.
- Consider the weaknesses of single anti-malware systems.
- Look for anti-malware solutions that cooperate to have greater coverage.
- Implement firewalls using whitelisting to allow certain ports or traffic while blocking the rest.
- Alternatively, block certain ports or traffic known to be malicious.
- Contract out preventative security measures to a third party if it is more cost feasible and fits within your risk appetite.

ACTIVITY 7-5
Discussing Preventative Measures

Data Files

C:\093024Data\Security Operations\School-logical-network.pdf

Before You Begin

Review the scenario and the network diagram in the **School-logical-network.pdf** file from the previous activity "Discussing Logging and Monitoring."

Scenario

In addition to monitoring, the school's administration is interested in exploring other preventative security measures. They have asked you to explain different concepts and to give your opinion on the suitability of different preventative technologies for the school.

---

1. School management is concerned about the amount of spam its email server is receiving. Would either whitelisting or blacklisting be a useful tool?

2. Management would like some of the production servers to host virtual machines and virtual applications. What role does sandboxing play in virtualization and how is that useful from a security perspective?

3. If you were to deploy a honeypot, where would you place it?

4. What devices should have anti-malware installed?

5. The school currently has a hardware-based firewall protecting the network. Would it be useful to also install personal (software-based) firewalls on all of the computers?

TOPIC F

Resource Provisioning and Protection

Rather than providing assets and services to users on a case-by-case basis, your business operations will be much more efficient with a scalable system that provisions resources when needed. But with this ease of provisioning comes the need for careful management of the provisioning process and protection for the resources themselves.

Purpose of Provisioning

When you provision something, you provide it or make it available. In IT, provisioning typically means you configure a system to provide its service to the end user. Often, this is accompanied by issuing the user equipment (such as a mobile device or laptop) to access that service. The service can be anything the user wants access to, including:

- Local area network access.
- Wireless network access.
- Mobile network access.
- All of the as-a-service services (SaaS, PaaS, IaaS, IDaaS, etc.).
- Any other service.
- Network share files.
- Application software.
- Removable media.
- Hard copy records.
- Any other resource.

Preferably, provisioning should be as automated as possible. Once the user has been approved and authorized, and any necessary equipment issued, the request for service should then be configured and supplied automatically. The Services Provisioning Markup Language (SPML) is a programming language used to automate all the steps necessary for providing that service. It is used to help coordinate efforts by all the systems involved in providing that service to set up, configure, and grant or revoke user access to the service.

 Note: Although service provisioning is usually granted to end users, it can also be provided to devices, processes, or systems.

Configuration Management

One of the most common mechanisms for provisioning, especially operating systems, software, and patches, is to use a *Configuration Management (CM)* application. This tool can automatically inventory and keep track of hardware and software assets on the network, including versions and licensing. It can deploy operating systems to bare metal boxes (new computers that have no operating system), install or update applications on computers, and deploy service packs and security patches to those devices.

CMs can collect statistics about every system on the network, including uptime, current patch levels, and system health status. They are an excellent tool to keep systems in compliance with regulatory or organizational baselines. They can also be used to help automate software testing and version control. The more expensive CMs are fully automated, though they have the ability to integrate manual deployment as needed.

A CM can automatically inventory practically everything on a system, including:

- Make.

- Model.
- MAC address.
- Serial number.
- Operating system version.
- BIOS/Firmware version.
- Location.
- BIOS passwords.
- IP addresses.
- Asset tags and bar codes.
- Installed software name, vendor, and version.
- Keys and activation codes.
- License type.
- License expiration date.
- License portability.
- Software usage (metering).
- Organization software asset number and contact.
- Service pack/patch level.
- Local users and groups.
- Files and folders.
- Registry settings.
- Services.
- Firewall status.
- Antivirus update level.
- Endpoint protection.
- Any additional configuration information.

This provides the administrator with a complete view of all systems on the network. Additionally, systems that are brought online only occasionally will also be detected, inventoried, and managed by the CM.

CMDB

Another common component of IT Asset Management is the *Configuration Management Database (CMDB)* This is a central repository that stores information about all the significant items in your IT environment. The items are called *Configuration Items (CI)*. They are IT assets that are related to IT processes. Examples of CIs include hardware, software, documents, models, plans, even people.

On the surface, a CMDB seems like just another database that tracks assets. The difference, however, is that a CMDB tracks the interrelations between the CIs. A good CMDB product will provide analytics and a relationship map showing dependencies between CIs. This helps the business analyze any impact a CI might have on a business process.

For example, a web application might obtain its data by reading a table from a particular instance of an Oracle database. This database might in turn depend on a piece of hardware to perform well. A CMDB can discover these relationships. If there are perpetual issues faced by a business process, relevant CIs and their relationships are discovered automatically by the CMDB, and the root cause of the problem identified. The business can then take measures to eliminate the problem.

CMDBs are especially useful in large, complex IT environments. The constant updates to the database give organizations greater insight and control over their environment, which in turn can lead to greater information security.

CM Policies

Like many other security systems, a CM is only as successful as its policy enables it to be. The policy needs to define how the CM process is carried out and how it will benefit the organization. Some of the items that make up a good CM policy include:

- A list of configuration items that are under the CM's control.
- How these items are named.
- How these items are added and removed from the CM's control.
- How the items are subject to change within the CM.
- How the same item is versioned if it appears multiple times in the CM.
- How the CM is enforced within the organization.

CM Practices

Once a policy is in place, a CM in any organization will benefit from certain practices. The *Capability Maturity Model Integration (CMMI)* program developed by Carnegie Mellon University suggests the following:

- Identify configuration items and any related assets that will be placed in control of the CM.
- Describe each item's characteristics in the CM.
- Implement configuration and change management processes for items controlled by the CM.
- Establish baselines for both internal and customer use.
- Ensure that requests to change items are tracked.
- Ensure any changes to items are controlled by the CM.
- Audit the baselines established for the CM items.

Asset Concerns in CM

In order for your configuration management system to be effective, you need to be able to describe an asset's characteristics, including:

- Any compliance requirements the asset is subject to while being managed.
- Any specific concerns related to the asset's implementation.
- The owner(s) of the asset.
- The user(s) of the asset.
- When the asset must be available to its users.
- How users will access the asset.
- Where the asset is stored.
- The business need that the asset addresses.

The last item is the most important—why exactly does this particular asset need to be provisioned? What purpose does it being provisioned serve? Answering these questions is crucial in ensuring that the provisioning process maintains the CIA of the asset.

Asset Inventory

A key aspect of providing service to your users is to know what assets you have that you can give the users. This is especially important when you need to issue laptops, mobile devices, or software licenses. A small organization can periodically conduct a physical count of its assets. A large organization, however, will need a more automated mechanism for tracking its inventory of assets.

Asset inventory does not simply refer to keeping a spreadsheet of what you have. It also refers to what assets have been issued to users, if they are still in use, if they have been lost, if they need replacement, and if they need to be taken out of service (decommissioned). A good asset management system will proactively track the age of assets, and alert the asset management team when it is time to upgrade or replace user devices.

Physical Assets

A physical asset is any hardware the company owns. In IT, it can include computers, servers, mobile devices, desktop phones, computer peripherals, server room racks, routers, switches, security appliances, modems, antennas, cabling—any physical device that is used on the network.

In terms of provisioning, you might have to issue a physical asset to a user as well as configure the system to provide service to the user. For example, when you provision mobile phone service to a user, you would issue the physical mobile device to the user, register the device with the telecommunications provider, and configure your mobile device web server to allow mobile phone wi-fi or incoming Internet connections to the company's network.

Virtual Assets

Virtual assets are not only servers deployed as virtual machines, but they can also be desktop images, guest operating systems, virtual SANs, configuration files, software-defined networking capabilities, cluster resources—anything that is software-based.

With virtual assets, the user already has access to the network and simply wants some service to be stood up quickly for use. The service is typically a virtual machine with a specified operating system, resources, and pre-installed applications.

Before virtualization, departments in a large organization that wanted a server often had to wait a month to get it. Servers were not simply sitting on a shelf in a warehouse waiting to be issued. The request would go through many steps, starting with approving the purchase order, ordering the hardware, waiting for the hardware to be delivered by the vendor, waiting for the server team to install an operating system and the desired applications on the hardware, and then finally delivering the server to the department.

With virtual assets, the department can simply go to the company's intranet portal, place the desired system in a shopping cart, and then submit the request. Criteria for approving such purchases would usually be predetermined, so the provisioning process would happen within minutes. The department that previously had to wait a month to get their server, could usually have it ready for use within an hour.

As with physical assets, virtual assets provide a service and have a lifecycle. The host systems that run virtual assets are periodically upgraded, usually to improve performance or security. At some point, the guest operating system or application running in a virtual machine will no longer be supported by the host, and will have to be decommissioned. Or, the needs of the department may evolve, so that the old sales application that worked so well for the past 10 years no longer does what the business requires. Or possibly no one has used that old virtual machine for the past six months, and it is time to take it down. Virtual assets need to be inventoried, have their usage (and usefulness) tracked, and their lifecycle managed.

Cloud Assets

Cloud assets are virtual assets hosted by a third party on the Internet. As with internally managed virtual assets, they provide tools and platforms for productivity and operations. Organizations often move their virtual assets to the cloud to transfer the cost and complexity of maintaining such assets to another. When inventorying a company's assets, cloud assets must be counted along with all the others.

Because the organization is offloading a lot of management and technical responsibility to the provider, there is often a tendency to forget about the liabilities associated with that asset. Organizations must inventory their cloud assets, track the usefulness of those assets, and manage the lifecycle of those assets as if they were internally managed.

Some examples of cloud assets include:

- Cloud services, like email, collaboration tools, etc.
- Cloud storage.
- Cloud-based virtual machines.
- Cloud-based networking components.

Applications

Applications are also company assets. Whether the software was purchased off-the-shelf (COTS) or developed in-house, it has business value and must be counted in the inventory. This is especially true for software that requires licensing. If you automatically deploy applications such as Microsoft Office to users, you must also track usage and licensing. Most vendors have some mechanism to enforce license compliance. With Microsoft, software licenses must be activated (either online or by telephone call to Microsoft). Failure to do so in a timely manner will cause the application to stop working, or to work in a limited manner (such as users can read but not edit documents).

Some examples of application-based assets include:

- Application processing workloads in a private cloud environment.
- Web services based on protocols like Extensible Markup Language (XML) and Simple Object Access Protocol (SOAP).
- Software as a Service (SaaS) like Microsoft Office Online and Salesforce customer relationship management (CRM).

Hardware Asset Management

While it may seem obvious that physical hardware requires physical security, it also requires appropriate care to maximize its value over its lifetime. Employees are less inclined to take care of equipment that they did not pay for. If you have a formal system in place for tracking hardware assets and tying them to a specific business unit, or even a specific user, it becomes easier to hold that business unit or user accountable. This is especially true when assets are mobile such as laptops and phones.

As always, follow the principle of least privilege and make people accountable for the hardware assets they use. Access to hardware and special areas should be limited to individuals who have an authorized need for them. Printers should be placed close to the people who need to print. Network devices should be stored in data centers and server rooms, and communications closets need to be protected from unauthorized access. Consider using biometric locks with cameras to help protect the sensitive areas.

Companies are well served by creating a clear hardware lifecycle policy. This helps with asset tracking. If implemented properly, it ensures that old hardware is cycled out when its usefulness has passed. It also assures employees that their computer will be replaced or their phone will be upgraded on a regular basis, such as every two or three years.

Software Asset Management

Software management has its own challenges. Uses may try to appropriate or copy software for their own personal use. In addition, managers might not properly store or track software licenses. They might throw out old files when cleaning out a cabinet, not realizing that those bits of paper are necessary to prove that the company owns the software that it is using. It particularly becomes an issue when one suddenly needs tech-support on a crashed system.

Many software vendors including Microsoft, Adobe, and others have put systems in place to help alleviate this problem. Now the licensing is tracked online by the vendor. Records can be accessed later in case the original emails or paper licenses that contain the product keys are lost. For this system to work, however, you generally have to register your company and/or the system serial number that uses the software. You have to create a user account to access these records, and you have to have a mechanism for transferring access to others.

If you have original copies of software, they should be in the custody of a media librarian who will control access to them, maintaining their integrity and limiting their availability. Software that has been installed should be protected at the system level to prevent its binaries (executable files) from being overwritten by viruses and malicious code. The way to do this is to digitally sign these files (most operating systems have this capability) and to apply vendor patches in a timely manner.

Media Management

Most media is in the form of tape, removable drive, or optical disk such as CD and DVD. These can be easily stolen, erased, or damaged in some way. As such, it should be encrypted and not allowed to just lay around. If you send your backups off-site, you should use a bonded courier service. These security methods should be part of a larger media management program that helps the organization identify, track, and control how media is used in the organization.

In particular, a media management program should account for removable media. Removable media is probably the greatest source of media vulnerability to companies today. When users can insert a thumb drive into a system, they can inadvertently (or purposely) introduce a virus or leak information out of the company. The company would not know that its information has been breached, and the user is not likely to report the breach. Another vulnerability of removable media is in its very portable nature: it becomes much easier for anyone, legitimate user or not, to physically move a thumb drive and have it connect to many different interfaces.

In response to these vulnerabilities, a number of vendors sell flash drives that use biometrics to unlock the device, digitally signing and encrypting the contents to help maintain confidentiality and integrity. You can also put technical controls on systems to disallow flash drives from accessing a system, even if they are physically plugged in.

Keep in mind that media need not only be electronic or magnetic. It can also be paper- or film/microfiche-based. This kind of information can be even more vulnerable because it can be read by the casual observer without the aid of any computer system. It could also be photocopied. In the age of camera-based phones, you should particularly protect nonmagnetic media from unauthorized access.

Media Protection Methods

The following protection methods may be valuable to your media management program.

Media Protection Method	Description
Two-man rule	The *two-man rule* is a technique that requires the presence of two individuals at all times to monitor behavior when certain criteria are met. These criteria vary and can include: • The nature of the information being accessed. • When certain activities are underway. • When particular systems or media are in use.
Media inventories	Frequent media-specific inventories will help identify missing items.
Media storage access	Logging access to media storage areas helps identify who might be responsible for media removal.
Portable media encryption	Any protected information that is transferred onto portable media must be encrypted, making unauthorized access to that stored information more difficult.

Media Protection Method	Description
Portable media status	The status and whereabouts of any portable media containing secured information must be carefully tracked and logged.

Hard Copy Records

It's not just hardware, software, and electronic media that the organization needs to protect—even in our digital world, many organizations still retain hard copies of sensitive documents and other data. A records and information management (RIM) system can help you identify hard copies that need protecting, as well as what level of protection each copy requires. RIM programs can also assist the disaster recovery process as vital documents are often kept in hard copy form.

However, like any physical object, hard copies of business documents are vulnerable to floods, fires, and many other types of natural disasters. In the face of these events, you should securely store hard copies in containers that can keep out the elements. There are storage containers available that have at least some measure of protection against fire and water, so place any mission critical copies in these.

You should also make physical backups of these hard copies and secure them in an offsite location. It may also be beneficial to go digital with your backups and convert the hard copies into protected PDFs. This way, it'll be easier to set up redundancy mechanisms, and may it be easier to access the document should a disaster occur.

Guidelines for Provisioning and Protecting Resources

Use the following guidelines when provisioning and protecting resources:

- Implement a configuration management (CM) system to track useful information about the assets in your organization.
- Store CM information in a configuration management database (CMDB).
- Incorporate CM policies that define how items should be named, added, removed, changed, and more.
- Incorporate CMMI practices in your CM such as establishing and auditing baselines of items tracked.
- Ensure that you cover important asset details in your CM, such as who owns the asset and who uses it.
- Clearly define for each asset what use it provides to the business.
- When provisioning physical assets, ensure they are configured properly before the user takes control of them.
- Observe the lifecycle of virtual assets, as they require updating and decommissioning from time to time.
- Ensure that your cloud assets are carefully managed, even if they seem out of your direct control.
- Track usage and licensing of software products.
- Follow the principle of least privilege with regard to hardware access.
- Assign a custodian role to software assets so someone can maintain their integrity and availability.
- Create a media management program that can identify, track, and control access and use of media like DVDs, USBs, etc.
- Implement various media protection methods like the two-man rule and portable media encryption.
- Ensure that your hard copy records are kept physically safe from natural disasters like flood and fire.
- Keep physical backups of sensitive hard copies offsite, or transform them into digital PDFs.

ACTIVITY 7-6
Analyzing Resource Provisioning and Protection

Scenario

In this activity, you will assess your understanding of resource provisioning and protection.

---

1. **What is the Services Provisioning Markup Language (SPML) used for?**
   - ○ It is used to replace XML and websites.
   - ○ It is used to provide security such as authentication in websites.
   - ○ It is used for editing service configuration documents.
   - ○ It is used to help automate the steps necessary to provision a service.

2. **How is a configuration management database (CMDB) different from a regular asset tracking database?**
   - ○ The configuration management database is part of a larger software suite that tracks all items in your network.
   - ○ The configuration management database tracks interrelationships and dependencies between assets.
   - ○ An asset tracking database keeps much greater detail about assets in the network.
   - ○ There's essentially no difference. Vendors use both terms interchangeably.

3. **When tracking assets, what is the single most important characteristic of an asset that you can record?**
   - ○ Its business purpose.
   - ○ Its serial number.
   - ○ Its product key.
   - ○ Its purchase price.

4. **Which of the following considerations is the most important for making an effective configuration management policy?**
   - ○ Its focus on the configuration management process.
   - ○ Its enforceability throughout the company.
   - ○ Its level of detail.
   - ○ Its adherence to good standards.

5. **What are the most fundamental goals of the configuration management process?**
   - ○ Capture as much detail about your assets as possible.
   - ○ Capture as much detail about your processes as possible.
   - ○ Limit which personnel are permitted to change company assets.
   - ○ List your assets in their baseline state, then capture and control all changes to those assets.

6. **What is the single most important concern in asset provisioning?**
   - ○ Identifying why the asset needs to be provisioned in the first place.
   - ○ Identify when the asset was provisioned.
   - ○ Identify how the asset was provisioned.
   - ○ Identify the cost of provisioning the asset.

7. Why is it important for the asset management system to alert managers when it is time to upgrade the asset?

   ○ Because departments need to spend their budget before the fiscal year ends.

   ○ Because managing the lifecycle of any asset includes tracking its age and useful life expectancy.

   ○ Because there should be consistency across deployed assets.

   ○ Because older, slower equipment hurts productivity.

8. When issuing a physical asset, what might you provision besides the device itself?

   ○ Documentation for the device.

   ○ A virtual version of the device as a backup for the physical device.

   ○ A configuration or service provided by the device.

   ○ A website for the device to receive updates from.

9. Why are virtual assets considered to be legitimate company assets, just like physical assets?

   ○ Because they provide a service and have a lifecycle just like a physical asset.

   ○ Because it costs time and money to create a virtual asset, just as it does a physical asset.

   ○ Because the software used in a virtual deployment has to be licensed, just like in a physical deployment.

   ○ Because both virtual and physical assets provide benefit to the company.

10. Why must an organization inventory and track cloud assets, even if a third party is managing those assets?

    ○ Because the organization may have to later take over management of the cloud asset.

    ○ Because the organization will want to verify that the service provider is adhering to the SLA.

    ○ Because the organization will want to track the usefulness of the asset.

    ○ Because the organization will periodically need to verify that the asset is functioning properly.

11. Why is an application also considered to be a company asset?

    ○ Because it provides business value.

    ○ Because its licensing costs money.

    ○ Because it will be part of a physical deployment.

    ○ Because it requires support like other assets.

12. What benefit does a hardware lifecycle policy provide a company?

    ○ It allows a company to deploy consistent hardware across the enterprise.

    ○ It ensures that users have the latest equipment to work with.

    ○ It helps track lost, stolen, or broken equipment.

    ○ It ensures that old equipment is cycled out when its usefulness has passed.

13. Why should a media librarian take custody of original software copies?

    ○ So that the original is not lost.

    ○ So that appropriate backups can be maintained.

    ○ So that all software can be organized into a central location.

    ○ So that the risk of users making illegal copies is reduced.

14. How do flash drives pose a risk to the organization?
- ○ Their use is hard to control.
- ○ They are portable, easy to steal, and are a common way to spread computer viruses.
- ○ Once erased, their data is irretrievable.
- ○ It is hard to put technical controls on the use of flash drives.

15. Why is portable media encryption a good practice to implement?
- ○ Even if the drive or disk is stolen, its contents cannot be easily accessed.
- ○ Users are forced to be more careful when they must encrypt portable media.
- ○ Portable media is less likely to carry a virus when its contents are encrypted.
- ○ The software that encrypts the contents can also be used to inventory and track the device.

16. What steps can be taken to protect hard copies of sensitive data? (Choose two.)
- ☐ Scan the hard copy so that you also have an electronic backup.
- ☐ Carefully file the hard copy in a well-documented filing system.
- ☐ Store multiple copies of the file around the office in case the original is lost.
- ☐ Store copies offsite or in a secure container.

TOPIC G

Patch and Vulnerability Management

A significant part of any system's operational lifecycle is maintaining the system through patch and vulnerability management. New vulnerabilities and software bugs are discovered daily, and you need a process in place to implement patches when they become available.

Patch Management Systems

Unless your network has only a few computers, it is difficult to keep all of your systems updated and patched in a timely manner. Most administrators depend on some sort of patch management system to keep their computers updated.

Although you can configure your computers to get their updates directly from the vendor's website on the Internet, this can clog your Internet link as thousands of computers simultaneously download their updates. Additionally, most administrators prefer to test updates before allowing them to be deployed.

A good patch management system will have the following capabilities:

*   Manage updates for all manner of computers, devices, applications, servers, and server services.
*   Approve or disapprove updates before they are deployed.
*   Automatically register client computers and servers and group them according to need and type.
*   Schedule update deployments to client computers and servers.
*   Schedule update downloads from the vendor's website.
*   Forward approved updates to downstream patch management servers in a hierarchical, distributed manner.

Using a patch management system gives you control over when, how, and which updates go to client computers and servers.

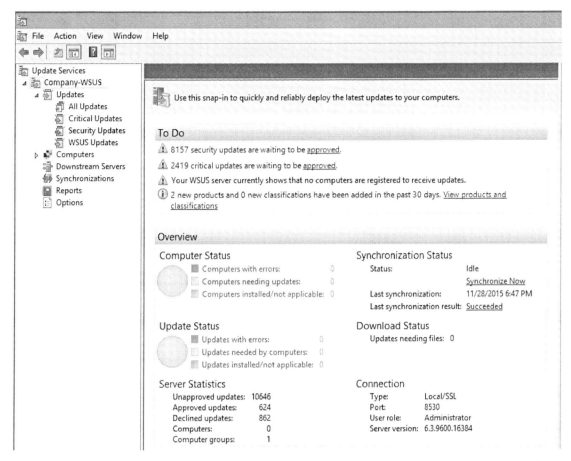

Figure 7–7: The Microsoft Windows Server Update Services (WSUS) Patch Management Console.

Patch Management Sources

Initially, client computers retrieve patches and updates directly from the vendor across the Internet. If you deploy a patch management solution, you will want to configure your clients to retrieve their updates from your server, not the vendor. Your patch management system may get its updates from a single vendor or several vendors. There are many commercially available patch management systems. There are also a number of good free ones as well, though they tend to have a more narrow feature set and less sophisticated interface. Many organizations, especially those with more skilled IT support staff, find that the free systems are quite sufficient for their use.

 Note: Microsoft Windows Server Update Services (WSUS) is a free patch management system that downloads updates from the Microsoft update site, and then distributes them to computers on the local network. If you use Microsoft Active Directory as your directory service, you can create a group policy that configures clients and servers to automatically retrieve patches and updates from the WSUS server.

Additionally, you may choose to use cloud-based patch management. This allows client computers from your organization to retrieve updates that you have tested and approved from anywhere with access to the Internet. Of course, cloud-based patch management is only effective if both you and your clients have sufficient access to the Internet. If you have a global organization, some regions may not have sufficient Internet access for cloud-based patch management to be practical. In those regions, the patch management source for your clients may have to be your local server. The server itself can be scheduled to retrieve updates during off hours when the Internet link is not busy. Most patch management systems will also permit you to side-load the updates (download the updates elsewhere and transfer them via removable media to the patch management server).

Patch Testing

Because a patch intended to fix one problem may inadvertently create another problem, most administrators prefer to test patches before deploying them into production.

While you might think that a single vendor could avoid creating problems within its own software systems, the reality is that many product teams are used to create different parts of a single operating system or large application. They perform integration to make sure that their modules work together, but with the overall products containing millions of lines of code, it is impossible to catch every possible permutation and potential issue up front. This is especially true if your system also has third party applications installed on it. So testing patches before you deploy them to all your users can help prevent service desk calls.

Most patch management systems provide a mechanism for testing patches beforehand on a test machine, approving or disapproving specific patches, and then choose which patches should be deployed to which systems and when.

Guidelines for Patch and Vulnerability Management

Use the following guidelines when implementing patch and vulnerability management:

* Have a system in place that can perform patch and vulnerability management.
* Ensure that this management system has the ability to determine what systems need to be patched, how to deliver those patches, and when to deliver them.
* Consider configuring the patch management system to deploy patches to your computers from an internal server, rather than forcing those computers to retrieve patches directly from the Internet or another vendor.
* If your client machines are on an Active Directory domain, consider pushing out updates to them via Windows Server Update Services (WSUS).
* When possible, test new patches on non-production systems before deploying them across the organization.
* Incorporate a testing process into your patch management system.

ACTIVITY 7-7

Discussing Patch and Vulnerability Management

Scenario

You are the information security consultant for a local school. The school has 20 classrooms, each with computers in them. There are about 400 computers total in the school. Students log on to these computers during lecture, and also to complete assignments. Because students need to be able to download and upload files, they are permitted to plug flash drives into the computers. The operating systems are Windows 7, 8, or 10 Professional, and all belong to a Microsoft Active Directory domain. The school also has several Windows Server 2012 servers that have a minimal to modest load. Management has asked you to recommend a patch management solution to minimize the risk of computer viruses.

1. Which patch management system would be a better choice for the school, a locally deployed server, or a cloud-based system?

2. Should the school purchase a commercial patch management system, or will the free Microsoft version be sufficient?

3. Should the school test patches, even critical security updates, before deploying them?

TOPIC H

Change Management

You know that vulnerabilities in software require patch management, but what about all of the other sources of change in your operations? Systems, policies, processes, procedures—none of these important elements are static. Factors both internal and external will prompt you to adjust these elements to keep them secure and supporting business objectives.

Change Management

Change management, also known as *change control*, encompasses a series of process phases that are used to ensure that a system's confidentiality, integrity, and availability (CIA) triad is well maintained. Even a small organization benefits from change management. If you allow IT personnel and software developers to arbitrarily make changes to a system, network, or application, at best it will create an undocumented system that someone else will have to figure out later. At worst it can take down a system or application, wreaking havoc in your production network with no documentation available to quickly undo the change.

Change management should be a structured, well-understood process like the organization's SDLC choice. People should know their roles and understand what to expect in change management.

Change Management Structure

Your change management structure should contain steps or phases that everyone adheres to. Unless you want to waste time later trying to figure out what someone did, your developers, administrators, and support personnel should not vary from this structure.

Change Control Phase	Description
Requesting the change	The change request requires justification that supports the potential change and a full explanation of the change.
Approving the change	The Change Control Board (CCB) evaluates the change request and approves the change. No change can continue until it is approved.
Communicating the change	Communicate the change and its intended impact.
Documenting the change	The change is recorded and scheduled in the change log.
Testing and reporting results	The CCB should confirm that adequate testing has occurred before approving the change implementation. A backout or failure recovery plan must be in place.
Implementing the change	Changes are implemented within scheduled parameters including date, time, by whom, and so on.
Reporting the change	Successful or unsuccessful changes should always be reported to management so that progress is recognized.

Information Technology Infrastructure Library

The newest development in change control is the development and adoption of the *Information Technology Infrastructure Library (ITIL)*. The ITIL® structure includes a definition and a procedure for change control. It provides concepts and techniques for conducting development, infrastructure, and operations management for information technology.

ITIL is published and circulated in a book series that covers IT management. The name ITIL is a registered trademark of the United Kingdom's Office of Government Commerce (OGC). Other international governmental and commercial organizations are quickly embracing and implementing the ITIL structure.

Change Management Components

The following table describes three major components of a change management system. These components, in their own way, help ensure a smooth transition between different states of the object being changed.

Change Management Component	Importance
Baselining	Without a baseline to compare against, it'll be very difficult for you to confirm that a change is meeting certain standards. Your change must not only add value to the object and thus the organization, but it shouldn't contradict the security requirements you've worked hard to define.
	For example, you may be upgrading the authentication mechanism used by your remote access server. This new mechanism may be more secure and easier to configure, making it easier for your network admins to maintain. However, your access control policy has set a baseline for mandatory access control (MAC) that must be enforced organization wide. What if this new authentication mechanism doesn't use MAC by default? You need to be wary of how changes like this might interfere with your established standards for operation security.
Versioning	Keeping track of versioning information is essential to the change management process for two main reasons. The first is that you can capture the current state of an object and more easily compare that version against your proposed changes. This will give you a better picture of how the object will change and what effect it might have on other objects in the organization.
	For example, assume you need to change how the roles in an RBAC system are structured. If you compare this proposed change with the current or even past versions, you can see how certain users might be given more or less access than they need as a result of this change.
	The other strength of versioning is the ability to quickly and painlessly roll back a change. After all, even when you put changes through a significant amount of tests, there may still be issues that crop up from time to time. Saving past versions of an object will enable you to bring that object back to a state that you know is stable.

Change Management Component	Importance
Security impact analysis (SIA)	Similar to a business impact analysis (BIA), a security impact analysis (SIA) determines how changes to an object will impact the existing state of security in the organization. Some changes in the organization may seem to have no relevance to security at first, but there is always the potential for security operations to be weakened as a result of even the most benign change. The SIA requires critical and creative thinking to envision potential scenarios in which a change could negatively affect security. For example, onboarding a new employee may not seem like an overt risk, but when you consider that new employees aren't ingrained in your security culture, don't necessarily have the same level of training and awareness as others, and are yet another attack vector for social engineers to target, you begin to see how even one more staff member might weaken operational security. Ultimately, an SIA should assess impact as well as provide recommendations to resolve risk, if needed.

Guidelines for Implementing Change Management

Use the following guidelines when implementing a change management process:

- Use change management to avoid not knowing how to address problems that may result from changes to your systems.
- Establish a change management structure that goes through the following phases:
  1. Request
  2. Approval
  3. Communication
  4. Documentation
  5. Testing
  6. Implementation
  7. Reporting
- Implement a baseline to ensure that any changes meet this standard at the very least.
- Use versioning to compare the current state of an object to the proposed change.
- Use versioning to have a quick and easy method for rolling back problematic changes.
- Perform a security impact analysis (SIA) to evaluate how a change may alter security in the organization.

ACTIVITY 7-8
Analyzing Change Management

Scenario
In this activity, you will assess your understanding of change management.

1. **What is the ultimate goal of change management?**
   - ○ To track all changes in the network.
   - ○ To continue to uphold the confidentiality, integrity, and availability of the organization's systems.
   - ○ To control all changes to devices and processes in the network.
   - ○ To simplify administration.

2. **Why should a Change Control Board (CCB) approve a change before it is implemented?**
   - ○ To maintain discipline in the organization.
   - ○ To maintain centralized control.
   - ○ To ensure that the change is appropriate for the entire enterprise.
   - ○ To prevent ad-hoc solutions based on individual preference.

3. **What role does a Security Impact Analysis (SIA) play in change management?**
   - ○ To determine possible risk and offer mitigations.
   - ○ To determine possible cost and offer cost reductions.
   - ○ To determine possible cause and offer counter-effects.
   - ○ To determine possible alternate scenarios and offer a recommendation.

TOPIC I

Incident Response

Despite your best efforts, incidents can and will happen. Whatever the size and impact of the incident, you need to have a plan in place to respond, otherwise you'll be scrambling to keep your operations out of harm's way.

Incident Response Process

From the perspective of the security operations team, incident response is now becoming a large part of their duties. Cyber attacks are constantly evolving and increasing in sophistication. In order to be able to effectively respond to incidents, the security operations team will need to continuously update their own skills, including the ability to recognize and respond to incidents. No matter the form that incidents will take, incident response has these basic steps:

1. Detect a problem.
2. Evaluate and analyze the problem.
3. Mitigate the damage.
4. Recover systems and remediate the problem.
5. Report details of the incident.
6. Determine any lessons learned.
7. Implement preventive controls.

Resources

The following organizations can assist you in developing an incident response framework for your own organization:

- Computer Emergency Response Team Coordination Center (CERT/CC)
- AusCERT
- Forum of Incident Response Teams (FIRST)
- NIST
- British Computing Society
- Canadian Communications Security Establishment (CSE)

IRT Roles and Responsibilities

In the realm of cyber security, there are a number of roles people play. If you intend to have your own Incident Response Team (IRT), it must be adequately staffed, properly trained, and sufficiently funded.

Within your own company, the following departments should be represented on the incident response team:

- IT
- Information security
- Physical/corporate security
- Executive management
- Human resources
- Legal
- Internal audit
- Media/Public relations

In addition to your own internal team members, incident response may include any of the following specialty roles. These can come from your organization or external agencies:

* **Computer Forensics Analyst** : Someone who tries to uncover digital data such as emails or erased files.
* **White Hat**: Someone who conducts vulnerability assessments or penetration tests of systems. They use the same techniques that real hackers would use to uncover system or process vulnerabilities.
* **Information Security Manager**: This is usually someone who was a digital forensics investigator for a number of years and now manages a forensics team.
* **Special Agent**: Someone who works in the cybercrimes or anti-terrorism unit of a government agency such as the military, the FBI, the Secret Service, the Department of Homeland Security, or others.

Incident Response Management

The incident response team won't do you much good unless they've been trained to both handle specific incidents and uphold your organization's specific security requirements. A successful team also needs to be managed closely to prevent a situation from becoming worse. What should the team be allowed to do? What should they not? Who will make these decisions, and are they absolute or on a case-by-case basis? These are the questions that an incident response management program needs to answer to ensure a smooth recovery of operations.

For example, one of the most critical roles is that of first responder. Because computer evidence is usually intangible and can be easily damaged, the first responder needs to take special precautions to prevent intentional or accidental deletion or damage to this evidence. Shutting down a server to stop hacking attack would probably destroy the evidence. Accessing files to look at them would change the last-accessed or last-modified timestamps of files, damaging the integrity and authenticity of the evidence. This in turn could destroy its usefulness in court or even for the company's internal purposes. Proper management procedures will ensure that first responders take correct action that will both keep business operations running, while retaining evidence of an attack.

Additionally, incident response management needs to provide the team with all of the tools and resources they need to get the job done. You don't want to wait until an incident is underway to find the right application to perform the analysis. Instead, have a plan in place to identify and evaluate potential resources, and then select the best ones based on your evaluation.

Detection

In the detection phase, the first hints that something might be occurring start to surface. Sometimes a non-technical staff member will notice something that doesn't seem quite right. The organization should have a clear escalation procedure so that the IT team is immediately notified. If necessary, that team can then escalate to a more specialized incident response team.

The following table lists some of the common sources, both technical and non-technical, that can detect an incident or assist in detection.

Source	Indicator Example
Anti-malware software	An alert generated when a virus signature is detected on a host system.
Network intrusion detection system/network intrusion prevention system (NIDS/NIPS)	An alert generated after an automated port scan is detected.
Host intrusion detection system/host intrusion prevention system (HIDS/HIPS)	An alert generated after the cryptographic hash of an important file no longer matches its known, accepted value.

Source	Indicator Example
System logs	An entry in the operating system event log indicates when a user has signed in to a host.
Network device logs	An entry in the firewall log indicates a dropped connection intended for a blocked port.
Security information and event management (SIEM)	An alert is generated if anomalous behavior is detected in any relevant logs.
Flow control device	A higher amount of traffic across the network than normal indicates an attempted Denial of Service (DoS) condition.
Internal personnel	Employee testimony indicates that they may have witnessed a breach in progress.
People outside the organization	An external party claiming to be responsible for an attack indicates that this is the case.
Research	Third-party research and vulnerability database information indicates a new threat that could be targeting your organization.

Evaluation and Analysis

Evaluation and analysis efforts can be challenging. Even beyond the huge number of detection alerts generated daily, many of these alerts may end up being false positives. In the analysis phase, you must be able to separate false positives from a real indicator of an incident.

Even if an alert or log entry is not a false positive and actually indicates something adverse has occurred, this does not necessarily mean this is the result of an incident. Servers fail, workstations crash, and files are modified due to errors caused by both machines and humans. Yet, these do not automatically tell you whether your organization has just suffered a significant attack or an accident.

In many cases, it comes down to your own judgment as a professional and the consensus of your team. To aid you in making these judgments, you should not only consult with other security professionals, but you should also correlate alerts, log entries, and other potential indicators. A strong correlation will go a long way toward indicating either that an incident has occurred or convincing you that one has not.

An incident analysis can benefit from the following:

- Document all systems within your organization, including hardware, software, utilities, and so on. This will ensure that nothing slips past your analysis.
- Set a baseline for normal behavior. This way, you'll be able to compare a system as it currently exists against the baseline, and if something is off, it will be easier to analyze the divergence.
- Retain logs from all sources. Incidents are sometimes identified months after the fact. Not having these logs will severely impact your analysis efforts.
- Correlate events, alerts, and other potential indicators across all sources. Finding a pattern of action that is replicated in both a NIDS and a host's system log will making it easier to determine the method of an attack.
- Research reputable Internet sources for information. Consulting security industry websites and security-centered forums may provide valuable insight into an incident.
- Filter out irrelevant or inconsequential sources of information. Too many sources with too much data can complicate your efforts.
- Properly document analysis findings in a database. Being able to quickly refer back to your previous results may help you correlate and evaluate data as efficiently as possible.

Response and Mitigation

When first responding to an incident, you should immediately assess your priorities so you can mitigate the damage. What requires immediate attention, and what can wait? *Triage* is a medical term that indicates the priority of patient treatment. In an emergency room, the most severe cases are seen first.

In a computer incident scenario, once the team has analyzed the situation and determined the incident, they implement a triage approach by responding to the situation based on criticality. If multiple events are occurring, the most serious event will be handled first and the remaining events will be intercepted based on risk priority.

The tricky part of any stage of your response is that you may inadvertently contaminate a crime scene. If you don't care about potentially prosecuting hackers are cyber criminals, then you can simply focus on containing the damage, discovering the problem, and bringing the system back online.

Recovery and Remediation

Recovery can range from something very basic, such as restoring an operating system image to a computer, to a very complex process that involves moving all personnel to a new location and setting up operations there. It might also not be possible to recover damaged data, especially if there is no backup. In that case, suitable contingencies to continue business operations must proceed. Before you recover a system, you must make sure that it will not be vulnerable to the same attack or loss that took it down in the first place. This might require patching the replacement, or relocating it to a more secure environment.

When you do recover your system, you almost certainly will want to improve its configuration to minimize the risk that a repeat incident will happen in the future. This could be as simple as applying new patches, tightening access control rules, or changing the antivirus software. Consider allowing a different team to conduct a vulnerability assessment on the system once you've patched it. Fresh sets of eyes and a different perspective are generally more effective in finding any overlooked weaknesses.

Remediation goes beyond simply recovering the system. In remediation, you are trying to stop or reverse the damage caused by the incident. It may require special efforts to bring business productivity to its original level. If the incident was publicly damaging to the company, remediation could include PR to restore an organization's reputation or customer service levels.

Remediation also tries to analyze the incident to discover its root cause (or causes) so that the incident can be prevented from happening again. By following investigative steps, working your way backwards, you can trace the series of events that led to the incident back to its root cause. Once you know the root cause, you can (hopefully) put controls in place to prevent the root cause, and thus the chain of events that led to the incident, from occurring again.

Consider Investigations

Because you want to be able to restore business functionality after an incident, special attention should be paid to the recovery phase. If you intend to investigate the incident as a computer crime, especially if you intend to prosecute based on your findings, you need to make sure that all evidence has been collected, documented, and is in proper custody before you recover the system.

In some cases, it may be necessary to completely preserve the system as evidence in an investigation. In that case, you would have to recover the service that system offered by setting up a whole new server, install and configure the operating system and any software as necessary, and restore backups to that new server. Many IT departments now use virtual machine copies of critical servers to quickly restore service.

Reporting and Documentation

After you consider the incident to be closed, you need to document it and report on it to upper management so that the impact to the business is known and resources can be allocated to help prevent it from happening in the future. Other than business impact, a typical incident report will detail what is known about an incident, including:

- The source(s) of the incident.
- The vectors used to trigger the incident.
- What systems were targeted in the incident.
- The specific impact and change to each system.
- The actions taken by the incident responders to mitigate the incident.
- The actions taken by the incident responders to recover systems and business operations.
- The actions taken by the incident responders to mitigate any lingering effects of the incident.
- The current state of the systems and if there are any unresolved issues.
- Lessons learned as a result of the incident and the organization's response.

Keep in mind that you may need to tailor your reports to different audiences. Upper management is likely not interested in this level of detail, so you should speak directly to what they are interested in —the financial impact of the incident, as well as its effect on how the organization is perceived by its customers.

Regulatory Reporting

In addition to reporting incidents to management, some organizations may be required to report incidents to a government agency or law enforcement. For example, any U.S. civilian government office is required to report personal privacy breaches to the U.S. Computer Emergency Response Team (CERT) within an hour of discovery. Other industries such as energy, financial, healthcare, construction, tobacco, food and drug, and others will have their own regulatory bodies that the organization must comply with.

The security professional must know what response types are required by both organization management and law. The company's security policy should clearly spell out conditions that require reporting, as well as the target, scope, type, and timing of that reporting.

Lessons Learned

Not only should you document what happened during an incident and how you responded, but you should also document afterwards what this incident means for your security. A *lessons learned report (LLR)* includes an analysis of security events and incidents that can provide insight into directions you may take to enhance security for the future.

Essentially, you will be identifying the elements of your security that need improving, and how you can go about improving them in the best way possible. The more you learn from your successes and mistakes, the more fine-tuned your judgment will be. This is an invaluable skill to have, especially if you're called on to solve complex, open-ended problems.

The majority of the LLR comes in answering a few simple questions. The following are just a few of the questions that you should ask when writing an LLR:

- What actions did you take, and how effective were they?
- Is this the optimal solution? In other words, is the solution that you used a stop-gap measure, or is this something that you could reproduce consistently and use as a policy?
- Are there more capable solutions out there?
- How did the teams react to the issue? Could they have solved the incident more quickly or efficiently?
- What did this incident cost the organization, in terms of both money and time?
- In the event of the same or a similar incident occurring, how would you respond differently?

* Do the answers to these questions necessitate a change in your security policy?

Make sure that management then acts upon the recommendations from the lessons learned. It is very demoralizing to staff to have the team uncover the root cause of an incident, making recommendations for preventing the incident from happening again, only to have management ignore the report's findings.

Guidelines for Implementing Incident Response

Use the following guidelines when responding to incidents:

* Follow a step-by-step incident response plan, making sure to take action for each step.
* Ensure that all relevant departments are included in the incident response process in some way.
* Incorporate specialty roles like white hat pen testers when appropriate during an incident.
* Ensure that incident responders are carefully managed and are given the tools they need to do their jobs.
* Consult various sources of detection inside and outside of the organization to identify an incident.
* Evaluate and analyze a potential incident to determine if a response is warranted.
* Set baselines, correlate event logs, and implement other analysis tasks to help make this determination.
* Triage the effects of an incident to handle the most serious issues first.
* Strengthen an affected system while recovering it to ensure it is not still vulnerable.
* Use remediation to go beyond recovery and reverse the damage of an incident.
* Report the details of the incident and its response to management.
* If necessary, draft a report to any legal or regulatory agencies that require it.
* Follow up the main report with a lessons learned report (LLR).
* Document what went right, what went wrong, and what can be improved in the LLR.

ACTIVITY 7-9
Discussing Incident Response

Scenario

You are the information security officer of a pharmaceutical company. The company has just developed a formula that could be a game changer in curing the common cold. Test batches of the formula have been created and have been put in the laboratory vault, where they are guarded by a time lock that requires two people to simultaneously open it. The company CEO is planning to hold a press conference about the drug the next day.

The night before the announcement, one of the guards hears a noise in the corridor by the server room and goes to investigate. Suddenly, an alarm sounds at the security desk. Someone has pressed the hostage sequence on the laboratory door's cipher lock. The guard at the desk scans the monitors to see what's going on, only to find that the ones showing the lab area are blank. Someone has cut the CCTV feed from those cameras. Knowing the situation might be very dangerous, the guards wait for law enforcement to arrive.

When the police officers approach the lab, they find the door is ajar. Laboratory and computer equipment lay strewn about the floor. The sound of frantic hammering and shouts for help come from a nearby closet. One of the scientists is locked inside. Once released, he tells the police that two masked gunmen forced him at gunpoint to open the laboratory door. They inserted a thumb drive into his computer and made him give them a copy of the formula. They also tried to get him to open the vault. Angry that the vault would not open with only one person, they shoved him into the closet and proceeded to ransack the lab. By the time the police arrived, the gunmen had fled.

You have been called to the scene to assess the technical damage and to help mitigate loss. Senior managers have also arrived to hear the story and survey the damage. To everyone's relief, you remind people that, although the formula appeared unencrypted on the scientist's computer when the gunmen took a copy, it was protected by digital rights management. This was a safeguard that you, the CISSP, instituted months ago. Any copy made to an external drive or sent by email attachment would be protected by 256-bit encryption. It would be essentially unusable to a thief. You also point out that any additional unauthorized activities on the computer will have been logged by the computer's host intrusion detection system—another safeguard that you insisted on when the computer was first issued to the scientist.

1. While the nature of this attack was mostly physical, what cyber damage will you look for?

2. Are there any additional incident response team members that might become involved besides the company's internal team?

3. As a first responder, what must you be particularly careful about when gathering computer evidence?

4. How can you detect any cyber theft or cyber damage to the computer?

5. As you evaluate and analyze damage to the computer, what will you do to ensure that any discoveries can be easily accessed for further examination?

6. As you initially respond to the damage, what will you firmly keep in mind as you perform your triage?

7. Will there be any need for remediation as you recover the computer system?

8. What level of reporting and documentation should you provide in your investigation?

9. Will the company need to report the incident to a regulatory body?

10. When listing lessons learned in your report, what is the single most important thing you can do?

TOPIC J

Investigations

Forensic investigations go hand-in-hand with incident response. Not only must you stop an incident, but you'll also want to determine who or what is responsible, as well as how exactly it was carried out. Following proper forensic procedures is a must for any organization that seeks to prosecute a computer crime.

Investigative Procedures

In an investigation, you are seeking to acquire, examine, and report on information found on computer systems and networks that might pertain to a criminal or civil matter. When investigating potential cyber crimes, it's important to remember that nearly anything someone does on a computer or network will leave a trace. This could include deleting files, changing registry entries, or sending instant messages. Operating system and application logs, the browser cache, even the files and drives themselves can give clues as to what happened, how the information traveled, and what systems are affected.

When investigating computer crime, your investigative technique is not merely a matter of using some software or hardware device to discover evidence. Your investigation is a set of procedures and protocols that are:

- **Methodical**. They are comprehensive, able to cover all manner of incidents and attacks. They also have a specific purpose and prevent the investigator from being careless with the investigation.
- **Verifiable**: They are able to objectively assess a situation without bias, conflict of interest, or anything else that might taint the investigation. Without accurate, verifiable data, your investigation will go nowhere.
- **Auditable**: A third party can easily confirm the legitimacy of your investigation and its tactics. This will help solidify your investigation's integrity, ensuring greater success.

Your investigative technique will follow four basic steps:

1. Discover evidence.
2. Collect the evidence.
3. Analyze the evidence.
4. Present findings.

Investigation Types

There are several investigation types.

Type	Description
Operational	Operational investigation seeks to discover the root cause of why or how something happened within an organization so that updated controls can be put in place. When there is a cybercrime, there can always be lessons learned that are applied to security operations to help minimize the chance that the same incident will happen again.
	In all cases of operational investigation, you must be able to refer to your existing operations manual to see if process and procedure was followed properly. You might discover that procedure was followed, but the procedures themselves were inadequate. Conducting a methodical review of how operations should run versus how they ran when the incident occurred will help you discover gaps in personnel training, security controls, and policy.
Criminal	In a criminal investigation, you are collecting clues and evidence to determine if a crime has been committed. You uncover and present the facts in a way to identify a criminal and prove that they broke the law. These laws could be everything from local to federal. If the organization decides that it wants the perpetrator to be brought to justice, it must contact law enforcement and file a police report.
	In a criminal investigation, the police or other government agencies will be involved, and will take over the investigation from the organization. At this point the organization will have to cooperate with law enforcement, including possibly surrendering servers, mobile devices, and other equipment that may have been involved in the crime. High impact cyber crimes in the United States are investigated by the FBI and the Department of Homeland Security (U.S. Secret Service and U.S. Immigration and Customs Enforcement).
	For cybercrime, local police departments are only just beginning to catch up in their ability to handle and respond to incidents. The Department of Homeland Security has published a document called the *Law Enforcement Cyber Incident Reporting resource* which provides information on when, what, and how law enforcement should report a cyber incident to a federal entity.
Civil	A civil investigation is one in which you collect data and supporting materials to present in a non-criminal court action. This could take the form of a lawsuit between two parties, investigation of insurance fraud, child support claims, and other noncriminal matters. Companies that cannot criminally prosecute someone for hacking or other wrongdoing might seek civil damages against that individual instead. Most civil damages are in the form of financial payments.
Regulatory	Regulatory investigation is handled by a government agency. Administrative law, or regulatory law, is that which is created by the legislature. These laws can be at the local, county, state, or federal level. These government agencies have been empowered to determine what is or is not legal activity. Each agency or law governs a particular industry or area of public concern. Examples include food and drug safety, pollution control, worker wages, market entries, and the export of goods.
	An example of how regulatory law might impact cybersecurity is the recent move by the US Department of Commerce to restrict the export of hacking tools. The intent of the regulation is to help keep hacking technology out of the hands of international attackers and repressive regimes, but this move has strong opposition from some in the cybersecurity industry.

Note: For more information on the Department of Homeland Security's efforts to combat cybercrime, see the website "Combating Cyber Crime" at **www.dhs.gov/topic/combating-cyber-crime**.

> **Note:** For more information on new anti-hacking regulations, see the article at **http:// thehill.com/regulation/cybersecurity/248579-cyber-industry-assails-anti-hacking-regulations**.

E-Discovery and Digital Forensics

Electronic discovery (e-discovery) is the process of looking for, locating, securing, and searching through electronic data in the hopes of finding evidence that can be used in a civil or criminal trial. It can be performed on a specific server, or across a network. It can also be court ordered. E-discovery is often performed by a white hat working for or alongside the organization.

When you're performing e-discovery for a forensic investigation, all manner of data is potential evidence: text files, images, calendar files, databases, audio files, video files, animations, websites, email, programs—if it's electronic, it can be discovered and searched. This can even include malware and spyware. What makes e-discovery so interesting is that people are often more careless with electronic information than they are with hard copy information such as memos and postal letters.

Digital forensics, also called *computer forensics*, follows e-discovery. It is a specialized field dedicated to the analysis of computer-based evidence that has been identified in the e-discovery process.

Digital forensics has been used to convict many criminals including terrorists, sexual predators, and murderers. A terrorist may use the Internet to recruit. A predator may use social networking sites to stalk prey. A murderer may brag about their activities online, or post blogs or rants that reveal their intent to kill others. In most cases, criminals who use technology usually fail to adequately cover their tracks afterwards. They don't realize that even if they delete files on their hard drive, a magnetic imprint will still exist, or some server on the Internet will still have a copy.

Evidence Collection Process

Once a crime has been committed, if evidence is uncovered, it must be secured and properly recorded and collected.

Evidence will be both physical and virtual. Physical evidence will include hardware and devices such as servers, workstations, laptops, mobile phones, cabling, network devices, and so on.

Virtual evidence will be files or code running in memory. As such it is trickier to handle, because it would be easy to destroy virtual evidence without realizing it. If the evidence is a malicious process running on the network, you certainly don't want to unplug the network or shut off the server that is running that process.

Evidence collection involves the gathering and processing of evidence. A piece of evidence can potentially go through these steps:

1. Discovery and recognition.
2. Protection.
3. Recording.
4. Collection.
5. Identification.
6. Storage and preservation.
7. Transportation.
8. Presentation in court.
9. Return to victim or owner.

Evidence Collection Techniques

Forensic experts can use numerous methods to obtain evidence specific to computer systems. These include:

- Analyzing software for the presence of viruses or worms.

- Obtaining forensic copies of disk drives.
- Analyzing disk drive areas for hidden information including slack space, deleted files, and unallocated space.
- Analyzing network traffic to locate criminal activity.

Cybercrime Evidence Collection

Because so much of the evidence is volatile, collecting evidence about cybercrimes requires special training and collection methods that differ from physical crimes.

If possible, even before the investigation begins, it is necessary to secure the scene. No one should approach computers, touch keyboards, nor turn on or off any device. Doing so may damage or contaminate evidence. You should also not disconnect any wires, remove any peripheral devices, connect or disconnect related systems, or do anything to change configurations or shut down operating systems. Trained investigators understand how to capture evidence from systems without compromising the system security or damaging evidence.

A complete copy of memory, cache memory, and disk must be made first. That copy should then be examined, and not the original. The original system must be photographed, tagged, bagged, and tracked.

When examining the copy for evidence, the most volatile evidence, such as processes running in RAM, must be captured first. This task is best left to professionals who have been trained in the proper practices. What is important for the CISSP to know is what *not* to do: do not attempt to undertake a digital investigation until you are properly trained and certified. Novices can often damage or remove all traces of evidence if they approach evidence gathering the wrong way.

Whole courses and certifications exist that focus solely on digital forensics. Trained investigators know that everything is evidence. They are cautious and careful about what they collect and how they collect it. They know that the courts typically view digital evidence as hearsay evidence or as corroborating evidence for expert witness testimony. The slightest question raised by the defence about the integrity of digital evidence can render that evidence inadmissible in court.

Rules of Digital or Electronic Evidence

Digital evidence is much more fragile and volatile than other types of criminal evidence such as fingerprints, hair, bullets, and fibers. Digital evidence can be easily erased, damaged, forged, or altered. Evidence of any kind should follow these rules:

- **Be relevant**. The evidence must pertain to the case at hand.
- **Be probative**. The evidence needs to help prove a fact.
- **Be authentic**. The source of evidence should not be called into question, raising doubts about your investigation.
- **Be accurate**. Inaccurate evidence will compromise the integrity of your investigation.
- **Be complete**. You don't want to miss key information that could change your understanding of the situation.
- **Be convincing**. Your goal in a criminal proceeding is not to convince yourself, but to convince others.
- **Be admissible**. Evidence must be collected according to all laws or it may be deemed invalid in court.

Chain of Custody

The *chain of custody* is the record of evidence history from collection, to presentation in court, to return or disposal. In security terms, the chain of evidence is used as a legal control to provide for the accountability and integrity of evidence. If it is small enough, physical evidence is often bagged and sealed to protect it.

The record should contain information about the evidence, such as the description, dimensions, markings, and serial numbers, who obtained the evidence, what the evidence is, when and where the evidence was obtained, who secured the evidence, and who had possession of the evidence.

The improper handling of evidence or the destruction of the chain of custody information may lead to the inadmissibility of the evidence in court.

Analyze and Store

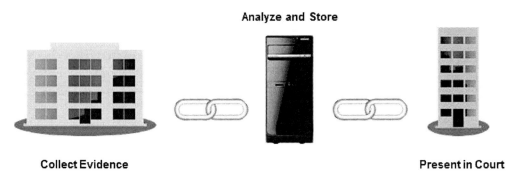

Collect Evidence   **Present in Court**

Figure 7-8: The chain of custody.

Example: Computer Removal

When computer crimes are reported, one of the first response activities is removing computers from the crime location. They are tagged with a chain of custody record to begin the process of making the evidence secure for future presentation in court.

Forensics Admissibility Guidelines

For evidence to be admissible in court, certain rules must be followed. However, the rules of evidence are not consistent among countries or even among various court systems in the United States. There are five common rules that govern the admissibility of evidence in both criminal and civil court proceedings.

Common Rule of Evidence	Description
Reliable	The evidence presented is consistent and can lead to a common conclusion.
Preserved	The chain of custody should record how evidence is kept safe from tampering.
Relevant	The evidence must pertain to the case at hand.
Properly identified	The evidence is not mistaken for something it is not.
Legally permissible	Determined by the judge and the rules of evidence of a particular court.

 Note: For more information regarding U.S. Federal Rules of Evidence, visit www.law.cornell.edu/rules/fre/.

Admissibility Considerations

For evidence to be used, it must be collected in legal ways. If law enforcement agencies are involved in gathering evidence, the collection must not violate the 4th Amendment to the U.S. Constitution. Illegal search and seizure is not allowed. If evidence is gathered internally, the 4th Amendment does not apply, but the court must be assured that the collection practices safeguard the accuracy and integrity of the evidence.

The courts prefer original documents. However, if an original document has been destroyed or damaged, or cannot be obtained for legal reasons, the court may admit copies of documents.

If a company uses monitoring to collect evidence on their employees, the provisions of the Electronic Communications Privacy Act (ECPA) apply. Employees must be notified in advance of the monitoring practice and agree in writing to the monitoring. ECPA violations can result in criminal prosecution of the monitoring organization.

Log files are often the foundation of electronic evidence. The admissibility of log files is dependent upon their protection from modification. A simple way to ensure that protection is to write the log files to restricted volumes with limited access. Another method is to create a hash of the log files to prove that they have not been altered. Additionally, log files must be evaluated and reviewed periodically to be used as evidence. Log files that have not been audited and verified will be excluded from the court.

 Note: For an authoritative reference guide on cyber forensics, see the *Official (ISC)² Guide to the CCFP CBK*. This is the official guidebook for the Certified Cyber Forensics Professional.

Root Cause Analysis

Not all investigations look for malicious intent. Some incidents may be caused by an accident or a chain of unforeseen events. Root cause analysis (RCA) seeks to uncover that ultimate cause of an incident.

The most straightforward way to find the root cause is to keep asking the question "what was the immediate thing that allowed this to happen?". With each answer, you again ask the same question: what is the immediate thing that allowed that to happen? You keep asking this question, working your way backwards. Typically, the root cause can be uncovered in about six questions. And typically, there will be more than one root cause. In most cases, the root cause or root causes ultimately fall on management, with insufficient process or controls in place.

For example, say a server was stolen over the weekend. Ask the team what was the immediate circumstance that allow the server to be stolen? The answer might be something like "on Sunday, the server room door was left ajar." The next question would be then "why was the server room door left ajar?" The next answer could be something like "because it was too hot." You would then in your interviews ask "who determined that it was too hot?" Then perhaps someone would answer "Joe made that decision." You would then interview Joe. He would tell you that while he was working in the server room he was sweating and he noticed the temperature was over 90 degrees. Your obvious next question would be "why would the server room ever reach that kind of temperature?"

In asking questions backwards you find out eventually that the alarm system which controls and reports on the HVAC system wasn't working properly. You find out that Joe attempted to follow protocol when environmental controls are not functioning properly, but the guard, whom he was supposed to notify, was away from his post, and when Joe repeatedly called his manager, there was no answer. At some point, you have enough information to determine where the process broke down.

Evidence Analysis

Analyzing evidence to determine information about an incident is the main goal of digital forensics. The methods you use to analyze evidence will vary based on the nature of the incident, the evidence that was discovered and collected, and what type of investigation you're performing. However, there are four general analysis methods that cover most investigations.

Analysis Method	Description
Media	This involves the recovery of information on DVDs, CDs, tapes, hard drives, and other storage media. Some of these media are more susceptible to physical destruction than others, and a knowledgeable attacker may be able to inflict logical damage on all of them. Specialized tools may be required to extract data from such damaged media.
Network	Network logs and other activity records can be analyzed to identify the source of an attack, the pattern it took, and other useful information about the way it was transmitted across the organization. Because the original evidence (network traffic) is not truly stored in the sense that media is, the logs that describe this traffic need to be robust.
Software	This can include the examination of code that may be harmful or used as a vector in an attack. Reverse engineering malware may lead the investigator to discover more about the malware's origins, purpose, and methods. These can be used to determine who wrote the malware and how it was used in an incident, and what other lingering affects it may have.
Hardware/embedded device	This can include mobile devices as well as standard computing hardware and embedded systems. Specialized tools can create a forensic image of a device's firmware. However, some embedded devices cannot be easily imaged without compromising the integrity of the device itself.

Investigation Reports

After collecting and analyzing evidence, you'll need to report your findings to the authorities, management, and possibly other stakeholders. While some forensic tools may have reports built in, this is often insufficient to present as an official report to a wider audience. Tool-assisted reports can be overly technical and fail to get to the point. That's why you should consider manually writing your reports based on the results of your investigation. To be effective, these reports must answer the following five questions:

- **Who was tasked with the investigation?**

  This establishes a clear authority upfront. Investigations are not guaranteed to be quick; on the contrary, many are very slow to progress. Without a record, you may forget; this is especially true if personnel change in the interim or if the company is part of a merger or other change in ownership.

- **What was the investigator tasked with?**

  Use this question to avoid any confusion or dispute at the end of an investigation. You need to define a clear focus of the investigation. Failing to do so may compromise the investigation by bogging it down in irrelevant details or by making it seem incoherent.

- **What was investigated?**

  Use this question to outline all of the actual objects of the investigation, including technology (such as workstations, network appliances, and so on.) and people (such as witnesses, suspects, etc.). It very important that your record of these objects is comprehensive; instead of simply stating that you reviewed "an employee's workstation," you should instead say: "A Dell Inspiron Desktop with serial number 12345 running Windows 8.1, assigned to Aaron Jones on February 9th, 2012 by the company."

- **What was found?**

  You must record all significant events, files, images, machines, testimony, etc., that are relevant to the investigation. This report is not just to help you remember, but also will likely need to be geared toward an audience, like a boss or the arbiter(s) of the court case. That's why you need to write plainly, practically, and avoid using jargon. For example: "The login records show that a user was signed in under the account A. Jones while the incident took place."

- **What does it all mean?**

  This last question prompts you to piece all of the findings together to offer up a conclusion. What do you believe happened, how did it happen, and who do you think is responsible? You cannot necessarily rely on the audience of this report to draw their own conclusions; they'll likely be looking for you to do that, so they can verify the validity of those conclusions. Although these conclusions may be subject to bias, if you support them with evidence, the arbiter(s) of the case will be more inclined to agree.

Guidelines for Conducting Investigations

Use the following guidelines when performing a forensic investigation:

- Follow an investigative process of discover, collection, analysis, and reporting of results.
- Make sure your investigation is methodical, verifiable, and auditable.
- Select the right type of investigation based on the nature of the incident, your business needs, and organizational capacity.
- Follow a process of evidence collection from discovery all the way to presentation and return of the evidence to its owner.
- When seizing digital evidence, make sure that no action changes the evidence.
- If you must access original digital evidence, use a person who is trained specifically for that purpose.
- Completely document and preserve all activities related to the seizure, access, storage, and transfer of evidence; ensure that this documentation is available for review.
- Recognize that when digital evidence is in your possession, you are completely responsible for all actions taken in the integrity of that evidence (that is, follow the chain of custody).
- Ensure that anyone involved in seizing, accessing, storing, and transferring digital evidence remains in compliance with the above principles.
- Ensure that evidence is admissible within your jurisdiction.
- Attempt to determine the root cause of an incident by continually asking, "What led to this action?"
- Understand that special tools may be required to recover media like DVDs and hard drives.
- Ensure that network logs are robust and accurate to help you analyze traffic that occurred at a certain point in time.
- Reverse engineer malware to determine its origin and attack methods.
- Take an image of a hardware device's firmware, but be careful not to jeopardize the original's integrity in doing so.
- Draft a report that answers fundamental questions about the investigation, such as what was investigated, what was found, and what all of the evidence points to.

ACTIVITY 7-10
Discussing Investigations

Scenario

You are an information security consultant for a financial lending institution. As you walk into work one morning, users tell you that something is not right with the customer database. A large number of records seem to be missing or modified. Nearly all of the users have an application that maintains a persistent connection to the database server, and they have all noticed the anomaly. As you examine the server logs, you notice there has been activity on the server since 3:00 that morning, and the activity is still ongoing. The network appears to be in the middle of a cyber attack.

Because a lot of financial records and personal information are involved, management is also considering treating this as a criminal matter. Management is also wondering if an unhappy employee who recently aired his grievances against the company on social media might be responsible. You immediately call a forensic investigator and make ready to assist that person in the investigation.

---

1. **While you are waiting for the forensic investigator to arrive, what should you tell users to do?**
   ○ Tell them they can go about their regular duties, but to stay away from the server.
   ○ Tell them to not touch anything, including their own computers, until the server's connectivity can be safely isolated from the rest of the network.
   ○ Tell them that they can enter new records, but not access existing records in the customer database.
   ○ Tell them they can go about their regular duties, but to not talk about the incident until the CEO makes a public statement.

2. **At what point should you involve law enforcement?**
   ○ As soon as you uncover sufficient evidence for prosecution.
   ○ The moment the organization decides it wants to criminally prosecute the perpetrator.
   ○ After you have examined the server's hard drive for evidence of wrongdoing.
   ○ The moment you discover that something is wrong.

3. **Why should the investigative process be auditable?**
   ○ You want to make sure the investigator does not get careless.
   ○ You want to make sure that the investigation maintains its legitimacy.
   ○ You want to make sure that your findings are without bias.
   ○ You want to make sure that the investigation does not contaminate evidence.

4. **Under what conditions might your organization file a civil complaint against the hacker?**
   ○ When it cannot file a criminal complaint, but still wants to seek damages.
   ○ After the criminal case concludes.
   ○ Before the criminal case begins.
   ○ When the organization wants to avoid the scandal of a public trial.

5. Would your investigation benefit from e-discovery?

6. What must be done with any electronic evidence that is uncovered?
   - ○ A copy of the evidence must be made.
   - ○ The evidence must be secured, and properly collected and recorded.
   - ○ The evidence must be photographed and tagged.
   - ○ The evidence must be immediately placed in a locked room.

7. The forensic investigator reminds you that any evidence you find must be probative. What does that mean?
   - ○ It must be authentic.
   - ○ It must be admissible in court.
   - ○ It must help prove a fact.
   - ○ It must be complete.

8. When is it permissible for there to be a time gap in the evidence chain of custody log?
   - ○ Never.
   - ○ When you and the forensic investigator are examining the evidence.
   - ○ When the evidence has been turned over to law enforcement.
   - ○ When the evidence is finally presented to a judge.

9. What does the forensic investigator mean by saying that any evidence you find must be preserved?
   - ○ Good clean copies must be made of it.
   - ○ The original must be kept intact.
   - ○ The chain of custody log must show how the evidence was kept safe from tampering.
   - ○ The operating system must not be shut down until the contents of memory are first dumped to a file.

10. If you find emails or log files that might incriminate the unhappy employee, what can you do to preserve those files to ensure that they are not tampered with later?

11. Might the Electronic Communications Privacy Act (ECPA) apply to this investigation?

12. Would root cause analysis (RCA) be useful in this investigation?

13. Can network evidence analysis be useful in this investigation?

14. **When you are through with the investigation and you finally write the investigation report, what must you always keep in mind?**

○   Your report must have sufficient evidence to prove a person's guilt.

○   You must ensure that the evidence remains intact in case the reader wants more information.

○   You must show how all the evidence you have gathered fits together to support your conclusion.

○   You must provide enough proof for law enforcement to want to become involved.

TOPIC K

Disaster Recovery Planning

Whether the result of a computer crime incident or not, disasters can and will hit the organization. It's tempting to try to put all of your efforts toward preventing disasters, but this isn't entirely feasible. Planning for adverse events will ensure that you're as ready as you'll ever be, and not hopelessly unprepared to return your operations to normal.

Disaster Recovery Planning Process

The disaster recovery process can be outlined as follows:

1. Identify recovery strategies.
2. Document these strategies in a plan.
3. Provide training on the plan.
4. Assess the plan.
5. Update and maintain the plan.

DRPs

A *Disaster Recovery Plan (DRP)* is a policy that defines how people and resources will be protected in case of a natural or man-made disaster, and how the organization will recover from the disaster. The DRP can include a list of individuals responsible for recovery, an inventory of hardware and software, and a series of steps to take to respond to the disaster and rebuild affected systems.

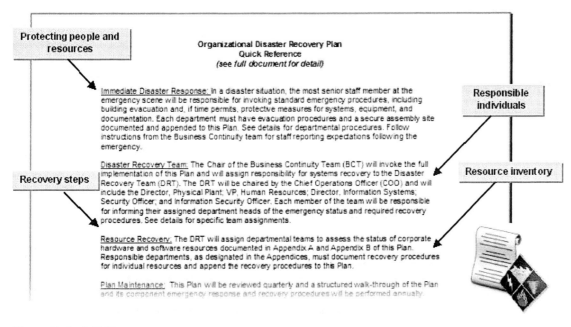

Figure 7-9: A DRP.

The disaster recovery response plan should be based on a disaster recovery policy established by the Board of Directors and upper management. That policy must include testing, evaluation, and fine-tuning for effectiveness before disaster strikes. The plan needs to be well documented, and staff trained to respond automatically in case of an emergency. It's hard enough to restore a server that just went up in flames. It's extremely challenging if not impossible to restore a data center without a well documented and well rehearsed plan in place.

DRP vs. BCP

Whereas the Business Continuity Plan (BCP) determines how to eliminate or mitigate risks, threats, and vulnerabilities, the DRP focuses on responses to circumstances that have caused a disastrous event. For example, an organization may be aware that a flood washed out a major bridge in its business area 10 years ago. Therefore, a DRP might be created that addresses flood possibilities and implements an expected organizational response system. The plan may designate a solution wherein two alternate travel routes are suggested when such a disaster is declared. If this is the case, the plan should include an effective communication scheme (such as a "phone tree") to inform all employees, business partners, customers, and suppliers of possible washout delays and commuting alternatives.

DRP Requirements

The following requirements should be part of any disaster recovery plan:

*   The strategy must be consistent regardless of the type of emergency.
*   There must be a process for assessing the effectiveness of the plan.
*   Certain personnel must be identified to own the disaster event and recovery process.
*   Management and response teams need to be identified and trained.
*   There needs to be a process for assembling key decision-makers during the disaster.
*   Internal communications protocols as well as communications with the media and general public must be predetermined.

It's critical that the disaster recovery response plan be carefully documented, with the location of these documents well known and easily accessible. You might not be able to depend on personnel that have rehearsed exactly what to do to be available during the disaster. In that case, other staff will have to be able to find these documents and follow their clearly written procedures to take over. The goal of a full written plan should be that any staff member with a similar skill set, who has never seen the plan before, should be able to read, understand, and effectively execute that plan.

As you make your disaster recovery plan, be sure to include the small things that users will need to do their daily jobs. Not everything that needs to be recovered for business continuity will be a server or network. Often it is as simple as having enough batteries, chairs, pens and paper, or a postage meter. It might involve having throwaway cellular phones with sufficient talk time for temporary use.

Be sure to involve all departments when determining your disaster recovery response. Ask every business unit/department manager, "If your entire team had to pick up and move to another location, what would they need to be able to function at the other location?" The list will include items that most IT people would not think of.

Disaster Recovery Strategy Considerations

There are several factors to take into consideration when an organization develops a disaster recovery strategy.

Disaster Recovery Factor	Description
Risks	As a DRP is created, residual risks must be considered.
	• People: The DRP must, at all costs, ensure the safety of the organization's people. Employee-related issues such as transportation, housing, food, sanitation, heating, cooling, and so on should always be considered. Failure to include these factors may decrease morale and counteract cooperation when needed.
	• Places: Determining a relocation scheme, if and when needed, is also an issue. While a backup site might be inexpensive, it may also present a high risk if it is located in a less desirable area, or if it is lacking the same protection profile as the original site. Transportation and utilities that match those used at the original site should be acquired for the backup location.
	• Things: Essential items such as office supplies, information technology (IT) equipment, and raw materials need to be protected to ensure and sustain individual performance, productivity, and efficiency as well as the continuation of business operations.
Cost vs. benefits	A recovery strategy may be highly effective but include a cost factor that the organization cannot afford. On the other hand, a simple, cost-effective solution may be found if the organization expends more time and effort up front. Goals and cost factors should be carefully weighed and considered to ensure an effective DRP.
Prioritization	When making a recovery decision, business needs should be ranked in order of importance to prioritize recovery efforts. Because business-critical processes are determined during BCP preparation, the DRP can use the same list to identify which processes to recover first.
	The prioritization list should be widely published so that there are no surprises when disaster strikes. Disasters can bring out the best in and the worst in people. If the owner of a critical system finds out during the disaster that their particular system has been rated low priority and they are going to have to wait hours—and possibly even days—to get up and running, it can make a difficult situation nearly intolerable.

Disaster Recovery Priority Levels

Each DRP should define the immediacy and priority of a particular incident to initiate the appropriate level of response.

Priority Level	Description
Short-term	This priority level prompts a rapid response. In most cases, short-term responses are necessary for business-critical processes. For example, in a production facility, if a production line is unavailable, it must be possible for staff to continue receiving orders so that products can be shipped upon availability.
Mid-term	This priority level initiates a quick response. For example, during a flood, four tractor-trailer rigs are damaged. Although these vehicles are necessary for product shipments, the organization has 18 more operational rigs that can deliver manufactured goods.

Priority Level	Description
Long-term	This priority level suspends response efforts for a period of time. For example, an organization may determine that, over time, it will be necessary to renovate the company cafeteria. However, given all the other existing issues that require urgent attention, management decides that the renovation project is not an immediate priority and puts it on hold.
Not required	This priority level defers response efforts indefinitely. For example, an employee basketball court that is used during the lunch hour for recreation is not a critical resource. Because this is an optional activity that does not require a prioritized response assignment, it should not be included in a priority list.

DRP Personnel Roles and Responsibilities

Disaster recovery planning requires the following roles and responsibilities to be determined and allocated.

Role	Description
Executive emergency management team	Senior managers who have the overall responsibility for restoring the organization services. This team does not directly manage the organization's normal day-to-day operations. During the disaster, it will be concerned with strategic and not tactical issues. It will respond to and assist in resolving issues that occurred during the crisis. They will be the organization's spokespeople to the news media and will make decisions on how to manage business impact of the disaster. The executive team leads the organization through the disaster, but does not manage the actual crisis itself.
Command center team	This team takes its direction from the executive team, and controls all communications both within the organization and to the outside world during the crisis. The command center team should have copies of all plans, procedures, and other documents required for recovery.
Emergency management team	This team is responsible for the tactical response during the disaster. This team manages the actual crisis, directing the emergency response teams.
Emergency response teams	There will be a number of teams and sub teams responsible for performing specific recovery tasks. These tasks can include: <ul><li>Retrieve records and backups from off-site storage.</li><li>Execute recovery procedures.</li><li>Identify problems that need to be escalated to management.</li><li>Report to the appropriate site or alternate site as laid out in the recovery procedure manual.</li><li>Communicate the status of recovery to the command center in a timely an ongoing manner.</li><li>Establish shifts for team members to support the recovery effort round-the-clock.</li><li>Confer with alternate site personnel as needed.</li><li>Help return operations to normal.</li><li>Reestablish support operations that have been affected by the disaster.</li><li>Identify equipment or software that needs to be replaced during the recovery effort.</li></ul>

Role	Description
End users	The goal of disaster response is to restore critical business operations as quickly as possible. This means that even end users have a role to play. They will need to be able to work effectively under reduced circumstances, understanding that they may have to make do with whatever is at hand. They should communicate their needs to their department manager, and not directly with the emergency response teams. This is especially important to help control confusion and minimize distractions for the emergency response teams.

RPOs

DRPs also instruct the organization on how to meet certain disaster recovery objectives. The *Recovery Point Objective (RPO)* is one such example. The RPO is the point in time, relative to a disaster, where the data recovery process will begin. In IT systems, it is often the point in time when the last successful backup is performed before the disruptive event occurs. It is the amount of time or data that you can afford to lose. It is important to individually determine an acceptable RPO for different systems and data stores.

For example, if the last backup was executed Sunday afternoon and the failure occurs on the following Tuesday, then the RPO is Sunday afternoon. The latest backup is restored and processing begins to recover all activity from Sunday afternoon to the Tuesday failure point.

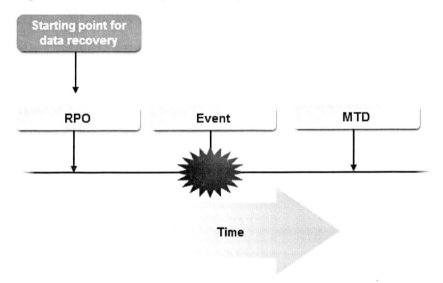

Figure 7-10: An RPO.

MTD

As mentioned in the Security and Risk Management lesson, Maximum Tolerable Downtime (MTD) is the longest period of time that a business outage may occur without causing serious business failures. When planning recovery point and recovery time objectives, your decisions should always be driven by the overall MTD of the service or process.

RTOs

The *Recovery Time Objective (RTO)* is the length of time within which normal business operations and activities can be restored following a disturbance. It includes the necessary recovery time to return to the RPO point, and reinstate the system and processing to their current status. The RTO must be achieved before the maximum tolerable downtime (MTD).

Mean time to recovery (MTTR) is the average time taken for a business to recover from an incident or failure and is an offset of the RTO. If MTTR exceeds the given RTO, then business operations need to switch to an alternate site.

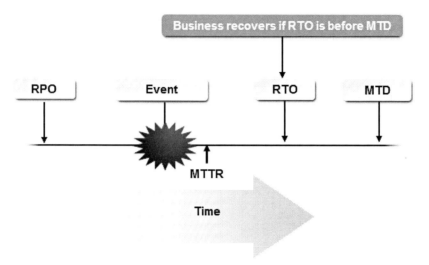

Figure 7–11: An RTO.

RPO/RTO Optimization

Ideally, the RPO and RTO should be zero or as near to zero as is economically feasible. That is, a failure can be immediately recovered. Although a near-zero RPO/RTO solution is extremely expensive, it is necessary in some circumstances. Airline reservation systems and stock market trading systems require the implementation of a near-zero RPO/RTO solution. In other cases, if the impact of a loss is less severe, a lower-cost solution can be used.

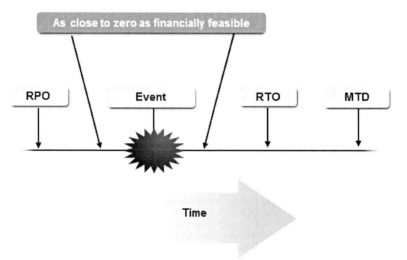

Figure 7–12: RPO/RTO optimization.

Cost of Recovery vs. Cost of Loss

When determining disaster response, the cost of recovery should be weighed against the cost of loss. In many cases, it is not justifiable to spend much on system recovery if the cost of system loss is minimal. Although recovery costs should be need based, they should not, necessarily, exceed the cost of loss.

However, the cost of loss is often difficult to identify. While it might be possible to quantify the loss in sales of non-produced items, there may be other areas of loss that are not as obvious, such as:

- Failing to maintain competitive advantages.
- Contract violations and associated penalties.
- Failing to maintain reputation.
- Revenue loss.
- Productivity loss.
- Delayed income.
- Failing to meet legal requirements.

A complete analysis should include these types of issues when determining recovery requirements.

DRP Training

For any plan to be effective, all involved personnel must be properly trained. In addition, the training needs be refreshed and tested on a regular basis. In fact, if appropriate training is not provided, C-level officers could be held liable for not performing due diligence.

Disaster recovery needs to be part of the culture of the organization. The security professional must make sure that sufficient training and awareness programs exist that involve all stakeholders. Is very likely that, as the security professional, you will have to introduce the idea of training and sell management on it.

Different teams require different levels of training. Common training for disaster recovery includes:

- Crisis leadership for senior management.
- Business continuity training for department managers.
- Technical training and logistics training for the technical teams.
- What to do and what NOT to do during a crisis training for end-users.

If your company has an intranet, it can be a good place to disseminate this information. However, do not expect end-users to simply read and understand any information you may have posted on an internal website. In addition, do not expect end-users to comply with instructions that they receive in an email. It is very important that their managers make sure that they have received the necessary training and can respond accordingly in the event of a disaster.

You should have regular training exercises for those responsible for disaster recovery. You might also consider having a business continuity section that includes end-user DRP information in the employee handbook, or in new employee orientation sessions. This will help employees to understand what to do in case of an event, and how they can obtain additional information.

DRP Test Strategy

Your DRP development process should include an assessment phase to ensure its effectiveness. You can use evaluation techniques similar to those used to evaluate a BCP. After the plan has been completed, you should review it at least yearly and make any maintenance-level changes required based on the results of the review as well as the results of periodic testing. You should certainly review the plan after you have had an event.

Before you actually test your plan, you should have a strategy for the test that includes the following:

- Testing scope and objectives.
- What functions, processes, and systems will be tested.
- An assurance that the test will not jeopardize normal business operations.
- Expectations of the test process for all departments and lines of business.
- A description of each test and how it will impact each department and business operations.
- The level of involvement of the staff, technologies, and facilities.
- Expectations of the test output.
- A measurement to determine the success of each test.

- Ability to identify any interdependencies (internal and external) that may impact the success of the test.
- Be able to uncover and rectify gaps in the testing process itself.
- Be able to tolerate deviating from the test script and injecting unplanned events such as the loss of key personnel, services, or equipment.
- Use a sufficient volume and range of transactions to provide an adequate representative sample in the test output.

It is important during the testing to validate recovery point and recovery time objectives (RPOs and RTOs). Testing will help you determine if these are reasonable and attainable.

As you perform your tests, you should start simply. Gradually you can increase the complexity and scope of the test. Eventually you can have your tests expand to encompass entire enterprise as well as your interaction with vendors and key external participants.

DRP Test Plan

Once you have a test strategy in place, you can develop a test plan. Your strategy will drive the actual plan. The plan should clearly communicate the testing scope and objectives and provide all participants with the appropriate information, including:

- A master schedule that lists all of the tests.
- A description of the test objectives and methods.
- A list of all test participants.
- The roles and responsibilities of all test participants, including support personnel.
- The decision-makers and their successors.
- Test locations.
- Test escalation conditions.
- Contact information.

DRP Test Types

There are several different types of tests for DRPs.

Type	Description
Read-Through	In a read-through, an individual or small team reads the plan to begin to familiarize themselves with its contents. This can be done before the larger team performs the test in earnest. Read-throughs are just a preliminary assessment and shouldn't take the place of more thorough tests, when possible.
Structured Walkthrough	Walkthroughs specifically focus on each DRP process phase. Planners and testers walk through the individual steps to validate the logical flow of the sequence of events.
	A structured walk-through is considered to be only the first step in the testing process. It can be used for training, but is not a preferred testing method. Its main objective is to ensure that key personnel are familiar with the BCP and DRP.
	A walkthrough is sometimes called a table top exercise.

Type	Description
Simulation	Simulations effectively test the validity and compliance of the DRP. In a simulation, each part of the planning process is exercised, with the exception of replicating and causing an outage. Although calls are made and specific actions are taken, the real event response is simulated. Participants choose a specific event or scenario and conduct a drill, playing out that event to identify gaps.
	Simulations will include the following:
	• Participation by all operational and support personnel who will be responsible for implementing the DRP and BCP.
	• Practice of specific responses, and validation of those responses.
	• Demonstrate required knowledge and skills, team dynamics, and decision-making.
	• Role playing to act out critical steps, recognize difficulties, and practice resolving problems.
	• Mobilization of management teams to practice coordination.
	• Some level of actual notification and resource mobilization.
	Simulations are instrumental in verifying design flaws, recovery requirements, and implementation errors. By identifying these solution discrepancies, process improvements can be applied that help ensure high-level plan maintenance.
Parallel	This test is used to ensure that systems perform adequately at the alternate offsite facility, without taking the main site offline. In a parallel test, data, equipment, and personnel can be temporarily set up at the alternate site.
	A parallel test includes:
	• A full test of the DRP/BCP.
	• Involvement of all employees.
	• Demonstrating emergency management capabilities.
	• Practice of interactions including assessment, control, and direction.
	• Testing of medical response.
	• Testing of warning procedures.
	• Testing of communications.
	• Actual or simulated relocation to alternate facilities.
	• Mobilization of personnel across geographical sites.
Full Interrupt	This test mimics an actual business disruption by shutting down the original site to test transfer and migration procedures to the alternate site, and to test operations in the presence of an emergency.
	A full interrupt test may require enterprise-wide participation, so that business units in other geographical locations can temporarily divide the workload from the affected site amongst themselves. A full interrupt can validate the organization's ability to respond to a crisis, especially if unplanned variations are introduced into the exercise. It can demonstrate, and identify, gaps in:
	• Management response and decision making capability.
	• Coordination of decision making roles.
	• Actual notifications.
	• Actual mobilization of resources.
	• Unexpected challenges encountered at actual response locations and facilities.
	• Actual data restores.

Update and Maintenance

The final phase of the disaster recovery planning process is to update and maintain your plan. The results of the plan assessment you perform will likely drive these changes, especially if the assessment reveals any major weaknesses. No plan is perfect on the first draft, and most will benefit greatly from several revisions.

However, it's not just your tests that should drive the maintenance of your plan. You should strive to review and potentially update your plan once every three months. This will ensure that the plan stays current with regard to your operations. After all, most successful organizations do not stay static, but change in a variety of meaningful ways. The size of the organization can change overnight, both financially and personnel-wise, so the recovery processes you planned out half a year ago may no longer be feasible or even relevant. And that's just one dimension of how the organization can change—think of how dynamic technology can be in any industry, and what a profound effect it can have on business operations. Your DRP needs to adapt in order to stay useful.

Guidelines for Planning for Disaster Recovery

Use the following guidelines when planning for disaster recovery:

- Follow the disaster recovery planning process.
- Document the disaster recovery plan based on input from executive-level management.
- Keep the disaster recovery plan (DRP) where it is easily accessible by those that need access to it.
- Consider even the smallest element of business operations to include in the DRP.
- Consider the risks, cost/benefit analysis, and prioritization required in the disaster recovery process.
- Qualify potential incidents in the DRP in terms of priority levels.
- Differentiate various roles and responsibilities for all levels of staff that are affected by the disaster recovery process.
- Include steps to measure recovery point objective (RPO) and recovery time objective (RTO) in your DRP.
- Optimize RPO and RTO to be as close to zero as possible.
- Train all affected staff on their role in the disaster recovery process.
- Apply different levels of training to different levels of staff.
- Incorporate regular training exercises into business operations.
- Assess the DRP to determine its effectiveness and any areas that could use improvement.
- Define the scope and expectations of your tests.
- Conduct a test type that is most appropriate and beneficial to the organization without adversely affecting business operations.
- Use the results of your assessment to improve your DRP and patch up any vulnerabilities.
- Review the DRP for maintenance every three months.

ACTIVITY 7-11
Analyzing Disaster Recovery Planning

Scenario
In this activity, you will assess your understanding of disaster recovery planning.

1. **Why is it necessary to train people when you develop a disaster recovery plan?**
   - ○ So that they can earn company continuing education credits.
   - ○ So that they know the company's DR strategy.
   - ○ So that they can uphold the CIA triad.
   - ○ So that they know how to respond in the event of a real disaster.

2. **Why should a disaster recovery plan (DRP) spell out recovery steps?**
   - ○ To make the recovery process as guided and straightforward as possible.
   - ○ To satisfy due diligence requirements.
   - ○ To assist management in directing user activity during a disaster.
   - ○ To provide IT traceability to business continuity planning steps.

3. **Why must you involve all departments when developing a disaster recovery response?**
   - ○ Because end users from each department will have to implement the response should disaster strike.
   - ○ Because a balanced plan involves all stakeholders.
   - ○ Because you will need end user buy-in from all the departments for your plan.
   - ○ Because the priorities of each department during a disaster might be very different from what the IT department expects.

4. **When creating your DRP, why should you publish a priority list of which systems will be brought online first after a disaster?**
   - ○ So that there are no disappointing surprises when a real disaster strikes.
   - ○ So that you can satisfy due care and due diligence.
   - ○ So that the IT team will be clear on what tasks to perform first.
   - ○ So that the management team can create a clear step-by-step recovery plan.

5. **When assigning disaster recovery priority levels, why might some systems be excluded from the disaster recovery list?**
   - ○ This may happen to systems that are optional and not required for the business to operate.
   - ○ This may happen to systems that are too expensive to restore.
   - ○ This may happen to individual systems that are considered too insignificant to list.
   - ○ This may happen to old systems that should be replaced, rather than restored, in the event of a disaster.

6. Who should speak to the news media in the event of a disaster?
   - ○ The command center team.
   - ○ The executive emergency management team.
   - ○ The receptionist assigned to answer the phone.
   - ○ The company attorney.

7. How is a Recovery Point Objective (RPO) different from a Recovery Time Objective (RTO)? (Choose two.)
   - ☐ The RTO attempts to restore a system to a specific state before the disaster.
   - ☐ The RPO attempts to restore a system within a specific amount of time.
   - ☐ The RPO attempts to restore a system to a specific state before the disaster.
   - ☐ The RTO attempts to restore a system within a specific amount of time.

8. Is a near-zero RTO/RPO always feasible?
   - ○ No, because your backups might not always survive a disaster.
   - ○ No, because it may simply be too expensive to implement.
   - ○ No, because your spare hardware might not always survive a disaster.
   - ○ Yes, because that is the goal of RTO and RPO.

9. What should a typical disaster recovery end-user training include?
   - ○ What to do and what not to do.
   - ○ Steps to take to recover your department's systems.
   - ○ Steps to take to recover your department's business flow.
   - ○ How to prevent department data from being destroyed during a disaster.

10. What is the ultimate goal of a disaster recovery test?
    - ○ To ensure that your recovery point and recovery time objectives are reasonable and attainable.
    - ○ To uncover and rectify gaps in the testing process itself.
    - ○ To make sure that loss of life is minimized.
    - ○ To provide an assurance that the test will not jeopardize normal business operations.

11. What is the next logical step after creating a test strategy?
    - ○ Conduct the test.
    - ○ Train all personnel.
    - ○ Document the strategy.
    - ○ Create the test plan.

12. Which test type will most thoroughly test your disaster recovery capabilities?
    - ○ Structured walkthrough.
    - ○ Parallel.
    - ○ Full Interrupt.
    - ○ Simulation.

13. Why should you regularly update your disaster recovery plan?

○   To keep your plan current with the changing technologies you use.

○   To continue to perform due diligence.

○   To keep users engaged and interested.

○   To keep management current on the latest recovery techniques.

TOPIC L

Disaster Recovery Strategies

Now that you've followed the planning process, you'll need to review the various recovery strategies available to you. Not all of the following strategies will be viable in your organization, but they are some of the most effective ways of returning the organization to normal operations.

Recovery Strategies

A successful DRP will outline several recovery strategies, including:

- The decision-makers and how to contact them.
- Where and how data is backed up.
- If any fault tolerance or redundancy mechanisms can restore data.
- The location of alternate sites and the services and technology that operates at those sites.
- Travel and accommodation services, as well as infrastructure and supply options at the alternate site.
- The recovery strategy for the organization in each specific technology.
- Where people should assemble if they cannot reenter the building.
- The process for declaring a disaster for a specific site.

Data Backup

A *data backup* is a second copy of data captured at a point in time and stored in a secure area as a precautionary safeguard in case of a disaster. Backups can use a variety of media copy mechanisms and different methods for selecting the data to back up. These variables affect the amount of data stored and the amount of time and media required for the backup. You can use any of the following as storage for backups:

- Magnetic tape.
- Fixed hard disk.
- Removable hard disk.
- Removable flash drive.
- CD/DVD.
- A dedicated file server such as a Network Attached Storage (NAS) device.
- Storage Area Network (SAN).
- Cloud storage.
- Remote servers that host the same service (such as database, email, directory service, and so on).

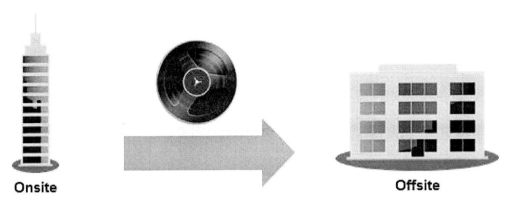

Figure 7-13: Data backup.

Example: Magnetic Tape Database Backup

Organizations often back up databases to magnetic tape on a regular basis and then transport the tapes to an offsite, secure storage facility for protection. This affords protection in case of catastrophic losses at the original location. Even though the industry has relied on tapes for years, many organizations are moving to disk-to-disk and online backups.

Backup Considerations

When implementing a backup solution, you should not simply backup your data and keep a copy somewhere. You should instead have a backup strategy that is driven by both your recovery time objective and your recovery point objective. Unless you're willing to spend a lot of money, you generally have to make a trade-off between how quickly you can backup your data versus how quickly you can restore it.

Ask yourself and management: "is it more important to be able to back up these huge amounts of data every night quickly, or is it more important to be able to bring that data immediately back online in case of an incident?" The data might be archival, such as past sales and old records, meaning that it is not so critical to bring it back online immediately. On the other hand, the data might need to be immediately available. It might be pending customer orders or lab results of a patient in intensive care.

If management wants to have both fast backup and fast restore, then you are better off investigating different types of redundant and fault-tolerant systems. Most organizations benefit by having both redundant systems and backups.

When considering how long it will take to restore a backup, also consider where you will store that backup. If you store your backups off-site, it may take a day or two just to retrieve backup media. On the other hand, if you store your backups in the server room, a fire could destroy the backups as well as the equipment. A good strategy is to have multiple copies of the backup: one taken offsite for safety, and one left onsite for convenience.

Another thing to consider is the availability of the technology needed for restoring your data. Replacing a server can be pretty quick, especially if you rent one. But if you striped your backups across multiple tape machines, can you get the same number of replacement tape machines to perform the restore? Your tape machines might be obsolete, and no one stocks them anymore. With the cost of disk storage and Internet access being so low these days, many companies now opt to back up to a removable drive or the cloud.

Keep in mind that backups should not only be for data. You should also backup the following:

- Source code.
- Configuration files.
- Application software.
- Server and desktop images and virtual machines.

- Utility software.
- License keys.
- Any other information you would need in a disaster recovery scenario.

Data Backup Methods

There are several standardized data backup methods.

Data Backup Method	Description
Full backup	A *full backup* is a method that backs up all selected files. It is used as a starting point for all backup activities. As the name suggests, all information is copied to the backup media.
	Microsoft® operating systems use the archive bit to identify modified files. Other backup software keeps track of modifications internally. When a file is modified, the archive bit is turned on. The full backup then clears the archive bit, making it easier to identify files needing backup and those that have not been modified.
Incremental backup	An *incremental backup* clears the archive bit and reduces backup time and media. An incremental backup copies files and databases that have been modified since the last full backup.
	Restoring an incremental backup requires the copying of the last full backup plus all incremental backups in the sequence in which they were created.
Differential backup	A *differential backup* copies all modifications since the last full backup to the backup media. It does not turn off the archive bit; over a period between full backups, the amount of media required for a differential backup continues to grow.
	Restoring the differential backup requires copying the last full and last differential backups.
Remote journaling	*Remote journaling* is a method wherein real-time copies of database transactions are stored in journals at a remote location. Journals can be replayed to transfer a database back to normal conditions.
	Should a disaster occur, the latest copy of the database is restored and the database then reprocesses the remote journal up to the last successfully completed transaction.
Electronic vaulting	*Electronic vaulting* is used to copy modified files to an offsite location. It is not done in real time like remote journaling.
	To restore an electronic vault after failure recovery, the files are copied back to the failed site over the network.

Redundancy and Fault Tolerance

In addition to a recovery site, most organizations will want to implement some form of redundancy or fault tolerance in their network infrastructure. *Redundancy* ensures that data exists in an additional form so that it can be used to correct corruption or loss of the data. *Fault tolerance* ensures that a system will still be operational even when parts of the system fail.

While a recovery site helps a business return to normal operations after a disaster or major incident, redundancy and fault tolerance keep the network infrastructure running despite small occurrences such as disk crashes, server crashes, or network link failures.

Common examples of redundancy and fault tolerance include:

- RAID arrays.
- Duplicate network links.
- Duplicate servers and network devices.
- Duplicate power supplies in a device.
- Uninterruptible power supply (UPS).
- Distributed network services.
- Duplicate backup copies.

The whole point of redundancy and fault tolerance is to automatically or semi-automatically recover from the failure of a single device or system. The data or system never goes off-line, or it goes off-line only very briefly. Because time is money, and downtime equals loss of productivity and profits, most businesses want to be able to continue to run even if one or several devices, or part of the infrastructure, fails.

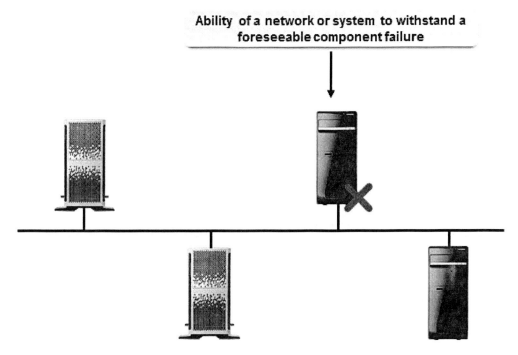

Figure 7-14: Fault tolerance.

Hot, Warm, and Cold Spares

You can have fault tolerant equipment that is hot spare, warm spare, or cold spare. Hot spare equipment is already installed, and will assume control automatically if the original device fails. A warm spare usually just requires an operator to press a button for the functionality to fail over.

A cold spare is not inserted into the system. It might have to be taken out of storage, unpacked, and installed into the system or rack. If it is a rack-mounted device such as a switch or server, it might already be mounted into the rack and pre-configured, but not plugged in or turned on. Should the original device fail, an operator would have to unplug all of the network cables from the original device, plug them into the cold spare, and start the cold spare. Once booted up, it will probably also require an update to its configuration and a backup restore to make it up-to-date and bring it to the same level of functionality as the original. In the case of operating systems and servers, it is now very common to use virtual machines to host server services. Copies of the virtual machine (VM) can be saved every day for quick failover to a cold spare.

High Availability

Hand in hand with redundancy and fault tolerance is the concept of high availability. Availability is one of three pillars of the CIA triad. When maintaining a secure network, you need to ensure that the services users need to perform their jobs or maintain business processes can be accessed whenever and however needed. High availability of a service depends on redundant and fault-tolerant hardware and systems.

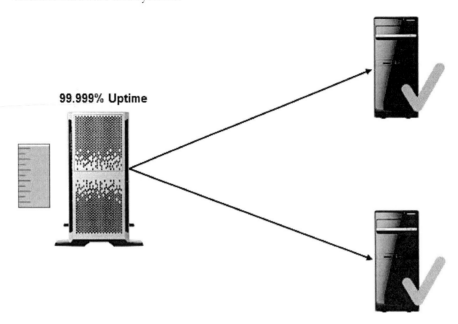

Figure 7–15: High availability.

RAID

Redundant Array of Independent Disks (RAID), or Redundant Array of Inexpensive Disks, is used to provide better disk performance or data redundancy depending on the implemented RAID type. RAID systems can incorporate striping, mirroring, and parity to provide high availability.

- RAID can be used to increase performance if striping is implemented. *Striping* is a disk-performance-enhancement feature in which data is spread across multiple drives to improve read and write access speeds. By distributing data among drives, the disk-platter rotation and disk-actuator movement that controls the read/write head can be optimized. Striping offers no protection to data if a drive is lost.
- To improve data redundancy, RAID may be used to automatically *mirror* information written on one drive to a second drive. If the first drive fails, the second drive is automatically put in service.
- *Duplexing* is the additional protection of having multiple hard drive controllers.
- *Parity* is another method that can improve redundancy. With a parity system, data is written as if it were being striped, but one of the volumes contains information that will allow the re-creation of lost data if a drive fails.

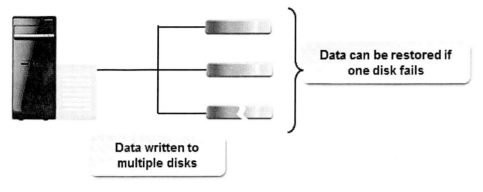

Figure 7-16: RAID.

RAID Levels

Many types of RAID have been tried over the years. Some like RAID 0,1, and 5 have become industry standards. RAID 2, 3, and 4 were not widely adopted but still helped to define techniques used today. The CISSP candidate should be familiar with all of the following RAID levels.

RAID Level	Description
Level 0	Striping of data on multiple disk drives for better performance. Provides no redundancy.
Level 1	Mirroring or duplexing of data on drives for redundancy. In mirroring, the two disks share a drive controller. In duplexing, each disk has its own drive controller, so the controller card does not impose a failure. Data is written to both halves of the mirror simultaneously.
	Disk write performance may be negatively impacted but disk reads may be slightly improved. This increases hardware costs because you will need to purchase two drives for every single device equivalent.
Level 2	Striping of data with an error correction code (ECC) for redundancy. It is not commercially viable.
Level 3	Striping of data at the byte level with parity information on a single drive for redundancy. It does not improve performance. The dedicated parity disk can be a bottleneck when implementing RAID 3. The single parity disk is also a risk to redundancy if the drive fails.
Level 4	Striping of data at the block level with the parity information on a single drive for redundancy. It does not improve performance. As with RAID 3, the dedicated parity disk can be a bottleneck when implementing RAID 4. The single parity disk is also a risk to redundancy if it is the drive that fails.
Level 5	Striping of the data and the parity information spread across all drives for redundancy. RAID 5 tolerates a single drive failure without forcing a recovery. Distributing parity in RAID 5 removes the bottlenecks seen in RAID 3 and 4. It requires a minimum of three drives. It has a higher hardware cost than RAID 0 but less than RAID 1.
Level 6	Striping of data with two levels of parity calculation and parity information spread across drives for redundancy. RAID 6 tolerates two drives failing without forcing a recovery.

RAID Level	Description
Level 10	A combination of RAID level 1 and RAID level 0. Data is first mirrored onto the RAID drives for redundancy. Each mirrored set is then striped for performance. This provides the best of both performance and fault tolerance. This is sometimes referred to as nested RAID. You might also see it as RAID 1 + 0 or RAID 5 + 0.

SAN, NAS, and RAIT

Storage Area Networks (SANs) and *Network Attached Storage (NAS)* devices will include many different options to allow for redundancy. Many of these are built on the concepts of RAID. The concepts of RAID can also be extended to tape drives, in which case it is referred to as *Redundant Array of Independent Tapes (RAIT)*.

 Note: The idea of presenting multiple disks to the operating system as a single disk or volume, as in RAID, is also referred to as concatenation.

Recovery Sites

As part of a DRP, an organization can maintain various types of alternate, or backup, recovery sites that can be used to restore system functioning. Recovery sites are especially useful in the case of a major disaster that makes the main place of business unusable. The disaster could be a natural disaster such as an earthquake, flood, tornado, or hurricane. It could also be the result of an accident, gas leak, environmental contamination, or terrorist attack. The disaster could also be infrastructure-related: a sinkhole that blocks the access road, loss of the power grid in that area—anything that prevents the business from conducting normal operations at the main site.

Alternate Site Type	Description
Dual data center	A dual data center is one in which two separate sites operate simultaneously. The business application is split across both sites. For companies that cannot tolerate any downtime or decrease in performance, both sites will have the capacity to carry the full load in case one site is down (surviving site strategy). Real-time trading and financial institutions use dual data centers. They also perform failover checks for all operations between the sites on a regular schedule to ensure full functionality and readiness at all times. Advantages of a dual data center: • Very little or no downtime. • Ease of maintenance. • No recovery required. Disadvantages of a dual data center: • This is the costliest option. • Requires redundant hardware, networks, personnel. • Distance between sites introduces technical and latency challenges.

Alternate Site Type	Description
Hot site/Mirror site	A *hot site*, or *mirror site*, is a fully configured alternate network that can be quickly put online after a disaster. A hot site is an exact duplicate of the primary processing location.
	In most cases, staffing at the hot site will be similar if not identical to the primary site. The viability of a hot site is tested by disconnecting the primary site from the hot site and observing whether the processing switchover is successful. Airline reservation centers, stock brokerages, and clearinghouses require the use of hot sites because they cannot tolerate any extended downtime and need a Recovery Point Objective (RPO) of nearly zero.
	An example of a hot site would be a secondary operations center that is fully staffed and in constant network contact with the primary center under normal conditions.
	A hot site can be internally owned or externally owned.
	Advantages of a hot site:
	• Recovery can be tested.
	• Highly available.
	• Site can be up and running within hours.
	Disadvantages of a hot site:
	• Expensive (especially an internal hot site).
	• Requires extra care that hardware and software between sites is compatible.
Warm site	A *warm site* is a location that is dormant or performs non-critical functions under normal conditions, but which can be rapidly converted to a key operations site if needed.
	Warm sites are often provided as a service with high investment costs by third-party vendors that own the hardware and operating location. Communications capabilities should match those of the primary site as closely as possible. The viability of a warm site is tested by confirming the successful transportation and installation of software and data from the primary site. The RPO can be days long or up to a week depending on the traveling distance and time required for installation.
	An example of a warm site might be a customer service center that could be quickly converted into a network-maintenance facility,if needed.
	Advantages of a warm site:
	• Less expensive than a hot site.
	• Faster recovery time than a cold site.
	• Available for longer recovery time.
	Disadvantages of a warm site:
	• Not readily available.
	• Not convenient to fully test.

Alternate Site Type	Description
Cold site	A *cold site* is a predetermined alternate location where a network can be rebuilt after a disaster.
	A cold site can be a space in a facility with appropriate power, environmental controls, and communications facilities. To use a cold site, an organization should order and install new hardware, transport the data and software to the location, hook up communications, and then begin operation.
	The RPO for a cold site can be up to weeks or months depending on hardware availability and installation speed. Although this is the least expensive alternative, it does present serious implementation problems. There is generally no effective way to test a cold site installation.
	An example of a cold site might be nothing more than a rented warehouse with available power and network hookups, where key equipment could be moved and installed in the event of a disaster.
	Advantage of a cold site:
	• Least expensive of the sites.
	Disadvantage of a cold site:
	• Will require days or even weeks to become operational.
Portable site	A *portable site* is a mobile site that can be operated anywhere should a disaster occur. It houses computer hardware, networking capabilities, and communications equipment to restore and maintain business operations. It may be located outside the primary site while it is in repair and recovery mode, which minimizes travel for employees who are involved in a disaster.
	For instance, large vans and trailers are often used as portable sites in which mirroring is performed to maintain up-to-date data in installed hardware. When a disaster is imminent, the computers can be relocated to a designated alternate location.
	In most cases, portable sites only support extremely critical applications. The downside is the high cost factor of acquiring and maintaining the vans and trailers, as well as the limited recovery capability presented by this solution.
	Advantages of a portable site:
	• Highly mobile and relatively easy to transport.
	• Modular design is flexible and extensible.
	• Does not require a building to house equipment and staff.
	Disadvantages of a portable site:
	• You must make sure ahead of time that there will be space to park the site.
	• The container might be challenging to upgrade or customize.
	• Maintaining a contract with a shipping company to move the container during a disaster may be expensive.

Recovery Site Strategies

No matter how big or small, each disaster requires an appropriate response approach to mitigate the impact on business process, service, people, data, and equipment. There are a number of strategies that can be taken for recovery.

Recovery Strategies	Description
Surviving Site	You can have several geographically dispersed locations that are fully equipped and staffed, and perform the same function. Should one site go down, the other site can continue. Although productivity output would be reduced, as a business you would still be open and offering goods and services to your customers.
Self-Service	If you have different offices or facilities, you can transfer the most time-sensitive work to a different location during the interruption.
Internal Arrangement	Cafeterias, training centers, meeting rooms, and recreation areas could be temporarily repurposed to accommodate staff from the affected site or other sites. This might mean the suspension of non-critical activities during the outage.
Reciprocal Agreement	You could have a standing agreement with a competitor to allow each other to run reduced operations at the other's location. Traditionally, newspapers had reciprocal agreements to allow each other to print limited runs. The risk of a reciprocal agreement is that both sides are not likely to have much space or capacity for each other's staff and operations. Additionally, reciprocal agreements cannot be enforced.
Dedicated Alternate Sites	Hot, warm, or cold sites built by the company to accommodate disasters.
Work from Home	With telecommuting becoming so popular, many employees might be able to work from home while the office is unusable. The risk of this arrangement is that the network that would ordinarily allow users to log in remotely might also be affected, or might not have the capacity to handle a sudden large influx of remote users.
External Suppliers	Some companies specialize in providing mobile offices or disaster area communications. These companies can respond quickly, bringing a fully loaded office trailer to the parking lot of an affected site, or dropping a self-contained communications center in a disaster area. In a natural disaster or terrorist attack, your employees might not be able to get to the job site. Many external suppliers can also provide temporary staff to assist with the work.
Outsourcing	Some of your work can be outsourced to vendors during disaster recovery. This will most likely cost more than doing the work in-house, but may be your only alternative if infrastructure or staff capabilities are limited.
No Arrangement	If the business function is low priority, the cost of the other solutions might not be justified. Any business considering to have a No Arrangement disaster recovery strategy should at least itemize the business functions that need to continue during a disaster, have at least a basic plan, and determine the cost of implementing that plan.

Guidelines for Selecting Disaster Recovery Strategies

Use the following guidelines when considering disaster recovery strategies:

* Ensure that you have a data backup strategy that supports your RPO and RTO.
* Consider where you will store your backups for optimum recovery.
* Consider what you'll need to back up—source code, application software, configuration files, and anything else that is essential to your business operations.
* Evaluate which data backup method is most appropriate for your needs. Consider using different methods for different data or systems.
* Implement redundancy and fault tolerance by using RAID, UPSes, duplicate network links, and so on.

- Choose a RAID solution that strikes a balance between fault tolerance and availability, both compared with your business needs.
- Consider having a hot, warm, or cold backup site ready in case of a disaster.
- Understand the major expense involved in maintaining any of these sites—assess if the cost outweighs the value.
- Consider various recovery site strategies, like having personnel work from home, or contracting with external suppliers.

ACTIVITY 7-12
Analyzing Disaster Recovery Strategies

Scenario
In this activity, you will assess your understanding of disaster recovery strategies.

1. **Which of the following can be used as backup media? (Choose four.)**
   - ☐ Magnetic tape
   - ☐ Removable disk
   - ☐ Internal hard drive
   - ☐ Cloud
   - ☐ SAN

2. **In addition to data, what else should you back up? (Choose four.)**
   - ☐ License keys
   - ☐ Source code
   - ☐ Server and desktop images and virtual machines
   - ☐ Web services
   - ☐ Configuration files

3. **How is remote journaling different from electronic vaulting?**
   - ○ Both send backups to offsite locations, but electronic vaulting is done in real time.
   - ○ Both send backups to offsite locations, but remote journaling is done in real time.
   - ○ Remote journaling sends backups to a remote location, whereas electronic vaulting sends backups to another server in the same site.
   - ○ Electronic vaulting sends backups to a remote location, whereas remote journaling sends backups to another server in the same site.

4. **What is the goal of redundancy and fault tolerance?**
   - ○ To provide load balancing in case of a denial of service attack.
   - ○ To provide network re-routing in case of a device failure.
   - ○ To reduce desktop downtime.
   - ○ To automatically or semi-automatically recover from the failure of a single device or system.

5. **With regard to RAID, how is mirroring different from parity?**
   - ○ Mirroring stripes data across multiple disks, whereas parity creates a complete duplicate of the original disk.
   - ○ Mirroring creates a complete duplicate of the original disk, whereas parity stripes data across multiple disks.
   - ○ Mirroring is a fault tolerant method, whereas parity is not.
   - ○ Parity is a fault tolerant method, whereas mirroring is not.

6. Of all the RAID levels, which one best provides both performance and fault tolerance?
   - ○ RAID 1
   - ○ RAID 5
   - ○ RAID 6
   - ○ RAID 10

7. Which recovery site type would be the most appropriate for a large financial center that performs millions of credit card transactions every day?
   - ○ Warm site.
   - ○ Cold site.
   - ○ Hot site.
   - ○ Dual data center.

8. What is the risk of allowing users to work from home after a disaster?
   - ○ They might not want to return to work when operations return to normal.
   - ○ They might not be able to return to work until roads and other civic infrastructure are restored.
   - ○ Too many remote connections might overwhelm the company network.
   - ○ Damaged power lines and limited telecom might restrict the effectiveness of users working from home.

TOPIC M

Disaster Recovery Implementation

After you've gone through the planning stages and formulated strategies specific to your organization, you can begin to implement your disaster recovery plan. Effective implementation is only possible when all levels in the organization coordinate; with this coordination comes the eventual return of business operations to normal.

Event Management

Events can be small or major. They can be the beginning of a disaster, or they might be very small (such as a water leak or a small fire in one area) that can be contained and quickly dealt with.

An event is the starting moment of whatever causes a business interruption. It could be a hardware failure, a power outage, a terrorist attack, a natural disaster, or anything else that potentially could significantly disrupt an organization. The trigger will cause the event management process to begin. Depending on the type of event, different teams might be the owners. A power failure or fire at a facility would have a different owner than a network outage.

When an event occurs, the team that owns the event will have certain goals to make recovery a success. These are:

- First and foremost, protect human life. Ensure that all personnel are able to evacuate safely.
- Ensure that there is only one source of information, for staff, the news media, and the general public.
- Ensure good communications and control rumors.
- During the early stages, quickly triage to determine what issues take priority.
- Be able to quickly and effectively escalate responses, especially if the event becomes a full blown disaster.
- Make sure that problems are managed in a consistent manner.
- Ensure that everyone knows exactly what to do.
- Allow those who must solve problems to do so without interference or interruption.
- Know when to declare that the event has become a disaster and initiate disaster recovery and/or business continuity processes.
- Maintain an operations procedure manual (playbook) that documents key roles and responsibilities, as well as processes that must be done, listed in the order of priority.

Whoever owns the event must know when it is necessary to escalate to the next level of management. It may be that a water leak can be sufficiently contained and managed without the need to wake up the CEO in the middle of the night. On the other hand, if a hurricane floods a major data center, the CEO and all other C-level officers will have to be alerted and kept updated as events unfold so that contingency plans across the company can be put into action.

Security Concessions in the Face of Disaster

A disaster is an especially vulnerable time for security. People will be so busy just trying to contain damage and bring systems back online by any means possible, that little attention will be paid to making sure that those systems are also secure. Very often, expected infrastructure will not be available. For example, during the terrorist attacks of 9/11, telecommunications companies resorted to running fiber optic cable out of hotel windows onto the sidewalk just to restore some semblance of communications at the disaster site. These cables, of course, were not protected in any way. Nor did the technicians have much attention to spare to provide security for the network equipment that they set up in those hotel rooms.

Event Management Categorization

When an event or disaster is underway, you will have to be able to continuously make decisions regarding the status and severity of the event. You'll have to determine the impact of a specific event on the organization and determine the right response.

One thing that will help is to categorize events, as outlined in the following table.

Event Type	Description
Non-Incident	This is a system malfunction or human error that results in minor disruption of service. The downtime is minimal and alternate processing or storage facilities do not need to be utilized.
Incident	This is an event that will cause an entire service or facility to stop working for a significant period of time. An incident will trigger the disaster recovery process.
Severe Incident	This is an event that causes destruction and a more severe interruption of the organization's mission, facilities, and personnel. It will trigger the disaster recovery process, and may require building a new primary facility. It will also require crisis management.

Disaster Recovery Response

Creating a good disaster recovery response is a process that many businesses do not spend enough time on. This requires full support by upper management to be effective. The goals of disaster recovery response are:

- Restore critical business IT systems to acceptable levels as quickly as possible.
- Prioritize recovery stages to support business continuity.
- Eventually transition from contingency operations to full recovery.
- Have a well-documented plan that everyone understands and can execute rather than making ad-hoc decisions.

Disaster Recovery Response Approaches

No matter how big or small, each disaster requires an appropriate response approach to mitigate the impact on people, data, and equipment.

Response Approach	Description
Short-term	Some solutions are considered short-term if they represent a stop-gap measure to be replaced in the future.
	• Mirrored sites: A mirrored site has all the features and functions of the primary site. Because the mirrored site has the current hardware, software, and data, if the primary site fails, the mirrored site can resume operations with a minimum RTO, often in seconds.
	• Shared location: In a shared location, the company shares processing capabilities with another company. Because the site is not owned by the company with the disaster, the shared location may not be available when needed.
	In either a mirrored site or shared location, the objective is to use the site temporarily and return to normal production as soon as possible.

Response Approach	Description
Long-term	Long-term approaches are useful when a decision is made to return to business as usual. To complete long-term approaches, a substantial investment in time and resources is necessary. • Relocation: Relocating to a completely different facility may be necessary if the damage to the primary site is extensive. As a long-term solution, this is beneficial if the new site is compatible with the old site; that is, if it has similar transportation and infrastructure support and the employees collectively agree with the move. • Rebuilding: Rebuilding the primary site is typically a costly and time-consuming proposition. The old site must be cleared and declared free of environmental issues. Building plans are then created and the local zoning board grants their approval. Once the building is complete, business operations can resume.

Communication with Stakeholders

Once the event has been recognized and event management has been triggered, the communications team must take over all communications both internal and external, and upper management must be notified immediately. There must always be failsafe operators who are on duty and can be contacted at any time day or night. The last thing you want is a fire to break out in a warehouse, and the manager on duty to not answer his phone, with no backup manager to call.

Communications are especially critical during a disaster. It is very easy during the initial confusion for rumors and misinformation to run rampant. This can put people's lives at risk and further damage the company. When approached by the news media, every employee should automatically refer any questions to the communications team.

The communications team must be able to notify all stakeholders. These include:

• Employees and their families.
• Vendors, contractors, and business partners.
• Facility and site managers.
• Department managers.
• Senior managers and Board of Directors.
• News media.
• Law enforcement.
• Emergency responders.
• Insurance companies.
• Suppliers and distributors.
• Customers.
• Government regulators.
• Competitors.
• Unions.
• Internet users.
• The general public or line-of-business related communities.
• Industry groups.

It's very important that all staff members who communicate with any outside entity listed above be given a regularly updated list of things to say, so that they provide the same, consistent message. It is human nature to embellish in an emotional situation, or to jump to conclusions without verifying facts. It is very easy during a disaster for a frightened or excited staff member to miscommunicate recovery status to a stakeholder. This can add to the impact of the disaster and make containment that much more difficult.

Communication Flow

Any personnel on an emergency notification list should be contacted directly by the responsible management team member. That manager should not delegate the task to another, to minimize inaccuracies in the message. While a single manager calling all team members would ensure a consistent message, it would be too time-consuming. Instead, a "call tree" should be established, with each team member in the tree directly responsible for calling a few people. The tree should not be more than three levels deep. In this way, all team members can be notified in a timely manner.

The security professional will need to document the communications procedure, including any call trees, to make sure there are no gaps and to make sure that risks are minimized. It may also be helpful to establish conference bridges specifically for recovery efforts. Be aware, however, that the technologies used may themselves be hampered by the situation. You might establish a conference bridge and phone number, only to have the entire phone system be down. Make sure that you use technologies that are in themselves fault tolerant, and provide alternates in case some do not work.

To ensure that all employees know what number to call in case of disaster, one common technique is to put a sticker with phone numbers on employee badges and refrigerator magnets that employees can refer to at home. The same number can also be used to notify employees of site closures, announcements, late start and early release notifications in case of severe weather, or any disasters they may see on the news.

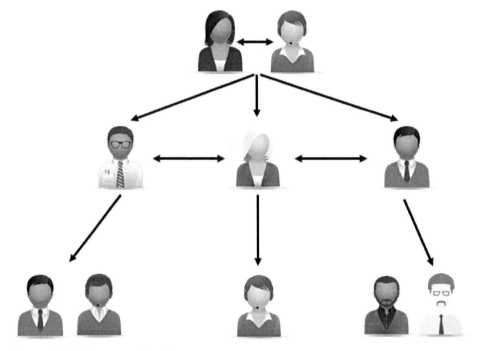

Figure 7-17: An example call tree.

Restoration

Restoration is the final part of disaster recovery, and should be part of the disaster recovery plan. In restoration, the primary working facility and environment has gone back to normal. Part of your staff might be functioning in an alternate site, but your recovery staff will be focusing on what is necessary to restore the primary facility. It is likely that the management team that owns this process will be a coordinated effort between facility staff and the technology team.

Transitioning to full normal operations is a planned activity. It can include returning all at once to the original location and/or service-level, moving to a new location and/or service-level, or incrementally moving to either.

In addition to recovering functionality in service, the organization's legal team and insurance agent should always play a role in restoration and recovery. The legal team can advise management and how to minimize damage while staying in compliance with regulators. The insurance agent can secure finances for the organization if it is covered under an applicable policy.

Guidelines for Disaster Recovery Implementation

Use the following guidelines when implementing the disaster recovery plan:

*   Ensure that the team managing an event can act quickly, consistently, and without interference.
*   Ensure that the team can escalate issues to higher levels of management, when applicable.
*   Categorize potential events as non-incidents, incidents, or severe incidents, depending on their context.
*   Implement a disaster recovery response that can quickly restore critical systems to normal functionality.
*   Choose a short term or long term approach to your recovery response, depending the incident's severity and your organization's business needs.
*   Establish a single, clear line of communications with stakeholders.
*   Ensure that any internal personnel refer outside parties with questions to the communications team.
*   Use a call tree line of communication to accurately and efficiently spread information to personnel.
*   Document all communication procedures to ensure there are no gaps or undue risks.
*   Ensure that legal counsel and insurance agents are consulted during the restoration process.

ACTIVITY 7-13
Discussing Disaster Recovery Implementation

Scenario

You are the CISO for a popular regional bank that serves a large island nation. The bank has many dozens of ATM machines across the island. A good part of the population depends on these machines to get cash for the weekend.

On Thursday, weather forecasters warn that a powerful storm, typhoon Nancy, will hit the island. Everyone is told to stay indoors. Those nearest the coast are encouraged to board up their windows and move to higher ground until the storm subsides. You and the rest of the bank's emergency response team are on duty at the corporate network operations center, monitoring the situation as well as the bank's infrastructure. As the storm approaches, you are alert but confident. After all, as a CISSP you have properly prepared your team for this kind of incident.

---

1. During the storm, what should be your first priority?
   - ○ To initiate the call tree.
   - ○ To establish a command center.
   - ○ To grab the backup tapes from the server room.
   - ○ To protect human life.

2. What immediate event management responses will this event trigger?

3. What critical systems will you want to restore as soon as the storm has passed?

4. Will your disaster recovery response have a short term approach, or a long term approach?

5. Once your communications center is established, what are the first messages you would send out to internal staff? To customers?

6. In case the phone system is knocked out by the storm, what alternatives can you use to keep communications flowing?

7. After the immediate danger has passed, what must the bank always keep in mind as it restores facilities and operations?

_____

Summary

In this lesson, you discussed the various ways in which security is integral to your business operations. When you apply continuous monitoring, disaster recovery and incident response, change management, and many more key practices to your operations, you'll help ensure that business runs smoothly and with a minimal amount of disruption.

What sort of preventative measures do you incorporate in your environment? How effective are they?

Have you ever been involved in responding to an incident or recovering from a disaster? If so, what steps did you take to mitigate its effects on the organization? Is there anything you would do differently?

 Note: Check your CHOICE Course screen for opportunities to interact with your classmates, peers, and the larger CHOICE online community about the topics covered in this course or other topics you are interested in. From the Course screen you can also access available resources for a more continuous learning experience.

8 Software Development Security

Lesson Time: 3 hours

Lesson Objectives

In this lesson, you will:

- Identify basic security principles in the system lifecycle.

- Specify security principles for the software development lifecycle.

- Determine database security best practices in software development.

- Identify security controls in the development environment.

- Specify best practices in software security effectiveness assessment.

Lesson Introduction

In the last lesson, you learned about security operations. Many organizations not only manage their network infrastructure and systems, but also develop software. This can be for in-house use, or to sell to customers. In this final lesson, you will learn about developing software securely.

TOPIC A

Security Principles in the System Lifecycle

The first thing you must know is what the system lifecycle is. In this topic, you will learn about the system lifecycle, what it shares in common with the software development lifecycle, and how it is different.

 Note: To learn more, view the LearnTO presentations from the **LearnTO** tile on the CHOICE course screen.

The System Lifecycle

It is important to recognize the difference between the overall system lifecycle (SLC) and the system development lifecycle. They sound very similar and are related, but it is important to remember that the SLC is a more all-encompassing process that includes the important phases after system development, particularly operation, maintenance, and disposal.

From a security standpoint, it is extremely important to account and plan for the disposal of the system even before it is built. Many systems are going to create tremendous amounts of data, and the proper protection and disposal of the data and the system is essential to maintaining confidentiality and integrity.

System development activities use many different processes, but most will encompass certain prescribed phases. The following is a commonly referenced SLC implemented by the U.S. Department of Justice (DOJ).

Phase	Description
Project Initiation	Research the general needs and feasibility of the project when a business need is identified and obtain management approval to continue system development.
System concept Development	Once the business need and project are validated, the ideas for fulfilling the need are evaluated. Start to develop funding support. Begin scope documents.
Planning	Review concept integration into existing process. Look for existing or overlapping projects. Determine the functions to be performed during the project and prepare a project plan.
Requirements Analysis	Define functional requirements. Consider user requirements. Create a Functional Requirements Document.
System Design	Proposed user inputs are reviewed by future end users of the system to see if they provide the desired functions.
System Development	Perform the actual programming activities to support the design. Acquire other hardware and software to support the application. This phase includes unit testing of specific modules as they are developed.
Integration and Test	Components are brought together and tested. Quality assurance (QA) testing is performed. Possible certifications and accreditations are obtained.

Phase	Description
Implementation	Prior to installation, evaluate the quality of the system using a separate QA group. Conduct user testing and acceptance, followed by user training. System is installed following the change management group's approval.
Operations/ Maintenance	Conduct a post-implementation review. Continue the operation and maintenance of the system. Changes to the system must be coordinated through the change control function. In-process reviews are ongoing.
Disposal	Terminate the system usage. Determine if the information in this soon-to-be disposed system needs to be brought forward or not. Dispose of the system. Ensure the security of the associated information in the system during and after the disposal phase.

Security in the System Development Processes

Whereas system development processes may have different numbers of steps, different names, and in some cases, different step definitions, it is imperative to deal with security issues as early in the process as possible. Ideally, security personnel should assist in the process from project initiation through the disposal phase.

Security that is implemented late in the development cycle will be less effective than security that is created early in the design phases, when it is developed as part of the overall solution. Security that is introduced late in the project will also be disruptive and likely more expensive. Security professionals are also responsible for ensuring that information confidentiality exists during the disposal phase of any system.

Integrated Product Team

Integrated product and process development (IPPD) is a technique for using multidisciplinary teams to optimize design, development, and deployment. Integrated Product Teams (IPTs) work together to build a program, identify and resolve issues, and make timely decisions. Team members are not necessarily dedicated to a single IPT. Their coordinated effort produces a more balanced and holistic product.

IPTs are assembled by the Program Manager, and may include members from a variety of teams, including:

- Design engineering.
- Development and manufacturing.
- Systems engineering.
- Test and evaluation.
- Contractors.
- Contract administration.
- Quality assurance.
- Training.
- Finance.
- Operations and maintenance.
- Procurement.
- Suppliers.
- Customers.

Another name for IPPD is DevOps. It is based on a lean and agile approach to system and software development. Rather than a daisy chain of one team handing off to the next, all teams are involved from the beginning and throughout the process so any potential issues encountered by one team can be addressed before they even arise.

Maturity Models

A *maturity model* is a framework for assessing the level of sophistication of an organization's processes. In the context of IT, it refers to the degree of formality and optimization of the organization's IT processes. Lower levels of maturity are reactive and ad-hoc. At lower maturity levels, the IT team is mostly "putting out fires." As the IT process becomes more mature, formally defined and repeatable steps are implemented. Metrics are used to measure results. Ultimately, as the overall system fully matures, all IT processes become proactive and optimized.

CMM

The *Capability Maturity Model (CMM)* is a process capability model that evaluates the levels of sophistication or maturity found in an organization's software development process. The model was developed by the Software Engineering Institute (SEI) at Carnegie Mellon University (CMU) in the 1990s. Common use of the CMM® has since expanded to include an organization's general IT operations.

CMM describes five levels of maturity, from lowest to highest, which include:

- Level 1: Initial. Processes are ad hoc and chaotic. It is a starting point.
- Level 2: Managed. Processes are established to track cost, schedule, and functionality. Processes can be repeated.
- Level 3: Defined. Processes are defined and part of standard procedure.
- Level 4: Quantitatively Managed. Processes are quantitatively managed and understood. Metrics are in place.
- Level 5: Optimizing. Process optimization. Continual process improvement.

Each maturity level includes key practices that an organization must exhibit. The levels provide a path to improve development projects. Levels cannot be skipped; they must be achieved in order.

The target maturity level for most organizations is Level 3, where the organization exhibits well-defined processes, solid communications practices, and reviews of output by coworkers. CMM can be used to measure your internal development staff as well as to evaluate a potential outsource vendor.

Operations and Maintenance

After the system has been developed and deployed into production, it must be maintained. From a security perspective, a new team is now responsible for running the system.

The team that developed the system, in conjunction with the business analysts, must create documentation and an operations procedure manual (run book) for the operations team to use and maintain the product. All too often, the team that creates the system may simply pass it off to the team that has to manage it without indicating exactly how to use it. This can of course introduce security vulnerabilities as well as user confusion and loss of productivity. The documentation must also include controls that should be in place. These controls should not only be for when a user uses the product, but also for the types of logging performed by the product as well as a way of maintaining and managing product versions.

The security professional should already have a list of potential vulnerabilities and things to watch for in the system's normal operations. This can include known issues that have not yet been addressed, the need for regular patching, and potential risks that the security practitioner has been documenting throughout the SLC. The CISSP must ensure that the operations team understands these potential risks and incorporates managing them as they operate and maintain the system.

Change Management as an Administrative Control

Change management is a formal process for handling changes to the organization's IT environment. It is an administrative control that seeks to provide efficient handling of changes in a controlled manner. The term change is very broad. It refers to any modification to an existing system including adding user accounts, upgrading the operating system, applying service packs and patches, installing software, or modifying the configuration in any way.

An effective change management system has process and procedures in place. No ad-hoc changes are permitted. Potential changes are first tested and approved. Everything is documented. Backups are made, and a rollback plan is in place in case something goes awry. When the change is implemented, it is done in a controlled and consistent manner so that there are no surprises and no mysteries to disrupt operations. The goal of change management is to reduce the risk associated with changes to systems and infrastructure.

Tests and Integrity Checks

Systems that have been put into production should be periodically tested for continued proper functionality and process integrity. These tests are used to make sure the system or software continues to operate as expected. There should be tests and integrity checks for:

- The program itself.
- Operating instructions.
- Any software utilities that go with the program.
- User skills and requirements.
- Any privileged functions or superuser capabilities.
- The hardware and software system that the program will run on.
- The jobs that will be run on the program.
- Components of the program including files, databases, and reports.
- Any edits to the software, including syntax, sanity checks, range checks, and check digits.
- Data both before and after processing, including counts, batch totals, hashes, and total numbers of transactions.
- Parameter checking for both input and output.
- Valid and legal memory address references.
- Completion codes.
- Peer review between programmers.
- Data library functions, including automated control systems, versioning, and change control.
- Erroneous transaction review and resolution.

Guidelines for Applying Security Principles in the System Lifecycle

 Note: All of the Guidelines for this lesson are available as checklists from the **Checklist** tile on the CHOICE Course screen.

Here are some guidelines you can use to understand security principles in the system lifecycle:

- Keep in mind that the system lifecycle is more comprehensive than the system development lifecycle. It includes operations/maintenance as well as disposal.
- When working on an IT project, consider using integrated product teams to create a more balanced and holistic product.
- Strive to continuously improve IT processes, making them more and more mature.
- Ensure that system development teams create a run book that the operations team can use to manage a system once it is in production.

- Institute a change management process to reduce risk when the IT environment changes.
- Perform periodic integrity checks to make sure the system is still functioning as expected.

ACTIVITY 8-1
Analyzing Security Principles in the System Lifecycle

Scenario

In this activity, you will assess your understanding of security principles in the system lifecycle.

1. How is the system lifecycle different from the system development lifecycle?

   ○ The system lifecycle is more comprehensive than the system development lifecycle, including phases for operations, maintenance, and disposal.

   ○ The system development lifecycle is more comprehensive than the system lifecycle, including phases for operations, maintenance, and disposal.

   ○ There is no difference. You can use the terms system lifecycle and system development lifecycle interchangeably.

   ○ The system lifecycle focuses on creating computer systems, whereas the system development lifecycle focuses on creating applications.

2. How can an integrated product team assist with product development?

3. At which CMM level does an organization have standardized processes?

   ○ Level 1

   ○ Level 2

   ○ Level 3

   ○ Level 4

4. What is the point of a run book?

   ○ It describes how to load and run a program on a mainframe platform.

   ○ It provides the developer team with instructions for deploying an application.

   ○ It is a set of operating instructions written by the developer team for the operations team to use in deployment.

   ○ It is a set of explicit instructions on how to compile an application's source code into an executable.

5. How can implementing change management help raise an organization's CMM level?

6. As you perform periodic tests and integrity checks, what type of non-technical checks should you perform and why?

TOPIC B

Security Principles in the Software Development Lifecycle

Now that you have an understanding of the system lifecycle, it is time to focus on software development. In this topic, you will learn about security concepts in the software development lifecycle.

Programming Basics

Although it is not an expectation of the CISSP® exam that candidates need to know how to program, having a basic understanding of programming terminology and practices will make you a better security professional. It may one day be your job to manage a development project and having a basic understanding of programming and software concepts will make the job easier and the organization more secure.

Machine Language, Assembly Language, and Source Code

Machine language or *machine code* is the lowest level of code, getting right down to the zeros and ones that a computer's central processing unit (CPU) will execute.

Assembly language is a low-level programming language that needs to be processed by an assembler utility to be converted to machine code. Code written in assembly language is highly efficient. It also takes considerably more effort to learn the language. Today's compilers remove the requirement for programmers to learn to write in assembly language. Developers can program in the higher languages more quickly.

Source code is a higher level programing language that is generally human readable; it has enough text-like qualities to start to recognize the intent of the program. Source code needs to be compiled in order for the CPU to recognize it as machine code. A compiler takes the source code and converts it to the assembly language appropriate for the CPU type. The output is an executable file. In Windows, it usually has an .exe extension. In Linux, the extension can be anything, but usually executables have no extension at all.

In addition to source code that is compiled, there are also interpreted languages in which the source code is interpreted directly into machine code at program runtime. This interpretation happens with each execution, as compared to the compiled code that is permanently changed by the compile process.

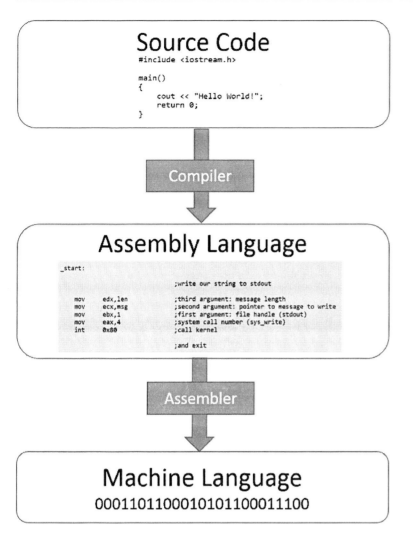

Figure 8-1: Code at different levels.

Program Language Types

There are many ways to categorize programming languages. The most common categorizations are compiled versus interpreted, and procedural versus object oriented. The following provides a high-level overview of some of the different types of languages used in application development.

Program Language Type	Description
Compiled languages	A *compiler* is a program that transforms the source of code of a higher-level language to object code that is understood by the device or operating system. It is often used to create an executable file. Once source code has been compiled into an executable, it can be run many times without the need to compile again. Common compiled languages include Fortran, COBOL, C, C++, C#, Objective-C, and Java. Compiled code is generally considered faster than interpreted code.

Program Language Type	Description
Interpreted languages	Interpreted languages are not put through a compiler but rather use an interpreter that translates the code line by line into machine code each time the application is run. Interpreted languages are usually scripting languages. Common interpreted languages include Perl, Javascript, Postscript, Python, Ruby, PHP, VBScript, Smalltalk, and PowerShell. Interpreted code has an advantage over compiled code because it can run on any machine that has an interpreter, thus providing write once, run many efficiencies.
Procedural languages	Procedural languages use routines, subroutines, methods, and functions. Writing an application involves writing thousands of lines of code. It is considered linear programming. Examples include C, Pascal, Fortran, and COBOL.
Object Oriented Programming (OOP)	OOP creates reusable objects that combine methods and data. The reusable nature of OOP offers potential cost savings and also potential security enhancements. If an object has been deemed secure, it can be re-used with confidence. Examples of object-oriented programming languages include Java, C++, C#, Objective-C, Python, Ruby, Swift, and Smalltalk.

Object Oriented Database

An Object Oriented Database (OOD) is a database management system in which data is represented as objects in order to make programming easier. Developers can work with objects in the database, rather than having to know the traditional database structured query language (SQL).

OOP Terminology

OOP uses objects to perform functions or house information and includes a series of specific terms.

OOP Term	Description/Example
Class	**Description:** A *class* defines the general characteristics of a type of object, including attributes, fields, and operations. A class should be somewhat self-defining. **Example:** The idea of a restaurant could be considered a class. The attributes are the menu items. The operations are the methods of food preparation and service. The allowed inputs are the raw materials, cooks, food servers, and customers. The allowed outputs are the meals that are produced from the menu, which will vary.
Object	**Description:** An *object* is a specific instance of a class. An object is a specific implementation of a class. It inherits its attributes from the class and defines specific values for each attribute. **Example:** Using the restaurant class as an example, a particular restaurant object might be a pizza parlor or an Asian restaurant. They are both restaurants in the general sense, but they produce completely different results.

OOP Term	Description/Example
Modularity	**Description:** *Modularity* isolates all object processes within the object. For programming implementation, the object becomes a single testing entity. If the module works as described in the specification, it is assumed that it will work well with other modules that call upon its services. **Example:** In the restaurant example, modularity assumes that all food is prepared on site. If you have to wait for food to be prepared in another restaurant and then be delivered to your eating location, you would not be pleased.
Method	**Description:** The *method* describes an object's abilities—what the object can do. In OOP, a method generally affects only one particular object. **Example:** The cook method in a pizza parlor will result in a different product set than that created when the cook method is executed in an Asian restaurant.
Encapsulation	**Description:** *Encapsulation* conceals or masks the functional details of a class from the calling objects. **Example:** Most restaurants do not readily release their recipes. When you go to a restaurant, you order the food from the menu. The processes used in food preparation are hidden from view.
Abstraction	**Description:** *Abstraction* generalizes classes to the highest, most appropriate level needed to use them. **Example:** If you are hungry, you might choose to go to a restaurant. If you are craving Northern Italian-style pizza, you would modify the level of abstraction to meet your needs for the specific type of pizza you desire. If you have no preference and want any variety of pizza, your highest level of abstraction would be a pizza parlor.
Polymorphism	**Description:** *Polymorphism* occurs when classes are treated as equivalents and are referred to in identical terms. **Example:** The class might have a method to order_food(). The order_food() method used in a restaurant with a wait staff involves communicating to the server in person. In a restaurant without servers, such as a carry-out restaurant, you communicate through the telephone. The resulting service is the same, but the implementation of the order_food() method is different.

OOP Term	Description/Example
Polyinstantiation	**Description:** *Polyinstantiation* is when a single class is instantiated into multiple independent instances. This can be used for security purposes when you want two different users of the system to get different answers even if they ask the same question. **Example:** Two customers come into your restaurant and both order sausage pizzas. One is a good friend so you make a wonderful Chicago-style deep-dish sausage pizza. The other is your competitor from up the street, so even though he ordered the same thing, you bake up a frozen pizza so he cannot learn your trade secrets.

Cohesion and Coupling

Cohesion is the level of independence of software modules of the same application. A highly cohesive module is highly independent from other modules. It can perform its function with little interaction from other modules. The more a module can do on its own the better, because it makes it more independent in terms of modifications; in other words, it would not affect other modules.

Coupling is the degree and complexity of interaction among modules in an application. When a module has to interact with other modules, which always happens in software, coupling can be low or high. Low coupling means a simple exchange of information in terms of amount and complexity. High coupling implies a higher level of dependencies between the modules. Higher levels of dependencies can create additional complexity, and in general, complexity is the enemy of security. Low coupling is better because it means more independence between modules and simpler software.

Distributed Programming Techniques

There are several distributed programming techniques:

- *Object Request Brokers (ORBs)* can be used to locate objects and can act as middleware for connecting programs.
- *Component Object Model (COM)* and *Distributed Component Object Model (DCOM)* are two Microsoft ORB tools. COM can discover objects on a local system and DCOM can discover objects on the network.
- *Common Object Request Broker Architecture (CORBA)* is an open source ORB framework. CORBA seeks to separate the interface from the instance. This can provide flexibility in design but also provides encapsulation so the client is not able to see all the details of the object.
- *Enterprise JavaBean (EJB)* is a tool from Sun Microsystems that allows for a distributed multi-tier application in Java.

SDLC

The Software Development Lifecycle (SDLC) involves more than simply writing code. Like the system development lifecycle, it has a number of stages:

- Concept and Initiation.
- Requirements.
- Design.
- Build.
- Test.
- Deploy.

You will notice that the SDLC does not include a management or decommissioning phase. This is because the focus is not on software lifecycle *en toto*, but on its development for implementation into production. After the software is developed and put into production, there will be these additional phases within the system lifecycle:

- Operations and Maintenance.
- Revision, Replacement, and Decommissioning.

Security in the SDLC

Because the business will be focused on functionality, and not security, the security professional should be involved in all of the SDLC stages, to ensure that the business considers security from the very beginning of the process. Developers in particular will not be focused on security. They will be under pressure to simply produce working code.

The security professional must be especially aware that embedding security in code is a lot more work for the developer, and will increase the size of the code. In addition, most developers actually do not know how to write code from a security perspective. The CISSP must work with the development team lead and development manager to ensure that developers are given the time, training, and resources necessary to instill security into the products they're creating.

Concept and Initiation

Concept and Initiation is the first stage in the software development lifecycle. In this stage, management lays out its vision for the software it wants to have developed. There is usually a kickoff meeting, and initial funding is granted to perform a feasibility study or create a proof of concept or prototype product.

During this phase, the security practitioner must ensure that the following questions are addressed:

- Will this product or the information it manages have any special value or sensitivity, and therefore special protection needs?
- Will the product itself have any proprietary functionality, and thus be company intellectual property, that will need to be protected in addition to the data that it is processing?
- Has the information owner determined the value of the information?
- If the original data is of low sensitivity, does the result have higher value or sensitivity?
- Are there any regulatory or compliance requirements for this product?
- Has the product received any assigned classifications or categorizations?
- Will use of the product introduce risk or potentially expose sensitive information?
- Will the output or reporting of this product require any special security measures?
- Will any of the data being processed by this product traverse a public or semi public network, and therefore require additional security controls?
- Will the use of the product require any specially secured areas for user interaction or operation?
- What is the potential impact of the product on the organization's operations or culture?
- Is there a risk that the company could become dependent on this product, and therefore will any special support be needed for the product in terms of business continuity?

Requirements

In this stage, all of the business requirements for the functionality of the software are determined. Gathering the requirements can be done through a number of methods, including management directives, user surveys, and focus groups. It is generally the role of the business analyst to gather these requirements from the different stakeholders within the company. End-users will typically want features that are outside the scope of the project or not tenable to implement. Departments will have competing needs. Ultimately, management will decide the final scope and requirements for the project.

The security practitioner must be part of the requirements gathering process, to note potential security risks and to help guide users in their thinking from a security perspective. It is at this stage that risk analysis, both for the software being developed and the project itself, is performed.

Design

During the design stage, the business requirements that were gathered during the requirements phase are translated into functional requirements (features) and nonfunctional requirements (infrastructure requirements to support the software). The security practitioner must be especially aware of how these requirements are being articulated, because they will be used directly by the software development team to actually code the products.

Build

During the build phase the software development team writes code. The security practitioner must insist that testing begins even during the build phase in order to minimize security risks. It is software bugs, from improperly tested code, that introduce security vulnerabilities in software. Most developers are focused on creating functionality.

The most secure way to develop code is to perform unit testing. In a unit test, the developer writes a simple pass/fail test for a single block of code before writing the code itself. At first the code block is expected to fail the test because the code itself has not actually been written. The developer then writes the code and runs the test again. If the developer has written the code block properly, it will pass. If the code does not pass the test, the developer must fix the problem. This method is known as test-driven development. Although it seems like unnecessary work, it assures that every line of code in the software performs exactly what it is supposed to do. This dramatically reduces the amount of bugs in software, and the expense of rework trying to fix those bugs later after the code becomes more complex.

From a security perspective, test driven development provides considerably more assurance that the code is secure because the expectation that security is a priority is understood on a line by line basis. It is software bugs, from improperly tested code, that introduce security vulnerabilities in software. Additionally, the development team can assert with certainty that they have 100% test coverage in their code.

As each developer works on his or her own piece of the software (module), they will start to test functionality between their separate modules. This is known as a system test. Then as the larger software is ready to test with other systems, including connecting to a network or a website, the developers test the software functionality with other teams. This is known as integration testing. At every stage of this testing, the security practitioner must ask the development leads to demonstrate that all known security vulnerabilities have been addressed.

Test

During the test phase, the product is almost ready to deploy. Special groups of users are asked to try the software to see if they like it. This is called acceptance testing. In addition, they test the software to see if it performs properly. Users are especially good at inadvertently discovering faults and flaws, because in their unfamiliarity with the product they will attempt all sorts of unexpected procedures. By observing user interaction during acceptance testing, the security practitioner can be alert for potential vulnerabilities with regard to user interaction. The end of the test phase results in certification and accreditation.

Certification and Accreditation

The final result of the test phase is certification and accreditation. In an enterprise, this will be a formal process that should be concluded before the system or product is put into production.

Certification is essentially a risk evaluation of the final product. The technical team certifies that the product does technically what it's supposed to do.

Accreditation is the formal acceptance of the certification (including any accompanying risk) by the Designated Approving Authority (DAA). The DAA is typically upper management that signs off on the product.

Any system used by the U.S. federal government must have a C&A process performed successfully before it receives approval to operate. The NIST Special Publication 800-37 "Guide for Applying the Risk Management Framework to Federal Information Systems" provides instruction and guidance on certification and accreditation.

The phases of the security C&A process include:

1. Establishing a preferred level of security.
2. Defining a specific environment for system use.
3. Evaluating individual system security.
4. Evaluating network system security.
5. Evaluating physical security.
6. Comparing evaluations to security requirements.
7. Approving the system for a specific time period if the system meets requirements.
8. Evaluating and approving operation if substantial system changes occur before expiration.

Deploy

During this stage, the software is ready to be rolled out into production. It is usually done in two stages: a limited pilot test, and then the general deployment. At this phase, the development team has handed off the product to the deployment team. However, the development team is standing by to fix any problems that might arise, and to warranty the product for a period of time.

During the deployment phase, the security practitioner must not only be on the lookout for software vulnerabilities within the environment, but also any security risks during the deployment process itself. For example, the software might not be patched while it is being rolled out. The deployment team that must make sure it is rolled out in a way that viruses are not introduced before the software is patched in the production environment.

Software Development Methodologies

Over the years, many different software development methods have been created to address the needs of large complex projects. Some of these have been adapted from other project management initiatives. Now, some of the tools developed for software development are also finding their way into project management. One of the more important components of the different methods is how they recognize and allow for security.

Common software development methodologies include:

- Waterfall
- Cleanroom
- Agile
- Prototyping
- Spiral

The Waterfall Model

The *waterfall software development model* creates software projects that flow from one defined phase to the next, as water flows from one level of a waterfall to another. The waterfall method was first used in manufacturing and was adapted for software development in the 1970s.

The term is often used derisively to refer to a rigid, flawed model, but because so many other methods were derived from the waterfall method, it is important to understand. It is considered flawed because in the true waterfall, it is only possible to go down the falls. Once a step has been completed, it is nearly impossible to go back up the falls. In some development projects, this is thought to be an advantage because many checks exist before moving to the next stage, which could actually result in a more secure system or application. In actual implementation, it is typically okay to go back one step. This is sometimes referred to as the modified waterfall. Most waterfall diagrams fail to provide for disposal, which is another concern.

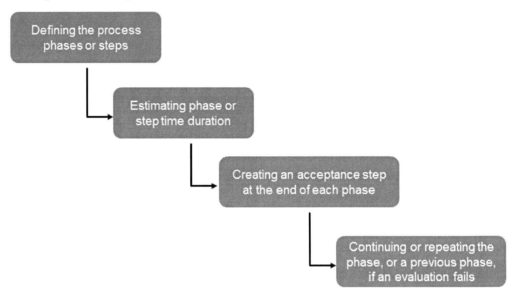

Figure 8–2: A waterfall software development model.

To help control software development, the waterfall model is implemented through a series of stages, which include:

1. Defining the process phases or steps.
2. Estimating the phase or step time duration to determine the project length.
3. Creating an acceptance step at the end of each phase; this is known as a milestone. The project status is evaluated during meetings held at the conclusion of each phase. Approval to proceed must be obtained before the project continues to the next step.
4. Continuing or repeating the phase, or a previous phase, if an evaluation fails.

Security, like functionality, must be deliberately included to appear in the program. If a feature was not specified in the design, it likely won't appear in the final product. Also, by the time the product is finally finished, it might not be what the customer wants or needs, or a changing market might have already made the product obsolete. Even so, there are many projects that are very large and complex, involving sign-off at each stage from many lines of business across the organization. These projects are still best served by the waterfall method.

The Cleanroom Model

The *cleanroom model* takes its name from the cleanroom that chip manufacturers use. It is based on the idea that it is easier and cheaper to keep dust out of the manufacturing process up front by building a cleanroom than it is to eliminate dust after the manufacturing.

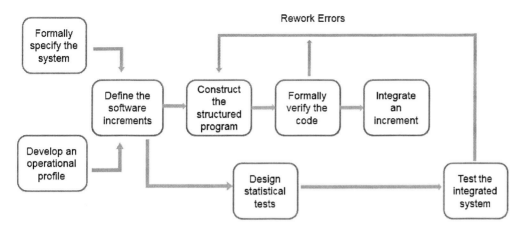

Figure 8-3: The cleanroom process.

In the cleanroom software development method, the goal is to write code correctly the first time, focusing on preventing bugs, rather than removing them after the fact. In this way, cleanroom development is highly security oriented. Cleanroom principles include:

- The software must be formally specified.
- The development is performed incrementally.
- Use a limited number of constructs (basic elements or commands).
- Statistically verify the software using rigorous tests.
- Statistically test the system to determine its reliability.

Agile Software Development

Agile software development was another response to the inflexibility of the waterfall method. Agile embraces flexibility, fast turnaround, frequent input from the customers, and constant improvement.

The key to Agile is that it has short development cycles called *sprints*. A sprint is a short length of time, typically 2 or 4 weeks. The length of a sprint is a fixed time box that cannot be changed. It forces the developers to take on limited, manageable chunks of work, and to stay focused. The goal of each sprint is to produce something—even just a single feature—that is production ready.

At the beginning of each sprint, in the planning phase, the developer team examines the list of desired features (also known as stories), and then informs the customer how much work can be accomplished in that sprint. The customer then prioritizes which stories it wants done first. During the sprint, the entire team works on a single story until it is done. If there is time, the team then moves on to the next story. When the time period for the sprint is done, the team stops, even if it is in the middle of a story.

At the end of each sprint is a retrospective review in which the team determines what went well, and what can be improved in the next sprint. In this way, Agile has built-in process improvement. The deliverable of each sprint is a feature (or even a whole product) that can be put into production.

Note: Just because a sprint produces a production-ready piece of code, this does not mean the code will necessarily be released immediately. Management may choose to wait until a sufficient number of production-ready features are done before releasing a group of features into production.

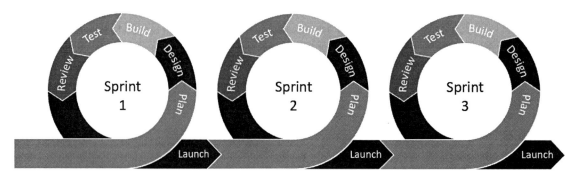

Figure 8-4: The Agile process.

Advantages of Agile include:

- Development periods are highly focused.
- Scope and cost are limited by time.
- The customer quickly realizes which features are unnecessary, and discards them.
- The end of each sprint produces a deliverable that is production ready (though it might not actually be put into production until later).

From a security perspective, the risk with Agile is that focus will be on features and not security. The security practitioner must work with product management to ensure that the stories given to the developer team include security requirements. This is especially true if some of those requirements are compliance-related.

 Note: Some mistakenly think that Agile is a series of mini-waterfalls. This is not the case. With waterfall, there is little or no restriction on time. Scope is pre-determined, and the project does not move on to the next stage until the present stage is complete. With Agile, the strict timebox means that scope expands and contracts based on available time. With each sprint, scope is always focused on the highest priority items, with lower priority items being pushed off until the next sprint, or even discarded completely.

Choosing Agile Over Waterfall

Most organizations are moving their software development process to Agile. If the project is highly complex, however, the strict formality of waterfall might still be a better choice. After all, waterfall was used to put a man on the moon. Agile would not be suitable for such an endeavor. Nonetheless, the constant changing nature of the software industry, and the demand to get product to market quickly makes Agile the methodology of choice for most software development projects today.

The Agile Manifesto

The "Agile Manifesto" was written in 2001 by a group of 17 software developers and is available on the Internet at **http://agilemanifesto.org/**.

It states: "We are uncovering better ways of developing software by doing it and helping others. Through this work, we have come to value:

- Individuals and interactions over processes and tools.
- Working software over comprehensive documentation.
- Customer collaboration over contract negotiation.
- Responding to change over following a plan.

That is, while there is value in the items on the right, we value the items on the left more."

Agile Methodologies

There are several variations of the agile software development model.

Item	Description
SCRUM	*SCRUM* is a variation of Agile. The original authors referred to it in terms of a "holistic or rugby approach." They went on to describe the idea of a group that "tries to go the distance as a unit, passing the ball back and forth." Another author then used the rugby term "scrum" to describe this group and the term stuck. SCRUM uses "sprints to finish components of a project. Each sprint starts with a meeting and ends with a review." Scrum methodology is able to scale to multiple teams in very large organizations.
XP	*Extreme Programming (XP)* focuses on delivering high-quality working software quickly and continuously. Planning is done using a "planning game" that involves the customer. XP uses test-driven development (where the unit test is written first and then the code is written and refined until it passes the test), uses coding standards, and maintains a sustainable pace.
Lean	*Lean* methodology focuses on eliminating waste. It selects only the truly valuable features, prioritizing them, and then producing them in small batches. It emphasizes concurrent work effort while minimizing intra-team dependencies.
Kanban	*Kanban* focuses on continual delivery, while not overburdening the development team. It emphasizes visualizing the day's workflow, limiting the amount of work in progress, and enhancing the flow from one task to the next.
DSDM	*Dynamic Systems Development Method (DSDM)* grew out of the Rapid Application Development (RAD) method. It was designed to address RAD's unstructured approach, providing a framework for planning, managing, executing, and scaling application development using Agile techniques.
Crystal	*Crystal* is one of the most lightweight of the Agile methodologies. It actually uses a family of methodologies to address the unique characteristics of different projects. It is especially focused on adaptability and the removal of bureaucracy and distractions.

 Note: There are many more software development models and methods and there are sure to be more developed in the future. It is important for companies to find a model to that will support their business and security objectives.

The Prototyping Model

The *prototyping model* attempts to address the concerns of the waterfall method by providing early prototypes for users to see and test. The presumption behind prototyping is that the customer is not completely clear on what they want.

A prototype is created and presented to the customer, who then critiques the prototype. From that feedback, a new prototype is created. This process is repeated until the customer is happy with the results.

The four basic steps of the prototype method are:

1. Identify basic requirements.
2. Develop an initial prototype.
3. Review the prototype.
4. Revise and enhance the prototype.

Prototyping is an excellent iterative way to develop software when requirements are not clear. The risk to prototyping, however, is that other important functionality, such as error-checking and security, are typically ignored. The customer may think that a working prototype is a nearly completed product, when in fact it is only a surface display of the product's features. Both the developer and the security practitioner must manage customer expectations during prototyping, making sure that the customer understands that a good prototype is only a sketch of the finished product, and that a lot more coding must be added to ensure stability, performance, and security.

 Note: Creating a prototype is reminiscent of using a police sketch artist to create an image of a suspect. The witness keeps providing feedback to the sketch artist until the right image is created.

The Spiral Model

In the *spiral model,* software development is an iterative process that always starts with risk analysis. At the start of each iteration, a risk analysis is performed. Then the iteration is planned, executed, and tested. As the project matures, the length of each step increases and the project focuses on the solution that meets requirements.

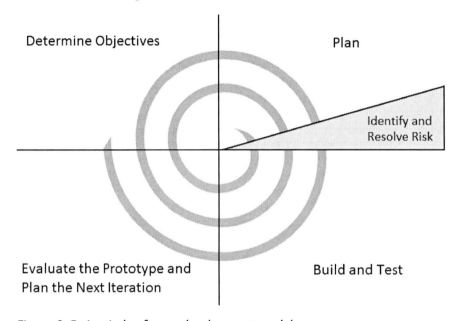

Figure 8-5: A spiral software development model.

The guiding principles for the spiral model include:

- Continuously analyzing risk.
- Establishing a full development team that includes users throughout the process.
- Creating stepped-out requirements and specifications.
- Developing software from the beginning to the end of the project, starting with prototypes and ending with the finished product.
- Alleviating unnecessary backtracking if something is unacceptable; objectionable design or software elements are remedied in the next spiral cycle.

The spiral model is good for large mission-critical projects where risk evaluation is important. The security implication of using the spiral model is that the project is highly dependent on effective risk analysis. The security practitioner must ensure that the organization has sufficient expertise to conduct an effective risk analysis.

Other Development Models

In addition to the development models previously described, there are other models that an organization can benefit from. The following table summarizes the more popular ones.

Model	Description
RAD	Rapid Application Development (RAD) was popular in the 1990's. It is a form of prototyping that sets strict time limits on creating a prototype. It also depends heavily on tools that can speed up the development process. Because it is a fairly unstructured approach, if decisions are made too quickly, it can lead to poor design.
JAD	Joint Analysis Development (JAD). Developed in the 1970's by IBM, this methodology was originally meant for developing large mainframe systems. It uses a management process that allows developers to work directly with users to jointly create a working application. JAD is now used in RAD, web development, and other methods. It is successful when key players communicate at critical phases of the project. Because so many stakeholders participate in JAD, as long as one of the people is security-oriented, JAD can address security requirements in the planning stage.
Exploratory Model	This model is a variation of prototyping in which few or none of the requirements are known ahead of time. Most of the initial specifications are educated guesses. Different designs are tried until one seems appropriate to develop. A rudimentary first generation system is developed and tested. Based on feedback and proposed improvements, a second generation system is developed. The process continues until the user is satisfied, or the project is considered unworkable. Because of the lack of structure, security requirements might be ignored in favor of enhancements.
Component-Based Development	This model uses standard building blocks to assemble a product. It does not build from scratch. The components can be standardized data that has been encapsulated into sets and standard processing methods for working with the data. From a security perspective, this method has the advantage of using components that have already been security tested.
Reuse Model	In this model, the application is built from components that already exist. It is best suited for object-oriented programming. Objects that were developed for other applications can be exported, modified, and reused for the new application. From a security perspective, the developer already knows the security issues of the objects that are being reused. Some objects can even be chosen based on their known security characteristics.

Structured Development

Structured development is based on structured programming concepts that require a careful combination of sequencing, selection, and iteration. It is possible to do structured programming in any language, though it is frequently used with a procedural programming language. By adhering strictly to the techniques of sequencing, selection, and iteration, and avoiding GOTO statements, the code can be made very tight, making it easy to verify and test. It is usually deployed in a top-down model where developers map out the overall program and then break it into modules that can be independently tested. These modules can then be used by other programs and can possibly save costs and development time in future projects.

GOTO Statements

The GOTO statement is used to quickly jump around a program. You essentially go to another line or point in the program. If there are too many such commands, you are left with "spaghetti" code, a derisive term for a program that is hard to follow. "Hard to follow" also means "hard to evaluate" from a security standpoint.

CASE

Computer-Aided Software Engineering (CASE) is not so much a model or a methodology but the adoption of tools and techniques to help with large-scale software projects. It can involve programming tools and computer utilities to help with projects that have many components and lots of people. As large projects are broken apart and assigned to different individuals scattered throughout an organization, the effort to put that all back together into a cohesive program is extremely challenging. CASE tools and training can help.

Guidelines for Implementing Security in the SDLC

Here are some guidelines you can use for implementing security in the software development lifecycle:

- Although the CISSP is not expected to be a programmer, be sure to familiarize yourself with programming basics and terminology to facilitate communication with developers.
- Make sure that initial security questions (ones that will impact the company) are addressed during the Concept and Initiation phase of the SDLC.
- In the Requirements phase of the SDLC, use a variety of methods to gather requirements, especially from end users who will have to use the product.
- In the Design phase of the SDLC, make sure that security requirements are properly articulated and included in the design.
- In the Build phase of the SDLC, make sure that developers unit test as much of their code as possible to minimize errors later on.
- In the Test phase of the SDLC, make sure that end users not only like the product, but that they are also utilized to see if they discover any additional bugs in the software.
- During the Deploy phase of the SDLC, try a limited pilot deployment first before conducting a full-scale rollout of the product.
- Use the waterfall model if your project is big and complex.
- Use the cleanroom model if your project is highly security-oriented, and you are willing to spend the time and resource to write code correctly the first time.
- Use an Agile model if you want to create high quality code in a time-boxed, focused manner.
- Use the prototyping model if the customer is not sure exactly what they want.
- Use the spiral model if you want to iteratively develop software while performing a risk analysis at the start of each iteration.
- If none of the above software development models works for you, consider other models such as RAD, JAD, Exploratory, Component-based, or reuse.
- Use structured development if you want code that is easy to verify and test.
- Use CASE tools to help automate your application development.

ACTIVITY 8-2
Discussing Security Principles in the Software Development Cycle

Scenario

You work as the CISO in a global technology company. The organization has thousands of application developers spread out across three continents working on many projects. For two decades, the company used the Waterfall model to develop software. Over the past few years, internal pressure to remain competitive drove some departments to try other software development models. Lately, there has been growing support for a company-wide move towards Agile. The CIO is trying to determine the business case for each of the methodologies. She has asked you to survey the company's various development projects to gain insights into the benefits of the various techniques being used. She is especially interested in any security considerations associated with each method.

1. Why are most developers writing in higher level languages instead of assembly language, considering that code written in assembly is so much more efficient?

2. What is the biggest benefit of using an interpreted language over a compiled language?

3. How does encapsulation in object-oriented programming promote information security?
    - ○ It encrypts the data inside to protect it from accidental disclosure.
    - ○ It divides the code into discrete parts so that it cannot be easily reassembled by a malicious process.
    - ○ It generalizes a class to the highest level necessary for use.
    - ○ It hides the code details of a class from other objects trying to use that class.

4. What is the value of using CORBA?
    - ○ It allows for a distributed multi-tier application in Java.
    - ○ It provides flexibility and encapsulation.
    - ○ It can discover objects on the network.
    - ○ It can be used to locate objects and can act as middleware for connecting programs.

5. What phases of a product's lifecycle are not addressed by the SDLC? (Choose two.)
    - ☐ Concept and Initiation
    - ☐ Revision, Replacement, and Decommissioning
    - ☐ Operations and Maintenance
    - ☐ Build and Test

6. From a security perspective, what is the greatest risk in any software development project?

   ○ There will be insufficient testing.

   ○ The development methodology will not include enough encapsulation of object classes.

   ○ The business will be focused on functionality to the exclusion of most other considerations.

   ○ The development environment will not be secure.

7. What are some security considerations that must be addressed at the Concept and Initiation phase?

8. At what phase of the SDLC should risk assessment be conducted?

   ○ Concept and Initiation

   ○ Requirements

   ○ Design

   ○ Build

9. What security considerations should be addressed in the SDLC Design phase?

   ○ Risk assessment should be conducted during this phase.

   ○ Security requirements should be clearly articulated during this phase.

   ○ Security testing should be conducted during this phase.

   ○ Security documentation should be developed at this phase.

10. How can test driven development (TDD) provide security during the Build phase?

11. How can users help with the security aspect of the Test phase in the SDLC?

12. What is the difference between certification and accreditation in software development?

   ○ Certification results from a technical test, whereas accreditation results from management acceptance.

   ○ Accreditation results from a technical test, whereas certification results from management acceptance.

   ○ There is no difference. The two refer to the same thing.

   ○ Accreditation is a necessary step that must be achieved before certification.

13. What security considerations must be addressed during the Deploy phase of the SDLC?

14. Is there still a use case for using the waterfall model to develop software?

15. From a security perspective, what makes cleanroom a desirable development methodology?

16. From a security perspective, what is the greatest risk of using Agile methodology to develop software?

17. Does Agile methodology ignore documentation?

18. If the development team wanted to especially involve the customer, which version of Agile should it use?
   - ○ SCRUM
   - ○ XP
   - ○ Lean
   - ○ Kanban

19. If the development team uses the prototyping model, why must the security practitioner manage customer expectations during development?

20. From a security perspective, what is the benefit of using the spiral development model?

21. Which of the following is especially suited to addressing security requirements during the planning stage?
   - ○ RAD
   - ○ JAD
   - ○ Exploratory Model
   - ○ Component-Based Development

22. How does using Structured Development techniques support code security?

23. How can using Computer Aided Software Engineering (CASE) assist in developing a complex application?

TOPIC C

Database Security in Software Development

No software development lesson would be complete without also studying database security. Many applications must access some kind of database to obtain needed data. In this topic, you will learn about database security in software development.

Database Systems

A *database system* is a set of related information within a software framework that is organized for ease of access and reporting. The information can be added to, edited, or deleted. It uses a Database Management System (DBMS) to oversee data. The DBMS also provides the commands for performing functions to the data.

A modern database system provides many features, which include:

*   A data definition language to create the structure of various tables.
*   A query language to access the information in the database.
*   Indexes or keys for efficient access to the information in the database.
*   A security structure to limit access based on pre-defined criteria.
*   Built-in bounds and limits checking.
*   Enforcement of data content rules within the database. This backstops poor programming practices with database rule implementation.
*   Internal integrity checks.

 Note: Oracle and Microsoft® SQL Server are both examples of a database system.

Database System Models

There are several database system models that each define how data is stored and accessed.

Database System Model	Description
Hierarchical Database Model	In this model, data is implemented in a tree-like structure. Relationships are created with a parent-child view. A single parent can have many children but each child can only have a single parent. These are largely legacy databases.
Network Database Model	This model is a type of hierarchical database implemented using pointers to other database elements so that traversing information in the database requires the use of pointers to locate subsequent entries. Children can have many parents. It refers to networks of data relationships and is not related to communication networking.
Relational Database Model	This model allows a designer to create relationships among the various database components. Multiple tables are defined and the relationships between them are established through structured methods. This is the most common database model at this point.

Database System Model	Description
Object-Oriented Database Model	The Object Oriented Database Model (OODBM) uses object-oriented programming (OOP) techniques with database technology. In object-oriented databases, the clients' access to the data is obtained by gaining entry to the database object in a closed environment. Programmers have limited control over the database. The object defines what may be accessed and how database access is accomplished.

Data Warehousing

A *data warehouse* is a pre-processed database that contains information about a specific subject from various sources, and is used for subsequent reporting and analysis. When developing an application, you will often write code that queries a data warehouse for information as opposed to querying a single database.

When creating warehouses, it is often necessary to pre-process the information to create data-consistent coding. For example, one information source in the warehouse might store telephone numbers as alphabetic data that include dashes, such as 212-555-1123. Another data source might store phone numbers in a numeric format, such as 2125551123. By pre-processing the information, a consistent phone number storage arrangement is determined and implemented.

Once data warehouses are created, they are not updated. If updates are required, another warehouse is created. This is to protect the value of the data if subsequent comparison reports are necessary.

Example: Voter Information

Political parties often create data warehouses containing voter information. This information is obtained from voter registration files. It is combined with census information, property tax information, vehicle registration information, and other data sources. This warehouse can then be used to perform an analysis of voting populations within precincts to create lists for political canvassing and other uses.

Data Mining Techniques

Data mining is the practice of analyzing large amounts of data to locate previously unknown or hidden information. As you develop your application, you might include code that performs data mining. Although inference and aggregation are attack techniques used by hackers, you can also use them legitimately to glean more information from the data than would normally be apparent. This allows you to make better decisions, so you can provide the best products and services. The following table gives examples of using data mining in your application.

Data Mining Technique	Description
Inference	A data miner reviews data trends and formulates predictions about the subject matter.
	For example, inference can be used to study the incidence of cancer in large populations. By comparing symptoms and disease incidents, it is possible to infer that some symptoms are better indicators of the disease's presence than others.

Data Mining Technique	Description
Aggregation	The summarization of information found in the data repository can be used for different purposes. Summarizing information rather than exposing the data directly enables different groups of users to make inferences by only looking at information they are authorized to see.
	For example, aggregation can also help in the study of a population's cancer incidence. By examining patient data and aggregating mortality information, it is possible to ascertain the average remaining lifetime of the population when considering the overall life span determined from the aggregation.
	Users are collecting data classified at a lower level to make inferences about data that would be classified at a higher level.

Database Vulnerabilities

An array of database vulnerabilities should be considered to avert disclosure risks, maintain confidentiality, and ensure data integrity. Software developers will often be required to write applications that retrieve data from databases. As a CISSP you should be aware of common database vulnerabilities so that you can help the development team make sure that your organization's application does not inadvertently contribute to those vulnerabilities.

Database Vulnerability	Cause(s)
Access control bypass	Database administrators (DBAs) can bypass normal application security and gain direct access to database information. This presents a security risk as unaudited and unedited updates might occur.
Aggregation	As mentioned previously, aggregation is the combination of nonsensitive data from separate sources to create sensitive data. Although you may need to use aggregation to better analyze data so the company can make more informed decisions, you must be careful that your application does not improperly disclose any sensitive data produced by aggregation. In practice, it is very difficult to completely de-identify data. Data that has had too much personally identifiable information removed or masked usually becomes too generic. It ceases to accurately represent the population, thus losing its analytical value.
Improper view restrictions	A *view* is a user portal into a database. Views are often restricted based on need to know or least privilege. With databases, there may be a way to negotiate an established view for a group of users by using programming techniques, such as an SQL injection attack, to gain access when it is not authorized.
DoS	When massive databases are scanned row by row in search of nonexistent data, a denial of service (DoS) outcome may be produced. This type of vulnerability can be threatened either intentionally or inadvertently. Poorly designed queries may result in a DoS when an unexpected system load occurs.

Database Vulnerability	Cause(s)
Deadlocks	A *deadlock* occurs when one transaction requires the use of a resource that is locked by another transaction. This often transpires when two or more transactions are waiting on resources locked by a separate transaction.
	If a program reads a row in update mode, the row is locked until the update is complete. Other users have to wait until the lock is released. Deadlocks can also occur if two transactions are waiting on each other's locked rows.

Database Controls

Database systems contain various embedded security features that help deter unauthorized database access. You may be asked to help guide the development team in creating an application that allows a user to enter or retrieve data from a database. In that case, they will need to include security controls in the code to protect the data from unauthorized modification or disclosure. The following table summarizes common database security mechanisms.

Database Security Mechanism	Description
Lock controls	*Lock controls* temporarily give exclusive access to a record to a single user or process. This prevents confusion when two people or processes are trying to update the same record. With a lock, only one can update a record at a time. Though necessary, lock controls can also produce deadlocks. Ensure that, as you write your application, any process that needs to change a record locks the record during the transaction so that no other process can modify it.
View-based access controls	A *view-based access control* is one in which a user is limited to viewing only certain fields (columns) in a record. Often a table will contain fields that have different levels of sensitivity. For example, an employee record will have regular information such as first name, last name, and employee ID. But it may also contain sensitive information such as salary, Social Security number, age, and other PII. You can use view-based access controls in your application to limit what fields a user can see, based on the user's role. For example, a data entry clerk should be restricted to only seeing non-sensitive fields, but a manager may need to see all fields in the employee record.
Grant and revoke access controls	*Grant and revoke access controls* extend the right to give access to others. Access controls on a database need not be limited to just entering and viewing information. Your application might need to give certain users the right to grant access to other people. For example, you might have an application that lets a student share his or her academic transcript with others. In that case, the student needs to have the ability to grant read access to the transcript record. Similarly, that same student should have the right to revoke (remove) any access that has been granted.
Security for object-oriented databases	Object-oriented databases have characteristics that make them very different from traditional relational database management systems (RDBMS). An OODBMS can use the same concepts for security that are the hallmark of object-oriented programming: encapsulation, inheritance, information hiding, and methods. You can also classify the sensitivity of an object through the use of class and instance. When an instance of a class is created, the object can automatically inherit the security level of its parent class.

Database Security Mechanism	Description
Metadata controls	*Metadata* is information that describes specific characteristics of data, such as origin, condition, content, and/or quality. In object-oriented systems, controlling access to metadata limits what users can discover about information available through objects.
Data contamination controls	Bounds checking, data typing, data length restrictions, and well-formed transactions are all methods used to control data contamination in the database.
OLTP controls	*Online transaction processing (OLTP)* presents issues related to concurrency and atomicity. If a user attempts to buy the last copy of a book at an online bookstore at the same time another user is making the same purchase, who gets the book? Row locking, atomicity, and logging are all used to ensure that only one book is sold and that the record of that sale is permanently recorded should the system fail.
Noise and perturbation	Artificial data is inserted to act as noise in order to confuse the users that should not have access. Legitimate users will have the noise filtered out. *Perturbation* is the intentional addition of spurious data into database fields with the intention of defeating inference attacks.
Cell suppression	*Cell suppression* involves intentionally hiding cells containing highly confidential information. The cells may be suppressed for everyone or they might be suppressed based on the ID of the user accessing the data. The database needs to allow for statistical analysis without allowing access to personally identifiable information (PII) so a certain amount of cell suppression is enforced.
Partitioning	The logical splitting apart of a database into independent parts. This is sometimes done for performance but it can also increase security by limiting what information is made available.

Guidelines for Implementing Database Security in Software Development

Here are some guidelines you can use for database security in software development:

*   If you have to design the database yourself, choose the database model that is most appropriate for your data. In most cases, it will be relational or object-oriented.
*   If your application must retrieve data from a data warehouse, you may have to pre-process the information to keep the data consistent.
*   Your application may have to use data mining techniques such as inference and aggregation in order to better analyze the data. Be careful to not inadvertently disclose any sensitive data obtained from these techniques.
*   Become familiar with common database vulnerabilities, and make sure that your code does not inadvertently contribute to these vulnerabilities.
*   Become familiar with database controls so that you can use them effectively in your application.

ACTIVITY 8–3
Discussing Database Security in Software Development

Scenario

You are an information security consultant for a Non-Governmental Organization (NGO) in a developing nation. The organization's major project for the past seven years has been to collect medical records from millions of patients around the country. The goal has been to track public health trends and to determine what impact, if any, public policy has had on stemming the rising epidemics of maternal mortality and drug-resistant tuberculosis.

For years, patient data had been duly recorded by health professionals into SQL databases around the country. That data was eventually rolled up to the district, provincial, and then finally the national level. Until recently, however, the technology did not exist in the country to deeply analyze the millions of records and terabytes of raw data that had been captured. The data is still housed in multiple databases. Despite efforts to standardize the data format, different organizations made their own variations in the data format.

The government wants to bring all of this disparate data together to take advantage of new data warehousing and mining techniques. The NGO developer team, while skilled in the C# programming language, has only basic experience in working with databases. Most of the developers do not know the SQL language, and have no idea what security capabilities exist in a database engine. The NGO, bound by the rules of PII, wants to make sure that the data is used both effectively and ethically. They have asked you to assist the developer team in keeping the data secure while mining it for public health information.

---

1. What general security features can you insist that the database developers include in the database to help protect the data?

2. Would this project benefit from using an object-oriented database model?

3. What will probably have to be done to the data before attempting to combine all of the databases into a single data warehouse?

4. What data mining technique can be used to help predict health trends across the nation, based on the existing data?
   - ○ Data warehousing
   - ○ Data mining
   - ○ Inference
   - ○ Aggregation

5. What data mining technique can be used to view trends without exposing individual health records?

   ○ Data warehousing

   ○ Data mining

   ○ Inference

   ○ Aggregation

6. What is the risk of using aggregation in your data mining process?

7. The developer team recently wrote some code to aggregate national data into summary reports. Initial tests using a few thousand records performed perfectly. However, when the reports were run against the production database with its millions of records, the database crashed.

   What do you think might have happened?

8. Various government agencies want to be able to query the database in an ad-hoc manner. You need to ensure that users can only see data that is appropriate for their need, and no more.

   What security techniques can you use to ensure that the amount and type of data users see is limited to their job requirement, especially if the application uses an object-oriented database model?

TOPIC D

Security Controls in the Development Environment

It is difficult if not impossible to produce a clean product in a dirty work environment. In order to develop secure software, you will need to implement security controls in the development environment itself.

Software Categories

There are two types of software categories that are used by organizations. As you develop your software, you will have to choose whether to make it proprietary or open source.

Software Category	Description
Proprietary software	*Proprietary software* is software that is developed by an organization that does not disclose the source code. From a security perspective, proprietary software is a black box. The proprietary vendor's claims of security are validated by testing, but cannot be evaluated by code inspection. On some occasions security may be validated with a third party testing lab or the product may have achieved Common Criteria or other assurances already. This can still leave the software open to undisclosed or unexpected vulnerabilities. A well-known example of proprietary software is Microsoft® Windows®.
Open source software	*Open source software* is software that is provided to a buyer with a complete copy of the source code. Purchasers can evaluate the security of open source software by examining the code provided. Although code inspection may not result in the discovery of all vulnerabilities, the purchaser has the opportunity to analyze the software rather than trust the vendor to supply vulnerability information. Since everyone in the open source community can look at the code, many believe that all errors will be discovered eventually. This is sometimes referred to as Linus' Law, which states, with sufficiently many eyeballs looking at the code, all bugs will become apparent. While this sounds good, it is also possible that a dishonest user will see the error and not report it until they know that customers are using the code. Then, when they reveal the bug, they will be compromising the company using the software. A well-known example of open source software is Linux. Linus' Law is a reference to the creator of Linux, Linus Torvalds.

Values of Proprietary vs. Open Source Software

Proprietary software, because of the closed nature of the system, presents an evaluation problem for security professionals. Open source software removes the evaluation limitations of proprietary software, yet hackers and other malware creators also have access to the open source and can create exploits based on their own code analyses. Each type of software has its own benefits; however, security professionals continue to struggle with the limitations of each.

Software Environment Security

In a computing environment, most user activity involves some sort of software. It's crucial that all software, including the operating systems that applications run on, uphold the CIA triangle. It's also crucial that all software development processes operate with security in mind. If applications are not developed properly, there's a very great risk that data can become corrupt or information can be leaked to the outside world.

This is especially true in today's environment where a lot of computing is done in a distributed manner. Today's systems are becoming increasingly more complex and virtualized. Heterogeneous systems are now being connected between partners and vendors. For example, when you buy airline tickets, your frequent flyer membership can lead you to third-party websites for special offers including car rentals, hotels, gifts, and other awards. These sites are not maintained by the airline. Today's online applications not only involve the hardware and operating system of a specific machine, but will also most likely involve one or more virtual machines running on another server, a network operating system and utilities, remote procedure calls and automated access to other websites, an object request broker between disparate systems, database and Web servers, and a variety of APIs between processes.

Since most of these processes are automated, requiring proprietary software that works between organizations, developing that software in a secure manner is the single most important thing you can do. The difficulty will be setting an enforceable standard for secure software development. In most cases this will require changing the developer culture in the organization, including management's expectations and requirements on the developer teams.

The security professional must get management to understand that proper business functionality (and sometimes even the survival of the company itself) depends on how well systems run. If these systems are built in-house, development practices must be centered around security, and not simply include security as an after-thought. There must be a clear, thoughtful, enforceable security policy when it comes to software development. Developers must be trained in writing secure code. There must be rigorous testing of the software before it is put into production. And management must give developers the time and resources necessary to write that secure code.

Best Practices for Secure Software Development

(ISC)[2] lists 10 best practices for secure software development:

- Protect the Brand Your Customers Trust.
- Know Your Business and Support it with Secure Solutions.
- Understand the Technology of the Software.
- Ensure Compliance to Governance, Regulations, and Privacy.
- Know the Basic Tenets of Software Security.
- Ensure the Protection of Sensitive Information.
- Design Software with Secure Features.
- Develop Software with Secure Features.
- Deploy Software with Secure Features.
- Educate Yourself and Others on How to Build Secure Software.

Note that in the above list, there is no mention of a specific technology or product to use. This of course is because technologies and products will constantly change. What you must set is a secure mindset in the business and the software development department. Make sure always that software development is driven by the idea that only authorized subjects (persons, systems, and other processes) can access your system and information, and only in the level necessary to complete the task.

 Note: For more information on the ISC(2) 10 best list, see the article "The 10 best practices for secure software development" at **https://www.isc2.org/uploadedfiles/ (isc)2_public_content/certification_programs/csslp/isc2_wpiv.pdf.**

Source Code Analysis Tools

Using source code analysis tools will help automate the process of reviewing code for software flaws. They are fast, can be run repeatedly, and can scan millions of lines of code much faster than any development team. However, do not assume that they will find all weaknesses. Additionally, many of these tools will inundate you with false positives. Consider source code analysis tools to be one of a number of mechanisms for ensuring a secure software environment.

There are many source code analysis tools available, both free and commercial. The following table lists some open source/free examples.

Tool	Description
Google CodeSearchDiggity	Uses Google Code Searches to find vulnerabilities in open source code. Will check projects hosted by Google Code, MS CodePlex, Source Forge, GitHub, and more.
FindBugs	Locates bugs and some security flaws in Java.
FXCop	Examines code assemblies in Microsoft.net and provides recommendations for design, localization, performance, and security improvements.
PreFast	Identifies defects in C/C++ programs.
RATS	Analyzes C, C++, HP, PYTHON, and Perl source code for buffer overflows and Time of Check/Time of Use (TOC/TOU) race conditions.
Brakeman	Vulnerability scanner for Ruby on Rails applications.

Note: Another excellent resource for discovering vulnerabilities in your code is the OWASP project. This is an international non-profit organization whose sole mission is to help developers improve software security. For more information about OWASP, visit their website at **www.owasp.org**.

Source Code Weakness

Source code is the original software code that developers can modify to create or implement a new product. Since source code is software in itself, it can have all of the software vulnerabilities that have already been described. Security professionals should be particularly concerned about any vulnerabilities in source code, because developers in your organization will use that source code as the foundation for developing new products. Source code must be thoroughly tested to make sure that it has no known vulnerabilities, so that developers can use it with confidence.

Disclosure

So what do you do when you have found a bug or security flaw in a vendor's piece of hardware or software?

Full disclosure involves releasing the information immediately and publicly. It is obviously controversial, but some feel that if they found it, others could have too, and everybody should know as quickly as possible. There are even publicly available websites dedicated to full disclosure. Most organizations would consider full disclosure unethical.

Partial disclosure, sometimes referred to as responsible disclosure, involves sharing the information with the hardware or software vendor first. This gives them a chance to fix the problem and release a patch. In some cases, if the reporting person feels the company is not taking them seriously or is taking too long to release a patch, the individual may resort to revealing the flaw publicly.

Software Vulnerabilities and Mitigation

There are many different software vulnerabilities to pay attention to during development. The following table lists the vulnerabilities and mitigation techniques.

Software Vulnerability	Description and Mitigation
Buffer overflow	Buffer overflows happen when more data is sent than the buffer is designed to accept and no boundary checking is in place. When the program writes the data that is beyond the buffer, it can result in existing information being overwritten, memory corruption, or in a worse-case scenario, the execution of unapproved code. To prevent buffer overflow exploitations, programmers should perform length checking or bounds checking on fields within a program.
Citizen programmers	These unskilled programmers create scripts and macros during their daily tasks and are often unaware of the risks triggered by their activities. Modern word processing applications and spreadsheets include scripting languages that give end users a lot of power. These activities can, subsequently, cause unnecessary problems with programming results. Be sure that you employ professional programmers and designers on your projects who have appropriate training and experience and follow commonly accepted best practices for application security design.
Covert channel	Unskilled programmers and designers often introduce and exploit covert channels in their designs and programs through unsound security practices. Be sure that the programmers and designers who work on your projects are well trained and adhere to the proper standards and specifications.
Malware	Programmers and designers must defend against malware when designing and writing systems. Internal program integrity checks can determine whether unwanted program additions have occurred through the emergence of the following types of malware: • Viruses • Worms • Hoaxes • Trojans • Remote Access Trojans (RATS) • Distributed denial of service (DDoS) zombies Furthermore, programming supervisory staff must review code prior to its release to confirm that none of the following malware has been introduced by programmers: • Logic bombs • Spyware • Adware • Easter eggs Be sure to run integrity checks and conduct code reviews to make sure that malware has not entered your code.
Malformed input	Programmers have an obligation to ensure that information entered into fields is properly formatted; if not, it must be rejected. Allowing numeric input when alphabetic information is required is a form of malformed input. This may cause failures in programs accessing the defective data. Make sure that your code validates input before accepting it.

Software Vulnerability	Description and Mitigation
Object reuse	Programmers should verify that previously recorded disk space or memory addresses are cleared and returned to the operating system when no longer needed. Make sure your application releases these resources as part of its cleanup process.
Executable/ mobile code	Web browsers suffer from failures such as the unexpected implementation of executable content or mobile codes on a server that has been injected into a Uniform Resource Locator (URL). *Mobile code* refers to executable software that is obtained from remote systems and installed on a local system without the recipient's knowledge, consent, or doing. Mobile code can include scripts, Adobe Flash® animations, Microsoft® ActiveX® controls, Java™ applets, Adobe® Shockwave® files, and macros. Be cognizant of these limitations and verify that system input does not contain unexpected information that may be executable and present a security risk.
Social engineering	To protect against social engineering attacks, such as shoulder surfing, make sure that you employ simple programming techniques that circumvent echoing passwords or that mask password entries with characters such as asterisks (*).
Time of check/ time of use	Programmers must be sensitive to the problems inherent in time of check/ time of use (TOC/TOU) situations. TOC/TOU requires that certain things happen in a certain order. For example, it is important that the system checks a user's credentials before using those credentials for access. Early data and data access edits and checks may lead to an insecure situation if the data is then accessed or applied at a later time. Make sure that the check of data and the use of data must be performed within a minimal interval of time.
Trapdoors and backdoors	These common techniques for acquiring unauthorized program or system access during program development and testing are security risks at the system production phase. Make sure that all trapdoors and backdoors are removed before system implementation.

Software Security Controls

An operating system or application environment contains various software control functions that help to secure systems during software development. The following table summarizes the most common control types.

Software Control	Description
Security kernel	The part of the operating system that enforces the reference monitor (RM).
Processor privilege state	Ensures that only operating system functions are executed in the privileged or supervisory state of the CPU and that user programs do not access privileged instructions.
Buffer overflow security	Internal operating system or application controls on bounds that reduce the likelihood of buffer overflows.
Incomplete parameter	Embedded controls in an operating system or application that verify the usage of proper data types in system calls.
Memory protection	An application must not be able to access the memory area of another application or the operating system. The memory mapping function of the central processing unit (CPU) enforces this restriction.

Software Control	Description
Covert channel controls	Covert channel tools, such as the Information Flow Model, that perform a thorough system design analysis.
Cryptography	Encrypting information stored in online or offline media for data confidentiality and integrity protection. Encrypting data in transit with IP security (IPSec).
Password protection	Passwords must be protected through encryption techniques, such as hashing, when stored on computer systems. Both operating systems and applications use passwords.
Granularity of controls	Providing a sufficient level of access control limitations in both the operating system and the application increases data protection. Applications can enforce their own access controls or integrate with single sign-on (SSO) options that may be available.
Environment separation	Just as separation of duties (SoD) provides additional security, controlling the software environment and separating information into views for different types of users also amplifies security.
Backups	Having backups available can protect the availability of data in the event of a disaster.
Training	Training developers and users of the application.
Scanning	Periodic scans and reviews of the applications to make sure there have been no modifications.

APIs

An Application Programming Interface (API) is a set of functions provided by the developer of an application or application module. Other developers who are writing other software or modules can have their code "talk" to the API to invoke those functions. APIs make code modular. A developer needs only write a piece of code and then create an API that exposes the functions of that code (but not the code itself) so that other developers can have their software or system interact with the module. Nearly all modern operating systems and applications use APIs.

From a security perspective, an API can introduce security risks, mainly because functionality of the module is being exposed to the general public and can be accessed by other unknown systems that are written to talk to that API.

The most common way that a hacker can try to break into a software module is to "provoke" the API with unexpected content. The hope is that the unexpected input into that API will cause the software module to handle the content incorrectly, returning error messages that teach the malicious developer about the internal workings of the software module that he or she is trying to break into. For example, if the API indicates that there is a database hidden behind it, the hacker might try using SQL injection or some other database attack.

The security professional should test (or get a competent developer to test) target systems by attacking the APIs, trying to get them to behave in a way that helps you discover and fix their vulnerabilities.

Code Repositories

A code repository is a file archive that stores source code for development projects. The repository can be publicly or privately available, either online or on a private server. Typically when a team works on creating software, different developers are assigned different modules or tasks to work on. A code repository allows the entire project to be stored in a centralized location. Developers check out their part of the code, work on it, and then check it back in. Having a single code repository also allows code version control as well as general oversight by peer reviewers and developer leads. The security professional should be able to also access the code repository to see what tests have been run on the code and to see the progress different developers are making.

The code repository should be secured just like any other system that stores intellectual property. This includes physical security of the server, patching and hardening of the operating system, and access controls on the repository. It also includes secure mechanisms for accessing the system locally or over the network, checking out, and checking in the software from the repository. There should be regular backups of the repository and a disaster recovery plan in case of failure. Again, only authorized individuals should be permitted to access the repository, and only so far as they require for their jobs.

There are many code repository hosting services available online. Some popular ones include:
- GitHub
- Assembla
- Visual Studio Online

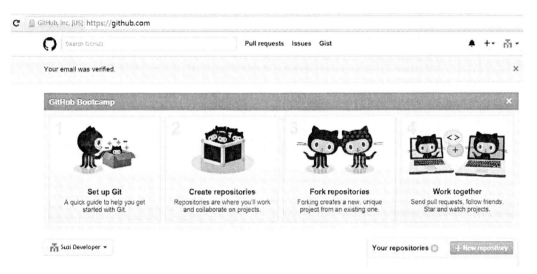

Figure 8-6: GitHub.

 Note: Many repositories are cloud-based so you will want to check their security polices since you won't be in control of the physical server.

Software Escrow

When proprietary software is used, access to the source code is not available. If the vendor stops supporting the product with patches—or worse, goes out of business—risk increases. It is possible to work with the vendor to use a *software escrow* agent to hold onto a copy of the source code. There will be rules and restrictions around how and when access to the source code is granted, but it could protect the company, especially if the company plans to use the software for a long time.

Secure Configuration Management

In software development, configuration management means more than controlling the version of software under development or release to production. The software should maintain its integrity and availability. All components of the software product should be the correct version including the code itself, its documentation, any design documents, and related control files. As with any configuration and change management system, your software configuration management system should first identify any changes that have been made.

These changes must be reviewed and authorized. In addition, any changes must be verified to ensure that the correct change was made. The configuration management process itself should be secured so that it follows an auditable, consistent, verifiable process.

The whole point of configuration management is to eliminate any confusion or error introduced by different versions of the code, or parts of the code. You do not want to allow different team members to unintentionally use the wrong version of the code or introduce wrong versions of the code into the final product.

Guidelines for Enforcing Security Controls in the Development Environment

Here are some guidelines you can use to enforce security controls in the development environment:

- Develop proprietary software when you do not wish to disclose the source code.
- Develop open source software when you wish to share the source code with others or invite peer review by other developers around the world.
- When you develop software, start with a secure mindset. Use that same mindset to drive everything you do.
- Use source code analysis tools to help automate the process of reviewing your code. However, do not assume that an automated tool will discover all weaknesses.
- Thoroughly test your source code so that other developers can use it with confidence.
- If you discover a flaw in an application, notify the vendor first to give the vendor a chance to patch it, rather than immediately publishing the flaw online.
- Become familiar with common software vulnerabilities. Make sure your own code includes parameter checking, input validation, and other controls to mitigate those vulnerabilities.
- Use code reviews to help discover bugs in your software.
- Use APIs to control the level of access other processes have to your application.
- Use a code repository to centralize the source code and control of your development project.
- Consider using software escrow to ensure that a customer has access to code that is under development, even if the vendor goes out of business.
- Use secure configuration management to protect your code versions and documentation.

ACTIVITY 8-4

Discussing Security Controls in the Development Environment

Before You Begin

Review the scenario in the activity titled "Discussing Database Security in Software Development."

Scenario

You are an information security consultant for a Non-Governmental Organization (NGO) in a developing nation. The developer team has been working on creating data mining software for the national health record database. There has been fierce debate over whether or not to make the application proprietary or open-source. There also has been much discussion over the need to implement security controls in the development environment. The developer team has always focused on functionality, and has not thought much about security as they develop code. Management has turned to you to help identify security risks and mitigation techniques that can be implemented in the development environment.

---

1. What can you tell management about the risks of developing proprietary versus open source software?

2. Why is it important to implement security in the software development environment?

3. What is the key message behind (ISC)²'s Best Practices for Secure Software Development?

4. Why must you not depend on automated source code analysis tools to catch all errors in your code?

5. A rival organization is developing a similar system that they hope to sell to the government. Competition is fierce for limited funding. Your team wants to publicly expose code flaws in the rival's product to discredit the other group and increase your group's chances of getting the funding. Some are suggesting holding a press conference to demonstrate the other application's security flaws.

   How should you respond to this suggestion?

6. The application may have to make a connection across the network to obtain data. Why is it important to keep the length of time between time of check and time of use (TOC/TOU) to a minimum?

7. When might it be desirable to implement granularity of access controls?

8. An API is generally considered to be a security enhancement because it protects the inner workings of a software module from casual observation. When would an API also be a security risk?

9. What are the decision points when considering using a public versus private code repository?

10. Should the government insist on software escrow for this project?

TOPIC E

Software Security Effectiveness Assessment

You have learned how to securely create software, including secure database access and keeping your developer environment secure. Now you must learn how to verify that your software security is actually working.

Software Audits

In a software audit, independent auditors conduct a review of the software development organization to see if that organization's software development process is in compliance with whatever specifications, standards, or contractual agreements apply to it.

A software audit is different from a software peer review or software management review because the assessment is done by an independent body that is concerned with compliance of the product or process rather than the technical content or quality.

The software auditing team can have the following roles:

- **Initiator**: Typically a manager, customer, or representative of the audited organization that decides there's a need for an audit
- **Lead auditor**: An individual responsible for administrative tasks such as preparing an audit plan, organizing the audit team, and making sure the audit meets its objectives. This person must be free from bias or any influence that could impact their ability to lead an independent, objective evaluation.
- **Recorder**: This person documents any decisions, recommendations, anomalies, or action items that the audit team discovers
- **Auditors**: These people examine the product that is defined in the audit plan. They document their findings and make recommendations for corrective action. The audit team might only have a single auditor.
- **Audited Organization**: The group or company that is being audited. They will provide someone to liaise with the audit team and provide all information requested by the auditors. When the audit is completed, the audited organization should implement any recommendations or corrective actions.

 Note: Do not mistake a software audit in this context for a software licensing audit. Software companies such as Microsoft, Oracle, SAP, and IBM will also audit companies to ensure that all installations of the software that company uses is paid for and licensed.

Software Change Logs

A change log in software development allows managers, security professionals, and contributors to see what notable changes have been made to the software. The change log should be a feature of the code repository. A good change log should adhere to the following:

- Keep it readable by humans.
- Easily link to any section of the code.
- Maintain one subsection for every version of code.
- List the releases in reverse chronological order, with the latest on top.
- Write all dates in a common, consistent format (for example YYYY-MM-DD).
- Explicitly mention if the project follows Semantic Versioning.

The security practitioner must ensure that changes are properly logged and periodically audited.

Change Log Labeling

Semantic Versioning is a strict method for expressing software versions. It follows this structure: MAJOR.MINOR.PATCH. For example, 1.3.15.

You increment each under the following conditions:

1. MAJOR version when you make an incompatible API change.
2. MINOR version when you add functionality in a backwards-compatible manner.
3. PATCH version when you make backwards-compatible bug fixes.

Risk Analysis and Mitigation

Risk analysis and mitigation is the process of trying to anticipate and minimize threats before they occur. Your risk analysis and mitigation strategy should:

- Be integrated throughout the SDLC.
- Be integrated throughout your change management process.
- Use standardized methods.
- Use published risk management frameworks from groups such as the ISO, NIST, ANSI, ISACA, and (ISC)².
- Track and manage vulnerabilities discovered during the risk assessment.
- Ensure that decisions based on the risk assessment are implemented, enforced, and remembered by the organization.

Software Testing and Verification

Whenever you implement a mitigation, you need to test and verify its effectiveness first. In an SDLC environment, this will be done by the quality assurance team. The QA team must perform the test as if it has no knowledge of the application or its functionality. This means that the test must be written very carefully, step by step, with clear instructions and clearly expected results. The QA team must follow these instructions to the letter, with no coaching or assistance from the developer team. Otherwise, test results could be skewed and not truly representative of the real capabilities of the application. The QA team will go through a pass/no pass checklist of features, including security functions. The results of this test will then be given to the developer team.

The developer team must address any failed functionality or security findings in the same way they would any other change request. Once the flaw has been fixed, the QA team or some other independent party must validate that it resolved the problem. The developer must not be the one to declare that a problem has been fixed.

You can digitally sign your code so that others can verify its integrity. Others who download the code can verify your digital signature (you'll have to make your public key available) to ensure that the code has not been modified. Of course, signing your code does not guarantee that it is free of flaws. It only gives others a mechanism for proving that someone else has not modified it since you released it.

Acceptance Testing

During acceptance testing, an independent group of users will try out the software. The software has already gone through a quality assurance process, where QA officers have tested it for exact functionality. But in acceptance testing, you want to see if the end-users can actually use this product. You want to make sure that the software you developed actually fulfills the business requirements of the organization.

From a security perspective, you might have security acceptance testing that is separate from end user acceptance testing. You want to make sure that the software meets all of the security requirements and specifications for the organization. In security testing you will try to uncover any design or implementation flaws that could allow an end-user to violate the organization's software security policy.

As the software goes through acceptance testing, the test process itself should have controls in place. These include:

- Using test data that pushes (and even exceeds) the boundaries of acceptable input ranges (for example, a person's age being 200).
- Testing data that is illegal (for example, letters in the ZIP Code, or a person's age being -5).
- Using test data that has known values and is known to be good and clean (no redundancy in a database, and no illegal values).
- Testing data that does not violate privacy policies.
- If you must use live production data to test, make an off-line copy of that data, sanitize the copy so that there is no risk of leaking sensitive data, and strictly control all copies of that data to prevent exposure or leakage to the outside world.
- Validating the data before and after the test, to make sure that it is as expected.
- Performing boundary checking on the input to see if you can cause buffer overflows.

To ensure the validity of your test, you should test the application in both the production environment and a test environment that stimulates the production environment. Acceptance testing is generally considered to be the first part of certification and accreditation. Once QA and acceptance testing are completed, the technical team can certify that the application does what it was designed to do. Management can then accept the certification and accredit the application, thus designating it as officially accepted for deployment into production.

Software Assurance for Software Acquisition

When a company purchases *commercial off-the-shelf (COTS)* software, or subcontracts software development to a vendor, there is a risk that the software will come with vulnerabilities and malicious code. *Software assurance (SwA)* is designed to help minimize these risks.

When a supplier implements proper software assurance, they will have implemented the following:

- Safety, security, and competence in their workforce.
- Safety and security risk management and mitigation during the development process.
- Independent safety and security reporting.
- The establishment of a qualified work environment, including proper development tools.
- A mechanism to ensure integrity and safety of the information.
- A system for monitoring the customer experience and reporting problems with the software in the customer environment back to the vendor.
- A business continuity process.

Software Acquisition

When acquiring software from a vendor, follow these best practices. They will lead to consistency and reduced risk:

- Make sure the vendor has a software assurance process.
- Implement a risk management strategy for acquiring software.
- Have a clear definition of what constitutes cyber security when it comes to acquisition.
- Have baseline cyber security requirements as a condition for awarding a contract.
- Require your vendor to train their personnel in your own cyber security requirements.
- Only purchase software or equipment from original equipment manufacturers (OEMs), their authorized partners and resellers, and other trusted sources.
- Incorporate cyber risk management into the overall enterprise risk management plan, and hold key decision-makers accountable for managing the risks of cyber security during software acquisition.

Guidelines for Assessing Software Security Effectiveness

Here are some guidelines you can follow for assessing software security effectiveness:

- Engage external software auditors to ensure that your product complies with the stated requirements.
- Use MAJOR.MINOR.PATCH labeling for software version change management.
- Integrate risk management throughout the SDLC.
- Use a QA team or some other independent party to test and verify your code.
- Use end user acceptance testing to verify that your product is usable and useful to end users.
- If your software requires formal testing and management acceptance, include a certification and accreditation process as part of your final testing.
- When buying software from a vendor, ensure that the vendor has a software assurance program in place.

ACTIVITY 8-5
Discussing the Assessment of the Effectiveness of Software Security

Before You Begin

Review the scenarios from the activities titled "Discussing Database Security in Software Development" and "Discussing Security Controls in the Development Environment."

Scenario

You are an information security consultant for a Non-Governmental Organization (NGO) in a developing nation. The NGO's developer team has finished creating a data mining application for the country's national health database. This application will access and analyze millions of health records gathered over the years from people all over the country. Because the project was funded by the U.S. government, it must adhere to some strict auditing and testing standards to determine how effective its security measures are. It must also be certified and accredited before it can be put into production. As the resident CISSP, you have been asked to help the team understand what to expect during the auditing and testing process.

---

1. An independent software auditing team has been brought in to review the system. One of the developers is wondering how this is different from the exhaustive peer review that was conducted earlier.

   What do you tell him?

2. The auditors are asking if the application change log follows Semantic Versioning. The lead developer has assured the lead auditor that it does. The NGO's country director is wondering what the implications will be of that type of labeling.

   What do you tell her?

3. The auditors are trying to determine if your risk analysis and mitigation strategy has followed best practice. What would this entail?

4. What can you do to verify that the software performs as expected, and has not been modified inappropriately? (Choose two.)

   ☐ The developer can run unit and system tests on the application.

   ☐ Different developer teams can run integration tests on the application.

   ☐ An independent QA team can test the software according to a strict step-by-step process.

   ☐ The developer team can digitally sign the code before release.

5. Once the application passes QA testing, what should be done next?

   ○ End users should be brought in to acceptance test the application.

   ○ The technical team can certify the application.

   ○ Management can accredit the application.

   ○ The code should be made ready for deployment into production.

6. After the application passes both security and end user acceptance testing, what should be done next?

   ○ The technical team can certify the application.

   ○ Management can accredit the application.

   ○ The code should be made ready for deployment into production.

   ○ The code version number should be changed.

7. What is the final step that should happen before the application is placed into production?

   ○ The technical team can certify the application.

   ○ Management can accredit the application.

   ○ The code version number should be changed.

   ○ End users can verify that the product satisfies a business need.

8. The application has passed all required tests. As a last requirement, the government is asking the NGO if it can provide software assurance for the application. The NGO's country director has asked you what this means.

   What do you tell her?

Summary

In this lesson, you learned about developing software securely. You started with an overview of the system lifecycle. You then went on to study security in the software development lifecycle, as well as the principles of database security in software development. You also learned about implementing security controls in the development environment and how to assess software security effectiveness.

What software development model is most appropriate for your environment?

What aspect of secure software development do you think will be the most challenging in your environment?

 Note: Check your CHOICE Course screen for opportunities to interact with your classmates, peers, and the larger CHOICE online community about the topics covered in this course or other topics you are interested in. From the Course screen you can also access available resources for a more continuous learning experience.

Course Follow-Up

Congratulations! You have completed the *Certified Information Systems Security Professional (CISSP®): Fourth Edition* course. You have gained the information you will need to successfully design, engineer, implement, and manage security in complex organizational environments.

You also covered the objectives that you will need to prepare for the (ISC)^2 CISSP exam. If you combine this class experience with review, private study, and hands-on experience, you will be well prepared to demonstrate your advanced security expertise both through professional certification and solid technical competence on the job.

What's Next?

Your next step after completing this course will probably be to prepare for and obtain your CISSP certification. You might also wish to pursue further technology-specific training in operating system or network design, implementation and support, or in application development and implementation.

You are encouraged to explore computer and network security further by actively participating in any of the social media forums set up by your instructor or training administrator through the **Social Media** tile on the CHOICE Course screen.

A | Mapping Course Content to (ISC)² Certified Information Systems Security Professional (CISSP®) 2015 Exam

Obtaining CISSP certification requires candidates to pass the CISSP 2015 exam. This table describes where the objectives for the exam are covered in this course.

Domain and Objective	Covered In
Domain 1.0 Security and Risk Management (e.g., Security, Risk, Compliance, Law, Regulations, Business Continuity)	Lesson 1
A. Understand and apply concepts of confidentiality, integrity, and availability	Lesson 1, Topic A
B. Apply security governance principles through:	Lesson 1, Topic A
• B.1 Alignment of security function to strategy, goals, mission, and objectives (e.g., business case, budget and resources)	Lesson 1, Topic A
• B.2 Organizational processes (e.g., acquisitions, divestitures, governance committees)	
• B.3 Security roles and responsibilities	
• B.4 Control frameworks	
• B.5 Due care	
• B.6 Due diligence	
C. Compliance	Lesson 1, Topic B
• C.1 Legislative and regulatory compliance	Lesson 1, Topic B
• C.2 Privacy requirements compliance	
D. Understand legal and regulatory issues that pertain to information security in a global context	Lesson 1, Topic B

Domain and Objective	Covered In
• D.1 Computer crimes • D.2 Licensing and intellectual property (e.g., copyright, trademark, digital-rights management) • D.3 Import/export controls • D.4 Trans-border data flow • D.5 Privacy • D.6 Data breaches	Lesson 1, Topic B
E. Understand professional ethics	Lesson 1, Topic C
• E.1 Exercise (ISC)² Code of Professional Ethics • E.2 Support organization's code of ethics	Lesson 1, Topic C
F. Develop and implement documented security policy, standards, procedures, and guidelines	Lesson 1, Topic D
G. Understand business continuity requirements	Lesson 1, Topic G
• G.1 Develop and document project scope and plan • G.2 Conduct business impact analysis	Lesson 1, Topic G
H. Contribute to personnel security policies	Lesson 1, Topic I
• H.1 Employment candidate screening (e.g., reference checks, education verification) • H.2 Employment agreements and policies • H.3 Employment termination processes • H.4 Vendor, consultant, and contractor controls • H.5 Compliance • H.6 Privacy	Lesson 1, Topic I
I. Understand and apply risk management concepts	Lesson 1, Topic E
• I.1 Identify threats and vulnerabilities • I.2 Risk assessment/analysis (qualitative, quantitative, hybrid) • I.3 Risk assignment/acceptance (e.g., system authorization) • I.4 Countermeasure selection • I.5 Implementation • I.6 Types of controls (preventive, detective, corrective, etc.) • I.7 Control assessment • I.8 Monitoring and measurement • I.9 Asset valuation • I.10 Reporting • I.11 Continuous improvement • I.12 Risk frameworks	Lesson 1, Topic E
J. Understand and apply threat modeling	Lesson 1, Topic F

Domain and Objective	Covered In
• J.1 Identifying threats (e.g., adversaries, contractors, employees, trusted partners) • J.2 Determining and diagramming potential attacks (e.g., social engineering, spoofing) • J.3 Performing reduction analysis • J.4 Technologies and processes to remediate threats (e.g., software architecture and operations)	Lesson 1, Topic F
K. Integrate security risk considerations into acquisition strategy and practice	Lesson 1, Topic H
• K.1 Hardware, software, and services • K.2 Third-party assessment and monitoring (e.g., on-site assessment, document exchange and review, process/ policy review) • K.3 Minimum security requirements • K.4 Service-level requirements	Lesson 1, Topic H
L. Establish and manage information security education, training, and awareness	Lesson 1, Topic J
• L.1 Appropriate levels of awareness, training, and education required within the organization • Periodic reviews for content relevancy	Lesson 1, Topic J
Domain 2 Asset Security (Protecting Security of Assets)	Lesson 2
A. Classify information and supporting assets (e.g., sensitivity, criticality)	Lesson 2, Topic A
B. Determine and maintain ownership (e.g., data owners, system owners, business/mission owners)	Lesson 2, Topic A
C. Protect Privacy	Lesson 2, Topic B
• C.1 Data owners • C.2 Data processors • C.3 Data remanence • C.4 Collection limitation	Lesson 2, Topic B
D. Ensure appropriate retention (e.g., media, hardware, personnel)	Lesson 2, Topic C
E. Determine data security controls (e.g., data at rest, data in transit)	Lesson 2, Topic D
• E.1 Baselines • E.2 Scoping and tailoring • E.3 Standards selection • E.4 Cryptography	Lesson 2, Topic D
F. Establish handling requirements (markings, labels, storage, destruction of sensitive information)	Lesson 2, Topic E
Domain 3 Security Engineering (Engineering and Management of Security)	Lesson 3

Domain and Objective	Covered In
A. Implement and manage engineering processes using secure design principles	Lesson 3, Topic A
B. Understand the fundamental concepts of security models (e.g., Confidentiality, Integrity, and Multi-level Models)	Lesson 3, Topic C
C. Select controls and countermeasures based upon systems security evaluation models	Lesson 3, Topic C
D. Understand security capabilities of information systems (e.g., memory protection, virtualization, trusted platform module, interfaces, fault tolerance)	Lesson 3, Topic B
E. Assess and mitigate the vulnerabilities of security architectures, designs, and solution elements	Lesson 3, Topic F
• E.1 Client-based (e.g., applets, local caches) • E.2 Server-based (e.g., data flow control) • E.3 Database security (e.g., inference, aggregation, data mining, data analytics, warehousing) • E.4 Large-scale parallel data systems • E.5 Distributed systems (e.g., cloud computing, grid computing, peer to peer) • E.6 Cryptographic systems • E.7 Industrial control systems (e.g., SCADA)	Lesson 3, Topic F
F. Assess and mitigate vulnerabilities in web-based systems (e.g., XML, OWASP)	Lesson 3, Topic G
G. Assess and mitigate vulnerabilities in mobile systems	Lesson 3, Topic G
H. Assess and mitigate vulnerabilities in embedded devices and cyber-physical systems (e.g., network-enabled devices, Internet of Things (IoT))	Lesson 3, Topic G
I. Apply cryptography	Lesson 3, Topic H, I
• I.1 Cryptographic lifecycle (e.g., cryptographic limitations, algorithm/protocol governance) • I.2 Cryptographic types (e.g., symmetric, asymmetric, elliptic curves) • I.3 Public Key Infrastructure (PKI) • I.4 Key management practices • I.5 Digital signatures • I.6 Digital rights management • I.7 Non-repudiation • I.8 Integrity (hashing and salting) • I.9 Methods of cryptanalytic attacks (e.g., brute force, cipher-text only, known plaintext)	Lesson 3, Topic H, I
J. Apply secure principles to site and facility design	Lesson 3, Topic J
K. Design and implement physical security	Lesson 3, Topic K

Domain and Objective	Covered In
• K.1 Wiring closets	Lesson 3, Topic K
• K.2 Server rooms	
• K.3 Media storage facilities	
• K.4 Evidence storage	
• K.5 Restricted and work area security (e.g., operations centers)	
• K.6 Data center security	
• K.7 Utilities and HVAC considerations	
• K.8 Water issues (e.g., leakage, flooding)	
• K.9 Fire prevention, detection, and suppression	

Domain 4 Communication and Network Security (Designing and Protecting Network Security) — Lesson 4

A. Apply secure design principles to network architecture (e.g., IP & non-IP protocols, segmentation) — Lesson 4, Topic A

- A.1 OSI and TCP/IP models — Lesson 4, Topic A
- A.2 IP networking
- A.3 Implications of multi-layer protocols (e.g., DNP3)
- A.4 Converged protocols (e.g., FCoE, MPLS, VoIP, iSCSI)
- A.5 Software-defined networks
- A.6 Wireless networks
- A.7 Cryptography used to maintain communication security

B. Secure network components — Lesson 4, Topic B

- B.1 Operation of hardware (e.g., modems, switches, routers, wireless access points, mobile devices) — Lesson 4, Topic B
- B.2 Transmission media (e.g., wired, wireless, fiber)
- B.3 Network access control devices (e.g., firewalls, proxies)
- B.4 Endpoint security
- B.5 Content-distribution networks
- B.6 Physical devices

C. Design and establish secure communication channels — Lesson 4, Topic C

- C.1 Voice — Lesson 4, Topic C
- C.2 Multimedia collaboration (e.g., remote meeting technology, instant messaging)
- C.3 Remote access (e.g., VPN, screen scraper, virtual application/desktop, telecommuting)
- C.4 Data communications (e.g., VLAN, TLS/SSL)
- C.5 Virtualized networks (e.g., SDN, virtual SAN, guest operating systems, port isolation)

D. Prevent or mitigate network attacks — Lesson 4, Topic D

Domain 5 Identity and Access Management (Controlling Access and Managing Identity) — Lesson 5

A. Control physical and logical access to assets — Lesson 5, Topic A

Domain and Objective	Covered In
• A.1 Information • A.2 Systems • A.3 Devices • A.4 Facilities	Lesson 5, Topic A
B. Manage identification and authentication of people and devices	Lesson 5, Topic B
• B.1 Identity management implementation (e.g., SSO, LDAP) • B.2 Single/multi-factor authentication (e.g., factors, strength, errors, biometrics) • B.3 Accountability • B.4 Session management (e.g., timeouts, screensavers) • B.5 Registration and proofing of identity • B.6 Federated identity management (e.g., SAML) • B.7 Credential management systems	Lesson 5, Topic B
C. Integrate identity as a service (e.g., cloud identity)	Lesson 5, Topic C
D. Integrate third-party identity services (e.g., on-premise)	Lesson 5, Topic C
E. Implement and manage authorization mechanisms	Lesson 5, Topic D
• E.1 Role-Based Access Control (RBAC) methods • E.2 Rule-based access control methods • E.3 Mandatory Access Control (MAC) • E.4 Discretionary Access Control (DAC)	Lesson 5, Topic D
F. Prevent or mitigate access control attacks	Lesson 5, Topic E
G. Manage the identity and access provisioning lifecycle (e.g., provisioning, review)	Lesson 5, Topic A
Domain 6 Security Assessment and Testing (Designing, Performing, and Analyzing Security Testing)	Lesson 6
A. Design and validate assessment and test strategies	Lesson 6, Topic A
B. Conduct security control testing	Lesson 6, Topic A
• B.1 Vulnerability assessment • B.2 Penetration testing • B.3 Log reviews • B.4 Synthetic transactions • B.5 Code review and testing (e.g., manual, dynamic, static, fuzz) • B.6 Misuse case testing • B.7 Test coverage analysis • B.8 Interface testing (e.g., API, UI, physical)	Lesson 6, Topic A
C. Collect security process data (e.g., management and operational controls)	Lesson 6, Topic C

Domain and Objective	Covered In
• C.1 Account management (e.g., escalation, revocation) • C.2 Management review • C.3 Key performance and risk indicators • C.4 Backup verification data • C.5 Training and awareness • C.6 Disaster recovery and business continuity	Lesson 6, Topic C
D. Analyze and report test outputs (e.g., automated, manual)	Lesson 6, Topic B
E. Conduct or facilitate internal and third party audits	Lesson 6, Topic D
Domain 7 Security Operations (e.g., Foundational Concepts, Investigations, Incident Management, Disaster Recovery)	Lesson 7
A. Understand and support investigations	Lesson 7, Topic J
• A.1 Evidence collection and handling (e.g., chain of custody, interviewing) • A.2 Reporting and documenting • A.3 Investigative techniques (e.g., root-cause analysis, incident handling) • A.4 Digital forensics (e.g., media, network, software, and embedded devices)	Lesson 7, Topic J
B. Understand requirements for investigation types	Lesson 7, Topic J
• B.1 Operational • B.2 Criminal • B.3 Civil • B.4 Regulatory • B.5 Electronic discovery (eDiscovery)	Lesson 7, Topic J
C. Conduct logging and monitoring activities	Lesson 7, Topic D
• C.1 Intrusion detection and prevention • C.2 Security information and event management • C.3 Continuous monitoring • C.4 Egress monitoring (e.g., data loss prevention, steganography, watermarking)	Lesson 7, Topic D
D. Secure the provisioning of resources	Lesson 7, Topic F
• D.1 Asset inventory (e.g., hardware, software) • D.2 Configuration management • D.3 Physical assets • D.4 Virtual assets (e.g., software-defined network, virtual SAN, guest operating systems) • D.5 Cloud assets (e.g., services, VMs, storage, networks) • D.6 Applications (e.g., workloads or private clouds, web services, software as a service)	Lesson 7, Topic F
E. Understand and apply foundational security operations concepts	Lesson 7, Topic A

Domain and Objective	Covered In
• E.1 Need to know/least privilege (e.g., entitlement, aggregation, transitive trust) • E.2 Separation of duties and responsibilities • E.3 Monitor special privileges (e.g., operators, administrators) • E.4 Job rotation • E.5 Information lifecycle • E.6 Service-level agreements	Lesson 7, Topic A
F. Employ resource protection techniques	Lesson 7, Topic F
• F.1 Media management • F.2 Hardware and software asset management	Lesson 7, Topic F
G. Conduct incident management	Lesson 7, Topic I
• G.1 Detection • G.2 Response • G.3 Mitigation • G.4 Reporting • G.5 Recovery • G.6 Remediation • G.7 Lessons learned	Lesson 7, Topic I
H. Operate and maintain preventative measures	Lesson 7, Topic E
• H.1 Firewalls • H.2 Intrusion detection and prevention systems • H.3 Whitelisting/Blacklisting • H.4 Third-party security services • H.5 Sandboxing • H.6 Honeypots/Honeynets • H.7 Anti-malware	Lesson 7, Topic E
I. Implement and support patch and vulnerability management	Lesson 7, Topic G
J. Participate in and understand change management processes (e.g., versioning, baselining, security impact analysis)	Lesson 7, Topic H
K. Implement recovery strategies	Lesson 7, Topic K, L
• K.1 Backup storage strategies (e.g., off-site storage, electronic vaulting, tape rotation) • K.2 Recovery site strategies • K.3 Multiple processing sites (e.g., operationally redundant systems) • K.4 System resilience, high availability, quality of service, and fault tolerance	Lesson 7, Topic K, L
L. Implement disaster recovery processes	Lesson 7, Topic M

Domain and Objective	Covered In
• L.1 Response • L.2 Personnel • L.3 Communications • L.4 Assessment • L.5 Restoration • L.6 Training and awareness	Lesson 7, Topic M
M. Test disaster recovery plans	Lesson 7, Topic K
• M.1 Read-through • M.2 Walkthrough • M.3 Simulation • M.4 Parallel • M.5 Full interruption	Lesson 7, Topic K
N. Participate in business continuity planning and exercises	Lesson 1, Topic G
O. Implement and manage physical security	Lesson 7, Topic B
• O.1 Perimeter (e.g., access control and monitoring) • O.2 Internal security (e.g., escort requirements/visitor control, keys and locks)	Lesson 7, Topic B
P. Participate in addressing personnel safety concerns (e.g., duress, travel, monitoring)	Lesson 7, Topic C
Domain 8 Software Development Security (Understanding, Applying, and Enforcing Software Security)	Lesson 8
A. Understand and apply security in the software development lifecycle	Lesson 8, Topic A, B
• A.1 Development methodologies (e.g., Agile, Waterfall) • A.2 Maturity models • A.3 Operation and maintenance • A.4 Change management • A.5 Integrated product team (e.g., DevOps)	Lesson 8, Topic A, B
B. Enforce security controls in development environments	Lesson 8, Topic D
• B.1 Security of the software environments • B.2 Security weaknesses and vulnerabilities at the source-code level (e.g., buffer overflow, escalation of privilege, input/output validation) • B.3 Configuration management as an aspect of secure coding • B.4 Security of code repositories • B.5 Security of application programming interfaces	Lesson 8, Topic D
C. Assess the effectiveness of software security	Lesson 8, Topic E

Domain and Objective	Covered In
• C.1 Auditing and logging of changes • C.2 Risk analysis and mitigation • C.3 Acceptance testing	Lesson 8, Topic E
D. Assess security impact of acquired software	Lesson 8, Topic E

Mastery Builders

Mastery Builders are provided for certain lessons as additional learning resources for this course. Mastery Builders are developed for selected lessons within a course in cases when they seem most instructionally useful as well as technically feasible. In general, Mastery Builders are supplemental, optional unguided practice and may or may not be performed as part of the classroom activities. Your instructor will consider setup requirements, classroom timing, and instructional needs to determine which Mastery Builders are appropriate for you to perform, and at what point during the class. If you do not perform the Mastery Builders in class, your instructor can tell you if you can perform them independently as self-study, and if there are any special setup requirements.

Mastery Builder 1-1
Assessing Security and Risk Management

Activity Time: 1 hour

Scenario

In this Mastery Builder, you will assess security and risk management.

---

1. Which statement about guidelines is correct?
   - ○ They describe the steps required to complete an activity.
   - ○ They describe a required use of specific tools.
   - ○ They are recommended settings or actions.
   - ○ They specify the minimum security required for a system.

2. The use of a security policy to define management intention is an example of which access control type?
   - ○ Administrative
   - ○ Physical
   - ○ Technical
   - ○ Preventative

3. The CIA triad is considered central to security. Which option best describes what it helps protect against?
   - ○ Disclosure, loss, and leakage
   - ○ Destruction, alteration, and disclosure
   - ○ Confidentiality, integrity, and availability
   - ○ Unavailability, downtime, and destruction

4. Which statement best describes security policies?
   - ○ They are operational instructions for implementing security.
   - ○ They document high level expectations from senior management.
   - ○ They detail tactical instructions for implementing security.
   - ○ They are work procedures specified by senior management.

5. The first step in risk analysis is to:
   - ○ Conduct a threat assessment.
   - ○ Identify assets and their value.
   - ○ Identify potential vulnerabilities.
   - ○ Identify the countermeasures.

6. Due to increased news coverage of significant data breaches at major corporations, your company's Board of Directors instructed the CEO to conduct a thorough risk assessment. As a result, the company hired its first CIO, who is tasked with carrying out the risk assessment. The CIO assembled a team to assist with the risk assessment processes, and they began by taking a complete inventory of all assets. Once the inventory was complete, a series of vulnerability assessments were conducted, and historical data regarding earlier security incidents was collected. You have been asked to use that historical information, as well as trends and threat forecasts from security research firms, to develop concrete figures to allow management to understand the costs associated with each risk. What type of risk analysis have you been asked to complete?

   ○ Cost-driven

   ○ Quantitative

   ○ Qualitative

   ○ Semi-quantitative

7. A business impact analysis (BIA) often includes which of the following security processes?

   ○ A vulnerability assessment.

   ○ Installing network countermeasures.

   ○ Training of key personnel.

   ○ A disaster recovery process.

8. Which statement best describes the primary purpose of a business continuity plan?

   ○ To ensure that the company will recover from one-time disasters.

   ○ To ensure business processes may continue after a disruption or crisis.

   ○ To identify key players in the business and enable succession planning.

   ○ To keep key business documents available when and where they are needed.

9. What is the best way to justify a request for funding for business continuity efforts?

   ○ Detail how a BCP protects the organization's ability to continue generating revenue.

   ○ Describe how a BCP allows the organization to more quickly achieve RPOs.

   ○ Describe how a DRP protects the organization's ability to continue generating revenue.

   ○ Describe how a BCP protects the organization against specific disaster scenarios.

10. Which of the following demonstrate the legal concept of due care? (Choose two.)

    ☐ Providing appropriate security training for all employees.

    ☐ Performing background checks on all prospective employees.

    ☐ Securing customers' personal information on the organization's servers.

    ☐ Performing risk assessments on network systems.

11. Your company recently acquired a smaller organization in the same industry. Which of the following is the most significant security risk as a result of this acquisition?

    ○ The other organization may have a different C-level structure than yours.

    ○ There may be a disparity between each organization's levels of security.

    ○ The other organization may use different access control mechanisms than yours.

    ○ There may be a disparity between each organization's security budget.

12. Which of the following is a privacy law that protects users' financial information when it is held by banks and other financial institutions?

   ○ Sarbanes-Oxley Act (SOX)

   ○ Electronic Communications Privacy Act (ECPA)

   ○ Federal Information Security Management Act (FISMA)

   ○ Gramm-Leach-Bliley Act (GLBA)

13. True or False? Patent protection is stronger and lasts longer than copyright protection.

   ☐ True

   ☐ False

14. Which of the following is a comprehensive set of processes that can increase the effectiveness and decrease the complexity of security-focused operations?

   ○ Governance, risk management, and compliance.

   ○ Governance, risk analysis, and risk mitigation.

   ○ Governance, risk management, and training

   ○ Risk management, compliance, and training

15. Which of the following are goals of the (ISC)^2 Code of Ethics canon? (Choose three.)

   ☐ Behaving responsibly, justly, honestly, honorably, and legally.

   ☐ Improving, enhancing, and protecting the profession.

   ☐ Ensuring, enabling, and supporting the exchange of free information.

   ☐ Providing adept, competent, and assiduous service to principals.

16. A user breaches a company's private file servers, but only glances at a couple of files before disconnecting. The user argues that they have not behaved unethically because they only viewed a relatively small amount of information. Additionally, they didn't leak the information to the public, so the company couldn't have suffered any significant harm. What fallacy or faulty reasoning has this user committed?

   ○ The ends justify the means.

   ○ Information yearns to be free.

   ○ If the act is easy and security is poor, the company can't find fault with the user.

   ○ The company's computer systems are shatterproof.

17. Which of the following are key tasks in upholding organizational ethics? (Choose three.)

   ☐ Weighing ethical actions in relation to cost or benefit to the organization.

   ☐ Hiring and retaining employees that have a strong ethical background.

   ☐ Acting responsibly to the organization's stakeholders and to the public.

   ☐ Adhering to established standards and laws that outline ethical behavior.

18. You want to write into your security documentation that all employee accounts must use a minimum of eight characters in their passwords. Any accounts that currently have a password shorter than eight characters should be disabled until the password is updated to comply with the eight character minimum. What type of security document would this apply to?

   ○ Guideline

   ○ Process

   ○ Standard

   ○ Baseline

19. True or False? In a Platform as a service (PaaS) model, the responsibility for security is on the vendor.

☐ True

☐ False

20. The company you acquired had its own set of security policies that governed its operations. What is the most important thing to consider regarding these policies?

○ Make sure the acquired company's policies don't contradict your own.

○ Make sure the acquired company's policies are written in your style.

○ Make sure the acquired company's policies address all of your systems.

○ Make sure your policies incorporate every item from the acquired company's policies.

21. Your company is in talks to form a partnership with another company in the same industry. You will be routinely sharing sensitive data and systems with the other company. You want to ensure that your data and systems are kept safe during and after this sharing process, and failure to do so by either party should result in legal penalties. Which of the following types of agreements should you draft?

○ Service-level agreement (SLA)

○ Memorandum of understanding (MOU)

○ Interconnection security agreement (ISA)

○ Business partnership agreement (BPA)

22. Which of the following is a rating system that determines the impact of a threat?

○ Damage, interruption, reproducibility, exploitability (DIRE)

○ Harm, affected users, reproducibility, manageability (HARM)

○ Tampering, harm, reproducibility, exploitability, affected users, thoroughness (THREAT)

○ Damage, reproducibility, exploitability, affected users, discoverability (DREAD)

23. The STRIDE acronym is a threat classification that includes which of the following?

○ Spoofing, tampering, reflection, integrity violation, denial of service, escalation

○ Spoofing, tampering, repudiation, information disclosure, denial of service, elevation of privilege

○ Systems hacking, threatening, restructuring, information disclosure, destruction, elevation of privilege

○ Systems hacking, tampering, repudiation, impersonation, destruction, elevation of privilege

24. What is the typical flow of a threat tree diagram, from top (beginning) to bottom (end)?

○ Identify the threat, identify how to mitigate the threat, identify who or what should implement the mitigation

○ Identify the threat, identify how the threat can occur, identify how to mitigate the threat

○ Identify how the threat can occur, identify what systems are vulnerable, identify how to mitigate the threat

○ Identify how the threat can occur, identify the source of the threat, identify how to mitigate the threat

25. What is an employee's sensitivity profile?

○ A description of the employee's technical level of access to sensitive systems.

○ A description of the employee's trustworthiness with regard to keeping sensitive information secure.

○ A description of the employee's need-to-know information based on their job role.

○ A description of the employee's need-to-know information based on them as an individual.

26. As a hiring manager charged with screening potential candidates, you need to ensure that you've done your due diligence. You need to make sure that a candidate has no criminal record, that the candidate has credentials and certifications relevant to the job, and that they can verify their prior work history. Which of the following practice should you incorporate into the hiring process to guarantee that these issues aren't missed with any candidate?

○ Mandate that each candidate sign a sworn agreement before being put through the interview process.

○ Create a baseline for the company's hiring process.

○ Remind each interviewer in-person before each interview they conduct.

○ Rely on the candidate to provide this information.

27. A disgruntled employee was recently terminated from your organization. He was given this notification at noon on Wednesday. His supervisor contacted you about an hour later to tell you of the termination, and you promptly disabled the employee's access. Other personnel that worked near the terminated employee stated that they saw him leave his cubicle and walk out the front door at about 2:00 p.m. that day. What should you have done differently to minimize the risk of the disgruntled employee causing harm to your organization? (Choose two.)

☐ Send security to escort the employee out of the building immediately after his termination.

☐ Conduct an exit interview with the terminated employee to find out what he has access to.

☐ Request that all supervisors notify you of unfriendly terminations first so you can disable access before the employee learns of his termination.

☐ Closely monitor the systems that the employee has access to after his termination.

28. When providing security training to senior management and the board of directors, what should be the primary focus of this training?

○ Basic computer security practices like using strong passwords and browsing the web safely.

○ The details of security documents like policies, procedures, and guidelines.

○ The importance of security in supporting business objectives, legal compliance, and shareholder expectations.

○ The latest knowledge of the various threats and controls that affect information security.

29. At minimum, how often should staff undergo security awareness training?

○ Six months

○ One year

○ Two years

○ Five years

30. As part of a security training program, which of the following is the most important for all staff to learn?

○ Best practices for VPN usage.

○ How to clean an infected computer.

○ How to properly wipe sensitive data.

○ How to identify social engineering attempts.

Mastery Builder 2-1
Assessing Asset Security

Activity Time: 1 hour

Scenario

In this Mastery Builder, you will assess your knowledge of information assets and data security.

---

1. Your company is preparing to begin a project that will update its aging infrastructure. As a security practitioner, which answer best describes what your primary concern should be before the project begins?

   ○ The cost associated with protecting the data.

   ○ The data management policy may need to be updated to address changes in the infrastructure.

   ○ The retention schedule for the protected information assets may need to change.

   ○ The project manager 's familiarity with current security policy.

2. Your company recently spent a significant amount of funds to acquire a database of product sales data from a data reseller. Who would be the best person to determine the data risk?

   ○ Data custodian

   ○ Senior management

   ○ Data owner

   ○ Database administrator

3. Which of these media would *not* be affected by degaussing?

   ○ Hard drive

   ○ Backup tape

   ○ CD-ROM

   ○ Floppy disk

4. As a data custodian, you are tasked with securely destroying data on a hard drive. The data on the drive is no longer needed, but the system owner wants to retain the entire drive itself for reuse. Which method of destruction should you choose to securely erase the data?

   ○ Physically destroy the drive.

   ○ Degauss the drive.

   ○ Overwrite the drive.

   ○ Encrypt the drive.

5. Which of the following is not a typical consideration when developing data management policies?

   ○ The financial impact of acquiring and protecting the data.

   ○ Performing a risk analysis to determine appropriate processes for access.

   ○ Current contracts with continuity service providers.

   ○ Potential conflicts with other existing policies.

6. Data that is at rest is:
   ○ More secure than data in transit.
   ○ No longer a risk to the organization.
   ○ Susceptible to both physical and logical loss.
   ○ Contained within the trusted network.

7. To support data integrity, data owners require training in which process?
   ○ Procurement
   ○ Data destruction
   ○ Data loss prevention
   ○ Quality control

8. Your company is interested in encrypting all the traffic between your branch office and headquarters. Which of these would be the best option?
   ○ End-to-end encryption
   ○ SSL VPN
   ○ Link encryption
   ○ IPSec

9. Data errors of commission are:
   ○ Errors that affect commissions payed to salespeople.
   ○ Errors leading to data being left out.
   ○ Errors leading to wrong information being added.
   ○ None of the above.

10. The responsibilities of a data custodian include which of the following?
    ○ Making sure users comply with all data access policies.
    ○ Assuring the quality of the data to data consumers.
    ○ Knowing the cost of the data, whether acquired or created.
    ○ Understanding legal or regulatory issues with the data.

11. Which of the following are among the benefits of defining and maintaining data standards?
    ○ Data is less expensive to acquire.
    ○ It ensures that data at rest is secure.
    ○ The accuracy and quality of the data may improve.
    ○ It greatly reduces the chance of data leakage.

12. Which of the following is not typically part of an organization's data handling policies and processes?
    ○ Access control systems
    ○ Asset management
    ○ Data disposal process
    ○ Data classification systems

13. A company's data classification policy describes four levels: Public, Internal, Management, and Secret. An older research and development database system has been retired. The records in the database were labeled Secret. What should happen to the data now that the database has been retired?

   ○ Since the database has been retired, the data should be destroyed.

   ○ The data should be exported to another system, retaining the Secret designation.

   ○ Its classification should be reviewed with the data owner to determine if a change is warranted.

   ○ It should be made Public and added to the historical archives of the company.

14. Which is not an example of data at rest?

   ○ Data on a web server hard disk.

   ○ Downloading a financial statement.

   ○ Backup media at a continuity site.

   ○ A printed copy of a classified document.

15. What methods or technologies are associated with data in transit?

   ○ Full disk encryption

   ○ Data recovery plans

   ○ SSL

   ○ Documented locations for removable media

16. Which set of statements best describe data management policies?

   ○ Data management policies must address matters of confidentiality, integrity, and availability from requisition to disposal. Policies should be reviewed at least annually. Care must be taken to address any applicable legal and/or regulatory requirements. Policies should not be adopted without considering the cost of implementing them.

   ○ Data management policies must address matters of confidentiality, integrity, and availability from data acquisition through data disposal. They must be flexible enough to adapt to changes in the business and data environments. Care must be taken to address any applicable legal or regulatory requirements. They should be reviewed at least annually, or when there are significant changes in the business, data, or regulatory environments. They should not be adopted without considering the cost of implementing them.

   ○ Data management policies must address matters of confidentiality, integrity, and availability from data acquisition through data disposal. They should be reviewed periodically, as changes to the business dictate. All legal and/or regulatory requirements must be addressed. Policies should be defined before costs are quantified, so that all costs may be addressed when budgeting.

   ○ Data management policies should define data owners and custodians. They should define data classification systems, data handling procedures, and standards for data destruction. They should be reviewed at least annually, so that outdated portions may be deleted. They should be modeled after specific published frameworks, like FIPS or SP-800-60.

17. Data policies should be reviewed at least:

   ○ Weekly

   ○ Monthly

   ○ Quarterly

   ○ Yearly

18. Data owners can be made up of which of these? (Choose two.)

   ☐ Security practitioners

   ☐ Groups of people

   ☐ Data creators

   ☐ Data custodians

19. True or False? It is OK for data policies to dictate a company's business initiatives

☐ True

☐ False

20. What role is responsible for managing access control requirements for data?

○ Data owner

○ Senior management

○ Data custodian

○ Human resources

21. Which of the following is a way that Asset Management supports the primary objectives of Information Security?

○ It allows asset owners to be provided with copies of the company's security policies.

○ It helps the company to understand how much is spent on hardware and software, so they'll know how much is left available for security countermeasures.

○ Only assets identified through Asset Management are subject to Information Security policies.

○ It separates data ownership from data custodianship.

22. Unlabelled data that is found should initially be given what level of protection?

○ None

○ Lowest level

○ Medium Level

○ Highest level

23. Who owns private data?

○ The person the data is about.

○ The company that stores the data.

○ The person that processes the data on a daily basis.

○ Ownership is shared between private citizens and organizations.

24. You're overseeing information security for a study that will collect and analyze information on the dietary habits of random individuals. Each individual will self-report their own information over a period of ten years. After ten years, their dietary habits will be compared to their medical issues or lack thereof in an attempt to find a correlation between eating habits and health. In upholding privacy requirements, which of the following information should you make sure is *not* collected?

○ The daily caloric intake of each individual.

○ Any existing medical conditions that are present at the start of the study.

○ Each individual's health insurance information.

○ The specific type of food ingested by each individual.

25. In your organization, you've had problems with operational knowledge being kept only in the minds of one or two individuals who have since left the company. What are some of the ways you can prevent this "siloing" of important business information? (Choose three.)

☐ Conduct an exit interview with each terminated employee to learn what you can.

☐ Make sure that all operational knowledge is documented.

☐ Employ job rotation so that multiple people are exposed to specific business operations.

☐ Plan a personnel retention policy that upholds continuity of operations after personnel leave the organization.

26. As part of your media retention policy, you store backup hard drives in a locked storage room. This locked room is about the size of a closet, and is completely sealed, with no vents, windows, or other ways of entry besides the locked door. The only things you store in this room are hard drives. One day, you begin your backup testing procedures and remove the drives from storage. During the test, you discover that some of the drives have failed. The failed drives show signs of physical warping. What is the most likely culprit?

○ Someone has maliciously damaged the drives.

○ The drives were exposed to excessive heat, causing them to fail.

○ The drives were not stacked properly, causing them to fall and receive damage.

○ The drives were subjected to magnetic interference, causing them to fail.

Mastery Builder 3-1
Assessing Security Engineering

Activity Time: 1 hour

Scenario

In this Mastery Builder, you will assess your knowledge of security engineering.

1. Which of the following is *not* a good security foundation principle as established by the NIST SP 800-27 engineering framework?

   ○ Establish a good security policy as a foundation for design.

   ○ Incorporate security into the overall system design.

   ○ Define clear physical and logical boundaries governed by policy.

   ○ Incorporate security into a system when necessary.

2. Which of the following is *not* a good ease of use principle as established by the NIST SP 800-27 engineering framework?

   ○ Base security on open standards, when possible.

   ○ Use organization-specific language when defining security requirements.

   ○ Design security for easier adoption of new technologies.

   ○ Incorporate a logical update process for technology.

3. Which of the following phases of the security engineering lifecycle includes security testing for certification and accreditation?

   ○ Implementation

   ○ Operations/maintenance

   ○ Development/acquisition

   ○ Initiation

4. Which of the following best describes a Direct Memory Access (DMA) attack?

   ○ An attacker uses a computer's insecure operating system to retrieve data from RAM.

   ○ An attacker uses a hardware bus to bypass operating system security and retrieve data from RAM.

   ○ An attacker exploits a virtual hypervisor to retrieve data from RAM used by a virtual guest.

   ○ An attacker exploits faulty firmware in hard drives to retrieve data from stored memory.

5. Which of the following are recommended ways to harden an operating system? (Choose three.)

   ☐ Disable all unused accounts.

   ☐ Run vulnerability assessment software on a regular basis.

   ☐ Disable vendor-issued update services.

   ☐ Change all default passwords.

6. The Trusted Platform Module (TPM) uses which of the following cryptographic algorithms?
   ○ Triple DES
   ○ AES-256
   ○ Twofish
   ○ RSA

7. Which of the following security models addresses conflicts of interest in access rights?
   ○ Graham-Denning
   ○ Brewer-Nash
   ○ Clark-Wilson
   ○ Biba

8. Which of the following is a security model that provides strict rules for what behavior is or is not allowed between data and users?
   ○ Lattice Model
   ○ Non-interference Model
   ○ Information Flow Model
   ○ State Machine Model

9. Which of the following access control categories is most commonly used on firewalls and routers to control network traffic?
   ○ Role-based Access Control
   ○ Discretionary Access Control
   ○ Rule-based Access Control
   ○ Mandatory Access Control

10. Which of the following enterprise security architecture (ESA) frameworks focuses on best practices for security governance in four domains: plan and organize, acquire and implement, deliver and support, and monitor and evaluate?
    ○ COBIT
    ○ ITIL
    ○ ISO/IEC 27001
    ○ PCI DSS

11. When it comes to incorporating security zones in your ESA, what is important to remember?
    ○ The zones must all adhere to the same security policies.
    ○ The zones must all have the same level of trust.
    ○ The zones may connect to one another, requiring some method of boundary control.
    ○ The zones must be kept independent of one another, requiring some method of boundary control.

12. When it comes to auditing and monitoring in your ESA, which of the following is a best practice?
    ○ Keep the logs of each system separate.
    ○ Forward all logs to a centralized system.
    ○ Log all possible activity.
    ○ Parse logs manually rather than rely on automated tools.

13. Which of the following is an intended function of keeping system code separate from user code?

   ○   The system code is assigned less resources, lowering its processing footprint.

   ○   The user code is assigned less resources, lowering its processing footprint.

   ○   The system code is fully trusted, whereas user code has less privileges.

   ○   The user code is fully trusted, whereas the system code has less privileges.

14. Which of the following services does a Trusted Platform Module (TPM) provide? (Choose three.)

   ☐   Full disk encryption

   ☐   Digital rights management (DRM)

   ☐   File-level access control

   ☐   Password-based authentication

15. You want to ensure that the servers in your organization are fault tolerant. In particular, the servers you want to protect serve up static content to employees on your intranet. Which of the following is the best technique to ensure these servers' fault tolerance under heavy traffic?

   ○   Replication

   ○   Clustering

   ○   Network load balancing

   ○   Virtualization

16. Which of the following controls allows clients to access your public-facing servers while keeping them isolated from your internal network?

   ○   Reverse proxy

   ○   Demilitarized zone (DMZ)

   ○   Intrusion prevention system (IPS)

   ○   Fault tolerance

17. Which of the following are vulnerabilities of cloud services? (Choose two.)

   ☐   You must depend on the security policies and practices of the cloud provider.

   ☐   You don't retain full ownership of the data hosted on cloud services.

   ☐   You don't have direct control over the security of the cloud-based systems that manage your data.

   ☐   You don't have any assurances of data availability in the cloud.

18. Which of the following best describes a covert timing vulnerability?

   ○   A process may be able to determine information about data based on the amount, type, and order in which another process accesses the data.

   ○   A process may be able to determine information about data based on the existence of a stored file that holds the data.

   ○   A process may be able to directly read data based on the amount, type, and order in which another process accesses the data.

   ○   A process may be able to directly read data based on the existence of a stored file that holds the data.

19. Remote users access your internal network through a VPN. Which of the following security concerns does the VPN *not* protect against?

   ○ Tampering of the remote user's traffic.

   ○ Disclosure of the remote user's traffic.

   ○ The remote user's computer being infected with malware.

   ○ The remote user's computer logging in without the proper credentials.

20. Which of the following mobile device management (MDM) strategies prevents users from obtaining high level privileges on their mobile device?

   ○ Remotely locking a device.

   ○ Protection against jailbreaking or rooting of a device.

   ○ Device enrollment.

   ○ Implementing encrypted containers on the device.

21. What is a difference between a stream cipher and a block cipher?

   ○ Block ciphers are faster and more secure than stream ciphers.

   ○ Stream ciphers are faster and more secure then block ciphers.

   ○ Block ciphers are faster, but less secure than stream ciphers.

   ○ Stream ciphers are faster, but less secure than block ciphers.

22. Which of the following is the primary goal of hashing?

   ○ Confidentiality

   ○ Integrity

   ○ Non-repudiation

   ○ Authentication

23. What is the relationship between a cipher and a cryptographic key?

   ○ The key determines which cipher is chosen (3DES, RSA, etc.).

   ○ The key determines the type of cipher chosen (stream or block).

   ○ The key determines the contents of the plaintext.

   ○ The key determines the result of the ciphertext.

24. How does a salt value help strengthen hashing?

   ○ A salt adds random data to the resulting hash value, making it different each time.

   ○ A salt subtracts data from the resulting hash value, making it different each time.

   ○ A salt adds random data to plaintext, producing a different hash result for the same plaintext value.

   ○ A salt adds random data to the hashing algorithm, producing a different result each time the hash is run.

25. Which of the following best describes a digital signature?

   ○ A message hash that has been encrypted with a public key.

   ○ A message hash that has been encrypted with the user's private key.

   ○ A document that associates credentials with a public key.

   ○ A document that associates credentials with the user's private key.

26. Which of the following best describes the process of hybrid cryptography?

○ A symmetric key encrypts the data, then an asymmetric key pair encrypts the symmetric key.

○ An asymmetric key pair encrypts the data, then a symmetric key encrypts the asymmetric key pair.

○ A symmetric key encrypts the data, which is then encrypted by another symmetric key.

○ An asymmetric key pair encrypts the data, which is then encrypted by another asymmetric key pair.

27. You are conducting a site vulnerability assessment on one of your office buildings, and so far you've covered the building's physical systems, the computer facilities housed in the building, and the various networking equipment that keeps your organization connected. What key area is missing from this site assessment?

○ Critical infrastructure security.

○ Personnel safety.

○ Perimeter security.

○ Business process security.

28. Which of the following are examples of good crime prevention through environmental design (CPTED)? (Choose two.)

☐ Place windows where they overlook sidewalks.

☐ Have multiple points of access and egress to and from a building.

☐ Limit the amount of benches, gazebos, and other outdoor shared seating areas.

☐ Keep bushes and tall trees away from surveyed areas.

29. In the event of a power failure, the biometric access control system to your data center will activate a failsecure process. Which of the following describes what will happen when the power fails?

○ The doors to the data center will open from the outside, but not the inside.

○ The doors to the data center will open from the inside, but not the outside.

○ The doors to the data center will not open from either the inside or outside.

○ The doors to the data center will open from both the inside and outside.

30. Which of the following handheld fire extinguishers is best used to extinguish an electrical fire?

○ Class A

○ Class B

○ Class C

○ Class D

31. Which of the following types of glass is resistant to impact from blunt objects?

○ Wired glass

○ Tempered glass

○ Laminated glass

○ Float glass

Mastery Builder 4-1
Assessing Communications and Network Security

Activity Time: 1 hour

Scenario

In this Mastery Builder, you will assess your knowledge of communications and network security.

1. Which layer of the OSI Model ensures that the receiver can properly interpret the transmitted information?
   - ○ Layer 7: Application
   - ○ Layer 6: Presentation
   - ○ Layer 5: Session
   - ○ Layer 3: Network

2. Which statement describes a characteristic of Internet Protocol (IP)?
   - ○ It is a proprietary, routable protocol.
   - ○ It is a connection-oriented protocol.
   - ○ It is a non-proprietary, routable protocol.
   - ○ It resides at Layer 4 of the OSI Model.

3. In the OSI Model, which of the following is *not* a valid Layer 7 protocol?
   - ○ HTTP
   - ○ SMTP
   - ○ ARP
   - ○ FTP

4. Which of the following protocols used by the original WPA standard has proven to be insecure and vulnerable to attack?
   - ○ CRC-32
   - ○ CCMP
   - ○ TKIP
   - ○ IPSec

5. Which of the following negative effects of a VoIP connection occurs when packet delays vary?
   - ○ Packet loss
   - ○ Sequence errors
   - ○ Poor codec quality
   - ○ Jitter

6. Which of the following is *not* true regarding the use of spread spectrum techniques with wireless networks? (Choose two.)

   ☐   Intercepting messages becomes more difficult.

   ☐   Transmission performance may be improved.

   ☐   It does not interfere with wireless encryption.

   ☐   It makes encryption unnecessary on wireless networks.

7.

   Which answer best describes the topology presented in the above images?

   ○   A: Physical ring | B: Logical bus

   ○   A: Physical star | B: Logical bus

   ○   A: Physical star | B: Logical ring

   ○   A: Physical star | B: Logical star

8. Your company is going through a period of rapid growth, and is currently developing plans to build out three new locations. You have been asked to meet with the project manager and network architects to ensure that security is considered during the design phase. The project team is currently considering the network topology and various physical layer options for the new locations, including shielded twisted pair (STP) cabling, fiber-optic cabling, and wireless networking options. Which options best represent your primary security concerns? (Choose three.)

   ☐   The design should consider the risk of wireless interference.

   ☐   The design should include secure locations for networking gear.

   ☐   The design should incorporate existing security policy.

   ☐   The design should address confidentiality, availability, and integrity.

   ☐   The design should meet business needs.

   ☐   Routers should be deployed using modern routing protocols.

9. Which of the following are good approaches to securing physical devices on your network? (Choose three.)

   ☐   Ensure that input devices cannot be conveniently connected to servers.

   ☐   Store non-rack-mountable equipment at the bottom of an equipment rack.

   ☐   Mount power adapters so that they are off the ground and easily visible.

   ☐   Use cable locks on laptops and small PCs.

10. Which of the following network devices retrieves content from outside the network on behalf of an internal client?

○ Proxy

○ Reverse proxy

○ Front-end processor

○ Concentrator

11. Which of the following firewall solutions can determine a packet's relationship to an earlier packet?

○ Packet filtering

○ Stateful inspection

○ Proxy

○ Screening host

12. Which statement best describes how Network Address Translation (NAT) supports confidentiality?

○ It allows outbound traffic to a specific Internet host to be returned to a specific internal node without needing to assign a public IP address to the internal node.

○ It encrypts traffic so it may not be accessed while in transit.

○ It hides the addresses of private network hosts from threat agents on the Internet.

○ NAT tables are refreshed regularly, so stored addresses are not likely to leak.

13. Which statement about IPSec is incorrect?

○ It provides anti-replay protection.

○ It has two modes.

○ It operates at Layer 4 of the OSI model.

○ Before a tunnel is created, the two ends must agree on the level of service.

14. A long-time vendor has a dedicated line in place between their headquarters and your data center. When outages occur, they typically are resolved by the vendor's telecom provider. Network diagnostic tools like tracert consistently report the same number of hops and latency figures show little fluctuation. Which network type is most likely in place?

○ Fiber-optic

○ Packet-switched

○ Circuit-switched

○ Virtual Private Network (VPN)

15. Which statement best describes the purpose of methods like CSMA/CD and CSMA/CA on data networks?

○ These methods make sure only nodes bearing the proper token initiate communications.

○ These methods reduce latency.

○ These methods manage media access for all nodes on a network.

○ These methods make sure data collisions are avoided.

16. The primary risk of a remote access server (RAS) is:

○ It typically does not offer authentication for users.

○ It typically does not allow you to configure services and protocols.

○ It typically does not allow you to enforce access policies.

○ It typically bypasses the network firewall.

17. Which of the following IPSec modes encapsulates data from endpoint to endpoint?

   ○ Tunnel

   ○ Transport

   ○ Transit

   ○ Bridge

18. Employees at your organization use company-issued smartphones in their day-to-day work. Your employees use these phones to conduct confidential calls with clients and other staff members. To prevent an IMSI-catcher from eavesdropping on these calls and tracking the employees' movement as they go mobile, what should you do?

   ○ Configure the phones to not negotiate encryption with cell towers.

   ○ Configure the phones to not broadcast their IMSI number.

   ○ Configure the phones to automatically drop a call upon detecting unusual activity.

   ○ Configure the phones to disable their GPS capabilities.

19. Which of the following is true regarding the Layer 2 Tunneling Protocol (L2TP)? (Choose two.)

   ☐ It is less secure than the Point-to-Point Tunneling Protocol (PPTP).

   ☐ Every packet is digitally signed.

   ☐ Data is natively encrypted.

   ☐ Data is not natively encrypted.

20. Which statement about Defense in Depth (DiD) is correct?

   ○ Once adopted, it provides perfect forward security.

   ○ It guarantees the security of information assets.

   ○ It is intended to create multiple layers of defenses, so that if any one defense mechanism is defeated, others remain in place to protect resources.

   ○ It mandates the use of perimeter firewalls, security zones, and endpoint protection.

21. Which of the following describes a smurf denial of service (DoS) attack?

   ○ The attacker sends ICMP packets to multiple nodes, spoofing the victim's IP address as the source. The nodes then reply to the spoofed address, causing the victim's device to overload.

   ○ The attacker sends UDP packets to multiple nodes, spoofing the victim's IP address as the source. The nodes then reply to the spoofed address, causing the victim's device to overload.

   ○ The attacker sends excessively large ICMP packets to a victim. The victim's device attempts to break down these packets, but in doing so, exceeds the size limit, causing the device to crash.

   ○ The attacker attempts to repeatedly synchronize with a victim. The attacker's device does not send an acknowledgement after receiving the victim's acknowledgement, causing the victim's device to leave open multiple connections. The victim's device becomes too busy to handle normal requests.

22. What is the most significant risk of an IPS generating a false alarm?

○ The alerts generated by the IPS will make its logs more complex and difficult to audit.

○ The IPS will actively block legitimate traffic, impacting network and system availability.

○ The IPS will normalize this behavior and continue to generate false alarms under similar circumstances.

○ The IPS will over-correct this behavior and fail to generate true alarms under similar circumstances.

23. Which of the following best describes the four stages of a network attack?

○ Target analysis, target acquisition, target access, target appropriation.

○ Target acquisition, target analysis, target access, target appropriation.

○ Target acquisition, target access, target analysis, target appropriation.

○ Target analysis, target access, target acquisition, target appropriation.

24. Which of the following best describes Address Resolution Protocol (ARP) spoofing?

○ The attacker is able to create IP packets with a forged source IP address to mask the sender's identity.

○ The attacker is able to replace Media Access Control (MAC) entries on a router so that traffic will be sent to the attacker's device, rather than its intended destination.

○ The attacker substitutes a different IP address for a domain name in the network's Domain Name System (DNS) entries in order to intercept traffic.

○ The attacker injects malicious code on a victim's device, allowing the attacker to assume that device's identity on the network.

Mastery Builder 5-1
Assessing Identity and Access Management

Scenario

In this Mastery Builder, you will assess your knowledge of identity and access management.

---

1. Which one of the following access control services determines what a subject may do when accessing an object?
    - ○ Accountability
    - ○ Authorization
    - ○ Audit
    - ○ Identification and authentication (I&A)

2. Which of the following are characteristics of a reference monitor? (Choose three.)
    - ☐ It must always be invoked.
    - ☐ It must terminate processes in the event of a failure.
    - ☐ It must be tamper-proof.
    - ☐ It must default to allowing access.

3. You've been asked to help secure logical access to your organization's new facilities. These new facilities are very large, and each will need a Wi-Fi network that covers the entire building so that users will have network access no matter where they are on the premises. As far as logical access to your network goes, which of the following is a major security concern about this initiative?
    - ○ Remote users accessing the network through a VPN.
    - ○ The actual range that your Wi-Fi signals extend to.
    - ○ The rules that determine when employees can and cannot access network resources.
    - ○ The channel that each access point broadcasts on.

4. Which one of the following access control administration methods involves assigning the processes to localized parts of the enterprise?
    - ○ Centralized
    - ○ Hybrid
    - ○ Collective
    - ○ Decentralized

5. The manual review of audit logs is associated with which risk?
    - ○ Brute force password attacks may go unnoticed.
    - ○ External attacks may not be reflected in the log files.
    - ○ Reviews may be ineffective because of the volume of data.
    - ○ Bad data may be input into the various log files.

6. Which one of the following authentication methods is best for safeguarding systems and facilities in high-security environments?
   - ○ A token.
   - ○ A PIN.
   - ○ Biometrics.
   - ○ Multifactor authentication.

7. Which of the following are characteristics of a single sign-on (SSO) environment? (Choose three.)
   - ☐ It is a cryptographic system composed of certificate authorities, digital certificates, and cryptographic algorithms.
   - ☐ Users need only one ID and password to access all systems and services.
   - ☐ If an SSO identity is compromised, all associated systems and services are at risk.
   - ☐ SSO can be extended beyond an entity's own network through federated trusts.
   - ☐ It is a synonym for authentication methods that require only a single authentication factor.

8. Which of the following are components of Kerberos? (Choose three.)
   - ☐ Access Ticket
   - ☐ Key Distribution Server
   - ☐ Service Ticket
   - ☐ Ticket Revocation Service
   - ☐ Ticket Granting Ticket

9. Which concept refers to a means of allowing internal users to present their internal credentials for access to external sites and services?
   - ○ Mutual authentication
   - ○ Identity federation
   - ○ Directory synchronization
   - ○ Kerberos

10. In order to save funds on office space, and to increase employee satisfaction, your company has decided to offer telework options to most staff. To facilitate access to company resources, those staff will connect remotely using a virtual private network. In order to connect to the workplace network using the VPN, staff must enter an alphanumeric value that displays on a small digital device and changes frequently. Staff who do not have a code may still access webmail. The device required to access the VPN is an example of a(n):
    - ○ Logical token
    - ○ Smart card
    - ○ Synchronous token
    - ○ Asynchronous token

11. Though single sign-on is convenient, what is a potential security concern?
    - ○ One compromised account grants access to all systems.
    - ○ It can allow hackers through the firewall.
    - ○ It can allow an unauthenticated user access to secure facilities.
    - ○ One forgotten password requires many password resets.

12. Agreements with cloud service providers should include terms that allow for:
   - ○ Federated identity.
   - ○ Indemnity for the service provider.
   - ○ Auditing the service provider.
   - ○ Voice recognition.

13. True or False? IDaaS is Internet-based but may provide authentication for both internal and external resources.
   - ☐ True
   - ☐ False

14. Which of the following identity federation systems asks a user what institution they are from before it grants the user access?
   - ○ WAYF
   - ○ SAML
   - ○ OpenID
   - ○ Shibboleth

15. Shibboleth uses which XML-based framework to send authentication information?
   - ○ XACML
   - ○ SAML
   - ○ DITA
   - ○ SPML

16. Which of the access control models is generally considered the most restrictive?
   - ○ Discretionary Access Control (DAC)
   - ○ Rule-based Access Control (RBAC)
   - ○ Mandatory Access Control (MAC)
   - ○ Role-based Access Control

17. Which of the following access control methods allow an object owner to assign access?
   - ○ Mandatory Access Control (MAC)
   - ○ Discretionary Access Control (DAC)
   - ○ Rule-based Access Control (RBAC)
   - ○ Role-based Access Control

18. Restricting access to objects based on the sensitivity of the information contained in the objects is an example of:
   - ○ Mandatory Access Control (MAC)
   - ○ Discretionary Access Control (DAC)
   - ○ Rule-based Access Control (RBAC)
   - ○ Role-based Access Control

19. Mandatory Access Control (MAC) requires the use of:
   - ○ Access control matrices.
   - ○ Permissions such as read, write, and modify.
   - ○ Security labels.
   - ○ Security parameters.

20. The type of access control used on a router or firewall to limit network activity is generally:
    ○ Discretionary.
    ○ Rule-based.
    ○ Role-based.
    ○ Mandatory.

21. Which of the following automated attack methods typically is the fastest way to obtain passwords?
    ○ Brute force
    ○ Rainbow tables
    ○ Shoulder surfing
    ○ Dictionary attack

22. A disgruntled employee grabbed his manager's cell phone from his office desk and correctly guessed the device's PIN. The disgruntled employee was then able to access the manager's company email account from the phone and sent out a malicious message to the company from the manager's account. What type of attack is this?
    ○ Software-based
    ○ Social engineering
    ○ Human-based
    ○ Physical

23. An executive at your organization recently had his corporate identity compromised. The attacker was able to use the executive's credentials to access and leak sensitive trade secrets to a competitor. The attacker obtained these credentials by pretending to be an IT employee in an e-mail. The e-mail message requested that the executive provide his credentials so that the IT employee could reset them for security reasons, and the executive complied. What type of attack is this?
    ○ Software-based
    ○ Social engineering
    ○ Human-based
    ○ Physical

24. Which of the following are general best practices for access control attack mitigation? (Choose three.)
    ☐ Implement Mandatory Access Control (MAC) on all systems.
    ☐ Routinely audit access control mechanisms to ensure their effectiveness.
    ☐ Continuously monitor access from both object and subject perspectives.
    ☐ Keep all staff well-trained on security policies and best practices.

25. Which of the following is the most effective way to evaluate your staff's weaknesses to social engineering attacks?
    ○ Review suspicious behavior that staff members have reported encountering.
    ○ Evaluate staff members' scores on a multiple choice exam that focuses on social engineering.
    ○ Conduct a social engineering penetration test on general staff.
    ○ Monitor staff members' external communications.

26. Technical access controls are also known as which of the following?
    ○ Discretionary access controls
    ○ Physical access controls
    ○ Logical access controls
    ○ Mandatory access controls

Mastery Builder 6-1
Assessing Security Assessment and Testing

Activity Time: 45 minutes

Scenario

In this Mastery Builder, you will assess your knowledge of security assessment and testing.

---

1. Which of the following are risks involved in security assessments? (Choose two.)
   - ☐ The testing process may end up finding nothing substantial, wasting time and money.
   - ☐ The testing process may disrupt normal operations.
   - ☐ Recommendations may be improperly implemented.
   - ☐ Recommendations may be too cost prohibitive.

2. Which of the following occasions should prompt you to conduct a vulnerability assessment? (Choose three.)
   - ☐ You need to document the current state of your systems.
   - ☐ A security breach has occurred.
   - ☐ After you've conducted a penetration test.
   - ☐ You're about to deploy a system for the first time.

3. Which of the following vulnerability scanning tools gathers information about users and groups on a network without authenticating to devices?
   - ○ Network enumerator
   - ○ Protocol scanner
   - ○ Protocol analyzer
   - ○ Packet analyzer

4. As the CISO of your organization, you have the go ahead from your CEO to begin planning a penetration test on your systems. So far, you've designated which of your security professionals will conduct the test, what types of tests they'll conduct, and what tools they'll use in the process. What other preparatory step are you missing?
   - ○ Designating an executive who will commission the test.
   - ○ Determining who will be responsible if something goes wrong during the test.
   - ○ Setting any necessary limitations on the test.
   - ○ Informing general staff about the test.

5. Which of the following best describes the disadvantage of a white box penetration test?
   ○ You may not have a complete view of the systems you're testing.
   ○ You may not be accurately simulating a real-world attack.
   ○ You may not be able to inform key personnel about the test.
   ○ You may be overly complicating the test.

6. What are the advantages of centralizing event log collection? (Choose two.)
   ☐ It reduces network load on generating and transmitting log data.
   ☐ It simplifies collection and analysis of logs.
   ☐ It makes it harder for attackers to cover their tracks.
   ☐ Centralization is easily integrated with all types of devices.

7. What is the primary challenge of event log collection?
   ○ Event logging is only available on a small number of device types.
   ○ Event logging is too inconsistent between the different operating systems.
   ○ Event logs often aren't detailed enough and may miss key occurrences.
   ○ Event logs often are too detailed and may make analysis more difficult.

8. What is the primary purpose of a synthetic transaction?
   ○ It enables professionals to craft an event for a specific use case.
   ○ It enables professionals to craft random event data.
   ○ It enables professionals to mimic an attack on their systems.
   ○ It enables professionals to introduce a vulnerability into their systems.

9. Which of the following software vulnerabilities is the result of an application failing to free up memory when it is no longer required?
   ○ Buffer overflow
   ○ Session fixation
   ○ Memory leak
   ○ Integer overflow

10. Which of the following software exploits enables an attacker to inject a malicious link into a website's forums so that users will click the link?
    ○ Reflected XSS attack
    ○ Stored XSS attack
    ○ DOM-based XSS attack
    ○ XSRF attack

11. Which of the following software testing techniques is best for detecting root problems that may not appear during a test of the running application?
    ○ Manual testing
    ○ Dynamic testing
    ○ Automated testing
    ○ Static testing

12. Which of the following software test types determines whether or not a small piece of code runs properly in isolation?
    ○ Integration test
    ○ Unit test
    ○ Functional test
    ○ Regression test

13. Which of the following are web-based input validating techniques? (Choose two.)
    ☐ Inputting massive amounts of random data into a web form.
    ☐ Editing client-side JavaScript in a web form.
    ☐ Attempting to open a secure web page without first authenticating.
    ☐ Leaving input fields empty in a web form.

14. Which of the following is the most important metric in determining test coverage of source code?
    ○ A specific percentage of total code you can afford to test.
    ○ The percentage of code that contains mostly user-facing functionality.
    ○ The amount of code that contains most of the application's logic.
    ○ The amount of code that was given the least amount of time for development.

15. Which of the following should be included in an Information Security Continuous Monitoring (ISCM) implementation? (Choose three.)
    ☐ Configuration management and change control processes throughout all phases of the system's lifecycle.
    ☐ Frequent assessment of security controls on low-impact systems.
    ☐ Active involvement from upper management.
    ☐ Management receiving up-to-date alerts.

16. Management wants to determine how effective their security awareness programs are for general staff. Which of the follow key performance indicators (KPIs) will be most useful in collecting data on the effectiveness of these programs?
    ○ How many failed authentication attempts users make before and after training.
    ○ How many help desk service requests users make before and after training.
    ○ The number of users that pass an awareness quiz before and after training.
    ○ The number of users that fall for a phishing penetration test before and after training.

17. Which of the following key performance indicators (KPIs) is the most useful in collecting data about the effectiveness of disaster recovery and business continuity processes?
    ○ The number of recorded incidents.
    ○ Response and resolution time for incidents.
    ○ The success rate of determining the source or cause of an incident.
    ○ The time span between incidents.

18. Which type(s) of service organizational control (SOC) is intended primarily for organizations that deal with financial reporting?
    ○ SOC 1
    ○ SOC 2
    ○ SOC 3
    ○ SOC 2 and SOC 3

19. What is the major difference between SOC 2 and SOC 3 reports?

○   SOC 2 reports focus on assurances of confidentiality, integrity, availability, and privacy, whereas SOC 3 reports do not.

○   SOC 3 reports focus on assurances of confidentiality, integrity, availability, and privacy, whereas SOC 2 reports do not.

○   SOC 3 reports provide less detail than SOC 2 reports and are intended for a more general audience.

○   SOC 2 reports provide less detail than SOC 3 reports and are intended for a more general audience.

20. Which of the following circumstances is most likely to require auditing by an external party?

○   The organization's compliance with its own security policies.

○   The organization's compliance with an industry standard risk management framework.

○   The organization's compliance with applicable laws and regulations.

○   The organization's compliance with general best practices for information security.

Mastery Builder 7-1
Assessing Security Operations

Activity Time: 1 hour, 20 minutes

Scenario

In this Mastery Builder, you will assess your knowledge of security operations.

1. Whose responsibility is it to implement proper data archiving and retention procedures during the information lifecycle?
   - ○ Data owner
   - ○ Data user
   - ○ Data custodian
   - ○ Data auditor

2. In order to uphold operational resilience, who should you consult with to determine which processes are the most important to the business?
   - ○ General staff
   - ○ IT staff
   - ○ Department managers
   - ○ Board of directors

3. Which of the following account management practices uphold the principle of least privilege? (Choose two.)
   - ☐ Setting expiration times for user accounts.
   - ☐ Enforcing password length and complexity requirements.
   - ☐ Enforcing password reuse requirements.
   - ☐ Automatically reviewing members in administrator groups.

4. According to UL 325, which of the following classes of fence gates would be most appropriate for a public parking lot entrance?
   - ○ Class I
   - ○ Class II
   - ○ Class III
   - ○ Class IV

5. What is an advantage of using guards over non-human physical controls? (Choose two.)
   - ☐ Guards are more reliable.
   - ☐ Guards are often more of a visual deterrent.
   - ☐ Guards can apply their own knowledge and intuition to a situation.
   - ☐ Guards are more cost-effective.

6. Which of the following assurances can a good lighting system provide? (Choose three.)

   ☐ It can act as a deterrent.

   ☐ It can aid in identifying attackers.

   ☐ It can interfere with an attacker's vision.

   ☐ It can be a useful alarm system.

7. Which of the following is the most helpful way to train personnel to uphold privacy?

   ○ Present a real-world scenario and ask them what they'd do in response.

   ○ Engage in a penetration test that targets the user's privacy.

   ○ Present personnel with a list of what they should and shouldn't do.

   ○ Mandate that personnel sign the organization's privacy policy.

8. Which of the following is *not* a best practice to secure privacy of information while traveling?

   ○ Avoid transporting electronic devices in checked baggage.

   ○ Only connect to open Wi-Fi networks you trust.

   ○ Clear your browser cache, history, and cookies after each use.

   ○ Be aware of your surroundings while entering a password.

9. You're putting together mock scenarios for your team to participate in. These scenarios focus on what personnel should do in the face of duress, such as a hostage-taking situation. You've trained your team to comply with the attackers' demands, how to stay calm, and how to get the attackers what they want so the situation can end quickly. Which of the following is an important step that your training program is missing?

   ○ How to minimize financial loss to the organization.

   ○ How to break free from the attackers' control.

   ○ How someone can alert the authorities.

   ○ How best to negotiate with the attackers.

10. Your intrusion prevention system (IPS) detected a port scan being conducted on your remote access server. As you investigate, you learn that one of your security professionals was conducting a routine vulnerability assessment of key systems, including this RAS server. Which of the following best describes the alert generated by the IPS?

    ○ True positive.

    ○ True negative.

    ○ False positive.

    ○ False negative.

11. You have a system in place that monitors email transmissions in your organization and automatically removes any attachments. What type of system is this?

    ○ Intrusion detection system (IDS).

    ○ Intrusion prevention system (IPS).

    ○ Data loss prevention (DLP).

    ○ Security information and event management (SIEM).

12. How can steganography be used to evade egress monitoring controls?

    ○ An attacker can physically move data to outside of the network.

    ○ The attacker can encrypt data packets and send them through an allowed protocol.

    ○ The attacker can initiate a DoS condition on the egress monitoring system.

    ○ The attacker can hide sensitive data in other media as it travels outside the network.

13. What is an advantage of whitelisting over blacklisting?

- ○ Whitelists are less restrictive.
- ○ Whitelists can protect against threats you don't know about.
- ○ Whitelists are more cost-effective.
- ○ Whitelists are easier to maintain.

14. What are the advantages to using virtual machine sandboxes? (Choose two.)

- ☐ The user can't interfere with the host.
- ☐ The user has greater control over their environment.
- ☐ The sandboxes are easily provisioned to multiple users.
- ☐ The sandboxes minimize network load.

15. When constructing honeypots and honeynets, you need to be aware of enticement and entrapment concerns. Which of the following are key differences between enticement and entrapment? (Choose two.)

- ☐ Enticement is legal, entrapment is not.
- ☐ Entrapment is legal, enticement is not.
- ☐ Enticement is luring someone to commit a crime they would not have otherwise committed.
- ☐ Entrapment is luring someone to commit a crime they would not have otherwise committed.

16. What is the most important asset characteristic you should describe in a configuration management (CM) system?

- ○ Who owns the asset.
- ○ Who uses the asset.
- ○ Where the asset is stored.
- ○ How the asset fulfills business needs.

17. Which of the following is a software asset management practice that ensures malicious code won't compromise an application's binaries?

- ○ Implement a digital watermark in the binaries.
- ○ Digitally sign the binaries.
- ○ Encrypt the binaries.
- ○ Use steganography to hide the binaries.

18. Which of the following best describes the two-man rule as it applies to media management?

- ○ No two people should have an equivalent level of access to media.
- ○ Only two people should have an equivalent level of access to media.
- ○ There must be two authorized people at all time to monitor media use.
- ○ Monitoring duties must rotate between two authorized people.

19. Which of the following are major reasons why you should implement a patch management system? (Choose two.)

☐ It relieves you of the burden of having to schedule updates.

☐ It allows you to develop in-house patches for external proprietary software.

☐ Default patch downloading from the Internet can negatively impact network bandwidth.

☐ Patches should not go untested before being deployed.

20. If Internet connectivity is an issue in your organization, which of the following ways could you configure your patch management servers to mitigate this issue? (Choose two.)

☐ Side-load vendor patches into the patch management servers.

☐ Schedule downloading of vendor patches during normal work hours.

☐ Schedule downloading of vendor patches during off hours.

☐ Schedule distribution of vendor patches during normal work hours.

21. What is the primary reason why a patch management system should include patch testing functionality?

○ Vendor patches may add new, unwanted features.

○ Vendor patches may fix one bug, but introduce another.

○ The contents of a vendor patch may become corrupted during transmission.

○ The patch management system may not distribute the patch properly.

22. You recently went through the change management process in order to update your workstations' operating systems from Windows 7 to Windows 10. In this process: you requested the change from the Change Control Board (CCB); the CCB approved the change; you informed IT personnel and staff about the impending move to the new OS; you thoroughly tested all of your production software on the new Windows 10 environment and determined that it was all compatible; you then had your IT staff update all available workstations; and lastly you reported to your CIO and the CCB that the operating system update was a success. Which key step did you forget to include in this change management process?

○ Reporting the success of the change to the Board of Directors.

○ Documenting the change in a change log.

○ Automating the process of updating the workstations from Windows 7 to 10.

○ Obtaining majority buy-in from the staff members that use the workstations.

23. Which of the following are the main reasons why versioning is so important to the change management process? (Choose two.)

☐ To establish a single baseline to compare all future versions against.

☐ To capture an object's current state and compare that version against the proposed changes.

☐ To quickly and easily roll back changes that introduce problems.

☐ To establish non-repudiation for changes.

24. Aside from assessing a change's impact to operational security, what else should a security impact analysis (SIA) provide?

○ An assessment of the change's affect on business models.

○ An assessment of the change's affect on personnel productivity.

○ Recommendations on how best to implement the change quickly and with minimal effort.

○ Recommendations on how to resolve any risk the change introduces.

25. Which of the following describes the process of triage as it relates to incident response?
    - ○ Identifying the best method for responding to an incident.
    - ○ Identifying which systems have been hit the hardest in an incident.
    - ○ Identifying the most critical systems to respond to first.
    - ○ Identifying the source of an incident.

26. Which of the following scenarios exhibits the remediation process in incident response?
    - ○ Restoring functionality to web servers that were DDoSed.
    - ○ Engaging in a public relations campaign to restore client confidence in the organization after an incident.
    - ○ Moving all personnel to an alternate site at which they will continue business operations.
    - ○ Cleaning malicious software from a user's workstation.

27. What is the ultimate goal of drafting a lessons learned report (LLR) after responding to an incident?
    - ○ Providing a well-reasoned justification for the actions taken during the response.
    - ○ Ensuring that recommendations in the LLR are implemented in the organization.
    - ○ Absolving the organization of legal liability with regards to the response.
    - ○ Providing a framework for legal prosecution of a suspected crime.

28. Which of the following characteristics describe what an investigation *must* be? (Choose three.)
    - ☐ Methodical
    - ☐ Extensible
    - ☐ Auditable
    - ☐ Verifiable

29. Which of the following forensic practices ensure that log files are admissible in court? (Choose two.)
    - ☐ Writing logs to access controlled volumes.
    - ☐ Hashing the log files.
    - ☐ Encrypting the contents of log files.
    - ☐ Defining a single authorized individual as the log owner.

30. What is a security concern involved with obtaining forensic evidence from an embedded device?
    - ○ Taking an image of the device's firmware may alter that firmware.
    - ○ A device's firmware changes too often to be of any forensic value.
    - ○ Evidence obtained from certain embedded devices is not admissible in court.
    - ○ Few tools are available that can accurately obtain evidence from embedded devices.

31. For IT systems, a Recovery Point Objective (RPO) is often reflected by which one of the following?
    - ○ The date of the last successful system restoration process.
    - ○ The point in time at which the last system failure occurred.
    - ○ The number of days the business can function without the system.
    - ○ The date of the last successful backup of the affected system.

32. Which of the following disaster recovery plan (DRP) test types is preliminary and should not replace more substantial tests?
   - ○ Simulation
   - ○ Full interrupt
   - ○ Parallel
   - ○ Readthrough

33. How often should you update and maintain your DRP?
   - ○ Every month
   - ○ Every 3 months
   - ○ Every year
   - ○ Every 2 years

34. Which of the following RAID levels allows two drives to fail without needing to recover?
   - ○ RAID 0
   - ○ RAID 1
   - ○ RAID 5
   - ○ RAID 6

35. Which of the following is a disadvantage of a hot site?
   - ○ The site cannot test recovery.
   - ○ The site cannot guarantee high availability.
   - ○ The site is expensive.
   - ○ The site takes a long time to get up and running.

36. Which of the following data backup methods clears the archive bit to reduce backup time and storage?
   - ○ Incremental
   - ○ Differential
   - ○ Remote journaling
   - ○ Electronic vaulting

37. Which of the following best describe an event categorized as a severe incident? (Choose two.)
   - ☐ It will trigger the disaster recovery process.
   - ☐ It will not require crisis management.
   - ☐ It may require building a new facility.
   - ☐ It has only natural causes.

38. Which of the following statements about a call tree are accurate when it applies to disaster recovery communications? (Choose two.)
   - ☐ It speeds up the communication process.
   - ☐ It slows down the communication process.
   - ☐ It should not be more than two levels deep.
   - ☐ It should not be more than three levels deep.

39. Why is it important to include the legal team in the restoration process after a disaster?

○ The legal team can secure financial aid for the restoration process.

○ The legal team can prepare the organization's defense in case it is held liable for damages.

○ The legal team can advise management on how to stay compliant during restoration efforts.

○ The legal team can help prepare the organization to press charges.

Mastery Builder 8-1
Assessing Software Development Security

Activity Time: 50 minutes

Scenario
In this Mastery Builder, you will assess your knowledge of software development security.

---

1. Which of the following phases of the systems lifecycle (SLC) occur after development? (Choose two.)
   - ☐ Implementation
   - ☐ Disposal
   - ☐ Maintenance
   - ☐ Requirements analysis

2. Which of the following is the ideal SLC phase to start incorporating security into?
   - ○ Planning
   - ○ System design
   - ○ Initiation
   - ○ Testing

3. Which of the following best describes a maturity model?
   - ○ A framework for assessing the organization's presence in a long-standing industry.
   - ○ A framework for assessing the organization's long-term goals.
   - ○ A framework for assessing the comprehensiveness of an organization's policy.
   - ○ A framework for assessing the sophistication level of an organization's processes.

4. Which of the following describe the Capability Maturity Model (CMM)? (Choose two.)
   - ☐ Maturity levels can be skipped.
   - ☐ Maturity levels cannot be skipped.
   - ☐ The target maturity level for most organizations is Level 3: Defined.
   - ☐ The target maturity level for most organizations is Level 4: Quantitatively Managed.

5. Which of the following best describes an Integrated Product Team (IPT)?
   - ○ Staff members from multiple disciplines work together to develop systems and programs.
   - ○ Staff members from similar disciplines work together to develop systems and programs.
   - ○ A dedicated team develops systems and programs so that they more efficiently work with existing systems and programs.
   - ○ A dedicated team identifies how new products may be integrated into existing systems and programs.

6. Which of the following best describes an interpreted language?

   ○ Source code is transformed into object code that is understood by the operating system.

   ○ Source code is translated line by line into machine code every time the program is run.

   ○ It enables the creation of reusable objects in source code.

   ○ It is faster than compiled code.

7. Which of the following software development models makes it impossible to go back to previous phases in the model?

   ○ Agile

   ○ Prototyping

   ○ Waterfall

   ○ Spiral

8. Which of the following best describe the software certification and accreditation process? (Choose two.)

   ☐ Certification is a risk evaluation of the software.

   ☐ Accreditation is a risk evaluation of the software.

   ☐ Management certifies the software does what it's supposed to do; the technical team accredits this certification.

   ☐ The technical team certifies the software does what it's supposed to; management accredits this certification.

9. Which of the following software development models attempts to find and correct security issues from the onset of writing source code, rather than afterward?

   ○ Agile

   ○ Cleanroom

   ○ Waterfall

   ○ Prototyping

10. Your organization is finishing development on a smartphone app that allows employees to quickly view the product store when they're on the go, such as when salespeople meet with clients. After you push the app onto each employee's company-provided phone, you get reports from users of the app crashing when they attempt to view pricing information for certain products. According to your development team, this exact error was reported on and fixed during the beta testing phase. However, the IT team that installed the app on users' phones was unaware of any such fix. What is the most likely explanation for this availability-compromising issue?

    ○ You failed to ensure that measures to uphold availability were incorporated in the design phase.

    ○ You failed to ensure that this issue was caught during the testing phase.

    ○ You failed to ensure that the patched and most up-to-date version of the software was used during the deployment phase.

    ○ You failed to ensure that the developers wrote security-conscious source code during the build phase.

11. Which of the database models requires pointers to locate other entries in the database?

- ○ Object-oriented
- ○ Network
- ○ Hierarchical
- ○ Relational

12. You organization has sales record databases that track sales across the world. However, a potential conflict arises between these databases when it comes to the date of each sale: dates in the United States follow the MM/DD/YYYY format, whereas dates in Europe follow the DD/MM/YYYY format. Which of the following techniques helps mitigate this conflict to create consistent data coding?

- ○ Pre-processing with a data warehouse.
- ○ Aggregation with data mining.
- ○ Curation with a data archive.
- ○ Collation with a relational database.

13. Which of the following are characteristics of a data warehouse? (Choose two.)

- ☐ They are typically not updated.
- ☐ They are frequently updated.
- ☐ They contain information about a subject from a single source.
- ☐ They contain information about a subject from various sources.

14. Which of the following is the most significant vulnerability of data aggregation?

- ○ Aggregated data may oversimplify or misrepresent disparate data sets.
- ○ Too much aggregated data may disclosure sensitive information.
- ○ Aggregated data views cannot be access controlled.
- ○ Aggregating too much data can cause a DoS condition.

15. You have a web-based storefront for customers to purchase your products. Because you have a limited supply of certain products, what type of database control can help limit conflicts that arise when two different people attempt to purchase the last item in stock at the same time?

- ○ Perturbation
- ○ Cell suppression
- ○ Partitioning
- ○ Online transaction processing (OLTP) controls

16. Which of the following are advantages of open source software over proprietary software? (Choose two.)

- ☐ Open source software has more people reviewing the code, spotting vulnerabilities.
- ☐ Open source software often undergoes an intensive testing process.
- ☐ Open source software can be repurposed for an organization's specific functional or security needs.
- ☐ Open source software is constantly and reliably updated.

17. Why might someone who finds a software vulnerability choose full disclosure rather than partial disclosure? (Choose two.)

☐ They believe in giving the vendor a chance to fix the vulnerability before it's known publicly.

☐ They believe that the vendor does not or will not take them seriously.

☐ They believe that everyone affected should know about the vulnerability as quickly as possible.

☐ They believe that only releasing part of what they know about a vulnerability to the public won't adequately explain its significance.

18. How can a programer protect against a buffer overflow vulnerability?

○ Ensure that backdoors are removed from the application before implementation.

○ Perform integrity checks for unwanted additions to the program.

○ Perform bounds checking on the program's fields.

○ Ensure that the time period between checking data and using data is minimal.

19. Why should a source code analysis tool be only one component of a larger system for identifying and correcting software security issues? (Choose two.)

☐ They operate slowly.

☐ There are all prohibitively expensive.

☐ They are at risk of producing false negatives.

☐ They are at risk of producing false positives.

20. An application that uses password masking protects against which type of attack?

○ Brute force password cracking.

○ Shoulder surfing.

○ Password guessing.

○ Rainbow tables.

21. Which of the following are best practices for software development change logs? (Choose three.)

☐ They should list version releases with the most recent on top.

☐ Every version of the code should have its own subsection.

☐ They should be written to be more machine readable than human readable.

☐ They should easily link to any section of code.

22. Which of the following best describe a software audit? (Choose two.)

☐ Audits are concerned with the technical accuracy of the software.

☐ Audits are not concerned with the technical accuracy of the software.

☐ Audits are performed by an independent body.

☐ Audits are performed by the development team.

23. When implementing Semantic Versioning, which of the following best describes a "MINOR" revision to software?

○ When you add backward-compatible functionality.

○ When you make a backward-compatible bug fix.

○ When you make a backward-incompatible API change.

○ When you make a backward-incompatible security fix.

24. Which of the following is *not* included as part of a software security acceptance test?

   ○   Testing for input that exceeds normal boundaries.

   ○   Testing for security policy violations.

   ○   Testing for end user productivity impact.

   ○   Testing illegal input.

25. Which of the following are best practices for acquiring software from a third party vendor? (Choose three.)

   ☐   Ensure that the vendor has trained their personnel on their own security requirements.

   ☐   Only contract out to vendors who meet your security baseline standards.

   ☐   Ensure the vendor has a software assurance process in place.

   ☐   Implement a risk management strategy for acquiring software.

Solutions

ACTIVITY 1-1: Discussing Security Governance Principles

1. Do you think that the CIO has performed due care and due diligence in sending an organization-wide email requiring all employees to comply with the new security policy? Why or why not?

   A: Answers will vary. Simply sending an email and expecting people to read, understand, and comply with it is not performing proper due care and due diligence. This is especially true for an organization that was not previously focused on information security, where employees were not required to think about security before. The receptionist's response demonstrates that she wasn't even aware that the email was sent or that it contained anything important. So as far as the employees you interviewed are concerned, the email did not meet its objective.

2. Based on the scenario, what gaps in the company's security governance would you immediately focus on?

   A: Answers will vary. One of the first things you might want to focus on is making sure that upper management actually understands the purpose and nature of security governance. It's clear that upper management thinks information security is necessary, but it is also clear that they do not understand what is involved or how to go about it. You will then want to help management create an appropriate security policy for the company. You'll have to help the organization change its culture regarding security. You will also want to assist management in understanding information security roles, and the responsibilities of the chief officers. From there you may also wish to help the company choose a control framework to base their security on. You may also wish to insist that the information security group be given more clear direction in their level of autonomy and authority.

ACTIVITY 1-2: Discussing Compliance

1. What compliance issues does the training company have?

   A: Answers will vary. Since the company is publicly traded in the U.S., it immediately is out of compliance with Sarbanes-Oxley for not keeping finance-related emails. The enrollment officer put PII at risk by keeping customer financial data on her laptop. It is likely that both U.S. and international privacy laws were broken, as well as possibly trans-border data flow regulations.

2. How can you help the organization stay in compliance with regulations?

   A: Answers will vary. The company could certainly use role-specific compliance training, as well as have some controls put in place to keep the company in compliance. It also probably needs a more involved legal department.

ACTIVITY 1-3: Discussing Professional Ethics in Security

1. **How should you answer the technician's suggestion of using the downloaded software in the library?**

   A: Answers will vary. It is obviously wrong to use unlicensed downloaded software, even if the college is strapped for cash. You might suggest looking for an open source (free) version of the software that will do the same job or a discounted academic license for the commercial version. You might also assist the college in prioritizing their software purchases.

2. **How should you address the president's concern about you having administrative access to the college financial database?**

   A: You can assure the president and the board that as a CISSP, you are bound by oath to uphold professional ethics, to behave honorably, and to provide competent and assiduous service. You can also remind the board and president that you cannot put effective controls in place on the database if you do not have administrative rights.

3. **From what you can see in the scenario, what are the larger information security issues, and how might you help the college address them?**

   A: Answers will vary. It is clear from the absence of procedure that the college does not yet have an IT governance infrastructure. Management probably does not yet know what this entails. The fact that the librarian is used to just asking for software, with the technician offering to install a downloaded copy, suggests that there is no approval process in place, no change control in place, and possibly no budget prioritization for legitimate software purchases. It also suggests that there are no controls in place for managing software installation and usage. From the president's behavior, there are signs of corruption and favoritism in the organization, which not only goes against CISSP professional ethics, but also will hurt the overall security posture of the college. This is as much a human and cultural issue as a professional issue. You will need to help the president overcome his disappointment and bias against you by demonstrating that good IT governance and adherence to professional ethics (including resisting corruption and favoritism) actually helps the college by focusing on best practice rather than personal gain. When designing and instituting IT security governance for the college, involve the president and senior management. Get them to participate as governance steering committee members, or in focus groups, under your guidance, to design and implement proper IT governance for the school. Get the legal department to identify any regulatory requirements, and include them in the focus group or steering committee.

ACTIVITY 1-4: Discussing Security Documentation

1. **What issues at the college would a security policy address?**

   A: Answers will vary. First and foremost, it would address the chaos that exists due to lack of structure and IT governance. If implemented thoughtfully, it would help shift the culture away from that of being self-serving to that of supporting the greater good, which would also improve the college's efforts at sustainability. It would help move the college IT department away from crisis management and putting out fires to being more proactive.

2. How can each of the security document types help the college?

   A: Answers will vary. The policy would establish the framework for governance and set the stage for cultural change. The standards document would help the college stay focused on their security targets. The guidelines would reinforce security thinking wherever there is not a specific mandate, but provide best practice. The procedures manual would give the IT staff clear step-by-step instructions on how to execute the standards. The baseline document would spell out the minimum acceptable level of security for the various systems and networks.

3. In what way would each document type inform (drive) the other document types?

   A: The policy document sets the high level objectives. It is aimed at management and governance and is not technical in nature. The policy document is then used by the standards document to outline specific objectives on a more technical level. The procedures document then lists exact steps for achieving the required standards. The standards document also sets the context for choosing and listing best practice in the guidelines document and the baseline document.

4. How can the problem of using illegitimate software be addressed in strategic planning? In tactical planning? In operational planning?

   A: Strategic planning can shift the thinking away from using random, pirated, and untested software to clean, licensed, virus-free software. It can align software acquisition with business needs, and make management conscious of the need to allocate budget for legitimate software purchases. It can set the tone for using software in a way that benefits the business. Tactical planning can prioritize software purchases and actually allocate budget, as well as reinforce the need for change control. Operational planning can require the IT team to follow specific procedures and not obtain software in a random or ad-hoc manner.

ACTIVITY 1–5: Discussing Risk Management

---

1. With regard to Incident #1, the information leakage event, would training the staff be a cost effective measure to mitigate future incidents?

   A: Answers will vary. If reducing the risk by half equals saving $250,000 annually, then yes. A $50,000 per year investment will preserve $200,000 per year in sales. However, one could argue that reducing the risk by half does not directly equate to reducing the lost sales by half. Training would make it 50% less likely that future information will be leaked. But the risk of leakage is still high. If the information still gets leaked and the competitor brings its own version to market first, the company may still lose $500,000 annually in lost sales on the new product.

2. With regard to Incident #2, the virus attack, would purchasing the antivirus license be a cost effective solution?

   A: For a single similar incident, no. The production floor produces $3,650,000 worth of goods per year ($10,000 x 365). The virus attack had a SLE of $10,000 ($10,000 per day x 2 days x 50% exposure = $10,000). The antivirus solution would cost $20,000, which is a net loss of $10,000 for this scenario. However, viruses are a daily threat. This incident is probably not the only one. There are likely many other virus-related incidents that were not as high profile as this, and thus probably not considered in the scenario. The company should reassess the real cost of having an out-of-date antivirus program, and perform the risk analysis again in that light.

3. With regard to Incident #3, which scenario (earthquakes or wildfires) should management devote more of its resources towards mitigating? What would be an appropriate risk response?

   A: Answers will vary. This scenario has no clear dollar value assigned to the two risks. A qualitative risk analysis will produce varying opinions of probability and impact. The wildfires happen more frequently, though the level of impact so far seems lower. The earthquake has a considerably lower frequency of occurrence, but the impact is likely to be dramatically higher. In either event, the appropriate response is to transfer the risk by buying insurance.

ACTIVITY 1-6: Discussing Threat Modeling

1. **Which of the three threat agents might have played a role in the information leakage incident?**

   A: Answers will vary. Since a rival company was able to quickly release a competing product, it looks like corporate espionage was at play. However, the rival company could have also employed a malicious hacker to help steal the plans for XYZ's new product. Additionally, inept users could have played an inadvertent role in assisting with the attack.

2. **What possible threat agent actions occurred during the information leakage incident?**

   A: Answers will vary. Certainly there was unauthorized access and disclosure to unauthorized users. There might also have been misuse by authorized users.

3. **Based on the DREAD acronym, how would you rate the impact of this threat?**

   A: This threat had a high impact in all areas: damage, reproducibility, exploitability, affected users, and discoverability.

4. **How do you think the product plans were stolen? What do you think were the possible avenues of attack?**

   A: Answers will vary. Infected flash drives could have been scattered in the parking lot, and unwary users could have inserted them in their machines. A hacker could have found and exploited vulnerabilities in the network to gain access. Corporate spies could have also gained access and stolen the plans.

5. **What recommendations would you make to mitigate this risk for the upcoming product?**

   A: Answers will vary. User education would reduce inadvertent participation by inept users. You might also want to create a more in-depth attack diagram to look for points of weakness, and then address those vulnerabilities accordingly.

ACTIVITY 1-7: Discussing Business Continuity Plan Fundamentals

1. **What business continuity disasters do the XYZ Group face?**

   A: Answers will vary. Natural disasters such as earthquake and fire are obvious choices. There might also be another major hacking attack against the production facility that shuts down operations. Also notice that senior managers like to attend events together. Although an incident during travel is less likely, it's still a risk to have so many high level officials travel together in the same plane or vehicle.

2. **What are some of the critical business processes that XYZ needs to sustain during a disaster?**

   A: Answers will vary. Because it manufactures and sells widgets, XYZ will need to maintain some level of production, distribution, sales, and accounting. It will also need to maintain some level of customer service. In addition to attending to customer needs, XYZ (actually any company) will also need to maintain HR, payroll, and personnel support.

3. **Which processes do you think XYZ should recover first?**

   A: Answers will vary. Probably the HR-related processes need to be attended to first so that the company has the human resources needed to survive the disaster. There needs to be a BIA performed for each of the processes, as well as have the maximum tolerable downtime for each determined.

4. After developing the BCP, what do you think will be the most critical exercise to perform to ensure that the BCP will save the company during a disaster?

    A: Answers will vary. You must test, evaluate, and maintain/update your BCP to ensure its effectiveness. But testing would come first.

5. How can you ensure that the BCP will be executed properly during the disaster?

    A: Answers will vary. You must train all of your staff to implement the BCP in case of a disaster. You must also make sure your BCP is written in plain language so that any intelligent person can follow its directions. Additionally, make sure that success of the BCP does not depend on any one person. For example, if the BCP calls for communicating through a phone tree, make sure that the plan does not depend on a single person to initiate the chain of phone calls.

ACTIVITY 1-8: Discussing Acquisition Strategy and Practice

1. Of all the concepts discussed in this topic, which do you consider to be the most important when evaluating the three competing vendors? Why?

    A: You should start with your strategy first. This will inform and drive all implementation processes.

2. What items would you require in the vendor's SLA? Why?

    A: Answers will vary. An SLA should at least outline what the service will be, the level of service provided, and the penalties for not providing the service as required.

3. Would you handle your evaluation of the offshore vendors differently from the local vendor? If so, what would you focus on the most and why?

    A: Because of distance, language barriers, and cultural differences, using an offshore vendor is generally a more risky choice than a local vendor. The offshore vendor will need to be vetted more carefully, possibly with the help of other parties.

ACTIVITY 1-9: Discussing Personnel Security Policies

1. As the company prepares to rapidly expand, which personnel security practice do you think should be implemented first and why?

    A: A policy should always be in place first to guide all other processes.

2. Of all the employee roles mentioned, which ones do you think require the most job position sensitivity profiling and why?

    A: Answers will vary. IT probably needs the most sensitivity profiling as people are moved into new (and more restrictive) positions. You will also want to engage personnel during the transition, helping them to understand their new role in the big picture.

3. How would you mitigate risk when reassigning, demoting, or terminating under-performing staff?

    A: Answers will vary. You'll need to implement clear policy, procedures, and controls to protect the network, company property, and other personnel in case employees become disgruntled or alienated. Involve the legal and HR departments to make sure transitions are done appropriately and as smoothly as possible. It will also take some psychology and interpersonal skills to help users transition to a new (more appropriate) role or out of the company. One good strategy is to give an employee you are keeping "ownership" of something that they can handle. It makes people feel valued and less likely to become a negative factor. If you must terminate the individual, do so in as graceful a manner as possible to help them accept the change and leave peacefully.

ACTIVITY 1-10: Discussing Security Awareness and Training

1. **What security issues need to be addressed in this training program?**

   A: Answers may vary, but the threat of social engineering and poor user security practices is potentially a huge risk to the organization. The organization needs to empower its staff with basic security know-how to avoid the human factor being the biggest threat to business continuity. Additionally, the organization should seek to build a security culture that it currently lacks.

2. **What are the objectives and expected outcomes for the training?**

   A: Answers will vary. Overall objectives may include: equipping users with the tools they need to do their jobs securely; providing users with best practices that relate to their job functions; ensuring that users know who to contact when they have security-related questions or concerns; and ensuring that everyone in the organization, no matter their position, is contributing to the collective security culture.

3. **What are the key points that your training should include for general staff?**

   A: Answers will vary. Some key points include: ways to identify and deny social engineering attempts; ways to secure communications, especially email and other messaging protocols the organization users; ways to safely surf the web; how to avoid malware from infecting their computers; how to keep sensitive company date confidential; paying special attention to the security challenges of BYOD; and more.

4. **Other than general staff, how would you customize the training program for different job roles/levels (e.g., board of directors, management, IT staff, security personnel, etc.)?**

   A: Senior management and members of the Board of Directors need to be trained on the importance of security assuring business objectives and the importance of legal and regulatory compliance. Middle management needs to be well-versed in policies, procedures, guidelines, and other documentation, ensuring that their employees are complying with them. IT staff need to be trained on the proper procedures for implementing technology in a secure way. Security professionals need constant training to keep up with the latest threat landscape, as well as the latest risk management processes as mandated by management. General staff should receive more user-focused training, like best practices for computer and Internet usage, and how to avoid social engineering attacks.

Mastery Builder 1-1: Assessing Security and Risk Management

1. **Which statement about guidelines is correct?**
   - ○ They describe the steps required to complete an activity.
   - ○ They describe a required use of specific tools.
   - ◉ They are recommended settings or actions.
   - ○ They specify the minimum security required for a system.

2. The use of a security policy to define management intention is an example of which access control type?

   - ⦿ Administrative
   - ○ Physical
   - ○ Technical
   - ○ Preventative

3. The CIA triad is considered central to security. Which option best describes what it helps protect against?

   - ○ Disclosure, loss, and leakage
   - ⦿ Destruction, alteration, and disclosure
   - ○ Confidentiality, integrity, and availability
   - ○ Unavailability, downtime, and destruction

4. Which statement best describes security policies?

   - ○ They are operational instructions for implementing security.
   - ⦿ They document high level expectations from senior management.
   - ○ They detail tactical instructions for implementing security.
   - ○ They are work procedures specified by senior management.

5. The first step in risk analysis is to:

   - ○ Conduct a threat assessment.
   - ⦿ Identify assets and their value.
   - ○ Identify potential vulnerabilities.
   - ○ Identify the countermeasures.

6. Due to increased news coverage of significant data breaches at major corporations, your company's Board of Directors instructed the CEO to conduct a thorough risk assessment. As a result, the company hired its first CIO, who is tasked with carrying out the risk assessment. The CIO assembled a team to assist with the risk assessment processes, and they began by taking a complete inventory of all assets. Once the inventory was complete, a series of vulnerability assessments were conducted, and historical data regarding earlier security incidents was collected. You have been asked to use that historical information, as well as trends and threat forecasts from security research firms, to develop concrete figures to allow management to understand the costs associated with each risk. What type of risk analysis have you been asked to complete?

   - ○ Cost-driven
   - ⦿ Quantitative
   - ○ Qualitative
   - ○ Semi-quantitative

7. A business impact analysis (BIA) often includes which of the following security processes?

   - ⦿ A vulnerability assessment.
   - ○ Installing network countermeasures.
   - ○ Training of key personnel.
   - ○ A disaster recovery process.

8. Which statement best describes the primary purpose of a business continuity plan?
   - ○ To ensure that the company will recover from one-time disasters.
   - ◉ To ensure business processes may continue after a disruption or crisis.
   - ○ To identify key players in the business and enable succession planning.
   - ○ To keep key business documents available when and where they are needed.

9. What is the best way to justify a request for funding for business continuity efforts?
   - ◉ Detail how a BCP protects the organization's ability to continue generating revenue.
   - ○ Describe how a BCP allows the organization to more quickly achieve RPOs.
   - ○ Describe how a DRP protects the organization's ability to continue generating revenue.
   - ○ Describe how a BCP protects the organization against specific disaster scenarios.

10. Which of the following demonstrate the legal concept of due care? (Choose two.)
    - ☑ Providing appropriate security training for all employees.
    - ☐ Performing background checks on all prospective employees.
    - ☑ Securing customers' personal information on the organization's servers.
    - ☐ Performing risk assessments on network systems.

11. Your company recently acquired a smaller organization in the same industry. Which of the following is the most significant security risk as a result of this acquisition?
    - ○ The other organization may have a different C-level structure than yours.
    - ◉ There may be a disparity between each organization's levels of security.
    - ○ The other organization may use different access control mechanisms than yours.
    - ○ There may be a disparity between each organization's security budget.

12. Which of the following is a privacy law that protects users' financial information when it is held by banks and other financial institutions?
    - ○ Sarbanes-Oxley Act (SOX)
    - ○ Electronic Communications Privacy Act (ECPA)
    - ○ Federal Information Security Management Act (FISMA)
    - ◉ Gramm-Leach-Bliley Act (GLBA)

13. True or False? Patent protection is stronger and lasts longer than copyright protection.
    - ☐ True
    - ☑ False

14. Which of the following is a comprehensive set of processes that can increase the effectiveness and decrease the complexity of security-focused operations?
    - ◉ Governance, risk management, and compliance.
    - ○ Governance, risk analysis, and risk mitigation.
    - ○ Governance, risk management, and training
    - ○ Risk management, compliance, and training

15. Which of the following are goals of the (ISC)2 Code of Ethics canon? (Choose three.)

- ☑ Behaving responsibly, justly, honestly, honorably, and legally.
- ☑ Improving, enhancing, and protecting the profession.
- ☐ Ensuring, enabling, and supporting the exchange of free information.
- ☑ Providing adept, competent, and assiduous service to principals.

16. A user breaches a company's private file servers, but only glances at a couple of files before disconnecting. The user argues that they have not behaved unethically because they only viewed a relatively small amount of information. Additionally, they didn't leak the information to the public, so the company couldn't have suffered any significant harm. What fallacy or faulty reasoning has this user committed?

- ○ The ends justify the means.
- ○ Information yearns to be free.
- ○ If the act is easy and security is poor, the company can't find fault with the user.
- ◉ The company's computer systems are shatterproof.

17. Which of the following are key tasks in upholding organizational ethics? (Choose three.)

- ☐ Weighing ethical actions in relation to cost or benefit to the organization.
- ☑ Hiring and retaining employees that have a strong ethical background.
- ☑ Acting responsibly to the organization's stakeholders and to the public.
- ☑ Adhering to established standards and laws that outline ethical behavior.

18. You want to write into your security documentation that all employee accounts must use a minimum of eight characters in their passwords. Any accounts that currently have a password shorter than eight characters should be disabled until the password is updated to comply with the eight character minimum. What type of security document would this apply to?

- ○ Guideline
- ○ Process
- ○ Standard
- ◉ Baseline

19. True or False? In a Platform as a service (PaaS) model, the responsibility for security is on the vendor.

- ☐ True
- ☑ False

20. The company you acquired had its own set of security policies that governed its operations. What is the most important thing to consider regarding these policies?

- ◉ Make sure the acquired company's policies don't contradict your own.
- ○ Make sure the acquired company's policies are written in your style.
- ○ Make sure the acquired company's policies address all of your systems.
- ○ Make sure your policies incorporate every item from the acquired company's policies.

21. Your company is in talks to form a partnership with another company in the same industry. You will be routinely sharing sensitive data and systems with the other company. You want to ensure that your data and systems are kept safe during and after this sharing process, and failure to do so by either party should result in legal penalties. Which of the following types of agreements should you draft?

- ○ Service-level agreement (SLA)
- ○ Memorandum of understanding (MOU)
- ◉ Interconnection security agreement (ISA)
- ○ Business partnership agreement (BPA)

22. Which of the following is a rating system that determines the impact of a threat?

   ○ Damage, interruption, reproducibility, exploitability (DIRE)

   ○ Harm, affected users, reproducibility, manageability (HARM)

   ○ Tampering, harm, reproducibility, exploitability, affected users, thoroughness (THREAT)

   ◉ Damage, reproducibility, exploitability, affected users, discoverability (DREAD)

23. The STRIDE acronym is a threat classification that includes which of the following?

   ○ Spoofing, tampering, reflection, integrity violation, denial of service, escalation

   ◉ Spoofing, tampering, repudiation, information disclosure, denial of service, elevation of privilege

   ○ Systems hacking, threatening, restructuring, information disclosure, destruction, elevation of privilege

   ○ Systems hacking, tampering, repudiation, impersonation, destruction, elevation of privilege

24. What is the typical flow of a threat tree diagram, from top (beginning) to bottom (end)?

   ○ Identify the threat, identify how to mitigate the threat, identify who or what should implement the mitigation

   ◉ Identify the threat, identify how the threat can occur, identify how to mitigate the threat

   ○ Identify how the threat can occur, identify what systems are vulnerable, identify how to mitigate the threat

   ○ Identify how the threat can occur, identify the source of the threat, identify how to mitigate the threat

25. What is an employee's sensitivity profile?

   ○ A description of the employee's technical level of access to sensitive systems.

   ○ A description of the employee's trustworthiness with regard to keeping sensitive information secure.

   ◉ A description of the employee's need-to-know information based on their job role.

   ○ A description of the employee's need-to-know information based on them as an individual.

26. As a hiring manager charged with screening potential candidates, you need to ensure that you've done your due diligence. You need to make sure that a candidate has no criminal record, that the candidate has credentials and certifications relevant to the job, and that they can verify their prior work history. Which of the following practice should you incorporate into the hiring process to guarantee that these issues aren't missed with any candidate?

   ○ Mandate that each candidate sign a sworn agreement before being put through the interview process.

   ◉ Create a baseline for the company's hiring process.

   ○ Remind each interviewer in-person before each interview they conduct.

   ○ Rely on the candidate to provide this information.

27. A disgruntled employee was recently terminated from your organization. He was given this notification at noon on Wednesday. His supervisor contacted you about an hour later to tell you of the termination, and you promptly disabled the employee's access. Other personnel that worked near the terminated employee stated that they saw him leave his cubicle and walk out the front door at about 2:00 p.m. that day. What should you have done differently to minimize the risk of the disgruntled employee causing harm to your organization? (Choose two.)

- ☑ Send security to escort the employee out of the building immediately after his termination.

- ☐ Conduct an exit interview with the terminated employee to find out what he has access to.

- ☑ Request that all supervisors notify you of unfriendly terminations first so you can disable access before the employee learns of his termination.

- ☐ Closely monitor the systems that the employee has access to after his termination.

28. When providing security training to senior management and the board of directors, what should be the primary focus of this training?

- ○ Basic computer security practices like using strong passwords and browsing the web safely.

- ○ The details of security documents like policies, procedures, and guidelines.

- ◉ The importance of security in supporting business objectives, legal compliance, and shareholder expectations.

- ○ The latest knowledge of the various threats and controls that affect information security.

29. At minimum, how often should staff undergo security awareness training?

- ○ Six months

- ◉ One year

- ○ Two years

- ○ Five years

30. As part of a security training program, which of the following is the most important for all staff to learn?

- ○ Best practices for VPN usage.

- ○ How to clean an infected computer.

- ○ How to properly wipe sensitive data.

- ◉ How to identify social engineering attempts.

ACTIVITY 2-1: Analyzing Asset Classification

1. What must Sharon do first in order to classify her data?

- ○ She must determine if the access controls will be mandatory or discretionary.

- ○ She must determine who the data owner will be.

- ◉ She must determine the sensitivity, purpose, value, and criticality of the data.

- ○ She must determine who the data custodian will be.

2. In this scenario, which of the follow statements is true?

- ○ Sharon is both the data owner and the data custodian.

- ◉ Sharon is the data owner and Robbie is the data custodian.

- ○ Sharon is the data custodian and Robbie is the data owner.

- ○ Robbie is both the data owner and the data custodian.

3. Which of the following classifications would be a good choice for Sharon's data?

   ○ Top Secret

   ○ Client confidential

   ⦿ Corporate confidential

   ○ Unclassified

4. What additional recommendations would you make to Sharon to help her classify her data?

   A: Answers will vary. You might want to make sure she creates a classification policy to inform all classification procedures. You might also ask her if she knows who the system owner will be, and if she will have to work with that person to help implement a classification process at the operating system level.

ACTIVITY 2-2: Discussing Privacy Protection

1. What errors were made regarding due care and due diligence?

   A: Answers will vary. Due care was most definitely not practiced to protect patient privacy. The development team failed to consider the consequences of keeping copies of PII on devices that were in several different physical locations. They also failed to put a plan in place for the complete destruction of this PII when they were done handling it.

2. What privacy laws apply to this scenario?

   A: In the United States, HIPAA laws were broken. In the developing nation, it is possible that no laws were broken, though you would have to check with local agencies to be sure.

3. What recommendations could you make to the field office with regard to balancing security versus convenience?

   A: Answers will vary. You would need clear guidance from management (and probably the legal department) as to what jurisdiction this scenario falls under, U.S. or the local government. Even if it turns out that no actual laws were broken, the spirit of protecting privacy was suspended for expediency. If it is permissible to use private patient data, it must be handled with the understanding that private medical information belongs to the patient, and not to the organization developing the application. In that case, the information requires special handling to keep it private, especially when developers are taking live patient data home to work on the products. The developer who gave away the laptop was well-meaning but clearly negligent. You would need to determine what procedures are required to scrub the data from the hard drive before giving the laptop away.

ACTIVITY 2-3: Analyzing Asset Retention

1. For how long should a company retain its records?

   ○ 1 year

   ○ 5 years

   ○ 7 years

   ⦿ Whatever length of time is appropriate

2. What should be the very first step in drafting a records retention policy?

- ⦿ Evaluate statutory requirements, litigations obligations, and business needs.
- ○ Assign retention periods.
- ○ Meet with data owners.
- ○ Have the Chief Information Security Officer (CISO) announce the policy.

3. What is the most appropriate storage media for this company?

- ○ Optical disks
- ○ Removable flash drives
- ○ Tape
- ⦿ Cloud

4. In what ways could hardware and personnel impact records retention?

A: Answers will vary. If your hardware breaks down and cannot be replaced, you might not be able to retrieve your data later. Also, if only one person knows how to store or retrieve the data, you again could be at risk of not being able to retain your records properly. You must make sure that you have the appropriate hardware (such as the right drives) to adequately store the data and then retrieve it later. You must also make sure that any operational procedures, such as how to operate a specific tape drive, are documented and known by more than one person.

ACTIVITY 2-4: Analyzing Data Security Controls

1. Which of the following are examples of data at rest? (Choose two.)

- ☐ Data being written to a backup tape.
- ☑ Files on a computer's hard drive.
- ☑ Data backed up to a cloud storage repository.
- ☐ Hard copy files being transported to off-site storage.

2. True or False? Data that is at rest is probably secure because it is most likely kept on a computer with a firewall.

- ☐ True
- ☑ False

3. Which of the following is true regarding data standards? (Choose two.)

- ☑ A data standard promotes data integrity.
- ☐ A data standard is a requirement mandated by government.
- ☑ A data standard is an agreement between organizations.
- ☐ A data standard is an enforceable guideline.

4. What are some of the potential benefits of defining and maintaining data standards?

A: Potential benefits may include (but are not limited to): They can help ensure consistent data formats between different sources and systems. They can improve data quality, accuracy, and availability. They can improve interoperability. Defined naming standards can improve useability and availability. They can help ensure consistent formatting (for example, the **last name** field in each system has the same name and field length).

5. **What role can encryption play in a data security baseline?**

    A: Answers will vary. Since encryption is the best security control you can place on your data, it will often be listed in a baseline. In your baseline, you might specify if encryption is optional, recommended, or required under various conditions.

ACTIVITY 2-5: Discussing Secure Data Handling

1. **Under what conditions do you think unqualified people might handle your data?**

    A: Answers will vary. The courier service that carries your backup tapes to a storage facility might hire drivers that are not bonded or properly trained. The unqualified person could include your own receptionist, who might keep the package containing the backups on her desk until the courier service arrives. A manager or junior technician might also take possession of the backup or some other copy of the data at some point.

2. **What sort of ways would you mark and label the data on this network share?**

    A: Answers will vary. It might be beneficial to add watermarks to the files so that it will be easier to prevent them from being tampered with. Additionally, the files and folders should be labeled with the appropriate level of access to keep non-project members from accessing the data. It's also helpful to ensure that all labels and markings are recorded with the data they are assigned, and the person or group that assigned them.

3. **How does the rise of mobility and bring your own device (BYOD) computing affect data remanence concerns?**

    A: Concerns may include (but are not limited to): Staff-owned devices may leave with company data still on them. Remote wipe processes may not work in all cases. Are devices properly sanitized when staff get rid of them (for example, when upgrading to a newer phone)? Will more devices be lost? Will IT be notified in the event of a device loss or theft?

4. **What do you think can be done to reduce the risks related to data remanence?**

    A: Answers will vary. Setting clear policies and educating users would address much of the problem. Establishing a stronger security culture at the organization will also help people to be mindful. You might even require that all devices and storage media at the end of their lifecycle be handed over to the security team for sanitization.

Mastery Builder 2-1: Assessing Asset Security

1. **Your company is preparing to begin a project that will update its aging infrastructure. As a security practitioner, which answer best describes what your primary concern should be before the project begins?**

    ○   The cost associated with protecting the data.

    ◉   The data management policy may need to be updated to address changes in the infrastructure.

    ○   The retention schedule for the protected information assets may need to change.

    ○   The project manager 's familiarity with current security policy.

2. Your company recently spent a significant amount of funds to acquire a database of product sales data from a data reseller. Who would be the best person to determine the data risk?

   ○ Data custodian

   ○ Senior management

   ◉ Data owner

   ○ Database administrator

3. Which of these media would not be affected by degaussing?

   ○ Hard drive

   ○ Backup tape

   ◉ CD-ROM

   ○ Floppy disk

4. As a data custodian, you are tasked with securely destroying data on a hard drive. The data on the drive is no longer needed, but the system owner wants to retain the entire drive itself for reuse. Which method of destruction should you choose to securely erase the data?

   ○ Physically destroy the drive.

   ○ Degauss the drive.

   ◉ Overwrite the drive.

   ○ Encrypt the drive.

5. Which of the following is not a typical consideration when developing data management policies?

   ○ The financial impact of acquiring and protecting the data.

   ○ Performing a risk analysis to determine appropriate processes for access.

   ◉ Current contracts with continuity service providers.

   ○ Potential conflicts with other existing policies.

6. Data that is at rest is:

   ○ More secure than data in transit.

   ○ No longer a risk to the organization.

   ◉ Susceptible to both physical and logical loss.

   ○ Contained within the trusted network.

7. To support data integrity, data owners require training in which process?

   ○ Procurement

   ○ Data destruction

   ○ Data loss prevention

   ◉ Quality control

8. Your company is interested in encrypting all the traffic between your branch office and headquarters. Which of these would be the best option?

   ○ End-to-end encryption

   ○ SSL VPN

   ◉ Link encryption

   ○ IPSec

9. Data errors of commission are:
   ○ Errors that affect commissions payed to salespeople.
   ○ Errors leading to data being left out.
   ◉ Errors leading to wrong information being added.
   ○ None of the above.

10. The responsibilities of a data custodian include which of the following?
    ◉ Making sure users comply with all data access policies.
    ○ Assuring the quality of the data to data consumers.
    ○ Knowing the cost of the data, whether acquired or created.
    ○ Understanding legal or regulatory issues with the data.

11. Which of the following are among the benefits of defining and maintaining data standards?
    ○ Data is less expensive to acquire.
    ○ It ensures that data at rest is secure.
    ◉ The accuracy and quality of the data may improve.
    ○ It greatly reduces the chance of data leakage.

12. Which of the following is not typically part of an organization's data handling policies and processes?
    ○ Access control systems
    ◉ Asset management
    ○ Data disposal process
    ○ Data classification systems

13. A company's data classification policy describes four levels: Public, Internal, Management, and Secret. An older research and development database system has been retired. The records in the database were labeled Secret. What should happen to the data now that the database has been retired?
    ○ Since the database has been retired, the data should be destroyed.
    ○ The data should be exported to another system, retaining the Secret designation.
    ◉ Its classification should be reviewed with the data owner to determine if a change is warranted.
    ○ It should be made Public and added to the historical archives of the company.

14. Which is not an example of data at rest?
    ○ Data on a web server hard disk.
    ◉ Downloading a financial statement.
    ○ Backup media at a continuity site.
    ○ A printed copy of a classified document.

15. What methods or technologies are associated with data in transit?
    ○ Full disk encryption
    ○ Data recovery plans
    ◉ SSL
    ○ Documented locations for removable media

16. Which set of statements best describe data management policies?

○ Data management policies must address matters of confidentiality, integrity, and availability from requisition to disposal. Policies should be reviewed at least annually. Care must be taken to address any applicable legal and/or regulatory requirements. Policies should not be adopted without considering the cost of implementing them.

○ Data management policies must address matters of confidentiality, integrity, and availability from data acquisition through data disposal. They must be flexible enough to adapt to changes in the business and data environments. Care must be taken to address any applicable legal or regulatory requirements. They should be reviewed at least annually, or when there are significant changes in the business, data, or regulatory environments. They should not be adopted without considering the cost of implementing them.

◉ Data management policies must address matters of confidentiality, integrity, and availability from data acquisition through data disposal. They should be reviewed periodically, as changes to the business dictate. All legal and/or regulatory requirements must be addressed. Policies should be defined before costs are quantified, so that all costs may be addressed when budgeting.

○ Data management policies should define data owners and custodians. They should define data classification systems, data handling procedures, and standards for data destruction. They should be reviewed at least annually, so that outdated portions may be deleted. They should be modeled after specific published frameworks, like FIPS or SP-800-60.

17. Data policies should be reviewed at least:
   ○ Weekly
   ○ Monthly
   ○ Quarterly
   ◉ Yearly

18. Data owners can be made up of which of these? (Choose two.)
   ☐ Security practitioners
   ☑ Groups of people
   ☑ Data creators
   ☐ Data custodians

19. True or False? It is OK for data policies to dictate a company's business initiatives
   ☐ True
   ☑ False

20. What role is responsible for managing access control requirements for data?
   ○ Data owner
   ○ Senior management
   ◉ Data custodian
   ○ Human resources

21. Which of the following is a way that Asset Management supports the primary objectives of Information Security?
   ○ It allows asset owners to be provided with copies of the company's security policies.
   ○ It helps the company to understand how much is spent on hardware and software, so they'll know how much is left available for security countermeasures.
   ○ Only assets identified through Asset Management are subject to Information Security policies.
   ◉ It separates data ownership from data custodianship.

22. Unlabelled data that is found should initially be given what level of protection?

○ None

○ Lowest level

○ Medium Level

◉ Highest level

23. Who owns private data?

◉ The person the data is about.

○ The company that stores the data.

○ The person that processes the data on a daily basis.

○ Ownership is shared between private citizens and organizations.

24. You're overseeing information security for a study that will collect and analyze information on the dietary habits of random individuals. Each individual will self-report their own information over a period of ten years. After ten years, their dietary habits will be compared to their medical issues or lack thereof in an attempt to find a correlation between eating habits and health. In upholding privacy requirements, which of the following information should you make sure is not collected?

○ The daily caloric intake of each individual.

○ Any existing medical conditions that are present at the start of the study.

◉ Each individual's health insurance information.

○ The specific type of food ingested by each individual.

25. In your organization, you've had problems with operational knowledge being kept only in the minds of one or two individuals who have since left the company. What are some of the ways you can prevent this "siloing" of important business information? (Choose three.)

☐ Conduct an exit interview with each terminated employee to learn what you can.

☑ Make sure that all operational knowledge is documented.

☑ Employ job rotation so that multiple people are exposed to specific business operations.

☑ Plan a personnel retention policy that upholds continuity of operations after personnel leave the organization.

26. As part of your media retention policy, you store backup hard drives in a locked storage room. This locked room is about the size of a closet, and is completely sealed, with no vents, windows, or other ways of entry besides the locked door. The only things you store in this room are hard drives. One day, you begin your backup testing procedures and remove the drives from storage. During the test, you discover that some of the drives have failed. The failed drives show signs of physical warping. What is the most likely culprit?

○ Someone has maliciously damaged the drives.

◉ The drives were exposed to excessive heat, causing them to fail.

○ The drives were not stacked properly, causing them to fall and receive damage.

○ The drives were subjected to magnetic interference, causing them to fail.

ACTIVITY 3-1: Analyzing Security in the Engineering Lifecycle

1. Your company is developing a product that is being held to high security standards. At what point in the security engineering lifecycle would you attempt to certify and accredit the product?

   ○ Operations and maintenance

   ○ Development and acquisitions

   ◉ Implementation

   ○ Concept and initiation

2. You're considering using security framework to help you apply security principles in your engineering lifecycle. Which of the frameworks operates at the organization level for developing new policies and practices?

   ○ Common Criteria

   ○ NIST SP800-27

   ◉ NIST SP800-14

   ○ SDLC

3. You work for a government agency that is developing a secure system. At which point in the engineering lifecycle would you conduct an impact analysis to see if you are in compliance with FISMA?

   ○ Certification and accreditation

   ○ Testing

   ◉ Initiation

   ○ Development/Acquisition

ACTIVITY 3-2: Analyzing System Component Security

1. What is the greatest security concern with regard to storage?

   ◉ Viruses from removable drives

   ○ Information leakage across the network

   ○ Hardware crash

   ○ Media sanitization before disposal

2. What rule can you follow to minimize the risk of using any new software?

   ○ Ensure that it is clean and paid for.

   ○ Ensure that it is installed from original media.

   ○ Ensure that it was not downloaded from the Internet.

   ◉ Ensure that it is properly licensed and digitally signed.

3. What is the greatest security concern regarding device drivers?

   ○ They could contain malicious code.

   ○ They could be applied to the wrong hardware.

   ◉ They could be poorly written and destabilize a critical system.

   ○ They could damage the device.

4. **What do you think might be causing the problem? (Choose two.)**

   ☑ The application driver that controls the X-ray machine was not well-written.

   ☐ The application is using the wrong computer bus to access the CPU.

   ☐ The application should not be using an X-ray machine as a peripheral.

   ☑ The application is launching in system privilege level, and then becoming unstable.

5. **What do you think may have happened?**

   ○ You have run out of disk space.

   ○ The server is too busy monitoring the network to respond to the mouse.

   ○ The application is replicating itself across the network.

   ◉ The application has consumed all of the server's memory and virtual memory, causing a denial-of-service attack on the server.

6. **What do you think may have happened?**

   ○ The daughter figured out her dad's device password.

   ○ The device needs more RAM to run the games properly.

   ◉ The daughter rooted the device to bypass firmware security controls.

   ○ The games were designed to be played on a laptop, and not a mobile device.

ACTIVITY 3-3: Discussing Security Models

1. **What security model do you use in your current work environment and why?**

   A: Answers will vary. Most environments today use Common Criteria, or a model based on it. This is because TCSEC, ITSEC, CTCPEC, and other early models have been superseded by common criteria.

2. **Under which conditions would it be preferable to use mandatory access control? Discretionary access control?**

   A: It would be preferable to use mandatory access control in a military or otherwise highly secure installation. MAC is the best choice when you do not want administrators using their own discretion to apply security to users. Discretionary access control is preferable in a commercial environment where it is necessary to apply different levels of security based on the individual, situation, or context.

ACTIVITY 3-4: Discussing Controls and Countermeasures in ESA

1. **Your organization is attempting to start a security project involving many different groups. The groups come from different organizations that have never worked together before, but would like to create a security product that can benefit all of them. Of the various ESA frameworks you have studied, which framework would be a good choice to use and why?**

   A: Zachman would be an excellent choice in the scenario. The groups have never worked together, and the strength of Zachman is that it specifies who plays what role in the project. Objectives are matched to specific roles, and technologies are mapped to business objectives.

2. You are implementing your company's Information Security Management System. The desired end result is formal verification of compliance. Which of the ESA frameworks that you have studied would be an appropriate choice in this case?

   A: ISO 27001 would be a good choice for this project. Because it is a formal standard, the company can choose to be audited as part of the process to assure compliance.

3. Of the five ESA building blocks, which provide both physical and logical controls? (Choose two.)

   ☐ Integrity

   ☐ Cryptography

   ☑ Auditing and monitoring

   ☑ Boundary control

ACTIVITY 3–5: Analyzing Information System Security Capabilities

1. How do you think virtualization could benefit security in your own environment?

   A: Answers will vary. One great feature of virtualization from both a systems administration and security perspective is the ability to very easily keep processes separate from each other. If in application running in a virtual machine becomes compromised, it would be very easy to suspend its processes to contain the damage. Virtualization also makes it very easy to monitor and manage whole systems from a central console. You could quickly destroy a compromised system, and replace it with a clean copy.

2. How can implementing TPM benefit security in your own environment?

   A: Answers will vary. A very common implementation of TPM is to protect laptops that are issued by the company to workers. TPM allows the hard drive of a laptop to remain encrypted, even when the operating system is booted. You can also use the boot restrictions capability of TPM to require a user to use a combination of RSA token and PIN to even boot the laptop.

3. Server fault tolerance techniques might you use to enhance security in your own environment?

   A: Answers will vary. With virtualization, server redundancy, whether by clustering or NLB, becomes easy to deploy. If you have specific server services running such as email or database, you can also use the native replication capabilities of that application to maintain copies of your data on other servers, both physical and virtual.

ACTIVITY 3-6: Discussing Design and Architecture Vulnerability Mitigation

1. **What potential architecture vulnerabilities do you think may exist in the system, and how would you mitigate them?**

   A: Answers will vary. Industrial Control Systems by their very nature have thousands of potential entry points for attack. Every power substation could potentially be open to security breach. Since this was a highly publicized rollout, everyone knows about the system. It could become a target. The first thing to investigate is whether or not the ICS has been patched against known security risks. Based on the scenario, the country does not appear to be wealthy. It is quite likely that it does not have the resources to deploy expensive technology to secure the system. The substations scattered around the country are quite possibly not well secured physically either. It is also quite likely that, since this technology is new to this country, power officials are not familiar with its vulnerabilities and how to protect it. You would want to make sure that the government has clear policies in place for Industrial Control Systems. You would also want to make sure that every available vulnerability mitigation practice that does not require extensive investment is deployed. This would include changing defaults, implementing strong passwords, using roles to restrict user privileges, providing physical access control, patching systems in a timely manner, and even deploying less expensive firewall and VPN solutions.

2. **What do you think happened? What are the gaps that allowed this situation to happen?**

   A: Answers will vary. Users obviously had too much privilege on production machines. They were able to install torrent clients and indulge in peer-to-peer file downloading on mission-critical computers. At least one of the downloads must have contained a virus, which spread to systems in the command-and-control center, taking down production machines and causing the ICS central console to stop responding. The gaps are as much human-based as technical. There were clearly gaps in security policy or at least lapses in enforcing the policy. Workers were also obviously not well educated in managing risks to the new ICS system. It also looks as though fault tolerance was not used effectively. Had a redundant ICS command center been deployed, it might have been able to take over when the first system failed.

3. **What do you think is going on? Could these unusual packets be a security risk?**

   A: Answers will vary. The contents of normal network packets should not have anything unusual about them. It's possible that they are being used as a covert channel by a malicious program to send unauthorized commands to the production computers. If that's the case, then they are very much a security risk.

4. **What additional security risks do you think the managers could be introducing into the network? What evidence would you look for to validate your concerns?**

   A: Answers will vary. Unsecured clients can infect computers on the internal network when they make remote connections to the network. Check the managers' laptops for signs of viruses and malware. Make sure the laptops have updated antivirus programs and proper personal firewall settings. See if there is any network access control on the network that requires remote clients to be healthy before they connect. Verify that servers are patched and hardened as much as possible, and require strong authentication from remote clients.

5. If the emails were not leaked by plant personnel, how could the newspapers get copies? How can future risks be mitigated?

   A: Answers will vary. If the plant's email is indeed being hosted by a local cloud provider, that provider could well be the source of the leak. You need to first inspect the email logs to see who received copies of the leaked memos. You then need to review the security controls placed on the email system, including verifying that strong authentication and encryption is required for sending and receiving email. If the email is hosted by a third-party provider, especially a small local company, the provider's internal security procedures and SLA with the power plant needs to be reviewed and possibly improved.

6. Figuring out that hidden data exists in a database, even though you cannot see it, is known as:
   ○ Data mining
   ○ Aggregation
   ○ Data analytics
   ● Inference

7. Using multiple data sources to figure out what is likely to happen is known as:
   ○ Data mining
   ○ Aggregation
   ● Data analytics
   ○ Inference

8. Which statement best describes the security concerns of a distributed system?
   ○ Multiple computers could crash simultaneously
   ● Messages between participating systems could become compromised
   ○ An overall profile of an individual can be created from many sources
   ○ A consumer's spending habits can be predicted before the actual event

9. What is currently the biggest risk associated with Big Data?
   ○ Shared files are likely to have viruses
   ○ Lack of standard public key encryption could compromise the data
   ○ The ability of computers to automatically mesh together could form bottlenecks
   ● There is no unified security model

ACTIVITY 3-7: Discussing Vulnerability Mitigation in Embedded, Mobile, and Web-Based Systems

1. What are the risks in this scenario, and how would you mitigate them?

   A: Answers will vary. There are several issues at stake. The fact that the blackhats were able to wrest control of a lethal weapon was a great concern in itself. The device depended on wireless connectivity, a technology with a history of security vulnerabilities, to distinguish friendly from unfriendly fire. Clearly the developers of the embedded app did not use safe coding practice, thus allowing malicious code injection.

2. **What are the ethical considerations in this scenario?**

   A: Answers will vary. The vendor handled the situation poorly, starting with being dismissive of any public criticism. (The vendor was also foolish to disparage that particular group of individuals). Rather than taking responsibility for risks to public safety, the vendor chose to put the blame on those who exposed the product's weaknesses. It also continued to insist that its product was safe, even though the opposite was proven. The vendor seemed to be more interested in public image and sales than the safety of its product. The blackhats also engaged in questionable behavior. Their reaction was as much a matter of ego as any real concern for public safety. Their assertion that they did not have any true malicious intent does not negate the fact that their hack might still have caused grave harm. Had the gun been loaded, the scenario could have ended in tragedy.

3. **If you were in the blackhats' position, and had discovered how to compromise the targeting system, how would you as a CISSP have handled the situation?**

   A: Answers will vary. A CISSP, who is bound by oath to behave "responsibly, justly, honestly, honorably, and legally," would not endanger lives to prove a point.

4. **From a security perspective, why is jailbreaking or rooting a mobile device the most damaging thing you can do to that device?**

   A: Answers will vary. When you root or jailbreak a device, you are bypassing integrity checks built into the firmware. This means that you could install an application that introduces viruses and malware, and possibly even replaces parts of the operating system with malicious code.

5. **In what way do web-based systems increase the risks associated with mobile devices?**

   A: Answers will vary. Web-based systems provide mobile devices access to internal servers, including email, database, file and print, unified communications, directory services, and others.

6. **How do OAuth 2.0 and OpenID Connect work together to protect web apps?**

   A: OpenID Connect uses the underlying services of OAuth 2.0 to simplify secure authentication for a wide range of devices.

ACTIVITY 3-8: Analyzing Cryptography Concepts

---

1. **Why are encryption methods used for data in transit often not suitable for data at rest?**

   ○ They require other networking protocols for support.

   ○ Encryption methods for data in transit always rely on weak keys.

   ⦿ Data in transit is vulnerable for a very short time (i.e., the life of a packet), but data at rest may be around for a long time, increasing the chance that the cryptographic methods used may be defeated as technology progresses.

   ○ Such distinctions are a myth—encryption technologies are always equally appropriate for data at rest and data in transit.

2. Which answer choice best describes the process of digitally signing a message?

○ The sender requests the public key of the recipient. The sender generates a symmetric key and uses it to encrypt a message. The sender encrypts the symmetric key with the recipient's public key. The encrypted symmetric key and message are sent to the recipient.

◉ The sender creates a message. The sender creates a hash of that message. The sender encrypts the hash of the message with his/her private key. The message, the encrypted hash, and the sender's public key are sent to the recipient.

○ The sender creates a message. The sender creates a hash of that message. The sender encrypts the hash of the message with the recipient's public key. The message and the encrypted hash are sent to the recipient.

○ The sender creates a message. The sender creates a hash of that message. The sender encrypts the hash of the message with his/her public key. The message, the encrypted hash, and the sender's private key are sent to the recipient.

3. How can key escrow protect against abuse of decryption keys?

A: Answers will vary. Key escrow splits a key into multiple parts, placing each part under the guardianship of a different organization. It would require collusion between many unrelated organizations to reassemble a key in an unauthorized manner.

4. When would you choose to use a stream cipher over a block cipher?

○ When you need to quickly encrypt large files on your hard drive.

◉ When you need to quickly encrypt data in realtime.

○ When you need to run multiple encryption permutations over the same file.

○ When you need to introduce randomness into your encryption process.

5. In what way could steganography aid a terrorist group?

A: Answers will vary. A terrorist group (or anyone else for that matter) could use steganography to hide secret information in plain sight on their website. They could embed plans for the next attack in their images, or issue commands to affiliates and sleeper cells.

6. Why must a security professional never assume that even a strong cryptosystem will remain unbroken indefinitely?

A: Answers will vary. Not only has raw computing power increased exponentially over the years, but weak implementations of a strong algorithm, or as-yet undiscovered side-channel attacks, could make the cryptosystem vulnerable to successful cryptanalysis.

7. Why does cryptography so often depend on prime factors?

○ Because very large numbers are harder to guess.

○ Because RSA set a precedent using prime factors that the rest of the world followed.

○ Because prime factors are easy to multiply and divide.

◉ Because prime factors have no internal repeat pattern, making them harder to analyze.

8. Does a replay attack require that the password ever be discovered?

○ Yes, this is what allows the replay to occur.

○ Yes, because that is the ultimate goal of a replay attack.

○ No, because there is a 50% chance that two different inputs will produce the same result.

◉ No, because the attacker uses data that has already been authenticated.

ACTIVITY 3-9: Analyzing Cryptography Techniques

1. Which of the following statements is true?
   - ⦿ Symmetric encryption is faster than asymmetric encryption.
   - ○ Asymmetric encryption is faster than symmetric encryption.
   - ○ Symmetric and asymmetric encryption have equally fast performance.
   - ○ Both symmetric and asymmetric encryption have slow performance.

2. Moo and Lily use asymmetric encryption to send secret messages to each other. If Moo wants to send Lily a message that only Lily can read, which key should he use?
   - ○ Moo's public key
   - ○ Moo's private key
   - ⦿ Lily's public key
   - ○ Lily's private key

3. How does a salt improve a hash?
   - ○ It makes the key longer.
   - ⦿ It adds randomness.
   - ○ It makes the output longer.
   - ○ It doubles the algorithm strength.

4. What role did the initialization vector (IV) play in the eventual downfall of WEP as a wireless protection mechanism?
   - ⦿ It used a keyspace that was too short.
   - ○ It slowed down the encryption process enough that a hacker could exploit the delay.
   - ○ It facilitated replay attacks against the wireless access point.
   - ○ It was especially susceptible to dictionary and rainbow attacks.

5. What is the benefit of making your own CA subordinate to a commercial trusted root CA?
   - ○ You can request the trusted root to issue end user certificates on your behalf.
   - ○ You can obtain substantial cost savings by issuing certificates on behalf of the trusted root.
   - ○ You can save money by not having to install your own trusted root CA.
   - ⦿ You can save money by freely issuing any number of certificates that will still be trusted by the outside world.

6. How is a digital signature different from a digital certificate?
   - ⦿ A digital signature is a message digest created by using a private key to ensure the authenticity of a file or transmission, whereas a digital certificate is a public key embedded into a file.
   - ○ A digital certificate is a message digest created by using a private key to ensure the authenticity of a file or transmission, whereas a digital signature is a public key embedded into a file.
   - ○ There is no real difference. They both refer to the same thing.
   - ○ Digital signatures are based on symmetric encryption, whereas digital certificates are based on asymmetric encryption.

7. What consideration(s) must you weigh when deciding whether or not to use Perfect Forward Secrecy (PFS) on your website?

○ You have to determine if the benefit of using PFS is worth its licensing cost.

⦿ You have to decide if the additional performance overhead of PFS is substantial enough to restrict its use.

○ You have to decide if you have the resources to support a proprietary technology.

○ You have to decide if you have the resources to support an open-source technology.

ACTIVITY 3-10: Discussing Site and Facility Design for Physical Security

1. From the scenario, what external threats do you identify?

   A: Answers will vary. Graffiti, bars, and broken windows indicate this is a rough part of town, probably with a high crime rate. Despite the convenience of the freeway and train track, the building's close proximity to both, as well as the airport, leave it vulnerable to traffic accidents from all three.

2. What natural threats do you identify?

   A: Answers will vary. The location is in a region known for its earthquakes. The overhead freeway could also send heavy debris falling on the facility during a temblor or aftershocks.

3. Is there any suitable place for the data center, restricted work area, or to house critical equipment?

   A: Answers will vary. There are no rooms on the ground floor, but you might be able to convert the raised offices to suit your needs. Otherwise, you would have to construct rooms for your critical areas, restricted work areas, and data center.

4. Do you think that power disruptions are likely at this location?

   A: Answers will vary. Many businesses routinely maintain backup power generators. Since this building is in a well-developed urban area, the power grid is probably fairly stable. Nonetheless, you would have to investigate the building's power system as well as the reliability of power in that area to be sure.

5. Does the building appear to have any environmental conditions that could threaten computer equipment?

   A: Answers will vary. Depending on the type of manufacturing, there could be a high dust level. There could also be a high heat level if ventilation is inadequate. What conditions the former occupant experienced might not translate directly to your own operations. You can address potential environmental threats during renovation.

ACTIVITY 3-11: Discussing Site and Facility Physical Security Implementation

1. When would it be useful to deploy both a backup power generator and a UPS for your server room?

   A: Answers will vary. The UPS will supply power for short periods of time, usually no more than 2 hours. The generator will supply power for as long as it has fuel. Usually you would use the UPS to provide power for the few minutes it takes to manually switch over to the generator.

2. How do you think that a data center can benefit from racks that have self-contained air cooling systems?

   A: Answers will vary. If implemented properly, limiting air conditioning to the rack itself will save money. A self-contained air cooling system will also help to keep dust and contaminants out of the servers in the rack.

3. What type of glass would you use in a restroom window at your facility?

   A: Answers will vary. The window will probably be small, high up on the wall, and used for ventilation. You want the glass to be tamper resistant, and aesthetics would not be a consideration. In that case, wired glass would be a good choice.

4. What steps can you take to maintain security while minimizing the risk in case of fire?

   A: Answers will vary. Ensure that you do not create any unnecessary fire hazards in the server room, such as storing paint, paper, or cleaning supplies with the equipment. Make sure that all wiring is rated for the current it will carry, is firmly plugged in to power outlets, and is in good repair with no frays or exposed wires. Make sure that equipment is not crowded together or arranged in a way that is likely to create excessive amounts of heat. Make sure the HVAC keeps the room cool. If you can afford it, implement a gas-based fire suppression system. Implement some type of monitoring system, including cameras, for on-site security staff to monitor for signs of fire. Make sure that staff knows what to do in case of fire, such as immediately cutting the power and notifying the fire department.

5. In what ways can hand-held fire extinguishers and sprinkler systems enhance fire suppression in a data center?

   A: Answers will vary. You would obviously not install water-based systems where the equipment is, but you could have water-based systems in other areas such as hallways, storage rooms, offices, etc. Hand held class C extinguishers would be handy, even in the equipment room itself, to quickly put out a small fire.

6. If you choose to install a water-based system at a data center, which one would be appropriate?

   A: Answers will vary. Probably a dry pipe or preaction system would be the best choice.

Mastery Builder 3–1: Assessing Security Engineering

---

1. Which of the following is not a good security foundation principle as established by the NIST SP 800-27 engineering framework?

   ○ Establish a good security policy as a foundation for design.

   ○ Incorporate security into the overall system design.

   ○ Define clear physical and logical boundaries governed by policy.

   ◉ Incorporate security into a system when necessary.

2. Which of the following is not a good ease of use principle as established by the NIST SP 800-27 engineering framework?

   ○ Base security on open standards, when possible.

   ◉ Use organization-specific language when defining security requirements.

   ○ Design security for easier adoption of new technologies.

   ○ Incorporate a logical update process for technology.

3. Which of the following phases of the security engineering lifecycle includes security testing for certification and accreditation?

   ◉ Implementation

   ○ Operations/maintenance

   ○ Development/acquisition

   ○ Initiation

4. Which of the following best describes a Direct Memory Access (DMA) attack?

   ○ An attacker uses a computer's insecure operating system to retrieve data from RAM.

   ⦿ An attacker uses a hardware bus to bypass operating system security and retrieve data from RAM.

   ○ An attacker exploits a virtual hypervisor to retrieve data from RAM used by a virtual guest.

   ○ An attacker exploits faulty firmware in hard drives to retrieve data from stored memory.

5. Which of the following are recommended ways to harden an operating system? (Choose three.)

   ☑ Disable all unused accounts.

   ☑ Run vulnerability assessment software on a regular basis.

   ☐ Disable vendor-issued update services.

   ☑ Change all default passwords.

6. The Trusted Platform Module (TPM) uses which of the following cryptographic algorithms?

   ○ Triple DES

   ○ AES-256

   ○ Twofish

   ⦿ RSA

7. Which of the following security models addresses conflicts of interest in access rights?

   ○ Graham-Denning

   ⦿ Brewer-Nash

   ○ Clark-Wilson

   ○ Biba

8. Which of the following is a security model that provides strict rules for what behavior is or is not allowed between data and users?

   ⦿ Lattice Model

   ○ Non-interference Model

   ○ Information Flow Model

   ○ State Machine Model

9. Which of the following access control categories is most commonly used on firewalls and routers to control network traffic?

   ○ Role-based Access Control

   ○ Discretionary Access Control

   ⦿ Rule-based Access Control

   ○ Mandatory Access Control

10. Which of the following enterprise security architecture (ESA) frameworks focuses on best practices for security governance in four domains: plan and organize, acquire and implement, deliver and support, and monitor and evaluate?

   ⦿ COBIT

   ○ ITIL

   ○ ISO/IEC 27001

   ○ PCI DSS

11. When it comes to incorporating security zones in your ESA, what is important to remember?

   ○ The zones must all adhere to the same security policies.

   ○ The zones must all have the same level of trust.

   ◉ The zones may connect to one another, requiring some method of boundary control.

   ○ The zones must be kept independent of one another, requiring some method of boundary control.

12. When it comes to auditing and monitoring in your ESA, which of the following is a best practice?

   ○ Keep the logs of each system separate.

   ◉ Forward all logs to a centralized system.

   ○ Log all possible activity.

   ○ Parse logs manually rather than rely on automated tools.

13. Which of the following is an intended function of keeping system code separate from user code?

   ○ The system code is assigned less resources, lowering its processing footprint.

   ○ The user code is assigned less resources, lowering its processing footprint.

   ◉ The system code is fully trusted, whereas user code has less privileges.

   ○ The user code is fully trusted, whereas the system code has less privileges.

14. Which of the following services does a Trusted Platform Module (TPM) provide? (Choose three.)

   ☑ Full disk encryption

   ☑ Digital rights management (DRM)

   ☐ File-level access control

   ☑ Password-based authentication

15. You want to ensure that the servers in your organization are fault tolerant. In particular, the servers you want to protect serve up static content to employees on your intranet. Which of the following is the best technique to ensure these servers' fault tolerance under heavy traffic?

   ○ Replication

   ○ Clustering

   ◉ Network load balancing

   ○ Virtualization

16. Which of the following controls allows clients to access your public-facing servers while keeping them isolated from your internal network?

   ○ Reverse proxy

   ◉ Demilitarized zone (DMZ)

   ○ Intrusion prevention system (IPS)

   ○ Fault tolerance

17. Which of the following are vulnerabilities of cloud services? (Choose two.)

☑ You must depend on the security policies and practices of the cloud provider.

☐ You don't retain full ownership of the data hosted on cloud services.

☑ You don't have direct control over the security of the cloud-based systems that manage your data.

☐ You don't have any assurances of data availability in the cloud.

18. Which of the following best describes a covert timing vulnerability?

◉ A process may be able to determine information about data based on the amount, type, and order in which another process accesses the data.

○ A process may be able to determine information about data based on the existence of a stored file that holds the data.

○ A process may be able to directly read data based on the amount, type, and order in which another process accesses the data.

○ A process may be able to directly read data based on the existence of a stored file that holds the data.

19. Remote users access your internal network through a VPN. Which of the following security concerns does the VPN not protect against?

○ Tampering of the remote user's traffic.

○ Disclosure of the remote user's traffic.

◉ The remote user's computer being infected with malware.

○ The remote user's computer logging in without the proper credentials.

20. Which of the following mobile device management (MDM) strategies prevents users from obtaining high level privileges on their mobile device?

○ Remotely locking a device.

◉ Protection against jailbreaking or rooting of a device.

○ Device enrollment.

○ Implementing encrypted containers on the device.

21. What is a difference between a stream cipher and a block cipher?

○ Block ciphers are faster and more secure than stream ciphers.

○ Stream ciphers are faster and more secure then block ciphers.

○ Block ciphers are faster, but less secure than stream ciphers.

◉ Stream ciphers are faster, but less secure than block ciphers.

22. Which of the following is the primary goal of hashing?

○ Confidentiality

◉ Integrity

○ Non-repudiation

○ Authentication

23. What is the relationship between a cipher and a cryptographic key?

○ The key determines which cipher is chosen (3DES, RSA, etc.).

○ The key determines the type of cipher chosen (stream or block).

○ The key determines the contents of the plaintext.

◉ The key determines the result of the ciphertext.

24. How does a salt value help strengthen hashing?
    ○ A salt adds random data to the resulting hash value, making it different each time.
    ○ A salt subtracts data from the resulting hash value, making it different each time.
    ◉ A salt adds random data to plaintext, producing a different hash result for the same plaintext value.
    ○ A salt adds random data to the hashing algorithm, producing a different result each time the hash is run.

25. Which of the following best describes a digital signature?
    ○ A message hash that has been encrypted with a public key.
    ◉ A message hash that has been encrypted with the user's private key.
    ○ A document that associates credentials with a public key.
    ○ A document that associates credentials with the user's private key.

26. Which of the following best describes the process of hybrid cryptography?
    ◉ A symmetric key encrypts the data, then an asymmetric key pair encrypts the symmetric key.
    ○ An asymmetric key pair encrypts the data, then a symmetric key encrypts the asymmetric key pair.
    ○ A symmetric key encrypts the data, which is then encrypted by another symmetric key.
    ○ An asymmetric key pair encrypts the data, which is then encrypted by another asymmetric key pair.

27. You are conducting a site vulnerability assessment on one of your office buildings, and so far you've covered the building's physical systems, the computer facilities housed in the building, and the various networking equipment that keeps your organization connected. What key area is missing from this site assessment?
    ○ Critical infrastructure security.
    ◉ Personnel safety.
    ○ Perimeter security.
    ○ Business process security.

28. Which of the following are examples of good crime prevention through environmental design (CPTED)? (Choose two.)
    ☑ Place windows where they overlook sidewalks.
    ☐ Have multiple points of access and egress to and from a building.
    ☐ Limit the amount of benches, gazebos, and other outdoor shared seating areas.
    ☑ Keep bushes and tall trees away from surveyed areas.

29. In the event of a power failure, the biometric access control system to your data center will activate a failsecure process. Which of the following describes what will happen when the power fails?
    ○ The doors to the data center will open from the outside, but not the inside.
    ○ The doors to the data center will open from the inside, but not the outside.
    ◉ The doors to the data center will not open from either the inside or outside.
    ○ The doors to the data center will open from both the inside and outside.

30. Which of the following handheld fire extinguishers is best used to extinguish an electrical fire?
    - ○ Class A
    - ○ Class B
    - ◉ Class C
    - ○ Class D

31. Which of the following types of glass is resistant to impact from blunt objects?
    - ◉ Wired glass
    - ○ Tempered glass
    - ○ Laminated glass
    - ○ Float glass

ACTIVITY 4-1: Analyzing Network Protocol Security

1. On 802.11-based wireless networks, what method is used to prevent nodes from transmitting at the same time?
   - ○ CSMA/CD
   - ○ Token-passing
   - ◉ CSMA/CA
   - ○ POTS

2. Which statement best describes the primary purpose of the OSI model?
   - ○ It allows network gear manufacturers to target their products to specific network types.
   - ○ To facilitate interoperability between networking products.
   - ◉ It serves as a platform-independent reference detailing how network applications and devices communicate.
   - ○ While once a useful tool, the OSI model serves no purpose in modern networks.

3. At which layer of the OSI model does segmentation occur?
   - ◉ Layer 4: Transport
   - ○ Layer 3: Network
   - ○ Layer 3: Transport
   - ○ Layer 4: Network

4. How are the OSI model and the TCP/IP model related?
   - ◉ While they share similarities (for example, an Application layer) and are both used as frameworks for understanding network communications, they are distinct models that are not related to each other.
   - ○ The TCP/IP model is used for networking in Microsoft Windows networks. The OSI model is used with non-Windows networks.
   - ○ The OSI model is used by hardware designers. The TCP/IP model is used exclusively by software developers.
   - ○ The TCP/IP model may be viewed as a simplification of the OSI model, since the layers in the TCP/IP model may be mapped to layers within the OSI model.

5. What are among the benefits of IPv6 networking? (Choose three.)

   ☑ Integrated security

   ☐ Improved media streaming

   ☑ Improved routing

   ☑ Very large address space

   ☐ Faster network speeds

   ☐ Eliminates anonymous traffic

6. What are the steps involved with automatic IP addressing using DHCP on IPv4 networks?

   ○ Discover – Request – Offer – Acknowledge

   ○ Find – Request – Offer – Accept

   ◉ Discover – Offer – Request – Acknowledge

   ○ Request – Lease – Acknowledge – Renew

7. What is the best definition of "Convergence"?

   ◉ Combining formerly distinct voice and data networks on a single IP network.

   ○ Reducing network traffic by eliminating duplicate transmissions.

   ○ Combining many smaller networks into one larger network.

   ○ The migration of IPv4 networks to IPv6.

8. Which of the following protocols are connectionless? (Choose two.)

   ☐ DNS

   ☐ TCP

   ☑ IP

   ☑ UDP

   ☐ SMTP

   ☐ ICMP

9. What is the primary difference between FCoE and iSCSI?

   ○ While they both can save money, iSCSI is suitable for long distances over existing infrastructure.

   ◉ FCoE cannot use an Ethernet network, whereas iSCSI can only travel on Ethernet.

   ○ iSCSI is meant for distances under 30 meters, whereas FCoE can travel much greater distances.

   ○ They are both basically the same; choosing between them is mostly a matter of preference.

10. What is the primary advantage of MPLS?

    ○ Improved performance on a LAN

    ◉ Improved performance on a MAN

    ○ Improved performance on an FCoE link

    ○ Improved performance on a VoIP network

11. What made WEP such a weak wireless security mechanism?

○ Its use of weak passwords.

○ The fact that it used only 40 bit encryption.

○ Its poor use of signaling efficiency.

◉ Its use of a short-length initialization vector.

12. While cryptography and encryption are valuable tools for securing network communications, what other factors should be considered to ensure a sound approach to communications security?

A: Students may raise ideas or concepts from their own experience, or from earlier topics. Some considerations may include: user training, data classifications, specialized technologies (like Data Loss Prevention), and limiting access to sensitive data. [This is, by no means, an exhaustive list.]

ACTIVITY 4-2: Analyzing Network Components Security

1. How can a hub help a hacker eavesdrop on the network?

○ It could be used to capture and redirect traffic flowing through it to a single unauthorized destination.

◉ It repeats all traffic out every port.

○ It can intelligently forward traffic to the port the hacker is using.

○ It has a MAC address table of all devices that the hacker can easily download.

2. Your network comprises a wired Ethernet network and one wireless access point (WAP). When clients access resources on the wired LAN after connecting through the WAP, what is the most appropriate term to describe the role of the WAP?

○ Firewall

○ Switch

○ Choke Point

◉ Gateway

3. Which statements about network hardware are correct? (Choose two.)

☐ Routers use protocols like RIP, BGP, and EIGRP to communicate with client systems.

☐ Routers operate at Layers 2 through 4 of the OSI model.

☑ Firewalls may be implemented as hardware or software, and may operate at Layers 2 through 7 of the OSI model.

☑ Switches use Media Access Control (MAC) addresses to forward frames to destination ports.

4. Which statement best describes a physical star-logical bus topology?

○ All nodes are connected by a singular, linear data path, but all communications are distributed through one central device.

◉ All nodes are connected to a central device, but communications between nodes are as if they are all connected to a singular, linear data path.

○ Each node connects directly to two other nodes, but communications between nodes are as if they are all connected to a singular, linear data path.

○ All nodes are connected to a central device, but communications are as if all nodes are directly connected to all other nodes.

5. Which statement is true regarding circuit-switched and packet-switched networks? (Choose two.)

☑ Of the two, a circuit-switched network is more secure.

☑ Of the two, a packet-switched network is more secure.

☐ In terms of bandwidth utilization, a circuit-switched network is more efficient.

☐ In terms of bandwidth utilization, a packet-switched network is more efficient.

6. A security zone that allows some hosts within it to be accessible from the Internet is called which of the following? (Choose two.)

☑ DMZ

☐ Proxy firewall

☐ NAT

☑ Screened subnet

☐ Bastion host

☐ PAT

7. True or False? Stateful Inspection Firewalls are the basis of many web application proxy servers.

☐ True

☑ False

8. How could a router be used to eavesdrop on a network?

○ It could be used to capture traffic into a log file for later unauthorized review.

○ It could be used to block legitimate traffic so a sniffer can capture that traffic.

◉ It could be used to capture and redirect traffic flowing through it to an unauthorized destination.

○ It can be planted like a bug on the network.

9. You are the network security consultant for a small college. Recently, students have been hacking into the school's database to change their records. How can you use VLANs to help mitigate this?

○ You can use VLANs to encrypt the database.

◉ You can use VLANs to isolate the database from the rest of the network.

○ You can use VLANs to apply sensitivity labels to your data.

○ You can use VLANs to facilitate intrusion detection on your network.

10. How can you use a content delivery network to conduct a denial-of-service attack on a company server?

○ You can configure CDN servers to bombard Internet root DNS servers with requests for lookups to the original content server.

○ You can configure CDN servers to withhold lookup results from clients.

◉ You can configure CDN servers to bombard the source server with random content requests.

○ You can configure CDN servers to withhold client lookup requests from the source server.

11. What is the purpose of a switch?

   ○ Connects multiple networks that share common protocols.

   ◉ Delivers frames to destination ports based on MAC addresses.

   ○ Analyzes traffic against rules based on source and/or destination address, port numbers, and/or protocol type.

   ○ Converts data between disparate systems.

ACTIVITY 4-3: Analyzing Communication Channel Security

---

1. Your security policy states that all internal network traffic must be encrypted. It also requires authenticated connections between devices. To meet these requirements, you decide to implement IPSec. Which features of IPSec may be used to meet the policy requirements? (Choose two.)

   ☐ AH only

   ☑ ESP only

   ☑ AH and ESP

   ☐ ESP to send, AH to receive

2. What steps may be taken to secure collaboration products? (Choose two.)

   ☑ Keep the collaboration software updated/patched.

   ☐ Run collaboration products on Honeynets.

   ☐ Use CSMA/CD.

   ☑ Train users on the proper use of the collaboration products.

3. What aspect of remote access makes it particularly vulnerable to attack?

   ○ It is usually deployed in a DMZ or perimeter network, instead of behind the internal firewall

   ○ It mostly accepts dial-up connections with no firewall.

   ◉ It is usually deployed in parallel to the firewall, thus bypassing firewall protections.

   ○ The fact that it uses older technology that is less secure.

4. What feature of an SSL VPN makes it easier to deploy? (Choose two.)

   ☑ It uses an SSL connection, which most firewalls are already configured to permit.

   ☑ It allows clients to use browsers to connect.

   ☐ It allows administrators to use existing routers to terminate the connection.

   ☐ It uses PPTP protocols, which are already built into most client and server systems.

5. What feature of a software-defined network makes it more intelligent than traditional networks?

   ○ It decentralizes switching and routing decisions, making the network more responsive.

   ◉ It uses an architecture that monitors and manages traffic from a higher level.

   ○ It uses whitebox switches that can work with any system.

   ○ It uses generic components that are cheaper, thus allowing you to deploy a fuller infrastructure for the same amount of money.

6. What is the fundamental difference between a VLAN and a PVLAN?

○ A PVLAN is a VLAN that has its own IP addressing scheme.

○ A PVLAN is a type of VLAN that has been specially designed for hotels and other customer-facing implementations.

○ A PVLAN is a virtual network implementation, whereas a VLAN is a physical network implementation.

◉ A PVLAN is a subdivision of a VLAN.

ACTIVITY 4-4: Discussing Network Attack Mitigation

---

1. What do you think happened, and how can this issue be resolved?

A: The users were victims of ransomware. The first thing to do is to make sure that the users do not pay, click the link, or call the phone number. Explain to them that they have been victimized by a malicious virus and that they should not respond in any way. You should then go to your antivirus provider's website to see if there is a removal tool for the ransomware. Make sure that all systems are updated at once. If necessary, restore the systems from backup.

2. Is this legitimate traffic to your website, or should you be concerned?

A: Answers will vary. It looks like someone was mirroring your site. This is quite unusual and could be reconnaissance against your site.

3. What do you think is going on, and what can you do about it?

A: It looks like a port scan that has been slowed down to evade detection. There is no legitimate reason for a client to make these kind of incomplete connection attempts. This is probably reconnaissance against those servers. You can attempt to trace packets back to the actual source. If the person is being this cautious, conducting an attack this slowly, they have probably taken other precautions to hide their identity. Be extra vigilant. Use an IDS to monitor the situation. Make sure the servers are locked down as much as possible.

4. What is going on, and how can you mitigate the problem?

A: Someone is trying to crack their passwords. Check the audit logs to see what computer name/IP address the failed login attempts are coming from. If really necessary, change the way in which those officials log on, such as switching them to using smart cards or tokens.

5. What do you think is happening, and what can you do about it?

A: It looks like an attacker from overseas has compromised the web server, and is running arbitrary code on it. The fact that the web server is initiating connections on its own to an overseas IP address is highly suspicious. Web servers simply do not initiate their own connections to anyone. They wait for connections to come to them. Implement intrusion detection or deep packet inspection to see if the signature (and vulnerability) can be identified. Perhaps it is malicious code injection or a buffer overflow. Possibly the logs have been altered to cover the attacker's tracks. If the outbound connections are to the same IP address, consider blocking that address on your firewall. Reboot the web server and apply the latest security patches on it, though you might want to back up the web server first.

6. What do you think is happening, and how can the problem be addressed?

A: Answers will vary. They could be experiencing cross-site scripting attacks on those social media sites. Update their antivirus and disallow scripts from running on their browsers.

7. **What do you think could be causing the slowdown, and how would you fix the problem?**

   A: Answers will vary. Assuming there is no other explanation such as short spikes in utilization, the server might be experiencing a denial of service attack. Since there does not seem to be heavy network traffic, perhaps it is an IP fragment attack or some other malformed network packet that is keeping the CPU busy for short intervals. Try to capture the traffic to the server to see if any client is sending just a few packets to the server when it freezes. Especially look for packets where the client makes no attempt to log on to the server.

8. **Did the troops pass the test? If not, why not, and what can be done?**

   A: They most definitely failed. You social engineered them into revealing sensitive information. Those staffers need training on how to recognize and defend themselves against social engineering.

9. **What steps can you take to protect the phone?**

   A: Implement good endpoint security. Disable unnecessary services, particularly Bluetooth. Require strong authentication and encryption. Use mobile device management and tracking to keep track of the device. Educate the CEO on how to keep her phone safe from hacking.

10. **Would you recommend a Network-based or Host-based IDS? Why? What factors may influence the effectiveness of an IDS solution?**

    A: Students who prefer network-based IDS may cite potential attacks originating from the Internet, or the potential of data exfiltration. A properly configured network-based IDS can identify many different types of attacks, and can have rules that generate alerts based on specific types of traffic traversing the network. Students who prefer host-based IDS may cite the ability to protect against attacks that specifically target the software on the database server, such as SQL injection attack and other application code exploits. A properly configured host-based IDS can identify many different types of attacks and can have rules that generate alerts based on specific rules that reflect the host environment. Factors that may influence the effectiveness of an IDS solution include: maintaining current threat signatures, the tuning period required for behavior-based systems, and administrative processes for reviewing and responding to generated alerts.

11. **Discuss the potential benefits and drawbacks of adopting a Defense in Depth approach to security.**

    A: Potential benefits include: slowing attacker progress, maintaining acceptable levels of security even if some defenses are compromised, giving the security professional more opportunities to identify attacks. Potential drawbacks include: lack of senior management support, increased costs (in money and other resources) for additional security controls, and increased complexity in the security and operational environments.

Mastery Builder 4–1: Assessing Communications and Network Security

1. **Which layer of the OSI Model ensures that the receiver can properly interpret the transmitted information?**

   ○ Layer 7: Application

   ◉ Layer 6: Presentation

   ○ Layer 5: Session

   ○ Layer 3: Network

2. **Which statement describes a characteristic of Internet Protocol (IP)?**

   ○ It is a proprietary, routable protocol.

   ○ It is a connection-oriented protocol.

   ◉ It is a non-proprietary, routable protocol.

   ○ It resides at Layer 4 of the OSI Model.

3. In the OSI Model, which of the following is not a valid Layer 7 protocol?

   ○ HTTP

   ○ SMTP

   ◉ ARP

   ○ FTP

4. Which of the following protocols used by the original WPA standard has proven to be insecure and vulnerable to attack?

   ○ CRC-32

   ○ CCMP

   ◉ TKIP

   ○ IPSec

5. Which of the following negative effects of a VoIP connection occurs when packet delays vary?

   ○ Packet loss

   ○ Sequence errors

   ○ Poor codec quality

   ◉ Jitter

6. Which of the following is not true regarding the use of spread spectrum techniques with wireless networks? (Choose two.)

   ☑ Intercepting messages becomes more difficult.

   ☐ Transmission performance may be improved.

   ☐ It does not interfere with wireless encryption.

   ☑ It makes encryption unnecessary on wireless networks.

7. Which answer best describes the topology presented in the above images?

   ○ A: Physical ring | B: Logical bus

   ◉ A: Physical star | B: Logical bus

   ○ A: Physical star | B: Logical ring

   ○ A: Physical star | B: Logical star

8. Your company is going through a period of rapid growth, and is currently developing plans to build out three new locations. You have been asked to meet with the project manager and network architects to ensure that security is considered during the design phase. The project team is currently considering the network topology and various physical layer options for the new locations, including shielded twisted pair (STP) cabling, fiber-optic cabling, and wireless networking options. Which options best represent your primary security concerns? (Choose three.)

   ☐ The design should consider the risk of wireless interference.

   ☐ The design should include secure locations for networking gear.

   ☑ The design should incorporate existing security policy.

   ☑ The design should address confidentiality, availability, and integrity.

   ☑ The design should meet business needs.

   ☐ Routers should be deployed using modern routing protocols.

9. Which of the following are good approaches to securing physical devices on your network? (Choose three.)

   ☑ Ensure that input devices cannot be conveniently connected to servers.

   ☐ Store non-rack-mountable equipment at the bottom of an equipment rack.

   ☑ Mount power adapters so that they are off the ground and easily visible.

   ☑ Use cable locks on laptops and small PCs.

10. Which of the following network devices retrieves content from outside the network on behalf of an internal client?

    ◉ Proxy

    ○ Reverse proxy

    ○ Front-end processor

    ○ Concentrator

11. Which of the following firewall solutions can determine a packet's relationship to an earlier packet?

    ○ Packet filtering

    ◉ Stateful inspection

    ○ Proxy

    ○ Screening host

12. Which statement best describes how Network Address Translation (NAT) supports confidentiality?

    ○ It allows outbound traffic to a specific Internet host to be returned to a specific internal node without needing to assign a public IP address to the internal node.

    ○ It encrypts traffic so it may not be accessed while in transit.

    ◉ It hides the addresses of private network hosts from threat agents on the Internet.

    ○ NAT tables are refreshed regularly, so stored addresses are not likely to leak.

13. Which statement about IPSec is incorrect?

    ○ It provides anti-replay protection.

    ○ It has two modes.

    ◉ It operates at Layer 4 of the OSI model.

    ○ Before a tunnel is created, the two ends must agree on the level of service.

14. A long-time vendor has a dedicated line in place between their headquarters and your data center. When outages occur, they typically are resolved by the vendor's telecom provider. Network diagnostic tools like tracert consistently report the same number of hops and latency figures show little fluctuation. Which network type is most likely in place?

    ○ Fiber-optic

    ○ Packet-switched

    ◉ Circuit-switched

    ○ Virtual Private Network (VPN)

15. Which statement best describes the purpose of methods like CSMA/CD and CSMA/CA on data networks?

    ○ These methods make sure only nodes bearing the proper token initiate communications.

    ○ These methods reduce latency.

    ◉ These methods manage media access for all nodes on a network.

    ○ These methods make sure data collisions are avoided.

16. The primary risk of a remote access server (RAS) is:
    ○ It typically does not offer authentication for users.
    ○ It typically does not allow you to configure services and protocols.
    ○ It typically does not allow you to enforce access policies.
    ⦿ It typically bypasses the network firewall.

17. Which of the following IPSec modes encapsulates data from endpoint to endpoint?
    ○ Tunnel
    ⦿ Transport
    ○ Transit
    ○ Bridge

18. Employees at your organization use company-issued smartphones in their day-to-day work. Your employees use these phones to conduct confidential calls with clients and other staff members. To prevent an IMSI-catcher from eavesdropping on these calls and tracking the employees' movement as they go mobile, what should you do?
    ⦿ Configure the phones to not negotiate encryption with cell towers.
    ○ Configure the phones to not broadcast their IMSI number.
    ○ Configure the phones to automatically drop a call upon detecting unusual activity.
    ○ Configure the phones to disable their GPS capabilities.

19. Which of the following is true regarding the Layer 2 Tunneling Protocol (L2TP)? (Choose two.)
    ☐ It is less secure than the Point-to-Point Tunneling Protocol (PPTP).
    ☑ Every packet is digitally signed.
    ☐ Data is natively encrypted.
    ☑ Data is not natively encrypted.

20. Which statement about Defense in Depth (DiD) is correct?
    ○ Once adopted, it provides perfect forward security.
    ○ It guarantees the security of information assets.
    ⦿ It is intended to create multiple layers of defenses, so that if any one defense mechanism is defeated, others remain in place to protect resources.
    ○ It mandates the use of perimeter firewalls, security zones, and endpoint protection.

21. Which of the following describes a smurf denial of service (DoS) attack?
    ⦿ The attacker sends ICMP packets to multiple nodes, spoofing the victim's IP address as the source. The nodes then reply to the spoofed address, causing the victim's device to overload.
    ○ The attacker sends UDP packets to multiple nodes, spoofing the victim's IP address as the source. The nodes then reply to the spoofed address, causing the victim's device to overload.
    ○ The attacker sends excessively large ICMP packets to a victim. The victim's device attempts to break down these packets, but in doing so, exceeds the size limit, causing the device to crash.
    ○ The attacker attempts to repeatedly synchronize with a victim. The attacker's device does not send an acknowledgement after receiving the victim's acknowledgement, causing the victim's device to leave open multiple connections. The victim's device becomes too busy to handle normal requests.

22. What is the most significant risk of an IPS generating a false alarm?
- ○ The alerts generated by the IPS will make its logs more complex and difficult to audit.
- ◉ The IPS will actively block legitimate traffic, impacting network and system availability.
- ○ The IPS will normalize this behavior and continue to generate false alarms under similar circumstances.
- ○ The IPS will over-correct this behavior and fail to generate true alarms under similar circumstances.

23. Which of the following best describes the four stages of a network attack?
- ○ Target analysis, target acquisition, target access, target appropriation.
- ◉ Target acquisition, target analysis, target access, target appropriation.
- ○ Target acquisition, target access, target analysis, target appropriation.
- ○ Target analysis, target access, target acquisition, target appropriation.

24. Which of the following best describes Address Resolution Protocol (ARP) spoofing?
- ○ The attacker is able to create IP packets with a forged source IP address to mask the sender's identity.
- ◉ The attacker is able to replace Media Access Control (MAC) entries on a router so that traffic will be sent to the attacker's device, rather than its intended destination.
- ○ The attacker substitutes a different IP address for a domain name in the network's Domain Name System (DNS) entries in order to intercept traffic.
- ○ The attacker injects malicious code on a victim's device, allowing the attacker to assume that device's identity on the network.

ACTIVITY 5-1: Analyzing Physical and Logical Access Control

1. Which statement is true regarding subjects and objects?
- ○ An entity can be either a subject or an object, but not both.
- ○ An object can be any entity attempting to access a subject.
- ◉ A subject can be any entity attempting to access an object.
- ○ Subjects can be people and processes, but not systems.

2. Which of the following choices best represent special concerns to address when considering physical access controls in the leased space? (Choose two.)
- ☐ The presence of smoke detectors and sprinkler systems.
- ☐ The availability of a front desk attendant and tenant list.
- ☑ The architecture may not adequately isolate the leased space.
- ☐ Emergency stairwells have push-bar doors.
- ☐ Stairs and elevators start in the lowest parking levels.
- ☑ Elevator riders may currently stop on any floor.

3. Which one of the following is generally considered to be the first physical layer of defense in a layered protection scheme?
- ○ Device locks
- ○ Secured area access
- ○ Facility access
- ◉ Perimeter access

4. Which of the following is not a physical security control?
   - ○ Employee entrance
   - ⊙ Encrypted hard disk
   - ○ Chain link fences
   - ○ Device cable locks

5. Which of the following is not a valid access control service?
   - ○ Identification
   - ⊙ Activation
   - ○ Authentication
   - ○ Audit

6. Which statement best describes a characteristic of centralized access control administration?
   - ⊙ A single group of administrators handles requests at a single site.
   - ○ Access control decisions occur closer to the subjects requesting access.
   - ○ It leverages centralized functions with local administration.
   - ○ Local administrator actions may be overridden by central administrators.

7. A local administrator persuaded to violate policy is a risk of which access control method?
   - ○ Centralized
   - ○ Local
   - ⊙ Decentralized
   - ○ Convergent

8. True or False? Access control monitoring is often called auditing.
   - ☑ True
   - ☐ False

9. Why should you periodically review your organization's access controls?

   A: Answers will vary. The first reason is to determine if existing controls are still applicable. Another reason is to determine how effective your access controls are. Reviewing access controls can also help uncover privilege abuse.

10. Why is it a good idea to isolate your database from the rest of the network?

    A: Answers will vary. A database usually contains sensitive information and is thus a high value target. Isolating it from the rest of the network provides an extra layer of protection for it.

11. Why would you follow an administrative access control policy with a technical access control policy?

    A: Answers will vary. The administrative policy drives and informs the technical policy. In complement to that, the technical policy gives you a concrete way to implement the administrative policy.

ACTIVITY 5-2: Analyzing Identification, Authentication, and Authorization

1. What are the three steps of identity management?
   - ○ Authentication, Authorization, Accounting
   - ○ Authentication, Authorization, Auditing
   - ○ Identification, Authorization, Accounting
   - ◉ Identification, Authentication, Authorization

2. Which protocol is most often associated with Challenge and Response?
   - ○ RADIUS
   - ○ RDP
   - ◉ CHAP
   - ○ TACACS

3. What is a potential weakness of using email for identification?

   A: Answers will vary. It does not provide any independent verification of identity. It assumes that the person using the email is the actual person being identified.

4. What types of attacks represent specific weaknesses to identification? (Choose two.)
   - ☑ Shoulder surfing
   - ☐ Bluejacking
   - ☑ Social engineering
   - ☐ Worms

5. Your organization recently updated its security policies, requiring all users to be issued new ID cards that carry digital certificates. Card readers are being installed at each workstation, and in the server room. Users will still be required to enter a user ID and password, but will also insert the smart card into a reader before logon will be successful. This is an example of what?
   - ○ Single sign-on
   - ◉ Two-factor authentication
   - ○ Something you have authentication
   - ○ Something you know authentication

6. Which of the following are not typical biometric authentication methods? (Choose two.)
   - ☐ Retinal scan
   - ☐ Facial recognition
   - ☐ Fingerprint
   - ☑ Geolocation
   - ☑ Signature
   - ☐ Hand geometry

7. When is it permissible to share your password with another?
   - ○ When you need them to do some work on your behalf.
   - ○ When they are your boss.
   - ○ When they are a system administrator.
   - ◉ Never.

8. Which statement is true regarding biometric crossover error rate (CER)?

   ○ Of false acceptance and false rejection, CER is the lower of the two.

   ○ Of false acceptance and false rejection, CER is the higher of the two.

   ⊙ CER is the intersection of false acceptance and false rejection rates.

   ○ CER is the lowest point of either false acceptance or false rejection errors.

9. True or False? Smart cards cannot be used for authentication at an endpoint.

   ☐ True

   ☑ False

10. Which term refers to methods that allow a single instance of identification and authentication to be applied to many systems or services?

    ○ Session Layer

    ○ Split-token

    ⊙ Session Management

    ○ Multi-factor

11. Which statement best describes a federated identity?

    ○ Using a single identity across your enterprise.

    ⊙ Using a single identity across multiple identity management systems.

    ○ Using a user name and password implemented in one system, and a smart card implemented in another system.

    ○ Using the same authentication server to authenticate users in different organizations.

12. What is the value of using a directory service?

    A: Answers will vary. It provides authentication consistency across your organization. It also is most likely to be standards-based and thus compatible with other systems.

13. What value does LDAP add to a directory service?

    A: Answers will vary. It provides a standard way for clients to search for (query) and find objects in a directory service database. It also provides a standard way for directory services to communicate (synchronize) with each other.

14. How might you use organizational units in Active Directory to enhance security?

    A: Answers will vary. Since you can use OUs to logically group objects together, you can place users or computers with the same security requirements into the same OU. You can then apply a policy to the OU, or assign an administrator to manage it.

15. What is the value of using time-sensitive tickets in Kerberos?

    A: Answers will vary. Time-sensitive tickets expire after awhile, requiring the user or computer to reauthenticate on a regular basis. This minimizes the risk of unauthorized users or systems getting on the network for very long. Additionally, the five minute permitted time skew between clocks makes it much more difficult to perform a replay attack against Kerberos.

16. Under what conditions could Single Sign-On become a security risk?

    A: Answers will vary. If an SSO login becomes compromised in one system, it might potentially compromise the other systems. Additionally, if an SSO server becomes unavailable, the user might not be able to authenticate anywhere in the enterprise.

17. How can the use of RADIUS enhance remote access security?

A: Answers will vary. Being able to centralize authentication, authorization, and accounting allows you to provide a consistent remote access login experience across your enterprise. It also makes it harder to compromise the authentication database because that database is kept separate from the remote access servers.

ACTIVITY 5-3: Analyzing Identity as a Service

1. What is the primary trade-off in using IDaaS?
   - ○ You are trading your existing centralized system for a vendor's decentralized system.
   - ◉ You are giving up control in exchange for convenience.
   - ○ You are reducing cost in exchange for security.
   - ○ You are increasing complexity in exchange for security.

2. What is required for a federated trust to work?
   - ○ A reciprocal agreement between participating organizations.
   - ○ A trust between the root CAs of the federated partners.
   - ◉ A third party certifier that both sides recognize.
   - ○ A single directory service that the federated partners share.

3. Which SAML-based authentication system is often used by universities?
   - ○ OpenID
   - ○ SAML
   - ○ WAYF
   - ◉ Shibboleth

4. How can granular authorization control assist with this program?
   - ○ It can use different databases to keep information about the clients separate from information about the service providers.
   - ◉ It can provide different types of service providers (volunteers, contractors, internal county employees, etc.) levels of access appropriate to their role.
   - ○ It can provide clients with access to information about the program.
   - ○ It can provide policy makers with access to information about the program.

ACTIVITY 5-4: Discussing Authorization Mechanisms

1. If Bob belongs to all three groups, what is his effective permission on the folder?
   - ○ He can only read.
   - ◉ He can only write.
   - ○ He can read and write.
   - ○ He cannot access the folder in any way.

2. Why is mandatory access control not widely deployed in private, commercial organizations?

   A: Answers will vary. Most commercial firms need the flexibility to assign access control in a variety of ways as needed. Most commercial firms are more focused on maintaining data integrity, rather than confidentiality. The primary focus of mandatory access control is to maintain confidentiality and secrecy.

3. Why is discretionary access control not widely deployed in the military?

   A: Answers will vary. The military depends on very strict information control to ensure success in its operations. Discretionary access control offers too many opportunities for information disclosure due to the fact that the information owner or administrator can change permissions at will.

4. What is the primary difference between role-based access control and rule-based access control?

   A: Answers will vary. Role-based access control assigns permissions based on a user's role. Roles are usually implemented in the form of groups, which users then become members of. Rule-based access control is not dependent on user or group identity. It grants or denies access based on conditions, regardless of the identity of the subject.

5. In what situations would non-RBAC be a preferred architecture model?

   A: Answers will vary. Non-RBAC assigns permissions to individuals, rather than the groups they belong to. This might be desirable in a very small organization, where creating groups is not necessary or practical.

6. In what situations would time-based access control be useful?

   A: Answers will vary. The most likely scenario is to prevent access during non-business hours, when legitimate users are likely to be logged off. It could also be used to help prevent access by hackers from other parts of the globe. Those individuals would have to access the system during hours when the administrator is on duty and more likely to notice the unauthorized access attempts.

ACTIVITY 5-5: Discussing Access Control Attack Mitigation

1. What do you think happened, and how can this be avoided in the future?

   A: Answers will vary. Object reuse (selling old devices) allowed someone to exploit data remanence. It would seem that the IT department did not do a sufficient job in sanitizing the hard drives of the devices. To be completely secure, the devices should have their hard drives removed and destroyed. This is difficult or impossible with mobile devices. One way to help mitigate the problem is to encrypt the data and then reset the device to factory default. The IT department really needs a better QA process.

2. How is it possible that the access control system is not accurately tracking student attendance?

   A: Answers will vary. Most likely the students are tailgating when entering classrooms. One student unlocks the door and a number of students follow. Consider putting a camera outside the door to verify that this is the problem.

3. **What do think has happened, and how could this have been prevented?**

   A: It looks like there was a physical attack during the weekend. An intruder entered through the restroom window, climbed up on the sink, lifted ceiling tiles on both sides of the wall and climbed down into the server room to steal the router. The window should have been locked to prevent entry. More than that, however, the drop ceiling poses a serious security risk for the server room. As is evidenced by the attack, an intruder can gain access by climbing through the false ceiling from another room. You might consider raising the walls around the server room to extend into the false ceiling up to the real ceiling.

4. **What methods might you suggest to mitigate the risk?**

   A: Answer will vary. A hostage situation is very dangerous, as it could quickly get out of control. Consider placing multiple physical controls in strategic locations leading up to the secure room. This could include several guard checkpoints, cameras that are remotely monitored, silent alarms, hostage codes on locks, and the like. Work with law enforcement to develop clear protocols to keep a hostage situation from escalating. Make sure personnel are highly trained to adhere to these protocols in a high-stress moment like a hostage situation.

5. **What can you do to mitigate the risks associated with dumpster diving?**

   A: Answers will vary. Lock the trash bins, or place them in a locked area/cage. Thoroughly shred any papers or disks before throwing them in the trash or recycle bin.

Mastery Builder 5-1: Assessing Identity and Access Management

1. **Which one of the following access control services determines what a subject may do when accessing an object?**
   - ○ Accountability
   - ⊙ Authorization
   - ○ Audit
   - ○ Identification and authentication (I&A)

2. **Which of the following are characteristics of a reference monitor? (Choose three.)**
   - ☑ It must always be invoked.
   - ☑ It must terminate processes in the event of a failure.
   - ☑ It must be tamper-proof.
   - ☐ It must default to allowing access.

3. **You've been asked to help secure logical access to your organization's new facilities. These new facilities are very large, and each will need a Wi-Fi network that covers the entire building so that users will have network access no matter where they are on the premises. As far as logical access to your network goes, which of the following is a major security concern about this initiative?**
   - ○ Remote users accessing the network through a VPN.
   - ⊙ The actual range that your Wi-Fi signals extend to.
   - ○ The rules that determine when employees can and cannot access network resources.
   - ○ The channel that each access point broadcasts on.

4. Which one of the following access control administration methods involves assigning the processes to localized parts of the enterprise?

   ○ Centralized

   ○ Hybrid

   ○ Collective

   ◉ Decentralized

5. The manual review of audit logs is associated with which risk?

   ○ Brute force password attacks may go unnoticed.

   ○ External attacks may not be reflected in the log files.

   ◉ Reviews may be ineffective because of the volume of data.

   ○ Bad data may be input into the various log files.

6. Which one of the following authentication methods is best for safeguarding systems and facilities in high-security environments?

   ○ A token.

   ○ A PIN.

   ○ Biometrics.

   ◉ Multifactor authentication.

7. Which of the following are characteristics of a single sign-on (SSO) environment? (Choose three.)

   ☐ It is a cryptographic system composed of certificate authorities, digital certificates, and cryptographic algorithms.

   ☑ Users need only one ID and password to access all systems and services.

   ☑ If an SSO identity is compromised, all associated systems and services are at risk.

   ☑ SSO can be extended beyond an entity's own network through federated trusts.

   ☐ It is a synonym for authentication methods that require only a single authentication factor.

8. Which of the following are components of Kerberos? (Choose three.)

   ☐ Access Ticket

   ☑ Key Distribution Server

   ☑ Service Ticket

   ☐ Ticket Revocation Service

   ☑ Ticket Granting Ticket

9. Which concept refers to a means of allowing internal users to present their internal credentials for access to external sites and services?

   ○ Mutual authentication

   ◉ Identity federation

   ○ Directory synchronization

   ○ Kerberos

10. In order to save funds on office space, and to increase employee satisfaction, your company has decided to offer telework options to most staff. To facilitate access to company resources, those staff will connect remotely using a virtual private network. In order to connect to the workplace network using the VPN, staff must enter an alphanumeric value that displays on a small digital device and changes frequently. Staff who do not have a code may still access webmail. The device required to access the VPN is an example of a(n):

- ○ Logical token
- ○ Smart card
- ◉ Synchronous token
- ○ Asynchronous token

11. Though single sign-on is convenient, what is a potential security concern?

- ◉ One compromised account grants access to all systems.
- ○ It can allow hackers through the firewall.
- ○ It can allow an unauthenticated user access to secure facilities.
- ○ One forgotten password requires many password resets.

12. Agreements with cloud service providers should include terms that allow for:

- ○ Federated identity.
- ○ Indemnity for the service provider.
- ◉ Auditing the service provider.
- ○ Voice recognition.

13. True or False? IDaaS is Internet-based but may provide authentication for both internal and external resources.

- ☑ True
- ☐ False

14. Which of the following identity federation systems asks a user what institution they are from before it grants the user access?

- ◉ WAYF
- ○ SAML
- ○ OpenID
- ○ Shibboleth

15. Shibboleth uses which XML-based framework to send authentication information?

- ○ XACML
- ◉ SAML
- ○ DITA
- ○ SPML

16. Which of the access control models is generally considered the most restrictive?

- ○ Discretionary Access Control (DAC)
- ○ Rule-based Access Control (RBAC)
- ◉ Mandatory Access Control (MAC)
- ○ Role-based Access Control

17. Which of the following access control methods allow an object owner to assign access?
- ○ Mandatory Access Control (MAC)
- ◉ Discretionary Access Control (DAC)
- ○ Rule-based Access Control (RBAC)
- ○ Role-based Access Control

18. Restricting access to objects based on the sensitivity of the information contained in the objects is an example of:
- ◉ Mandatory Access Control (MAC)
- ○ Discretionary Access Control (DAC)
- ○ Rule-based Access Control (RBAC)
- ○ Role-based Access Control

19. Mandatory Access Control (MAC) requires the use of:
- ○ Access control matrices.
- ○ Permissions such as read, write, and modify.
- ◉ Security labels.
- ○ Security parameters.

20. The type of access control used on a router or firewall to limit network activity is generally:
- ○ Discretionary.
- ◉ Rule-based.
- ○ Role-based.
- ○ Mandatory.

21. Which of the following automated attack methods typically is the fastest way to obtain passwords?
- ○ Brute force
- ◉ Rainbow tables
- ○ Shoulder surfing
- ○ Dictionary attack

22. A disgruntled employee grabbed his manager's cell phone from his office desk and correctly guessed the device's PIN. The disgruntled employee was then able to access the manager's company email account from the phone and sent out a malicious message to the company from the manager's account. What type of attack is this?
- ○ Software-based
- ○ Social engineering
- ◉ Human-based
- ○ Physical

23. An executive at your organization recently had his corporate identity compromised. The attacker was able to use the executive's credentials to access and leak sensitive trade secrets to a competitor. The attacker obtained these credentials by pretending to be an IT employee in an e-mail. The e-mail message requested that the executive provide his credentials so that the IT employee could reset them for security reasons, and the executive complied. What type of attack is this?

○ Software-based

◉ Social engineering

○ Human-based

○ Physical

24. Which of the following are general best practices for access control attack mitigation? (Choose three.)

☐ Implement Mandatory Access Control (MAC) on all systems.

☑ Routinely audit access control mechanisms to ensure their effectiveness.

☑ Continuously monitor access from both object and subject perspectives.

☑ Keep all staff well-trained on security policies and best practices.

25. Which of the following is the most effective way to evaluate your staff's weaknesses to social engineering attacks?

○ Review suspicious behavior that staff members have reported encountering.

○ Evaluate staff members' scores on a multiple choice exam that focuses on social engineering.

◉ Conduct a social engineering penetration test on general staff.

○ Monitor staff members' external communications.

26. Technical access controls are also known as which of the following?

○ Discretionary access controls

○ Physical access controls

◉ Logical access controls

○ Mandatory access controls

ACTIVITY 6-1: Discussing System Security Control Testing

1. What is the single most important output of a security assessment?

○ A comprehensive analysis of the vulnerability state of the network.

○ A report on the overall security posture of the organization.

◉ A report that turns technical findings into risk mitigating actionable items.

○ A complete list of IP addresses, ports, and protocols in use on the network, as well as the results of a vulnerability scan of every system.

2. With regards to an administrative assessment, what is the security relationship between policy/documentation and observed activity?

A: Answers will vary. Policy and documentation describes what management and users should be doing. Observed activity produces an eyewitness record of what they actually are doing. Users and managers that are not following policy and documented procedures might be violating company or regulatory requirements, and might be contributing to security vulnerabilities.

3. **Why would unused user accounts present a security vulnerability?**

   A: Answers will vary. The goal of hardening a system is to remove or reduce every possible avenue of attack. This means eliminating anything that is not absolutely necessary for the proper operation of the system. If you're not using certain services, protocols, configurations, or even user accounts, don't leave them in. They only provide a hacker more opportunity to attack the system.

4. **Why should you perform a vulnerability assessment when you first deploy a new system?**

   A: Answers will vary. You want to first make sure the new system has few if any known vulnerabilities. You also want to know its starting security level (baseline) to see if it complies with company or regulatory requirements.

5. **When conducting a penetration test, why is it necessary to outline the rules of engagement first?**

   A: Answers will vary. Because the pen tester will use the same techniques as a hacker to vulnerability test the network, it is important to identify scope and boundaries. This helps keep the engagement controlled and professional by limiting the risk of destabilizing or damaging any production systems.

6. **Why would a pen tester want to install a backdoor in a vulnerable system as part of the test?**

   A: Answers will vary. Leaving something like a backdoor, where the attacker can freely return to cause more damage, clearly demonstrates the seriousness of the vulnerability.

7. **Why is a blackbox approach to penetration testing so effective?**

   A: Answers will vary. Since an outside attacker will start with little or no knowledge of the target system, a blackbox approach most closely represents a real attack.

8. **How can having a system event log actually hurt security efforts?**

   A: Answers will vary. Unless logging events causes a serious performance problem, the log itself will not hurt security efforts. Quite the opposite, it will contain evidence of attacks or attempted attacks. Where the problem comes in is when the size of the log is so big that it cannot be effectively analyzed for useful information.

9. **How can having a centralized logging system help reduce an attacker's ability to hide evidence of the attack?**

   A: Answers will vary. Centralized logging collects events that have been forwarded by individual systems. Since an attacker will want to erase evidence of their activities, the most common thing to do is to compromise the log itself and selectively delete log entries that indicate the attack. If a copy of the same log is sent to an unknown central location, then it makes it much harder for an attacker to discover where that copy is and to delete it.

10. **How can log management policy and procedures help increase network security?**

    A: Answers will vary. Policy helps you focus your log implementation on what is important, the potential attacks you want to monitor for. Procedure helps the IT department manage the log effectively.

11. **How could a synthetic transaction be used in a penetration test?**

    A: Answers will vary. A synthetic transaction can be used to simulate a malicious action to see how the system responds, and how much the system can be compromised by such activity.

ACTIVITY 6-2: Discussing Software Security Control Testing

1. **What concerns, if any, do you have regarding the test coverage? What else might you require of the developer team?**

   A: Answers will vary. Ideally there should be 100% test coverage, but this is usually not practical. You will want to make sure that the existing 70% coverage tests all of the code that provides the program's logic. Because this is a critical application, you might require additional unit testing (code-based testing) or code review. You might write extra test cases to ensure that all processing paths the application can take have been tested or verify that an automated testing suite was used to check test coverage.

2. **What testing needs to be performed to make sure that the bank's system works with the cellular provider's system?**

   A: Answers will vary, but at the very least integration and interface testing between the bank's application and the cellular company's application needs to be performed. User acceptance and system testing needs to be performed as well.

3. **What positive test cases might you write for the bank's ATM application?**

   A: Answers will vary. Happy paths could include logging a customer on when they enter the correct PIN number, correctly displaying the account balance when requested, correctly verifying that the phone number entered in the recipient field belongs to a registered mobile customer, or correctly debiting the account when the transaction is complete.

4. **What negative test cases might you write for the bank's ATM application?**

   A: Answers will vary. Unhappy paths for this application could include leaving required fields blank, entering letters in the recipient's mobile phone number field, entering letters or negative amounts in the money field, and repeatedly pressing random keys.

ACTIVITY 6-3: Discussing Security Process Data Collection

1. **What key performance indicators should be included in your monitoring process?**

   A: Answer will vary. You'll want a broad range of KPIs for security, network performance, and student attendance. KPIs could include: number of students attending class by time of day; number of security incidents per month; average cost of each security incident; number of help desk calls per month; time required for a help desk call to be resolved and satisfactorily closed; time spent on maintenance of computer lab machines; wireless network throughput by time of day; and more.

2. **What training KPIs could you include?**

   A: Answers will vary. You could have a KPI to track the number of staff trained to use the equipment. You could also have a KPI to track pre- and post-assessment scores to verify comprehension after each training. This should be followed up by tracking the number of help desk calls/classroom assistance calls related to using the new equipment.

3. **Will you implement an ISCM as part of your monitoring process?**

   A: Answers will vary. Some version of ISCM would be useful. However, this is not a large organization, so any ISCM would probably be scaled down to be appropriate for the school. Additionally, management is trusting you to take care of the network, so their ability to be actively involved might be limited.

4. **Would you use NIST SP 800-137 to guide your ISCM implementation?**

   A: Answers will vary. The college is not a federal agency, so you would not use the document in its entirety. However, there are some elements that could be useful to you, particularly those that address implementing metrics, assessing security controls, IT asset management, and updated awareness of threats and vulnerabilities.

5. Do you see a need for collecting/reporting on data from DR/BCP and backups?

A: Answers will vary. These are important, but they were not addressed in management's original request for KPIs. You will probably want to recommend to management that DR/BCP also be addressed, and that they should be aware of the team's readiness to respond to a disaster.

ACTIVITY 6-4: Discussing Audits

---

1. What topics should be addressed in the pre-audit meeting?

A: Answers will vary. You should identify the scope, objectives, and timeline of the audit. You will need to explain what an internal audit entails, including examining logs and observing existing processes to see if they are in compliance with requirements. You will need to point out to management that any audit requires their backing, including providing whatever cooperation or facility is needed to conduct the audit.

2. With regard to the web-based payment processing system, what specific standards should be implemented for the audit?

A: The audit needs to use SOC 2 standards. You might also want to include SOC 3 for simpler reporting.

3. Would this company benefit from an external audit?

A: Most definitely. You have already indicated that you are not an IS auditor. Your role will be limited to verifying technical controls and configurations. Since the company is concerned about compliance, they will need to engage an external auditor who specializes in financial systems.

4. When conducting the internal IT audit, what steps will you include?

A: Answers will vary. You'll need to have an overall plan, as well as a clear understanding of the scope and limits of the audit. You'll want to collect data ahead of time,review and test all systems, interview data handlers and other key personnel, and record your findings against a checklist. You'll want your report to make recommendations on how to fix any issues you many find. Before you finalize your report, you should review the draft with management.

Mastery Builder 6-1: Assessing Security Assessment and Testing

---

1. Which of the following are risks involved in security assessments? (Choose two.)

☐ The testing process may end up finding nothing substantial, wasting time and money.

☑ The testing process may disrupt normal operations.

☑ Recommendations may be improperly implemented.

☐ Recommendations may be too cost prohibitive.

2. Which of the following occasions should prompt you to conduct a vulnerability assessment? (Choose three.)

    ☑ You need to document the current state of your systems.

    ☑ A security breach has occurred.

    ☐ After you've conducted a penetration test.

    ☑ You're about to deploy a system for the first time.

3. Which of the following vulnerability scanning tools gathers information about users and groups on a network without authenticating to devices?

    ◉ Network enumerator

    ○ Protocol scanner

    ○ Protocol analyzer

    ○ Packet analyzer

4. As the CISO of your organization, you have the go ahead from your CEO to begin planning a penetration test on your systems. So far, you've designated which of your security professionals will conduct the test, what types of tests they'll conduct, and what tools they'll use in the process. What other preparatory step are you missing?

    ○ Designating an executive who will commission the test.

    ○ Determining who will be responsible if something goes wrong during the test.

    ◉ Setting any necessary limitations on the test.

    ○ Informing general staff about the test.

5. Which of the following best describes the disadvantage of a white box penetration test?

    ○ You may not have a complete view of the systems you're testing.

    ◉ You may not be accurately simulating a real-world attack.

    ○ You may not be able to inform key personnel about the test.

    ○ You may be overly complicating the test.

6. What are the advantages of centralizing event log collection? (Choose two.)

    ☐ It reduces network load on generating and transmitting log data.

    ☑ It simplifies collection and analysis of logs.

    ☑ It makes it harder for attackers to cover their tracks.

    ☐ Centralization is easily integrated with all types of devices.

7. What is the primary challenge of event log collection?

    ○ Event logging is only available on a small number of device types.

    ○ Event logging is too inconsistent between the different operating systems.

    ○ Event logs often aren't detailed enough and may miss key occurrences.

    ◉ Event logs often are too detailed and may make analysis more difficult.

8. What is the primary purpose of a synthetic transaction?

    ◉ It enables professionals to craft an event for a specific use case.

    ○ It enables professionals to craft random event data.

    ○ It enables professionals to mimic an attack on their systems.

    ○ It enables professionals to introduce a vulnerability into their systems.

9. Which of the following software vulnerabilities is the result of an application failing to free up memory when it is no longer required?

   ○ Buffer overflow

   ○ Session fixation

   ◉ Memory leak

   ○ Integer overflow

10. Which of the following software exploits enables an attacker to inject a malicious link into a website's forums so that users will click the link?

    ○ Reflected XSS attack

    ◉ Stored XSS attack

    ○ DOM-based XSS attack

    ○ XSRF attack

11. Which of the following software testing techniques is best for detecting root problems that may not appear during a test of the running application?

    ○ Manual testing

    ○ Dynamic testing

    ○ Automated testing

    ◉ Static testing

12. Which of the following software test types determines whether or not a small piece of code runs properly in isolation?

    ○ Integration test

    ◉ Unit test

    ○ Functional test

    ○ Regression test

13. Which of the following are web-based input validating techniques? (Choose two.)

    ☑ Inputting massive amounts of random data into a web form.

    ☐ Editing client-side JavaScript in a web form.

    ☐ Attempting to open a secure web page without first authenticating.

    ☑ Leaving input fields empty in a web form.

14. Which of the following is the most important metric in determining test coverage of source code?

    ○ A specific percentage of total code you can afford to test.

    ○ The percentage of code that contains mostly user-facing functionality.

    ◉ The amount of code that contains most of the application's logic.

    ○ The amount of code that was given the least amount of time for development.

15. Which of the following should be included in an Information Security Continuous Monitoring (ISCM) implementation? (Choose three.)

    ☑ Configuration management and change control processes throughout all phases of the system's lifecycle.

    ☐ Frequent assessment of security controls on low-impact systems.

    ☑ Active involvement from upper management.

    ☑ Management receiving up-to-date alerts.

16. Management wants to determine how effective their security awareness programs are for general staff. Which of the follow key performance indicators (KPIs) will be most useful in collecting data on the effectiveness of these programs?

   ○   How many failed authentication attempts users make before and after training.

   ○   How many help desk service requests users make before and after training.

   ○   The number of users that pass an awareness quiz before and after training.

   ◉   The number of users that fall for a phishing penetration test before and after training.

17. Which of the following key performance indicators (KPIs) is the most useful in collecting data about the effectiveness of disaster recovery and business continuity processes?

   ○   The number of recorded incidents.

   ◉   Response and resolution time for incidents.

   ○   The success rate of determining the source or cause of an incident.

   ○   The time span between incidents.

18. Which type(s) of service organizational control (SOC) is intended primarily for organizations that deal with financial reporting?

   ◉   SOC 1

   ○   SOC 2

   ○   SOC 3

   ○   SOC 2 and SOC 3

19. What is the major difference between SOC 2 and SOC 3 reports?

   ○   SOC 2 reports focus on assurances of confidentiality, integrity, availability, and privacy, whereas SOC 3 reports do not.

   ○   SOC 3 reports focus on assurances of confidentiality, integrity, availability, and privacy, whereas SOC 2 reports do not.

   ◉   SOC 3 reports provide less detail than SOC 2 reports and are intended for a more general audience.

   ○   SOC 2 reports provide less detail than SOC 3 reports and are intended for a more general audience.

20. Which of the following circumstances is most likely to require auditing by an external party?

   ○   The organization's compliance with its own security policies.

   ○   The organization's compliance with an industry standard risk management framework.

   ◉   The organization's compliance with applicable laws and regulations.

   ○   The organization's compliance with general best practices for information security.

ACTIVITY 7-1: Discussing Security Operations Concepts

---

1.   Why is maintaining operational resilience a core theme of security operations?

   A: Answers will vary. Operational resilience and security operations share a primary goal: to keep the business functioning, even in the face of negative events.

2.   Why is it that you cannot set and forget permissions levels?

   A: Answers will vary. Most networks and systems are too dynamic to be able to set permissions once. Adding users, changing requirements, and new emerging threats are but a few examples that require permissions to be periodically reviewed and possibly changed.

---

3. Why is separation of duties so important in security operations?

    A: Because it reduces the risk of malicious activity. Separating duties (and their subsequent powers) would require collusion between two or more people to carry out a malicious action.

4. What are some risks associated with service accounts?

    A: Answers will vary. Service accounts often have more privilege than standard users. At the same time, because services generally cannot change their own passwords, service account passwords are set to never expire and be unchangeable.

5. How is the security benefit of job rotation different from that of separation of duties?

    A: Answers will vary. Job rotation is used to uncover fraud and abuse that has already happened. Separation of duties is used to discourage fraud and abuse from happening.

6. What are some security concerns associated with the destruction phase of the information lifecycle?

    A: Answers will vary. Mostly you want to make sure that sensitive data is not accidentally disclosed.

7. Why should security be a key metric in an SLA?

    A: Answers will vary. You want to make sure that the organization you are outsourcing to also follows good security principles, so that they can protect your data and processes.

ACTIVITY 7-2: Discussing Physical Security

1. Does the physical layout of the facility lend itself to good layered security?

    A: No, not really. The building is a low-security office in an upscale neighborhood. Its design did not consider physical security. There is currently no perimeter security at all.

2. What type of fencing would you install?

    A: Answers will vary. 8 feet high with a Class II commercial gate is a good choice. It would need to be high enough that it could not easily be scaled. You would have to determine if additions such as razor wire or barbed wire are necessary.

3. Where would you place lighting?

    A: Answers will vary. You would probably want to provide lighting around the entire facility, especially around the trees. You would also want to light the driveway, parking lot, and entrances.

4. Are bollards necessary?

    A: Answers will vary. They probably would not be useful, considering that the parking lot is already close to the building. Drivers enter parallel to the building. It would be difficult to run into the building at high speed.

5. Which internal areas do you think are sensitive or high-risk?

    A: Answers will vary. The Server Room, Records Room, and Offices for sure. The Test and Production areas are also sensitive.

6. Where would you place cameras?

    A: Answers will vary. The most likely places are the parking lot and surrounding property area, building entrances/exits, hallways, in the Records Room, and the Server Room.

7. Would you install any other types of surveillance?

   A: Answers will vary. The property is rather small, so it would be fairly easy for guards to patrol it visually. You might consider putting sensors on the fence. You probably don't need to eavesdrop on anyone, so audio is probably not necessary.

8. What security recommendations would you make regarding any windows and doors?

   A: Answers will vary. They must be sturdy enough so that they cannot be easily broken into. The location suggests that more obvious window security such as bars are unnecessary, and would even be out of place in that neighborhood.

9. On which doors might you put a biometric/card access lock?

   A: Answers will vary. Good candidates include the exterior door and the Server Room. You might also consider the Records Room, since it contains electronic copies of completed projects.

10. Would you place a cipher lock on any of the doors?

    A: Answers will vary. You might consider putting a cipher lock where development (Production Areas) and testing occur. These require some level of security, but not as much as, say, the server room.

11. Do you think a mantrap would be useful anywhere?

    A: Answers will vary. Probably not. The business has some government security clearances, but the nature of the business makes it a less likely target for armed robbery than a bank or some other high-security facility.

12. Where might you post guards?

    A: Answers will vary. The facility is small and does not require much armed patrol. You might put a guard shack at the front gate.

13. Would you install a PIDS anywhere?

    A: Answers will vary. The facility and its surrounding area is rather small, and would therefore be fairly easy to patrol visually. Guards and cameras might be sufficient, unless there are areas that guards will not be able to visually monitor.

14. What types of secure storage would you provide for copies of completed products?

    A: Answers will vary. If XYZCo is required to keep disk-based copies of the products it creates, it will want to store them securely, especially if they are for sensitive purposes. A locked cabinet might not be sufficient in those cases. It might be necessary to create a secure room that has strong access control. Depending on the value of the products, it might even be necessary to install a safe or a vault.

15. What type of alarm system might you install?

    A: Answers will vary. If there is guard presence at all times, you could have an alarm for local response. You might also want the local response alarm to alert the guard company's remote office. If there is no guard presence, then you'll need an alert that calls for remote response or law enforcement response.

16. How can you automatically update and maintain physical access logs?

    A: Answers will vary. The only way to automate physical access logs is to use electronic access control methods such as card entry or biometrics. Otherwise, if you have a visitor's log book or some manual system, you will have to manually transfer entries into a database (which you probably will not do).

ACTIVITY 7-3: Discussing Personnel Security

---

1. In addition to physical well-being, what is the other goal of personnel safety?

   A: Personnel safety also seeks to maintain someone's mental well-being.

2. How is scenario-based training useful in raising privacy awareness in a company?

   A: Answers will vary. It allows you to creatively test users' understanding of privacy issues, and to correct any misconceptions they may have.

3. Why should corporate travelers be wary of using technology gifts they have received abroad?

   A: Answers will vary. It is quite possible that these gifts will be compromised and used for corporate or government espionage.

4. Why should an organization involve law enforcement or other experts when training staff to deal with duress?

   A: Answers will vary. When an employee is forced to do something under duress, the situation is very dangerous and can quickly become deadly. Staff must know how to protect themselves and keep the situation from getting out of hand.

ACTIVITY 7-4: Discussing Logging and Monitoring

1. Should the school use passive monitoring (intrusion detection) or active monitoring (intrusion prevention)?

   A: Answers will vary. Since the school wants malicious activity to be proactively stopped, intrusion prevention is preferable. This still requires monitoring by an network administrator, however, in case the IPS blocks the wrong traffic.

2. What is the biggest concern with implementing an IDS?

   A: False positives and false negatives. Of the two, false negatives are the worst because break-ins that are in progress go unreported.

3. Where would you place IDS sensors on the network?

   A: Answers will vary. Good locations include behind the firewall, in the perimeter network, behind the VPN server, next to the wireless access point, and next to the production servers.

4. In addition to the firewall, where might you implement data loss prevention?

   A: Answers will vary. The best locations are where the data resides, particularly at the production servers and the perimeter network.

5. Where should egress monitoring be implemented?

   A: Answers will vary. The best locations are wherever there is the likelihood of data leaving the network, particularly at the VPN server and the firewall. The wireless access point is another possible target for egress monitoring, as a wireless signal is unbound and therefore by its very nature not completely contained within the internal network.

6. How might a hacker evade egress monitoring?

   A: Answers will vary. Encryption is the most common method. Steganography is another way if the hacker can hide sensitive data in seemingly innocuous images or other files. Once can always, of course, use sneakernet by copying sensitive files onto a flash drive.

7. If you were to implement a SIEM system, where would you put the central console and where would you place the data collection agents?

   A: Answers will vary. The most common place to put the central SIEM system would be in the same network as the production servers. The data collection agents, if possible, should be placed on every computer device in the network.

ACTIVITY 7-5: Discussing Preventative Measures

1. School management is concerned about the amount of spam its email server is receiving. Would either whitelisting or blacklisting be a useful tool?

   A: Answers will vary. Whitelisting is useful if email only comes from known domains, which is not likely. The school would be best served by subscribing to a blacklisting service.

2. Management would like some of the production servers to host virtual machines and virtual applications. What role does sandboxing play in virtualization and how is that useful from a security perspective?

   A: Answers will vary. Sandboxing seeks to keep virtual machines or applications separate from each other. This reduces the possibility of attack from one VM or application on others or on the host server.

3. If you were to deploy a honeypot, where would you place it?

   A: Answers will vary, but the most common place is in the perimeter network (DMZ). You could also place a honeynet outside the firewall to distract hackers from trying to enter any part of the network.

4. What devices should have anti-malware installed?

   A: Answers will vary. Preferably every desktop, server, and mobile device should have anti-malware software installed.

5. The school currently has a hardware-based firewall protecting the network. Would it be useful to also install personal (software-based) firewalls on all of the computers?

   A: Yes, though you will want to configure the servers to allow client connections for specific services, as well as configure the clients to allow servers to make management connections.

ACTIVITY 7-6: Analyzing Resource Provisioning and Protection

1. What is the Services Provisioning Markup Language (SPML) used for?
   - ○ It is used to replace XML and websites.
   - ○ It is used to provide security such as authentication in websites.
   - ○ It is used for editing service configuration documents.
   - ◉ It is used to help automate the steps necessary to provision a service.

2. How is a configuration management database (CMDB) different from a regular asset tracking database?
   - ○ The configuration management database is part of a larger software suite that tracks all items in your network.
   - ◉ The configuration management database tracks interrelationships and dependencies between assets.
   - ○ An asset tracking database keeps much greater detail about assets in the network.
   - ○ There's essentially no difference. Vendors use both terms interchangeably.

3. When tracking assets, what is the single most important characteristic of an asset that you can record?
   - ◉ Its business purpose.
   - ○ Its serial number.
   - ○ Its product key.
   - ○ Its purchase price.

---

4. **Which of the following considerations is the most important for making an effective configuration management policy?**
   - ⦿ Its focus on the configuration management process.
   - ○ Its enforceability throughout the company.
   - ○ Its level of detail.
   - ○ Its adherence to good standards.

5. **What are the most fundamental goals of the configuration management process?**
   - ○ Capture as much detail about your assets as possible.
   - ○ Capture as much detail about your processes as possible.
   - ○ Limit which personnel are permitted to change company assets.
   - ⦿ List your assets in their baseline state, then capture and control all changes to those assets.

6. **What is the single most important concern in asset provisioning?**
   - ⦿ Identifying why the asset needs to be provisioned in the first place.
   - ○ Identify when the asset was provisioned.
   - ○ Identify how the asset was provisioned.
   - ○ Identify the cost of provisioning the asset.

7. **Why is it important for the asset management system to alert managers when it is time to upgrade the asset?**
   - ○ Because departments need to spend their budget before the fiscal year ends.
   - ⦿ Because managing the lifecycle of any asset includes tracking its age and useful life expectancy.
   - ○ Because there should be consistency across deployed assets.
   - ○ Because older, slower equipment hurts productivity.

8. **When issuing a physical asset, what might you provision besides the device itself?**
   - ○ Documentation for the device.
   - ○ A virtual version of the device as a backup for the physical device.
   - ⦿ A configuration or service provided by the device.
   - ○ A website for the device to receive updates from.

9. **Why are virtual assets considered to be legitimate company assets, just like physical assets?**
   - ⦿ Because they provide a service and have a lifecycle just like a physical asset.
   - ○ Because it costs time and money to create a virtual asset, just as it does a physical asset.
   - ○ Because the software used in a virtual deployment has to be licensed, just like in a physical deployment.
   - ○ Because both virtual and physical assets provide benefit to the company.

10. Why must an organization inventory and track cloud assets, even if a third party is managing those assets?

- ○ Because the organization may have to later take over management of the cloud asset.
- ○ Because the organization will want to verify that the service provider is adhering to the SLA.
- ◉ Because the organization will want to track the usefulness of the asset.
- ○ Because the organization will periodically need to verify that the asset is functioning properly.

11. Why is an application also considered to be a company asset?

- ◉ Because it provides business value.
- ○ Because its licensing costs money.
- ○ Because it will be part of a physical deployment.
- ○ Because it requires support like other assets.

12. What benefit does a hardware lifecycle policy provide a company?

- ○ It allows a company to deploy consistent hardware across the enterprise.
- ○ It ensures that users have the latest equipment to work with.
- ○ It helps track lost, stolen, or broken equipment.
- ◉ It ensures that old equipment is cycled out when its usefulness has passed.

13. Why should a media librarian take custody of original software copies?

- ◉ So that the original is not lost.
- ○ So that appropriate backups can be maintained.
- ○ So that all software can be organized into a central location.
- ○ So that the risk of users making illegal copies is reduced.

14. How do flash drives pose a risk to the organization?

- ○ Their use is hard to control.
- ◉ They are portable, easy to steal, and are a common way to spread computer viruses.
- ○ Once erased, their data is irretrievable.
- ○ It is hard to put technical controls on the use of flash drives.

15. Why is portable media encryption a good practice to implement?

- ◉ Even if the drive or disk is stolen, its contents cannot be easily accessed.
- ○ Users are forced to be more careful when they must encrypt portable media.
- ○ Portable media is less likely to carry a virus when its contents are encrypted.
- ○ The software that encrypts the contents can also be used to inventory and track the device.

16. What steps can be taken to protect hard copies of sensitive data? (Choose two.)

- ☑ Scan the hard copy so that you also have an electronic backup.
- ☐ Carefully file the hard copy in a well-documented filing system.
- ☐ Store multiple copies of the file around the office in case the original is lost.
- ☑ Store copies offsite or in a secure container.

ACTIVITY 7-7: Discussing Patch and Vulnerability Management

1. Which patch management system would be a better choice for the school, a locally deployed server, or a cloud-based system?

   A: Answers will vary. Unless the school has a large Internet connection, it would probably make sense to have a locally deployed server.

2. Should the school purchase a commercial patch management system, or will the free Microsoft version be sufficient?

   A: Answers will vary. The school will have to consider its budget and the level of IT skill available onsite. Commercial systems are usually easier to use, but the free Microsoft patch management system is quite sufficient if there is enough available IT skill to operate it.

3. Should the school test patches, even critical security updates, before deploying them?

   A: Answers will vary. If you can spare the time and resources, patches should be tested before being deployed. This is true even of critical security updates.

ACTIVITY 7-8: Analyzing Change Management

1. What is the ultimate goal of change management?
   - ○ To track all changes in the network.
   - ◉ To continue to uphold the confidentiality, integrity, and availability of the organization's systems.
   - ○ To control all changes to devices and processes in the network.
   - ○ To simplify administration.

2. Why should a Change Control Board (CCB) approve a change before it is implemented?
   - ○ To maintain discipline in the organization.
   - ○ To maintain centralized control.
   - ◉ To ensure that the change is appropriate for the entire enterprise.
   - ○ To prevent ad-hoc solutions based on individual preference.

3. What role does a Security Impact Analysis (SIA) play in change management?
   - ◉ To determine possible risk and offer mitigations.
   - ○ To determine possible cost and offer cost reductions.
   - ○ To determine possible cause and offer counter-effects.
   - ○ To determine possible alternate scenarios and offer a recommendation.

ACTIVITY 7-9: Discussing Incident Response

1. While the nature of this attack was mostly physical, what cyber damage will you look for?

   A: Answers will vary. In addition to assessing the physical damage to the computer equipment, you will also want to determine how much data loss or data compromise has occurred.

2. Are there any additional incident response team members that might become involved besides the company's internal team?

   A: Answers will vary. Because this is partly a high value cyber crime, a special agent from a government agency such as the FBI might become involved.

3. As a first responder, what must you be particularly careful about when gathering computer evidence?

   A: Answers will vary. You especially want to make sure that you don't accidentally delete or damage any of the computer evidence.

4. How can you detect any cyber theft or cyber damage to the computer?

   A: Answers will vary. Assuming that the computer still functions and was not physically damaged, you can look at its host intrusion detection log to see what files were accessed, copied, modified, or deleted.

5. As you evaluate and analyze damage to the computer, what will you do to ensure that any discoveries can be easily accessed for further examination?

   A: Answers will vary. Document carefully and thoroughly, and store your findings in a database that is easy to query and refer to.

6. As you initially respond to the damage, what will you firmly keep in mind as you perform your triage?

   A: Answers will vary. You'll want to contain the damage, and if necessary prevent any further damage to the system. Additionally, you'll want to look for evidence that can be used in prosecuting the case. You'll also want to make sure that the evidence is not contaminated or damaged, thus making it unusable in a criminal prosecution.

7. Will there be any need for remediation as you recover the computer system?

   A: Answers will vary. This was an unusual physical attack. There might not be any computer vulnerabilities that need to be remediated. You already ensured that critical data could not leave the system by implementing strong encryption and digital rights management ahead of time. You also installed a host-based intrusion detection system so that you could assess the level of activity on the computer.

8. What level of reporting and documentation should you provide in your investigation?

   A: Answers will vary. You will want to provide as much detail as possible to be thorough. Your report should be guided by company security policy, regulatory requirements, and any requirements for a criminal investigation. You will need to include any unresolved issues in your report, as well as lessons learned and recommendations for mitigating similar incidents in the future.

9. Will the company need to report the incident to a regulatory body?

   A: Answers will vary. Most likely yes. In the United States, the pharmaceutical industry is heavily regulated by the Food and Drug Administration (FDA). Many other countries have a similar regulatory agency.

10. When listing lessons learned in your report, what is the single most important thing you can do?

   A: Answers will vary. Make sure you spell out recommendations that management can follow to mitigate future risks. Consider including a time frame in which your recommendations should be implemented. Follow up with management when that time frame has elapsed to see if those recommendations were implemented.

ACTIVITY 7-10: Discussing Investigations

1. While you are waiting for the forensic investigator to arrive, what should you tell users to do?

   ○ Tell them they can go about their regular duties, but to stay away from the server.

   ◉ Tell them to not touch anything, including their own computers, until the server's connectivity can be safely isolated from the rest of the network.

   ○ Tell them that they can enter new records, but not access existing records in the customer database.

   ○ Tell them they can go about their regular duties, but to not talk about the incident until the CEO makes a public statement.

2. At what point should you involve law enforcement?

   ○ As soon as you uncover sufficient evidence for prosecution.

   ◉ The moment the organization decides it wants to criminally prosecute the perpetrator.

   ○ After you have examined the server's hard drive for evidence of wrongdoing.

   ○ The moment you discover that something is wrong.

3. Why should the investigative process be auditable?

   ○ You want to make sure the investigator does not get careless.

   ◉ You want to make sure that the investigation maintains its legitimacy.

   ○ You want to make sure that your findings are without bias.

   ○ You want to make sure that the investigation does not contaminate evidence.

4. Under what conditions might your organization file a civil complaint against the hacker?

   ◉ When it cannot file a criminal complaint, but still wants to seek damages.

   ○ After the criminal case concludes.

   ○ Before the criminal case begins.

   ○ When the organization wants to avoid the scandal of a public trial.

5. Would your investigation benefit from e-discovery?

   A: Answers will vary. If you suspect that the unhappy employee had something to do with the attack, you might check both internal company records as well as social media to see if threats had been made or there was activity that could aid in an attack later.

6. What must be done with any electronic evidence that is uncovered?

   ○ A copy of the evidence must be made.

   ◉ The evidence must be secured, and properly collected and recorded.

   ○ The evidence must be photographed and tagged.

   ○ The evidence must be immediately placed in a locked room.

7. The forensic investigator reminds you that any evidence you find must be probative. What does that mean?

   ○ It must be authentic.

   ○ It must be admissible in court.

   ◉ It must help prove a fact.

   ○ It must be complete.

8. When is it permissible for there to be a time gap in the evidence chain of custody log?

   ⦿ Never.

   ○ When you and the forensic investigator are examining the evidence.

   ○ When the evidence has been turned over to law enforcement.

   ○ When the evidence is finally presented to a judge.

9. What does the forensic investigator mean by saying that any evidence you find must be preserved?

   ○ Good clean copies must be made of it.

   ○ The original must be kept intact.

   ⦿ The chain of custody log must show how the evidence was kept safe from tampering.

   ○ The operating system must not be shut down until the contents of memory are first dumped to a file.

10. If you find emails or log files that might incriminate the unhappy employee, what can you do to preserve those files to ensure that they are not tampered with later?

    A: Answers will vary. One thing you can do is to hash the files to prove their integrity later.

11. Might the Electronic Communications Privacy Act (ECPA) apply to this investigation?

    A: Answers will vary. If you end up monitoring employee activity to search for clues, then yes, the ECPA would definitely apply.

12. Would root cause analysis (RCA) be useful in this investigation?

    A: Answers will vary. Because you are looking for evidence of a deliberate act, then RCA is not the right approach. RCA might be useful if you are trying to determine the conditions that permitted the attacker to succeed in the attack.

13. Can network evidence analysis be useful in this investigation?

    A: Answers will vary. If the source of the attack is from another device across the network (or even the Internet), then analyzing network evidence would be very valuable. Of course, the network logs would have to contain sufficient information to provide clues as to the origin of the attack.

14. When you are through with the investigation and you finally write the investigation report, what must you always keep in mind?

    ○ Your report must have sufficient evidence to prove a person's guilt.

    ○ You must ensure that the evidence remains intact in case the reader wants more information.

    ⦿ You must show how all the evidence you have gathered fits together to support your conclusion.

    ○ You must provide enough proof for law enforcement to want to become involved.

ACTIVITY 7-11: Analyzing Disaster Recovery Planning

1. Why is it necessary to train people when you develop a disaster recovery plan?

   ○ So that they can earn company continuing education credits.

   ○ So that they know the company's DR strategy.

   ○ So that they can uphold the CIA triad.

   ⦿ So that they know how to respond in the event of a real disaster.

2. Why should a disaster recovery plan (DRP) spell out recovery steps?

   ⦿ To make the recovery process as guided and straightforward as possible.

   ○ To satisfy due diligence requirements.

   ○ To assist management in directing user activity during a disaster.

   ○ To provide IT traceability to business continuity planning steps.

3. Why must you involve all departments when developing a disaster recovery response?

   ○ Because end users from each department will have to implement the response should disaster strike.

   ○ Because a balanced plan involves all stakeholders.

   ○ Because you will need end user buy-in from all the departments for your plan.

   ⦿ Because the priorities of each department during a disaster might be very different from what the IT department expects.

4. When creating your DRP, why should you publish a priority list of which systems will be brought online first after a disaster?

   ⦿ So that there are no disappointing surprises when a real disaster strikes.

   ○ So that you can satisfy due care and due diligence.

   ○ So that the IT team will be clear on what tasks to perform first.

   ○ So that the management team can create a clear step-by-step recovery plan.

5. When assigning disaster recovery priority levels, why might some systems be excluded from the disaster recovery list?

   ⦿ This may happen to systems that are optional and not required for the business to operate.

   ○ This may happen to systems that are too expensive to restore.

   ○ This may happen to individual systems that are considered too insignificant to list.

   ○ This may happen to old systems that should be replaced, rather than restored, in the event of a disaster.

6. Who should speak to the news media in the event of a disaster?

   ○ The command center team.

   ⦿ The executive emergency management team.

   ○ The receptionist assigned to answer the phone.

   ○ The company attorney.

7. How is a Recovery Point Objective (RPO) different from a Recovery Time Objective (RTO)? (Choose two.)

   ☐ The RTO attempts to restore a system to a specific state before the disaster.

   ☐ The RPO attempts to restore a system within a specific amount of time.

   ☑ The RPO attempts to restore a system to a specific state before the disaster.

   ☑ The RTO attempts to restore a system within a specific amount of time.

8. Is a near-zero RTO/RPO always feasible?

   ○ No, because your backups might not always survive a disaster.

   ⦿ No, because it may simply be too expensive to implement.

   ○ No, because your spare hardware might not always survive a disaster.

   ○ Yes, because that is the goal of RTO and RPO.

9. What should a typical disaster recovery end-user training include?
   - ⊙ What to do and what not to do.
   - ○ Steps to take to recover your department's systems.
   - ○ Steps to take to recover your department's business flow.
   - ○ How to prevent department data from being destroyed during a disaster.

10. What is the ultimate goal of a disaster recovery test?
   - ⊙ To ensure that your recovery point and recovery time objectives are reasonable and attainable.
   - ○ To uncover and rectify gaps in the testing process itself.
   - ○ To make sure that loss of life is minimized.
   - ○ To provide an assurance that the test will not jeopardize normal business operations.

11. What is the next logical step after creating a test strategy?
   - ○ Conduct the test.
   - ○ Train all personnel.
   - ○ Document the strategy.
   - ⊙ Create the test plan.

12. Which test type will most thoroughly test your disaster recovery capabilities?
   - ○ Structured walkthrough.
   - ○ Parallel.
   - ⊙ Full Interrupt.
   - ○ Simulation.

13. Why should you regularly update your disaster recovery plan?
   - ○ To keep your plan current with the changing technologies you use.
   - ⊙ To continue to perform due diligence.
   - ○ To keep users engaged and interested.
   - ○ To keep management current on the latest recovery techniques.

ACTIVITY 7–12: Analyzing Disaster Recovery Strategies

1. Which of the following can be used as backup media? (Choose four.)
   - ☑ Magnetic tape
   - ☑ Removable disk
   - ☐ Internal hard drive
   - ☑ Cloud
   - ☑ SAN

2. In addition to data, what else should you back up? (Choose four.)
   - ☑ License keys
   - ☑ Source code
   - ☑ Server and desktop images and virtual machines
   - ☐ Web services
   - ☑ Configuration files

3. How is remote journaling different from electronic vaulting?

   ○ Both send backups to offsite locations, but electronic vaulting is done in real time.

   ⦿ Both send backups to offsite locations, but remote journaling is done in real time.

   ○ Remote journaling sends backups to a remote location, whereas electronic vaulting sends backups to another server in the same site.

   ○ Electronic vaulting sends backups to a remote location, whereas remote journaling sends backups to another server in the same site.

4. What is the goal of redundancy and fault tolerance?

   ○ To provide load balancing in case of a denial of service attack.

   ○ To provide network re-routing in case of a device failure.

   ○ To reduce desktop downtime.

   ⦿ To automatically or semi-automatically recover from the failure of a single device or system.

5. With regard to RAID, how is mirroring different from parity?

   ○ Mirroring stripes data across multiple disks, whereas parity creates a complete duplicate of the original disk.

   ⦿ Mirroring creates a complete duplicate of the original disk, whereas parity stripes data across multiple disks.

   ○ Mirroring is a fault tolerant method, whereas parity is not.

   ○ Parity is a fault tolerant method, whereas mirroring is not.

6. Of all the RAID levels, which one best provides both performance and fault tolerance?

   ○ RAID 1

   ○ RAID 5

   ○ RAID 6

   ⦿ RAID 10

7. Which recovery site type would be the most appropriate for a large financial center that performs millions of credit card transactions every day?

   ○ Warm site.

   ○ Cold site.

   ○ Hot site.

   ⦿ Dual data center.

8. What is the risk of allowing users to work from home after a disaster?

   ○ They might not want to return to work when operations return to normal.

   ○ They might not be able to return to work until roads and other civic infrastructure are restored.

   ⦿ Too many remote connections might overwhelm the company network.

   ○ Damaged power lines and limited telecom might restrict the effectiveness of users working from home.

ACTIVITY 7-13: Discussing Disaster Recovery Implementation

1. During the storm, what should be your first priority?
   - ○ To initiate the call tree.
   - ○ To establish a command center.
   - ○ To grab the backup tapes from the server room.
   - ◉ To protect human life.

2. What immediate event management responses will this event trigger?

   A: This is a severe incident. It should trigger the disaster recovery process and crisis management.

3. What critical systems will you want to restore as soon as the storm has passed?

   A: Answers will vary. Because large parts of the population will depend on getting money immediately after the disaster, you would probably want to restore internal company communications, basic networking, and as many ATM machines as possible.

4. Will your disaster recovery response have a short term approach, or a long term approach?

   A: Answers will vary. If the corporate office or any branch offices are damaged in the storm, you'll need to have a short term approach to get those facilities up and running. If any locations are seriously damaged, you may have to relocate or rebuild those facilities.

5. Once your communications center is established, what are the first messages you would send out to internal staff? To customers?

   A: Answers will vary. You'll want to initiate your call tree to make sure all personnel are safe and accounted for. You'll also want to give instructions to bank personnel on what to do. Some people will be needed during the disaster response process, while others may be told to stay at home for awhile. You will most definitely want to communicate to your customers which ATM machines they can get cash from, and if other ATMs are expected to come back online soon.

6. In case the phone system is knocked out by the storm, what alternatives can you use to keep communications flowing?

   A: Answers will vary. Most people will turn to their cell phones to make calls, send messages, or get online during a disaster. Many communities also tune in to radio or television stations for news and announcements as well. Your communications team might be able to get a local broadcasting station to make announcements to both your customers and staff.

7. After the immediate danger has passed, what must the bank always keep in mind as it restores facilities and operations?

   A: Answers will vary. Restoration will have to be done based on priority. Getting core operations and service to customers restored will be the highest priority. Equipment salvage at damaged sites will be a much lower priority. HR processes, particularly providing payroll and benefits to staff, will be also be critical. Because this is a financial institution, the IT team will need to work with the legal department and government regulators to stay in compliance with applicable law.

Mastery Builder 7-1: Assessing Security Operations

1. Whose responsibility is it to implement proper data archiving and retention procedures during the information lifecycle?
   - ○ Data owner
   - ○ Data user
   - ⦿ Data custodian
   - ○ Data auditor

2. In order to uphold operational resilience, who should you consult with to determine which processes are the most important to the business?
   - ○ General staff
   - ○ IT staff
   - ⦿ Department managers
   - ○ Board of directors

3. Which of the following account management practices uphold the principle of least privilege? (Choose two.)
   - ☑ Setting expiration times for user accounts.
   - ☐ Enforcing password length and complexity requirements.
   - ☐ Enforcing password reuse requirements.
   - ☑ Automatically reviewing members in administrator groups.

4. According to UL 325, which of the following classes of fence gates would be most appropriate for a public parking lot entrance?
   - ○ Class I
   - ⦿ Class II
   - ○ Class III
   - ○ Class IV

5. What is an advantage of using guards over non-human physical controls? (Choose two.)
   - ☐ Guards are more reliable.
   - ☑ Guards are often more of a visual deterrent.
   - ☑ Guards can apply their own knowledge and intuition to a situation.
   - ☐ Guards are more cost-effective.

6. Which of the following assurances can a good lighting system provide? (Choose three.)
   - ☑ It can act as a deterrent.
   - ☑ It can aid in identifying attackers.
   - ☐ It can interfere with an attacker's vision.
   - ☑ It can be a useful alarm system.

7. Which of the following is the most helpful way to train personnel to uphold privacy?
   - ⦿ Present a real-world scenario and ask them what they'd do in response.
   - ○ Engage in a penetration test that targets the user's privacy.
   - ○ Present personnel with a list of what they should and shouldn't do.
   - ○ Mandate that personnel sign the organization's privacy policy.

8. Which of the following is not a best practice to secure privacy of information while traveling?
   - ○ Avoid transporting electronic devices in checked baggage.
   - ◉ Only connect to open Wi-Fi networks you trust.
   - ○ Clear your browser cache, history, and cookies after each use.
   - ○ Be aware of your surroundings while entering a password.

9. You're putting together mock scenarios for your team to participate in. These scenarios focus on what personnel should do in the face of duress, such as a hostage-taking situation. You've trained your team to comply with the attackers' demands, how to stay calm, and how to get the attackers what they want so the situation can end quickly. Which of the following is an important step that your training program is missing?
   - ○ How to minimize financial loss to the organization.
   - ○ How to break free from the attackers' control.
   - ◉ How someone can alert the authorities.
   - ○ How best to negotiate with the attackers.

10. Your intrusion prevention system (IPS) detected a port scan being conducted on your remote access server. As you investigate, you learn that one of your security professionals was conducting a routine vulnerability assessment of key systems, including this RAS server. Which of the following best describes the alert generated by the IPS?
    - ○ True positive.
    - ○ True negative.
    - ◉ False positive.
    - ○ False negative.

11. You have a system in place that monitors email transmissions in your organization and automatically removes any attachments. What type of system is this?
    - ○ Intrusion detection system (IDS).
    - ○ Intrusion prevention system (IPS).
    - ○ Data loss prevention (DLP).
    - ◉ Security information and event management (SIEM).

12. How can steganography be used to evade egress monitoring controls?
    - ○ An attacker can physically move data to outside of the network.
    - ○ The attacker can encrypt data packets and send them through an allowed protocol.
    - ○ The attacker can initiate a DoS condition on the egress monitoring system.
    - ◉ The attacker can hide sensitive data in other media as it travels outside the network.

13. What is an advantage of whitelisting over blacklisting?
    - ○ Whitelists are less restrictive.
    - ◉ Whitelists can protect against threats you don't know about.
    - ○ Whitelists are more cost-effective.
    - ○ Whitelists are easier to maintain.

14. What are the advantages to using virtual machine sandboxes? (Choose two.)
    - ☑ The user can't interfere with the host.
    - ☐ The user has greater control over their environment.
    - ☑ The sandboxes are easily provisioned to multiple users.
    - ☐ The sandboxes minimize network load.

15. When constructing honeypots and honeynets, you need to be aware of enticement and entrapment concerns. Which of the following are key differences between enticement and entrapment? (Choose two.)

    ☑ Enticement is legal, entrapment is not.

    ☐ Entrapment is legal, enticement is not.

    ☐ Enticement is luring someone to commit a crime they would not have otherwise committed.

    ☑ Entrapment is luring someone to commit a crime they would not have otherwise committed.

16. What is the most important asset characteristic you should describe in a configuration management (CM) system?

    ○ Who owns the asset.

    ○ Who uses the asset.

    ○ Where the asset is stored.

    ◉ How the asset fulfills business needs.

17. Which of the following is a software asset management practice that ensures malicious code won't compromise an application's binaries?

    ○ Implement a digital watermark in the binaries.

    ◉ Digitally sign the binaries.

    ○ Encrypt the binaries.

    ○ Use steganography to hide the binaries.

18. Which of the following best describes the two-man rule as it applies to media management?

    ○ No two people should have an equivalent level of access to media.

    ○ Only two people should have an equivalent level of access to media.

    ◉ There must be two authorized people at all time to monitor media use.

    ○ Monitoring duties must rotate between two authorized people.

19. Which of the following are major reasons why you should implement a patch management system? (Choose two.)

    ☐ It relieves you of the burden of having to schedule updates.

    ☐ It allows you to develop in-house patches for external proprietary software.

    ☑ Default patch downloading from the Internet can negatively impact network bandwidth.

    ☑ Patches should not go untested before being deployed.

20. If Internet connectivity is an issue in your organization, which of the following ways could you configure your patch management servers to mitigate this issue? (Choose two.)

    ☑ Side-load vendor patches into the patch management servers.

    ☐ Schedule downloading of vendor patches during normal work hours.

    ☑ Schedule downloading of vendor patches during off hours.

    ☐ Schedule distribution of vendor patches during normal work hours.

21. What is the primary reason why a patch management system should include patch testing functionality?

   ○ Vendor patches may add new, unwanted features.

   ◉ Vendor patches may fix one bug, but introduce another.

   ○ The contents of a vendor patch may become corrupted during transmission.

   ○ The patch management system may not distribute the patch properly.

22. You recently went through the change management process in order to update your workstations' operating systems from Windows 7 to Windows 10. In this process: you requested the change from the Change Control Board (CCB); the CCB approved the change; you informed IT personnel and staff about the impending move to the new OS; you thoroughly tested all of your production software on the new Windows 10 environment and determined that it was all compatible; you then had your IT staff update all available workstations; and lastly you reported to your CIO and the CCB that the operating system update was a success. Which key step did you forget to include in this change management process?

   ○ Reporting the success of the change to the Board of Directors.

   ◉ Documenting the change in a change log.

   ○ Automating the process of updating the workstations from Windows 7 to 10.

   ○ Obtaining majority buy-in from the staff members that use the workstations.

23. Which of the following are the main reasons why versioning is so important to the change management process? (Choose two.)

   ☐ To establish a single baseline to compare all future versions against.

   ☑ To capture an object's current state and compare that version against the proposed changes.

   ☑ To quickly and easily roll back changes that introduce problems.

   ☐ To establish non-repudiation for changes.

24. Aside from assessing a change's impact to operational security, what else should a security impact analysis (SIA) provide?

   ○ An assessment of the change's affect on business models.

   ○ An assessment of the change's affect on personnel productivity.

   ○ Recommendations on how best to implement the change quickly and with minimal effort.

   ◉ Recommendations on how to resolve any risk the change introduces.

25. Which of the following describes the process of triage as it relates to incident response?

   ○ Identifying the best method for responding to an incident.

   ○ Identifying which systems have been hit the hardest in an incident.

   ◉ Identifying the most critical systems to respond to first.

   ○ Identifying the source of an incident.

26. Which of the following scenarios exhibits the remediation process in incident response?

   ○ Restoring functionality to web servers that were DDoSed.

   ◉ Engaging in a public relations campaign to restore client confidence in the organization after an incident.

   ○ Moving all personnel to an alternate site at which they will continue business operations.

   ○ Cleaning malicious software from a user's workstation.

27. What is the ultimate goal of drafting a lessons learned report (LLR) after responding to an incident?

    ○ Providing a well-reasoned justification for the actions taken during the response.

    ◉ Ensuring that recommendations in the LLR are implemented in the organization.

    ○ Absolving the organization of legal liability with regards to the response.

    ○ Providing a framework for legal prosecution of a suspected crime.

28. Which of the following characteristics describe what an investigation must be? (Choose three.)

    ☑ Methodical

    ☐ Extensible

    ☑ Auditable

    ☑ Verifiable

29. Which of the following forensic practices ensure that log files are admissible in court? (Choose two.)

    ☑ Writing logs to access controlled volumes.

    ☑ Hashing the log files.

    ☐ Encrypting the contents of log files.

    ☐ Defining a single authorized individual as the log owner.

30. What is a security concern involved with obtaining forensic evidence from an embedded device?

    ◉ Taking an image of the device's firmware may alter that firmware.

    ○ A device's firmware changes too often to be of any forensic value.

    ○ Evidence obtained from certain embedded devices is not admissible in court.

    ○ Few tools are available that can accurately obtain evidence from embedded devices.

31. For IT systems, a Recovery Point Objective (RPO) is often reflected by which one of the following?

    ○ The date of the last successful system restoration process.

    ○ The point in time at which the last system failure occurred.

    ○ The number of days the business can function without the system.

    ◉ The date of the last successful backup of the affected system.

32. Which of the following disaster recovery plan (DRP) test types is preliminary and should not replace more substantial tests?

    ○ Simulation

    ○ Full interrupt

    ○ Parallel

    ◉ Readthrough

33. How often should you update and maintain your DRP?

    ○ Every month

    ◉ Every 3 months

    ○ Every year

    ○ Every 2 years

34. Which of the following RAID levels allows two drives to fail without needing to recover?
   - ○ RAID 0
   - ○ RAID 1
   - ○ RAID 5
   - ◉ RAID 6

35. Which of the following is a disadvantage of a hot site?
   - ○ The site cannot test recovery.
   - ○ The site cannot guarantee high availability.
   - ◉ The site is expensive.
   - ○ The site takes a long time to get up and running.

36. Which of the following data backup methods clears the archive bit to reduce backup time and storage?
   - ◉ Incremental
   - ○ Differential
   - ○ Remote journaling
   - ○ Electronic vaulting

37. Which of the following best describe an event categorized as a severe incident? (Choose two.)
   - ☑ It will trigger the disaster recovery process.
   - ☐ It will not require crisis management.
   - ☑ It may require building a new facility.
   - ☐ It has only natural causes.

38. Which of the following statements about a call tree are accurate when it applies to disaster recovery communications? (Choose two.)
   - ☑ It speeds up the communication process.
   - ☐ It slows down the communication process.
   - ☐ It should not be more than two levels deep.
   - ☑ It should not be more than three levels deep.

39. Why is it important to include the legal team in the restoration process after a disaster?
   - ○ The legal team can secure financial aid for the restoration process.
   - ○ The legal team can prepare the organization's defense in case it is held liable for damages.
   - ◉ The legal team can advise management on how to stay compliant during restoration efforts.
   - ○ The legal team can help prepare the organization to press charges.

ACTIVITY 8-1: Analyzing Security Principles in the System Lifecycle

1. **How is the system lifecycle different from the system development lifecycle?**

   ⦿ The system lifecycle is more comprehensive than the system development lifecycle, including phases for operations, maintenance, and disposal.

   ○ The system development lifecycle is more comprehensive than the system lifecycle, including phases for operations, maintenance, and disposal.

   ○ There is no difference. You can use the terms system lifecycle and system development lifecycle interchangeably.

   ○ The system lifecycle focuses on creating computer systems, whereas the system development lifecycle focuses on creating applications.

2. **How can an integrated product team assist with product development?**

   A: Answers will vary. Because an IPT is an interdisciplinary group with members from many different teams, it can leverage many perspectives and skill sets to create a more holistic and balanced product.

3. **At which CMM level does an organization have standardized processes?**

   ○ Level 1

   ○ Level 2

   ⦿ Level 3

   ○ Level 4

4. **What is the point of a run book?**

   ⦿ It describes how to load and run a program on a mainframe platform.

   ○ It provides the developer team with instructions for deploying an application.

   ○ It is a set of operating instructions written by the developer team for the operations team to use in deployment.

   ○ It is a set of explicit instructions on how to compile an application's source code into an executable.

5. **How can implementing change management help raise an organization's CMM level?**

   A: Answers will vary. Change management is a standardized procedure. While change management alone will not take an organization to a higher CMM level, it is one of several things an organization can do to move towards Level 3.

6. **As you perform periodic tests and integrity checks, what type of non-technical checks should you perform and why?**

   A: Answers will vary. Non-technical checks would include human interaction, including checking user skills requirements and verifying that users have those needed skills, and verifying that effective peer-based code reviews are happening.

ACTIVITY 8-2: Discussing Security Principles in the Software Development Cycle

1. Why are most developers writing in higher level languages instead of assembly language, considering that code written in assembly is so much more efficient?

   A: Answers will vary. Writing in assembly language does indeed make code much more efficient, but the language is much more difficult to master. With developers under pressure to be as productive as possible, almost all development is done in a high-level language.

2. What is the biggest benefit of using an interpreted language over a compiled language?

   A: Answers will vary. Mostly, it is the portability (platform independence) of an interpreted language that makes it so attractive. You can run the same interpreted language code on a variety of systems, as long as each has an interpreter to handle the code.

3. How does encapsulation in object-oriented programming promote information security?

   ○ It encrypts the data inside to protect it from accidental disclosure.

   ○ It divides the code into discrete parts so that it cannot be easily reassembled by a malicious process.

   ○ It generalizes a class to the highest level necessary for use.

   ◉ It hides the code details of a class from other objects trying to use that class.

4. What is the value of using CORBA?

   ○ It allows for a distributed multi-tier application in Java.

   ◉ It provides flexibility and encapsulation.

   ○ It can discover objects on the network.

   ○ It can be used to locate objects and can act as middleware for connecting programs.

5. What phases of a product's lifecycle are not addressed by the SDLC? (Choose two.)

   ☐ Concept and Initiation

   ☑ Revision, Replacement, and Decommissioning

   ☑ Operations and Maintenance

   ☐ Build and Test

6. From a security perspective, what is the greatest risk in any software development project?

   ○ There will be insufficient testing.

   ○ The development methodology will not include enough encapsulation of object classes.

   ◉ The business will be focused on functionality to the exclusion of most other considerations.

   ○ The development environment will not be secure.

7. What are some security considerations that must be addressed at the Concept and Initiation phase?

   A: Answers will vary. Some considerations include: does the information handled by the application have any special sensitivity/security needs, will it have any compliance requirements, and will using the product expose the data in any way?

8. At what phase of the SDLC should risk assessment be conducted?

   ○ Concept and Initiation

   ◉ Requirements

   ○ Design

   ○ Build

9. What security considerations should be addressed in the SDLC Design phase?

   ○ Risk assessment should be conducted during this phase.

   ◉ Security requirements should be clearly articulated during this phase.

   ○ Security testing should be conducted during this phase.

   ○ Security documentation should be developed at this phase.

10. How can test driven development (TDD) provide security during the Build phase?

    A: Answers will vary. TDD assures that the code performs exactly as required on a line-by-line basis, and that there are no surprises. Bugs and code instabilities are considerably reduced using this method.

11. How can users help with the security aspect of the Test phase in the SDLC?

    A: Answers will vary. Users, being unfamiliar with the software, will try unexpected actions that can help expose problems in the software.

12. What is the difference between certification and accreditation in software development?

    ◉ Certification results from a technical test, whereas accreditation results from management acceptance.

    ○ Accreditation results from a technical test, whereas certification results from management acceptance.

    ○ There is no difference. The two refer to the same thing.

    ○ Accreditation is a necessary step that must be achieved before certification.

13. What security considerations must be addressed during the Deploy phase of the SDLC?

    A: Answers will vary. The two biggest concerns are to watch for software vulnerabilities and to make sure that the deployment process itself does not introduce any risks.

14. Is there still a use case for using the waterfall model to develop software?

    A: Answers will vary. Some projects will be too large or complex to be sufficiently handled by other methodologies. In that case, waterfall is still the best approach.

15. From a security perspective, what makes cleanroom a desirable development methodology?

    A: Answers will vary. Cleanroom methodology is secure by design. Its goal is to write code that has no bugs to begin with.

16. From a security perspective, what is the greatest risk of using Agile methodology to develop software?

    A: Answers will vary. The greatest risk is that all of the focus will be on functionality, and that little or no consideration will be paid to security.

17. Does Agile methodology ignore documentation?

    A: Answers will vary. Agile values working software over extensive documentation, but it does not discard the need for documentation.

18. If the development team wanted to especially involve the customer, which version of Agile should it use?

    ○ SCRUM

    ◉ XP

    ○ Lean

    ○ Kanban

19. **If the development team uses the prototyping model, why must the security practitioner manage customer expectations during development?**

    A: Answers will vary. Customers will tend to see the prototype as a completed product, and not realize that considerably more work must go into the software to make it secure.

20. **From a security perspective, what is the benefit of using the spiral development model?**

    A: Answers will vary. The greatest benefit of using spiral is that a complete risk assessment is conducted at the beginning of every iteration of the software's development.

21. **Which of the following is especially suited to addressing security requirements during the planning stage?**

    ○ RAD

    ◉ JAD

    ○ Exploratory Model

    ○ Component-Based Development

22. **How does using Structured Development techniques support code security?**

    A: Answers will vary. It mostly makes the code easy to break into modules that can be easily verified and individually tested.

23. **How can using Computer Aided Software Engineering (CASE) assist in developing a complex application?**

    A: Answers will vary. If a complex project has been broken into many subparts for development by different teams, CASE helps keep the entire program cohesive.

ACTIVITY 8-3: Discussing Database Security in Software Development

1. **What general security features can you insist that the database developers include in the database to help protect the data?**

    A: Answers will vary. There are a number of things you can implement in a database to protect the data. These include access control, enforcing data content rules in the database, internal integrity checks, and built-in bounds and limit checking.

2. **Would this project benefit from using an object-oriented database model?**

    A: Answers will vary. Since the developer team doesn't know SQL, but are comfortable with object-oriented programming, an OODBM might be very useful. You will still need a SQL architect to set up the underlying database structure.

3. **What will probably have to be done to the data before attempting to combine all of the databases into a single data warehouse?**

    A: Answers will vary. One thing that definitely will have to happen is to make sure the data from all of the databases is in the same format. The data will need to be pre-processed to permit consistent coding.

4. **What data mining technique can be used to help predict health trends across the nation, based on the existing data?**

    ○ Data warehousing

    ○ Data mining

    ◉ Inference

    ○ Aggregation

5. What data mining technique can be used to view trends without exposing individual health records?

   ○ Data warehousing

   ○ Data mining

   ○ Inference

   ⦿ Aggregation

6. What is the risk of using aggregation in your data mining process?

   A: Answers will vary. Aggregation could inadvertently leak personal information. Conversely, de-identifying the data too much in the aggregation process could also strip it of any real analytical value.

7. What do you think might have happened?

   A: Answers will vary. It is quite possible that poor coding or inefficient SQL queries caused an inadvertent denial of service against the database.

8. What security techniques can you use to ensure that the amount and type of data users see is limited to their job requirement, especially if the application uses an object-oriented database model?

   A: Answers will vary. There are a number of techniques that can be used, depending on the requirement. If an object-oriented approach is used, then the classic OOP security mechanisms of encapsulation, inheritance, information hiding, and methods can be used. You can also use class and instance to classify data sensitivity. You can also use metadata controls to limit what users can discover about the data.

ACTIVITY 8-4: Discussing Security Controls in the Development Environment

---

1. What can you tell management about the risks of developing proprietary versus open source software?

   A: Answers will vary. If implemented properly, open-source software is likely to have fewer vulnerabilities because it will be more thoroughly tested and vetted by the open source community. On the other hand, making the source code open source means that you have no intellectual property rights. Other organizations can legally use the code to create competitive products. In a developing nation, where funding and other resources are scarce, open-source software would be a more sustainable choice.

2. Why is it important to implement security in the software development environment?

   A: Answers will vary. If you do not have a secure development process, you run the risk of introducing viruses or corrupting the source code during the development process. Since this application deals with personally identifiable information, you must take extra precautions to not put people's health records at risk.

3. What is the key message behind (ISC)2's Best Practices for Secure Software Development?

   A: You must start with a secure mindset in both the business and software development department. This is difficult to achieve when working with limited resources under tight deadlines.

4. Why must you not depend on automated source code analysis tools to catch all errors in your code?

   A: Answers will vary. No automated tool has proven to be 100% effective at catching all software errors. Many will report false positives. You must use automated code analysis tools as part of a larger strategy for testing source code.

5. How should you respond to this suggestion?

   A: Answers will vary. It will depend on the manner in which the other group's code flaws are exposed. A CISSP must always act honorably and discourage unprofessional behavior. The team should be able to demonstrate that the other application has security weaknesses to the appropriate decision-making body without resorting to unethical tactics such as a surprise public demonstration.

6. The application may have to make a connection across the network to obtain data. Why is it important to keep the length of time between time of check and time of use (TOC/TOU) to a minimum?

   A: Answers will vary. The longer the time between when a credential is checked and when it is used, the greater the opportunity for a rogue process to exploit the validated credential.

7. When might it be desirable to implement granularity of access controls?

   A: Answers will vary. You would want granularity of controls when different users have different requirements on a system.

8. An API is generally considered to be a security enhancement because it protects the inner workings of a software module from casual observation. When would an API also be a security risk?

   A: Answers will vary. If the API has not been well tested, an attacker might find a vulnerability that would cause the API to malfunction and disclose more than it should.

9. What are the decision points when considering using a public versus private code repository?

   A: Answers will vary. A public repository is convenient and easy for most people to access from anywhere. The security of a public repository, however, is only as good as the security practices of the hosting company. With a private repository, you are in control of the server and will (hopefully) have a more secure implementation by virtue of the fact that the server cannot be accessed by the general public. However, it is quite possible for a private implementation to be less secure than a public service.

10. Should the government insist on software escrow for this project?

    A: Answers will vary. Any time you are paying a third party to develop an application, it is always wise to have a provision in which you can retrieve the source code, even if it is unfinished. This is only good business practice. It does not imply mistrust of the vendor to require such a provision.

ACTIVITY 8-5: Discussing the Assessment of the Effectiveness of Software Security

1. What do you tell him?

   A: Answers will vary. A software auditing team is concerned with regulatory compliance and requirements fulfillment, rather than technical quality. Because this application deals with personal health records, it will have particular regulatory and business requirements that must be satisfied.

2. What do you tell her?

   A: Answers will vary. Mostly it means that every time there is a major or minor revision, the version number of the application must be changed before it is released. This will help reduce any confusion caused by mismatched versions.

3. The auditors are trying to determine if your risk analysis and mitigation strategy has followed best practice. What would this entail?

   A: Answers will vary. Mostly this means that you have included risk analysis and mitigation throughout the SDLC and change management process. You have followed recognized standards and frameworks. You have tracked and managed vulnerabilities discovered during risk analysis, and you have ensured that the organization remembers mitigation decisions made and why those decisions were made.

4. **What can you do to verify that the software performs as expected, and has not been modified inappropriately? (Choose two.)**

   ☐ The developer can run unit and system tests on the application.

   ☐ Different developer teams can run integration tests on the application.

   ☑ An independent QA team can test the software according to a strict step-by-step process.

   ☑ The developer team can digitally sign the code before release.

5. **Once the application passes QA testing, what should be done next?**

   ◉ End users should be brought in to acceptance test the application.

   ○ The technical team can certify the application.

   ○ Management can accredit the application.

   ○ The code should be made ready for deployment into production.

6. **After the application passes both security and end user acceptance testing, what should be done next?**

   ◉ The technical team can certify the application.

   ○ Management can accredit the application.

   ○ The code should be made ready for deployment into production.

   ○ The code version number should be changed.

7. **What is the final step that should happen before the application is placed into production?**

   ○ The technical team can certify the application.

   ◉ Management can accredit the application.

   ○ The code version number should be changed.

   ○ End users can verify that the product satisfies a business need.

8. **What do you tell her?**

   A: Answers will vary. It basically means that the NGO developed the application with safety and security in mind. Risk analysis and mitigation was an integral part of the development process, and there was always a mechanism to ensure integrity and security. The NGO also will provide a mechanism to collect end user feedback and problem reporting when the application goes into production.

Mastery Builder 8-1: Assessing Software Development Security

1. **Which of the following phases of the systems lifecycle (SLC) occur after development? (Choose two.)**

   ☐ Implementation

   ☑ Disposal

   ☑ Maintenance

   ☐ Requirements analysis

2. Which of the following is the ideal SLC phase to start incorporating security into?

○ Planning

○ System design

◉ Initiation

○ Testing

3. Which of the following best describes a maturity model?

○ A framework for assessing the organization's presence in a long-standing industry.

○ A framework for assessing the organization's long-term goals.

○ A framework for assessing the comprehensiveness of an organization's policy.

◉ A framework for assessing the sophistication level of an organization's processes.

4. Which of the following describe the Capability Maturity Model (CMM)? (Choose two.)

☐ Maturity levels can be skipped.

☑ Maturity levels cannot be skipped.

☑ The target maturity level for most organizations is Level 3: Defined.

☐ The target maturity level for most organizations is Level 4: Quantitatively Managed.

5. Which of the following best describes an Integrated Product Team (IPT)?

◉ Staff members from multiple disciplines work together to develop systems and programs.

○ Staff members from similar disciplines work together to develop systems and programs.

○ A dedicated team develops systems and programs so that they more efficiently work with existing systems and programs.

○ A dedicated team identifies how new products may be integrated into existing systems and programs.

6. Which of the following best describes an interpreted language?

○ Source code is transformed into object code that is understood by the operating system.

◉ Source code is translated line by line into machine code every time the program is run.

○ It enables the creation of reusable objects in source code.

○ It is faster than compiled code.

7. Which of the following software development models makes it impossible to go back to previous phases in the model?

○ Agile

○ Prototyping

◉ Waterfall

○ Spiral

8. Which of the following best describe the software certification and accreditation process? (Choose two.)

☑ Certification is a risk evaluation of the software.

☐ Accreditation is a risk evaluation of the software.

☐ Management certifies the software does what it's supposed to do; the technical team accredits this certification.

☑ The technical team certifies the software does what it's supposed to; management accredits this certification.

9. Which of the following software development models attempts to find and correct security issues from the onset of writing source code, rather than afterward?

   ○ Agile

   ◉ Cleanroom

   ○ Waterfall

   ○ Prototyping

10. Your organization is finishing development on a smartphone app that allows employees to quickly view the product store when they're on the go, such as when salespeople meet with clients. After you push the app onto each employee's company-provided phone, you get reports from users of the app crashing when they attempt to view pricing information for certain products. According to your development team, this exact error was reported on and fixed during the beta testing phase. However, the IT team that installed the app on users' phones was unaware of any such fix. What is the most likely explanation for this availability-compromising issue?

   ○ You failed to ensure that measures to uphold availability were incorporated in the design phase.

   ○ You failed to ensure that this issue was caught during the testing phase.

   ◉ You failed to ensure that the patched and most up-to-date version of the software was used during the deployment phase.

   ○ You failed to ensure that the developers wrote security-conscious source code during the build phase.

11. Which of the database models requires pointers to locate other entries in the database?

   ○ Object-oriented

   ◉ Network

   ○ Hierarchical

   ○ Relational

12. You organization has sales record databases that track sales across the world. However, a potential conflict arises between these databases when it comes to the date of each sale: dates in the United States follow the MM/DD/YYYY format, whereas dates in Europe follow the DD/MM/YYYY format. Which of the following techniques helps mitigate this conflict to create consistent data coding?

   ◉ Pre-processing with a data warehouse.

   ○ Aggregation with data mining.

   ○ Curation with a data archive.

   ○ Collation with a relational database.

13. Which of the following are characteristics of a data warehouse? (Choose two.)

   ☑ They are typically not updated.

   ☐ They are frequently updated.

   ☐ They contain information about a subject from a single source.

   ☑ They contain information about a subject from various sources.

14. Which of the following is the most significant vulnerability of data aggregation?

   ○ Aggregated data may oversimplify or misrepresent disparate data sets.

   ◉ Too much aggregated data may disclosure sensitive information.

   ○ Aggregated data views cannot be access controlled.

   ○ Aggregating too much data can cause a DoS condition.

15. You have a web-based storefront for customers to purchase your products. Because you have a limited supply of certain products, what type of database control can help limit conflicts that arise when two different people attempt to purchase the last item in stock at the same time?
   - ○ Perturbation
   - ○ Cell suppression
   - ○ Partitioning
   - ◉ Online transaction processing (OLTP) controls

16. Which of the following are advantages of open source software over proprietary software? (Choose two.)
   - ☑ Open source software has more people reviewing the code, spotting vulnerabilities.
   - ☐ Open source software often undergoes an intensive testing process.
   - ☑ Open source software can be repurposed for an organization's specific functional or security needs.
   - ☐ Open source software is constantly and reliably updated.

17. Why might someone who finds a software vulnerability choose full disclosure rather than partial disclosure? (Choose two.)
   - ☐ They believe in giving the vendor a chance to fix the vulnerability before it's known publicly.
   - ☑ They believe that the vendor does not or will not take them seriously.
   - ☑ They believe that everyone affected should know about the vulnerability as quickly as possible.
   - ☐ They believe that only releasing part of what they know about a vulnerability to the public won't adequately explain its significance.

18. How can a programer protect against a buffer overflow vulnerability?
   - ○ Ensure that backdoors are removed from the application before implementation.
   - ○ Perform integrity checks for unwanted additions to the program.
   - ◉ Perform bounds checking on the program's fields.
   - ○ Ensure that the time period between checking data and using data is minimal.

19. Why should a source code analysis tool be only one component of a larger system for identifying and correcting software security issues? (Choose two.)
   - ☐ They operate slowly.
   - ☐ There are all prohibitively expensive.
   - ☑ They are at risk of producing false negatives.
   - ☑ They are at risk of producing false positives.

20. An application that uses password masking protects against which type of attack?
   - ○ Brute force password cracking.
   - ◉ Shoulder surfing.
   - ○ Password guessing.
   - ○ Rainbow tables.

21. Which of the following are best practices for software development change logs? (Choose three.)
   - ☑ They should list version releases with the most recent on top.
   - ☑ Every version of the code should have its own subsection.
   - ☐ They should be written to be more machine readable than human readable.
   - ☑ They should easily link to any section of code.

22. Which of the following best describe a software audit? (Choose two.)

☐ Audits are concerned with the technical accuracy of the software.

☑ Audits are not concerned with the technical accuracy of the software.

☑ Audits are performed by an independent body.

☐ Audits are performed by the development team.

23. When implementing Semantic Versioning, which of the following best describes a "MINOR" revision to software?

◉ When you add backward-compatible functionality.

○ When you make a backward-compatible bug fix.

○ When you make a backward-incompatible API change.

○ When you make a backward-incompatible security fix.

24. Which of the following is not included as part of a software security acceptance test?

○ Testing for input that exceeds normal boundaries.

○ Testing for security policy violations.

◉ Testing for end user productivity impact.

○ Testing illegal input.

25. Which of the following are best practices for acquiring software from a third party vendor? (Choose three.)

☐ Ensure that the vendor has trained their personnel on their own security requirements.

☑ Only contract out to vendors who meet your security baseline standards.

☑ Ensure the vendor has a software assurance process in place.

☑ Implement a risk management strategy for acquiring software.

Glossary

2DES
(Double DES) The same symmetric encryption algorithm as DES with the exception that the encryption process is repeated twice in an attempt to strengthen the output.

3DES
(Triple DES) A symmetric encryption algorithm that uses the DES algorithm but employs three keys to encrypt the same information in three processes.

802.11i
See WPA2.

abstraction
As an OOP term, this is when classes are generalized to the highest, most appropriate level needed to use them.

acceptance
A risk management principle that retains losses when they occur and employs no countermeasures.

acceptance test
A software test where end users try the completed software to see if they like it, can easily use it, and if it satisfies their business requirements.

access control
The process of allowing only authorized users, programs, or other computer systems such as networks to observe, modify, or otherwise take possession of the resources of a computer system or physical property.

access control matrix
A technical access control consisting of a tabular display of access rights.

accountability
The concept of determining what entity can be held responsible for what action.

accounting system
An asset valuation method that references existing asset costs and quantifies potential risk based on logged expenses.

accreditation
The Designated Approving Authority's acceptance of system security risks.

ACID integrity
(atomicity, consistency, isolation, and durability) Database integrity that concentrates on four essential areas of integrity assurance.

ACL
(access control list) A list of permissions that is associated with each object, which specifies the subjects that can access the object and the subjects' level of access. It is used on routers and switches to filter protocols on interfaces, either inbound or outbound.

AD
(Active Directory) Microsoft's LDAP-compatible directory service.

addressing path
The third and last physical computer bus pathway that transfers information between a CPU and an I/O device.

administrative controls
A broad area of security, including policies and procedures, personnel security, monitoring, user and password management, and permission management.

administrative law
The laws set by regulatory agencies. Also known as regulatory law.

Advisory Committee–BCP team
A group of individuals from varying backgrounds within the community who collectively assemble to create the BCP and assist in plan maintenance.

AES
(Advanced Encryption Standard) A symmetric block cipher that has been approved by the U.S. government for encrypting Secret and Top Secret information.

aggregation
A data mining technique used to summarize information found in the data repository. The summarization can be implemented for different reasons.

agile software development
This model uses incremental and iterative rounds of development using cross-functional teams. It encourages short, iterative sessions over long life-cycle development.

AI
(artificial intelligence) A mechanism that attempts to mimic or emulate the process of human intelligence by implementing algorithms that cause the system to learn about its environment and make decisions based on its learning.

ALE
(Annualized Loss Expectancy) An equation factor used to determine risk by estimating the expected loss from each identified threat on an annual basis.

algorithm
In encryption, the rule, system, or mechanism used to encrypt data.

API
(Application Programming Interface) A set of functions an application developer adds to a module of code to allow other processes to request services from that code.

appliance
A specialized networking, single-purpose device with functionality limited to provide support for a single task.

Application layer
An OSI model layer (Layer 7) that provides services and utilities that enable application programs to send information into the communications network.

A TCP/IP model layer that is similar in function to the Session, Presentation, and Application layers of the OSI model. At this layer, application programs begin sending information, and end at the destination device or application.

application state
A CPU mode that can execute only non-privileged instructions, protecting the system from unauthorized activities by user programs.

ARO
(Annualized Rate of Occurrence) An equation percentage factor that determines the likelihood of events and the estimated number of times an identified incident or threat will occur within a year. Also known as Annual Rate of Occurrence.

ARP
(Address Resolution Protocol) A protocol used in the TCP/IP model to determine the MAC address for a known IP address.

ARP poisoning
When an attacker redirects an IP address to a MAC address that was not its intended destination.

array
A data structure that houses collections of primitives that are interrelated.

ASLR
(Address Space Layout Randomization) A security technique in which a data structure in memory is organized in a random manner to make it less predictable and thus harder to exploit.

assembly language
A low-level programming code. The code is processed by an assembler utility to create machine code.

asset
Anything of value that could be compromised, stolen, or harmed, including information, physical resources, and reputation.

asset management system
An asset valuation method that provides an asset value based on accounting principles, detailed records of corporate property, and similar assets.

asset valuation
A method of determining how much an asset is worth to an organization.

asymmetric encryption
A two-way encryption scheme that uses paired private and public keys.

asynchronous messaging
A data services function where the sender and receiver are not directly and simultaneously interacting, and some delay is included in the communication process. Email is an asynchronous messaging protocol.

asynchronous token system
The user is sent a small amount of text or a number. When the user enters it into a device, the device will create a separate code that the user then combines with his password to authenticate to the system.

ATM
(Asynchronous Transfer Mode) A protocol used to move all types of data at high speeds in a fiber-based network.

atomicity
The first component of ACID integrity that ensures the completion of all tasks associated with a particular transaction.

attack
The intentional act of attempting to bypass one or more security services or controls of an information system.

attribute
A column, or field, in a database.

audit committee
A structural faction of an organization that is responsible for ensuring legal adherence and regulation compliance.

audit log
In information security, an electronic record of operating system, application, and security information. Also known as an audit file.

AV
(Asset Value) An equation factor used to determine impact by containing the value of the asset prior to a damage-causing event.

availability
The fundamental principle of ensuring that systems operate continuously and that authorized persons can access data that they need.

avalanche effect
A process found in a cipher that causes a very small change in the plaintext to produce a very large change in the ciphertext.

avoidance
A risk management principle that eliminates threats through mitigation, thereby significantly reducing risk.

backdoor
A mechanism for gaining access to a computer that bypasses or subverts the normal method of authentication.

backdoor attack

A software attack where the attacker creates a software mechanism to gain access to a system and its resources. This can involve software or a bogus user account.

baiting

A form of social engineering in which an attacker leaves infected physical media in an area where a victim finds it and then inserts it into a computer.

bandwidth limiter

See traffic shaper.

baseline

A security document that specifies the minimum security required in a system or process.

bastion host

A server that provides a very special function with everything else stripped away. It is traditionally hardened to withstand attack.

BCP

(Business Continuity Plan) A policy that defines how normal day-to-day business will be maintained in the event of a business disruption or crisis.

best practices

Commonly accepted activities related to business operations.

BIA

(business impact analysis) A BCP phase that identifies present organizational risks and determines the impact to ongoing, business-critical operations if risks are actualized.

Biba Model

An integrity model that uses integrity levels to depict the trust level of the information.

Big Data

A general term that refers to data sets that are so huge and complex that they cannot be processed through traditional means.

birthday attack

A type of cryptographic attack that exploits weaknesses in the mathematical algorithms used to encrypt passwords, to take advantage of the probability of different password inputs producing the same encrypted output.

black box

A test in which the tester is given no information about the system being tested.

blacklisting

The process of blocking specific systems, software, services, etc., from using a resource. Anything not on the list is allowed.

blackout

A power failure in which all power is lost.

blind testing

A type of penetration test where the target organization is not aware of testing activities.

block cipher

A type of symmetric encryption that encrypts data a block at a time, often in 64-bit or 128-bit blocks. It is usually more secure, but is also slower, than stream ciphers.

Blowfish

A freely available 64-bit block cipher algorithm that uses a variable key length.

BLP Model

(Bell-LaPadula) A confidentiality model that limits the access to classified objects to those subjects with an equal or higher clearance.

bollard

An obstacle designed to stop a vehicle.

botnet

A group of computers or an entire network of computers that is taken over by malware without the knowledge of the network's owner.

BPA

(business partnership agreement) An agreement that defines how a business partnership will be conducted.

Brewer–Nash Model

A security model that relates to the control of the conflict of interest in a computer system.

brownout

A long-term, low-voltage power failure during which lights go dim for an extended period of time.

brute force

A type of password attack where an attacker uses an application to exhaustively try every possible alphanumeric combination to try to crack encrypted passwords and circumvent the authentication system.

buffer overflow

An attack against the buffers that are written into applications and hardware devices.

A TCB vulnerability that moves too much information into a program memory area.

bus topology

A network topology in which network nodes are arranged in a linear format.

CA

(certificate authority) A server that issues certificates and the associated public/private key pairs.

cable modem

A specialized interface device used in a cable television infrastructure to provide high-speed Internet access to homes and small businesses.

cache memory

A category of RAM used to expedite access to security instructions that require processing.

CAN

(campus area network) A network that covers an area equivalent to an academic or enterprise campus.

cardinality

In databases, the types of relationships that are available.

CASE

(Computer-Aided Software Engineering) The adoption of tools and techniques to help with large-scale software projects.

CAST-128

A symmetric encryption algorithm with a 128-bit key, named for its developers, Carlisle Adams and Stafford Tavares.

CBC

(Cipher Block Chaining) A block cipher mode wherein 64-bit plaintext blocks are XORed with a 64-bit IV and then encrypted using the key.

CCTV

(closed-circuit television) A visual recording device that uses video cameras to transmit images to monitors and video recorders. It is placed in strategic locations in an organization to record movement or actions of employees.

CDN

(content delivery network) A large distributed system of servers that serve web content to end users via the Internet.

cell

The intersection, or value, of a row and column in a database.

cell suppression

Intentionally hiding cells containing highly confidential information. The cells may be suppressed for everyone or they might be suppressed based on the ID of the user accessing the data.

centralized access control

The process of administering access controls at a centralized site.

CER

(crossover error rate) Where FRR and FAR biometric errors intersect on a graph; the biometric measurement with the lowest CER provides the best protection.

certificate management system

A system that provides the software tools to perform the day-to-day functions of the PKI.

certificate repository

A database containing digital certificates.

certification

A risk evaluation of information system security.

CFAA

(Computer Fraud and Abuse Act) Legislation passed in 1984 to protect government systems from illegal access or from exceeding access permissions. Amended in 1994, 1996, and 2001 to extend coverage to new types of attacks.

CFB

(Cipher FeedBack) A block cipher mode wherein the IV is first encrypted using the key and then XORed with the plaintext to create the ciphertext.

chain of custody

The record of evidence handling from collection through presentation in court.

chain of evidence

The record of evidence history from collection, to presentation in court, to disposal.

chaining

A method for strengthening block ciphers in which the results of one cipher step alter the encryption process for the subsequent step.

change control

A formal process of tracking hardware and software changes to ensure they are properly authorized and implemented and follow procedural specifications. Also see change management.

change management

The process through which changes to the configuration of information systems are monitored and controlled.

CHAP

(Challenge-Handshake Authentication Protocol) An encrypted remote-access authentication method that enables connections from any authentication method requested by the server, except for PAP unencrypted authentication.

CI

(configuration item) An asset stored in a configuration management database (CMDB).

CIA triad

(confidentiality, integrity, and availability) The same as the information security triad. Also called triple or triangle.

cipher

An algorithm used to encrypt, decrypt, or hash information.

ciphertext

The coded, encrypted form of data.

CIRT

(computer incident response team) A team comprising individuals from IT, HR, legal, and others trained to respond appropriately to security events.

civil law

The legal category that governs a wrong committed against a business or individual resulting in damage or loss to that business or individual.

Clark–Wilson Model

An integrity model that relates trust to the integrity of the processes surrounding the data.

class

As an OOP term, this defines the general characteristics of a type of object, including attributes, fields, and operations.

classification

A labeling scheme that measures the risk of information loss or modification.

cleanroom model

The idea that in software development, it is easier and cheaper to eliminate defects before code is written, rather than trying to remove them afterwards.

cleartext

The original form of a message. Also referred to as plaintext.

clickjacking

An attack that forces a user to unintentionally click a link. An attacker uses opaque layers or multiple transparent layers to trick a user.

clipping level

In security auditing, a logging technique that sets a limit on the number of log records created for a given incident.

closed shop

A security control method in which only authorized users are allowed access to system information.

CMDB

(Configuration Management Database) A central repository that stores information about all the significant items in an IT environment and configuration management information.

CMM

(Capability Maturity Model) An evaluation model that indicates the level of sophistication or maturity found in an organization's software development process.

CMMI

(Capability Maturity Model Integration) A process improvement project initiative that incorporates the different CMMs into one cohesive collection of integrated models.

COBIT 5

(Control Objectives for Information and related Technologies) A security framework for security governance best practices developed by the ISACA.

code book

An alternative cipher. A book or booklet that contains a series of codes that are used to represent common words or phrases that might be used in communication.

codification

Laws, rules, and regulations that are documented and grouped by subject.

cohesion

The level of independence of software modules of the same application. A highly cohesive module is highly independent from other modules.

cold site

A predetermined alternate location where a network can be rebuilt after a disaster.

collaboration

The use of technology to conduct virtual meetings between two or more participants, usually in different locations.

collision

When a hash function generates identical output from different input.

COM

(Component Object Model) A Microsoft technology used to create reusable software components that can be linked together to create applications. The links may be between one or more applications running on the same machine.

Common Criteria

A security standard where security targets can be submitted by consumers and describe system protection expectations. It was developed to replace TCSEC and ITSEC and published by the ISO/IEC.

common law

A set of unwritten but well-understood and normally accepted principles of justice.

compartmentalization

Complements least privilege and need to know by separating and isolating subjects that work on different projects.

compensating control

A control that is implemented when the system cannot provide protection required by policy in order to mitigate the risk down to an acceptable level.

compensating controls

In OPSEC, controls that mitigate the lack of another control.

compiled language

A program language where source code is run through a compiler.

compiler

A program that transforms the source of code of a higher level language to object code that is understood by the device or operating system.

compliance

The awareness of and adherence to relevant laws and regulations that are set forth by and apply to a particular corporation, public agency, or organizational entity.

computer bus

The set of physical connections between devices that are attached to a computer's motherboard.

computer crime

A criminal act that involves the use of a computer as the source or target, instead of an individual.

computer forensics

A skill that deals with analyzing data from storage devices, computer systems, networks, and wireless communications, and presenting this information as a form of evidence in a court of law.

concentrator

A network device that connects multiple links to a signal destination.

confidentiality

The fundamental principle of keeping information and communications private and protecting them from unauthorized access.

configuration management

The process used to track hardware and software components in an enterprise to ensure that existing configurations match implementation standards.

The process through which an organization's information systems components are kept in a controlled state that meets the organization's requirements, including those for security and compliance.

confusion

An encryption technique used to create a complex cipher by mixing up the key values.

consistency

The second component of ACID integrity that requires database stability before and after a transaction.

constrained interfaces access control

An access control technique that limits access to information by constraining the interface.

contact card

A smart card that has small metal contacts and must be used with its corresponding reader.

contactless card

A smart card that uses radio waves and must be used in close proximity to a reader.

content dependent access control

An access control technique that limits a subject's access to objects by examining object data to see if the subject has access rights.

context dependent access control

An access control technique where the context of the request is determined before processing.

continuous improvement

The ongoing effort to continually optimize policies and processes in order to identify and mitigate potential risks before they affect the organization.

control

A countermeasure that you put in place to avoid, mitigate, or counteract security risks due to threats or attacks.

control framework

A structure for organizing security controls in an organization.

cookie

A text file that a browser downloads from a website that is used to identify the same browser when the user visits the site later.

COPPA

(Children's Online Privacy Protection Act) Legislation passed in 1998 to protect the online privacy of children. Includes the right to opt out of any information sent by a provider, to limit the amount and type of information collected from children, and to require parental consent for any information provided to children.

copyright
Intellectual property law that protects original material created by an author or a musician.

CORBA
(Common Object Request Broker Architecture) An open, vendor-neutral object broker framework that provides functionality similar to DCOM.

corrective control
A control that responds to the security violation to reduce or completely eliminate the impact.

corrective controls
In OPSEC, controls such as file backup restorations that remedy problems caused by security setbacks.

COTS
(commercial off-the-shelf) A standard product that can be purchased from a retail channel.

coupling
The degree and complexity of interaction among modules in an application.

covert channel
An unauthorized communications path wherein unexpected data flows are detected by the Information Flow Model.

covert storage
A TCB vulnerability where a file saved by one process should be unavailable to another process, but the second process may be able to learn information just by seeing that a file exists.

covert timing
A TCB vulnerability where the watching process is able to monitor the traffic or CPU utilization and make determinations based on this information.

CPTED
(Crime Prevention Through Environmental Design) A technique that uses landscape design and physical layout to reduce crime.

CPU
(Central Processing Unit) The computer component that executes security instructions that allow a computer system to operate successfully.

CRC
(Cyclical Redundancy Check) A function used by Ethernet to detect transmission errors in the Data Link layer of the OSI model.

criminal law
The legal category that governs individual conduct violating government laws enacted for public or societal protection.

critical business process
An activity that, if not recovered, can lead to business loss or failure.

CRL
(Certificate Revocation List) A list of the serial numbers of revoked or otherwise invalid certificates that is maintained by a CA and made available to CA users.

cryptanalysis
The study of cryptosytems with the intent of breaking them.

cryptography
The analysis and practice of information concealment for the purpose of securing sensitive data transmissions.

cryptology
The study of both cryptography and cryptanalysis.

cryptosystem
The general term used or the hardware and/or software used to implement a cryptographic process.

crystal
An agile software development methodology that addresses the unique characteristics of different projects.

CSA
(Computer Security Act) Legislation passed in 1987 to protect computer systems and fulfill training needs and plan developments for

information and systems security. Replaced by FISMA in 2002.

CSMA
(Carrier Sense Multiple Access) A protocol used to determine if there is anyone else on the network as it gets ready to transmit data.

CSMA/CA
(Carrier Sense Multiple Access with Collision Avoidance) A mode of CSMA that will jam the transmission of other nodes in order to prevent collisions.

CSMA/CD
(Carrier Sense Multiple Access with Collision Detection) A mode of the CSMA protocol in which nodes listen for traffic before transmitting in order to avoid collisions.

CTCPEC
(Canadian Trusted Computer Product Evaluation Criteria) A publication released in 1992 by the Canadian System Security Centre (CSSC) to address gaps in the Orange Book.

CTR
(Counter) A block cipher mode where a counter provides the IV.

cyber-physical system
See embedded device.

DAC
(discretionary access control) A means of restricting access to objects based on the identity of the subjects and/or groups to which they belong.

data access service
A function that mediates the access of data over a network.

data at rest
Data that resides on a storage medium for long-term retention.

data backup
Copies of data captured at a point in time and stored in a secure area as a precautionary safeguard in case of a disaster.

data breach
An incident that results in the release or potential exposure of secure information.

data exchange service
A protocol that allows individuals to access information on a central server and, in some cases, transfer that information to the individuals' local computers.

data in transit
Data that moves from one type of medium to another.

Data Link layer
An OSI model layer (Layer 2) that organizes bits into frames. Most Data Link layer protocols define the structure of a frame.

data mining
The practice of analyzing large amounts of data to locate previously unknown or hidden information.

data network
A collection of hardware and software that allows the exchange of information between sending and receiving application processes.

data path
The first of three physical computer bus pathways that transfers information between a CPU and an I/O device.

data remanence
An electronic property where faulty information is left on media during the file erasure and deletion process.

data services
The functions that are provided and the applications that are accessible by connecting devices to a network.

data structure
A standardized format for storing information in a computer system so that this information can be efficiently accessed.

data warehouse
A pre-processed database that contains information about a specific subject from

various sources, and is used for subsequent reporting and analysis.

database
A data structure in which the data environment uses primitives, arrays, lists, and matrices to store and present data to applications.

database integrity
An assurance that data stored within a database is accurate and valid and not unknowingly altered or deleted. Also known as ACID integrity.

database system
A set of related information organized within a software framework for ease of access and reporting.

DCOM
(Distributed Component Object Model) A Microsoft extension of COM that allows for components to be located throughout the network.

DDoS
(distributed denial of service) A software attack that uses multiple source machines to perpetrate a logical DoS against a chosen victim.

deadlock
A database vulnerability wherein two or more competing processes are waiting for the other to release a particular resource.

decentralized access control
The process of administering access control elements that are found in distributed locations throughout the enterprise.

decipher
The same as decryption.

decryption
A security technique that transforms encrypted data into a readable form, revealing the content.

defense in depth
A risk concept that uses a layered approach to mitigate security threats at multiple levels within the networks and systems. Also known as layered defense.

degaussing
A purging technique that removes all data from magnetic media.

Delphi method
A systematic and interactive communication technique that involves iteratively questioning a panel of independent experts to obtain asset value forecasts.

deluge
A water-based extinguishing system wherein high output sprinklers in wet or dry pipe systems saturate the affected area.

demonstrative evidence
Evidence that is used to demonstrate or explain events, such as the use of a model to explain how a computer crime was committed.

DES
(Data Encryption Standard) A symmetric block algorithm that uses a 64-bit block and a 64-bit key.

detective control
A control that alerts the security professionals to the attempted security violation.

detective controls
In OPSEC, controls such as an IDS that discover the location of unauthorized access infiltration or unauthorized access attempts in a system.

deterrent control
A control that discourages individuals from violating security policies because of the effort to circumvent it or the negative consequences of doing so.

deterrent controls
In OPSEC, controls that encourage compliance with security guidelines and practices.

DH
(Diffie-Hellman) A cryptographic protocol that provides for secure key exchange.

DHCP
(Dynamic Host Configuration Protocol) A protocol used to assign IP addresses to devices in an IP network.

DHE
(Diffie-Hellman Ephemeral) A variant of DH that uses ephemeral keys to provide secure key exchange.

Diameter
An authentication protocol that allows for a variety of connection types, such as wireless.

dictionary attack
A type of cryptographic attack that automates password guessing by comparing encrypted passwords against a predetermined list of possible password values.

differential backup
A method that copies all modifications since the last full backup to the backup media.

diffusion
An encryption technique used to create a complex cipher by mixing up the plaintext.

digital certificate
An electronic document that associates credentials with a public key.

digital forensics
See computer forensics.

digital signature
An encrypted hash value that is appended to a message to identify the sender and the message.

digital watermarking
The steganographic process of embedding source data within media to enforce copyright protection.

direct evidence
Evidence received from the testimony of an individual who observed the crime or activity. Evidence that clearly indicates that the crime was committed and proves the case on its own merits.

directive control
A control that specifies expected employee behavior and can often take the form of policies and guidelines.

directive controls
In OPSEC, controls such as corporate security policies that provide guidance.

distributed system architecture
A network architecture that is used for systems in which a number of computers are networked together and share application processes and data.

DLP
(data loss prevention) Software that stops data in a system from being stolen.

DMZ
(demilitarized zone) A small section of a private network that is located between two routers and made available for secure public access.

DNP3
(Distributed Network Protocol) A communications protocol for industrial machinery and other automated systems.

DNS
(Domain Name Service) A protocol used to resolve or translate device and domain names into IP addresses using a central repository.

DNS cache poisoning
An attack that corrupts the lookup database of a local Domain Name System server, replacing correct IP addresses with false information, thus redirecting clients to fake web servers.

DNSSEC
(Domain Name System Security Extension) A set of specifications that provide authentication and other security mechanisms to DNS data.

DOM–based attack
(Direct Object Model-based attack) An attack where an attacker executes malicious scripts solely on the client of a web app that uses JavaScript.

DoS

(denial of service) Any attack that will render a service, server, or system unavailable. DoS can happen at the physical layer and/or the logical layer.

drivers

Software modules that interface between the operating system and the I/O devices.

DRM

(Digital Rights Management) A set of services used to protect intellectual property.

DRP

(Disaster Recovery Plan) A policy that defines how people and resources will be protected in case of a natural or man-made disaster, and how the organization will recover from the disaster.

dry pipe

A water-based extinguishing system wherein the pipes are not filled with water until a fire is detected. Sprinkler heads can be individually activated or activated by a system.

DS

(directory service) A data services technology used to provide information about users and resources in a computer network.

DSDM

(Dynamic Systems Development Method) An agile software development methodology that provides a framework for planning, managing, executing, and scaling application development.

DSL

(Digital Subscriber Line) An Internet access protocol that uses telephone lines and digital signaling at high frequencies to attach users to the telephone company-supplied ISPs.

dual-homed firewall

Hardware that has two network interfaces. It establishes the perimeter between the trusted and untrusted network.

due care

Establishes the generally recognized expectations of behavior that companies or entities in a given industry must adhere to when performing normal business functions.

due diligence

The research necessary for good decision making regarding preventive measures to avoid harm to other entities or their property

dumpster diving

A human-based attack where the goal is to reclaim important information by inspecting the contents of trash containers.

duplexing

Writing data to a disk using multiple drive controllers and multiple disks. It provides very high reliability, a higher cost, and slightly longer write times than striping.

durability

The fourth component of ACID integrity that ensures transaction stability upon notification to the user of transaction completion.

e-discovery

The process of identification, collection, and retention of electronic data to prepare for litigation.

EAP

(Extensible Authentication Protocol) An authentication protocol that enables systems to use hardware-based identifiers, such as fingerprint scanners or smart card readers, for authentication.

EAR

(Export Administration Regulations) A federal regulation that controls the export of certain technology.

ECB

(Electronic Code Book) A block cipher mode that breaks the plaintext down into 64-bit blocks and then encrypts each block separately.

ECC

(elliptic curve cryptography) A public-key, asymmetric encryption algorithm that is based on developments in discrete logs and requires short keys.

ECDHE

(Elliptic Curve Diffie-Hellman Ephemeral) A variant of DH that incorporates the use of ECC and ephemeral keys.

ECPA

(Electronic Communications Privacy Act) Legislation passed in 1986 to protect the privacy of educational information held in any federally funded institution of higher learning.

EF

(Exposure Factor) An equation factor used to determine impact by estimating the damage or loss caused by one event.

egress monitoring

The process of analyzing data sent outside the network to determine if the action is authorized.

EJB

(Enterprise JavaBean) A tool from Sun Microsystems that allows for distributed multi-tier application in Java.

electronic vaulting

A data backup method used to copy modified files to an offsite location.

Elgamal

A public-key, asymmetric encryption algorithm developed by Taher Elgamal.

emanation

A software attack where protected information is leaked through the natural process of electrons passing through a wire or over the radio.

embedded device

A small computer system that performs a dedicated function in a physical device. Also called a cyber-physical system.

encapsulation

As an OOP term, this is when the functional details of a class are concealed or masked from the calling objects.

encipher

The same as encrypt.

encryption

A security technique that converts data from its ordinary, intelligible state, or plaintext form, into coded, or ciphertext form so that only authorized parties with the necessary decryption information can decode and read the data.

endpoint security

A comprehensive solution that secures laptops and mobile devices as they remotely connect to the organization's network.

enticement

The practice of attracting criminals to repeat a particular illegal act as a means to catch them.

entity

A term of reference that identifies multiple things in security access control, such as a user or computer program.

entity integrity

This requires that each tuple in a database has a unique primary key that is not null, thereby assuring uniqueness.

entrapment

The practice of capturing an individual at a crime scene who did not have criminal intentions to perform an illegal act.

error handling

See exception handling.

ESA

(Enterprise Security Architecture) The part of your enterprise design that focuses on company-wide security.

Ethernet

A LAN and CAN protocol that supports communication between devices at the Physical and Data Link layers of the OSI model.

ethics

Pertaining to a profession or an organization, refers to the principles of acceptable and proper conduct as well as the internal moral value system.

event log
A file that contains detailed information about performance and security problems.

exception handling
The programming technique of responding to errors in execution.

expert system
An extended AI and KBS system that provides problem-solving assistance. Equipped with a knowledge base of information about a specific subject area such as a medical diagnosis.

exploit
A technique that takes advantage of a vulnerability to perform an attack.

extranet
See DMZ.

facility control system
A set of support information services that combine with physical security protection processes to protect and limit access to facilities.

factoring attack
A type of cryptographic attack that attempts to determine the prime numbers used in asymmetric encryption as a means to break cryptosystems.

Fair Cryptosystems
In cryptography, an escrow method that allows a key to be split into "N" parts that re-create the original key.

FAR
(false acceptance rate) A biometric error where an unauthorized individual is given access.

fault tolerance
A system property in which a single component fault does not cause a complete system failure. Often enabled through redundancy.

FCoE
(Fibre Channel over Ethernet) Fibre Channel implementations that use high-speed Ethernet networks to transmit and store data.

federated identity
A single identity that is propagated through multiple disparate systems.

FERPA
(Family Educational Rights and Privacy Act) Protects the privacy of educational information held in any federally funded institution of higher learning. Passed in the same session of Congress as the Privacy Act of 1974.

firewall
A software program or hardware device that protects networks from unauthorized data by blocking unsolicited traffic.

firmware
Small chips designed to hold a small set of instructions to assist devices.

FISMA
(Federal Information Security Management Act) Legislation passed in 2002 to remedy the evolutionary nature of information systems security in the federal government.

flat file
An early storage mechanism for computer data.

foreign key
In databases, a cell value in one table that refers to a unique key in a different table, thus enabling the creation of relations between tables.

frequency analysis
A method for breaking encryption when simple substitution algorithms are used. It is based on the fact that certain letters will statistically appear more often than others.

front-end processor
A device that is placed between an input or output device and the computer's central processor.

FRR
(false rejection rate) A biometric error where an authorized individual is denied access.

FTP
(File Transfer Protocol) A protocol that transfers files from one device to another over TCP/IP.

full backup
A method that backs up all selected files. It is used as a starting point for all backup activities that copies all information to the backup media.

full disclosure
This involves releasing information regarding security flaws immediately and publicly.

full-duplex
A Session-layer communication mode that allows for simultaneous, two-way data transmission.

function point
A unit of measurement used to size software applications and convey the quantity of business functionality that an information system offers its users.

functional test
A software test that tests a specific functionality in an application.

fuzzing
A testing method used to identify vulnerabilities and weaknesses in an application, by sending the application a range of random or unusual input data and noting failures and crashes.

gateway
A network device that converts data between incompatible systems.

generator
A power protection device that creates its own electricity through the use of motors.

GLBA
(Gramm-Leach-Bliley Act) Legislation passed in 1999 to protect the privacy of an individual's financial information that is held by financial institutions and others such as tax preparation companies.

governance
Pertaining to an organization, refers to the organization's methods of exercising authority or control as well as its system of management.

Graham-Denning Model
A security model that deals with the creation and deletion of objects and subjects, as well as the reading, granting, deleting, and transferring of access rights.

grant and revoke access control
Controls that extend the right to give access to others.

grey box test
A test in which the tester may have knowledge of internal architectures and systems, or other preliminary information about the system being tested.

guessing
A human-based attack where the goal is to guess a password or PIN through brute force means or by using deduction.

guideline
A security document that recommends or suggests a specific action, implementation, or use of tools as a best practice for meeting the policy standard.

half-duplex
A Session-layer communication mode where data transmission occurs in both directions, but is restricted to one direction at a time.

Harrison-Ruzzo-Ullman Model
A security model used for changing access rights and creating and deleting subjects or objects.

hash
The value that results from hashing encryption. The same as hash value and message digest.

hash value
The same as hash.

hashing
One-way encryption that transforms cleartext into ciphertext that is never decrypted.

HAVAL

A modified MD5 hash algorithm that produces 128-bit, 160-bit, 192-bit, 224-bit, and 256-bit hash values.

hearsay evidence

Evidence that is presented by an individual who was not a direct observer but who heard, or received word, about the event from others. Computer records are considered hearsay because they cannot directly testify.

heat detector

A perimeter IDS that is installed to measure temperature increases emitted from a heat source such as a human, fire, or animal.

HIDS

(host-based intrusion detection system) Software that is installed on a host computer to monitor and detect host and network traffic anomalies and report the anomalies to the network administrator.

Hierarchical Database Management Model

A database system model that is implemented in a tree-like structure with relationships that are created with a parent-child view.

hijacking

The act of taking the place of a client in a client/server session after the client has authenticated to the server.

HIPAA

(Health Insurance Portability and Accountability Act) Legislation passed in 1996 to protect people with health insurance when they transferred from one company to another. Modified in 2003 to add a privacy component that protects a class of information called the Protected Health Information (PHI).

HIPS

(host-based intrusion prevention system) An application that is installed on the host and is designed to monitor host and network activity that affects that host to block suspicious network and system traffic in real time and report findings to the network administrator.

HMAC

(Hash-based Message Authentication Code) An authentication code algorithm that creates a hash of a file that is then encrypted for transmission.

honeynet

An entire dummy network used to lure attackers.

honeypot

A security tool used to lure attackers away from the actual network components.

Host-to-Host layer

A TCP/IP model layer that is similar in function to the Transport layer of the OSI model. This layer's protocols support application-to-application information transfer using port numbers to identify applications.

hot site

A fully configured alternate network that can be online quickly after a disaster. Also known as a mirror site.

HTTP

(Hypertext Transfer Protocol) A protocol that transfers web page data from one device to another over TCP/IP.

HTTPS

(Hypertext Transfer Protocol Secure) A secure version of HTTP that supports web commerce by providing a secure connection between the web browser and server. It is a combination of HTTP and SSL/TLS. The SSL/TLS component will provide encryption and identification to the HTTP protocol, thereby providing secure communications between the connecting devices.

hub

A network device that transmits signals to every node in a network.

HVAC system

(heating, ventilation, and air conditioning) A physical system that controls the environment inside a building.

hybrid access control
The process of administering access controls in centralized and decentralized domains.

I/O
(input/output) Devices that provide input to and output from a computer system. Secondary storage is a form of I/O device.

IA
(interoperability agreement) The general term for any document that outlines a business partnership or collaboration in which all entities exchange some resources while working together.

ICMP
(Internet Control Message Protocol) A protocol used by operating systems and network devices to send error messages or relay messages back to devices that are available.

IDaaS
(Identity-as-a-Service) An authentication infrastructure that can be thought of as cloud-based single sign-on.

IDEA
(International Data Encryption Algorithm) A block cipher first proposed in 1991 that is used in Open PGP.

identity management
The process of controlling how users and other entities are recognized in various systems.

IDS
(intrusion detection system) A hardware or software solution that identifies and addresses potential attacks on a computer (or host) or a network.

IGMP
(Internet Group Management Protocol) A protocol used with IP multicasting to indicate when a device is joining a multicast-enabled application data stream.

IKE
(Internet Key Exchange) Used by IPSec to create a master key, which in turn is used to generate bulk encryption keys for encrypting data.

IM
(instant messaging) A synchronous messaging protocol where participants in the communication process are online and send and receive messages to and from each other at the same time.

IMAP
(Internet Message Access Protocol) An email retrieval protocol that allows a user to view the mail on the server and retrieve the mail from a host of their choosing.

in-rush
A surge or spike that is caused when a device is started that uses a great amount of current.

incremental backup
A method that clears the archive bit and reduces backup time and media by only copying files and databases that have been modified since the last full backup.

inference
A data mining technique used to review data trends and formulate predictions about the subject matter.

Information Flow Model
A security model that controls the direction of data flow among the various security levels when allowed.

information privacy law
Law protecting the information of private individuals from malicious disclosure or unintentional misuse.

information security triad
The three principles of security control and management: confidentiality, integrity, and availability. Also called the CIA triad or triple.

infrared device
A motion sensor that emits a beam of infrared light that is sensed by the receiver. Has a limited distance of operation.

initiator
An iSCSI client machine.

instruction path

The second of three physical computer bus pathways that transfers information between a CPU and an I/O device.

insurance valuation

An asset valuation method that relies on insurers to accept the risk of loss for the assets they insure and to perform an analysis of the risk associated with the policies they issue.

integer overflow

An attack in which a computed result is too large to fit in its assigned storage space, leading to crashing, corruption, or triggering a buffer overflow.

integration test

A software test in which individual components of a system are tested together to see if they interact as expected.

integrity

The fundamental principle of ensuring that electronic data is accurate and free of error or unauthorized modification.

In asymmetric encryption, it is supported when the sender encrypts using the sender's private key and the receiver decrypts with the sender's public key.

intellectual property law

Law that protects the rights of ownership of ideas through trademarks, patents, and copyrights, including the owners' right to transfer intellectual property and receive compensation for the transfer.

interface test

A type of software integration test that focuses on the interface between two systems/applications.

interpreted language

A program language that is not put through a compiler, but rather uses an interpreter that translates the code line by line into machine code each time the application is run.

IoT

(Internet of Things) A network of physical objects that includes more than just computing devices.

IP

(Internet Protocol) A protocol used to move information between nodes on an IP network.

IP fragmentation attack

An attack in which maliciously crafted pieces of an IP packet (IP fragments) are sent to the target.

IPPD

(integrated product and process development) A technique for using multidisciplinary teams to optimize design, development, and deployment.

IPS

(intrusion prevention system) A computer security monitoring device that tracks and blocks suspicious and malicious activities to prevent damage to a system or network.

IPSec

(Internet Protocol security) A set of open, non-proprietary standards that you can use to secure data as it travels across the network or the Internet through data authentication, hashing, and encryption.

iQN

(iSCSI Qualified Name) A unique identifier assigned to clients in an iSCSI architecture.

ISA

(interconnection security agreement) A agreement that focuses on securing technology in a business relationship.

ISCM

(Information Security Continuous Monitoring) The ongoing process of identifying controls, vulnerabilities, and threats as they relate to the organization's risk management policies.

iSCSI

(Internet Small Computer System Interface) A protocol that implements links between data storage networks using IP.

ISO 27002

This document is the current international standard for information systems security.

ISO/IEC 27001

A formal standard that is concerned with the standardization of a company's Information Security Management System (ISMS).

isolation

The third component of ACID integrity wherein transactions and database processes cannot discern the progress of other, simultaneous transactions.

ITAM

(IT Asset Management)The process of collecting inventory, financial, and contractual data to manage an IT asset throughout its lifecycle.

ITAR

(International Traffic in Arms Regulation) A federal regulation that controls the import and export of defense-related goods and services.

ITIL

(Information Technology Infrastructure Library) An IT management structure developed by the United Kingdom's OGC that includes concepts and techniques for conducting development, infrastructure, and operations management.

ITSEC

(Information Technology Security Evaluation Criteria) A security standard developed in Europe that evaluates systems based on targets provided by the customer, against the vendors.

IV

(initialization vector) A string of bits that is used with the cipher and the key to produce a unique result when the same key is used to encrypt the same cleartext.

JDBC

(Java Database Connectivity) A database interface language that allows Java-based programs to access databases transparently.

job rotation

A security principle that encourages organizations to build a highly qualified staff by exposing employees to different job areas.

kanban

An Agile software development methodology that focuses on continual delivery, while not overburdening the development team.

KBS

(knowledge-based system) A program that uses knowledge-based techniques to support human decision making, learning, and action.

Kerberos

A single sign-on (SSO) method where the user enters access credentials that are then passed to the Authentication Server (AS), which contains the allowed access credentials.

kernel mode

See supervisor state.

key

In cryptography, a specific piece of information that is used with an algorithm to perform encryption and decryption.

In databases, an attribute that provides a unique value in a tuple or row that uniquely identifies that row.

key clustering

An encryption anomaly in which two different keys generate the same ciphertext from the same plaintext.

key escrow

In cryptography, the process of splitting a key into two parts and storing each part with a different escrow agency.

key generation

A process of generating a public and private key pair using a specific application.

keyspace

Key size; the total number of keys available from a key of a given size. A 32-bit key allows for over four billion possible keys.

keystroke logging
An attack in which an attacker captures a user's keyboard input.

KPI
(key performance indicator) A quantifiable unit of measure (metric) that an organization uses to gauge its own performance.

L2TP
(Layer 2 Tunneling Protocol) A protocol that combines PPTP and L2F to provide for authentication but not for confidentiality. L2TP allows for the use of additional protocols like IPSec to provide encryption and confidentiality.

LAN
(local area network) A self-contained network that spans a small area, such as a single building, floor, or room.

Lattice Model
A security model used to implement mandatory access controls where data is classified or labeled and users are cleared for access.

layered protection
In computer architecture, the process of building security into various hardware, firmware, and software components. In physical security, a mechanism that begins from the perimeter, or outermost boundary of a facility, and continues inward through the building grounds, entry points, and interior. Also known as layered defense or defense in depth.

LDAP
(Lightweight Directory Access Protocol) A simple network protocol used to access network directory databases, which store information about authorized users and their privileges, as well as other organizational information.

LDAPS
(Lightweight Directory Access Protocol Secure or Secure LDAP) A method of implementing LDAP using SSL/TLS encryption.

lean
An Agile software development methodology that focuses on eliminating waste.

LEAP
(Lightweight Extensible Authentication Protocol) A protocol that establishes mutual authentication and generates WEP keys for wireless communication.

least privilege
A security principle that ensures employees and other system users have only the minimum set of rights, permissions, and privileges that they need to accomplish their jobs.

liability
A legal responsibility for any damage caused by one individual or company to another.

licensing
Intellectual property law that protects materials in use by an individual or organization other than the creator.

link encryption
An Internet security device that is attached to each end of a transmission line to encrypt and decrypt data.

list
A data structure that contains ordered arrays.

LLR
(lessons learned report) A document that provides an analysis of security events and incidents that can provide insight into directions you may take to enhance security for the future.

lock controls
Controls that temporarily give exclusive access to a record to a single user or process.

log management infrastructure
A software application that consolidates logs from all devices.

logic bomb
Malicious software that stays hidden and dormant on a system until an event such as a date or remote command detonates it.

MaaS

(Malware-as-a-Service) Anything that can be profitable for legitimate business that can be lucrative for criminals as well, offered by organized criminal groups.

MAC

(mandatory access control) A means of restricting access to objects based on the sensitivity of the information contained in the objects and the formal authorization of subjects to access information of such sensitivity.

MAC

(message authentication code) An authentication code algorithm that uses a shared secret key to encrypt a file, taking the last block of encrypted data and sending it as an authentication code with the unencrypted file.

MAC address

(Media Access Control) A unique, hardware-level address assigned to network access devices by its manufacturer.

machine code

See machine language.

machine language

The lowest level of code, down to the zeros and ones that a CPU executes.

magnetic detector

A perimeter IDS that is installed to measure changes in a magnetic field. Reacts to conductors like keys or coins.

magnetic stripe card

An access card that stores authentication data on a strip of magnetized metal that is swiped through a magnetic reader.

maintenance hook

Application and hardware developers create these shortcuts during development. If these are not removed before the product ships, they may lead to exploits.

malicious code attack

A type of software attack where an attacker inserts malicious software into a user's system to disrupt or disable the operating system or an application. A malicious code attack can also make an operating system or an application take action to disrupt or disable other systems on the same network or on a remote network.

malicious software

Unauthorized software that can cause system failures or malfunctions or other ill effects.

malware

Malicious code, such as viruses, Trojans, or worms.

MAN

(metropolitan area network) A network that covers an area equivalent to a city or other municipality.

man trap

A facility control device that is a physical entry portal with two doors on either end of a secure chamber.

man-in-the-middle attack

A network attack that occurs when an attacker interposes a device between two legitimate hosts to gain access to their data transmissions. The intruder device responds actively to the two legitimate hosts as if it were the intended source or destination.

matrix

A data structure that includes an array with more than one dimension.

maturity model

A framework for assessing the level of sophistication of an organization's processes.

MD2

(Message Digest 2) An early hash algorithm developed as part of the MD series that is optimized for 8-bit computers and produces a 128-bit hash value. Predecessor to MD4 and MD5.

MD4

(Message Digest 4) A hash algorithm developed as part of the MD series that is optimized for 32-bit computers and produces a 128-bit hash value. Predecessor to MD5.

MD5
(Message Digest 5) This hash algorithm, based on RFC 1321, produces a 128-bit hash value and is used in IPSec policies for data authentication. It provides a considerable amount of security over MD4.

MDC
(modification detection code) The same as MIC.

memory leak
The result of failing to release memory that is allocated by an application.

mesh topology
A network topology in which each node has a direct, point-to-point connection to every other node.

message digest
A specific application of hashing used to create cryptographic data that verifies the contents of a message that has not been altered. It is either keyed or non-keyed.

message hash
The same as message digest.

metadata
Information that describes specific data characteristics.

method
An OOP term that describes an object's abilities.

MIC
(message integrity code) An authentication code that does not imply the use of a secret key and therefore must be transmitted in encrypted form to ensure message integrity.

microwave system
A motion sensor that emits a narrow beam of low-intensity radio signals that are sensed by the receiver. Used in coverage areas that are too large for infrared device detection.

MIME
(Multipurpose Internet Mail Extension) An internal labeling process used to define email attachment types.

mirror
Data is written simultaneously to two drives, thereby protecting the data should either drive fail. It still relies on a single drive controller, which allows a single point of failure. It provides high availability but slightly longer write times than striping.

mirror site
See hot site.

misuse test
A software test that identifies vulnerabilities and weaknesses in applications by validating the input that the app accepts, as well as any other ways that an attacker could exploit the app's behavior.

mitigation
A risk management principle that curtails the severity of risk or lessens the probability of a loss occurrence.

mobile code
Executable software that is obtained from remote systems and installed on a local system sometimes without the recipient's knowledge, consent, or doing.

modem
A network device that converts digital signals to analog signals, and vice versa.

modularity
As an OOP term, this is when all object processes within the object are isolated.

motion sensor
A perimeter IDS that uses movement to detect an approach or presence inside a controlled area.

MOU
(memorandum of understanding) An informal business agreement that is not legally binding and does not involve the exchange of money.

MPLS

(Multiprotocol Label Switching) Aggregates different types of traffic onto a MPLS cloud. MPLS uses labels rather than addresses to move data efficiently through the network.

MTD

(maximum tolerable downtime) The longest period of time a business can be inoperable without causing the business to cease.

multifactor authentication

A system wherein more than one type of authentication is used in accessing a system or facility. Also called two-factor authentication.

multiplexer

A network device that combines multiple signals into one.

multiprocessing

A multiple processor technique that permits multitasking across numerous processors to reach optimal system performance.

multiprogramming

Allows for the simultaneous execution of more than one program.

multistate

A processor technique where different execution modes can be run.

multitasking

A single processor technique that allows more than one program to appear to be running at one time.

multithreading

A single processor technique that allows the parallel execution of multiple threads on a computer system.

NAP

(Network Access Protection) Microsoft Windows Server technology that uses RADIUS to evaluate the health state of a host in a network.

NAS

(Network Attached Storage) Dedicated devices that are connected to a network to provide data file storage and sharing functions.

NAT

(Network Address Translation) A simple form of Internet connection and security that conceals internal addressing schemes from the public Internet.

NDA

(non-disclosure agreement) An agreement that stipulates that entities will not share confidential information, knowledge, or materials with unauthorized third parties.

need to know

A security principle based on an individual's need to access classified data resources to perform a given task or job function.

NetBIOS

(Network Basic Input/Output System) An interface that allows applications to properly communicate over different computers in a network.

Network Access layer

A TCP/IP model layer that covers the physical networking requirements of generating frames on a cable, fiber, or wireless network.

Network Database Management Model

A type of hierarchical database system model that is implemented using pointers to other database elements.

Network layer

An OSI model layer (Layer 3) that uses logical networking addresses to represent network interfaces.

network scanning

A type of penetration test that uses a port scanner to identify devices attached to the target network and to enumerate the applications hosted on the devices.

network session

A logical communications connection between two hosts, or nodes.

network topology

The physical and logical arrangement of nodes in a network.

network virtualization

The concept of connecting one part of the physical network to another part, without interacting with the parts in between.

Networking layer

A TCP/IP model layer that creates logical networks using IP network addresses.

NFS

(Network File System) An older file sharing network protocol that is predominant in communicating with Linux/UNIX environments.

NIDS

(network intrusion detection system) A passive hardware system that uses sensors to monitor traffic on a specific segment of the network.

NIIPA

(National Information Infrastructure Protection Act) Legislation passed in 1996 to target new computer security threats. Created legal remedies for hacking, stealing trade secrets, and damaging systems and information.

NIPS

(network intrusion prevention system) An inline prevention control security device that monitors suspicious network and system traffic and reacts in real time to block it.

NIST SP 800 series

(National Institute of Standards and Technology Special Publication 800 series) Various publications that focus on establishing standards and models for many facets of computer security.

Non-Interference Model

A security model that limits the interference between elements at different security levels.

non-repudiation

The security goal of ensuring that the party that sent a transmission or created data remains associated with that data. In asymmetric encryption, it is supported when the sender's public key is used to decrypt the message.

normalization

A database design technique that reduces redundant information and duplication between tables to ensure that each table contains only the minimal number of rows and columns required to store information and retrieve it meaningfully.

NPS

(Network Policy Server) Microsoft's implementation of a RADIUS server that aids in administrating VPNs and wireless networks.

NTLM

(NT LAN Manager) An authentication protocol created by Microsoft for use in its products.

NTP

(Network Time Protocol) A network-based information service that allows network components to synchronize their clocks with a central clock source.

object

As an OOP term, this is a specific instance and implementation of a class. It inherits the class's attributes and defines specific values for each attribute.

The security entity being accessed.

object reuse

As a software attack, the act of reclaiming classified or sensitive information from media that has been erased.

Object-Oriented Database Model

A database system model that uses object-oriented programming techniques with database technology.

ODBC

(Open Database Connectivity) A database language that provides a standard application program interface (API) that allows programmers to access any database from any platform.

OFB

(Output FeedBack) A block cipher mode wherein the IV is encrypted with the key and then chained to the next block's encryption step.

offshoring
Outsourcing in another country.

OLA
(operating-level agreement) A business agreement that outlines the relationship between divisions or departments in an organization.

OLE DB
(Object Linking and Embedding Database) A database language that allows the linking and embedding of documents, graphics, sound files, and other formatted information into a parent document.

OLTP
(online transaction processing) A database security mechanism that presents issues related to concurrency and atomicity.

OOD
(Object Oriented Databases) The object oriented programming approach has been extended into database design with OOD.

OOP
(Object Oriented Programming) Program languages that create reusable objects that combine methods and data.

open source software
Software that is provided to a buyer with a complete copy of the source code.

OpenID
A method of authenticating users with a federated identity management system.

operational and project planning
A planning effort that deals with the near term, from the present to 12 months out.

OPSEC
(operations security) A process of denying adversaries information about business capabilities and plans by identifying, controlling, and protecting indicators associated with sensitive business activities.

ORBs
(Object Request Brokers) These tools are used to locate objects and can act as middleware for connecting programs.

organizational security model
The totality of information security implementations in an organization.

OSI model
(Open System Interconnection) A reference model for how data is exchanged between any two points in a telecommunications network.

OTP
(one-time pad) An alternative cipher containing a very long, non-repeating key that is the same length as the plaintext. The key is used one time only and then destroyed.

OU
(organizational unit) Analogous to folders on a hard drive.

outsourcing
Using a chosen partner organization for business processes previously done internally.

P-box
(permutation box) A component of symmetric-key algorithms that is used to arrange S-boxes by scrambling them.

packet filtering firewall
A firewall where decisions are made on packets as they pass through.

PAN
(personal area network) A very small network that might include a small office/home office (SOHO) network or a Bluetooth connection between a mobile phone and a headset.

PAP
(Password Authentication Protocol) A remote access authentication method that sends client IDs and passwords as plaintext.

parity
An error detection method in which the number of ones within a transmitted data word is compared with those received. If the count matches, the data is assumed to be valid.

partial disclosure

This involves sharing information regarding security flaws with hardware and software vendors before the general public.

password cracking

An attack in which an attacker seeks to retrieve a user's password.

PAT

(Port Address Translation) A type of NAT that uses port numbers, as a means of providing uniqueness, to allow hundreds of internal users to be serviced by a single, exterior IP address.

patent

A legal protection provided to unique inventions. Protects the item's creator from competition for a given period of time.

PBX

(Private Branch Exchange) A phone system used in larger organizations that has its own switching network and controls lines for both internal and external communications.

PCI DSS

(Payment Card Industry Data Security Standard) A proprietary standard that specifies how organizations should handle information security for major card brands.

PDU

(Protocol Data Unit) A unit of data as it appears at each layer of the OSI model.

PEAP

(Protected Extensible Authentication Protocol) A protocol that encapsulates EAP in an encrypted SSL tunnel.

peer-to-peer services

A data services application that does not use the typical client/server model for implementation; all participants in the application are considered equals.

PEM

(Privacy-Enhanced Mail) A standard that provides for secure exchange of email over the Internet and applies various cryptographic techniques to allow for confidentiality, sender authentication, and message integrity.

penetration test

The controlled use of attack methods to test the security of a system or facility.

perimeter network

An alternate type of DMZ.

perturbation

The intentional addition of spurious data into database fields with the intention of defeating inference attacks.

PFS

(perfect forward secrecy) A characteristic of session encryption that ensures that if a key used during a certain session is compromised, it should not affect previously encrypted data.

PGP

(Pretty Good Privacy) A method of securing emails created to prevent attackers from intercepting and manipulating email and attachments by encrypting and digitally signing the contents of the email using public-key cryptography.

phishing

A type of email-based social engineering attack in which the attacker sends email from a spoofed source to try to elicit private information from the victim.

photometric detector

A perimeter IDS that is installed to detect a change in light level in a designated area; specifically, a windowless room or area. Sounds an alarm if its emitted beam does not hit a receiver.

phreaking

An attack in which an attacker identifies the tones used to route long distance calls, enabling them to switch calls and use long distance services for free.

physical controls

These controls are used to limit an individual's physical access to protected information or facilities, such as locks, doors, fences, and perimeter defenses.

Physical layer

An OSI model layer (Layer 1) that transmits bits of data across a physical medium.

physical security

The implementation and practice of various control mechanisms that are intended to restrict physical access to facilities.

PIDS

(perimeter intrusion detection system) A control or group of controls that monitor for intrusions into a physical perimeter.

PII

(personally identifiable information) Any information that potentially could identify a single person.

ping of death

A type of IP fragmentation attack in which fragments of oversized ping packets are sent to a target, causing the target to crash as it tries to reconstruct the pieces.

PKI

(public key infrastructure) A cryptographic system that is composed of a CA, certificates, software, services, and other cryptographic components, for the purpose of enabling authenticity and validation of data and/or entities. For example, PKI can be used to secure transactions over the Internet.

plaintext

The original, unencrypted form of data. Also referred to as cleartext.

point-to-point topology

A network topology that is simply a link between two devices.

policy

A high-level security document that states management intentions.

polyinstantiation

As an OOP term, this is when a single class is instantiated into multiple independent instances.

polymorphism

As an OOP term, this occurs when classes are treated as equivalents and are referenced identically.

POP

(Post Office Protocol) An email retrieval protocol that generally pulls the mail from the server to whatever the device the user is currently utilizing.

portable site

A mobile site, such as a van or trailer, that can be operated anywhere should a disaster occur. It houses computer hardware, networking capabilities, and communications equipment to restore and maintain business operations.

POTS

(Plain Old Telephone System) A telephone system that uses analog signals to transmit voice.

power line monitor

A power protection device that is used to evaluate the source of electrical power.

PPP

(Point-to-Point Protocol) A remote access protocol used to support dial-up services and automatic configuration.

PPTP

(Point-to-Point Tunneling Protocol) An early remote access protocol used to implement VPNs.

preaction

A water-based, dry pipe extinguishing system that has special sprinkler heads that are heat sensitive. Water is discharged after the system is activated and the nozzles are activated.

precedent

A new or changed law, never before established, that is created by a judge to specifically pertain to a particular issue or case.

Presentation layer

An OSI model layer (Layer 6) that translates data so that the receiver can properly interpret the transmitted information.

pressure-sensitive sensor

A perimeter IDS that is used to detect pressure when weight, such as a human or animal body, is applied to the device.

preventative control

A control that stops a security incident.

preventative controls

In OPSEC, controls such as user IDs and passwords that prevent unauthorized access or data modification.

primary storage

A common term used for memory based on its immediate availability as an information storage location.

primitive

A data structure in which data elements are singular in nature and are not broken down into small components when accessed.

privacy

A legal principle that maintains the secrecy or protection of an individual's information.

Privacy Act of 1974

Protects the privacy of individual information held by the U.S. government. Mandated in response to the abuse of privacy during the Nixon administration.

private key

The component of asymmetric encryption that is kept secret by one party during two-way encryption.

procedural language

A program language that uses routines, subroutines, methods, and functions.

procedure

A security document that describes implementation practices and the steps taken to complete an activity.

program coordinator

The individual responsible for implementing and controlling an organization's BCP.

proprietary software

Software that is developed by organizations that do not disclose the source code.

protocol analyzer

A surveillance tool used to intercept and record computer network traffic. Also known as a sniffer.

prototyping model

A model that provides early prototypes for users to see and test. This early feedback from users can then be used to develop better products more quickly.

proximity detector

A perimeter IDS that is installed to emit a measurable electrical field while in use. Also called a capacitance detector.

proxy

A device that retrieves content from outside the network on behalf of an internal client.

proxy firewall

A firewall that acts as an intermediary server or gateway that will terminate a connection and then re-initiate it if the traffic is warranted.

proxy server

A server that caches (temporarily stores) content obtained from the original source server(s).

prudent man rule

Another name for the prudent person rule.

prudent person rule

A common law standard or principle that suggests that adequate protection is the protection that a prudent person would use in normal circumstances.

PSTN

(Public Switched Telephone Network) See POTS.

public key

The component of asymmetric encryption that can be accessed by anyone.

public–key cryptography

The same as public-key and asymmetric encryption.

QC

(quality control) The process of reviewing the accuracy, integrity, and reliability of an asset.

qualitative risk analysis

A best-guess estimate of risk occurrence that is not based on numerical analysis or history.

quantitative risk analysis

An estimate based on the historical occurrences of incidents and the likelihood of risk re-occurrence.

Quantum Cryptography

The practice of using quantum mechanics to perform cryptography.

RA

(registration authority) An authority in a network that processes requests for digital certificates from users.

race condition

A TCB vulnerability that occurs when two processes try to access and modify information at the same time.

RADIUS

(Remote Authentication Dial-in User Service) An authentication protocol used to authenticate and authorize dial-in users.

RAID

(Redundant Array of Independent Disks) A storage technology used to provide better disk performance or data redundancy depending on the implemented RAID type. Also called Redundant Array of Inexpensive Disks.

rainbow attack

Password guessing that is automated by comparing encrypted passwords against a predetermined list of possible password values.

rainbow table

A password cracking technique that uses sets of pre-computed passwords and their hashes stored in a file that dramatically reduce the time needed to crack a password.

RAIT

(Redundant Array of Independent Tapes) A storage technology used to provide better tape performance or data redundancy.

RAM

(Random Access Memory) A type of computer data storage that uses short-term memory to store program instructions and data for immediate use.

ransomware

Code that restricts the victim's access to their computer or the data on it. The attacker then demands a ransom be paid, usually through an online payment service like PayPal or Green Dot MoneyPak, under threat of keeping the restriction or destroying the information they have locked down.

RARP

(Reverse Address Resolution Protocol) A protocol that enables a device that knows its MAC address to request an IP address.

RAS

(Remote Access Service) A data service that provides access to a computer system or network from a separate location, often for administrative reasons.

RBAC

(role-based access control) An access control technique that is implemented when a subject's access to objects is based on the job performed by the subject.

RC algorithms

(Rivest Cipher) A series of variable key-length symmetric encryption algorithms developed by Ronald Rivest.

RDBMS

(Relational Database Management System) A collection of multiple tables that are related to one another through the use of the foreign key concept.

recovery control

A control that returns the system to an operational state after a failure to protect the CIA triad.

recovery controls

In OPSEC, controls such as trusted recovery that assist in correcting security problems by returning the system to a secure state.

recovery team

A group of designated individuals who implement recovery procedures and control the recovery operations in the event of an internal or external disruption to critical business processes.

redundancy

Using more than one resource to maintain availability.

referential integrity

A database that ensures the proper maintenance of all table values that are referenced by the foreign keys in other tables.

reflected attack

An attack where the attacker poses as a legitimate user and sends information to a web server in the form of a page request or form submission.

regression test

A software test in which the same set of tests are run after some component of the application has been changed or updated.

Relational Database Management Model

A database system model that allows a designer to create relationships among the various database components.

remote access

The ability to connect to a network from a remote location.

remote journaling

A data backup method wherein real-time copies of database transactions are stored in journals at a remote location. Journals can be replayed to transfer a database back to normal conditions.

repeater

A network device that is used to amplify signals as they normally degrade over long distances.

replay attack

A type of cryptographic attack that can be used to bypass the encryption protecting passwords while in transit.

retention

The act of storing a business asset.

reverse engineering

A cryptographic process of analyzing and determining the structure, function, and operation of a cryptosystem.

reverse proxy

A device that retrieves content from inside the network on behalf of external clients.

ring topology

A network topology in which all network nodes are connected in a continuous circle.

RIPEMD

(RACE Integrity Primitives Evaluation Message Digest) A message digest algorithm that is based along the lines of the design principles used in MD4.

risk

The likelihood of a threat exposing a vulnerability.

risk analysis

The security management process for addressing any risk or economic damages that affect an organization.

risk management

The process of assessing risk, reducing it to an acceptable level, and implementing systems to maintain that minimal level of risk.

RM

(reference monitor) A component of some types of access control systems that determines if the subject can access the object.

RNG

(random number generator) A device that is used to create keys and to perform cryptographic functions.

ROM

(Read-Only Memory) A type of computer data storage that uses long-term memory to store program information and configuration information used during the initiation process of a computer.

rootkit

Code that is intended to take full or partial control of a system at the lowest levels.

routable

A way of describing protocols that can forward packets from one network address to another.

router

A networking device used to connect multiple networks that employ the same protocol.

router redundancy

A technique for employing multiple routers in teams to limit the risk of routing failure should a router malfunction.

routing

A Network layer function that allows the devices in one network to send information to and receive information from other logical network devices.

RPC

(remote procedure call) A data services process used to cause the execution of a module, subroutine, or procedure at a remote location.

RPO

(Recovery Point Objective) The point in time, relative to a disaster, where the data recovery process begins.

RSA

(Rivest Shamir Adleman) The first successful asymmetric algorithm to be designed for public-key encryption. It is named for its designers, Rivest, Shamir, and Adleman.

RTO

(Recovery Time Objective) The length of time within which normal business operations and activities must be restored following a disturbance.

rule-based access control

An access control technique that is based on a set of operational rules or restrictions.

S-box

(substitution box) A component of symmetric-key algorithms that is used to camouflage plaintext-to-ciphertext relationships.

S-HTTP

(Secure Hypertext Transfer Protocol) A security protocol that is an alternate form of protecting HTTP data.

S/MIME

(Secure/MIME) An extension of MIME that prevents attackers from intercepting and manipulating email and attachments by encrypting and digitally signing the contents of the email using public-key cryptography.

sag

A momentary low-voltage power failure.

salvage team

A group of designated individuals who restore the primary site to its normal operating environment.

SAML

(Security Assertion Markup Language) An XML-based data format used to exchange authentication information between a client and a service.

SAN

(Storage Area Network) A specialized physical network that is made up of dedicated storage devices that perform block-level operations.

sashimi software development model

A modification of the waterfall model where there is an intentional overlap between phases.

SCADA

(supervisory control and data acquisition) A type of industrial control system that typically monitors water, gas, and electrical assets, and can issue remote commands to those assets.

scoping

The practice of determining how far reaching your security implementation will be.

screen scraping
A form of terminal emulation that allows you to access legacy programs on newer hardware.

screened subnet
See DMZ.

screening host
A router that protects the internal network with an ACL.

SCRUM
An Agile software development methodology that employs iterative and incremental development by using the timeboxed approach and emphasizing the importance of teamwork.

SDN
(software-defined networking) An approach to networking architecture that simplifies management by centralizing control over a network.

secondary storage
A means of storage that keeps information for long periods of time and in great volumes.

secret–key cryptography
The same as shared-key and symmetric encryption.

security auditing
The practice of recording security-relevant events in an audit file for future analysis.

security kernel
Implements the RM in an operating system.

security monitoring
The practice of monitoring operations controls to identify abnormal computer activity.

security perimeter
An imaginary line that surrounds the TCB and separates the trusted and untrusted parts of a computer system.

security profile
A description of the security-relevant information about each user or protected element in a system.

security violation
A breach of security regulations or policies that may or may not result in a system compromise.

segment
A small unit of information created by the Transport layer of the OSI model to control information flow to the layers above.

SEM
(security event management) The collection and analysis of security event logs from a wide variety of devices.

sensitivity profile
A security document that details the information an individual needs to know to effectively perform a specific job role.

SESAME
(Secure European System for Applications in a Multi-vendor Environment) A single sign-on (SSO) method created in Europe.

session fixation
An attack that forces a user to engage in a session that the attacker can later hijack.

Session layer
An OSI model layer (Layer 5) that establishes the startup, continuation, and termination of a network session. The Session layer supports full-duplex, half-duplex, and simplex data transmission.

session management
The process of describing how a single instance of identification and authentication is applied to a resource or group of resources.

session prediction
An attack in which an attacker can correctly guess a poorly generated session ID and hijack the session.

SHA
(Secure Hash Algorithm) This hash algorithm is modeled after MD5 and is considered the stronger of the two because it produces a 160-bit hash value. There is also SHA-256, SHA-384, and SHA-512, with the numbers representing the block size.

shared-key encryption
The same as symmetric encryption.

Shibboleth
A SAML-based federated identity management system used by universities and public service organizations.

shoulder surfing
A social engineering attack where the goal is to look over the shoulder of an individual as he or she enters password information or a PIN number.

SIA
(security impact analysis) The process of determining how changes to an object will impact the existing state of security in the organization.

side channel attack
A type of cryptographic attack that targets the cryptosystem by gathering information about the physical characteristics of the encryption and then exploiting them.

SIEM
(Security Information and Event Management) The collection and analysis of security event logs from a wide variety of devices including servers, routers, IDS, and IPS.

simplex
A Session-layer communication mode where the transmission of data occurs in only one direction.

single point of failure
Any device, circuit, or process that causes the unavailability of data upon failure.

SLA
(service level agreement) A business document that is used to define a pre-agreed level of performance for an activity or contracted service.

SLE
(Single Loss Expectancy) The estimated impact of an event.

SLIP
(Serial Line Internet Protocol) A simple remote access communications protocol that encapsulates IP datagrams carried over dial-up networks.

smart card
A credit-card-sized device that contains a chip that can provide storage and intelligence to the authentication process as "something you have."

SMTP
(Simple Message Transport Protocol) A protocol used for email delivery.

Smurf attack
An attack based on sending high volumes of ICMP ping packets to a target.

sneakernet
The process of physically carrying removable media into and out of a network.

sniffing
A software attack that uses special monitoring software to gain access to private communications on the network wire or across a wireless network. This type of attack is used either to steal the content of the communications itself or to gain information that will help the attacker later gain access to the network and resources. Also called eavesdropping.

SOC
(service organization control) An accounting standard used to assure customers who outsource their services to service providers.

social engineering
An attack where the goal is to obtain sensitive data, including user names and passwords, from network users through deception and trickery.

SoD
(separation of duties) A division of tasks between different people to complete a business process or work function.

software escrow
A service that holds onto a copy of software source code.

SONET
(Synchronous Optical Networking) A fiber-optic-based network that is used to move data at higher speeds than a traditional Ethernet.

source code
Higher-level programming language that is generally human readable.

SOX Act
(Sarbanes-Oxley) Legislation passed in 2002 to help control how corporations report about and audit themselves. Also referred to as Sarbox.

spam
An attack that causes network over-utilization by filling networks with unwanted email messages.

spike
A short-term, high-voltage power malfunction.

spiral software development model
A method of developing software iteratively through risk analysis, requirements specification, prototyping, and testing or implementation.

spoofing
A social engineering or software-based attack where the goal is to pretend to be someone else for the purpose of identity concealment. Spoofing can occur in IP addresses, MAC addresses, and email.

spyware
Code that is secretly installed on a user's computer to gather data about the user and relay it to a third party.

SQL
(Structured Query Language) A programming and query language common to many large-scale database systems.

SQL injection
An attack that injects a SQL query into the input data directed at a server by accessing the client side of the application.

SSH
(Secure Shell) An administrative services protocol that replaces Telnet and provides a secure, encrypted environment for command line access to devices for configuration purposes.

SSL
(Secure Sockets Layer) A security protocol used to provide confidentiality services to the IP protocol suite for information transfer.

SSO
(single sign-on) A method of access control wherein a single user ID and password will allow a user to access all of his or her applications.

standard
A security document that describes a required implementation or use of tools.

star topology
A network topology that uses a central connectivity device with separate point-to-point connections to each node.

State Machine Model
A security model that monitors the system as it moves from one state to another.

stateful inspection firewall
A firewall that determines the state of the packets as they pass through.

statutes
Laws enacted by the legislative branch of a government.

statutory law
Written law comprising statutes passed by federal, state, and local legislatures defining day-to-day laws and how bodies of government function.

steganography

An alternative cipher process that hides information by enclosing it in other files such as a graphic, movie, or sound file.

stored attack

An attack where an attacker injects malicious code or links into a website's forums, databases, or other data.

strategic planning

A long-range planning effort that reviews required security activities, focusing on major changes or improvements in the security posture of an organization.

stream cipher

A relatively fast type of symmetric encryption that encrypts data one bit at a time.

striping

A disk-performance-enhancement feature in which data is spread across multiple drives to improve read and write access speeds.

structured development

A development method based on structured programming concepts that require a careful combination of sequencing, selection, and iteration to achieve a desired result.

subject

The entity requesting security access.

substitution

A technique that replaces parts of a message or cryptographic output to hide the original information.

supervisor state

A CPU mode that can execute any security instructions that are available.

surge

A long-term, high-voltage power malfunction.

surge/spike protector

A power protection device that provides power protection circuits that can reduce or eliminate the impact of surges and spikes.

surveillance system

A physical security mechanism that monitors designated internal and external areas of a facility for unusual behavior or a potential intruder.

SwA

(software assurance) The process of minimizing security risks in software and ensuring that the software functions as intended.

switch

An interconnecting network device used to forward frames to the correct port based on MAC addresses. A switch can work with pairs of ports, connecting two segments as needed.

symmetric encryption

A two-way encryption scheme in which encryption and decryption are both performed by the same secret key.

SYN flood

In this DoS attack, an attacker sends countless requests for a TCP connection (as SYN messages) to a file transfer protocol (FTP) server, web server, or any other target system attached to the Internet. Because the attacker's message contains a spoofed IP, the target server is flooded with incomplete TCP connections.

SYN flood attack

A type of DoS attack in which the attacker sends multiple SYN messages initializing TCP connections with a target host.

synchronous messaging

Real-time communication between two or more people. IM is a synchronous messaging protocol.

synchronous token system

The time or counter on the user's device will need to be synchronized with the authentication server as it expects a particular code to be entered.

system test

A software test that tests a complete, integrated system to verify that it satisfies the original specified requirements.

table

A set of rows and columns in a database that contains related information.

TACACS

(Terminal Access Controller Access Control System) An authentication protocol that accepts login requests and authenticates the access credentials of the user.

tactical planning

A mid-term planning effort that is in-between operational and strategic in duration.

tailgating

A social engineering attack whereby an individual closely follows someone else into a secure environment with the intent of avoiding authentication by the control system.

tailoring

The practice of modifying an existing security practice to suit your particular needs.

target

An iSCSI storage device or application.

targeted testing

A type of penetration test where the target organization is informed of the test.

TCB

(Trusted Computing Base) The hardware, firmware, and software components of a computer system that implement the security policy of a system.

TCP

(Transmission Control Protocol) A connection-oriented transport protocol used in the TCP/IP model.

TCP/IP model

(Transmission Control Protocol/Internet Protocol) A model that represents a collection of communications protocols used to govern data exchange on the Internet.

TCSEC

(Trusted Computer System Evaluation Criteria) The first attempt at a system security evaluation process implemented by the U.S. Department of Defense.

technical controls

These controls are implemented in the computing environment, often in operating systems, application programs, database frameworks, firewalls, routers, switches, and wireless access points.

terminal emulation

Technology that allows you to open a console to interface with, usually from a remote machine.

test-driven development

A software development method in which the developer writes an automated test for a desired function or improvement. Because the code has not yet been written, the test will initially fail. The developer then writes the minimal amount of code required to pass the test.

theft

A human-based attack where the goal is to blatantly steal information and resources.

threading

A computing technique that enables a program to split itself into two or more concurrently running tasks.

threat

A potential danger caused by exploiting a vulnerability.

threat agent

An individual that will expose a vulnerability and cause harm.

threat modeling

A structured process of identifying and assessing the possible threat agents and attack vectors that might be used to target systems.

time-based access control

An access control technique that limits when an individual can access the system.

TKIP

(Temporal Key Integrity Protocol) A security protocol created as an improvement to the number of and usage of keys. It is an algorithm that secures wireless computer networks by changing the keys on packets for each packet exchange

TLS

(Transport Layer Security) A security protocol that is an updated version of SSL, with mutual authentication as an added service.

TOC/TOU

(time of check/time of use) Uses a weakness in the TCB where access is granted at one point in time and used much later on.

TOGAF

(The Open Group Architecture Framework) An open framework that provides common terms and methods that can be followed to create a secure organization.

tort law

The legal category that identifies what constitutes a legal harm and creates the means for recovering damages in the case of intentional malicious acts or accidents.

TPM

(Trusted Platform Module) An international standard for implementing a cryptographically secure processor on a computer motherboard.

trade secret

An item that requires protection that the loss of which will severely damage the business.

trademark

A design or phrase used to identify products or services.

traffic shaper

A device that limits the amount of bandwidth used by certain traffic in a network.

transfer

A risk management principle that reallocates risk acceptance to another party, such as an insurance company, by means of a contract.

Transport layer

An OSI model layer (Layer 4) that ensures reliable data transmission by breaking up big data blocks into segments that can be sent more efficiently on the network. The Transport layer also implements flow control

to preserve information from buffer overflows or other network problems.

transport mode

An IPSec mode that protects the information in a payload of an IP datagram.

transposition

The process of rearranging parts of a message or cryptographic output to hide the original information.

trapdoor attack

A software attack where a hidden entry point into a program or operating system bypasses the normal identification and authentication processes.

tree topology

A network topology in which all devices are connected to a branching cable.

triage

In incident response, the process of responding to the situation based on criticality. Typically known as a medical term that indicates the priority of patient treatment.

Trojan horse

Unauthorized software that masquerades as legitimate software. Also known as a Trojan program.

Trojan program

See Trojan horse.

trusted recovery

A protection mechanism used in data recovery that ensures the security of a computer system that crashes or fails by recovering security-relevant elements in a trusted or secure state.

tunnel mode

An IPSec mode that allows the encryption of the original IP datagram and the entire payload.

tuple

A row, or record, in a database.

two-man rule

A media protection technique that requires the presence of two individuals at all times to monitor behavior when certain criteria are met.

Twofish

A symmetric key block cipher, similar to Blowfish, consisting of a block size of 128 bits and key sizes up to 256 bits.

Type 1 error

See FRR.

Type II error

See FAR.

UDP

(User Datagram Protocol) A connectionless transport protocol, used in TCP/IP as an alternative to TCP, that supports process identification using port numbers and error detection.

unit test

A software test that is a simple "pass/no pass" for a small piece of code, typically an individual function that is run alone and isolated.

untrusted recovery

A data recovery level wherein a recovery process is performed that does not ensure that the result is a secure and trusted environment.

UPS

(Uninterruptible Power Supply) A device that continues to provide power to connected circuits when the main source of power becomes unavailable.

USA PATRIOT Act

(Uniting and Strengthening America by Providing Appropriate Tools Required to Intercept and Obstruct Terrorism) Legislation passed in 2001, following 9/11, that increased the governmental ability to wiretap and control financial transactions used to fund terrorism.

user state

A CPU mode that can execute only non-privileged instructions. Implements the same function as the application state.

versioning

The process of keeping track of a system's changing states.

vibration detector

A perimeter IDS that is installed to measure vibrations caused by breaking glass, collisions with solid objects, or footsteps.

view

A user portal into a database.

view-based access control

Controls in which a user is limited to viewing only certain fields (columns) in a record.

violation analysis

A security monitoring technique that tracks anomalies in user activity. Also called violation processing or violation tracking.

virtual memory

A category of storage that emulates physical memory by using random access disks to temporarily store information needed by the operating system and application programs.

virtual password

A long phrase known to a user that is entered into a password administration system. Also known as a passphrase.

virus

A malware or malicious program that attaches itself to another program.

VLAN

(virtual local area network) A point-to-point physical network that is created by grouping selected hosts together, regardless of their physical location.

VoIP

(Voice over IP) A data services protocol that implements the transmission of voice over the Internet Protocol.

VoIP

(Voice over IP) A term used for a technology that enables you to deliver telephony communications over a network by using IP.

A data services protocol that implements the transmission of voice over IP.

VPN

(Virtual Private Network) Creates a protected pathway secured with various means and used to move enterprise information between corporate locations using the Internet instead of private corporate resources.

vulnerability

Any weakness in a system or process that could lead to harm.

vulnerability assessment

An evaluation of a system's security and ability to meet compliance requirements based on the configuration state of the system

vulnerability scanning

A type of penetration test that exploits known weaknesses in operating systems and applications that were identified through reconnaissance and enumeration.

WAN

(wide area network) A network used to connect physically distributed networks over long, geographical distances.

WAP

(Wireless Access Protocol) A protocol associated with the implementation of mobile phone and PDA applications that access the Internet.

war dialing

A type of penetration test that uses a modem and software to dial a range of phone numbers to locate computer systems, PBX devices, and HVAC systems.

war driving

A type of penetration test that locates and attempts to penetrate wireless systems.

warm site

A location that is dormant or performs non-critical functions under normal conditions, but can be rapidly converted to a key operations site if needed.

Wassenaar Arrangement

A treaty observed by dozens of countries that promotes greater transparency in the transfer of weapons, technologies, and other goods.

waterfall software development model

A method of designing and creating software that has defined phases that flow from one to the next, as water flows from one level of a waterfall to another.

WAYF

(Where Are You From) A single sign-on system which verifies the institution a user is from before they can access a service.

WEP

(Wired Equivalent Privacy) Provides 64-bit, 128-bit, and 256-bit encryption using the RC4 algorithm for wireless communication.

wet pipe

A water-based extinguishing system wherein the pipes store water at all times. When a given temperature is reached, the system discharges the water.

white box

A test in which the tester knows about all aspects of the systems and understands the function and design of the system before the test is conducted.

whitelisting

The process of allowing specific systems, software, services, etc., to use a resource. Anything not on the list is blocked.

wireless router

A network device that acts as both a router and a wireless access point.

WLAN

(wireless local area network) A local area network that is implemented using wireless access points rather than Ethernet cabling.

work factor

The amount of time needed to break a cryptosystem.

worm

A malware program that does not require the support of a target program in the way a virus does.

WPA

(Wi-Fi Protected Access) A security standard that provides additional encryption capabilities for wireless transmissions.

WPA2

A wireless access protocol that is implemented with the AES encryption algorithm. Also known as 802.11i.

XaaS

(X-as-a-Service) This refers to "anything service" or "everything as a service" and is the growing number of services that can be delivered via the cloud.

XML

(eXtensible Markup Language) A document description language that simplifies the presentation of database information in various formats.

XP

(extreme programming) An Agile development methodology that focuses on delivering high-quality working software quickly and continuously.

XSRF

(cross-site request forgery) A type of attack where an attacker takes advantage of the trust established between an authorized user of a website and the website itself.

XSS

(cross-site scripting) A type of attack where the attacker takes advantage of scripting and input validation vulnerabilities in an interactive website to attack legitimate users.

Zachman

A security framework designed to get the different groups working on a project to communicate with each other; it is commonly associated with the who, what, when, how, where, and why of information security.

Index

(COBIT 5) *24*
(ISC)²
    Code of Ethics canons *29*
    Code of Ethics preamble *29*
    personnel safety *425*

2x8 rule *413*
3DES *208*
802.11i *258*
    See also WPA2
8x2 rule *413*

A

abstraction *523*
acceptance
    and risk *45*
acceptance test *384*
access control
    administration methods *316*
    bypass *540*
    card *414*
    grant and revoke *541*
    limitations *550*
    services implementation *315*
    service types *314*
    view-based *541*
access control matrix *351*
accountability *315, 332*
accounting system *40*
accreditation *527*
ACL *274*
Active Directory, *See* AD
AD *335*
addressing path *134*

Address Resolution Protocol, *See* ARP
Address Space Layout Randomization, *See* ASLR
administrative control *47, 49*
administrative services department *10*
Advanced Encryption Standard, *See* AES
Advisory Committee-BCP team
    responsibilities *63*
advisory security policy *34*
adware *548*
AES *208*
aggregation *169, 540*
Agile
    manifesto *530*
    software development *529*
AH *287, 288*
alarm systems *419*
ALE *44*
algorithm
    filtering *264*
alternate site *498*
American Standard Code for Information Interchange, *See* ASCII
Annualized/Annual Rate of Occurrence, *See* ARO
Annualized Loss Expectancy, *See* ALE
anomaly-based IDS *304*
API *156, 550*
appliance *265*
Application layer *241, 244*
application programming interface, *See* API
Application Programming Interface, *See* API
application protocol-based IDS *304*
application state *128*

approving the change phase *456*
architecture categories
    firmware *134*
argon *233*
ARO *43*
ARP *246*
ARP poisoning *298*
ASCII *241*
ASLR *156*
assembler *520*
Assembly language *520*
asset
    identification *39*
    management system *40*
    valuation *40*
    valuation methods *40*
Asset Value, *See* AV
asymmetric encryption
    algorithms *209*
asynchronous token system *329*
atomicity *542*
attack
    encryption-based *202*
audit *315*
auditors
    and the ISO *8*
Authentication Header, *See* AH
authentication protocols
    RADIUS configurations *338*
authentication types
    something you have *328*
    something you know *326*
authorization *315*
automatic access control *414*
AV *44*
availability *3*
avalanche effect *193*
avoidance
    and risk *45*
awareness program objectives *83*

B

backdoor attack *358, 549*
background check
    for information security *79*
background investigation
    for information security *79*
baiting *360*
bandwidth limiter *265*
baseline
    hiring procedures *79*

baselining *457*
bastion host *274*
BCP
    contents *60*
BCP team, *See* Advisory Committee-BCP team
Bell-LaPadula (BLP) Model *141*
best-guess estimate *42*
BIA
    organizational goals *65*
Biba Model
    impact *142*
Big Data *175*
biometric device
    acceptance *330*
    entry system *415*
    errors *331*
    types *329*
birthday attack *202*
bit patterns
    predefined *196*
    substitute *196*
black box *545*
black box test *373*
blacklisting *437*
blind testing *374*
block cipher *198, 211*
Blowfish *208*
Board of Directors *5, 6*
bollard *413*
bounds checking *548*
BPA *74*
Brewer-Nash Model *141*
bridge device *243*
brute force attack *296*
buffer overflow *297, 382, 548, 549*
built-in bounds *538*
business continuity
    and the ISO *8*
Business Continuity Plan, *See* BCP
business continuity process *68*
business partnership agreement, *See* BPA
business plan
    evaluation *67*
    maintenance *68*
    testing *67*
bus topology *268*

C

C&A *527*
CA *216*

cabled media *270*

cache memory *128*

campus area network, *See* CAN

CAN *266*

Canadian Trusted Computer Product
Evaluation Criteria, *See* CTCPEC

Capability Maturity Model, *See* CMM

card entry system *414*

Carrier Sense Multiple Access, *See* CSMA

Carrier Sense Multiple Access/Collision
Detect, *See* CSMA/CD

Carrier Sense Multiple Access with Collision
Avoidance, *See* CSMA/CA

CASE *534*

CCB *456*

CCTV *227, 418*

CDN *275*

cell suppression *542*

Center for the Study of Ethics in the
Professions, *See* CSEP

centralized access control *316*

Central Processing Unit, *See* CPU

CEO *6, 10*

CER *331*

certificate
information *213*
management system *213*
repository database *213*
revoked *215*
X.509 version 3 *213*

certificate authority, *See* CA

Certificate Revocation List, *See* CRL

certification *526*

certification and accreditation, *See* C&A

CFAA *20*

chain of custody *471*

Challenge Handshake Authentication Protocol,
See CHAP

change control
phase *456*
procedure, ITIL *456*
process *456*

Change Control Board, *See* CCB

change management *456*

change request *456*

CHAP *338*

Chief Executive Officer, *See* CEO

Chief Information Officer, *See* CIO

Children's Online Privacy Protection Act, *See*
COPPA

chlorofluorocarbons *233*

chosen ciphertext attack *203*

chosen plaintext attack *203*

CI *443*

CIA triad
and IPSec *288*

CIO *5*

cipher *192*

cipher keypad *414*

ciphertext *190*

ciphertext-only attack *203*

CIRT *8*

citizen programmer *548*

Clark-Wilson Model *141*

class *522*

classification
commercial *94*
military *94*
schemes *94*

classifications *92*

cleanroom model *528*

cleartext *190*
See also plaintext

clickjacking *299*

Client Confidential classification *95*

closed-circuit television, *See* CCTV

CM *442*

CMDB *443*

CMM *516*

COBIT *152*

coded text, *See* ciphertext

code injection *184*

cohesion *524*

cold site *500*

collaboration *282*

collision *209, 210*

COM *524*

combination lock *414*

commercial classification *94*

commercial off-the-shelf, *See* COTS

Common Criteria *144*

Common Object Request Broker Architecture,
See CORBA

communicating the change phase *456*

compensating security control *48*

compiled languages *521*

compliance *15*

Component Object Model, *See* COM

Computer-Aided Software Engineering, *See*
CASE

computer bus *133*

computer crime

law *19*
    overview *18*
computer ethics fallacies *28*
computer forensics *470*
    See also digital forensics
Computer Fraud and Abuse Act, *See* CFAA
computer game
    and ethics fallacies *28*
computer incident response team, *See* CIRT
Computer Security Act, *See* CSA
concealable transmitter *419*
concentrator *264*
concurrent access *542*
conduct *34*
Confidential *94*
confidentiality *2, 515*
Configuration Items, *See* CI
Configuration Management, *See* CM
Configuration Management Database, *See*
CMDB
consequences *34*
constrained interfaces access control *354*
content delivery network, *See* CDN
content dependent access control *354*
context dependent access control *354*
contingency plan *64*
continuous improvement *50*
control *3*
control framework *11*
Control Objectives for Information and
        related Technology
    Information Systems Audit and Control
    Association, *See* ISACA
    ISACA *152*
Control Objectives for Information and
Related Technology 5, *See* COBIT 5
control selection criteria *46*
cookie *299*
COPPA *17*
copyright *21*
CORBA *524*
Corporate Confidential classification *94*
corporate security *11*
corrective security control *49*
cost
    of loss *484*
    of recovery *484*
cost effectiveness
    and control selection *46*
cost vs. benefit
    and disaster recovery *481*

COTS *557*
countermeasure *305*
coupling *524*
covert channel
    and Information Flow Model *140*
    control *550*
    overview *164*
covert storage *164*
covert timing *164*
CPTED *221*
CPU *128*
CRC *243*
credit history review
    for information security *79*
Crime Prevention Through Environmental
Design, *See* CPTED
criminal history check
    for information security *79*
critical asset
    and improper risk management *38*
critical business process *65*
critical sub-processes *65*
CRL *215*
crossover error rate, *See* CER
cross-site request forgery, *See* XSRF
cross-site scripting, *See* XSS
cryptanalysis
    methodologies *203*
    overview *201*
cryptographic attack *203*
cryptographic weakness *202*
cryptography
    key management *195*
    secret-key *207*
cryptology *201*
cryptosystem
    and cryptanalysis *203*
    and factoring attack *203*
    overview *201*
    work factor *201*
Crystal *531*
CSA *20*
CSEP *27*
CSMA *251*
CSMA/CA *251*
CSMA/CD *251*
CSRF, *See* XSRF
CTCPEC *144*
cybercrime *471*
Cyclical Redundancy Check, *See* CRC

D

DAA *527*

DAC *350*

damages
    economic *39*

DARPA *244*

data
    backup *492*
    contamination control *542*
    content rules enforcement *538*
    definition language *538*
    integrity *540*
    path *134*
    repository *540*
    warehouse *539*

data at rest *109*

database
    security mechanisms *541*
    system models *538*
    system overview *538*
    vulnerabilities *540*

database administrator, *See* DBA

Database Management System, *See* DBMS

data breach *20*

data-consistent coding *539*

Data Encryption Standard, *See* DES

datagram fragmentation *247*

data in transit *110*

Data Link layer *243*, *267*

Data loss prevention, *See* DLP

data mining *539*

data network
    media types *270*
    topologies *267*
    topology types *268*
    types *265*

data recovery process *483*

data remanence *115*

DBA *540*

DBMS *538*

DCOM *524*

DDoS *301*, *548*

deadbolt lock *413*

deadlock *541*

decentralized access control *316*

decryption
    and cryptography *190*

Defense Advanced Research Projects Agency, *See* DARPA

defense in depth *4*, *305*

Defined maturity *516*

degaussing *116*

Delphi method *43*

deluge *235*

demilitarized zone, *See* DMZ

denial of service, *See* DoS

DES *208*

Designated Approving Authority, *See* DAA

detective
    security control *48*

determination factors *42*

deterrent
    security control *48*

device locks *414*

DH *209*

DHCP *246*

DHE *209*

Diameter *316*, *339*

dictionary attack *202*, *296*

differential backup *494*

Diffie-Hellman, *See* DH

Diffie-Hellman Ephemeral, *See* DHE

digital certificate *213*, *216*

digital forensics *470*
        See also computer forensics

Digital Rights Management, *See* DRM

digital signature
    hash *215*

digital transmitter *419*

digital watermarking *431*

directive
    security control *48*

Directive 95/46/EC *18*

Direct Object Model, *See* DOM

directory service, *See* DS

Disaster Recover Plan, *See* DRP

disaster recovery
    and the ISO *8*
    evaluation and maintenance *485*
    priority level *481*
    response approaches *500*, *506*
    strategy *480*

disaster response *484*

disclosure
    risk *540*

discretionary access control, *See* DAC

disk actuator movement *496*

disk-platter rotation *496*

disposal phase *515*

Distributed Component Object Model, *See* DCOM

distributed denial of service, *See* DDoS

Distributed Network Protocol 3, *See* DNP3
DLP *430*
DMZ *274*
DNP3 *251*
DNS *246*
DNS cache poisoning *298*
DNSSEC *258*
documentation
 of results *474*
  security-related *73*
documenting the change phase *456*
Domain Name Service, *See* DNS
Domain Name System Security Extension, *See*
DNSSEC
DOM-based attack *383*
doors *412*
DoS *215, 301, 304, 540*
driver *127*
drivers *134*
DRM *207*
DRP *68, 479*
drug use check
 for information security *79*
dry pipe *235*
DS *334*
DSDM *531*
dual-homed firewall *274*
due care , *See* due diligence
due diligence *12, 60*
dumpster diving *359*
duplexing *496, 497*
Dynamic Host Configuration Protocol, *See*
DHCP
Dynamic Systems Development Method, *See*
DSM

E

EAP *338*
EAR *23*
EBCDIC *241*
ECC *209, 497*
ECDHE *209*
echoing passwords *549*
economic damages *39*
ECPA *16, 473*
e-discovery *470*
EF *44*
egress monitoring *431*
EJB *524*
Electronic Communications Privacy Act, *See*
ECPA

electronic discovery, *See* e-discovery
electronic vaulting *494*
elliptic curve cryptography, *See* ECC
Elliptic Curve Diffie-Hellman Ephemeral, *See*
ECDHE
emanation *163*
embedded device *183*
embedded security features *541*
Encapsulated Security Payload, *See* ESP
encapsulation *523*
encipher *190*
encryption
 and cryptography *190*
 asymmetric algorithms *209*
 hashing algorithms *210*
 key *203*
 of the hash *215*
 shared-key *207*
 symmetric *207*
 symmetric algorithms *207*
encryption-based attack *202*
endpoint security *275*
ends justify the means
 and ethics fallacies *28*
Enigma *202*
Enterprise JavaBean, *See* EJB
Enterprise Security Architecture, *See* ESA
entity *314*
environmental
 controls *550*
error correction code, *See* ECC
error detection *245*
error handling *381*
ESA *147*
ESP *287, 288*
Ethernet
 LAN *265*
 NIC *265*
ethics
 and (ISC)² *29*
 and IAB *28*
 code *27*
 fallacies *28*
European Union
 privacy laws *18*
event log *374*
evidence
 collection techniques *471*
 rules of *472*
exception handling *381*
executable content *549*

exploit *3*
Export Administration Regulations, *See* EAR
Exposure Factor, *See* EF
Extended Binary Coded Decimal Information Code, *See* EBCDIC
Extensible Authentication Protocol, *See* EAP
external audit *397*
extranet *275*
Extreme Programming, *See* XP

F

facial recognition *33, 330*
facility
    control device *414*
    design *221*
factoring attack *203*
Fair Cryptosystem *195*
fair hiring regulations *79*
false acceptance rate, *See* FAR
false rejection rate, *See* FRR
Family Educational Rights and Privacy Act, *See* FERPA
FAR *331*
fault tolerance *494*
FCoE *252*
FE-13 *233*
feasibility *514*
Federal Information Security Management Act, *See* FISMA
federal sentencing guidelines *20*
federated identity *334*
fencing *412*
FERPA *16*
fiber optics *266*
Fibre Channel over Ethernet, *See* FCoE
File Transfer Protocol, *See* FTP
file transmission *211*
filtering algorithm *264*
financial history review
    for information security *79*
financial impact *39*
fingerprint scanner *330, 415*
fire
    code *412*
    prevention methods *233*
    protection level *412*
fire extinguisher
    hand-held *234*
    water-based *234*
firewall
    overview *264*

types *273*
FISMA *20*
flood impact *65*
FM-200 *233*
frame relay *266*
free information
    and ethics fallacies *28*
frequency analysis *203*
front-end processor *264*
FRR *331*
FTP *246*
full backup *494*
full disclosure *547*
full-duplex *242*
full interruption testing *68*
functional design analysis and planning phase *514*
functional test *384*
fuzzing *386*

G

gateway *263*
GLBA *16, 27*
governance *4, 5*
Graham-Denning Model *141*
Gramm-Leach-Bliley Act, *See* GLBA
granularity of controls *550*
grey box test *373*
guidelines
    and relationships *34*
    vs. standards *33*

H

hacker *28, 305, 545*
half-duplex *242*
Halon *233*
hand geometry sensor *330, 415*
hand-held fire extinguisher *234*
handprint *330*
hardware architecture components *127*
Harrison-Ruzzo-Ullman Model *141*
hash
    and digital signature *215*
    encryption *215*
    salting *211*
    value *209*
Hash-based Message Authentication Code, *See* HMAC
hashing
    and password protection *211*

encryption algorithms *210*
file verification *211*
HDLC *266*
Health Insurance Portability and Accountability Act, *See* HIPAA
Heartbleed bug *217*
heat detector *417*
heating, ventilation, and air conditioning system, *See* HVAC
HIDS *303*
Hierarchical Database Management Model *538*
High-Level Data Link Control, *See* HDLC
hijacking *298*
HIPAA *16*, *27*
hiring practice applications *78*
HMAC *211*
hoax *548*
honeynets *438*
honeypots *438*
host-based IDS *303*
   See also HIDS
Host-to-Host layer *244*
hot site *499*
HTTP *246*
hub *263*
HVAC *232*
hybrid access control *316*
hybrid IDS *304*
Hyper Text Transfer Protocol, *See* HTTP

I

I/O devices *133*
I&A *315*
IA *73*
IAB
   ethics *28*
   RFC 1087 *28*
ICMP *246*
IDaaS *167*, *343*
ID card *325*
identification and authentication, *See* I&A
identification types
   ID card *325*
   user ID *325*
   weaknesses *325*
Identity as a Service, *See* IDaaS
Identity-as-a-Service, *See* IDaaS
identity federation *334*
identity management *324*
IDS
   categories *303*

modes *303*
perimeter *416*
IGMP *247*
IMAP *247*
implementing the change phase *456*
incomplete parameter check/enforcement *549*
incremental backup *494*
index *538*
Inergen *233*
inference *168*, *539*
information
   concealment *190*
   privacy law *16*
Information Flow Model *140*, *550*
information security
   criminals *28*
   governance *5*
   reporting options *10*
   strategic alignment *4*
Information Security Continuous Monitoring, *See* ISCM
Information Systems Security Certification Consortium, *See* (ISC)²
Information Technology Security Evaluation Criteria, *See* ITSEC
informative security policy *34*
infrared devices *416*
initialization vector, *See* IV
Initial maturity *516*
input/output devices, *See* I/O devices
installation/implementation phase *515*
instruction path *134*
insurance
   department *11*
   valuation *40*
integer overflow *382*
integrated product and process development, *See* IPPD
Integrated Product Teams, *See* IPTs
integration test *384*
integrity *2*
intellectual property
   international protection *22*
   law *21*
intelligent keys *414*
interface test *384*
internal audit *397*
internal audit department *10*
internal integrity checks *538*
International Information Systems Security Certification Consortium, *See* (ISC)²

International Organization for Standardization, *See* ISO

International Traffic in Arms Regulations, *See* ITAR

Internet Architecture Board, *See* IAB

Internet Control Message Protocol, *See* ICMP

Internet Group Management Protocol, *See* IGMP

Internet Message Access Protocol, *See* IMAP

Internet of Things, *See* IoT

Internet Protocol security, *See* IPSec

Internet Small Computer System Interface, *See* iSCSI

interoperability agreement, *See* IA

interpreted languages *522*

intrusion detection system, *See* IDS

intrusion prevention system, *See* IPS

IoT *56*

IP *243, 245*

IP fragmentation attack *301*

IPPD *515*

IPS *303, 305*

IPSec
    overview *286*
    process *288*

IPTs *515*

iQN *253*

iris scanner *330, 415*

ISA *73*

ISC2, *See* (ISC)²

ISCM *389*

iSCSI *253*

iSCSI Qualified Name, *See* iQN

ISO
    responsibilities *8*
    roles *8*

ISO/IEC 27001 *24, 152*

ITAM *90*

ITAR *23*

IT Asset Management, *See* ITAM

IT department *10*

ITGI *4*

IT Governance Institute, *See* ITGI

ITIL *152, 456*

IT Infrastructure Library, *See* ITIL

ITSEC *143*

IV *211*

J

job position sensitivity profiling *78*

K

Kanban *531*

Kerberos *336*

kernel mode, *See* supervisor state

key
    clustering *194*
    escrow *195*
    management in cryptography *195*

keyless lock *413*

key lock *413*

key performance indicator, *See* KPI

keyspace *194*

keystroke logging *296*

known-plaintext attack *203*

KPI *392*

L

LAN *246, 265*

Lattice Model *140*

layered protection *411*

LDAP *247, 335*

LDAPS *335*

Lean *531*

LEAP *338*

least privilege *351, 540*

legal department *11*

length checking *548*

liability *12, 19*

licensing *22*

lie detector testing
    for information security *79*

lifetime control *245*

lighting *413*

Lightweight Directory Access Protocol, *See* LDAP

Lightweight Extensible Authentication Protocol, *See* LEAP

limits checking *538*

line workers *5*

Linux *545*

lithium transmitter *419*

local area network, *See* LAN

lock controls *541*

lock type *413*

log files *473*

logging *542*

logic bomb *297, 548*

log management infrastructure *375*

long-term priority *482*

long-term response *507*

long-term security goals, *See* strategic security goals

M

MaaS *167*
MAC *243*, *349*
MAC address *262*, *263*
machine code *520*
machine language *520*
magnetic detector *417*
magnetic stripe card *328*
magnetic tape
    data *190*
    database backup *493*
Maintenance hooks *358*
malformed input *548*
malicious code attack *296*
malware *296*, *305*, *545*, *548*
Malware-as-a-Service, *See* MaaS
MAN *266*
Managed maturity *516*
mandatory access control, *See* MAC
man-in-the-middle *298*
man-in-the-middle attack *203*
man-made disasters *42*
man trap *415*
masking passwords *549*
matrix organization *5*
maturity model *516*
maximum tolerable downtime, *See* MTD
MD4 *210*
MD5 *210*
mean time to recovery, *See* MTTR
media
    cabled *270*
    protection methods *447*
    wireless *270*
Media Access Control addresses, *See* MAC address
medium-term security goals, *See* tactical security goals
memorandum of understanding, *See* MOU
memory
    mapping *549*
    protection *549*
memory leaks *382*
mesh topology *269*
message digest
    and digital signature *215*
Message Digest 4, *See* MD4
Message Digest 5, *See* MD5

message hash, *See* message digest
metadata *542*
method *523*
metropolitan area network, *See* MAN
microwave systems *416*
mid-term priority *481*
milestone *528*
military classification *94*
mirror
    and RAID *497*
    overview *496*
    site *499*, *506*
misuse test *384*
mobile code *549*
modem *263*
modularity *523*
motion sensor *416*
MOU *74*
MPLS *254*
MTD *66*, *483*
MTTR *484*
multi-factor authentication *331*
multiplexer *264*
multiprocessing *130*
multiprogramming *129*
Multi-Protocol Label Switching, *See* MPLS
multistate *129*
multitasking *129*
multithreading *129*

N

NAP *339*
NAS *498*
NAT *275*
National Information Infrastructure Protection Act, *See* NIIPA
National Institute of Standards and Technology, *See* NIST
National Institute of Standards and Technology Special Publication 800 series, *See* NIST SP 800 series
national security *94*
natural disasters *41*
NDA *74*, *94*
need to know *78*, *351*, *540*
NetBIOS *247*
network
    architecture components *262*
    IDS *304*
    session *242*
Network Access layer *244*

Network Access Protection, *See* NAP
Network Address Translation, *See* NAT
Network Attached Storage, *See* NAS
Network-based Intrusion Detection System, *See* NIDS
Network Basic Input Output System, *See* NetBIOS
Network Database Management Model *538*
Network File System, *See* NFS
Networking layer *244*
network interface card, *See* NIC
Network layer *243*
Network Policy Server, *See* NPS
network scanning *374*
network virtualization, *See* NV
NFS *247, 299*
NIC *265*
NIDS *304*
NIIPA *20*
NIST
    contingency plan *64*
    overview *64*
    Pub 800–34 *64*
    SP 800 series *24*
noise and perturbation *542*
non-disclosure agreement, *See* NDA
no need to know *78*
Non-Interference Model *140*
non-repudiation *192*
not required priority *482*
NPS *339*
NT LAN Manager, *See* NTLM
NTLM *210*
NV *289*

O

object
    and access control *314*
    reuse *549*
Object Oriented Database, *See* OOD
Object-Oriented Database Model *539*
object-oriented programming, *See* OOP
Object Request Broker, *See* ORB
object reuse *358*
OCSP *215*
Office of Government Commerce, *See* OGC
OGC *457*
OLA *74*
OLTP *542*
Online Certificate Status Protocol, *See* OCSP
online transaction processing, *See* OLTP

OOD
    overview *522*
    security *541*
OOP *522, 539*
OpenID *345*
open source software *545*
OpenSSL *217*
Open System Interconnection model, *See* OSI model
operating-level agreement, *See* OLA
operational/maintenance phase *515*
operational and project planning *34*
operational security goals *11*
Optimizing maturity *516*
ORB *524*
organizational
    ethics *27*
    structure *5*
organizational units, *See* OU
OSI model
    and mnemonics *244*
    layers *241*
OU *335*

P

packet filtering firewalls *274*
PAN *266*
PAP *338*
parallel testing *67*
parity *496*
partial disclosure *547*
partitioning *542*
passive system IDS *303*
passphrase *326*
password
    administration *327*
    cracking *296*
    echoing *549*
    guessing *326*
    protection *550*
    protection, hashing *211*
    virtual *326*
Password Authentication Protocol, *See* PAP
PAT *275*
patent *21*
Payment Card Industry Data Security Standard, *See* PCI DSS
PBX *269*
PCI DSS
    definition of *23*
PDU *241, 243*

PEAP *338*
penetration testing
    and the ISO *8*
    definition of *371*
perfect forward secrecy, *See* PFS
performance measurement *4*
perimeter IDS *416*
perimeter network *274*
permission codes *351*
permutation, *See* transposition
Personal and Confidential classification *95*
personal area network, *See* PAN
personal identification number, *See* PIN
personal interview
    for information security *79*
personality screening
    for information security *79*
Personally Identifiable Information, *See* PII
personally identifying information, *See* PII
personnel safety issues *425*
PFS *216*
PGP *259*
phishing *359*
phone transmitter *419*
photometric detector *417*
phreaking *269*
physical access barrier *411*
physical access logs *420*
physical control *47, 49*
Physical layer *243*
physical protection areas *222*
physical security
    methods *227*
    overview *220*
PII *15, 16*
PIN *326*
ping of death *301*
PKI
    components *213*
    process *213*
Plain Old Telephone System, *See* POTS
plaintext *190*
    See also cleartext
point-to-point topology *268*
policy *32, 34*
polyinstantiation *524*
polymorphism *523*
POP *247*
POP3 *241*
portable site *500*
Port Address Translation, *See* PAT

position sensitivity screening *79*
Post Office Protocol, *See* POP
Post Office Protocol version 3, *See* POP3
POTS *269*
practicality
    and control selection *46*
preaction *235*
pre-processed structured database *539*
Presentation layer *241*
pressure-sensitive sensor *416*
Pretty Good Privacy, *See* PGP
preventative security control *48*
primary storage *131*
prioritization
    and disaster recovery *481*
    and the ISO *8*
Privacy Act of 1974 *16*
private branch exchange, *See* PBX
Private classification *95*
private key *215*
privileges
    with access control *314*
probability qualification *39*
probability quantification *39*
procedural languages *522*
procedure *32, 34*
processor privilege state *549*
program coordinator *62*
project initiation phase *514*
proper conduct, *See* ethics
proprietary software *545*
Protected Extensible Authentication Protocol,
See PEAP
protocol-based IDS *304*
Protocol Data Unit, *See* PDU
prototyping
    and the spiral model *532*
    model *531*
proximity
    card *328*
    detector *417*
proxy
    firewalls *274*
    overview *264*
    servers *275*
prudent person rule *12, 19*
PSTN *269*
public key infrastructure, *See* PKI
Public Switched Telephone Network, *See*
PSTN

Q

QA *514*
QC *116*
QoS *252*
qualitative risk analysis *42*
quality assurance, *See* QA
quality control, *See* QC
quality of service, *See* QoS
Quantitatively Managed maturity *516*
quantitative risk analysis *43*
quantum cryptography *196*
query language *538*

R

RA *213*
RACE Integrity Primitives Evaluation Message
Digest, *See* RIPEMD
RADIUS *33, 316, 337*
RAID
    levels *497*
    overview *496*
rainbow attack *202, 296*
rainbow table *358*
RAIT *498*
RAM *130*
Random Access Memory, *See* RAM
ransomware *297*
RARP *246*
RATS *548*
RBAC *352*
RC algorithm *208*
reactive system IDS *303*
Read-Only Memory, *See* ROM
rebuilding *507*
records management *60*
Recovery Point Objective, *See* RPO
recovery security control *49*
Recovery Time Objective, *See* RTO
reduction
    and risk *45*
redundancy *494*
Redundant Array of Independent/Inexpensive
Disks, *See* RAID
Redundant Array of Independent Tapes, *See*
RAIT
reference check
    for information security *79*
reference monitor *315, 549*
reflected attack *383*
registration authority, *See* RA

regression test *384*
regulatory security policy *34*
rehash *215*
Relational Database Management Model *538*
relocation *507*
remote access *284*
Remote Access Trojans, *See* RATS
Remote Authentication Dial-In User Service,
See RADIUS
remote journaling *494*
repeaters *264*
replay attack *203*
report documentation *474*
reporting the change phase *456*
reprimands *34*
requesting the change phase *456*
resource management *4*
restricted work area *227*
retention *101*
retina scanner *330, 415*
Reverse Address Resolution Protocol, *See*
RARP
reverse proxy *264*
RFC
    1087 *28*
    and TCP/IP *244*
ring topology *269*
RIPEMD *210*
risk
    and disaster recovery *481*
    countermeasure *305*
    minimizing *27*
    probability and prioritization *44*
    reallocation *45*
    types *41*
risk analysis *39, 44, 532*
risk management
    business documentation *73*
    department *11*
    improper *38*
    principles *45*
risk mitigation *4, 45, 480*
risk reduction
    and control selection *46*
Rivest Cipher, *See* RC algorithm
Rivest Shamir Adelman, *See* RSA
role-based access control, *See* RBAC
ROM *131*
rootkit *298*
routable *243*
routed network *267*

router *243, 262*
routing *243*
row locking *542*
RPO *483*
RPO/RTO optimization *484*
RSA *209*
RSA Factoring Challenge *203*
RTO *483*
rule-based access control *353*
rules of evidence *472*

S

S/MIME *259*
SA *287, 288*
SAML *345*
SAN *266, 498*
S-box *208*
SCADA *251*
scoping *108*
screened subnet *274*
screening host *274*
screen scraping *284*
SCRUM *531*
SDN *288*
secondary storage *132*
Secret classification *94*
secret-key cryptography *207*
Secure/Multipurpose Internet Mail Extensions, *See* S/MIME
Secure Hash Algorithm, *See* SHA
Secure LDAP, *See* LDAPS
Secure Shell, *See* SSH
Secure Sockets Layer and Transport Layer Security, *See* SSL/TLS
security
    dogs *419*
    facility design *221*
    features, embedded *541*
    goals *11, 34*
    guard *415*
    kernel *315, 549*
    patrol *418*
    physical *220*
    reporting options *10*
    structure *538*
    training *83*
security architecture frameworks *151*
Security Assertion Markup Language, *See* SAML
Security Association, *See* SA
security awareness

and the ISO *8*
    training *83*
security clearances
    for information security *79*
security control
    categories *46*
    types *49*
security impact analysis, *See* SIA
Security Information and Event Management, *See* SIEM
security policy
    objectives *34*
    organizational roles *6*
    process *34*
    types *32, 34*
segments *242*
SEI *516*
sensitivity profile *78*
service level agreement, *See* SLA
service organization control, *See* SOC
session
    fixation *383*
    prediction *383*
Session layer *242*
session management *332*
SHA *210*
shared-key encryption *207*
shared location *506*
shatterproof
    and ethics fallacies *28*
Shibboleth *345*
short-term priority *481*
short-term response *506*
short-term security goals, *See* operational security, goals
shoulder surfing *325, 359, 549*
SIA *458*
side-channel attack *203*
signature-based IDS *304*
Simple Mail Transport Protocol, *See* SMTP
Simple Message Transport Protocol, *See* SMTP
simplex *242*
simulations *67*
Single Loss Expectancy, *See* SLE
single sign-on, *See* SSO
SLA *72*
SLC *514*
SLE *44*
smart card *325, 328*
SMTP *241, 246*
smurf attack *301*

Sneakernet *432*
sniffing *296*
SOC *398*
social engineering *3, 325, 359, 374, 549*
SoD *10, 351, 550*
software
    categories *545*
    control types *549*
    escrow *551*
    values of categories *545*
Software assurance, *See* SwA
Software Defined Networking, *See* SDN
software development
    security considerations *548*
Software Engineering Institute, *See* SEI
something you are *326*
something you have *326, 328*
something you know *326*
SONET *266*
source code *520, 545*
SOX Act *17, 27*
spam *297*
spiral model *532*
spoofing *215, 298, 359*
spyware *357, 548*
SQL injection
    attack *540*
    overview *382*
SSH *258*
SSL/TLS *258*
SSO *337*
staff workers *5*
standards
    and relationships *34*
    overview *32*
    vs. guidelines *33*
star topology *268*
stateful inspection firewall *274, 305*
State Machine Model *140*
steganography *200*
storage area network, *See* SAN
Storage Area Network, *See* SAN
stored attack *383*
strategic alignment *4*
strategic planning *33*
strategic security goals *11*
stream cipher *197, 211*
striping *496*
structured development model *533*
Structured Query Language, *See* SQL
subject *314*

substitution *196*
supervisor state *128, 549*
Supervisory Control and Data Acquisition, *See*
SCADA
surveillance
    system *417*
    system types *418*
SwA *557*
switch *243, 263*
switched network *266*
symmetric encryption
    algorithms *207*
    and factoring attacks *203*
synchronized clocks *211*
Synchronous Optical Networking, *See* SONET
synchronous token *329*
SYN flood *301*
system design specifications phase *514*
system lifecycle, *See* SLC
system test *384*

T

TACACS *316*
tactical planning *33*
tactical security goals *11*
tagged *241*
tailgating *359*
tailoring *108*
taking candy from a baby
    and ethics fallacies *28*
targeted testing *374*
TCB *127*
TCP *242, 245*
TCP/IP
    model *244*
    protocols *245*
TCSEC *143*
technical control *47, 49*
Temporal Key Integrity Protocol, *See* TKIP
Terminal Access Controller Access Control
System, *See* TACACS
terminal emulation *284*
test-driven development *526*
testing and reporting results phase *456*
The Open Group Architecture Framework, *See*
TOGAF
threading *129*
threat
    agent *37*
    assessment *39*
    modeling *54*

time-based access control *354*
time factors *211*
TKIP *257*
TOC/TOU *549*
TOGAF *152*
token device *328*
tokens *329*
Top Secret classification *94*
TPM *157*
trademark *21*
Trade Secret classification *22, 95*
traffic shaper *265*
transfer
 and risk *45*
Transmission Control Protocol, *See* TCP
Transmission Control Protocol/Internet
Protocol, *See* TCP/IP
Transport layer *242*
transposition
 bit-based *197*
 character-based *197*
 simple *197*
trapdoor attack *358, 549*
tree structure *538*
tree topology *269*
Triple DES, *See* 3DES
Trojan horse *297, 548*
 See also Trojan program
Trojan program *297*
 See also Trojan horse
Trusted Computer System Evaluation Criteria,
See TCSEC
Trusted Computing Base, *See* TCB
Trusted Platform Module, *See* TPM
Twofish *208*
two-man rule *447*
Type 1 error, *See* FRR
Type II error, *See* FAR

U

UDP *242, 245*
unauthorized information disclosure *227*
Unclassified classification *94*
Uniform Resource Locator, *See* URL
unit test *384*
URL *549*
USA Patriot Act *17*
user
 ID *325*
 portal *540*
 state *128*

User Datagram Protocol, *See* UDP

V

value delivery *4*
versioning *457*
vibration detector *417*
view
 improper restrictions *540*
virtual
 memory *131*
 password *326*
virtual local area network, *See* VLAN
Virtual Private Network, *See* VPN
virus
 and mitigation *548*
 and penetration testing *297*
 detection software *305*
VLAN *263, 267*
Voice over Internet Protocol, *See* VoIP
voiceprint *330*
VoIP *255, 265*
vulnerability
 determination factors *42*
 identification *39*
 scanning *374*
vulnerability assessment
 definition of *369*

W

walkthrough *67*
walls *412*
WAN
 overview *266*
 technologies *267*
war dialing *374*
War driving *374*
warm site *499*
Wassenaar Arrangement *23*
water-based fire extinguisher *234*
waterfall software development model *527*
WAYF *345*
WEP *257*
wet pipe *234*
Where Are You From, *See* WAYF
white box test *373*
whitelisting *437*
wide area network, *See* WAN
Wi-Fi Protected Access, *See* WPA
windows *412*
WIPO *22*

Wired Equivalent Privacy, *See* WEP
wireless
    media *270*
    routers *262*
Wireless LANs, *See* WLANs
WLANs *265*
work factor *201*
work history verification
    for information security *79*
World Intellectual Property Organization, *See*
WIPO
worm *297, 548*
WPA *257*
WPA2 *258*
    See also 802.11i

X

X.25 *266*
x.509 version 3 certificate *213*
XaaS *167*
X-as-a-Service, *See* XaaS
XOR *198*
XP *531*
XSRF *299, 383*
XSS *299, 383*

Z

Zachman Framework *152*

093024S rev 1.0
ISBN-13 978-1-4246-2610-6
ISBN-10 1-4246-2610-2